FreeBSD Handbook

FreeBSD Handbook

Second Edition

The FreeBSD Documentation Project

FreeBSD Handbook, Second Edition
by The FreeBSD Documentation Project
Copyright © 1995, 1996, 1997, 1998, 1999, 2000, 2001, 2002 The FreeBSD Documentation Project
All rights reserved. Printed in the United States of America.

Published by FreeBSD Mall, Inc., 3623 Sanford Street, Concord, CA 94520

Editor, First Edition: Jim Mock.

Editors, Second Edition: Murray Stokely and Nik Clayton.

Associate Editor: Chern Lee.

Cover Designer and Illustrator: Michele Membrila.

Print History:

April, 2000	First Edition
November, 2001	Second Edition
May, 2002	Second Edition, Second Printing

ISBN: 1-57176-303-1

Table of Contents

List of Tables

List of Figures

List of Examples

Preface

Intended Audience

The FreeBSD newcomer will find that the first section of this book guides the user through the FreeBSD installation process, and gently introduces the concepts and conventions that underpin Unix. Working through this section requires little more than the desire to explore, and the ability to take on board new concepts as they are introduced.

Once you've have travelled this far, the second, far larger, section of the Handbook is a comprehensive reference to all manner of topics of interest to FreeBSD system administrators. Some of these chapters may recommend that you do some prior reading, and this is noted in the synopsis at the beginning of each chapter.

For a list of additional sources of information, please see Appendix B.

Changes from the First Edition

This second edition is the culmination of over two years of work by the dedicated members of the FreeBSD Documentation Project. The following are the major changes in this new edition:

- A complete Index has been added.
- All ASCII figures have been replaced by graphical diagrams.
- A standard synopsis has been added to each chapter to give a quick summary of what information the chapter contains, and what the reader is expected to know.
- The content has been logically reorganized into three parts: "Getting Started", "System Administration", and "Appendices".
- Chapter 2 ("Installing FreeBSD") was completely rewritten with many screenshots to make it much easier for new users to grasp the text.
- Chapter 3 ("Unix Basics") has been expanded to contain additional information about processes, daemons, and signals.
- Chapter 4 ("Installing Applications") has been expanded to contain additional information about binary package management.
- Chapter 5 ("The X Window System") has been completely rewritten with an emphasis on using modern desktop technologies such as KDE and GNOME on XFree86 4.X.
- Chapter 7 ("The FreeBSD Booting Process") has been expanded.
- Chapter 12 ("Storage") has been written from what used to be two separate chapters on "Disks" and "Backups". We feel that the topics are easier to comprehend when presented as a single chapter. A section on RAID (both hardware and software) has also been added.

- Chapter 15 ("Serial Communications") has been completely reorganized and updated for FreeBSD 4.X/5.X.
- Chapter 16 ("PPP and SLIP") has been substantially updated.
- Many new sections have been added to Chapter 17 ("Advanced Networking").
- Chapter 18 ("Electronic Mail") has been expanded to include more information about configuring **sendmail**.
- Chapter 20 ("Linux Compatibility") has been expanded to include information about installing **Oracle** and **SAP/R3**.
- The following new topics are covered in this second edition:
  - Configuration and Tuning (Chapter 6).
  - Sound (Chapter 14)

Organization of This Book

This book is split into three logically distinct sections. The first section, *Getting Started*, covers the installation and basic usage of FreeBSD. It is expected that the reader will follow these chapters in sequence, possibly skipping chapters covering familiar topics. The second section, *System Administration*, covers a broad collection of subjects that are of interest to more advanced FreeBSD users. Each section begins with a succinct synopsis that describes what the chapter covers and what the reader is expected to already know. This is meant to allow the casual reader to skip around to find chapters of interest. The third section contains appendices of reference information.

Chapter 1, Introduction

Introduces FreeBSD to a new user. It describes the history of the FreeBSD Project, the goals, development model, and everything else they've done for the FreeBSD project.

Chapter 2, Installation

Walks a user through the entire installation process. Some advanced installation topics, such as installing through a serial console, are also covered.

Chapter 3, Unix Basics

Covers the basic commands and functionality of the FreeBSD operating system. If you are familiar with Linux or another flavor of Unix then you can probably skip this chapter.

Chapter 4, Installing Applications

Covers the installation of third-party software with both FreeBSD's innovative "Ports Collection" and standard binary packages.

Chapter 5, The X Window System

Describes the X Window System in general and using XFree86 on FreeBSD in particular. Also describes common desktop environments such as KDE and GNOME.

Chapter 6, Configuration and Tuning

Describes the parameters available for system administrators to tune a FreeBSD system for optimum performance. Also describes the various configuration files used in FreeBSD and where to find them.

Chapter 7, Booting Process

Describes the FreeBSD boot process and explains how to control this process with configuration options.

Chapter 8, Users and Basic Account Management

Describes the creation and manipulation of user accounts. Also discusses resource limitations that can be set on users and other account management tasks.

Chapter 9, Configuring the FreeBSD Kernel

Explains why you might need to configure a new kernel and provides detailed instructions for configuring, building, and installing a custom kernel.

Chapter 10, Security

Describes many different tools available to help keep your FreeBSD system secure, including Kerberos, IPSec, OpenSSH, and network firewalls.

Chapter 11, Printing

Describes managing printers on FreeBSD, including information about banner pages, printer accounting, and initial setup.

Chapter 12, Storage

Describes how to manage storage media and filesystems with FreeBSD. This includes physical disks, RAID arrays, optical and tape media, memory-backed disks, and network filesystems.

Chapter 13, Localization

Describes how to use FreeBSD in languages other than English. Covers both system and application level localization.

Chapter 14, Sound

Shows how to setup sound support for your system. Also describes some sample audio applications.

Chapter 15, Serial Communications

Explains how to connect terminals and modems to your FreeBSD system for both dial in and dial out connections.

Chapter 16, PPP and SLIP

Describes how to use PPP, SLIP, or PPP over Ethernet to connect to remote systems with FreeBSD.

Chapter 17, Advanced Networking

Describes many networking topics, including sharing an Internet connection with other computers on your LAN, using network filesystems, sharing account information via NIS, setting up a name server, and much more.

Chapter 18, Electronic Mail

Explains the different components of an email server and dives into simple configuration topics for the most popular mail server software: **sendmail**.

Chapter 19, The Cutting Edge

Explains the different between FreeBSD-STABLE, FreeBSD-CURRENT, and FreeBSD releases. Describes which users would benefit from tracking a development system and outlines that process.

Chapter 20, Linux Binary Compatibility

Describes the Linux compatibility features of FreeBSD. Also provides detailed installation instructions for many popular Linux applications such as Oracle, SAP/R3, and Mathematica.

Appendix A, Obtaining FreeBSD

Lists different sources for obtaining FreeBSD media on CDROM or DVD as well as different sites on the Internet that allow you to download and install FreeBSD.

Appendix B, Bibliography

This book touches on many different subjects that may leave you hungry for a more detailed explanation. The bibliography lists many excellent books that are referenced in the text.

Appendix C, Resources on the Internet

Describes the many forums available for FreeBSD users to post questions and engage in technical conversations about FreeBSD.

Appendix D, PGP Keys

Lists the PGP fingerprints of several FreeBSD Developers.

Appendix E, Contributing Authors

We've attempted to list many of the authors responsible for writing this book along with a brief description of their contributions. Unfortunately, there are bound to be significant omissions from this list.

Conventions used in this book

To provide a consistent and easy to read text, several conventions are followed throughout the book.

Typographic Conventions

Italic

An *italic* font is used for filenames, URLs, emphasized text, and the first usage of technical terms.

`Monospace`

A `monospaced` font is used for error messages, commands, environment variables, names of ports, hostnames, user names, group names, device names, variables, and code fragments.

Bold

> A **bold** font is used for applications, commands, and keys.

User Input

Keys are rendered in **bold** to stand out from other text. Key combinations that are meant to be typed simultaneously are rendered with '+' between the keys, such as :

Ctrl+Alt+Del

Keys that are meant to be typed in sequence will be separated with commas, for example :

Ctrl+X, Ctrl+S

Would mean that the user is expected to type the **Ctrl** and **X** keys simultaneously and then to type the **Ctrl** and **S** keys simultaneously.

Examples

Examples starting with E:\> indicate a MS-DOS command. Unless otherwise noted, these commands may be executed from a "Command Prompt" window in a modern Microsoft Windows environment.

```
E:\> tools\fdimage floppies\kern.flp A:
```

Examples starting with # indicate a command that must be invoked as the superuser in FreeBSD. You can login as root to type the command, or login as your normal account and use **su** to gain superuser privileges.

```
# dd if=kern.flp of=/dev/fd0
```

Examples starting with % indicate a command that should be invoked from a normal user account. Unless otherwise noted, C-shell syntax is used for setting environment variables and other shell commands.

```
% top
```

Acknowledgments

The book you are holding represents the efforts of many hundreds of people around the world. Whether they sent in fixes for typos, or submitted complete chapters, all the contributions have been useful.

While it is impossible to list everyone involved in the Handbook here, we would like to single out a few people.

Chern Lee and Valentino Vaschetto at WindRiver Systems put in an inordinate amount of effort in the months leading up to publication. Chern wrote many sections, created all of the graphical figures, and made many sweeps throughout the book for spelling and grammatical errors. Val indexed half of the book and contributed to many sections.

Michele Membrila, also at WindRiver Systems, designed the beautiful artwork on the covers and inside this book.

Jim Mock, editor of the first edition, continues to contribute changes back, and through his FreeBSD 'zine[1] web site provides additional FreeBSD documentation.

---

1 http://www.freebsdzine.org/

Dima Dorfman relentlessly responded to submissions from FreeBSD users and integrated their feedback into the book you're now reading.

Satoshi Asami, Neil Blakey-Milner, Andrey Chernov, Matt Dillon, Jake Hamby, Brian Handy, Guy Helmer, Poul Henning-Kamp, Jordan Hubbard, Tom Hukins, Yoshinobu Inoue, Sean Kelly, Holger Kipp, Bill Lloyd, Marcel Moolenaar, Moses Moore, Rich Murphey, Mark Murray, Alex Nash, David O'Brien, Gary Palmer, Bill Paul, John Polstra, Randy Pratt, Chris Shumway, Mike Smith, Brian Somers, G. Adam Stanislav, Bill Swingle, Bob Van Valzah, Michael Wu, Jörg Wunsch, and Kazutaka Yokota have all contributed substantial amounts of text at one time or another.

Thanks to Wind River Systems for sponsoring this second printed edition by paying several authors, seeing the book through publication, and so on.

- Nik Clayton and Murray Stokely, October 15, 2001

I. Getting Started

This part of the FreeBSD Handbook is for users and administrators who are new to FreeBSD. These chapters will:

- Introduce you to FreeBSD
- Guide you through the installation process
- Teach you some Unix basics
- Show you how to install the wealth of third party applications available for FreeBSD
- Introduce you to X, the Unix windowing system, and detail how to configure a desktop environment that makes you more productive.

We have tried to keep the number of forward references in the text to a minimum so that you can read this section of the Handbook from front to back with the minimum of page flipping required.

Chapter 1

Introduction

1.1 Synopsis

Thank you for your interest in FreeBSD! The following chapter covers various items about the FreeBSD Project, such as its history, goals, development model, and so on.

After reading this chapter, you will know:

- How FreeBSD relates to other computer operating systems.
- The history of the FreeBSD Project.
- The goals of the FreeBSD Project.
- The basics of the FreeBSD open-source development model.
- And of course: where the name "FreeBSD" comes from.

1.2 Welcome to FreeBSD!

FreeBSD is a 4.4BSD-Lite based operating system for the Intel architecture (x86) and DEC Alpha based systems. Ports to other architectures are also underway. For a brief overview of FreeBSD, see the next section. If you are interested in contributing something to the Project (code, hardware, unmarked bills), see the Contributing to FreeBSD[1] article.

1.2.1 What Can FreeBSD Do?

FreeBSD has many noteworthy features. Some of these are:

- *Preemptive multitasking* with dynamic priority adjustment to ensure smooth and fair sharing of the computer between applications and users, even under the heaviest of loads.
- *Multi-user facilities* which allow many people to use a FreeBSD system simultaneously for a variety of things. This means, for example, that system peripherals such as printers and tape drives are properly shared between all users on the system or the network and that individual resource limits can be placed on users or groups of users, protecting critical system resources from over-use.

---

1 http://www.FreeBSD.org/doc/en_US.ISO8859-1/articles/contributing/article.html

- Strong *TCP/IP networking* with support for industry standards such as SLIP, PPP, NFS, DHCP, and NIS. This means that your FreeBSD machine can interoperate easily with other systems as well as act as an enterprise server, providing vital functions such as NFS (remote file access) and email services or putting your organization on the Internet with WWW, FTP, routing and firewall (security) services.

- *Memory protection* ensures that applications (or users) cannot interfere with each other. One application crashing will not affect others in any way.

- FreeBSD is a *32-bit* operating system (*64-bit* on the Alpha) and was designed as such from the ground up.

- The industry standard *X Window System* (X11R6) provides a graphical user interface (GUI) for the cost of a common VGA card and monitor and comes with full sources.

- *Binary compatibility* with many programs built for Linux, SCO, SVR4, BSDI and NetBSD.

- Thousands of *ready-to-run* applications are available from the FreeBSD *ports* and *packages* collection. Why search the net when you can find it all right here?

- Thousands of additional and *easy-to-port* applications are available on the Internet. FreeBSD is source code compatible with most popular commercial Unix systems and thus most applications require few, if any, changes to compile.

- Demand paged *virtual memory* and "merged VM/buffer cache" design efficiently satisfies applications with large appetites for memory while still maintaining interactive response to other users.

- *SMP* support for machines with multiple CPUs.

- A full complement of *C*, *C++*, *Fortran*, and *Perl* development tools. Many additional languages for advanced research and development are also available in the ports and packages collection.

- *Source code* for the entire system means you have the greatest degree of control over your environment. Why be locked into a proprietary solution at the mercy of your vendor when you can have a truly open system?

- Extensive *online documentation*.

- *And many more!*

FreeBSD is based on the 4.4BSD-Lite release from Computer Systems Research Group (CSRG) at the University of California at Berkeley, and carries on the distinguished tradition of BSD systems development. In addition to the fine work provided by CSRG, the FreeBSD Project has put in many thousands of hours in fine tuning the system for maximum performance and reliability in real-life load situations. As many of the commercial giants struggle to field PC operating systems with such features, performance and reliability, FreeBSD can offer them *now*!

The applications to which FreeBSD can be put are truly limited only by your own imagination. From software development to factory automation, inventory control to azimuth correction of remote satellite antennae; if it can be done with a commercial Unix product then it is more than likely that you can do it with FreeBSD too! FreeBSD also benefits significantly from the literally thousands of high quality applications developed by research centers and universities around the world, often available at little to no cost. Commercial applications are also available and appearing in greater numbers every day.

Because the source code for FreeBSD itself is generally available, the system can also be customized to an almost unheard of degree for special applications or projects, and in ways not generally possible with operating systems from most major commercial vendors. Here is just a sampling of some of the applications in which people are currently using FreeBSD:

- *Internet Services:* The robust TCP/IP networking built into FreeBSD makes it an ideal platform for a variety of Internet services such as:

  - FTP servers

  - World Wide Web servers (standard or secure [SSL])

  - Firewalls and NAT ("IP masquerading") gateways

  - Electronic Mail servers

  - USENET News or Bulletin Board Systems

  - And more...

  With FreeBSD, you can easily start out small with an inexpensive 386 class PC and upgrade all the way up to a quad-processor Xeon with RAID storage as your enterprise grows.

- *Education:* Are you a student of computer science or a related engineering field? There is no better way of learning about operating systems, computer architecture and networking than the hands on, under the hood experience that FreeBSD can provide. A number of freely available CAD, mathematical and graphic design packages also make it highly useful to those whose primary interest in a computer is to get *other* work done!

- *Research:* With source code for the entire system available, FreeBSD is an excellent platform for research in operating systems as well as other branches of computer science. FreeBSD's freely available nature also makes it possible for remote groups to collaborate on ideas or shared development without having to worry about special licensing agreements or limitations on what may be discussed in open forums.

- *Networking:* Need a new router? A name server (DNS)? A firewall to keep people out of your internal network? FreeBSD can easily turn that unused 386 or 486 PC sitting in the corner into an advanced router with sophisticated packet-filtering capabilities.

- *X Window workstation:* FreeBSD is a fine choice for an inexpensive X terminal solution, either using the freely available XFree86 server or one of the excellent commercial servers provided by X Inside. Unlike an X terminal, FreeBSD allows many applications to be run locally, if desired, thus relieving the burden on a central server. FreeBSD can even boot "diskless", making individual workstations even cheaper and easier to administer.

- *Software Development:* The basic FreeBSD system comes with a full complement of development tools including the renowned GNU C/C++ compiler and debugger.

FreeBSD is available in both source and binary form on CDROM and via anonymous FTP. Please see Appendix A for more information about obtaining FreeBSD.

1.2.2 Who uses FreeBSD?

FreeBSD is used to power some of the biggest sites on the Internet, including:

- Yahoo! (`http://www.yahoo.com/`)

- Apache (`http://www.apache.org/`)

- Be, Inc. (`http://www.be.com/`)

- Blue Mountain Arts (`http://www.bluemountain.com/`)
- Pair Networks (`http://www.pair.com/`)
- Whistle Communications (`http://www.whistle.com/`)
- Microsoft (`http://www.microsoft.com/`)
- Hotmail (`http://www.hotmail.com/`)
- Sony Japan (`http://www.sony.co.jp/`)

and many more.

1.3 About the FreeBSD Project

The following section provides some background information on the project, including a brief history, project goals, and the development model of the project.

1.3.1 A Brief History of FreeBSD

Contributed by Jordan Hubbard

The FreeBSD project had its genesis in the early part of 1993, partially as an outgrowth of the "Unofficial 386BSD Patchkit" by the patchkit's last 3 coordinators: Nate Williams, Rod Grimes and myself.

Our original goal was to produce an intermediate snapshot of 386BSD in order to fix a number of problems with it that the patchkit mechanism just was not capable of solving. Some of you may remember the early working title for the project being "386BSD 0.5" or "386BSD Interim" in reference to that fact.

386BSD was Bill Jolitz's operating system, which had been up to that point suffering rather severely from almost a year's worth of neglect. As the patchkit swelled ever more uncomfortably with each passing day, we were in unanimous agreement that something had to be done and decided to try and assist Bill by providing this interim "cleanup" snapshot. Those plans came to a rude halt when Bill Jolitz suddenly decided to withdraw his sanction from the project without any clear indication of what would be done instead.

It did not take us long to decide that the goal remained worthwhile, even without Bill's support, and so we adopted the name "FreeBSD", coined by David Greenman. Our initial objectives were set after consulting with the system's current users and, once it became clear that the project was on the road to perhaps even becoming a reality, I contacted Walnut Creek CDROM with an eye towards improving FreeBSD's distribution channels for those many unfortunates without easy access to the Internet. Walnut Creek CDROM not only supported the idea of distributing FreeBSD on CD but also went so far as to provide the project with a machine to work on and a fast Internet connection. Without Walnut Creek CDROM's almost unprecedented degree of faith in what was, at the time, a completely unknown project, it is quite unlikely that FreeBSD would have gotten as far, as fast, as it has today.

The first CDROM (and general net-wide) distribution was FreeBSD 1.0, released in December of 1993. This was based on the 4.3BSD-Lite ("Net/2") tape from U.C. Berkeley, with many components also provided by 386BSD and the Free Software Foundation. It was a fairly reasonable success for a first offering, and we followed it with the highly successful FreeBSD 1.1 release in May of 1994.

Around this time, some rather unexpected storm clouds formed on the horizon as Novell and U.C. Berkeley settled their long-running lawsuit over the legal status of the Berkeley Net/2 tape. A condition of that settlement was U.C. Berkeley's concession that large parts of Net/2 were "encumbered" code and the property of Novell, who had in turn acquired it from AT&T some time previously. What Berkeley got in return was Novell's "blessing" that the 4.4BSD-Lite release, when it was finally released, would be declared unencumbered and all existing Net/2 users would be strongly encouraged to switch. This included FreeBSD, and the project was given until the end of July 1994 to stop shipping its own Net/2 based product. Under the terms of that agreement, the project was allowed one last release before the deadline, that release being FreeBSD 1.1.5.1.

FreeBSD then set about the arduous task of literally re-inventing itself from a completely new and rather incomplete set of 4.4BSD-Lite bits. The "Lite" releases were light in part because Berkeley's CSRG had removed large chunks of code required for actually constructing a bootable running system (due to various legal requirements) and the fact that the Intel port of 4.4 was highly incomplete. It took the project until November of 1994 to make this transition, at which point it released FreeBSD 2.0 to the net and on CDROM (in late December). Despite being still more than a little rough around the edges, the release was a significant success and was followed by the more robust and easier to install FreeBSD 2.0.5 release in June of 1995.

We released FreeBSD 2.1.5 in August of 1996, and it appeared to be popular enough among the ISP and commercial communities that another release along the 2.1-STABLE branch was merited. This was FreeBSD 2.1.7.1, released in February 1997 and capping the end of mainstream development on 2.1-STABLE. Now in maintenance mode, only security enhancements and other critical bug fixes will be done on this branch (RELENG_2_1_0).

FreeBSD 2.2 was branched from the development mainline ("-CURRENT") in November 1996 as the RELENG_2_2 branch, and the first full release (2.2.1) was released in April 1997. Further releases along the 2.2 branch were done in the summer and fall of '97, the last of which (2.2.8) appeared in November 1998. The first official 3.0 release appeared in October 1998 and spelled the beginning of the end for the 2.2 branch.

The tree branched again on Jan 20, 1999, leading to the 4.0-CURRENT and 3.X-STABLE branches. From 3.X-STABLE, 3.1 was released on February 15, 1999, 3.2 on May 15, 1999, 3.3 on September 16, 1999, 3.4 on December 20, 1999, and 3.5 on June 24, 2000, which was followed a few days later by a minor point release update to 3.5.1, to incorporate some last-minute security fixes to Kerberos. This will be the final release in the 3.X branch.

There was another branch on March 13, 2000, which saw the emergence of the 4.X-STABLE branch, now considered to be the "current -stable branch". There have been several releases from it so far: 4.0-RELEASE came out in March 2000, 4.1 was released in July 2000, 4.2 in November 2000, 4.3 in April 2001, and 4.4 in September 2001. There will be more releases along the 4.X-stable (RELENG_4) branch well into 2002.

Long-term development projects continue to take place in the 5.0-CURRENT (trunk) branch, and SNAPshot releases of 5.0 on CDROM (and, of course, on the net) are continually made available from the snapshot server as work progresses[1].

1.3.2 FreeBSD Project Goals

The goals of the FreeBSD Project are to provide software that may be used for any purpose and without strings attached. Many of us have a significant investment in the code (and project) and would certainly not mind a little financial compensation now and then, but we are definitely not prepared to insist on it. We believe that our first and foremost "mission" is to provide code to any and all comers, and for whatever purpose, so that the code gets the widest

---

1. Snapshot releases may be downloaded from *ftp://current.freebsd.org/pub/FreeBSD/snapshots*

possible use and provides the widest possible benefit. This is, I believe, one of the most fundamental goals of Free Software and one that we enthusiastically support.

That code in our source tree which falls under the GNU General Public License (GPL) or Lesser General Public License (LGPL) comes with slightly more strings attached, though at least on the side of enforced access rather than the usual opposite. Due to the additional complexities that can evolve in the commercial use of GPL software we do, however, prefer software submitted under the more relaxed BSD copyright when it is a reasonable option to do so.

1.3.3 The FreeBSD Development Model

The development of FreeBSD is a very open and flexible process, FreeBSD being literally built from the contributions of thousands of people around the world, as can be seen from our our list of contributors[2]. We are constantly on the lookout for new developers and ideas, and those interested in becoming more closely involved with the project need simply contact us at the FreeBSD technical discussions mailing list `<freebsd-hackers@FreeBSD.org>`. The FreeBSD announcements mailing list `<freebsd-announce@FreeBSD.org>` is also available to those wishing to make other FreeBSD users aware of major areas of work.

Useful things to know about the FreeBSD project and its development process, whether working independently or in close cooperation:

The CVS repository

> The central source tree for FreeBSD is maintained by CVS [3] (Concurrent Versions System), a freely available source code control tool that comes bundled with FreeBSD. The primary CVS repository resides on a machine in Santa Clara CA, USA from where it is replicated to numerous mirror machines throughout the world. The CVS tree, as well as the -CURRENT and -STABLE trees which are checked out of it, can be easily replicated to your own machine as well. Please refer to Section 19.3 for more information about using the FreeBSD CVS repository.

The committers list

> The *committers* are the people who have *write* access to the CVS tree, and are thus authorized to make modifications to the FreeBSD source (the term "committer" comes from the cvs(1) `commit` command, which is used to bring new changes into the CVS repository). The best way of making submissions for review by the committers list is to use the send-pr(1) command, though if something appears to be jammed in the system then you may also reach them by sending mail to `<cvs-committers@FreeBSD.org>`.

The FreeBSD core team

> The *FreeBSD core team* would be equivalent to the board of directors if the FreeBSD Project were a company. The primary task of the core team is to make sure the project, as a whole, is in good shape and is heading in the right directions. Inviting dedicated and responsible developers to join our group of committers is one of the functions of the core team, as is the recruitment of new core team members as others move on. The current core team was elected from a pool of committer candidates in October 2000. Elections are held every 2 years.

---

2. For a partial list of the many thousands of individuals and organizations that have helped to create FreeBSD, please see *http://www.FreeBSD.org/doc/en_US.ISO8859-1/articles/contributors/index.html*
3. The BSD community pioneered the previously unheard of idea of allowing everyday users access to the source code repository. Previously, commit logs were considered a closely guarded secret even by otherwise open-source projects.

Some core team members also have specific areas of responsibility, meaning that they are committed to ensuring that some large portion of the system works as advertised. For a complete list of FreeBSD developers and their areas of responsibility, please see the *FreeBSD Contributors List*

> **Note:** Most members of the core team are volunteers when it comes to FreeBSD development and do not benefit from the project financially, so "commitment" should also not be misconstrued as meaning "guaranteed support." The "board of directors" analogy above is not actually very accurate, and it may be more suitable to say that these are the people who gave up their lives in favor of FreeBSD against their better judgment!

Outside contributors

Last, but definitely not least, the largest group of developers are the users themselves who provide feedback and bug fixes to us on an almost constant basis. The primary way of keeping in touch with FreeBSD's more non-centralized development is to subscribe to the FreeBSD technical discussions mailing list <freebsd-hackers@FreeBSD.org> (see Section C.1) where such things are discussed.

Providing code is not the only way of contributing to the project; for a more complete list of things that need doing, please refer to the FreeBSD Project web site[2].

In summary, our development model is organized as a loose set of concentric circles. The centralized model is designed for the convenience of the *users* of FreeBSD, who are thereby provided with an easy way of tracking one central code base, not to keep potential contributors out! Our desire is to present a stable operating system with a large set of coherent application programs (Chapter 4) that the users can easily install and use, and this model works very well in accomplishing that.

All we ask of those who would join us as FreeBSD developers is some of the same dedication its current people have to its continued success!

1.3.4 The Current FreeBSD Release

FreeBSD is a freely available, full source 4.4BSD-Lite based release for Intel i386, i486, Pentium, Pentium Pro, Celeron, Pentium II, Pentium III (or compatible) and DEC Alpha based computer systems. It is based primarily on software from U.C. Berkeley's CSRG group, with some enhancements from NetBSD, OpenBSD, 386BSD, and the Free Software Foundation.

Since our release of FreeBSD 2.0 in late 94, the performance, feature set, and stability of FreeBSD has improved dramatically. The largest change is a revamped virtual memory system with a merged VM/file buffer cache that not only increases performance, but also reduces FreeBSD's memory footprint, making a 5MB configuration a more acceptable minimum. Other enhancements include full NIS client and server support, transaction TCP support, dial-on-demand PPP, integrated DHCP support, an improved SCSI subsystem, ISDN support, support for ATM, FDDI, Fast

---

2 http://www.FreeBSD.org

and Gigabit Ethernet (1000Mbit) adapters, improved support for the latest Adaptec controllers, and many hundreds of bug fixes.

We have also taken the comments and suggestions of many of our users to heart and have attempted to provide what we hope is a more sane and easily understood installation process. Your feedback on this (constantly evolving) process is especially welcome!

In addition to the base distributions, FreeBSD offers a ported software collection with thousands of commonly sought-after programs. At the time of this printing, there were over 5,900 ports! The list of ports ranges from http (WWW) servers, to games, languages, editors, and almost everything in between. The entire ports collection requires approximately 100MB of storage, all ports being expressed as "deltas" to their original sources. This makes it much easier for us to update ports, and greatly reduces the disk space demands made by the older 1.0 ports collection. To compile a port, you simply change to the directory of the program you wish to install, type `make install`, and let the system do the rest. The full original distribution for each port you build is retrieved dynamically off the CDROM or a local FTP site, so you need only enough disk space to build the ports you want. Almost every port is also provided as a pre-compiled "package", which can be installed with a simple command (`pkg_add`) by those who do not wish to compile their own ports from source.

A number of additional documents which you may find very helpful in the process of installing and using FreeBSD may now also be found in the `/usr/share/doc` directory on any machine running FreeBSD. You may view the locally installed manuals with any HTML capable browser using the following local URLs:

The FreeBSD Handbook

> *file://localhost/usr/share/doc/handbook/index.html*

The FreeBSD FAQ

> *file://localhost/usr/share/doc/faq/index.html*

You can also view the master (and most frequently updated) copies at `http://www.FreeBSD.org/`.

Chapter 2
Installing FreeBSD

2.1 Synopsis

FreeBSD is provided with a text-based, easy to use installation program called **Sysinstall**. This is the default installation program for FreeBSD, although vendors are free to provide their own installation suite if they wish. This chapter describes how to use **Sysinstall** to install FreeBSD.

After reading this chapter, you will know:

- How to create the FreeBSD installation disks.
- How FreeBSD refers to, and subdivides, your hard disks.
- How to start **Sysinstall**.
- The questions **Sysinstall** will ask you, what they mean, and how to answer them.

Before reading this chapter, you should:

- Read the supported hardware list that shipped with the version of FreeBSD you are installing, and verify that your hardware is supported.

> **Note:** In general, these installation instructions are written for i386 ("PC compatible") architecture computers. Where applicable, instructions specific to other platforms (for example, Alpha) will be listed.

2.2 Pre-installation Tasks

2.2.1 Inventory Your Computer

Before installing FreeBSD you should attempt to inventory the components in your computer. The FreeBSD installation routines will show you the components (hard disks, network cards, CDROM drives, and so forth) with their model number and manufacturer. FreeBSD will also attempt to determine the correct configuration for these devices, which includes information about IRQ and IO port usage. Due to the vagaries of PC hardware this process is not always completely successful, and you may need to correct FreeBSD's determination of your configuration.

If you already have another operating system installed, such as Windows or Linux, it is a good idea to use the facilities provided by those operating systems to see how your hardware is already configured. If you are really not sure what settings an expansion card is using, you may find it printed on the card itself. Popular IRQ numbers are 3, 5, and 7, and IO port addresses are normally written as hexadecimal numbers, such as 0x330.

We recommend you print or write down this information before installing FreeBSD. It may help to use a table, like this:

Table 2-1. Sample Device Inventory

Device Name	IRQ	IO port(s)	Notes
First hard disk	N/A	N/A	4GB, made by Seagate, first IDE master
CDROM	N/A	N/A	First IDE slave
Second hard disk	N/A	N/A	2GB, made by IBM, second IDE master
First IDE controller	14	0x1f0	
Network card	N/A	N/A	Intel 10/100
Modem	N/A	N/A	3Com 56K faxmodem, on COM1:

. . .

2.2.2 Backup Your Data

If the computer you will be installing FreeBSD on contains valuable data then ensure you have it backed up, and that you have tested the backups before installing FreeBSD. The FreeBSD installation routine will prompt you several times before writing any data to your disk, but once that process has started it cannot be undone.

2.2.3 Decide Where to Install FreeBSD

If you want FreeBSD to use all your disk, then there is nothing more to concern yourself with at this point — you can skip to the next section.

However, if you need FreeBSD to co-exist with other operating systems then you need to have a rough understanding of how data is laid out on the disk, and how this affects you.

Disk Layouts for the i386

A PC disk can be divided in to discrete chunks. These chunks are called *partitions*. By design, the PC only supports four partitions per disk. These partitions are called *primary partitions*. To work around this limitation and allow more than four partitions, a new partition type was created, the *extended partition*. A disk may contain only one extended partition. Special partitions, called *logical partitions*, can be created inside this extended partition.

Each partition has a *partition ID*, which is a number used to identify the type of data on the partition. FreeBSD partitions have the partition ID 165.

In general, each operating system that you use will identify partitions in a particular way. For example, DOS, and its descendants, like Windows, assign each primary and logical partition a *drive letter*, starting with C:.

FreeBSD must be installed into a primary partition. FreeBSD can keep all its data, including any files that you create, on this one partition. However, if you have multiple disks, then you can create a FreeBSD partition on all, or some, of them. When you install FreeBSD, you must have one partition available. This might be a blank partition that you have prepared, or it might be an existing partition that contains data that you no longer care about.

If you are already using all the partitions on all your disks, then you will have to free one of them for FreeBSD using the tools provided by the other operating systems you use (e.g., fdisk on DOS or Windows).

If you have a spare partition then you can use that. However, you may need to shrink one or more of your existing partitions first.

A minimal installation of FreeBSD takes as little as 100MB of disk space. However, that is a *very* minimal install, leaving almost no space for your own files. A more realistic minimum is 250MB without a graphical environment, and 350MB or more if you want a graphical user interface. If you intend to install a lot of third party software as well, then you will need more space.

You can use a commercial tool such as **Partition Magic** to resize your partitions to make space for FreeBSD. The tools directory on the CDROM contains two free software tools which can carry out this task, **FIPS** and **PResizer**. Documentation for both of these is in the same directory.

> **Warning:** Incorrect use of these tools can delete the data on your disk. Be sure that you have recent, working backups before using them.

Example 2-1. Using an existing partition unchanged

Suppose that you have a computer with a single 4GB disk that already has a version of Windows installed, and you have split the disk in to two drive letters, C: and D:, each of which is 2GB in size. You have 1GB of data on C:, and 0.5GB of data on D:.

This means that your disk has two partitions on it, one per drive letter. You can copy all your existing data from D: to C:, which will free up the second partition, ready for FreeBSD.

Example 2-2. Shrinking an existing partition

Suppose that you have a computer with a single 4GB disk, that already has a version of Windows installed. When you installed Windows you created one large partition, giving you a C: drive that is 4GB in size. You are currently using 1.5GB of space, and want FreeBSD to have 2GB of space.

In order to install FreeBSD you will need to either:

1. Backup your Windows data, and then reinstall Windows, asking for a 2GB partition at install time.

2. Use one of the tools such as **Partition Magic**, described above, to shrink your Windows partition.

Disk Layouts for the Alpha

You will need a dedicated disk for FreeBSD on the Alpha. It is not possible to share a disk with another operating system at this time. Depending on the specific Alpha machine you have, this disk can either be a SCSI disk or an IDE disk, as long as your machine is capable of booting from it.

Following the conventions of the Digital / Compaq manuals all SRM input is shown in uppercase. SRM is case insensitive.

To find the names and types of disks in your machine, use the SHOW DEVICE command from the SRM console prompt:

```
>>>show device
dka0.0.0.4.0          DKA0        TOSHIBA CD-ROM XM-57  3476
dkc0.0.0.1009.0       DKC0               RZ1BB-BS       0658
dkc100.1.0.1009.0     DKC100        SEAGATE ST34501W    0015
dva0.0.0.0.1          DVA0
ewa0.0.0.3.0          EWA0          00-00-F8-75-6D-01
pkc0.7.0.1009.0       PKC0              SCSI Bus ID 7   5.27
pqa0.0.0.4.0          PQA0                PCI EIDE
pqb0.0.1.4.0          PQB0                PCI EIDE
```

This example is from a Digital Personal Workstation 433au and shows three disks attached to the machine. The first is a CDROM drive called DKA0 and the other two are disks and are called DKC0 and DKC100 respectively.

Disks with names of the form DKx are SCSI disks. For example DKA100 refers to a SCSI with SCSI target ID 1 on the first SCSI bus (A), whereas DKC300 refers to a SCSI disk with SCSI ID 3 on the third SCSI bus (C). Devicename PKx refers to the SCSI host bus adapter. As seen in the SHOW DEVICE output SCSI CDROM drives are treated as any other SCSI hard disk drive.

IDE disks have names similar to DQx, while PQx is the associated IDE controller.

2.2.4 Collect Your Network Configuration Details

If you intend to connect to a network as part of your FreeBSD installation (for example, if you will be installing from an FTP site, or an NFS server), then you need to know your network configuration. You will be prompted for this information during the installation so that FreeBSD can connect to the network to complete the install.

Connecting to an Ethernet Network, or Cable/DSL Modem

If you connect to an Ethernet network, or you have an Internet connection via cable or DSL, then you will need the following information:

1. IP address.

2. IP address of the default gateway.

3. Hostname.

4. DNS server IP addresses.

If you do not know this information, then ask your system administrator or service provider. They may say that this information is assigned automatically, using *DHCP*. If so, make a note of this.

Connecting Using a Modem

If you dial up to an ISP using a regular modem then you can still install FreeBSD over the Internet, it will just take a very long time.

You will need to know:

1. The phone number to dial for your ISP.

2. The COM: port your modem is connected to.

3. The username and password for your ISP account.

2.2.5 Check for FreeBSD Errata

Although the FreeBSD project strives to ensure that each release of FreeBSD is as stable as possible, bugs do occasionally creep in to the process. On very rare occasions those bugs affect the installation process. As these problems are discovered and fixed they are noted in the FreeBSD Errata, posted on the FreeBSD web site. You should check the errata before installing to make sure that there are no late-breaking problems which you should be aware of.

Information about all the releases, including the errata for each release, can be found on the release information[1] section of the FreeBSD web site[2].

2.2.6 Prepare the Boot Discs

FreeBSD can be installed from a number of different media; CDROM, DVD, FTP (both anonymous and non-anonymous), NFS, tape, or an existing MS-DOS partition.

> **Tip:** If you have FreeBSD on CDROM or DVD, and your computer allows you to boot from the CDROM or DVD (typically a BIOS option called "Boot Order" or similar) then you can skip this section. The FreeBSD CDROM and DVD images are bootable and can be used to install FreeBSD without any other special preparation.

The FreeBSD installation process is started by booting your computer into the FreeBSD installer—it is not a program you run within another operating system. To do this, you must create some floppy disks that can be booted from, and then boot from them.

If you are *not* installing directly from CDROM, DVD, or FTP then you are probably preparing your own installation media (e.g., an MS-DOS partition), which must be prepared before you install FreeBSD. This is a slightly more

---

1 http://www.FreeBSD.org/releases/index.html
2 http://www.FreeBSD.org/

advanced, infrequent activity, and is documented in Section 2.13. This includes the scenario where you want to create your own FTP site on your own network so that other computers can use your site as a FreeBSD FTP installation site.

In general, to create boot floppy images, follow these steps:

1. Acquire the Boot Floppy Images

   The boot discs are available on your installation media in the floppies directory, and can also be downloaded from the `floppies`[3] directory of the FreeBSD FTP sites.

   The floppy images have a `.flp` extension. The `floppies/` directory contains a number of different images, and the ones you will need to use depends on the version of FreeBSD you are installing, and in some cases, the hardware you are installing to. In most cases you will need two files, `kern.flp` and `mfsroot.flp`, but check `README.TXT` in the same directory to be sure.

   > **Important:** Your FTP program must use *binary mode* to download these disk images. Some web browsers have been known to use *text* (or *ASCII*) mode, which will be apparent if you cannot boot from the disks.

2. Prepare the Floppy Disks

   You must prepare one floppy disk per image file you had to download. It is imperative that these disks are free from defects. The easiest way to test this is to format the disks for yourself. Do not trust pre-formatted floppies.

   > **Important:** If you try to install FreeBSD and the installation program crashes, freezes, or otherwise misbehaves, one of the first things to suspect is the floppies. Try writing the floppy image files to some other disks and try again.

3. Write the Image Files to the Floppy Disks.

   The `.flp` files are *not* regular files you copy to the disk. Instead, they are images of the complete contents of the disk. This means that you *cannot* use commands like DOS' `copy` to write the files. Instead, you must use specific tools to write the images directly to the disk.

   If you are creating the floppies on a computer running DOS/Windows, then we provide a tool to do this called `fdimage`.

   If you are using the floppies from the CDROM, and your CDROM is the `E:` drive, then you would run this:

   ```
   E:\> tools\fdimage floppies\kern.flp A:
   ```

   Repeat this command for each `.flp` file, replacing the floppy disk each time, being sure to label the disks with the name of the file that you copied to them. Adjust the command line as necessary, depending on where you have placed the `.flp` files. If you do not have the CDROM, then `fdimage` can be downloaded from the `tools` directory[4] on the FreeBSD FTP site.

   If you are writing the floppies on a Unix system (such as another FreeBSD system) you can use the dd(1) command to write the image files directly to disk. On FreeBSD, you would run:

   ---

   3 ftp://ftp.FreeBSD.org/pub/FreeBSD/releases/i386/4.4-RELEASE/floppies/
   4 ftp://ftp.FreeBSD.org/pub/FreeBSD/tools/

```
# dd if=kern.flp of=/dev/fd0
```

On FreeBSD, /dev/fd0 refers to the first floppy disk (the A: drive). /dev/fd1 would be the B: drive, and so on. Other Unix variants might have different names for the floppy disk devices, and you will need to check the documentation for the system as necessary.

You are now ready to start installing FreeBSD.

2.3 Starting the Installation

Important: By default, the installation will not make any changes to your disk(s) until you see the following message.

```
Last Chance: Are you SURE your want continue the installation?

If you're running this on a disk with data you wish to save then WE
STRONGLY ENCOURAGE YOU TO MAKE PROPER BACKUPS before proceeding!

We can take no responsibility for lost disk contents!
```

The install can be exited at any time prior to the final warning without changing the contents of the hard drive. If you are concerned that you have configured something incorrectly you can just turn the computer off before this point, and no damage will be done.

2.3.1 Booting

Booting for the i386

1. Start with your computer turned off.

2. Turn on the computer. As it starts it should display an option to enter the system set up menu, or BIOS, commonly reached by keys like **F2**, **F10**, **Del**, or **Alt+S**. Use whichever keystroke is indicated on screen. In some cases your computer may display a graphic while it starts. Typically, pressing **Esc** will dismiss the graphic and allow you to see the necessary messages.

3. Find the setting that controls which devices the system boots from. This is commonly shown as a list of devices, such as Floppy, CDROM, First Hard Disk, and so on.

   If you needed to prepare boot floppies, then make sure that the floppy disk is selected. If you are booting from the CDROM then make sure that that is selected instead. In case of doubt, you should consult the manual that came with your computer, and/or its motherboard.

   Make the change, then save and exit. The computer should now restart.

4. If you needed to prepare boot floppies, as described in Section 2.2.6 then one of them will be the first boot disc, probably the one containing `kern.flp`. Put this disc in your floppy drive.

   If you are booting from CDROM, then you will need to turn on the computer, and insert the CDROM at the first opportunity.

   If your computer starts up as normal, and loads your existing operating system then either:

   1. The disks were not inserted early enough in the boot process. Leave them in, and try restarting your computer.

   2. The BIOS changes earlier did not work correctly. You should redo that step until you get the right option.

5. FreeBSD will start to boot. If you are booting from CDROM you will see a display similar to this:

   ```
   Verifying DMI Pool Data .......
   Boot from ATAPI CD-ROM :
    1. FD 2.88MB  System Type-(00)
   /boot.config: -P
   Keyboard: yes
   BTX loader 1.00 BTX version is 1.01
   Console: internal video/keyboard
   BIOS drive A: is disk0
   BIOS drive B: is disk1
   BIOS drive C: is disk2
   BIOS drive C: is disk3
   BIOS 639kB/64512kB available memory
   FreeBSD/i386 bootstrap loader, Revision 0.8
   (jkh@bento.freebsd.org, Mon Nov 20 11:41:23 GMT 2000)
   |
   Hit [Enter] to boot immediately, or any other key for command prompt.
   Booting [kernel] in 9 seconds... _
   ```

   If you are booting from floppy disc, you will see a display similar to this:

   ```
   Verifying DMI Pool Data .......

   BTX loader 1.00  BTX version is 1.01
   Console: internal video/keyboard
   BIOS drive A: is disk0
   BIOS drive C: is disk1
   BIOS 639kB/261120kB available memory

   FreeBSD/i386 bootstrap loader, Revision 0.8
    (jkh@narf.osd.bsdi.com, Sat Apr 21 08:46:19 GMT 2001)
   /kernel text=0x24f1bb data=0x307ac+0x2062c |

   Please insert MFS root floppy and press enter:
   ```

   Follow these instructions by removing the `kern.flp` disc, insert the `mfsroot.flp` disc, and press **Enter**.

6. Irrespective of whether you booted from floppy or CDROM, the boot process will then get to this point.

   ```
   Hit [Enter] to boot immediately, or any other key for command prompt.
   Booting [kernel] in 9 seconds... _
   ```

Either wait ten seconds, or press **Enter**. This will then launch the kernel configuration menu.

Booting for the Alpha

1. Start with your computer turned off.

2. Turn on the computer and wait for a boot monitor prompt.

3. If you needed to prepare boot floppies, as described in Section 2.2.6 then one of them will be the first boot disc, probably the one containing `kern.flp`. Put this disc in your floppy drive and type the following command to boot the disk (substituting the name of your floppy drive if necessary):

   ```
   >>>BOOT DVA0 -FLAGS " -FILE "
   ```

   If you are booting from CDROM, insert the CDROM into the drive and type the following command to start the installation (substituting the name of the appropriate CDROM drive if necessary):

   ```
   >>>BOOT DKA0 -FLAGS " -FILE "
   ```

4. FreeBSD will start to boot. If you are booting from a floppy disc, at some point you will see the message:

   ```
   Please insert MFS root floppy and press enter:
   ```

   Follow these instructions by removing the `kern.flp` disc, insert the `mfsroot.flp` disc, and press **Enter**.

5. Irrespective of whether you booted from floppy or CDROM, the boot process will then get to this point.

   ```
   Hit [Enter] to boot immediately, or any other key for command prompt.
   Booting [kernel] in 9 seconds... _
   ```

   Either wait ten seconds, or press **Enter**. This will then launch the kernel configuration menu.

2.3.2 Kernel Configuration

The *kernel* is the core of the operating system. It is responsible for many things, including access to all the devices you may have on your system, such as hard disks, network cards, sound cards, and so on. Each piece of hardware supported by the FreeBSD kernel has a driver associated with it. Each driver has a two or three letter name, such as sa for the SCSI sequential access driver, or sio for the Serial I/O driver (which manages COM ports).

When the kernel starts, each driver checks the system to see whether or not the hardware it supports exists on your system. If it does, then the driver configures the hardware and makes it available to the rest of the kernel.

This checking is commonly referred to as *device probing*. Unfortunately, it is not always possible to do this in a safe way. Some hardware drivers do not co-exist well together, and probing for one piece of hardware can sometimes leave another in an inconsistent state. This is a basic limitation of the design of the PC.

Many older devices are called ISA devices—as opposed to PCI devices. The ISA specification requires each device to have some information hard coded into it, typically the Interrupt Request Line number (IRQ) and IO port address that the driver uses. This information is commonly set by using physical *jumpers* on the card, or by using a DOS based utility.

This was often a source of problems, because it was not possible to have two devices that shared the same IRQ or port address.

Newer devices follow the PCI specification, which does not require this, as the devices are supposed to cooperate with the BIOS, and be told which IRQ and IO port addresses to use.

If you have any ISA devices in your computer then FreeBSD's driver for that device will need to be configured with the IRQ and port address that you have set the card to. This is why carrying out an inventory of your hardware (see Section 2.2.1) can be useful.

Unfortunately, the default IRQs and memory ports used by some drivers clash. This is because some ISA devices are shipped with IRQs or memory ports that clash. The defaults in FreeBSD's drivers are deliberately set to mirror the manufacturer's defaults, so that, out of the box, as many devices as possible will work.

This is almost never an issue when running FreeBSD day-to-day. Your computer will not normally contain two pieces of hardware that clash, because tone of them would not work (irrespective of the operating system you are using).

It becomes an issue when you are installing FreeBSD for the first time because the kernel used to carry out the install has to contain as many drivers as possible, so that many different hardware configurations can be supported. This means that some of those drivers will have conflicting configurations. The devices are probed in a strict order, and if you own a device that is probed late in the process, but conflicted with an earlier probe, then your hardware might not function or be probed correctly when you install FreeBSD.

Because of this, the first thing you have the opportunity to do when installing FreeBSD is look at the list of drivers that are configured in to the kernel, and either disable some of them, if you do not own that device, or confirm (and alter) the driver's configuration if you do own the device but the defaults are wrong.

This probably sounds much more complicated than it actually is.

Figure 2-1 shows the first kernel configuration menu. We recommend that you choose the Start kernel configuration in full-screen visual mode option, as it presents the easiest interface for the new user.

Figure 2-1. Kernel Configuration Menu

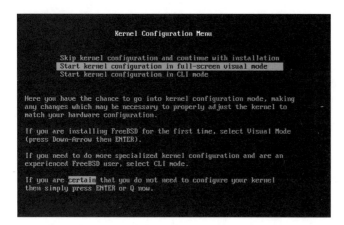

The kernel configuration screen (Figure 2-2) is then divided into four sections.

1. A collapsible list of all the drivers that are currently marked as "active", subdivided in to groups such as Storage, and Network. Each driver is shown as a description, its two three letter driver name, and the IRQ and memory port used by that driver. In addition, if an active driver conflicts with another active driver then CONF is shown next to the driver name. This section also shows the total number of conflicting drivers that are currently active.

2. Drivers that have been marked inactive. They remain in the kernel, but they will not probe for their device when the kernel starts. These are subdivided in to groups in the same way as the active driver list.

3. More detail about the currently selected driver, including its IRQ and memory port address.

4. Information about the keystrokes that are valid at this point in time.

Figure 2-2. The Kernel Device Configuration Visual Interface

At this point there will always be conflicts listed. Do not worry about this, it is to be expected; all the drivers are enabled, and as has already been explained, some of them will conflict with one another.

You now have to work through the list of drivers, resolving the conflicts.

Resolving Driver Conflicts

1. Press **X**. This will completely expand the list of drivers, so you can see all of them. You will need to use the arrow keys to scroll back and forth through the active driver list.

   Figure 2-3 shows the result of pressing **X**.

Figure 2-3. Expanded Driver List

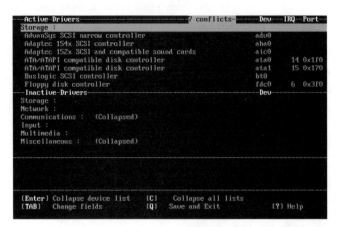

2. Disable all the drivers for devices that you do not have. To disable a driver, highlight it with the arrow keys and press **Del**. The driver will be moved to the Inactive Drivers list.

    If you inadvertently disable a device that you need then press **Tab** to switch to the Inactive Drivers list, select the driver that you disabled, and press **Enter** to move it back to the active list.

    > **Important:** Do not disable sc0. This controls the screen, and you will need this unless you are installing over a serial cable.

    > **Important:** Only disable atkbd0 if you are using a USB keyboard. If you have a normal keyboard then you must keep atkbd0.

3. If there are no conflicts listed then you can skip this step. Otherwise, the remaining conflicts need to be examined. If they do not have the indication of an "allowed conflict" in the message area, then either the IRQ/address for device probe will need to be changed, *or* the IRQ/address on the hardware will need to be changed.

    To change the driver's configuration for IRQ and IO port address, select the device and press **Enter**. The cursor will move to the third section of the screen, and you can change the values. You should enter the values for IRQ and port address that you discovered when you made your hardware inventory. Press **Q** to finish editing the device's configuration and return to the active driver list.

    If you are not sure what these figures should be then you can try using -1. Some FreeBSD drivers can safely probe the hardware to discover what the correct value should be, and a value of -1 configures them to do this.

    The procedure for changing the address on the hardware varies from device to device. For some devices you may need to physically remove the card from your computer and adjust jumper settings or DIP switches. Other cards may have come with a DOS floppy that contains the programs used to reconfigure the card. In any case, you should refer to the documentation that came with the device. This will obviously entail restarting your computer, so you will need to boot back in to the FreeBSD installation routine when you have reconfigured the card.

4. When all the conflicts have been resolved the screen will look similar to Figure 2-4.

Figure 2-4. Driver Configuration With No Conflicts

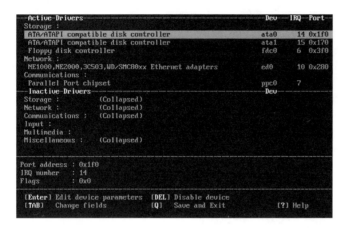

As you can see, the active driver list is now much smaller, with only drivers for the hardware that actually exists being listed.

You can now save these changes, and move on to the next step of the install. Press **Q** to quit the device configuration interface. This message will appear.

```
Save these parameters before exiting? ([Y]es/[N]o/[C]ancel)
```

Answer **Y** to save the parameters and the probing will start. After displaying the probe results in white on black text **Sysinstall** will start and display its main menu (Figure 2-5).

Figure 2-5. Sysinstall Main Menu

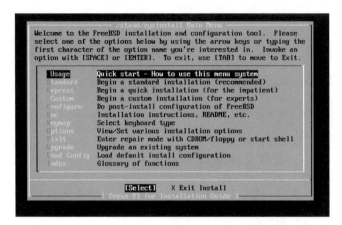

2.3.3 Reviewing the Device Probe Results

The last few hundred lines that have been displayed on screen are stored and can be reviewed.

To review the buffer, press **Scroll Lock**. This turns on scrolling in the display. You can then use the arrow keys, or **PageUp** and **PageDown** to view the results. Press **Scroll Lock** again to stop scrolling,

Do this now, to review the text that scrolled off the screen when the kernel was carrying out the device probes. You will see text similar to Figure 2-6, although the precise text will differ depending on the devices that you have in your computer.

Figure 2-6. Typical Device Probe Results

```
avail memory = 58880000 (57500K bytes)
Preloaded elf kernel "kernel" at 0xc065d000.
md1: Malloc disk
npx0: <math processor> on motherboard
npx0: INT 16 interface
pcib0: <Host to PCI bridge> on motherboard
pci0: <PCI bus> on pcib0
pcib1: <VIA 82C598MVP (Apollo MVP3) PCI-PCI (AGP bridge> at device 1.0 on pci0
pci1: <PCI bus> on pcib1
pci1: <Matrox MGA G200 AGP graphics accelerator> at 0.0 irq 11
isab0: <VIA 82C586 PCI-ISA bridge> at device 7.0 on pci0
isa0: <ISA bus> on isab0
atapci0: <VIA 82C586 ATA33 controller> port 0xe000-0xe00f at device 7.1 on pci0
ata0: at 0x1f0 irq 14 on atapci0
uhci0: <VIA 83C572 USB controller> port 0xe400-0xe41f irq 10 at device 7.2 on pci0
usb0: <VIA 83C572 USB controller> on uhci0
```

```
usb0: USB revision 1.0
uhub0: VIA UHCI root hub, class 9/0, rev 1.00/1.00, addr 1
uhub0: 2 ports with 2 removable, self powered
chip1: <VIA 82C586B ACPI interface> at device 7.3 on pci0
fdc0: <NEC 72065B or clone> at port 0x3f0-0x3f5,0x3f7 irq6 drq2 on isa0
fdc0: FIFO enabled, 8 bytes threshold
fd0: <1440-KB 3.5" drive> on fdc0 drive 0
atkbdc0: <keyboard controller (i8042)> at port 0x60-0x6f on isa0
atkbd0: <AT Keyboard> flags 0x1 irq 1 on atkbdc0
kbd0 at atkbd0
psm0: <PS/2 Mouse> irq 12 on atkbdc0
psm0: model Generic PS/2 mouse, device ID 0
vga0: <Generic ISA VGA> at port 0x3c0-0c3df iomem 0xa0000-0xbffff on isa0
sc0: <System console> at flags 0x100 on isa0
sc0: VGA <16 virtual consoles, flags-0x300>
sio0 at port 0x3f8-0x3ff irq 4 flags 0x10 on isa0
sio0: type 16550A
sio1: at port 0x2f8-0x2ff irq3 on isa0
sio1: type 16550A
ppc0: <Parallel port> at port 0x378-0x37f irq 7 on isa0
ppc0: SMC-like chipset (ECP/EPP/PS2/NIBBLE) in COMPATIBLE mode
ppc0: FIFO with 16/16/15 bytes threshold
ppi0: <Parallel I/O> on ppbus0
plip0: <PLIP network interface> on ppbus0
ad0: 8063MB <IBM-DHEA-38451> [16383/16/63] at ata0-master using UDMA33
acd0: CDROM <DELTA OTC-H101/ST3 F/W by OIPD> at ata0-slave using PIO4
Mounting root from ufs:/dev/md0c
/stand/sysinstall running as init on vty0
```

Check the probe results carefully to make sure that FreeBSD found all the devices you expected. If a device was not found, then it will not be listed. If the device's driver required configuring with the IRQ and port address then you should check that you entered them correctly.

If you need to make changes to the UserConfig device probing, its easy to exit the sysinstall program and start over again. Its also a good way to become more familiar with the process.

Figure 2-7. Select Sysinstall Exit

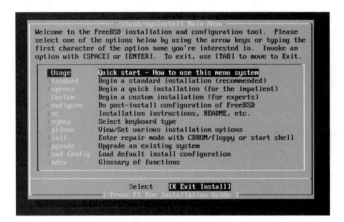

Use the arrow keys to select Exit Install from the Main Install Screen menu. The following message will display:

```
                  User Confirmation Requested
      Are you sure you wish to exit? The system will reboot
         (be sure to remove any floppies from the drives).

                        [ Yes ]     No
```

The install program will start again if the CDROM is left in the drive and [Yes] is selected.

If you are booting from floppies it will be necessary to remove the mfs.root floppy and replace it with kern.flp before rebooting.

2.4 Introducing Sysinstall

Sysinstall is the installation application provided by the FreeBSD Project. It is console based and is divided into a number of menus and screens that you can use to configure and control the installation process.

The **Sysinstall** menu system is controlled by the arrow keys, **Enter**, **Space**. and other keys. A detailed description of these keys, and what they do, is contained in **Sysinstall's** usage information.

To review this information, ensure that the Usage entry is highlighted and that the [Select] button is selected, as shown in Figure 2-8, then press **Enter**.

The instructions for using the menu system will be displayed. After reviewing them, press **Enter** to return to the Main Menu.

Figure 2-8. Selecting Usage From Sysinstall Main Menu

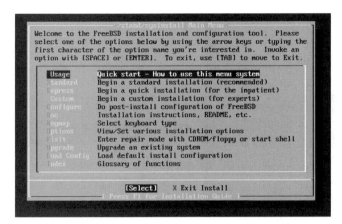

2.4.1 Selecting The Documentation Menu

From the Main Menu, select Doc with the arrow keys and press **Enter**.

Figure 2-9. Selecting Documentation Menu

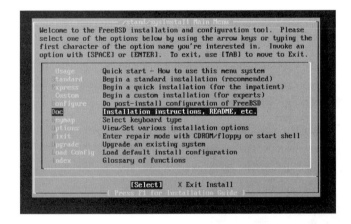

This will display the Documentation Menu.

Figure 2-10. Sysinstall Documentation Menu

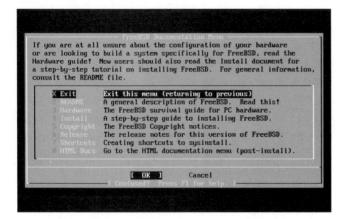

It is important to read the documents provided.

To view a document, select it with the arrow keys and press **Enter**. When finished reading a document, pressing **Enter** will return to the Documentation Menu.

To return to the Main Installation Menu, select Exit with the arrow keys and press **Enter**.

2.4.2 Selecting The Keymap Menu

To change the keyboard mapping, use the arrow keys to select Keymap from the menu and press **Enter**

Figure 2-11. Sysinstall Main Menu

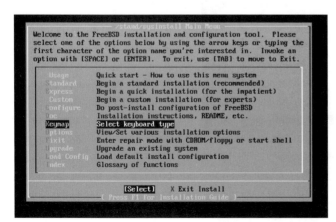

A different keyboard mapping may be chosen by selecting the menu item using up/down arrow keys and pressing **Space**. Pressing **Space** again will unselect the item. When finished, choose the [OK] using the arrow keys and press **Enter**.

Only a partial list is shown in this screen representation. Selecting [Cancel] will use the default keymap and return to the Main Install Menu.

Figure 2-12. Sysinstall Keymap Menu

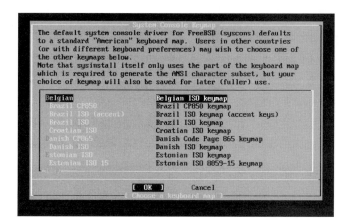

2.4.3 Installation Options Screen

Select Options and press **Enter**

Figure 2-13. Sysinstall Main Menu

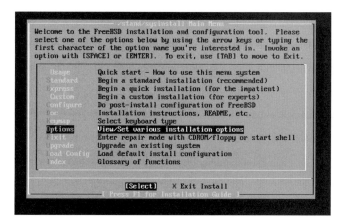

Figure 2-14. Sysinstall Options

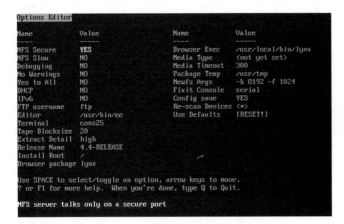

The default values are usually fine for most users and do not need to be changed.

The description of the selected item will appear at the bottom of the screen highlighted in blue. Notice that one of the options is Use Defaults to reset all values to startup defaults.

Press **F1** to read the help screen about the various options.

Pressing **Q** will return to the Main Install menu.

2.4.4 Begin A Standard Installation

The Standard installation is the option recommended for those new to Unix or FreeBSD. Use the arrow keys to select Standard and then press **Enter** to start the installation.

Figure 2-15. Begin Standard Installation

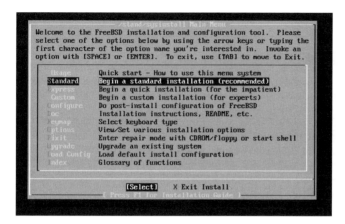

2.5 Allocating Disk Space

Your first task is to allocate disk space for FreeBSD, and label that space so that **Sysinstall** can prepare it. In order to do this you need to know how FreeBSD expects to find information on the disk.

2.5.1 BIOS Drive Numbering

Before you install and configure FreeBSD on your system, there is an important subject that you should be aware of, especially if you have multiple hard drives.

In a PC running a BIOS-dependent operating system such as MS-DOS or Microsoft Windows, the BIOS is able to abstract the normal disk drive order, and the operating system goes along with the change. This allows the user to boot from a disk drive other than the so-called "primary master". This is especially convenient for some users who have found that the simplest and cheapest way to keep a system backup is to buy an identical second hard drive, and perform routine copies of the first drive to the second drive using **Ghost** or **XCOPY** . Then, if the first drive fails, or is attacked by a virus, or is scribbled upon by an operating system defect, he can easily recover by instructing the BIOS to logically swap the drives. It is like switching the cables on the drives, but without having to open the case.

More expensive systems with SCSI controllers often include BIOS extensions which allow the SCSI drives to be re-ordered in a similar fashion for up to seven drives.

A user who is accustomed to taking advantage of these features may become surprised when the results with FreeBSD are not as expected. FreeBSD does not use the BIOS, and does not know the "logical BIOS drive mapping". This can lead to very perplexing situations, especially when drives are physically identical in geometry, and have also been made as data clones of one another.

When using FreeBSD, always restore the BIOS to natural drive numbering before installing FreeBSD, and then leave it that way. If you need to switch drives around, then do so, but do it the hard way, and open the case and move the jumpers and cables.

An Illustration from the Files of Bill and Fred's Exceptional Adventures:

Bill breaks-down an older Wintel box to make another FreeBSD box for Fred. Bill installs a single SCSI drive as SCSI unit zero and installs FreeBSD on it.

Fred begins using the system, but after several days notices that the older SCSI drive is reporting numerous soft errors and reports this fact to Bill.

After several more days, Bill decides it is time to address the situation, so he grabs an identical SCSI drive from the disk drive "archive" in the back room. An initial surface scan indicates that this drive is functioning well, so Bill installs this drive as SCSI unit four and makes an image copy from drive zero to drive four. Now that the new drive is installed and functioning nicely, Bill decides that it is a good idea to start using it, so he uses features in the SCSI BIOS to re-order the disk drives so that the system boots from SCSI unit four. FreeBSD boots and runs just fine.

Fred continues his work for several days, and soon Bill and Fred decide that it is time for a new adventure -- time to upgrade to a newer version of FreeBSD. Bill removes SCSI unit zero because it was a bit flaky and replaces it with another identical disk drive from the "archive." Bill then installs the new version of FreeBSD onto the new SCSI unit zero using Fred's magic Internet FTP floppies. The installation goes well.

Fred uses the new version of FreeBSD for a few days, and certifies that it is good enough for use in the engineering department...it is time to copy all of his work from the old version. So Fred mounts SCSI unit four (the latest copy of the older FreeBSD version). Fred is dismayed to find that none of his precious work is present on SCSI unit four.

Where did the data go?

When Bill made an image copy of the original SCSI unit zero onto SCSI unit four, unit four became the "new clone," When Bill re-ordered the SCSI BIOS so that he could boot from SCSI unit four, he was only fooling himself. FreeBSD was still running on SCSI unit zero. Making this kind of BIOS change will cause some or all of the Boot and Loader code to be fetched from the selected BIOS drive, but when the FreeBSD kernel drivers take-over, the BIOS drive numbering will be ignored, and FreeBSD will transition back to normal drive numbering. In the illustration at hand, the system continued to operate on the original SCSI unit zero, and all of Fred's data was there, not on SCSI unit four. The fact that the system appeared to be running on SCSI unit four was simply an artifact of human expectations.

We are delighted to mention that no data bytes were killed or harmed in any way by our discovery of this phenomenon. The older SCSI unit zero was retrieved from the bone pile, and all of Fred's work was returned to him, (and now Bill knows that he can count as high as zero).

Although SCSI drives were used in this illustration, the concepts apply equally to IDE drives.

2.5.2 Disk Organization

The smallest unit of organization that FreeBSD uses to find files is the filename. Filenames are case-sensitive, which means that `readme.txt` and `README.TXT` are two separate files. FreeBSD does not use the extension (`.txt`) of a file to determine whether the file is program, or a document, or some other form of data.

Files are stored in directories. A directory may contain no files, or it may contain many hundreds of files. A directory can also contain other directories, allowing you to build up a hierarchy of directories within one another. This makes it much easier to organize your data.

Files and directories are referenced by giving the file or directory name, followed by a forward slash, /, followed by any other directory names that are necessary. If you have directory `foo`, which contains directory `bar`, which contains the file `readme.txt`, then the full name, or *path* to the file is `foo/bar/readme.txt`.

Directories and files are stored in a filesystem. Each filesystem contains exactly one directory at the very top level, called the *root directory* for that filesystem. This root directory can then contain other directories.

So far this is probably similar to any other operating system you may have used. There are a few differences; for example, DOS uses \ to separate file and directory names, while MacOS uses :.

FreeBSD does not use drive letters, or other drive names in the path. You would not write `c:/foo/bar/readme.txt` on FreeBSD.

Instead, one filesystem is designated the *root filesystem*. The root filesystem's root directory is referred to as /. Every other filesystem is then *mounted* under the root filesystem. No matter how many disks you have on your FreeBSD system, every directory appears to be part of the same disk.

Suppose you have three filesystems, called A, B, and C. Each filesystem has one root directory, which contains two other directories, called A1, A2 (and likewise B1, B2 and C1, C2).

Call A the root filesystem. If you used the `ls` command to view the contents of this directory you would see two subdirectories, A1 and A2. The directory tree looks like this.

```
 /
 |
 +--- A1
 |
 '--- A2
```

A filesystem must be mounted on to a directory in another filesystem. So now suppose that you mount filesystem B on to the directory A1. The root directory of B replaces A1, and the directories in B appear accordingly.

```
 /
 |
 +--- A1
 |     |
 |     +--- B1
 |     |
 |     '--- B2
 |
 '--- A2
```

Any files that are in the B1 or B2 directories can be reached with the path /A1/B1 or /A1/B2 as necessary. Any files that were in /A1 have been temporarily hidden. They will reappear if B is *unmounted* from A.

If B had been mounted on A2 then the diagram would look like this;

```
 /
 |
```

and the paths would be /A2/B1 and /A2/B2 respectively.

Filesystems can be mounted on top of one another. Continuing the last example, the C filesystem could be mounted on top of the B1 directory in the B filesystem, leading to this arrangement.

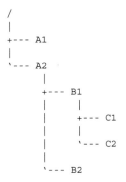

Or C could be mounted directly on to the A filesystem, under the A1 directory.

If you are familiar with DOS, this is similar, although not identical, to the join command.

This is not normally something you need to concern yourself with. Typically you create filesystems when installing FreeBSD and decide where to mount them, and then never change them unless you add a new disk.

It is entirely possible to have one large root filesystem, and not need to create any others. There are some drawbacks to this approach, and one advantage.

Benefits of multiple filesystems

- Different filesystems can have different *mount options*. For example, with careful planning, the root filesystem can be mounted read-only, making it impossible for you to inadvertently delete or edit a critical file.

- FreeBSD automatically optimizes the layout of files on a filesystem, depending on how the filesystem is being used. So a filesystem that contains many small files that are written frequently will have a different optimization to one that contains fewer, larger files. By having one big filesystem this optimization breaks down.

- FreeBSD's filesystems are very robust should you lose power. However, a power loss at a critical point could still damage the structure of the filesystem. By splitting your data over multiple filesystems it is more likely that the system will still come up, making it easier for you to restore from backup as necessary.

Benefit of a single filesystem

- Filesystems are a fixed size. If you create a filesystem when you install FreeBSD and give it a specific size, you may later discover that you need to make the partition bigger. This is not easily accomplished without backing up, recreating the filesystems with the size, and then restoring.

  Important: FreeBSD 5.0 will feature a new command, `growfs`, which will make it possible to increase the size of a filesystem on the fly, removing this limitation.

Filesystems are contained in partitions. This does not have the same meaning as the earlier usage of the term partition in this chapter, because of FreeBSD's Unix heritage. Each partition is identified by a letter, a through to h. Each partition can only contain one filesystem, which means that filesystems are often described by either their typical mount point on the root filesystem, or the letter of the partition they are contained in.

FreeBSD also uses disk space for *swap space*. Swap space provides FreeBSD with *virtual memory*. This allows your computer to behave as though it has much more memory than it actually does. When FreeBSD runs out of memory it moves some of the data that is not currently being used to the swap space, and moves it back in (moving something else out) when it needs it.

Some partitions have certain conventions associated with them.

Partition	Convention
a	Normally contains the root filesystem
b	Normally contains swap space
c	Normally the same size as the enclosing slice. This allows utilities that need to work on the entire slice (for example, a bad block scanner) to work on the c partition. You would not normally create a filesystem on this partition.
d	Partition d used to have a special meaning associated with it, although that is now gone. To this day, some tools may operate oddly if told to work on partition d, so **Sysinstall** will not normally create partition d.

Each partition-that-contains-a-filesystem is stored in what FreeBSD calls a *slice*. Slice is FreeBSD's term for what were earlier called partitions, and again, this is because of FreeBSD's Unix background. Slices are numbered, starting at 1, through to 4.

Slice numbers follow the device name, prefixed with an s, starting at 1. So "da0s*1*" is the first slice on the first SCSI drive. There can only be four physical slices on a disk, but you can have logical slices inside physical slices of the appropriate type. These extended slices are numbered starting at 5, so "ad0s*5*" is the first extended slice on a disk. These devices are used by file systems that expect to occupy a slice.

Slices, "dangerously dedicated" physical drives, and other drives contain *partitions*, which are represented as letters from a to h. This letter is appended to the device name, so "da0*a*" is the a partition on the first da drive, which is "dangerously dedicated". "ad1s3*e*" is the fifth partition in the third slice of the second IDE disk drive.

Finally, each disk on the system is identified. A disk name starts with a code that indicates the type of disk, and then a number, indicating which disk it is. Unlike slices, disk numbering starts at 0. Common codes that you will see are listed in Table 2-2.

When referring to a partition FreeBSD requires that you also name the slice and disk that contains the partition, and when referring to a slice you should also refer to the disk name. Do this by listing the disk name, s, the slice number, and then the partition letter. Examples are shown in Example 2-3.

Example 2-4 shows a conceptual model of the disk layout that should help make things clearer.

In order to install FreeBSD you must first configure the disk slices, then create partitions within the slice you will use for FreeBSD, and then create a filesystem (or swap space) in each partition, and decide where that filesystem will be mounted.

Table 2-2. Disk Device Codes

Code	Meaning
ad	ATAPI (IDE) disk
da	SCSI direct access disk
acd	ATAPI (IDE) CDROM
cd	SCSI CDROM
fd	Floppy disk

Example 2-3. Sample Disk, Slice, and Partition Names

Name	Meaning
ad0s1a	The first partition (a) on the first slice (s1) on the first IDE disk (ad0).
da1s2e	The fifth partition (e) on the second slice (s2) on the second SCSI disk (da1).

Example 2-4. Conceptual Model of a Disk

This diagram shows FreeBSD's view of the first IDE disk attached to the system. Assume that the disk is 4GB in size, and contains two 2GB slices (DOS partitions). The first slice contains a DOS disk, C:, and the second slice contains a FreeBSD installation. The FreeBSD installation has three partitions, and a swap partition.

The three partitions will each hold a filesystem. Partition a will be used for the root filesystem, e for the /var directory

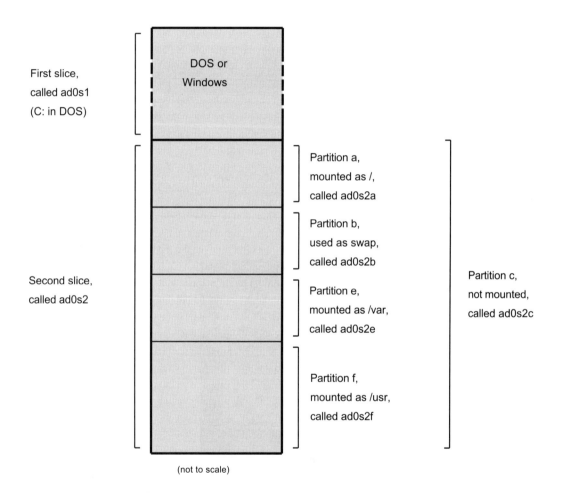

First slice,
called ad0s1
(C: in DOS)

DOS or
Windows

Second slice,
called ad0s2

Partition a,
mounted as /,
called ad0s2a

Partition b,
used as swap,
called ad0s2b

Partition e,
mounted as /var,
called ad0s2e

Partition f,
mounted as /usr,
called ad0s2f

Partition c,
not mounted,
called ad0s2c

(not to scale)

2.5.3 Creating Slices using FDisk

Note: No changes you make at this point will be written to the disk. If you think you have made a mistake and want to start again you can use the menus to exit **Sysinstall** and try again. If you get confused and can not see how to exit you can always turn your computer off.

After choosing to begin a standard installation in **Sysinstall** you will be shown this message.

```
                    Message
  In the next menu, you will need to set up a DOS-style ("fdisk")
  partitioning scheme for your hard disk. If you simply wish to devote
  all disk space to FreeBSD (overwriting anything else that might be on
  the disk(s) selected) then use the (A)ll command to select the default
  partitioning scheme followed by a (Quit. If you wish to allocate only
  free space to FreeBSD, move to a partition marked "unused" and use the
  (C)reate command.
                    [  OK  ]

             [ Press enter to continue ]
```

Press **Enter** as instructed. You will then be shown a list of all the hard drives that the kernel found when it carried out the device probes. Figure 2-16 shows an example from a system with two IDE disks. They have been called ad0 and ad2.

Figure 2-16. Select Drive for FDisk

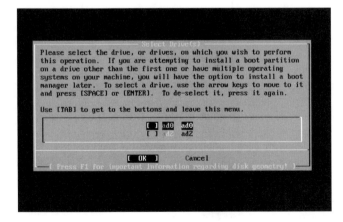

You might be wondering why ad1 is not listed here. Why has it been missed?

Consider what would happen if you had two IDE hard disks, one as the master on the first IDE controller, and one as the master on the second IDE controller. If FreeBSD numbered these as it found them, as ad0 and ad1 then everything would work.

But if you then added a third disk, as the slave device on the first IDE controller, it would now be ad1, and the previous ad1 would become ad2. Because device names (such as ad1s1a) are used to find filesystems, you may suddenly discover that some of your filesystems no longer appear correctly, and you would need to change your FreeBSD configuration.

To work around this, the kernel can be configured to name IDE disks based on where they are, and not the order in which they were found. With this scheme the master disk on the second IDE controller will *always* be ad2, even if there are no ad0 or ad1 devices.

This configuration is the default for the FreeBSD kernel, which is why this display shows ad0 and ad2. The machine on which this screenshot was taken had IDE disks on both master channels of the IDE controllers, and no disks on the slave channels.

You should select the disk on which you want to install FreeBSD, and then press [OK]. **FDisk** will start, with a display similar to that shown in Figure 2-17.

The **FDisk** display is broken in to three sections.

The first section, covering the first two lines of the display, shows details about the currently selected disk, including its FreeBSD name, the disk geometry, and the total size of the disk.

The second section shows the slices that are currently on the disk, where they start and end, how large they are, the name FreeBSD gives them, and their description and sub-type. This example shows two small unused slices, which are artifacts of disk layout schemes on the PC. It also shows one large FAT slice, which almost certainly appears as C: in DOS / Windows, and an extended slice, which may contain other drive letters for DOS / Windows.

The third section shows the commands that are available in **FDisk**.

Figure 2-17. Typical Fdisk Partitions Before Editing

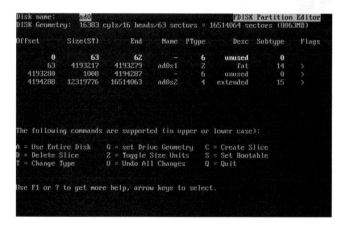

What you do now will depend on how you want to slice up your disk.

If you want to use FreeBSD for the entire disk (which will delete all the other data on this disk when you confirm that you want **Sysinstall** to continue later in the installation process) then you can press **A**, which corresponds to the Use Entire Disk option. The existing slices will be removed, and replaced with a small area flagged as unused (again, an artifact of PC disk layout), and then one large slice for FreeBSD. If you do this then you should then select the newly created FreeBSD slice using the arrow keys, and press **S** to mark the slice as being bootable. The screen will then look very similar to Figure 2-18. Note the A in the Flags column, which indicates that this slice is *active*, and will be booted from.

If you will be deleting an existing slice to make space for FreeBSD then you should select the slice using the arrow keys, and then press **D**. You can then press **C**, and be prompted for size of slice you want to create. Enter the appropriate figure and press **Enter**.

If you have already made space for FreeBSD (perhaps by using a tool such as **Partition Magic**) then you can press **C** to create a new slice. Again, you will be prompted for the size of slice you would like to create.

Figure 2-18. Fdisk Partition Using Entire Disk

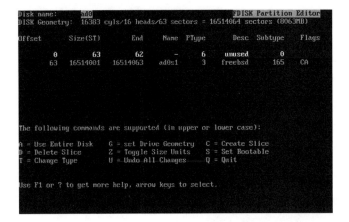

When finished, press **Q**. Your changes will be saved in **Sysinstall**, but will not yet be written to disk.

2.5.4 Install a Boot Manager

You now have the option to install a boot manager. In general, you should choose to install the FreeBSD boot manager if:

- You have more than one drive, and have installed FreeBSD onto a drive other than the first one.
- You have installed FreeBSD alongside another operating system on the same disk, and you want to choose whether to start FreeBSD or the other operating system when you start the computer.

Make your choice and press **Enter**.

Figure 2-19. Sysinstall Boot Manager Menu

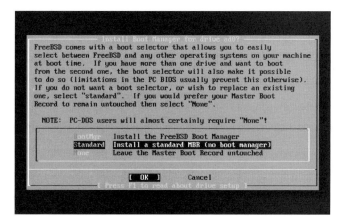

The help screen, reached by pressing **F1**, discusses the problems that can be encountered when trying to share the hard disk between operating systems.

2.5.5 Creating Slices on Another Drive

If there is more than one drive, it will return to the Select Drives screen after the boot manager selection. If you wish to install FreeBSD on to more than one disk, then you can select another disk here and repeat the slice process using **FDisk**,

Figure 2-20. Exit Select Drive

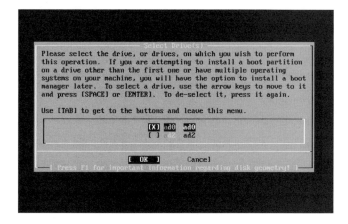

The **Tab** key toggles between the last drive selected, [OK], and [Cancel].

Press the **Tab** once to toggle to the [OK], then press **Enter** to continue with the installation.

2.5.6 Creating Partitions using Disklabel

You must now create some partitions inside each slice that you have just created. Remember that each partition is lettered, from a through to h, and that partitions b, c, and d have conventional meanings that you should adhere to.

Certain applications can benefit from particular partition schemes, especially if you are laying out partitions across more than one disk. However, for this, your first FreeBSD installation, you do not need to give too much thought to how you partition the disk. It is more important that you install FreeBSD and start learning how to use it. You can always re-install FreeBSD to change your partition scheme when you are more familiar with the operating system.

This scheme features four partitions—one for swap space, and three for filesystems.

Table 2-3. Partition Layout for First Disk

Partition	Filesystem	Size	Description
a	/	64MB	This is the root file system. Every other filesystem will be mounted somewhere under this one. 64MB is a reasonable size for this filesystem. You will not be storing too much data on it, as a regular FreeBSD install will put about 40MB of data here. The remaining space is for temporary data, and also leaves expansion space if future versions of FreeBSD need more space in /
b	N/A	2-3 x RAM	The system's swap space is kept on this partition. Choosing the right amount of swap space can be a bit of an art. A good rule of thumb is that you should have two or three times the amount of RAM as swap space. So if you have 64MB of RAM then you should have between 128MB and 196MB of swap. You should also have at least 64MB of swap, so if you have less than 32MB of RAM in your computer then set the swap amount to 64MB. If you have more than one disk then you can put swap space on each disk. FreeBSD will then use each disk for swap, which effectively speeds up the act of swapping. In this case, calculate the total amount of swap you need (e.g., 128MB), and then divide this by the number of disks you have (e.g., two disks) to give the amount of swap you should put on each disk, in this example, 64MB of swap per disk.
e	/var	50MB	The /var directory contains variable length files; log files, and other administrative files. Many of these files are read-from or written-to extensively during FreeBSD's day-to-day running. Putting these files on another filesystem allows FreeBSD to optimise the access of these files without affecting other files in other directories that do not have the same access pattern.

Partition	Filesystem	Size	Description
f	/usr	Rest of disk	All your other files will typically be stored in /usr, and its subdirectories.

If you will be installing FreeBSD on to more than one disk then you must also create partitions in the other slices that you configured. The easiest way to do this is to create two partitions on each disk, one for the swap space, and one for a filesystem.

Table 2-4. Partition Layout for Subsequent Disks

Partition	Filesystem	Size	Description
b	N/A	See description	As already discussed, you can split swap space across each disk. Even though the a partition is free, convention dictates that swap space stays on the b partition.
e	/disk*n*	Rest of disk	The rest of the disk is taken up with one big partition. This could easily be put on the a partition, instead of the e partition. However, convention says that the a partition on a slice is reserved for the filesystem that will be the root (/) filesystem. You do not have to follow this convention, but **Sysinstall** does, so following it yourself makes the installation slightly cleaner. You can choose to mount this filesystem anywhere; this example suggests that you mount them as directories /disk*n*, where *n* is a number that changes for each disk. But you can use another scheme if you prefer.

Having chosen your partition layout you can now create it using **Sysinstall**. You will see this message.

```
                              Message
      Now, you need to create BSD partitions inside of the fdisk
      partition(s) just created. If you have a reasonable amount of disk
      space (200MB or more) and don't have any special requirements, simply
      use the (A)uto command to allocate space automatically. If you have
      more specific needs or just don't care for the layout chosen by
      (A)uto, press F1 for more information on manual layout.

                             [  OK  ]
```

Press **Enter** to start the FreeBSD partition editor, called **Disklabel**.

Figure 2-21 shows the display when you first start **Disklabel**. The display is divided in to three sections.

The first few lines show the name of the disk you are currently working on, and the slice that contains the partitions you are creating (at this point **Disklabel** calls this the Partition name rather than slice name). This display also shows the amount of free space within the slice; that is, space that was set aside in the slice, but that has not yet been assigned to a partition.

The middle of the display shows the partitions that have been created, the name of the filesystem that each partition contains, their size, and some options pertaining to the creation of the filesystem.

The bottom third of the screen shows the keystrokes that are valid in **Disklabel**.

Figure 2-21. Sysinstall Disklabel Editor

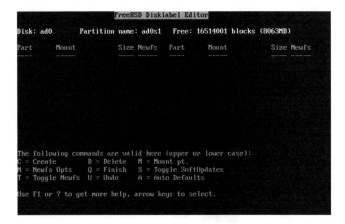

Disklabel can automatically create partitions for you and assign them default sizes. Try this now, by Pressing **A**. You will see a display similar to that shown in Figure 2-22. Depending on the size of the disk you are using the defaults may or may not be appropriate. This does not matter, as you do not have to accept the defaults.

Figure 2-22. Sysinstall Disklabel Editor With Auto Defaults

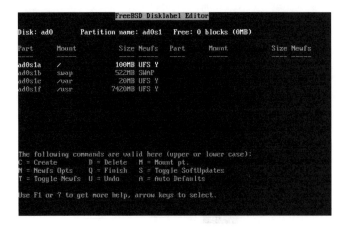

To delete the suggested partitions, and replace them with your own, use the arrow keys to select the first partition, and press **D** to delete it. Repeat this to delete all the suggested partitions.

To create the first partition (a, mounted as /), make sure the disk information at the top of the screen is selected, and press **C**. A dialog box will appear prompting you for the size of the new partition (as shown in Figure 2-23). You can enter the size as the number of disk blocks you want to use, or, more usefully, as a number followed by either M for megabytes, G for gigabytes, or C for cylinders.

Figure 2-23. Free Space For Root Partition

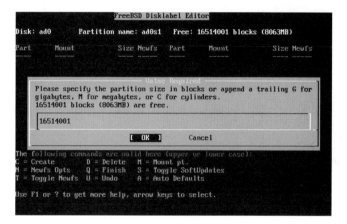

The default size shown will create a partition that takes up the rest of the slice. If you are using the partition sizes described earlier, then delete the existing figure using **Backspace**, and then type in **64M**, as shown in Figure 2-24. Then press [OK].

Figure 2-24. Edit Root Partition Size

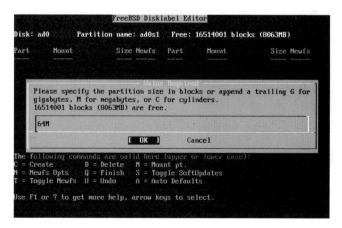

Having chosen the partition's size you will then asked whether this partition will contain a filesystem or swap space. The dialog box is shown in Figure 2-25. This first partition will contain a filesystem, so check that FS is selected and then press **Enter**.

Figure 2-25. Choose The Root Partition Type

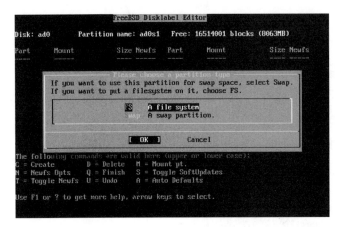

Finally, because you are creating a filesystem, you must tell **Disklabel** where the filesystem is to be mounted. The dialog box is shown in Figure 2-26. The root filesystem's mount point is /, so type /, and then press **Enter**.

Figure 2-26. Choose The Root Mount Point

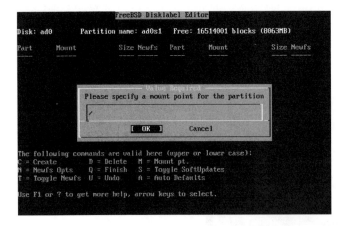

The display will then update to show you the newly created partition. You should repeat this procedure for the other partitions. When you create the swap partition you will not be prompted for the filesystem mount point, as swap partitions are never mounted. When you create the final partition, /usr, you can leave the suggested size as is, to use the rest of the slice.

Your final FreeBSD DiskLabel Editor screen will appear similar to Figure 2-27, although your values chosen may be different. Press **Q** to finish.

Figure 2-27. Sysinstall Disklabel Editor

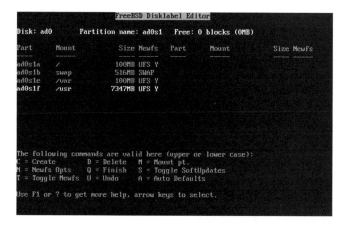

2.6 Choosing What To Install

2.6.1 Select The Distribution Set

Deciding which distribution set to install will depend largely on the intended use of the system and the amount of disk space available. The predefined options range from installing the smallest possible configuration to everything. Those who are new to Unix and/or FreeBSD should almost certainly select one of these canned options. Customizing a distribution set is typically for the more experienced user.

Press **F1** for more information on the distribution set options and what they contain. When finished reviewing the help, pressing **Enter** will return to the Select Distributions Menu.

If a graphical user interface is desired then a distribution set that is preceded by an X should be chosen. The configuration of XFree86 and selection of a default desktop is part of the post-installation steps.

The default XFree86 version installed is the 3.x branch. You should check to see whether your video card is supported at the XFree86[5] web site. If it is only supported under the 4.x branch, then you will need to install and configure XFree86 4.x after installation. Select a distribution without X and refer to Chapter 5 for more information.

If compiling a custom kernel is anticipated, select an option which includes the source code. For more information on why a custom kernel should be built or how to build a custom kernel see Chapter 9.

---

5 http://www.xfree86.org/

Obviously, the most versatile system is one that includes everything. If there is adequate disk space, select All as shown in Figure 2-28 by using the arrow keys and press **Enter**. If there is a concern about disk space consider using an option that is more suitable for the situation. Other distributions can be added after installation.

Figure 2-28. Choose Distributions

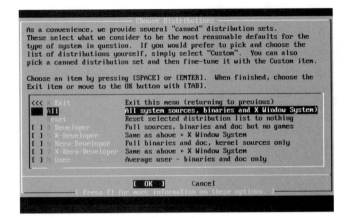

2.6.2 Installing The Ports Collection

After selecting the desired distribution, an opportunity to install the FreeBSD Ports Collection is presented. The ports collection is an easy and convenient way to install software. The ports collection does not contain the source code necessary to compile the software. It is a collection of files which automates the downloading, compiling and installation. Chapter 4 discusses how to use the ports collection.

The installation program does not check to see if you have adequate space. Select this option only if you have adequate hard disk space.

```
                   User Confirmation Requested
        Would you like to install the FreeBSD ports collection?

        This will give you ready access to over 5,900 ported software packages,
        at a cost of around 100MB of disk space when "clean" and possibly much
        more than that if a lot of the distribution tarballs are loaded
        (unless you have the extra CDs from a FreeBSD CD/DVD distribution
        available and can mount it on /cdrom, in which case this is far less
        of a problem).

        The ports collection is a very valuable resource and well worth having
        on your /usr partition, so it is advisable to say Yes to this option.

        For more information on the ports collection & the latest ports,
        visit:
```

```
http://www.freebsd.org/ports
```

```
                            [ Yes ]      No
```

Select [Yes] with the arrow keys to install the ports collection or [No] to skip this option. Press **Enter** to continue. The Choose Distributions menu will redisplay.

Figure 2-29. Confirm Distributions

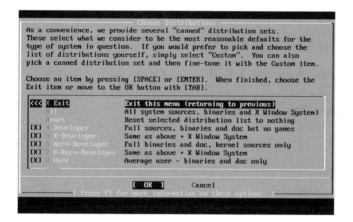

If satisfied with the options, select Exit with the arrow keys, ensure that [OK] is highlighted, and press **Enter** to continue.

2.7 Choosing Your Installation Media

If Installing from a CDROM, use the arrow keys to highlight Install from a FreeBSD CD/DVD. Ensure that [OK] is highlighted, then press **Enter** to proceed with the installation.

For other methods of installation, select the appropriate option and follow the instructions.

Press **F1** to display the Online Help for installation media. Press **Enter** to return to the media selection menu.

Figure 2-30. Choose Installation Media

FTP Installation Modes: There are three FTP installation modes you can choose from: active FTP, passive FTP, or via a HTTP proxy.

FTP Active, Install from an FTP server

> This option will make all FTP transfers use "Active" mode. This will not work through firewalls, but will often work with older FTP servers that do not support passive mode. If your connection hangs with passive mode (the default), try active!

FTP Passive, Install from an FTP server through a firewall

> This option instructs FreeBSD to use "Passive" mode for all FTP operations. This allows the user to pass through firewalls that do not allow incoming connections on random port addresses.

FTP via a HTTP proxy, Install from an FTP server through a http proxy

> This option instructs FreeBSD to use the HTTP protocol (like a web browser) to connect to a proxy for all FTP operations. The proxy will translate the requests and send them to the FTP server. This allows the user to pass through firewalls that do not allow FTP at all, but offer a HTTP proxy. In this case, you have to specify the proxy in addition to the FTP server.

For a proxy FTP server, you should usually give the name of the server you really want as a part of the username, after an "@" sign. The proxy server then "fakes" the real server. For example, assuming you want to install from `ftp.FreeBSD.org`, using the proxy FTP server `foo.example.com`, listening on port 1024.

In this case, you go to the options menu, set the FTP username to `ftp@ftp.FreeBSD.org`, and the password to your email address. As your installation media, you specify FTP (or passive FTP, if the proxy supports it), and the URL `ftp://foo.example.com:1234/pub/FreeBSD`.

Since /pub/FreeBSD from ftp.FreeBSD.org is proxied under foo.example.com, you are able to install from *that* machine (which will fetch the files from ftp.FreeBSD.org as your installation requests them).

2.8 Committing to the Installation

The installation can now proceed if desired. This is also the last chance for aborting the installation to prevent changes to the hard drive.

```
                    User Confirmation Requested
        Last Chance! Are you SURE you want to continue the installation?

        If you're running this on a disk with data you wish to save then WE
        STRONGLY ENCOURAGE YOU TO MAKE PROPER BACKUPS before proceeding!

        We can take no responsibility for lost disk contents!

                        [ Yes ]      No
```

Select [Yes] and press **Enter** to proceed.

The installation time will vary according to the distribution chosen, installation media used, and the speed of the computer. There will be a series of messages displayed indicating the status.

The installation is complete when the following message is displayed:

```
                              Message

        Congratulations! You now have FreeBSD installed on your system.

        We will now move on to the final configuration questions.
        For any option you do not wish to configure, simply select No.

        If you wish to re-enter this utility after the system is up, you may
        do so by typing: /stand/sysinstall .

                              [ OK ]

                  [  Press enter to continue  ]
```

Press **Enter** to proceed with post-installation configurations.

Selecting [No] and pressing **Enter** will abort the installation so no changes will be made to your system. The following message will appear :

```
                              Message
        Installation complete with some errors.  You may wish to scroll
        through the debugging messages on VTY1 with the scroll-lock feature.
        You can also choose "No" at the next prompt and go back into the
```

```
installation menus to try and retry whichever operations have failed.
```

[OK]

This message is generated because nothing was installed. Pressing **Enter** will return to the Main Installation Menu to exit the installation.

2.9 Post-installation

Configuration of various options follows the successful installation. An option can be configured by re-entering the configuration options before booting the new FreeBSD system or after installation using /stand/sysinstall and selecting Configure.

2.9.1 Network Device Configuration

If you previously configured PPP for an FTP install, this screen will not display and can be configured later as described above.

For detailed information on Local Area Networks and configuring FreeBSD as a gateway/router refer to the tutorial PPP- Pendantic PPP Primer[6].

```
                    User Confirmation Requested
      Would you like to configure Ethernet or SLIP/PPP network devices?

                         [ Yes ]    No
```

To configure a network device, select [Yes] and press **Enter**. Otherwise, select [No] to continue.

---

6 http://www.FreeBSD.org/tutorials/ppp/index.html

Figure 2-31. Selecting An Ethernet Device

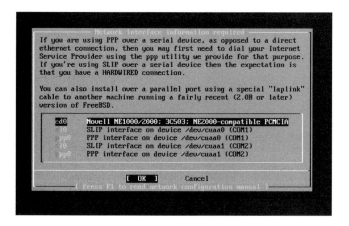

Select the interface to be configured with the arrow keys and press **Enter**.

```
                        User Confirmation Requested
              Do you want to try IPv6 configuration of the interface?

                              Yes    [ No ]
```

In this private local area network the current Internet type protocol (IPv4) was sufficient and [No] was selected with the arrow keys and **Enter** pressed.

If you want to try the new Internet protocol (IPv6), choose [Yes] and press **Enter**. It will take several seconds to scan for RA servers.

```
                        User Confirmation Requested
              Do you want to try DHCP configuration of the interface?

                              Yes    [ No ]
```

If DHCP (Dynamic Host Configuration Protocol) is not required select [No] with the arrow keys and press **Enter**.

Selecting [Yes] will execute **dhclient**, and if successful, will fill in the network configuration information automatically. Refer to Section 17.8 for more information.

The following Network Configuration screen shows the configuration of the Ethernet device for a system that will act as the gateway for a Local Area Network.

Figure 2-32. Set Network Configuration For ed0

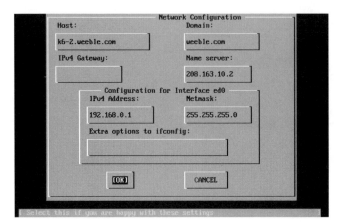

Use **Tab** to select the information fields and fill in appropriate information:

Host

The fully-qualified hostname, e.g. k6-2.example.com in this case.

Domain

The name of the domain that your machine is in, e.g. example.com for this case.

IPv4 Gateway

IP address of host forwarding packets to non-local destinations. Fill this in only if the machine is a node on the network. *Leave this field blank* if the machine is the gateway to the Internet for the network.

Name server

IP address of your local DNS server. There is no local DNS server on this private local area network so the IP address of the provider's DNS server (208.163.10.2) was used.

IPv4 address

The IP address to be used for this interface was (192.168.0.1).

Netmask

The address block being used for this local area network is a Class C block (192.168.0.0 - 192.168.255.255). The default netmask is for a Class C network (255.255.255.0).

Extra options to ifconfig

Any interface-specific options to ifconfig you would like to add. There were none in this case.

Use **Tab** to select [OK] when finished and press **Enter**.

```
                User Confirmation Requested
    Would you like to Bring Up the ed0 interface right now?

                        [ Yes ]    No
```

Choosing [Yes] and pressing **Enter** will bring the machine up on the network and be ready for use after leaving leaving the installation.

2.9.2 Configure Internet Services

```
                User Confirmation Requested
    Do you want to configure inetd and the network services that it provides?

                        Yes    [ No ]
```

If [No] is selected, various services such **telnetd** will not be enabled. This means that remote users will not be able to **telnet** into this machine. Local users will be still be able to access remote machines with **telnet**.

These services can be enabled after installation by editing /etc/inetd.conf with your favorite text editor. See Section 17.12.1 for more information.

Select [Yes] if you wish to configure these services during install. An additional confirmation will display.

```
                User Confirmation Requested
    The Internet Super Server (inetd) allows a number of simple Internet
    services to be enabled, including finger, ftp and telnetd.  Enabling
    these services may increase risk of security problems by increasing
    the exposure of your system.

    With this in mind, do you wish to enable inetd?

                        [ Yes ]    No
```

Select [Yes] to continue.

```
                User Confirmation Requested
    inetd(8) relies on its configuration file, /etc/inetd.conf, to determine
    which of its Internet services will be available.  The default FreeBSD
    inetd.conf(5) leaves all services disabled by default, so they must be
    specifically enabled in the configuration file before they will
    function, even once inetd(8) is enabled.  Note that services for
    IPv6 must be seperately enabled from IPv4 services.

    Select [Yes] now to invoke an editor on /etc/inetd.conf, or [No] to
    use the current settings.

                        [ Yes ]    No
```

Selecting [Yes] will allow adding services by deleting the # at the beginning of a line.

Figure 2-33. Editing `inetd.conf`

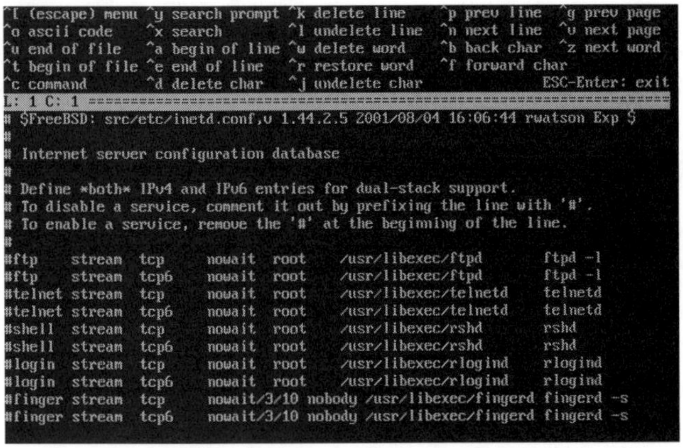

After adding the desired services, pressing **Esc** will display a menu which will allow exiting and saving the changes.

2.9.3 Configure Gateway

```
                 User Confirmation Requested
      Do you want this machine to function as a network gateway?

                      [ Yes ]    No
```

If the machine will be acting as the gateway for a local area network and forwarding packets between other machines then select [Yes] and press **Enter**. If the machine is a node on a network then select [No] and press **Enter** to continue.

2.9.4 Anonymous FTP

```
                 User Confirmation Requested
      Do you want to have anonymous FTP access to this machine?

                      Yes    [ No ]
```

Deny Anonymous FTP

Selecting the default [No] and pressing **Enter** will still allow users who have accounts with passwords to use FTP to access the machine.

Allow Anonymous FTP

Anyone can access your machine if you elect to allow anonymous FTP connections. The security implications should be considered before enabling this option. For more information about security see Chapter 10.

To allow anonymous FTP, use the arrow keys to select [Yes] and press **Enter**. The following screens (or similar) will display :

Figure 2-34. Default Anonymous FTP Configuration

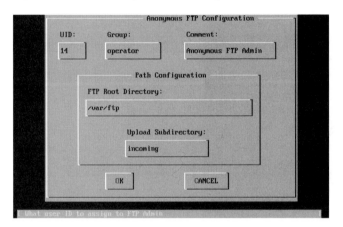

Pressing **F1** will display the help :

```
This screen allows you to configure the anonymous FTP user.

The following configuration values are editable:

UID:     The user ID you wish to assign to the anonymous FTP user.
         All files uploaded will be owned by this ID.

Group:   Which group you wish the anonymous FTP user to be in.

Comment: String describing this user in /etc/passwd


FTP Root Directory:

         Where files available for anonymous FTP will be kept.

Upload subdirectory:

         Where files uploaded by anonymous FTP users will go.
```

The ftp root directory will be put in /var by default. If you do not have enough room there for the anticipated FTP needs, the /usr directory could be used by setting the FTP Root Directory to /usr/ftp.

When you are satisfied with the values, press **Enter** to continue.

```
                    User Confirmation Requested
         Create a welcome message file for anonymous FTP users?

                         [ Yes ]      No
```

If you select [Yes] and press **Enter**, an editor will automatically start allowing you to edit the message.

Figure 2-35. Edit The FTP Welcome Message

This is a text editor called ee. Use the instructions to change the message or change the message later using a text editor of your choice. Note the file name/location at the bottom.

Press **Esc** and a pop-up menu will default to a) leave editor. Press **Enter** to exit and continue.

2.9.5 Configure Network File Services

Network File Services (NFS) allows sharing of files across a network. A machine can be configured as a server, a client, or both. Refer to Section 17.4 for a more information.

NFS Server

```
                    User Confirmation Requested
         Do you want to configure this machine as an NFS server?

                         Yes    [ No ]
```

If there is no need for a Network File System server or client, select [No] and press **Enter**.

If [Yes] is chosen, a message will pop-up indicating that the exports file must be created.

```
                            Message
  Operating as an NFS server means that you must first configure an
  /etc/exports file to indicate which hosts are allowed certain kinds of
  access to your local file systems.
  Press [Enter] now to invoke an editor on /etc/exports
                           [ OK ]
```

Press **Enter** to continue. A text editor will start allowing the exports file to be created and edited.

Figure 2-36. Editing the Exports File

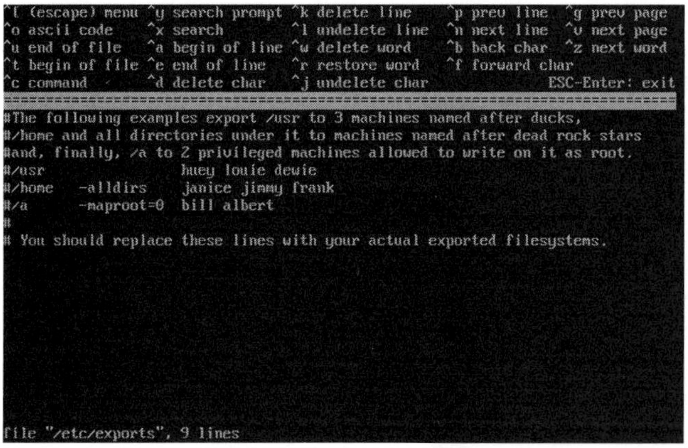

Use the instructions to add the actual exported filesystems now or later using a text editor of your choice. Note the filename/location at the bottom of the editor screen.

Press **Esc** and a pop-up menu will default to a) leave editor. Press **Enter** to exit and continue.

NFS Client

```
                      User Confirmation Requested
      Do you want to configure this machine as an NFS client?

                         Yes    [ No ]
```

With the arrow keys, select [Yes] or [No] as appropriate and press **Enter**.

2.9.6 Security Profile

A security profile is a set of configuration options that attempts to achieve the desired ratio of security to convenience by enabling and disabling certain programs and other settings.

More information about security profiles can be found in the FreeBSD FAQ[7].

```
                        User Confirmation Requested
      Do you want to select a default security profile for this host (select
      No for "medium" security)?

                            [ Yes ]      No
```

Selecting [No] and pressing **Enter** will set the security profile to medium.

Selecting [Yes] and pressing **Enter** will allow selecting a different security profile.

Figure 2-37. Security Profile Options

Press **F1** to display the help. Press **Enter** to return to selection menu.

Use the arrow keys to choose Medium unless your are sure that another level is required for your needs. With [OK] highlighted, press **Enter**.

An appropriate confirmation message will display depending on which security setting was chosen.

```
                            Message

      Moderate security settings have been selected.

      Sendmail and SSHd have been enabled, securelevels are
      disabled, and NFS server setting have been left intact.
      PLEASE NOTE that this still does not save you from having
      to properly secure your system in other ways or exercise
      due diligence in your administration, this simply picks
      a standard set of out-of-box defaults to start with.

      To change any of these settings later, edit /etc/rc.conf
```

---

7 http://www.FreeBSD.org/doc/en_US.ISO8859-1/books/faq/install.html#SECURITY-PROFILES

```
                              [OK]

                             Message

  Extreme security settings have been selected.

  Sendmail, SSHd, and NFS services have been disabled, and
  securelevels have been enabled.
  PLEASE NOTE that this still does not save you from having
  to properly secure your system in other ways or exercise
  due diligence in your administration, this simply picks
  a more secure set of out-of-box defaults to start with.

  To change any of these settings later, edit /etc/rc.conf

                              [OK]
```

Press **Enter** to continue with the post-installation configuration.

2.9.7 System Console Settings

There are several options available to customize the system console.

```
                    User Confirmation Requested
          Would you like to customize your system console settings?

                         [ Yes ]   No
```

To view and configure the options, select [Yes] and press **Enter**.

Figure 2-38. System Console Configuration Options

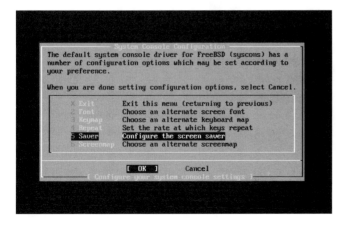

A commonly used option is the screensaver. Use the arrow keys to select Saver and then press **Enter**.

Figure 2-39. Screensaver Options

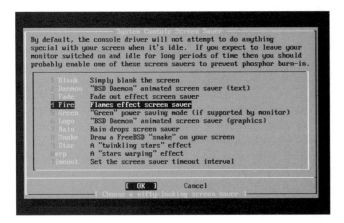

Select the desired screen saver using the arrow keys and then press **Enter**. The System Console Configuration menu will redisplay.

The default time interval is 300 seconds. To change the time interval, select Saver again. At the Screensaver Options menu, select Timeout using the arrow keys and press **Enter**. A pop-up menu will appear :

Figure 2-40. Screensaver Timeout

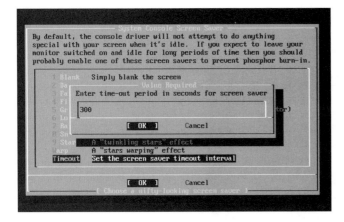

The value can be changed, then select [OK] and press **Enter** to return to the System Console Configuration menu.

Figure 2-41. System Console Configuration Exit

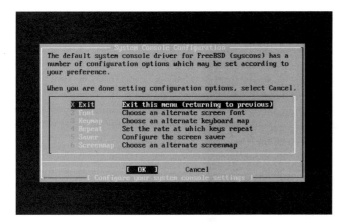

Selecting Exit and pressing **Enter** will continue with the post-installation configurations.

2.9.8 Setting The Time Zone

Setting the timezone for your machine will allow it to automatically correct for any regional time changes and perform other timezone related functions properly.

The example shown is for a machine located in the Eastern time zone of the United States. Your selections will vary according to your geographical location.

```
                     User Confirmation Requested
         Would you like to set this machine's time zone now?

                          [ Yes ]    No
```

Select [Yes] and press **Enter** to set the time zone.

```
                     User Confirmation Requested
     Is this machine's CMOS clock set to UTC? If it is set to local time
     or you don't know, please choose NO here!

                          Yes    [ No ]
```

Select [Yes] or [No] according to how the machine's clock is configured and press **Enter**.

Figure 2-42. Select Your Region

The appropriate region is selected using the arrow keys and then press **Enter**.

Figure 2-43. Select Your Country

Select the appropriate country using the arrow keys and press **Enter**.

Figure 2-44. Select Your Timezone

The appropriate time zone is selected using the arrow keys and pressing **Enter**.

```
               Confirmation
    Does the abbreviation 'EDT' look reasonable?

               [ Yes ]   No
```

Confirm the abbreviation for the time zone is correct. If it looks okay, press **Enter** to continue with the post-installation configuration.

2.9.9 Linux Compatibility

```
         User Confirmation Requested
   Would you like to enable Linux binary compatibility?

               [ Yes ]   No
```

Selecting [Yes] and pressing **Enter** will allow running Linux software on FreeBSD. The install will proceed to add the appropriate packages for Linux compatibility.

If installing by FTP, the machine will need to be connected to the Internet. Sometimes a remote ftp site will not have all the distributions like the Linux binary compatibility. This can be installed later if necessary.

2.9.10 Mouse Settings

This option will allow you to cut and paste text in the console and user programs with a 3-button mouse. If using a 2-button mouse, refer to manual page, moused(8), after installation for details on emulating the 3-button style. This example depicts a non-USB mouse.

```
                    User Confirmation Requested
         Does this system have a non-USB mouse attached to it?

                          [ Yes ]    No
```

Select [Yes] for a non-USB mouse or [No] for a USB mouse and press **Enter**.

Figure 2-45. Select Mouse Protocol Type

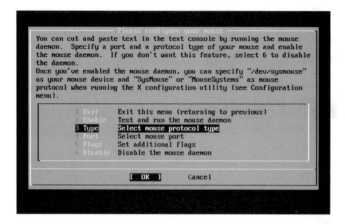

Use the arrow keys to select Type and press **Enter**

Figure 2-46. Set Mouse Protocol

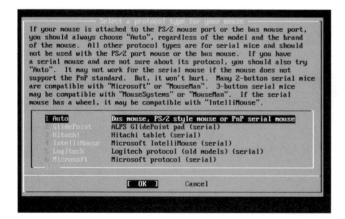

The mouse used in this example is a PS/2 type, so the default Auto was appropriate. To change protocol, use the arrow keys to select another option. Ensure that [OK] is highlighted and press **Enter** to exit this menu.

Figure 2-47. Configure Mouse Port

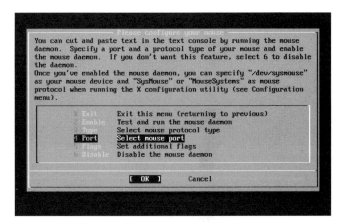

Use the arrow keys to select Port and press **Enter**.

Figure 2-48. Setting The Mouse Port

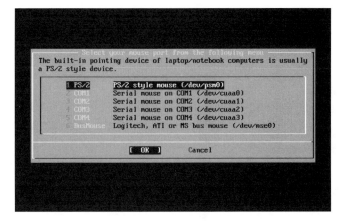

This system had a PS/2 mouse, so the default PS/2 was appropriate. To change the port, use the arrow keys and then press **Enter**.

Figure 2-49. Enable The Mouse Daemon

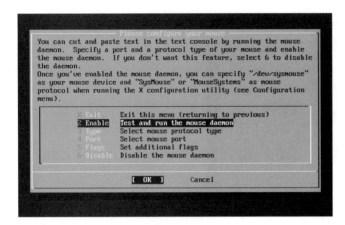

Last, the mouse daemon is enabled and tested.

Figure 2-50. Test The Mouse Daemon

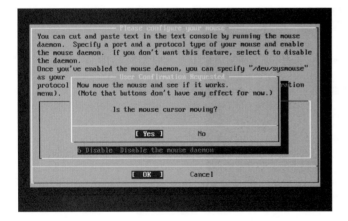

The cursor moved around the screen so the mouse daemon is running:

Select [Yes] to return to the previous menu then select Exit with the arrow keys and press **Enter** to return to continue with the post-installation configuration.

2.9.11 Configure X-Server

In order to use a graphical user interface such as **KDE**, **GNOME**, or others, the X server will need to be configured.

To see whether your video card is supported, check the XFree86[8] web site. If your video card is only supported under XFree86 4.x, refer to Chapter 5 for installation and configuration.

```
                    User Confirmation Requested
         Would you like to configure your X server at this time?

                           [ Yes ]    No
```

Warning: It is necessary to know your monitor specifications and video card information. Equipment damage can occur if settings are incorrect. If you do not have this information, select [No] and perform the configuration after installation when you have the information using /stand/sysinstall, selecting Configure and then XFree86.

If you have graphics card and monitor information, select [Yes] and press **Enter** to proceed with configuring the X server.

Figure 2-51. Select Configuration Method Menu

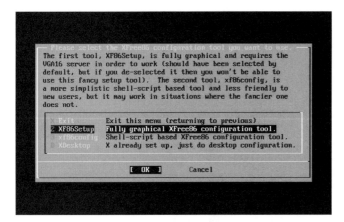

There are several ways to configure the X server. **XF86Setup** is fully graphical and probably the easiest. Use the arrow keys to select the XF86Setup and press **Enter**.

```
                              Message
         You have configured and been running the mouse daemon.
         Choose "/dev/sysmouse" as the mouse port and "SysMouse" or
         "MouseSystems" as the mouse protocol in the X configuration utility.

                              [ OK ]

                    [ Press enter to continue ]
```

---

8 http://www.xfree86.org/

This indicates that the mouse daemon previously configured has been detected. Press **Enter** to continue.

```
Press [Enter] to switch to graphics mode.

This may take a while...

[ OK ]
```

Press **Enter** to switch to the graphics mode and continue. It will *not* try to switch to the graphics mode until **Enter** is pressed. The screen will go black and then shortly a screen with a large X in the center will appear. Be patient and wait.

After a few more moments, the **XF86Setup** introduction will display. Read all instructions *carefully*. Press **Enter** to continue.

XF86Setup Overview

There are several areas of configuration to be completed. The configuration choices you make will depend on the hardware in the system so only a general overview can be given here.

Along the top of the configuration tool there are buttons indicating the areas to be configured. You should be able to use the mouse if it was previously configured and select each item by clicking on it. Review each area and make appropriate selections for your system.

1. Mouse

    The mouse is the first item to be configured. If you previously configured your mouse, the mouse daemon will already be running and should indicate SysMouse automatically for the mouse protocol. If you are use a two button mouse, you should also select Emulate3Buttons. There are other settings that can be tweaked if necessary.

    After completing your selections, click on the Apply and check the mouse actions are working properly. If further adjustment is needed, make them and recheck the operation by clicking on Apply again. When finished, move on to the next item.

2. Keyboard

    Select the appropriate keyboard model. The default keyboard is Generic 101-key PC.

    Select the language layout for your keyboard. The default layout is U.S. English. If you are not using a U.S. keyboard, you may need to additionally select a variant.

    There are other options under Group Shift/Lock behavior and Control Key Position that can be selected if desired. Generally the default settings are fine.

    After completing the keyboard configuration, click on Apply and move on to the next item.

3. Card

    Click on Read README file for additional help in configuring your video card.

    Select the appropriate video card from the list using the scrollbar. Clicking on your card will show as "Card selected:" above the list box.

    Next, the Detailed Setup was selected just to check details. Typically, if your video card was in the list, no changes will be needed here.

When finished, move on to the next item.

4. Monitor

   There are two ways to proceed. One method requires that you enter the horizontal and vertical sweep capabilities of your monitor in the text boxes.

   Choosing one of the monitor options listed that the monitor is the other method. After selecting a listed option, the horizontal and vertical sweep rates that will be used will display. Compare those to your monitor specifications. The monitor must be capable of using those ranges.

   Do not exceed the ratings of your monitor. Damage could occur. If you have doubts select **ABORT** and get the information. The remainder of the installation process will be unaffected and configuring the X-Server can be done later using /stand/sysinstall.

   When finished, move on to the next item.

5. Mode

   Select the video mode(s) that you want to use. You can select more than one option. Typically, useful ranges are 640x480, 800x600, and 1024x768 but those are a function of video card capability, monitor size, and eye comfort.

   Next, select the default color depth you want to use. Your choices are 8bpp, 16bpp, 24bpp, and 32bpp. Select the highest color depth that your video card will support.

   When finished, move on to the next item.

6. Other

   The default settings are reasonable values, so you probably will not need to change anything here.

   The default setting which allows the server to be killed with the hotkey sequence **Ctrl+Alt+Backspace** should be left on. This can be executed if something is wrong with the server settings and prevent hardware damage.

   The default setting that allows video mode switching will permit changing of the mode while running X with the hotkey sequence **Alt++** or **Alt+-**.

7. Testing the Server

   Verify all the settings once again and select Done and the following message will display :

   ```
   If you've finished configuring everything press the
   Okay button to start the X server using the configuration
   you've selected.  If you still wish to configure some things,
   press one of the buttons at the top and then press "Done" again,
   when you've finished.
   ```

   After selecting Okay, some messages will briefly appear advising to wait and attempting to start the X-server. This process takes a few moments, so be patient.

   The screen will go blank for a short period of time and then a screen will appear with the message "Congratulations, you've got a running server!"

   If nothing appears or the display is distorted, kill the X-server using **Ctrl+Alt+Backspace** and adjust the settings or revisit them after installation.

8. Running xvidtune

   The display can be adjusted for height, width, or centering by using **xvidtune**.

There are warnings that improper settings can damage your equipment. Heed them. If in doubt, do not do it. Instead, use the monitor controls to adjust the display for x-windows. There may be some display differences when switching back to text mode, but it is better than damaging equipment. **xvidtune** can be ran later using `/stand/sysinstall`.

Read the xvidtune(1) man page before making any adjustments.

9. Saving Configuration

   When you are satisfied, the configuration can now be saved. Select Save the configuration and Exit The configuration file will be saved to `/etc/XF86Config`.

Once the configuration is done, the installation program will need to create a link to the server :

```
        Do you want to create an 'X' link to the SVGA server?

            (the link will be created in the directory:
                    /usr/X11R6/bin) Okay?

                        [ Yes ]    No
```

Select [Yes] and press **Enter** to create the link.

```
                    Link created successfully.

                            [ OK ]
```

Press **Enter** to continue configuration.

2.9.12 Select Default X Desktop

There are a variety of window managers available. They range from very basic environments to full desktop environments with a large suite of software. Some require only minimal disk space and low memory while others with more features require much more. The best way to determine which is most suitable for you is to try a few different ones. Those are available from the ports collection or as packages and can be added after installation.

You can select one of the popular desktops to be installed and configured as the default desktop. This will allow you to start it right after installation.

Figure 2-52. Select Default Desktop

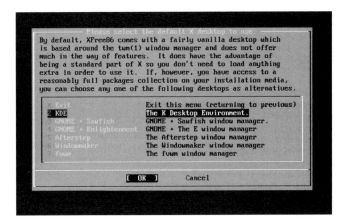

Use the arrow keys to select a desktop and press **Enter**. Installation of the selected desktop will proceed.

2.9.13 Install Packages

The packages are pre-compiled binaries and are a convenient way to install software.

Installation of one package is shown for purposes of illustration. Additional packages can also be added at this time if desired. After installation /stand/sysinstall can be used to add additional packages.

```
                    User Confirmation Requested
   The FreeBSD package collection is a collection of hundreds of
   ready-to-run applications, from text editors to games to WEB servers
   and more. Would you like to browse the collection now?

                         [ Yes ]    No
```

Selecting [Yes] and pressing **Enter** will be followed by the Package Selection screens:

Figure 2-53. Select Package Category

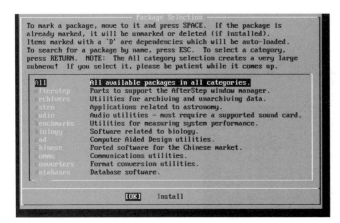

All packages available will be displayed if All is selected or you can select a particular category. Highlight your selection with the arrow keys and press **Enter**.

A menu will display showing all the packages available for the selection made.

Figure 2-54. Select Packages

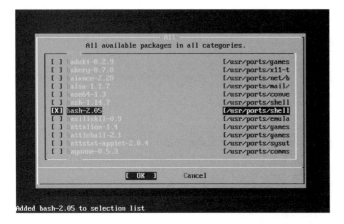

The **bash** shell is shown selected. Select as many as desired by highlighting the package and pressing the **Space**. A short description of each package will appear in the lower left corner of the screen.

Pressing the **Tab** key will toggle between the last selected package, [OK], and [Cancel].

When you have finished marking the packages for installation, press **Tab** once to toggle to the [OK] and press **Enter** to return to the Package Selection menu.

The left and right arrow keys will also toggle between [OK] and [Cancel]. This method can also be used to select [OK] and press **Enter** to return to the Package Selection menu.

Figure 2-55. Install Packages

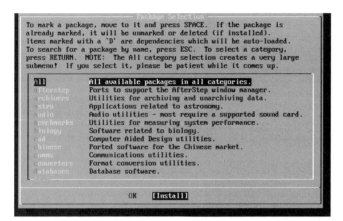

Use the arrow keys to select [Install] and press **Enter**. You will then need to confirm that you want to install the packages.

Figure 2-56. Confirm Package Installation

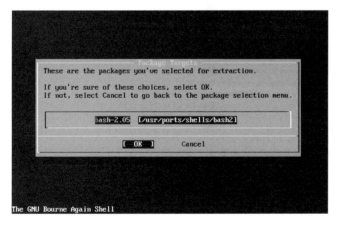

Selecting [OK] and pressing **Enter** will start the package installation. Installing messages will appear until completed. Make note if there are any error messages.

The final configuration continues after packages are installed.

2.9.14 Add User/Groups

You should add at least one user during the installation so that you can use the system without being logged in as root. The root partition is generally small and running applications as root can quickly fill it. A bigger danger is noted below :

```
                    User Confirmation Requested
    Would you like to add any initial user accounts to the system? Adding
    at least one account for yourself at this stage is suggested since
    working as the "root" user is dangerous (it is easy to do things which
    adversely affect the entire system).

                         [ Yes ]    No
```

Select [Yes] and press **Enter** to continue with adding a user.

Figure 2-57. Select Add User

Select Add User with the arrow keys and press **Enter**.

Figure 2-58. Add User Information

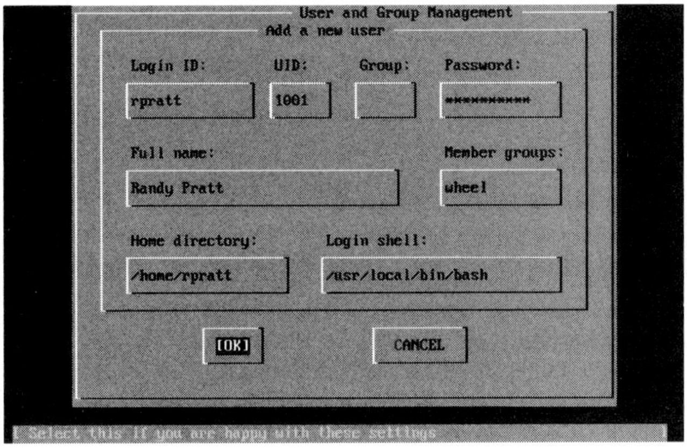

The following descriptions will appear in the lower part of the screen as the items are selected with **Tab** to assist with entering the required information.

Login ID

> The login name of the new user (mandatory)

UID

> The numerical ID for this user (leave blank for automatic choice)

Group

> The login group name for this user (leave blank for automatic choice)

Password

> The password for this user (enter this field with care!)

Full name

> The user's full name (comment)

Member groups

> The groups this user belongs to (i.e. gets access rights for)

Home directory

> The user's home directory (leave blank for default)

Login shell

> The user's login shell (leave blank for default). (`/bin/sh`)

The login shell was changed from /bin/sh to /usr/local/bin/bash to use the **bash** shell that was previously installed as a package. Do not try to use a shell that does not exist or you will not be able to login.

The user was also added to the group "wheel" to be able to become a superuser with root privileges.

When you are satisfied, press [OK] and the User and Group Management menu will redisplay.

Figure 2-59. Exit User and Group Management

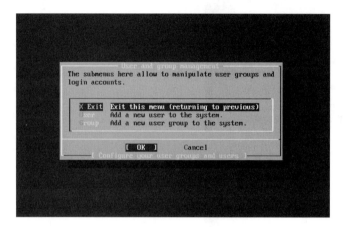

Groups could also be added at this time if specific needs are known. Otherwise, this may be accessed through using /stand/sysinstall after installation is completed.

When you are finished adding users, select Exit with the arrow keys and press **Enter** to continue the installation.

2.9.15 Set `root` Password

```
                        Message
Now you must set the system manager's password.
This is the password you'll use to log in as "root".

                       [ OK ]

             [ Press enter to continue ]
```

Press **Enter** to set the root password.

The password will need to be typed in twice correctly. Needless to say, make sure you have a way of finding the password if you forget.

```
Changing local password for root.
 New password :
 Retype new password :
```

The installation will continue after the password is successfully entered.

2.9.16 Exiting Install

If you need to configure additional network devices or to do any other configurations, you can do it at this point or after installation with /stand/sysinstall.

```
                    User Confirmation Requested
        Visit the general configuration menu for a chance to set any last
        options?

                          Yes    [ No ]
```

Selecting [No] with the arrow keys and pressing **Enter** returns to the Main Installation Menu

Figure 2-60. Exit Install

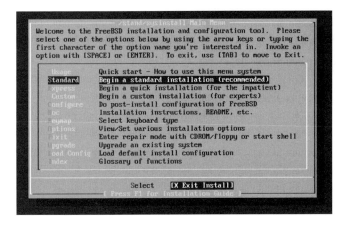

Select [X Exit Install] with the arrow keys and press **Enter**. You will be asked to confirm exiting the installation :

```
                    User Confirmation Requested
        Are you sure you wish to exit? The system will reboot (be sure to
        remove any floppies from the drives).

                          [ Yes ]    No
```

Select [Yes] and remove floppy if booting from floppy. The CDROM drive is locked until the machine starts to reboot. The CDROM drive is then unlocked and can be removed from drive (quickly).

The system will reboot so watch for any error messages that may appear.

2.9.17 FreeBSD Bootup

FreeBSD Bootup on the i386

If everything went well, you will see messages scroll off the screen and you will arrive at a login prompt. You can view the content of the messages by pressing **Scroll-Lock** and using **PgUp** and **PgDn**. Pressing **Scroll-Lock** again will return to the prompt.

The entire message may not display (buffer limitation) but it can be viewed from the command line after logging in by typing dmesg at the prompt.

Login using the username/password you set during installation (rpratt, in this example). Avoid logging in as root except when necessary.

Typical boot messages :

```
Copyright (c) 1992-2001 The FreeBSD Project.
Copyright (c) 1982, 1986, 1989, 1991, 1993, 1994
        The Regents of the University of California. All rights reserved.
FreeBSD 4.3-RELEASE #0: Sat Apr 21 10:54:49 GMT 2001
    jkh@narf.osd.bsdi.com:/usr/src/sys/compile/GENERIC
Timecounter "i8254"   frequency 1193182 Hz
CPU: AMD-K6(tm) 3D processor (300.68-MHz 586-class CPU)
  Origin = "AuthenticAMD"  Id = 0x580  Stepping = 0
  Features=0x8001bf<FPU,VME,DE,PSE,TSC,MSR,MCE,CX8,MMX>
  AMD Features=0x80000800<SYSCALL,3DNow!>
real memory  = 268435456 (262144K bytes)
config> di sn0
config> di lnc0
config> di le0
config> di ie0
config> di fe0
config> di cs0
config> di bt0
config> di ata1
config> di aic0
config> di aha0
config> di adv0
config> q
avail memory = 256983040 (250960K bytes)
Preloaded elf kernel "kernel" at 0xc044d000.
Preloaded userconfig_script "/boot/kernel.conf" at 0xc044d09c.
md0: Malloc disk
npx0: <math processor> on motherboard
npx0: INT 16 interface
pcib0: <Host to PCI bridge> on motherboard
pci0: <PCI bus> on pcib0
pcib1: <VIA 82C598MVP (Apollo MVP3) PCI-PCI (AGP) bridge> at device 1.0 on pci0
pci1: <PCI bus> on pcib1
pci1: <Matrox MGA G200 AGP graphics accelerator> at 0.0 irq 11
isab0: <VIA 82C586 PCI-ISA bridge> at device 7.0 on pci0
```

```
isa0: <ISA bus> on isab0
atapci0: <VIA 82C586 ATA33 controller> port 0xe000-0xe00f at device 7.1 on pci0
ata0: at 0x1f0 irq 14 on atapci0
ata1: at 0x170 irq 15 on atapci0
uhci0: <VIA 83C572 USB controller> port 0xe400-0xe41f irq 10 at device 7.2 on pci0
usb0: <VIA 83C572 USB controller> on uhci0
usb0: USB revision 1.0
uhub0: VIA UHCI root hub, class 9/0, rev 1.00/1.00, addr 1
uhub0: 2 ports with 2 removable, self powered
chip1: <VIA 82C586B ACPI interface> at device 7.3 on pci0
ed0: <NE2000 PCI Ethernet (RealTek 8029)> port 0xe800-0xe81f irq 9 at
device 10.0 on pci0
ed0: address 52:54:05:de:73:1b, type NE2000 (16 bit)
isa0: too many dependant configs (8)
isa0: unexpected small tag 14
fdc0: <NEC 72065B or clone> at port 0x3f0-0x3f5,0x3f7 irq 6 drq 2 on isa0
fdc0: FIFO enabled, 8 bytes threshold
fd0: <1440-KB 3.5" drive> on fdc0 drive 0
atkbdc0: <keyboard controller (i8042)> at port 0x60-0x6f on isa0
atkbd0: <AT Keyboard> flags 0x1 irq 1 on atkbdc0
kbd0 at atkbd0
psm0: <PS/2 Mouse> irq 12 on atkbdc0
psm0: model Generic PS/2 mouse, device ID 0
vga0: <Generic ISA VGA> at port 0x3c0-0x3df iomem 0xa0000-0xbffff on isa0
sc0: <System console> at flags 0x1 on isa0
sc0: VGA <16 virtual consoles, flags=0x300>
sio0 at port 0x3f8-0x3ff irq 4 flags 0x10 on isa0
sio0: type 16550A
sio1 at port 0x2f8-0x2ff irq 3 on isa0
sio1: type 16550A
ppc0: <Parallel port> at port 0x378-0x37f irq 7 on isa0
ppc0: SMC-like chipset (ECP/EPP/PS2/NIBBLE) in COMPATIBLE mode
ppc0: FIFO with 16/16/15 bytes threshold
ppi0: <Parallel I/O> on ppbus0
lpt0: <Printer> on ppbus0
lpt0: Interrupt-driven port
plip0: <PLIP network interface> on ppbus0
ad0: 8063MB <IBM-DHEA-38451> [16383/16/63] at ata0-master using UDMA33
ad2: 8063MB <IBM-DHEA-38451> [16383/16/63] at ata1-master using UDMA33
acd0: CDROM <DELTA OTC-H101/ST3 F/W by OIPD> at ata0-slave using PIO4
Mounting root from ufs:/dev/ad0s1a
swapon: adding /dev/ad0s1b as swap device
Automatic boot in progress...
/dev/ad0s1a: FILESYSTEM CLEAN; SKIPPING CHECKS
/dev/ad0s1a: clean, 70119 free (655 frags, 8683 blocks, 0.7% fragmentation)
/dev/ad0s1f: FILESYSTEM CLEAN; SKIPPING CHECKS
/dev/ad0s1f: clean, 6976313 free (51774 frags, 829297 blocks, 0.7% fragmentation)
/dev/ad0s1e: filesystem CLEAN; SKIPPING CHECKS
/dev/ad0s1e: clean, 97952 free (9 frags, 12381 blocks, 0.0% fragmentation)
Doing initial network setup: hostname.
lo0: flags=8049<UP,LOOPBACK,RUNNING,MULTICAST> mtu 16384
```

```
        inet6 fe80::1%lo0 prefixlen 64 scopeid 0x8
        inet6 ::1 prefixlen 128
        inet 127.0.0.1 netmask 0xff000000
Additional routing options: tcp extensions=NO IP gateway=YES TCP
keepalive=YES
routing daemons:.
additional daemons: syslogd.
Doing additional network setup: portmap.
Starting final network daemons: creating ssh RSA host key
Generating RSA keys:  Key generation complete.
Your identification has been saved in /etc/ssh/ssh_host_key.
Your public key has been saved in /etc/ssh/ssh_host_key.pub.
The key fingerprint is:
2d:02:37:d2:0e:68:93:8f:9c:46:de:92:f4:be:60:0a root@k6-2.example.com
 creating ssh DSA host key
Generating DSA parameter and key.
Your identification has been saved in /etc/ssh/ssh_host_dsa_key.
Your public key has been saved in /etc/ssh/ssh_host_dsa_key.pub.
The key fingerprint is:
38:af:d2:1f:63:14:00:d8:83:fd:dd:4b:97:1c:43:6d root@k6-2.example.com.
setting ELF ldconfig path: /usr/lib /usr/lib/compat /usr/X11R6/lib
/usr/local/lib
setting a.out ldconfig path: /usr/lib/aout /usr/lib/compat/aout
/usr/X11R6/lib/aout
starting standard daemons: inetd cron sendmail sshd usbd.
Initial rc.i386 initialization: linux.
rc.i386 configuring syscons: blank_time screensaver moused.
Additional ABI support: linux.
Local package initilization:.
Additional TCP options:.

FreeBSD/i386 (k6-2.example.com) (ttyv0)

login: rpratt
Password:
```

Generating the RSA and DSA keys may take some time on slower machines. This happens only on the initial boot-up of a new installation. Subsequent boots will be faster.

If the X server has been configured and a Default Desktop chosen, it can be started by typing `startx` at the command line.

Bootup of FreeBSD on the Alpha

Once the install procedure has finished, you will be able to start FreeBSD by typing something like this to the SRM prompt:

```
>>>BOOT DKC0
```

This instructs the firmware to boot the specified disk. To make FreeBSD boot automatically in the future, use these commands:

```
>>> SET BOOT_OSFLAGS A
>>> SET BOOT_FILE "
>>> SET BOOTDEF_DEV DKC0
>>> SET AUTO_ACTION BOOT
```

The boot messages will be similar (but not identical) to those produced by FreeBSD booting on the i386.

2.9.18 FreeBSD Shutdown

It is important to properly shutdown the operating system. Do not just turn off power. First, become a superuser by typing su at the command line and entering the root password. This will work only if the user is a member of the group wheel. Otherwise, login as root and use shutdown -h now.

```
The operating system has halted.
Please press any key to reboot.
```

It is safe to turn off the power after the shutdown command has been issued and the message "Please press any key to reboot" appears. If any key is pressed instead of turning off the power switch, the system will reboot.

2.10 Supported Hardware

FreeBSD currently runs on a wide variety of ISA, VLB, EISA, and PCI bus-based PCs with Intel, AMD, Cyrix, or NexGen "x86" processors, as well as a number of machines based on the Compaq Alpha processor. Support for generic IDE or ESDI drive configurations, various SCSI controllers, PCMCIA cards, USB devices, and network and serial cards is also provided. FreeBSD also supports IBM's microchannel (MCA) bus.

A list of supported hardware is provided with each FreeBSD release in the FreeBSD Hardware Notes. This document can usually be found in a file named HARDWARE.TXT, in the top-level directory of a CDROM or FTP distribution or in sysinstall's documentation menu. It lists, for a given architecture, what hardware devices are known to be supported by each release of FreeBSD.

2.11 Troubleshooting

The following section covers basic installation troubleshooting, such as common problems people have reported. There are also a few questions and answers for people wishing to dual-boot FreeBSD with MS-DOS.

2.11.1 What to Do If Something Goes Wrong...

Due to various limitations of the PC architecture, it is impossible for probing to be 100% reliable, however, there are a few things you can do if it fails.

Check the Hardware Notes document for your version of FreeBSD to make sure your hardware is supported.

If your hardware is supported and you still experience lock-ups or other problems, reset your computer, and when the visual kernel configuration option is given, choose it. This will allow you to go through your hardware and supply information to the system about it. The kernel on the boot disks is configured assuming that most hardware devices are in their factory default configuration in terms of IRQs, IO addresses, and DMA channels. If your hardware has been reconfigured, you will most likely need to use the configuration editor to tell FreeBSD where to find things.

It is also possible that a probe for a device not present will cause a later probe for another device that is present to fail. In that case, the probes for the conflicting driver(s) should be disabled.

> **Warning:** Do not disable any drivers you will need during the installation, such as your screen (sc0). If the installation wedges or fails mysteriously after leaving the configuration editor, you have probably removed or changed something you should not have. Reboot and try again.

In configuration mode, you can:

- List the device drivers installed in the kernel.
- Change device drivers for hardware that is not present in your system.
- Change IRQs, DRQs, and IO port addresses used by a device driver.

After adjusting the kernel to match your hardware configuration, type Q to boot with the new settings. Once the installation has completed, any changes you made in the configuration mode will be permanent so you do not have to reconfigure every time you boot. It is still highly likely that you will eventually want to build a custom kernel, which is described in Chapter 9.

2.11.2 MS-DOS User's Questions and Answers

Many users wish to install FreeBSD on PCs inhabited by MS-DOS. Here are some commonly asked questions about installing FreeBSD on such systems.

1. Help, I have no space! Do I need to delete everything first?

If your machine is already running MS-DOS and has little or no free space available for the FreeBSD installation, all hope is not lost! You may find the **FIPS** utility, provided in the tools directory on the FreeBSD CDROM or various FreeBSD FTP sites to be quite useful.

FIPS allows you to split an existing MS-DOS partition into two pieces, preserving the original partition and allowing you to install onto the second free piece. You first defragment your MS-DOS partition using the Windows **DEFRAG** utility (go into Explorer, right-click on the hard drive, and choose to defrag your hard drive), or Norton Disk Tools. You then must run **FIPS**. It will prompt you for the rest of the information it needs. Afterwards, you can reboot and install FreeBSD on the new free slice. See the *Distributions* menu for an estimate of how much free space you will need for the kind of installation you want.

There is also a *very* useful product from PowerQuest[9] called **Partition Magic**. This application has far more functionality than **FIPS**, and is highly recommended if you plan to often add/remove operating systems (like me). However, it does cost money, and if you plan to install FreeBSD once and then leave it there, **FIPS** will probably be fine for you.

2. Can I use compressed MS-DOS filesystems from FreeBSD?

No. If you are using a utility such as Stacker(tm) or DoubleSpace(tm), FreeBSD will only be able to use whatever portion of the filesystem you leave uncompressed. The rest of the filesystem will show up as one large file (the stacked/double spaced file!). *Do not remove that file or you will probably regret it greatly!*

It is probably better to create another uncompressed primary MS-DOS partition and use this for communications between MS-DOS and FreeBSD.

3. Can I mount my extended MS-DOS partition?

Yes. DOS extended partitions are mapped in at the end of the other "slices" in FreeBSD, e.g., your D: drive might be /dev/da0s5, your E: drive, /dev/da0s6, and so on. This example assumes, of course, that your extended partition is on SCSI drive 0. For IDE drives, substitute ad for da appropriately if installing 4.0-RELEASE or later, and substitute wd for da if you are installing a version of FreeBSD prior to 4.0. You otherwise mount extended partitions exactly like you would any other DOS drive, for example:

```
# mount -t msdos /dev/ad0s5 /dos_d
```

2.11.3 Alpha User's Questions and Answers

This section answers some commonly asked questions about installing FreeBSD on Alpha systems.

1. Can I boot from the ARC or Alpha BIOS Console?

No. FreeBSD, like Compaq Tru64 and VMS, will only boot from the SRM console.

2. Help, I have no space! Do I need to delete everything first?

Unfortunately, yes.

3. Can I mount my Compaq Tru64 or VMS filesystems?

No, not at this time.

---

9 http://www.powerquest.com/

2.12 Advanced Installation Guide

This section describes how to install FreeBSD in exceptional cases.

2.12.1 Installing FreeBSD on a System without a Monitor or Keyboard

This type of installation is called a "headless install", because the machine that you are trying to install FreeBSD on either does not have a monitor attached to it, or does not even have a VGA output. How is this possible you ask? Using a serial console. A serial console is basically using another machine to act as the main display and keyboard for a system. To do this, just follow these steps:

1. Fetch the Right Boot Floppy Images

   First you will need to get the right disk images so that you can boot into the install program. The secret with using a serial console is that you tell the boot loader to send I/O through a serial port instead of displaying console output to the VGA device and trying to read input from a local keyboard. Enough of that now, let's get back to getting these disk images.

   You will need to get kern.flp[10] and mfsroot.flp[11] from the floppies directory[12].

2. Write the Image Files to the Floppy Disks.

   The image files, such as `kern.flp`, are *not* regular files that you copy to the disk. Instead, they are images of the complete contents of the disk.

   This means that you can *not* use commands like DOS' `copy` to write the files. Instead, you must use specific tools to write the images directly to the disk.

   If you are creating the floppies on a computer running DOS then we provide a tool to do this called `fdimage`.

   If you are using the floppies from the CDROM, and your CDROM is the `E:` drive then you would run this:

   ```
   E:\> tools\fdimage floppies\kern.flp A:
   ```

   Repeat this command for each `.flp` file, replacing the floppy disk each time. Adjust the command line as necessary, depending on where you have placed the `.flp` files. If you do not have the CDROM then `fdimage` can be downloaded from the `tools` directory[13] on the FreeBSD FTP site.

   If you are writing the floppies on a Unix system (such as another FreeBSD system) you can use the dd(1) command to write the image files directly to disk. On FreeBSD you would run:

   ```
   # dd if=kern.flp of=/dev/fd0
   ```

   On FreeBSD `/dev/fd0` refers to the first floppy disk (the `A:` drive). `/dev/fd1` would be the `B:` drive, and so on. Other Unix variants might have different names for the floppy disk devices, and you will need to check the documentation for the system as necessary.

3. Enabling the Boot Floppies to Boot into a Serial Console

---

10 ftp://ftp.FreeBSD.org/pub/FreeBSD/releases/i386/4.4-RELEASE/floppies/kern.flp
11 ftp://ftp.FreeBSD.org/pub/FreeBSD/releases/i386/4.4-RELEASE/floppies/mfsroot.flp
12 ftp://ftp.FreeBSD.org/pub/FreeBSD/releases/i386/4.4-RELEASE/floppies/
13 ftp://ftp.FreeBSD.org/pub/FreeBSD/tools/

Warning: Do not try to mount the floppy if it is write-protected

If you were to boot into the floppies that you just made, FreeBSD would boot into its normal install mode. We want FreeBSD to boot into a serial console for our install. To do this, you have to mount the `kern.flp` floppy onto your FreeBSD system using the mount(8) command.

```
# mount /dev/fd0 /mnt
```

Now that you have the floppy mounted, you must change into the floppy directory

```
# cd /mnt
```

Here is where you must set the floppy to boot into a serial console. You have to make a file called `boot.config` containing "/boot/loader -h". All this does is pass a flag to the bootloader to boot into a serial console.

```
# echo "/boot/loader -h" > boot.config
```

Now that you have your floppy configured correctly, you must unmount the floppy using the umount(8) command

```
# cd /
# umount /mnt
```

Now you can remove the floppy from the floppy drive

4. Connecting Your Null Modem Cable

   You now need to connect a null modem cable between the two machines. Just connect the cable to the serial ports of the 2 machines. *A normal serial cable will not work here*, you need a null modem cable because it has some of the wires inside crossed over.

5. Booting Up for the Install

   It is now time to go ahead and start the install. Put the `kern.flp` floppy in the floppy drive of the machine you are doing the headless install on, and power on the machine.

6. Connecting to Your Headless Machine

   Now you have to connect to that machine with cu(1):

```
# cu -l /dev/cuaa0
```

That's it! You should be able to control the headless machine through your cu session now. It will ask you to put in the `mfsroot.flp`, and then it will come up with a selection of what kind of terminal to use. Just select the FreeBSD color console and proceed with your install!

2.13 Preparing Your Own Installation Media

Note: To prevent repetition, "FreeBSD disk" in this context means a FreeBSD CDROM or DVD that you have purchased, or produced yourself.

There may be some situations in which you need to create your own FreeBSD installation media and/or source. This might be physical media, such as a tape, or a source that **Sysinstall** can use to retrieve the files, such as a local FTP site, or an MS-DOS partition. For example;

- You have many machines connected to your local network, and one FreeBSD disk. You want to create a local FTP site using the contents of the FreeBSD disk, and then have your machines use this local FTP site instead of needing to connect to the Internet.
- You have a FreeBSD disk, FreeBSD does not recognize your CD/DVD drive, but DOS/Windows does. You want to copy the FreeBSD installations files to a DOS partition on the same computer, and then install FreeBSD using those files.
- The computer you want to install on does not have a CD/DVD drive, or a network card, but you can connect a "Laplink-style" serial or parallel cable to a computer that does.
- You want to create a tape that can be used to install FreeBSD.

2.13.1 Creating a Local FTP Site with a FreeBSD Disk

FreeBSD disks are laid out in the same way as the FTP site. This makes it very easy for you to create a local FTP site that can be used by other machines on your network when installing FreeBSD.

1. On the FreeBSD computer that will host the FTP site, ensure that the CDROM is in the drive, and mounted on /cdrom.

   ```
   # mount /cdrom
   ```

2. Create an account for anonymous FTP in /etc/passwd. Do this by editing /etc/passwd using vipw(8) and adding this line.

   ```
   ftp:*:99:99::0:0:FTP:/cdrom:/nonexistent
   ```

3. Ensure that the FTP service is enabled in /etc/inetd.conf.

Anyone with network connectivity to your machine can now chose a media type of FTP and type in **ftp://your machine** after picking "Other" in the FTP sites menu during the install.

> **Warning:** This approach is OK for a machine that is on your local network, and that is protected by your firewall. Offering up FTP services to other machines over the Internet (and not your local network) exposes your computer to the attention of crackers and other undesirables. We strongly recommend that you follow good security practices if you do this.

2.13.2 Creating Installation Floppies

If you must install from floppy disk (which we suggest you do *not* do), either due to unsupported hardware or simply because you insist on doing things the hard way, you must first prepare some floppies for the installation.

At a minimum, you will need as many 1.44MB or 1.2MB floppies as it takes to hold all the files in the `bin` (binary distribution) directory. If you are preparing the floppies from DOS, then they *MUST* be formatted using the MS-DOS `FORMAT` command. If you are using Windows, use Explorer to format the disks (right-click on the `A:` drive, and select "Format".

Do *not* trust factory pre-formatted floppies. Format them again yourself, just to be sure. Many problems reported by our users in the past have resulted from the use of improperly formatted media, which is why we are making a point of it now.

If you are creating the floppies on another FreeBSD machine, a format is still not a bad idea, though you do not need to put a DOS filesystem on each floppy. You can use the `disklabel` and `newfs` commands to put a UFS filesystem on them instead, as the following sequence of commands (for a 3.5" 1.44MB floppy) illustrates:

```
# fdformat -f 1440 fd0.1440
# disklabel -w -r fd0.1440 floppy3
# newfs -t 2 -u 18 -l 1 -i 65536 /dev/fd0
```

Note: Use `fd0.1200` and `floppy5` for 5.25" 1.2MB disks.

Then you can mount and write to them like any other filesystem.

After you have formatted the floppies, you will need to copy the files to them. The distribution files are split into chunks conveniently sized so that 5 of them will fit on a conventional 1.44MB floppy. Go through all your floppies, packing as many files as will fit on each one, until you have all of the distributions you want packed up in this fashion. Each distribution should go into a subdirectory on the floppy, e.g.: `a:\bin\bin.aa`, `a:\bin\bin.ab`, and so on.

Once you come to the Media screen during the install process, select "Floppy" and you will be prompted for the rest.

2.13.3 Installing from an MS-DOS Partition

To prepare for an installation from an MS-DOS partition, copy the files from the distribution into a directory on that partition. For example, `c:\freebsd`. The directory structure of the CDROM or FTP site must be partially reproduced within this directory, so we suggest using the DOS `xcopy` command if you are copying it from a CD. For example, to prepare for a minimal installation of FreeBSD:

```
C:\> md c:\freebsd
C:\> xcopy e:\bin c:\freebsd\bin\ /s
C:\> xcopy e:\manpages c:\freebsd\manpages\ /s
```

Assuming that `C:` is where you have free space and `E:` is where your CDROM is mounted.

If you do not have a CDROM drive, you can download the distribution from ftp.FreeBSD.org[14]. Each distribution is in its own directory; for example, the *bin* distribution can be found in the 4.4/bin[15] directory.

For as many distributions you wish to install from an MS-DOS partition (and you have the free space for), install each one under `c:\freebsd` — the `BIN` distribution is the only one required for a minimum installation.

---

14 ftp://ftp.FreeBSD.org/pub/FreeBSD/releases/i386/4.4-RELEASE/
15 ftp://ftp.FreeBSD.org/pub/FreeBSD/releases/i386/4.4-RELEASE/bin

2.13.4 Creating an Installation Tape

Installing from tape is probably the easiest method, short of an online FTP install or CDROM install. The installation program expects the files to be simply tarred onto the tape. After getting all of the distribution files you are interested in, simply tar them onto the tape;

```
# cd /freebsd/distdir
# tar cvf /dev/rwt0 dist1 ... dist2
```

When you go to do the installation, you should also make sure that you leave enough room in some temporary directory (which you will be allowed to choose) to accommodate the *full* contents of the tape you have created. Due to the non-random access nature of tapes, this method of installation requires quite a bit of temporary storage. You should expect to require as much temporary storage as you have stuff written on tape.

> **Note:** When starting the installation, the tape must be in the drive *before* booting from the boot floppy. The installation probe may otherwise fail to find it.

2.13.5 Before Installing over a Network

There are three types of network installations you can do. Serial port (SLIP or PPP), Parallel port (PLIP (laplink cable)), or Ethernet (a standard Ethernet controller (includes some PCMCIA)).

The SLIP support is rather primitive, and limited primarily to hard-wired links, such as a serial cable running between a laptop computer and another computer. The link should be hard-wired as the SLIP installation does not currently offer a dialing capability; that facility is provided with the PPP utility, which should be used in preference to SLIP whenever possible.

If you are using a modem, then PPP is almost certainly your only choice. Make sure that you have your service provider's information handy as you will need to know it fairly early in the installation process.

If you use PAP or CHAP to connect your ISP (in other words, if you can connect to the ISP in Windows without using a script), then all you will need to do is type in `dial` at the **ppp** prompt. Otherwise, you will need to know how to dial your ISP using the "AT commands" specific to your modem, as the PPP dialer provides only a very simple terminal emulator. Please refer to the user-ppp section (Section 16.2) and FAQ[16] entries for further information. If you have problems, logging can be directed to the screen using the command `set log local ...`.

If a hard-wired connection to another FreeBSD (2.0-R or later) machine is available, you might also consider installing over a "laplink" parallel port cable. The data rate over the parallel port is much higher than what is typically possible over a serial line (up to 50kbytes/sec), thus resulting in a quicker installation.

Finally, for the fastest possible network installation, an Ethernet adapter is always a good choice! FreeBSD supports most common PC Ethernet cards; a table of supported cards (and their required settings) is provided in the Hardware Notes for each release of FreeBSD. If you are using one of the supported PCMCIA Ethernet cards, also be sure that it is plugged in *before* the laptop is powered on! FreeBSD does not, unfortunately, currently support hot insertion of PCMCIA cards during installation.

---

16 http://www.FreeBSD.org/FAQ/ppp.html

You will also need to know your IP address on the network, the netmask value for your address class, and the name of your machine. If you are installing over a PPP connection and do not have a static IP, fear not, the IP address can be dynamically assigned by your ISP. Your system administrator can tell you which values to use for your particular network setup. If you will be referring to other hosts by name rather than IP address, you will also need a name server and possibly the address of a gateway (if you are using PPP, it is your provider's IP address) to use in talking to it. If you want to install by FTP via a HTTP proxy (see below), you will also need the proxy's address. If you do not know the answers to all or most of these questions, then you should really probably talk to your system administrator or ISP *before* trying this type of installation.

Before Installing via NFS

The NFS installation is fairly straight-forward. Simply copy the FreeBSD distribution files you want onto a server somewhere and then point the NFS media selection at it.

If this server supports only "privileged port" (as is generally the default for Sun workstations), you will need to set this option in the Options menu before installation can proceed.

If you have a poor quality Ethernet card which suffers from very slow transfer rates, you may also wish to toggle the appropriate Options flag.

In order for NFS installation to work, the server must support subdir mounts, e.g., if your FreeBSD 3.4 distribution directory lives on:`ziggy:/usr/archive/stuff/FreeBSD`, then `ziggy` will have to allow the direct mounting of `/usr/archive/stuff/FreeBSD`, not just `/usr` or `/usr/archive/stuff`.

In FreeBSD's `/etc/exports` file, this is controlled by the `-alldirs`. Other NFS servers may have different conventions. If you are getting "permission denied" messages from the server, then it is likely that you do not have this enabled properly.

Chapter 3
Unix Basics

3.1 Synopsis

The following chapter will cover the basic commands and functionality of the FreeBSD operating system. Much of this material is relevant for any Unix-like operating system. Feel free to skim over this chapter if you are familiar with the material. If you are new to FreeBSD, then you will definitely want to read through this chapter carefully.

After reading this chapter, you will know:

- How Unix file permissions work.
- What processes, daemons, and signals are.
- What a shell is, and how to change your default login environment.
- How to use basic text editors.
- How to read manual pages for more information.

3.2 Permissions

FreeBSD, being a direct descendant of BSD Unix, is based on several key Unix concepts. The first, and most pronounced, is that FreeBSD is a multi-user operating system. The system can handle several users all working simultaneously on completely unrelated tasks. The system is responsible for properly sharing and managing requests for hardware devices, peripherals, memory, and CPU time evenly to each user.

Because the system is capable of supporting multiple users, everything the system manages has a set of permissions governing who can read, write, and execute the resource. These permissions are stored as two octets broken into three pieces, one for the owner of the file, one for the group that the file belongs to, and one for everyone else. This numerical representation works like this:

Value	Permission	Directory Listing
0	No read, no write, no execute	---
1	No read, no write, execute	--x
2	No read, write, no execute	-w-
3	No read, write, execute	-wx
4	Read, no write, no execute	r--

Value	Permission	Directory Listing
5	Read, no write, execute	r-x
6	Read, write, no execute	rw-
7	Read, write, execute	rwx

You can use the -l command line argument to ls(1) to view a long directory listing that includes a column with information about a file's permissions for the owner, group, and everyone else. Here's how the first column of ls -l is broken up:

```
-rw-r--r--
```

The first character, from left to right, is a special character that tells if this is a regular file, a directory, a special character or block device, a socket, or any other special pseudo-file device. The next three characters, designated as rw- gives the permissions for the owner of the file. The next three characters, r-- gives the permissions for the group that the file belongs to. The final three characters, r--, gives the permissions for the rest of the world. A dash means that the permission is turned off. In the case of this file, the permissions are set so the owner can read and write to the file, the group can read the file, and the rest of the world can only read the file. According to the table above, the permissions for this file would be 644, where each digit represents the three parts of the file's permission.

This is all well and good, but how does the system control permissions on devices? FreeBSD actually treats most hardware devices as a file that programs can open, read, and write data to just like any other file. These special device files are stored on the /dev directory.

Directories are also treated as files. They have read, write, and execute permissions. The executable bit for a directory has a slightly different meaning than that of files. When a directory is marked executable, it means it can be searched into, for example, a directory listing can be done in that directory.

There are more to permissions, but they are primarily used in special circumstances such as setuid binaries and sticky directories. If you want more information on file permissions and how to set them, be sure to look at the chmod(1) man page.

3.3 Directory Structure

The FreeBSD directory hierarchy is fundamental to obtaining an overall understanding of the system. The most important concept to grasp is that of the root directory, "/". This directory is the first one mounted at boot time and it contains the base system necessary to prepare the operating system for multi-user operation. The root directory also contains mount points for every other file system that you may want to mount.

A mount point is a directory where additional file systems can be grafted onto the root file system. Standard mount points include /usr, /var, /mnt, and /cdrom. These directories are usually referenced to entries in the file /etc/fstab. /etc/fstab is a table of various file systems and mount points for reference by the system. Most of the file systems in /etc/fstab are mounted automatically at boot time from the script rc(8) unless they contain the noauto option. Consult the fstab(5) manual page for more information on the format of the /etc/fstab file and the options it contains.

A complete description of the filesystem hierarchy is available in hier(7). For now, a brief overview of the most common directories will suffice.

Directory	Description
`/`	Root directory of the filesystem.
`/bin/`	User utilities fundamental to both single-user and multi-user environments.
`/boot/`	Programs and configuration files used during operating system bootstrap.
`/boot/defaults/`	Default bootstrapping configuration files; see loader.conf(5).
`/dev/`	Device nodes; see intro(4).
`/etc/`	System configuration files and scripts.
`/etc/defaults/`	Default system configuration files; see rc(8).
`/etc/mail/`	Configuration files for mail transport agents such as sendmail(8).
`/etc/namedb/`	`named` configuration files; see named(8).
`/etc/periodic/`	Scripts that are run daily, weekly, and monthly, via cron(8); see periodic(8).
`/etc/ppp/`	`ppp` configuration files; see ppp(8).
`/mnt/`	Empty directory commonly used by system administrators as a temporary mount point.
`/proc/`	Process file system; see procfs(5), mount_procfs(8).
`/root/`	Home directory for the `root` account.
`/sbin/`	System programs and administration utilities fundamental to both single-user and multi-user environments.
`/stand/`	Programs used in a standalone environment.
`/tmp/`	Temporary files, usually a mfs(8) memory-based filesystem (the contents of `/tmp` are usually NOT preserved across a system reboot).
`/usr/`	The majority of user utilities and applications.
`/usr/bin/`	Common utilities, programming tools, and applications.
`/usr/include/`	Standard C include files.
`/usr/lib/`	Archive libraries.
`/usr/libdata/`	Miscellaneous utility data files.
`/usr/libexec/`	System daemons & system utilities (executed by other programs).
`/usr/local/`	Local executables, libraries, etc. Also used as the default destination for the FreeBSD ports framework. Within `/usr/local`, the general layout sketched out by hier(7) for `/usr` should be used. Exceptions are the man directory is directly under `/usr/local` rather than under `/usr/local/share`. Ports documentation is in `share/doc/port`.

Directory	Description
`/usr/obj/`	Architecture-specific target tree produced by building the `/usr/src` tree.
`/usr/ports`	The FreeBSD ports collection (optional).
`/usr/sbin/`	System daemons & system utilities (executed by users).
`/usr/share/`	Architecture-independent files.
`/usr/src/`	BSD and/or local source files.
`/usr/X11R6/`	X11R6 distribution executables, libraries, etc (optional).
`/var/`	Multi-purpose log, temporary, transient, and spool files.
`/var/log/`	Miscellaneous system log files.
`/var/mail/`	User mailbox files.
`/var/spool/`	Miscellaneous printer and mail system spooling directories.
`/var/tmp/`	Temporary files that are kept between system reboots.
`/var/yp`	NIS maps.

3.4 Mounting and Unmounting Filesystems

The filesystem is best visualized as a tree, rooted, as it were, at `/`. `/dev`, `/usr`, and the other directories in the root directory are branches, which may have their own branches, such as `/usr/local`, and so on.

There are various reasons to house some of these directories on separate filesystems. `/var` contains the directories `log/`, `spool/`, and various types of temporary files, and as such, may get filled up. Filling up the root filesystem is not a good idea, so splitting `/var` from `/` is often favorable.

Another common reason to contain certain directory trees on other filesystems is if they are to be housed on separate physical disks, or are separate virtual disks, such as Network File System (Section 17.4) mounts, or CDROM drives.

3.4.1 The `fstab` File

During the boot process (described in detail in Chapter 7), filesystems listed in `/etc/fstab` are automatically mounted (unless they are listed with the `noauto` option).

The `/etc/fstab` file contains a list of lines of the following format:

```
device      /mount-point fstype    options      dumpfreq     passno
```

device

A device name (which should exist), as explained in the Disk naming conventions section (Section 12.2).

mount-point

> A directory (which should exist), on which to mount the filesystem.

fstype

> The filesystem type to pass to mount(8). The default FreeBSD filesystem is ufs.

options

> Either rw for read-write filesystems, or ro for read-only filesystems, followed by any other options that may be needed. A common option is noauto for filesystems not normally mounted during the boot sequence. Other options are listed in the mount(8) manual page.

dumpfreq

> The number of days the filesystem should be dumped, and passno is the pass number during which the filesystem is checked during the boot sequence.

3.4.2 The mount Command

The mount(8) command is what is ultimately used to mount filesystems.

In its most basic form, you use:

```
# mount device mountpoint
```

There are plenty of options, as mentioned in the mount(8) manual page, but the most common are:

Mount Options

-a

> Mount all the filesystems listed in /etc/fstab. Exceptions are those marked as "noauto", excluded by the -t flag, or those that are already mounted.

-d

> Do everything except for the actual system call. This option is useful in conjunction with the -v flag to determine what the mount is actually trying to do.

-f

> Force the mount of an unclean filesystem (dangerous), or forces the revocation of write access when downgrading a filesystem's mount status from read-write to read-only.

-r

> Mount the filesystem read-only. This is identical to using the rdonly argument to the -o option.

`-t` *fstype*

> Mount the given filesystem as the given filesystem type, or mount only filesystems of the given type, if given the `-a` option.

> "ufs" is the default filesystem type.

`-u`

> Update mount options on the filesystem.

`-v`

> Be verbose.

`-w`

> Mount the filesystem read-write.

The `-o` option takes a comma-separated list of the options, including the following:

nodev

> Do not interpret special devices on the filesystem. This is a useful security option.

noexec

> Do not allow execution of binaries on this filesystem. This is also a useful security option.

nosuid

> Do not interpret setuid or setgid flags on the filesystem. This is also a useful security option.

3.4.3 The `umount` Command

The umount(8) command takes, as a parameter, one of a mountpoint, a device name, or the `-a` or `-A` option.

All forms take `-f` to force unmounting, and `-v` for verbosity.

`-a` and `-A` are used to unmount all mounted filesystems, possibly modified by the filesystem types listed after `-t`. `-A`, however, does not attempt to unmount the root filesystem.

3.5 Processes

FreeBSD is a multi-tasking operating system. This means that it seems as though more than one program is running at once. Each program running at any one time is called a *process*. Every command you run will start at least one new process, and there are a number of system processes that run all the time, keeping the system functional.

Each process is uniquely identified by a number called a *process ID*, or *PID*, and, like files, each process also has one owner and group. The owner and group information is used to determine what files and devices the process can open, using the file permissions discussed earlier. Most processes also have a parent process. The parent process is the process that started them. For example, if you are typing commands to the shell then the shell is a process, and any commands you run are also processes. Each process you run in this way will have your shell as its parent process. The exception to this is a special process called init. init is always the first process, so its PID is always 1. init is started automatically by the kernel when FreeBSD starts.

Two commands are particularly useful to see the processes on the system, ps(1) and top(1). The ps(1) command is used to show a static list of the currently running processes, and can show their PID, how much memory they are using, the command line they were started with, and so on. The top(1) command displays all the running processes, and updates the display every few seconds, so that you can interactively see what your computer is doing.

By default, ps(1) only shows you the commands that are running and are owned by you. For example;

```
% ps
  PID  TT  STAT     TIME COMMAND
  298  p0  Ss    0:01.10 tcsh
 7078  p0  S     2:40.88 xemacs mdoc.xsl (xemacs-21.1.14)
37393  p0  I     0:03.11 xemacs freebsd.dsl (xemacs-21.1.14)
48630  p0  S     2:50.89 /usr/local/lib/netscape-linux/navigator-linux-4.77.bi
48730  p0  IW    0:00.00 (dns helper) (navigator-linux-)
72210  p0  R+    0:00.00 ps
  390  p1  Is    0:01.14 tcsh
 7059  p2  Is+   1:36.18 /usr/local/bin/mutt -y
 6688  p3  IWs   0:00.00 tcsh
10735  p4  IWs   0:00.00 tcsh
20256  p5  IWs   0:00.00 tcsh
  262  v0  IWs   0:00.00 -tcsh (tcsh)
  270  v0  IW+   0:00.00 /bin/sh /usr/X11R6/bin/startx -- -bpp 16
  280  v0  IW+   0:00.00 xinit /home/nik/.xinitrc -- -bpp 16
  284  v0  IW    0:00.00 /bin/sh /home/nik/.xinitrc
  285  v0  S     0:38.45 /usr/X11R6/bin/sawfish
```

As you can see in this example, the output from ps(1) is organized in to a number of columns. PID is the process ID discussed earlier. PIDs are assigned starting from 1, go up to 65536, and wrap around back to the beginning when you run out. TT shows the tty the program is running on, and can safely be ignored for the moment. STAT shows the program's state, and again, can be safely ignored. TIME is the amount of time the program has been running on the CPU—this is not necessarily the elapsed time since you started the program, as some programs spend a lot of time waiting for things to happen before they need to spend time on the CPU. Finally, COMMAND is the command line that was used to run the program.

ps(1) supports a number of different options to change the information that is displayed. One of the most useful sets is auxww. a displays information about all the running processes, not just your own. u displays the username of the process' owner, as well as memory usage. x displays information about daemon processes, and ww causes ps(1) to display the full command line, rather than truncating it once it gets too long to fit on the screen.

The output from top(1) is similar. A sample session looks like this;

```
% top
last pid: 72257;  load averages:  0.13,  0.09,  0.03    up 0+13:38:33  22:39:10
```

```
47 processes:  1 running, 46 sleeping
CPU states: 12.6% user,  0.0% nice,  7.8% system,  0.0% interrupt, 79.7% idle
Mem: 36M Active, 5256K Inact, 13M Wired, 6312K Cache, 15M Buf,  408K Free
Swap: 256M Total, 38M Used, 217M Free, 15% Inuse

  PID USERNAME PRI NICE  SIZE    RES STATE   TIME   WCPU    CPU COMMAND
72257 nik       28   0  1960K  1044K RUN     0:00 14.86%  1.42% top
 7078 nik        2   0 15280K 10960K select  2:54  0.88%  0.88% xemacs-21.1.14
  281 nik        2   0 18636K  7112K select  5:36  0.73%  0.73% XF86_SVGA
  296 nik        2   0  3240K  1644K select  0:12  0.05%  0.05% xterm
48630 nik        2   0 29816K  9148K select  3:18  0.00%  0.00% navigator-linu
  175 root       2   0   924K   252K select  1:41  0.00%  0.00% syslogd
 7059 nik        2   0  7260K  4644K poll    1:38  0.00%  0.00% mutt
...
```

The output is split in to two sections. The header (the first five lines) shows the PID of the last process to run, the system load averages (which are a measure of how busy the system is), the system uptime (time since the last reboot) and the current time. The other figures in the header relate to how many processes are running (47 in this case), how much memory and swap space has been taken up, and how much time the system is spending in different CPU states.

Below that are a series of columns containing similar information to the output from ps(1). As before you can see the PID, the username, the amount of CPU time taken, and the command that was run. top(1) also defaults to showing you the amount of memory space taken by the process. This is split in to two columns, one for total size, and one for resident size—total size is how much memory the application has needed, and the resident size is how much it is actually using at the moment. In this example you can see that Netscape has required almost 30 MB of RAM, but is currently only using 9 MB.

top(1) automatically updates this display every two seconds; this can be changed with the s option.

3.6 Daemons, Signals, and Killing Processes

When you run an editor it is easy to control the editor, tell it to load files, and so on. You can do this because the editor provides facilities to do so, and because the editor is attached to a *terminal*. Some programs are not designed to be run with continuous user input, and so they disconnect from the terminal at the first opportunity. For example, a web server spends all day responding to web requests, it normally does not need any input from you. Programs that transport email from site to site are another example of this class of application.

We call these programs *daemons*. Daemons were characters in Greek mythology; neither good or evil, they were little attendant spirits that, by and large, did useful things for mankind. Much like the web servers and mail servers of today do useful things. This is why the BSD mascot has, for a long time, been the cheerful looking daemon with sneakers and a pitchfork.

There is a convention to name programs that normally run as daemons with a trailing "d". **BIND** is the Berkeley Internet Name Daemon (and the actual program that executes is called named), the **Apache** web server program is called httpd, the line printer spooling daemon is lpd and so on. This is a convention, not a hard and fast rule; for example, the main mail daemon for the **Sendmail** application is called sendmail, and not maild, as you might imagine.

Sometimes you will need to communicate with a daemon process. These communications are called *signals*, and you can communicate with daemons (or with any running process) by sending it a signal. There are a number of different signals that you can send—some of them have a specific meaning, others are interpreted by the application, and the application's documentation will tell you how that application interprets signals. You can only send a signal to a process that you own. If you try and send a signal to someone else's process it will be ignored. The exception to this is the root user, who can send signals to everyone's processes.

FreeBSD will also send applications signals in some cases. If an application is badly written, and tries to access memory that it is not supposed to, FreeBSD sends the process the *Segmentation Violation* signal (SIGSEGV). If an application has used the alarm(3) system call to be alerted after a period of time has elapsed then it will be sent the Alarm signal (SIGALRM), and so on.

Two signals can be used to stop a process, SIGTERM and SIGKILL. SIGTERM is the polite way to kill a process; the process can *catch* the signal, realize that you want it to shut down, close any log files it may have open, and generally finish whatever it is doing at the time before shutting down. In some cases a process may even ignore SIGTERM if it is in the middle of some task that can not be interrupted.

SIGKILL can not be ignored by a process. This is the "I do not care what you are doing, stop right now" signal. If you send SIGKILL to a process then FreeBSD will stop that process there and then[1].

The other signals you might want to use are SIGHUP, SIGUSR1, and SIGUSR2. These are general purpose signals, and different applications will do different things when they are sent.

Suppose that you have changed your web server's configuration file—you would like to tell the web server to re-read its configuration. You could stop and restart httpd, but this would result in a brief outage period on your web server, which may be undesirable. Most daemons are written to respond to the SIGHUP signal by re-reading their configuration file. So instead of killing and restarting httpd you would send it the SIGHUP signal. Because there is no standard way to respond to these signals, different daemons will have different behavior, so be sure and read the documentation for the daemon in question.

Signals are sent using the kill(1) command, as this example shows.

Sending a Signal to a Process

This example shows how to send a signal to inetd(8). The inetd(8) configuration file is /etc/inetd.conf, and inetd(8) will re-read this configuration file when it is sent SIGHUP.

1. Find the process ID of the process you want to send the signal to. Do this using ps(1) and grep(1). The grep(1) command is used to search through output, looking for the string you specify. This command is run as a normal user, and inetd(8) is run as root, so the ax options must be given to ps(1).

   ```
   % ps -ax | grep inetd
     198  ??  IWs    0:00.00 inetd -wW
   ```

   So the inetd(8) PID is 198. In some cases the grep inetd command might also occur in this output. This is because of the way ps(1) has to find the list of running processes.

2. Use kill(1) to send the signal. Because inetd(8) is being run by root you must use su(1) to become root first.

---

1. Not quite true—there are a few things that can not be interrupted. For example, if the process is trying to read from a file that is on another computer on the network, and the other computer has gone away for some reason (been turned off, or the network has a fault), then the process is said to be "uninterruptible". Eventually the process will time out, typically after two minutes. As soon as this time out occurs the process will be killed.

```
% su
Password:
# /bin/kill -s HUP 198
```

As is common with Unix commands, kill(1) will not print any output if it is successfully. If you try and send a signal to a process that you do not own then you will see `kill: PID: Operation not permitted`. If you mistype the PID you will either send the signal to the wrong process, which could be bad, or, if you are lucky, you will have sent the signal to a PID that is not currently in use, and you will see `kill: PID: No such process`.

> **Why Use** `/bin/kill`**?:** Many shells provide the `kill` command as a built in command; that is, the shell will send the signal directly, rather than running `/bin/kill`. This can be very useful, but different shells have a different syntax for specifying the name of the signal to send. Rather than try to learn all of them, it can be simpler just to use the `/bin/kill` ... command directly.

Sending other signals is very similar, just substitute TERM or KILL in the command line as necessary.

> **Important:** Killing random process on the system can be a bad idea. In particular, init(8), process ID 1, is very special. Running `/bin/kill -s KILL 1` is a quick way to shutdown your system. *Always* double check the arguments you run kill(1) with *before* you press **Return**.

3.7 Shells

In FreeBSD, a lot of everyday work is done in a command line interface called a shell. A shell's main job is to take commands from the input channel and execute them. A lot of shells also have built in functions to help everyday tasks such a file management, file globing, command line editing, command macros, and environment variables. FreeBSD comes with a set of shells, such as sh, the Bourne Shell, and csh, the C-shell. Many other shells are available from the FreeBSD Ports Collection that have much more power, such as tcsh and bash.

Which shell do you use? It is really a matter of taste. If you are a C programmer you might feel more comfortable with a C-like shell such as tcsh. If you have come from Linux or are new to a Unix command line interface you might try bash. The point is that each shell has unique properties that may or may not work with your preferred working environment, and that you have a choice of what shell to use.

One common feature in a shell is file-name completion. Given the typing of the first few letters of a command or filename, you can usually have the shell automatically complete the rest of the command or filename by hitting the **Tab** key on the keyboard. Here is an example. Suppose you have two files called `foobar` and `foo.bar`. You want to delete `foo.bar`. So what you would type on the keyboard is: `rm fo`[**Tab**]`.`[**Tab**].

The shell would print out `rm foo`[BEEP]`.bar`.

The [BEEP] is the console bell, which is the shell telling me it was unable to totally complete the filename because there is more than one match. Both `foobar` and `foo.bar` start with `fo`, but it was able to complete to `foo`. If you type in `.`, then hit **Tab** again, the shell would be able to fill in the rest of the filename for you.

Another function of the shell is environment variables. Environment variables are a variable key pair stored in the shell's environment space. This space can be read by any program invoked by the shell, and thus contains a lot of program configuration. Here is a list of common environment variables and what they mean:

Variable	Description
USER	Current logged in user's name.
PATH	Colon separated list of directories to search for binaries.
DISPLAY	Network name of the X11 display to connect to, if available.
SHELL	The current shell.
TERM	The name of the user's terminal. Used to determine the capabilities of the terminal.
TERMCAP	Database entry of the terminal escape codes to perform various terminal functions.
OSTYPE	Type of operating system. e.g., FreeBSD.
MACHTYPE	The CPU architecture that the system is running on.
EDITOR	The user's preferred text editor.
PAGER	The user's preferred text pager.
MANPATH	Colon separated list of directories to search for manual pages.

To view or set an environment variable differs somewhat from shell to shell. For example, in the C-Style shells such as `tcsh` and `csh`, you would use `setenv` to set and view environment variables. Under Bourne shells such as `sh` and `bash`, you would use `set` and `export` to view and set your current environment variables. For example, to set or modify the EDITOR environment variable, under `csh` or `tcsh` a command like this would set EDITOR to /usr/local/bin/emacs:

```
% setenv EDITOR /usr/local/bin/emacs
```

Under Bourne shells:

```
% export EDITOR="/usr/local/bin/emacs"
```

You can also make most shells expand the environment variable by placing a $ character in front of it on the command line. For example, `echo $TERM` would print out whatever $TERM is set to, because the shell expands $TERM and passes it on to echo.

Shells treat a lot of special characters, called meta-characters as special representations of data. The most common one is the `*` character, which represents any number of characters in a filename. These special meta-characters can be used to do file name globing. For example, typing in `echo *` is almost the same as typing in `ls` because the shell takes all the files that match `*` and puts them on the command line for echo to see.

To prevent the shell from interpreting these special characters, they can be escaped from the shell by putting a backslash (\) character in front of them. `echo $TERM` prints whatever your terminal is set to. `echo \$TERM` prints $TERM as is.

3.7.1 Changing Your Shell

The easiest way to change your shell is to use the chsh command. Running chsh will place you into the editor that is in your EDITOR environment variable; if it is not set, you will be placed in vi. Change the "Shell:" line accordingly.

You can also give chsh the -s option; this will set your shell for you, without requiring you to enter an editor. For example, if you wanted to change your shell to bash, the following should do the trick:

```
% chsh -s /usr/local/bin/bash
```

Running chsh with no parameters and editing the shell from there would work also.

> **Note:** The shell that you wish to use *must* be present in the /etc/shells file. If you have installed a shell from the ports collection (Chapter 4), then this should have been done for you already. If you installed the shell by hand, you must do this.
>
> For example, if you installed bash by hand and placed it into /usr/local/bin, you would want to:
>
> ```
> # echo "/usr/local/bin/bash" >> /etc/shells
> ```
>
> Then rerun chsh.

3.8 Text Editors

A lot of configuration in FreeBSD is done by editing text files. Because of this, it would be a good idea to become familiar with a text editor. FreeBSD comes with a few as part of the base system, and many more are available in the ports collection.

The easiest and simplest editor to learn is an editor called **ee**, which stands for easy editor. To start **ee**, one would type at the command line ee filename where filename is the name of the file to be edited. For example, to edit /etc/rc.conf, type in ee /etc/rc.conf. Once inside of ee, all of the commands for manipulating the editor's functions are listed at the top of the display. The caret ^ character means the control key on the keyboard, so ^e expands to pressing the control key plus the letter e. To leave **ee**, hit the escape key, then choose leave editor. The editor will prompt you to save any changes if the file has been modified.

FreeBSD also comes with more powerful text editors such as vi as part of the base system, and emacs and vim as part of the FreeBSD Ports Collection. These editors offer much more functionality and power at the expense of being a little more complicated to learn. However if you plan on doing a lot of text editing, learning a more powerful editor such as vim or emacs will save you much more time in the long run.

3.9 Devices and Device Nodes

A device is a term used mostly for hardware-related activities in a system, including disks, printers, graphics cards, and keyboards. When FreeBSD boots, the majority of what FreeBSD displays are devices being detected. You can look through the boot messages again by viewing `/var/run/dmesg.boot`.

For example, `acd0` is the first IDE CDROM drive, while `kbd0` represents the keyboard.

Most of these devices in a Unix operating system must be accessed through a special file called device nodes, which are located in the `/dev` directory.

3.9.1 Creating Device Nodes

When adding a new device to your system, or compiling in support for additional devices, a device driver often-times needs to be created.

MAKEDEV Script

On systems without DEVFS, device nodes are created using the MAKEDEV(8) script as shown below:

```
# cd /dev
# sh MAKEDEV ad1
```

This example would make the proper device nodes for the second IDE drive when installed.

devfs (Device File System)

The device file system, or devfs, provides access to kernel's device namespace in the global filesystem namespace. Instead of having to create and modify device nodes, devfs maintains this particular filesystem for you.

See the devfs(5) man page for more information.

devfs is used by default in FreeBSD 5.0.

3.10 For More Information...

3.10.1 Manual Pages

The most comprehensive documentation on FreeBSD is in the form of manual pages. Nearly every program on the system comes with a short reference manual explaining the basic operation and various arguments. These manuals can be viewed with the man command. Use of the man command is simple:

```
% man command
```

command is the name of the command you wish to learn about. For example, to learn more about `ls` command type:

```
% man ls
```

The online manual is divided up into numbered sections:

1. User commands.

2. System calls and error numbers.

3. Functions in the C libraries.

4. Device drivers.

5. File formats.

6. Games and other diversions.

7. Miscellaneous information.

8. System maintenance and operation commands.

9. Kernel developers.

In some cases, the same topic may appear in more than one section of the online manual. For example, there is a chmod user command and a chmod() system call. In this case, you can tell the man command which one you want by specifying the section:

```
% man 1 chmod
```

This will display the manual page for the user command chmod. References to a particular section of the online manual are traditionally placed in parenthesis in written documentation, so chmod(1) refers to the chmod user command and chmod(2) refers to the system call.

This is fine if you know the name of the command and simply wish to know how to use it, but what if you cannot recall the command name? You can use man to search for keywords in the command descriptions by using the -k switch:

```
% man -k mail
```

With this command you will be presented with a list of commands that have the keyword "mail" in their descriptions. This is actually functionally equivalent to using the apropos command.

So, you are looking at all those fancy commands in /usr/bin but do not have the faintest idea what most of them actually do? Simply do:

```
% cd /usr/bin
% man -f *
```

or

```
% cd /usr/bin
% whatis *
```

which does the same thing.

3.10.2 GNU Info Files

FreeBSD includes many applications and utilities produced by the Free Software Foundation (FSF). In addition to manual pages, these programs come with more extensive hypertext documents called `info` files which can be viewed with the `info` command or, if you installed **emacs**, the info mode of **emacs**.

To use the info(1) command, simply type:

```
% info
```

For a brief introduction, type `h`. For a quick command reference, type `?`.

Chapter 4

Installing Applications: Packages and Ports

4.1 Synopsis

FreeBSD is bundled with a rich collection of system tools as part of the base system. However, there is only so much one can do before needing to install an additional third-party application to get real work done. FreeBSD provides two complementary technologies for installing third party software on your system; the FreeBSD Ports Collection, and binary software packages. Either system may be used to install the newest version of your favorite applications from local media or straight off the network.

After reading this chapter, you will know:

- How to install third-party binary software packages.
- How to build third-party software from the ports collection.
- How to remove previously installed packages or ports.

4.2 Overview of Software Installation

If you have used a Unix system before you will know that the typical procedure for installing third party software goes something like this:

1. Download the software, which might be distributed in source code format, or as a binary.

2. Unpack the software from its distribution format (typically a tarball compressed with either compress(1) or gzip(1)).

3. Locate the documentation (perhaps a README file, or some files in a doc/ subdirectory) and read up on how to install the software.

4. If the software was distributed in source format, compile it. This may involve editing a Makefile, or running a configure script, and other work.

5. Test and install the software.

And that is only if everything goes well. If you are installing a software package that was not deliberately ported to FreeBSD you may even have to go in and edit the code to make it work properly.

Should you want to, you can continue to install software the "traditional" way with FreeBSD. However, FreeBSD provides two technologies which can save you a lot of effort; packages and ports. At the time of this printing, over 5,900 third party applications have been made available in this way.

For any given application, the FreeBSD package for that application is a single file which you must download. The package contains pre-compiled copies of all the commands for the application, as well as any configuration files or documentation. A downloaded package file can be manipulated with FreeBSD package management commands, such as pkg_add(1), pkg_delete(1), and pkg_info(1).

In this way, a new application can be installed with a single command.

A FreeBSD port for an application is a collection of files designed to automate the process of compiling an application from source code.

Remember that there are a number of steps you would normally carry out if you compiled a program yourself (unpacking, patching, compiling, installing). The files that make up a port contain all the necessary information to allow the system to do this for you. You run a handful of simple commands and the source code for the application is automatically downloaded, extracted, patched, compiled, and installed for you.

In fact, the ports system can also be used to generate packages which can later be manipulated with `pkg_add` and the other package management commands that will be introduced shortly.

Both packages and ports understand *dependencies*. Suppose you want to install an application that depends on a specific library being installed. Both the application and the library have been made available as FreeBSD ports and packages. If you use the `pkg_add` command or the ports system to add the application, both will notice that the library has not been installed, and the commands will install the library first.

Given that the two technologies are quite similar, you might be wondering why FreeBSD bothers with both. Packages and ports both have their own strengths, and which one you use will depend on your own preference.

Package Benefits

- A compressed package tarball is typically smaller than the compressed tarball containing the source code for the application.

- Packages do not require any additional compilation. For large applications, such as **Mozilla**, **KDE**, or **GNOME** this can be important, particularly if you are on a slow system.

- Packages do not require you to understand the process involved in compiling software on FreeBSD.

Ports Benefits

- Packages are normally compiled with conservative options, because they have to run on the maximum number of systems. By installing from the port, you can tweak the compilation options to (for example) generate code that is specific to a Pentium III or Athlon processor.

- Some packages have compile time options relating to what they can and cannot do. For example, **Apache** can be configured with a wide variety of different built-in options. By building from the port you do not have to accept the default options, and can set them yourself.

  In some cases, multiple packages will exist for the same application to specify certain settings. For example, **Ghostscript** is available as a `ghostscript` package and a `ghostscript-nox11` package, depending on whether or not you have installed an X11 server. This sort of rough tweaking is possible with packages, but rapidly becomes impossible if an application has more than one or two different compile time options.

- The licensing conditions of some software distributions forbid binary distribution. They must be distributed as source code.
- Some people do not trust binary distributions. At least with source code, you can (in theory) read through it and look for potential problems yourself.
- If you have local patches, you will need the source in order to apply them.
- Some people like having code around, so they can read it if they get bored, hack it, borrow from it (license permitting, of course), and so on.

To keep track of updated ports, subscribe to the `<freebsd-ports@freebsd.org>` mailing list.

The remainder of this chapter will explain how to use packages and ports to install and manage third party software on FreeBSD.

4.3 Finding Your Application

Before you can install any applications you need to know what you want, and what the application is called.

FreeBSD's list of available applications is growing all the time. Fortunately, there are a number of ways to find what you want.

- The FreeBSD web site maintains an up-to-date searchable list of all the available applications, at `http://www.FreeBSD.org/ports/`. The name space is divided in to categories, and you may either search for an application by name (if you know it), or you can list all the applications available in a category.
- Dan Langille maintains FreshPorts, at `http://www.FreshPorts.org/`. FreshPorts tracks changes to the applications in the ports tree as they happen, and allows you to "watch" one or more ports, and will send you an email when they are updated.
- If you do not know the name of the application you want, try using a site like FreshMeat (`http://www.freshmeat.net/`) or AppWatch (`http://www.appwatch.com/`) to find an application, then check back at the FreeBSD site to see if the application has been ported yet.

4.4 Using the Packages System

4.4.1 Installing a Package

You can use the pkg_add(1) utility to install a FreeBSD software package from a local file or from a server on the network.

Example 4-1. Downloading a Package and then Installing It Locally

```
# ftp -a ftp2.freebsd.org
Connected to ftp2.freebsd.org.
220 ftp2.freebsd.org FTP server (Version 6.00LS) ready.
331 Guest login ok, send your email address as password.
230-
230-      This machine is in Vienna, VA, USA, hosted by Verio.
230-          Questions? E-mail freebsd@vienna.verio.net.
230-
230-
230 Guest login ok, access restrictions apply.
Remote system type is UNIX.
Using binary mode to transfer files.
ftp> cd /pub/FreeBSD/ports/packages/sysutils/
250 CWD command successful.
ftp> get lsof-4.56.4.tgz
local: lsof-4.56.4.tgz remote: lsof-4.56.4.tgz
200 PORT command successful.
150 Opening BINARY mode data connection for 'lsof-4.56.4.tgz' (92375 bytes).
100% |*************************************************| 92375        00:00 ETA
226 Transfer complete.
92375 bytes received in 5.60 seconds (16.11 KB/s)
ftp> exit
# pkg_add lsof-4.56.4.tgz
```

If you do not have a source of local packages (such as a FreeBSD CDROM set) then it will probably be easier to use the -r option to pkg_add(1). This will cause the utility to automatically determine the correct object format and release and then to fetch and install the package from an FTP site.

```
# pkg_add -r lsof-4.56.4
```

The example above would download the correct package and add it without any further user intervention.

Package files are distributed in .tgz format. You can find them at ftp://ftp.FreeBSD.org/pub/FreeBSD/ports/packages/, or on the FreeBSD CDROM distribution. Every CD on the FreeBSD 4-CD set (and PowerPak, etc) contains packages in the /packages directory. The layout of the packages is similar to that of the /usr/ports tree. Each category has its own directory, and every package can be found within the All directory.

The directory structure of the package system is identical to that of the ports; they work with each other to form the entire package/port system.

4.4.2 Deleting a Package

To remove a previously installed software package, use the pkg_delete(1) utility.

```
# pkg_delete xchat-1.7.1
```

4.4.3 Managing Packages

pkg_info(1) is a utility that lists and describes the various packages installed.

```
# pkg_info
cvsup-16.1          A general network file distribution system optimized for CV
docbook-1.2         Meta-port for the different versions of the DocBook DTD
...
```

pkg_version(1) is a utility that summarizes the versions of all installed packages. It compares the package version to the current version found in the ports tree.

```
# pkg_version
cvsup                        =
docbook                      =
...
```

The symbols in the second column indicate the relative age of the installed version and the version available in the local ports tree.

Symbol	Meaning
=	The version of the installed package matches that of the one found in the local ports tree.
<	The installed version is older then the one available in the ports tree.
>	The installed version is newer than the one found in the local ports tree. (local ports tree is probably out of date)
?	The installed package cannot be found in the ports index.
*	There are multiple versions of the package.

4.4.4 Miscellaneous

All package information is stored within the /var/db/pkg directory. The installed file list and descriptions of each package can be found within files in this directory.

4.5 Using the Ports Collection

The following sections provide basic instructions on using the ports collection to install or remove programs from your system.

4.5.1 Installing Ports

The first thing that should be explained when it comes to the ports collection is what is actually meant by a "skeleton". In a nutshell, a port skeleton is a minimal set of files that are needed for a program to compile and install cleanly on FreeBSD. Each port skeleton includes:

- A `Makefile`. The `Makefile` contains various statements that specify how the application should be compiled and where it should be installed on your system

- A `distinfo` file. This file contains information about the files that must be downloaded to build the port, and checksums, to ensure that those files have not been corrupted during the download.

- A `files` directory. This directory contains patches to make the program compile and install on your FreeBSD system. Patches are basically small files that specify changes to particular files. They are in plain text format, and basically say "Remove line 10" or "Change line 26 to this ...". Patches are also known as "diffs" because they are generated by the **diff** program.

  This directory may also contain other files used in building the port.

- A `pkg-comment` file. This is a one-line description of the program.

- A `pkg-descr` file. This is a more detailed, often multiple-line, description of the program.

- A `pkg-plist` file. This is a list of all the files that will be installed by the port. It also tells the ports system what files to remove upon deinstallation.

Now that you have enough background information to know what the ports collection is used for, you are ready to install your first port. There are two ways this can be done, and each is explained below.

Before we get into that however, you will need to choose a port to install. There are a few ways to do this, with the easiest method being the ports listing on the FreeBSD web site[6]. You can browse through the ports listed there or use the search function on the site. Each port also includes a description so you can read a bit about each port before deciding to install it.

Another method is to use the `whereis` command. To use `whereis`, simply type "`whereis <program you want to install>`" at the prompt, and if it is found on your system, you will be told where it is, like so:

```
# whereis lsof
lsof: /usr/ports/sysutils/lsof
```

This tells us that `lsof` (a system utility) can be found in the `/usr/ports/sysutils/lsof` directory.

Yet another way of finding a particular port is by using the ports collection's built-in search mechanism. To use the search feature, you will need to be in the `/usr/ports` directory. Once in that directory, run `make search key=program-name` where "program-name" is the name of the program you want to find. For example, if you were looking for `lsof`:

```
# cd /usr/ports
# make search key=lsof
Port:    lsof-4.56.4
```

---

6 http://www.FreeBSD.org/ports/

```
Path:   /usr/ports/sysutils/lsof
Info:   Lists information about open files (similar to fstat(1))
Maint:  obrien@FreeBSD.org
Index:  sysutils
B-deps:
R-deps:
```

The part of the output you want to pay particular attention to is the "Path:" line, since that tells you where to find it. The other information provided is not needed in order to install the port directly, so it will not be covered here.

> **Note:** You must be the `root` user to install ports.

Now that you have found a port you would like to install, you are ready to do the actual installation.

Installing Ports from a CDROM

As you may have guessed from the title, everything described in this section assumes you have a FreeBSD CDROM set. If you do not, you can order one from the FreeBSD Mall[7].

Assuming that your FreeBSD CDROM is in the drive and is mounted on `/cdrom` (and the mount point *must* be `/cdrom`), you are ready to install the port. To begin, change to the directory where the port you want to install lives:

```
# cd /usr/ports/sysutils/lsof
```

Once inside the `lsof` directory, you will see the port skeleton. The next step is to compile (also called build) the port. This is done by simply typing `make` at the prompt. Once you have done so, you should see something like this:

```
# make
>> lsof_4.57D.freebsd.tar.gz doesn't seem to exist in /usr/ports/distfiles/.
>> Attempting to fetch from file:/cdrom/ports/distfiles/.
===>  Extracting for lsof-4.57
...
[extraction output snipped]
...
>> Checksum OK for lsof_4.57D.freebsd.tar.gz.
===>  Patching for lsof-4.57
===>  Applying FreeBSD patches for lsof-4.57
===>  Configuring for lsof-4.57
...
[configure output snipped]
...
===>  Building for lsof-4.57
...
[compilation snipped]
...
#
```

---

7 http://www.freebsdmall.com/

Take notice that once the compile is complete you are returned to your prompt. The next step is to install the port. In order to install it, you simply need to tack one word onto the make command, and that word is install:

```
# make install
===>   Installing for lsof-4.57
...
[install routines snipped]
...
===>   Generating temporary packing list
===>   Compressing manual pages for lsof-4.57
===>   Registering installation for lsof-4.57
===>   SECURITY NOTE:
       This port has installed the following binaries which execute with
       increased privileges.
#
```

Once you are returned to your prompt, you should be able to run the application you just installed. Since lsof is a program that runs with increased privileges, a security warning is shown. During the building and installation of ports, you should take heed of any other warnings that may appear.

Note: You can save an extra step by just running make install instead of make and make install as two separate steps.

Note: Please be aware that the licenses of a few ports do not allow for inclusion on the CDROM. This could be because a registration form needs to be filled out before downloading, redistribution is not allowed, and so on. If you wish to install a port not included on the CDROM, you will need to be online in order to do so (see the next section).

Installing Ports from the Internet

As with the last section, this section makes an assumption that you have a working Internet connection. If you do not, you will need to perform the CDROM installation.

Installing a port from the Internet is done exactly the same way as it would be if you were installing from a CDROM. The only difference between the two is that the program's source code is downloaded from the Internet instead of pulled from the CDROM.

The steps involved are identical:

```
# make install
>> lsof_4.57D.freebsd.tar.gz doesn't seem to exist in /usr/ports/distfiles/.
>> Attempting to fetch from ftp://ftp.FreeBSD.org/pub/FreeBSD/ports/distfiles/.
Receiving lsof_4.57D.freebsd.tar.gz (439860 bytes): 100%
439860 bytes transferred in 18.0 seconds (23.90 kBps)
===>   Extracting for lsof-4.57
...
```

```
[extraction output snipped]
...
>> Checksum OK for lsof_4.57D.freebsd.tar.gz.
===>   Patching for lsof-4.57
===>   Applying FreeBSD patches for lsof-4.57
===>   Configuring for lsof-4.57
...
[configure output snipped]
...
===>   Building for lsof-4.57
...
[compilation snipped]
...
===>   Installing for lsof-4.57
...
[install routines snipped]
...
===>   Generating temporary packing list
===>   Compressing manual pages for lsof-4.57
===>   Registering installation for lsof-4.57
===>   SECURITY NOTE:
       This port has installed the following binaries which execute with
       increased privileges.
#
```

As you can see, the only difference is the line that tells you where the system is fetching the port from.

That about does it for installing ports onto your system. In the next section you will learn how to remove a port from your system.

4.5.2 Removing Installed Ports

Now that you know how to install ports, you are probably wondering how to remove them, just in case you install one and later on you decide that you installed the wrong port. The next few paragraphs will cover just that.

Now we will remove our previous example (which was lsof for those of you not paying attention). As with installing ports, the first thing you must do is change to the port directory, which if you remember was /usr/ports/irc/lsof. After you change directories, you are ready to uninstall lsof. This is done with the make deinstall command:

```
# cd /usr/ports/irc/lsof
# make deinstall
===>   Deinstalling for lsof-4.57
```

That was easy enough. You have now managed to remove lsof from your system. If you would like to reinstall it, you can do so by running make reinstall from the /usr/ports/irc/lsof directory.

4.6 Troubleshooting

The following sections cover some of the more frequently asked questions about the ports collection and some basic troubleshooting techniques, and what do to if a port is broken.

4.6.1 Some Questions and Answers

1. I thought this was going to be a discussion about modems??!

Ah, you must be thinking of the serial ports on the back of your computer. We are using "port" here to mean the result of "porting" a program from one version of Unix to another.

2. What is a patch?

A patch is a small file that specifies how to go from one version of a file to another. It contains plain text, and basically says things like "delete line 23", "add these two lines after line 468", or "change line 197 to this". They are also known as diffs because they are generated by the **diff** program.

3. What is all this about tarballs?

It is a file ending in `.tar`, or with variations such as `.tar.gz`, `.tar.Z`, `.tar.bz2`, and even `.tgz`.

Basically, it is a directory tree that has been archived into a single file (`.tar`) and optionally compressed (`.gz`). This technique was originally used for *T*ape *AR*chives (hence the name `tar`), but it is a widely used way of distributing program source code around the Internet.

You can see what files are in them, or even extract them yourself by using the standard Unix `tar` program, which comes with the base FreeBSD system, like this:

```
% tar tvzf foobar.tar.gz
% tar xzvf foobar.tar.gz
% tar tvf foobar.tar
% tar xvf foobar.tar
```

4. And a checksum?

It is a number generated by adding up all the data in the file you want to check. If any of the characters change, the checksum will no longer be equal to the total, so a simple comparison will allow you to spot the difference.

5. I did what you said for compiling ports from a CDROM and it worked great until I tried to install the kermit port.

```
# make install
>> cku190.tar.gz doesn't seem to exist on this system.
```

```
>> Attempting to fetch from ftp://kermit.columbia.edu/kermit/archives/.
```

Why can it not be found? Have I got a dud CDROM?

As explained in the compiling ports from CDROM section, some ports cannot be put on the CDROM set due to licensing restrictions. Kermit is an example of that. The licensing terms for kermit do not allow us to put the tarball for it on the CDROM, so you will have to fetch it by hand—sorry!

The reason why you got all those error messages was because you were not connected to the Internet at the time. Once you have downloaded it from any of the MASTER_SITES (listed in the Makefile), you can restart the install process.

6. I did that, but when I tried to put it into /usr/ports/distfiles I got some error about not having permission.

The ports mechanism looks for the tarball in /usr/ports/distfiles, but you will not be able to copy anything there because it is symlinked to the CDROM, which is read-only. You can tell it to look somewhere else by doing:

```
# make DISTDIR=/where/you/put/it install
```

7. Does the ports scheme only work if you have everything in /usr/ports? My system administrator says I must put everything under /u/people/guests/wurzburger, but it does not seem to work.

You can use the PORTSDIR and PREFIX variables to tell the ports mechanism to use different directories. For instance,

```
# make PORTSDIR=/u/people/guests/wurzburger/ports install
```

will compile the port in /u/people/guests/wurzburger/ports and install everything under /usr/local.

```
# make PREFIX=/u/people/guests/wurzburger/local install
```

will compile it in /usr/ports and install it in /u/people/guests/wurzburger/local.

And of course,

```
# make PORTSDIR=../ports PREFIX=../local install
```

will combine the two (it is too long to write fully on the page, but it should give you the general idea).

Some ports that use imake(1) (a part of the X Windows System) do not work well with PREFIX, and will insist on installing under /usr/X11R6. Similarly, some Perl ports ignore PREFIX and install in the Perl tree. Making these ports respect PREFIX is a difficult or impossible job.

If you do not fancy typing all that in every time you install a port, it is a good idea to put these variables into your environment. Read the manual page for your shell for instructions on doing so.

8. I do not have a FreeBSD CDROM, but I would like to have all the tarballs handy on my system so I do not have to wait for a download every time I install a port. Is there any way to get them all at once?

To get every single tarball for the ports collection, do:

```
# cd /usr/ports
# make fetch
```

For all the tarballs for a single ports directory, do:

```
# cd /usr/ports/directory
# make fetch
```

and for just one port—well, you have probably guessed already.

9. I know it is probably faster to fetch the tarballs from one of the FreeBSD mirror sites close by. Is there any way to tell the port to fetch them from servers other than the ones listed in the MASTER_SITES?

Yes. If you know, for example, that `ftp.FreeBSD.org` is much closer to you than the sites listed in MASTER_SITES, do as follows:

```
# cd /usr/ports/directory
# make MASTER_SITE_OVERRIDE= \
ftp://ftp.FreeBSD.org/pub/FreeBSD/ports/distfiles/ fetch
```

10. I want to know what files `make` is going to need before it tries to pull them down.

`make fetch-list` will display a list of the files needed for a port.

11. Is there any way to stop the port from compiling? I want to do some hacking on the source before I install it, but it is a bit tiresome to watch it and hit control-C every time.

Doing `make extract` will stop it after it has fetched and extracted the source code.

12. I am trying to make my own port and I want to be able to stop it compiling until I have had a chance to see if my patches worked properly. Is there something like `make extract`, but for patches?

Yes, `make patch` is what you want. You will probably find the PATCH_DEBUG option useful as well. And by the way, thank you for your efforts!

13. I have heard that some compiler options can cause bugs. Is this true? How can I make sure that I compile ports with the right settings?

Yes, with version 2.6.3 of `gcc` (the version shipped with FreeBSD 2.1.0 and 2.1.5), the `-O2` option could result in buggy code unless you used the `-fno-strength-reduce` option as well. (Most of the ports do not use `-O2`). You *should* be able to specify the compiler options used by something like:

```
# make CFLAGS='-O2 -fno-strength-reduce' install
```

or by editing `/etc/make.conf`, but unfortunately not all ports respect this. The surest way is to do `make configure`, then go into the source directory and inspect the Makefiles by hand, but this can get tedious if the source has lots of sub-directories, each with their own Makefiles.

The default FreeBSD compiler options are quite conservative, so if you have not changed them you should not have any problems.

14. There are so many ports it is hard to find the one I want. Is there a list anywhere of what ports are available?

Look in the `INDEX` file in `/usr/ports`. If you would like to search the ports collection for a keyword, you can do that too. For example, you can find ports relevant to the LISP programming language using:

```
% cd /usr/ports
% make search key=lisp
```

15. I went to install the `foo` port but the system suddenly stopped compiling it and starting compiling the `bar` port. What is going on?

The `foo` port needs something that is supplied with `bar` — for instance, if `foo` uses graphics, `bar` might have a library with useful graphics processing routines. Or `bar` might be a tool that is needed to compile the `foo` port.

16. I installed the `grizzle` program from the ports and frankly it is a complete waste of disk space. I want to delete it but I do not know where it put all the files. Any clues?

No problem, just type:

```
# pkg_delete grizzle-6.5
```

Alternatively, you can type:

```
# cd /usr/ports/somewhere/grizzle
# make deinstall
```

17. Hang on a minute, you have to know the version number to use that command. You do not seriously expect me to remember that, do you?

Not at all, you can find it out by doing:

```
# pkg_info -I 'grizzle*'
Information for grizzle-6.5:
grizzle-6.5 - the combined piano tutorial, LOGO interpreter and shoot 'em up
arcade game.
```

The version number can also be found using the `pkg_info` or by typing: `ls /var/db/pkg`

18. Talking of disk space, the ports directory seems to be taking up an awful lot of room. Is it safe to go in there and delete things?

Yes, if you have installed the program and are fairly certain you will not need the source again, there is no point in keeping it hanging around. The surest way to do this is:

```
# cd /usr/ports
# make clean
```

which will go through all the ports subdirectories and delete everything except the skeletons for each port.

> **Tip:** It is possible to achieve the same effect without recursively calling each makefile. For example, you can delete all of the work subdirectories directly with the following command:
>
> ```
> # find /usr/ports -depth -name work -exec rm -rf {} \;
> ```

19. I tried that and it still left all those tarballs or whatever you called them in the `distfiles` directory. Can I delete those as well?

Yes, if you are sure you have finished with them, those can go as well. They can be removed manually, or by using `make distclean`.

20. I like having lots and lots of programs to play with. Is there any way of installing all the ports in one go?

Just do:

```
# cd /usr/ports
# make install
```

Be careful, as some ports may install files with the same name. If you install two graphics ports and they both install `/usr/local/bin/plot` then you will obviously have problems.

21. OK, I tried that, but I thought it would take a very long time so I went to bed and left it to get on with it. When I looked at the computer this morning, it had only done three and a half ports. Did something go wrong?

No, the problem is that some of the ports need to ask you questions that we cannot answer for you (e.g., "Do you want to print on A4 or US letter sized paper?") and they need to have someone on hand to answer them.

22. I really do not want to spend all day staring at the monitor. Any better ideas?

OK, do this before you go to bed/work/the local park:

```
# cd /usr/ports
# make -DBATCH install
```

This will install every port that does *not* require user input. Then, when you come back, do:

```
# cd /usr/ports
# make -DINTERACTIVE install
```

to finish the job.

23. At work, we are using `frobble`, which is in your ports collection, but we have altered it quite a bit to get it to do what we need. Is there any way of making our own packages, so we can distribute it more easily around our sites?

No problem, assuming you know how to make patches for your changes:

```
# cd /usr/ports/somewhere/frobble
# make extract
# cd work/frobble-2.8
[Apply your patches]
# cd ../..
# make package
```

24. This ports stuff is really clever. I am desperate to find out how you did it. What is the secret?

Nothing secret about it at all, just look at the `bsd.port.mk` and `bsd.port.subdir.mk` files in `/usr/ports/Mk/`.

(Readers with an aversion to intricate shell-scripts are advised not to look at the files in this directory.)

4.6.2 Help! This Port Is Broken!

If you come across a port that does not work for you, there are a few things you can do, including:

1. Fix it! The Porter's Handbook[8] includes detailed information on the "Ports" infrastructure so that you can fix the occasional broken port or even submit your own!

2. Gripe—*by email only!* Send email to the maintainer of the port first. Type `make maintainer` or read the `Makefile` to find the maintainer's email address. Remember to include the name and version of the port (send the `$FreeBSD:` line from the `Makefile`) and the output leading up to the error when you email the maintainer. If you do not get a response from the maintainer, you can use `send-pr` to submit a bug report.

3. Grab the package from an ftp site near you. The "master" package collection is on `ftp.FreeBSD.org` in the packages directory[9], but be sure to check your local mirror *first!* These are more likely to work than trying to compile from source and are a lot faster as well. Use the pkg_add(1) program to install the package on your system.

---

8 http://www.FreeBSD.org/porters-handbook/index.html
9 ftp://ftp.FreeBSD.org/pub/FreeBSD/ports/packages/

Chapter 5
The X Window System

5.1 Synopsis

FreeBSD uses XFree86 to provide users with a powerful graphical user interface. XFree86 is a open-source implementation of the X Window System. This chapter will cover installation and configuration of XFree86 on a FreeBSD system. For more information on XFree86 and video hardware that it supports, check the XFree86[1] web site.

After reading this chapter, you will know:

* The various components of the X window system, and how they interoperate.
* How to install and configure XFree86.
* How to install and use different window managers.
* How to use TrueType fonts in XFree86.
* How to setup your system for graphical logins (XDM).

Before reading this chapter, you should:

* Know how to install additional third-party software (Chapter 4).

5.2 Understanding X

Using X for the first time can be somewhat of a shock to someone familiar with other graphical environments, such as Microsoft Windows or MacOS.

It is not necessary to understand all of the details of various X components and how they interact, however, some basic knowledge makes it possible to take advantage of X's strengths.

5.2.1 Why X?

X is not the first window system written for Unix, but it is the most popular. X's original development team had worked on another window system before writing X. That system's name was "W" (for "Window"). X is just the next letter in the Roman alphabet.

---

1 http://www.XFree86.org/

X can be called "X", "X Window System", "X11", and other terms. "X Windows" is to be avoided wherever possible; see X(1) for more information.

5.2.2 The X Client/Server Model

X was designed from the beginning to be network-centric, and adopts a "client-server" model. In the X model, the "X server" runs on the computer that has the keyboard, monitor, and mouse attached. The server is responsible for managing the display, handling input from the keyboard and mouse, and so on. Each X application (such as **XTerm**, or **Netscape**) is a "client". A client sends messages to the server such as "Please draw a window at these coordinates", and the server sends back messages such as "The user just clicked on the OK button".

If there is only one computer involved, such as in a home or small office environment, the X server and the X clients will be running on the same computer. However, it is perfectly possible to run the X server on a less powerful desktop computer, and run X applications (the clients) on, say, the powerful and expensive machine that serves the office. In this scenario the communication between the X client and server takes place over the network.

This confuses some people, because the X terminology is exactly backward to what they expect. They expect the "X server" to be the big powerful machine down the hall, and the "X client" to be the machine on their desk.

Remember that the X server is the machine with the monitor and keyboard, and the X clients are the programs that display the windows.

There is nothing in the protocol that forces the client and server machines to be running the same operating system, or even to be running on the same type of computer. It is certainly possible to run an X server on Microsoft Windows or Apple's MacOS, and there are various free and commercial applications available that do exactly that.

The X server that ships with FreeBSD is called **XFree86**, and is available for free, under a license very similar to the FreeBSD license. Commercial X servers for FreeBSD are also available.

5.2.3 The Window Manager

The X design philosophy is much like the Unix design philosophy, "tools, not policy". This means that X does not try to dictate how a task is to be accomplished. Instead, tools are provided to the user, and it is the user's responsibility to decide how to use those tools.

This philosophy extends to X not dictating what windows should look like on screen, how to move them around with the mouse, what keystrokes to should use to move between windows (i.e., **Alt+Tab**, in the case of Microsoft Windows), what the title bars on each window should look like, whether or not they have close buttons on them, and so on.

Instead, X delegates this responsibility to an application called a "Window Manager". There are dozens of window managers available for X; **AfterStep**, **Blackbox**, **ctwm**, **Enlightenment**, **fvwm**, **Sawfish**, **twm**, **Window Maker**, and more. Each of these window managers provides a different look and feel; some of them support "virtual desktops"; some of them allow customized keystrokes to manage the desktop; some have a "Start" button or similar device; some are "themeable", allowing a complete change of look-and-feel by applying a new theme. These window managers, and many more, are available in the x11-wm category of the Ports Collection.

In addition, the **KDE** and **GNOME** desktop environments both have their own window managers which integrate with the desktop.

Each window manager also has a different configuration mechanism; some expect configuration file written by hand, others feature GUI tools for most of the configuration tasks; at least one (**sawfish**) has a configuration file written in a dialect of the Lisp language.

Focus Policy: Another feature the window manager is responsible for is the mouse "focus policy". Every windowing system needs some means of choosing a window to be actively receiving keystrokes, and should visibly indicate which window is active as well.

A familiar focus policy is called "click-to-focus". This is the model utilized by Microsoft Windows, in which a window becomes active upon receiving a mouse click.

X does not support any particular focus policy. Instead, the window manager controls which window has the focus at any one time. Different window managers will support different focus methods. All of them support click to focus, and the majority of them support several others.

The most popular focus policies are:

focus-follows-mouse

The window that is under the mouse pointer is the window that has the focus. This may not necessarily be the window that is on top of all the other windows. The focus is changed by pointing at another window, there is no need to click in it as well.

sloppy-focus

This policy is a small extension to focus-follows-mouse. With focus-follows-mouse, if the mouse is moved over the root window (or background) then no window has the focus, and keystrokes are simply lost. With sloppy-focus, focus is only changed when the cursor enters a new window, and not when exiting the current window.

click-to-focus

The active window is selected by mouse click. The window may then be "raised", and appear in front of all other windows. All keystrokes will now be directed to this window, even if the cursor is moved to another window.

Many window managers support other policies, as well as variations on these. Be sure to consult the documentation for the window manager itself.

5.2.4 Widgets

The X approach of providing tools and not policy extends to the widgets that seen on screen in each application.

"Widget" is a term for all the items in the user interface that can be clicked or manipulated in some way; buttons, check boxes, radio buttons, icons, lists, and so on. Microsoft Windows calls these "controls".

Microsoft Windows and Apple's MacOS both have a very rigid widget policy. Application developers are supposed to ensure that their applications share a common look and feel. With X, it was not considered sensible to mandate a particular graphical style, or set of widgets to adhere to.

As a result, do not expect X applications to have a common look and feel. There are several popular widget sets and variations, including the original Athena widget set from MIT, **Motif** (on which the widget set in Microsoft Windows was modeled, all bevelled edges and three shades of grey), **OpenLook**, and others.

Most newer X applications today will use a modern-looking widget set, either Qt, used by **KDE**, or **GTK**, used by the **GNOME** project. In this respect, there is some convergence in look-and-feel of the Unix desktop, which certainly makes things easier for the novice user.

5.3 Installing XFree86

Before installing XFree86, decide on which version to run. **XFree86 3.X** is a maintenance branch of XFree86 development. It is very stable, and it supports a huge number of graphics cards. However, no new development is being done on the software. **XFree86 4.X** is a complete redesign of the system with many new features such as better support for fonts and anti-aliasing. Unfortunately this new architecture requires that the video drivers be rewritten, and some of the older cards that were supported in 3.X are not yet supported in 4.X.

The FreeBSD setup program offers users the opportunity to install and configure XFree86 3.3.6 during installation (covered in Section 2.9.11). To run **XFree86 4.X**, wait until after the base FreeBSD system is installed, and then install XFree86. For example, to build and install **XFree86 4.X** from the ports collection:

```
# cd /usr/ports/x11/XFree86-4
# make all install clean
```

Alternatively, **XFree86 4.X** can be installed from a binary package with the `pkg_add` tool or directly from the FreeBSD binaries provided on the XFree86 web site[2].

The rest of this chapter will explain how to configure XFree86, and how to setup a productive desktop environment.

5.4 XFree86 Configuration

5.4.1 Before Starting

Before configuration of **XFree86 4.X**, the the following information about the target system is needed:

- Monitor specifications
- Video Adapter chipset
- Video Adapter memory

The specifications for the monitor are used by **XFree86** to determine the resolution and refresh rate to run at. These specifications can usually be obtained from the documentation that came with the monitor or from the manufacturer's website. There are two ranges of numbers that are needed, the horizontal scan rate and the vertical synchronization rate.

---

2 http://www.XFree86.org/

The video adapter's chipset defines what driver module **XFree86** uses to talk to the graphics hardware. With most chipsets, this can be automatically determined, but it is still useful to know in case the automatic detection does not work correctly.

Video memory on the graphic adapter determines the resolution and color depth the system can run at. This is important to know so the user knows the limitations of the system.

5.4.2 Configuring XFree86 4.X

Configuration of **XFree86 4.X** is a multi-step process. The first step is to build an initial configuration file with the `-configure` option to **XFree86**. As the super user, simply run:

```
# XFree86 -configure
```

This will generate a skeleton **XFree86** configuration file in the current working directory called `XF86Config.new`. The **XFree86** program will attempt to probe the graphics hardware on the system and will write a configuration file to load the proper drivers for the detected hardware on the target system.

The next step is to test the existing configuration to verify that **XFree86** can work with the graphics hardware on the target system. To preform this task, the user needs to run:

```
# XFree86 -xf86config XF86Config.new
```

If a black and grey grid and an X mouse cursor appears, then the configuration was successful. To exit the test, just press **Ctrl+Alt+Backspace** simultaneously.

Next, tune the `XF86Config.new` configuration file to taste. Open up the file in a text editor such as emacs(1) or ee(1). The first thing to do is is add the frequencies for the target system's monitor. These are usually expressed as a horizontal and vertical synchronization rate. These values are added to the `XF86Config.new` file under the "Monitor" section:

```
Section "Monitor"
        Identifier   "Monitor0"
        VendorName   "Monitor Vendor"
        ModelName    "Monitor Model"
        Horizsync    30-107
        VertRefresh  48-120
EndSection
```

The `Horizsync` and `VertRefresh` keywords may not exist in the configuration file. If they do not, they need to be added, with the correct horizontal synchronization rate placed after the `Horizsync` keyword and the vertical synchronization rate after the `VertRefresh` keyword. In the example above the target monitor's rates where entered.

While the `XF86Config.new` configuration file is still open in an editor, next select what the default resolution and color depth is desired. This is defined in the `Screen` section:

```
Section "Screen"
        Identifier "Screen0"
        Device     "Card0"
        Monitor    "Monitor0"
        DefaultColorDepth 24
```

```
        SubSection "Display"
                Depth     24
                Modes     "1024x768"
        EndSubSection
  EndSection
```

The `DefaultColorDepth` keyword describes the color depth to run at by default. This can be overridden with the `-bpp` command line switch to XFree86(1) The Modes keyword describes the resolution to run at for the given color depth. In the example above, the default color depth is twenty four bits per pixel. At this color depth, the accepted resolution is one thousand twenty four pixels by seven hundred and sixty eight pixels.

To run at a resolution of one thousand twenty four pixels by seven hundred sixty eight pixels at twenty four bits per pixel, then add the `DefaultColorDepth` keyword with the value of twenty four, and add to the `"Display"` subsection with the desired Depth the Modes keyword with the resolution the user wishes to run at. Note that only VESA standard modes are supported as defined by the target system's graphics hardware.

Finally, write out the configuration file and test it using the test mode given above. If all is well, then the configuration file needs to be installed in a common location where XFree86(1) can find it. This is typically `/etc/X11/XF86Config` or `/usr/X11R6/etc/X11/XF86Config`.

```
  # cp XF86Config.new /etc/X11/XF86Config
```

Once the configuration file has been placed in a common location, configuration is complete. In order to start **XFree86 4.X** with startx(1), install the `x11/wrapper` port. **XFree86 4.X** can also be started with xdm(1).

5.4.3 Advanced Configuration Topics

Configuration with Intel i810 Graphics Chipsets

Configuration with Intel i810 integrated chipsets requires the `agpgart` AGP programming interface for **XFree86** to to drive the card. To `agpgart`, the `agp.ko` kernel loadable module needs to be loaded into the kernel with kldload(8). This can be done automatically with the loader(8) at boot time. Simply add this line to `/boot/loader.conf`:

```
  agp_load="YES"
```

Next, a device node needs to be created for the programming interface. To create the AGP device node, run MAKEDEV(8) in the `/dev` directory:

```
  # cd /dev
  # sh MAKEDEV agpgart
```

This will allow configuration the hardware as any other graphics board.

5.5 Using Fonts in XFree86

5.5.1 Type1 Fonts

The default fonts that ship with **XFree86** are less than ideal for typical desktop publishing applications. Large presentation fonts show up jagged and unprofessional looking, and small fonts in Netscape are almost completely unintelligible. However, there are several free, high quality Type1 (PostScript) fonts available which can be readily used with **XFree86**, either version 3.X or version 4.X. For instance, the URW font collection (`x11-fonts/urwfonts`) includes high quality versions of standard type1 fonts (Times Roman, Helvetica, Palatino and others). The Freefont collection (`x11-fonts/freefont`) includes many more fonts, but most of them are intended for use in graphics software such as the Gimp, and are not complete enough to serve as screen fonts. In addition, **XFree86** can be configured to use TrueType fonts with a minimum of effort: see the section on TrueType fonts later.

To install the above Type1 font collections from the ports collection, run the following commands:

```
# cd /usr/ports/x11-fonts/urwfonts
# make install clean
```

And likewise with the freefont or other collections. To tell the X server that these fonts exist, add an appropriate line to the `XF86Config` file (in `/etc/` for **XFree86** version 3, or in `/etc/X11/` for version 4), which reads:

```
FontPath "/usr/X11R6/lib/X11/fonts/URW/"
```

Alternatively, at the command line in the X session run:

```
% xset fp+ /usr/X11R6/lib/X11/fonts/URW
% xset fp rehash
```

This will work but will be lost when the X session is closed, unless it is added to the startup file (`~/.xinitrc` for a normal `startx` session, or `~/.xsession` when logging in through a graphical login manager like **XDM**). A third way is to use the new `XftConfig` file: see the section on anti-aliasing.

5.5.2 TrueType Fonts

XFree86 4.X has built in support for rendering TrueType fonts. There are two different modules that can enable this functionality. The "freetype" module is used in this example because it is more consistent with the other font rendering back-ends. To enable the freetype module just add the following line to the module section of the `/etc/X11/XF86Config` file.

```
Load "freetype"
```

For **XFree86 3.3.X**, a separate TrueType font server is needed. **Xfstt** is commonly used for this purpose. To install **Xfstt**, simply install the port `x11-servers/Xfstt`.

Now make a directory for the TrueType fonts (for example, `/usr/X11R6/lib/X11/fonts/TrueType`) and copy all of the TrueType fonts into this directory. Keep in mind that TrueType fonts cannot be directly taken from a Macintosh; they must be in Unix/DOS/Windows format for use by **XFree86**. Once the files have been copied into this directory, use **ttmkfdir** to create a `fonts.dir` file, so that the X font renderer knows that these new files have been installed. `ttmkfdir` is available from the FreeBSD Ports Collection as `x11-fonts/ttmkfdir`.

```
# cd /usr/X11R6/lib/X11/fonts/TrueType
# ttmkfdir > fonts.dir
```

Now add the TrueType directory to the font path. This is just the same as described above for Type1 fonts, that is, use

```
% xset fp+ /usr/X11R6/lib/X11/fonts/TrueType
% xset fp rehash
```

or add a `FontPath` line to the `XF86Config` file.

That's it. Now **Netscape**, **Gimp**, **StarOffice**, and all of the other X applications should now recognize the installed TrueType fonts. Extremely small fonts (as with text in a high resolution display on a web page) and extremely large fonts (within **StarOffice**) will look much better now.

5.5.3 Anti-Aliased Fonts

Starting with version 4.0.2, **XFree86** supports anti-aliased fonts. Currently, most software has not been updated to take advantage of this new functionality. However, Qt (the toolkit for the **KDE** desktop) does; so if **XFree86 4.0.2** is used (or higher), Qt 2.3 (or higher) and **KDE**, all KDE/Qt applications can be made to use anti-aliased fonts.

To configure anti-aliasing, create (or edit, if it already exists) the file `/usr/X11R6/lib/X11/XftConfig`. Several advanced things can be done with this file; this section describes only the simplest possibilities.

First, tell the X server about the fonts that are to be anti-aliased. For each font directory, add a line similar to this:

```
dir "/usr/X11R6/lib/X11/Type1"
```

Likewise for the other font directories (URW, truetype, etc) containing fonts to be anti-aliased. Anti-aliasing makes sense only for scalable fonts (basically, Type1 and TrueType) so do not include bitmap font directories here. The directories included here can now be commented out of the `XF86Config` file.

Antialiasing makes borders slightly fuzzy, which makes very small text more readable and removes "staircases" from large text, but can cause eyestrain if applied to normal text. To exclude point sizes between 9 and 13 from anti-aliasing, include these lines:

```
match
  any size > 8
  any size < 14
edit
  antialias = false;
```

Spacing for some monospaced fonts may also be inappropriate with anti-aliasing. This seems to be an issue with **KDE**, in particular. One possible fix for this is to force the spacing for such fonts to be 100. Add the following lines:

```
match any family == "fixed"     edit family =+ "mono";
match any family == "console"   edit family =+ "mono";
```

(this aliases the other common names for fixed fonts as "mono"), and then add:

```
match any family == "mono" edit spacing = 100;
```

Supposing the `Lucidux` fonts as desired whenever monospaced fonts are required (these look nice, and do not seem to suffer from the spacing problem), replace that last line with these:

```
match any family == "mono"         edit family += "LuciduxMono";
match any family == "Lucidux Mono"     edit family += "LuciduxMono";
match any family == "LuciduxMono"      edit family =+ "Lucidux Mono";
```

(the last lines alias different equivalent family names).

Finally, it is nice to allow users to add commands to this file, via their personal `.xftconfig` files. To do this, add a last line:

```
includeif  "~/.xftconfig"
```

One last point: with an LCD screen, sub-pixel sampling may be desired. This basically treats the (horizontally separated) red, green and blue components separately to improve the horizontal resolution; the results can be dramatic. To enable this, add the line somewhere in the `XftConfig` file

```
match edit rgba=rgb;
```

(depending on the sort of display, the last word may need to be changed from from "rgb" to "bgr", "vrgb" or "vbgr": experiment and see which works best.)

Anti-aliasing should be enabled the next time the X server is started. However, note that programs must know how to take advantage of it. At the present time, the toolkit Qt does, so the entire **KDE** environment can use anti-aliased fonts (see Section 5.7.3.2 on **KDE** for details); there are patches for gtk+ to do the same, so if compiled against such a patched gtk+, the GNOME environment and Mozilla can also use anti-aliased fonts. In fact, there is now a port called `x11/gdkxft` which allows one to use antialiased fonts without recompiling: see Section 5.7.1.3 for details.

Anti-aliasing is still new to FreeBSD and **XFree86**; configuring it should get easier with time, and it will soon be supported by many more applications.

5.6 The X Display Manager

5.6.1 Overview

The X Display Manager (**XDM**) is an optional part of the X Window System that is used for login session management. This is useful for several types of situations, including minimal "X Terminals", desktops, and large network display servers. Since the X Window System is network and protocol independent, there are a wide variety of possible configurations for running X clients and servers on different machines connected by a network. **XDM** provides a graphical interface for choosing which display server to connect to, and entering authorization information such as a login and password combination.

Think of **XDM** as providing the same functionality to the user as the getty(8) utility (see Section 15.3.2 for details). That is, it performs system logins to the display being connected to and then runs a session manager on behalf of the user (usually an X window manager). **XDM** then waits for this program to exit, signaling that the user is done and should be logged out of the display. At this point, **XDM** can display the login and display chooser screens for the next user to login.

5.6.2 Using XDM

The **XDM** daemon program is located in `/usr/X11R6/bin/xdm`. This program can be run at any time as `root` and it will start managing the X display on the local machine. If **XDM** is to be run every time the machine boots up, a convenient way to do this is by adding an entry to `/etc/ttys`. For more information about the format and usage of this file, see Section 15.3.2.1. There is a line in the default `/etc/ttys` file for running the **XDM** daemon on a virtual terminal:

```
ttyv8 "/usr/X11R6/bin/xdm -nodaemon" xterm off secure
```

By default this entry is disabled, and in order to enable it change field 5 from `off` to `on` and then restart init(8) using the directions in Section 15.3.2.2. The first field, the name of the terminal this program will manage, is `ttyv8`. This means that **XDM** will start running on the 9th virtual terminal.

5.6.3 Configuring XDM

The **XDM** configuration directory is located in `/usr/X11R6/lib/X11/xdm`. In this directory there are several files used to change the behavior and appearance of **XDM**. Typically these files will be found:

File	Description
`Xaccess`	Client authorization ruleset.
`Xresources`	Default X resource values.
`Xservers`	List of remote and local displays to manage.
`Xsession`	Default session script for logins.
`Xsetup_*`	Script to launch applications before the login interface.
`xdm-config`	Global configuration for all displays running on this machine.
`xdm-errors`	Errors generated by the server program.
`xdm-pid`	The process ID of the currently running XDM.

Also in this directory are a few scripts and programs used to setup the desktop when **XDM** is running. The purpose of each of these files will be briefly described. The exact syntax and usage of all of these files is described in xdm(1)

The default configuration is a simple rectangular login window with the hostname of the machine displayed at the top in a large font and "Login:" and "Password:" prompts below. This is a good starting point for changing the look and feel of **XDM** screens.

Xaccess

The protocol for connecting to **XDM** controlled displays is called the X Display Manager Connection Protocol (XDMCP). This file is a ruleset for controlling XDMCP connections from remote machines. By default, it allows any client to connect, but that does not matter unless the xdm-config is changed to listen for for remote connections.

Xresources

This is an application-defaults file for the display chooser and the login screens. This is where the appearance of the login program can be modified. The format is identical to the app-defaults file described in the **XFree86** documentation.

Xservers

This is a list of the remote displays the chooser should provide as choices.

Xsession

This is the default session script for **XDM** to run after a user has logged in. Normally each user will have a customized session script in ~/.xsessionrc that overrides this script.

Xsetup_*

These will be run automatically before displaying the chooser or login interfaces. There is a script for each display being used, named Xsetup_ followed by the local display number (for instance Xsetup_0). Typically these scripts will run one or two programs in the background such as xconsole.

xdm-config

This contains settings in the form of app-defaults that are applicable to every display that this installation manages.

xdm-errors

This contains the output of the X servers that **XDM** is trying to run. If a display that **XDM** is trying to start hangs for some reason, this is a good place to look for error messages. These messages are also written to the user's ~/.xsession-errors file on a per-session basis.

5.6.4 Running a Network Display Server

In order for other clients to connect to the display server, edit the access control rules, and enable the connection listener. By default these are set to conservative values. To make **XDM** listen for connections, first comment out a line in the xdm-config file:

```
! SECURITY: do not listen for XDMCP or Chooser requests
! Comment out this line if you want to manage X terminals with xdm
DisplayManager.requestPort:    0
```

and then restart **XDM**. Remember that comments in app-defaults files begin with a "!" character, not the usual "#". More strict access controls may be desired. Look at the example entries in Xaccess file, and refer to the xdm(1) manual page.

5.6.5 Replacements for XDM

Several replacements for the default **XDM** program exist. One of them, **KDM** (bundled with **KDE**) is described later in this chapter. **KDM** offers many visual improvements and cosmetic frills, as well as the functionality to allow users to choose their window manager of choice at login time.

5.7 Desktop Environments

This section describes the different desktop environments available for X on FreeBSD. A "desktop environment" will mean anything ranging from a simple window manager, to a complete suite of desktop applications such as **KDE** or **GNOME**.

5.7.1 GNOME

About GNOME

GNOME is a user-friendly desktop environment that enables users to easily use and configure their computers. **GNOME** includes a panel (for starting applications and displaying status), a desktop (where data and applications can be placed), a set of standard desktop tools and applications, and a set of conventions that make it easy for applications to cooperate and be consistent with each other. Users of other operating systems or environments should feel right at home using the powerful graphics-driven environment that **GNOME** provides.

Installing GNOME

The easiest way to install **GNOME** is through the "Desktop Configuration" menu during the FreeBSD installation process as described in Chapter 2. They can also be easily installed from a package or the ports collection:

To install the **GNOME** package from the network, simply type:

```
# pkg_add -r gnome
```

To build **GNOME** from source, use the ports tree:

```
# cd /usr/ports/x11/gnome
# make install clean
```

Once **GNOME** is installed, the X server must be told to start **GNOME** instead of a default window manager. If a custom `.xinitrc` is already in place, simply replace the line that starts the current window manager with one that starts **/usr/X11R6/bin/gnome-session** instead. If nothing special has been done to configuration file, then it is enough to simply type:

```
# echo "/usr/X11R6/bin/gnome-session" > ~/.xinitrc
```

Next, type `startx`, and the **GNOME** desktop environment will be started.

> **Note:** If a display manager, like **XDM**, is being used, this will not work. Instead, create an executable `.xsession` file with the same command in it. To do this, edit the file and replace the existing window manager command with **/usr/X11R6/bin/gnome-session**:

```
# echo "#!/bin/sh" > ~/.xsession
# echo "/usr/X11R6/bin/gnome-session" >> ~/.xsession
# chmod +x ~/.xsession
```

Another option is to configure the display manager to allow choosing the window manager at login time; the section on KDE2 details explains how to do this for `kdm`, the display manager of **KDE**.

Anti-aliased fonts with GNOME

While anti-aliased fonts made their first appearance on XFree86 desktops in the KDE environment and are supported there in the standard installation, it is also possible to use them with gtk applications such as the GNOME environment. The most straightforward way is probably by using the **libgdkxft** library, in the `x11/gdkxft` port. After installing this port, read the `/usr/X11R6/share/doc/gdkxft/README` file carefully.

Then, all that is needed is to do is tell gtk applications to look for their font-rendering functions in `libgdkxft.so` before looking in the standard place, `libgdk.so`. This is easily accomplished by setting an environment variable to point to the right place; with the Bourne shell (**/bin/sh**) or similar shells, type the command (to start **The Gimp**, say)

```
% LD_PRELOAD=/usr/X11R6/lib/libgdkxft.so gimp
```

and with csh and similar shells, type

```
% setenv LD_PRELOAD /usr/X11R6/lib/libgdkxft.so
% gimp
```

Or, the commands

```
LD_PRELOAD=/usr/X11R6/lib/libgdkxft.so
```

```
export LD_PRELOAD
```

can be put into `.xinitrc`, `.xsession` or in the appropriate place(s) in `/usr/X11R6/lib/X11/xdm/Xsession`, depending on how X is normally started. However, this short-cut may cause problems if Linux GTK binaries are run.

5.7.2 KDE2

About KDE2

KDE is an easy to use contemporary desktop environment. Some of the things that **KDE** brings to the user are:

- A beautiful contemporary desktop
- A desktop exhibiting complete network transparency
- An integrated help system allowing for convenient, consistent access to help on the use of the **KDE** desktop and its applications
- Consistent look and feel of all **KDE** applications
- Standardized menu and toolbars, keybindings, color-schemes, etc.
- Internationalization: **KDE** is available in more than 40 languages
- Centralized consisted dialog driven desktop configuration
- A great number of useful **KDE** applications

KDE has an office application suite based on **KDE**'s "KParts" technology consisting of a spread-sheet, a presentation application, an organizer, a news client and more. **KDE** also comes with a web browser called **Konqeuror**, which represents a solid competitor to other existing web browsers on Unix systems. More information on **KDE** can be found on the KDE website.[3]

Installing KDE2

Just like with **GNOME** or any other desktop environment, the easiest way to install **KDE** is through the "Desktop Configuration" menu during the FreeBSD installation process as described in Chapter 2. Once again, the software can be easily installed from a package or from the ports collection:

To install the **KDE2** package from the network, simply type:

```
# pkg_add -r kde2
```

To build **KDE** from source, use the ports tree:

```
# cd /usr/ports/x11/kde2
# make install clean
```

---

3 http://www.kde.org/

After **KDE2** has been installed, the X server must be told to launch this application instead of the default window manager. This is accomplished by editing the `.xinitrc` file:

```
# echo "/usr/X11R6/bin/startkde" > ~/.xinitrc
```

Now, whenever invoke X-Windows with `startx`, **KDE2** will be the desktop.

If a display manager such as **xdm** is being used, then configuration is slightly different. Edit the `.xsession` file instead. Instructions for **kdm** are described later in this chapter.

5.7.3 More Details on KDE2

Now that **KDE2** is installed on the system, most things can be discovered through the help pages, or just by pointing and clicking at various menus. Windows or Mac users will feel quite at home.

The best reference for **KDE** is the on-line documentation. **KDE** comes with its own web browser, **Konqueror**, dozens of useful applications, and extensive documentation. The remainder of this section discusses the technical items that are difficult to learn by random exploration.

The KDE display manager

An administrator of a multi-user system may wish to have a graphical login screen to welcome users. `xdm` can be used, as described earlier. However, **KDE** includes an alternative, **KDM**, which is designed to look more attractive and include more login-time options. In particular, users can easily choose (via a menu) which desktop environment (**KDE2**, **GNOME**, or something else) to run after logging on.

To begin with, run the **KDE2** control panel, `kcontrol`, as `root`. It is generally considered unsafe to run the entire X environment as `root`. Instead, run the window manager as a normal user, open a terminal window (such as `xterm` or **KDE**'s `konsole`, become `root` with **su** (the user must be in the `wheel` group in `/etc/group` for this), and then type **kcontrol**.

Click on the icon on the left marked System, then on Login manager. On the right there are various configurable options, which the **KDE** manual will explain in greater detail. Click on sessions on the right. Click New type to add various window managers and desktop environments. These are just labels, so they can say **KDE** and **GNOME** rather than **startkde** or **gnome-session**. Include a label `failsafe`.

Play with the other menus as well, they are mainly cosmetic and self-explanatory. When are done, click on Apply at the bottom, and quit the control center.

To make sure **kdm** understands what the labels (**KDE**, **GNOME** etc) mean, edit the files used by xdm.

> Note: In **KDE 2.2** this has changed: **kdm** now uses its own configuration files. Please see the **KDE 2.2** documentation for details.

In a terminal window, as `root`, edit the file `/usr/X11R6/lib/X11/xdm/Xsession`. There is a section in the middle like this:

```
case $# in
1)
        case $1 in
        failsafe)
                exec xterm -geometry 80x24-0-0
                ;;
        esac
esac
```

A few lines need to be added to this section. Assuming the labels from used were "KDE2" and "GNOME", use the following:

```
case $# in
1)
        case $1 in
        KDE2)
                exec /usr/X11R6/bin/startkde
                ;;
        GNOME)
                exec /usr/X11R6/bin/gnome-session
                ;;
        failsafe)
                exec xterm -geometry 80x24-0-0
                ;;
        esac
esac
```

For the **KDE** login-time desktop background to be honored, the following line needs to be added to `/usr/X11R6/lib/X11/xdm/Xsetup_0`:

```
/usr/X11R6/bin/kdmdesktop
```

Now, make sure **kdm** is listed in `/etc/ttys` to be started at the next bootup. To do this, simply follow the instructions from the previous section on xdm and replace references to the `/usr/X11R6/bin/xdm` program with `/usr/local/bin/kdm`.

Anti-aliased Fonts

Starting with version 4.0.2, **XFree86** supports anti-aliasing via its "RENDER" extension, and starting with version 2.3, Qt (the toolkit used by **KDE**) supports this extension. Configuring this is described in Section 5.5.3 on antialiasing X11 fonts. So, with up-to-date software, anti-aliasing is possible on a **KDE2** desktop. Just go to the KDE2 menu, go to Preferences -> Look and Feel -> Style, and click on the check box "Use Anti-Aliasing for Fonts and Icons". For a Qt application which is not part of **KDE**, the environment variable QT_XFT needs to be set to true before starting the program.

5.7.4 XFCE

About XFCE

XFCE is a desktop environment based on the GTK toolkit used by **GNOME**, but is much more lightweight and meant for those who want a simple, efficient desktop which is nevertheless easy to use and configure. Visually, it looks very much like **CDE**, found on commercial Unix systems. Some of **XFCE**'s features are:

- A simple, easy-to-handle desktop
- Fully configurable via mouse, with drag and drop, etc
- Main panel similar to **CDE**, with menus, applets and app launchers
- Integrated window manager, file manager, sound manager, **GNOME** compliance module, and other things
- Themeable (since it uses GTK)
- Fast, light and efficient: ideal for older/slower machines or machines with memory limitations

More information on **XFCE** can be found on the XFCE website[4].

Installing XFCE

A binary package for **xfce** exists (at the time of writing). To install, simply type:

```
# pkg_add -r xfce
```

Alternatively, to build from source, use the ports collection:

```
# cd /usr/ports/x11-wm/xfce
# make install clean
```

Now, tell the X server to launch **XFCE** the next time X is started. Simply type this:

```
# echo "/usr/X11R6/bin/startxfce" > ~/.xinitrc
```

The next time X is started, **XFCE** will be the desktop. As before, if a display manager like xdm is being used, create an .xsession, as described in the section on GNOME, but with the /usr/X11R6/bin/startxfce command; or, configure the display manager to allow choosing a desktop at login time, as explained in the section on kdm.

---

4 http://www.xfce.org/

II. System Administration

The remaining chapters of the FreeBSD Handbook cover all aspects of FreeBSD system administration. Each chapter starts by describing what you will learn as a result of reading the chapter, and also details what you are expected to know before tackling the material.

These chapters are designed to be read when you need the information. You do not have to read them in any particular order, nor do you need to read all of them before you can begin using FreeBSD.

Chapter 6

Configuration and Tuning

6.1 Synopsis

Configuring a system correctly can substantially reduce the amount of work involved in maintaining and upgrading it in the future. This chapter describes some of the aspects of administrative configuration of FreeBSD systems.

This chapter will also describe some of the parameters that can be set to tune a FreeBSD system for optimum performance.

After reading this chapter, you will know:

- Why and how to efficiently size, layout, and place filesystems and swap partition on your hard drive.
- The basics of the `rc.conf` configuration and `/usr/local/etc/rc.d` startup systems.
- How to configure virtual hosts on your network device.
- How to use the various configuration files in `/etc`.
- How to tune FreeBSD using `sysctl` variables.
- How to tune disk performance and modify kernel limitations.

Before reading this chapter, you should:

- Understand the basics of Unix and FreeBSD (Chapter 3).
- Be familiar with keeping FreeBSD sources up to date (Chapter 19), and the basics of kernel configuration/compilation (Chapter 9).

6.2 Initial Configuration

6.2.1 Partition Layout

Base Partitions

When laying out your filesystem with disklabel(8) or sysinstall(8), it is important to remember that hard drives can transfer data at a faster rate from the outer tracks than the inner. Knowing this, you should place your smaller, heavily-accessed filesystems, such as root and swap, closer to the outside of the drive, while placing larger partitions, such as /usr, towards the inner. To do so, it is a good idea to create partitions in a similar order: root, swap, /var, /usr.

The size of your /var partition reflects the intended use of your machine. /var is primarily used to hold: mailboxes, print spool and log files. Mail boxes and log files, in particular, can grow to unexpected sizes based upon how many users are on your system and how long your log files are kept. If you intend to run a mail server, a /var partition of over a gigabyte can be suitable. Additionally, /var/tmp must be large enough to contain any packages you may wish to add.

The /usr partition holds the bulk of the files required to support the system and a subdirectory within it called /usr/local holds the bulk of the files installed from the ports(7) hierarchy. If you do not use ports all that much and do not intend to keep system source (/usr/src) on the machine, you can get away with a 1 gigabyte /usr partition. However, if you install a lot of ports (especially window managers and Linux binaries), we recommend at least a two gigabyte /usr and if you also intend to keep system source on the machine, we recommend a three gigabyte /usr. Do not underestimate the amount of space you will need in this partition, it can creep up and surprise you!

When sizing your partitions, keep in mind the space requirements for your system to grow. Running out of space in one partition while having plenty in another can lead to much frustration.

> **Note:** Some users who have used sysinstall(8)'s `Auto-defaults` partition sizer have found either their root or /var partitions too small later on. Partition wisely and generously.

Swap Partition

As a rule of thumb, your swap space should typically be double the amount of main memory. For example, if the machine has 128 megabytes of memory, the swap file should be 256 megabytes. Systems with lesser memory may perform better with a lot more swap. It is not recommended that you configure any less than 256 megabytes of swap on a system and you should keep in mind future memory expansion when sizing the swap partition. The kernel's VM paging algorithms are tuned to perform best when the swap partition is at least two times the size of main memory. Configuring too little swap can lead to inefficiencies in the VM page scanning code as well as create issues later on if you add more memory to your machine.

Finally, on larger systems with multiple SCSI disks (or multiple IDE disks operating on different controllers), it is strongly recommend that you configure swap on each drive (up to four drives). The swap partitions on the drives should be approximately the same size. The kernel can handle arbitrary sizes but internal data structures scale to 4 times the largest swap partition. Keeping the swap partitions near the same size will allow the kernel to optimally stripe swap space across the disks. Do not worry about overdoing it a little, swap space is the saving grace of Unix. Even if you do not normally use much swap, it can give you more time to recover from a runaway program before being forced to reboot.

Why Partition?

Why partition at all? Why not create one big root partition and be done with it? Then I do not have to worry about undersizing things!

There are several reasons this is not a good idea. First, each partition has different operational characteristics and separating them allows the filesystem to tune itself to those characteristics. For example, the root and `/usr` partitions are read-mostly, with very little writing, while a lot of reading and writing could occur in `/var` and `/var/tmp`.

By properly partitioning your system, fragmentation introduced in the smaller more heavily write-loaded partitions will not bleed over into the mostly-read partitions. Additionally, keeping the write-loaded partitions closer to the edge of the disk, for example before the really big partition instead of after in the partition table, will increase I/O performance in the partitions where you need it the most. Now it is true that you might also need I/O performance in the larger partitions, but they are so large that shifting them more towards the edge of the disk will not lead to a significant performance improvement whereas moving `/var` to the edge can have a huge impact. Finally, there are safety concerns. Having a small neat root partition that is essentially read-only gives it a greater chance of surviving a bad crash intact.

6.3 Core Configuration

The principal location for system configuration information is within `/etc/rc.conf`. This file contains a wide range of configuration information, principally used at system startup to configure the system. Its name directly implies this; it is configuration information for the `rc*` files.

An administrator should make entries in the `rc.conf` file to override the default settings from `/etc/defaults/rc.conf`. The defaults file should not be copied verbatim to `/etc` - it contains default values, not examples. All system-specific changes should be made in the `rc.conf` file itself.

A number of strategies may be applied in clustered applications to separate site-wide configuration from system-specific configuration in order to keep administration overhead down. The recommended approach is to place site-wide configuration into another file, such as `/etc/rc.conf.site`, and then include this file into `/etc/rc.conf`, which will contain only system-specific information.

As `rc.conf` is read by sh(1) it is trivial to achieve this. For example:

- rc.conf:

```
. rc.conf.site
hostname="node15.example.com"
network_interfaces="fxp0 lo0"
ifconfig_fxp0="inet 10.1.1.1"
```

- rc.conf.site:

```
defaultrouter="10.1.1.254"
saver="daemon"
blanktime="100"
```

The `rc.conf.site` file can then be distributed to every system using `rsync` or similar program, whilst the `rc.conf` file remains unique.

Upgrading the system using sysinstall(8) or `make world` will not overwrite the `rc.conf` file, so system configuration information will not be lost.

6.4 Application Configuration

Typically, installed applications have their own configuration files, with their own syntax, etc. It is important that these files be kept separate from the base system, so that they may be easily located and managed by the package management tools.

Typically, these files are installed in `/usr/local/etc`. In the case where an application has a large number of configuration files, a subdirectory will be created to hold them.

Normally, when a port or package is installed, sample configuration files are also installed. These are usually identified with a ".default" suffix. If there are no existing configuration files for the application, they will be created by copying the .default files.

For example, here is `/usr/local/etc/apache`:

```
-rw-r--r--  1 root   wheel    2184 May 20  1998 access.conf
-rw-r--r--  1 root   wheel    2184 May 20  1998 access.conf.default
-rw-r--r--  1 root   wheel    9555 May 20  1998 httpd.conf
-rw-r--r--  1 root   wheel    9555 May 20  1998 httpd.conf.default
-rw-r--r--  1 root   wheel   12205 May 20  1998 magic
-rw-r--r--  1 root   wheel   12205 May 20  1998 magic.default
-rw-r--r--  1 root   wheel    2700 May 20  1998 mime.types
-rw-r--r--  1 root   wheel    2700 May 20  1998 mime.types.default
-rw-r--r--  1 root   wheel    7980 May 20  1998 srm.conf
-rw-r--r--  1 root   wheel    7933 May 20  1998 srm.conf.default
```

It can be quickly seen that only the `srm.conf` file has been changed. A later update of the apache port would not overwrite this changed file.

6.5 Starting Services

It is common for a system to host a number of services. These may be started in several different fashions, each having different advantages.

Software installed from a port or the packages collection will often place a script in `/usr/local/etc/rc.d` which is invoked at system startup with a `start` argument, and at system shutdown with a `stop` argument. This is the recommended way for starting system-wide services that are to be run as `root`, or that expect to be started as `root`. These scripts are registered as part of the installation of the package, and will be removed when the package is removed.

A generic startup script in `/usr/local/etc/rc.d` looks like:

```
#!/bin/sh
echo -n ' FooBar'
```

```
case "$1" in
start)
        /usr/local/bin/foobar
        ;;
stop)
        kill -9 `cat /var/run/foobar.pid`
        ;;
*)
        echo "Usage: `basename $0` {start|stop}" >&2
        exit 64
        ;;
esac

exit 0
```

This script is called with `start` at startup, and the `stop` at shutdown to allow it to carry out its purpose.

Some services expect to be invoked by inetd(8) when a connection is received on a suitable port. This is common for mail reader servers (POP and IMAP, etc.). These services are enabled by editing the file `/etc/inetd.conf`. See inetd(8) for details on editing this file.

Some additional system services may not be covered by the toggles in `/etc/rc.conf`. These are traditionally enabled by placing the command(s) to invoke them in `/etc/rc.local`. As of FreeBSD 3.1 there is no default `/etc/rc.local`; if it is created by the administrator it will however be honored in the normal fashion. Note that `rc.local` is generally regarded as the location of last resort; if there is a better place to start a service, do it there.

> **Note:** Do *not* place any commands in `/etc/rc.conf`. To start daemons, or run any commands at boot time, place a script in `/usr/local/etc/rc.d` instead.

It is also possible to use the cron(8) daemon to start system services. This approach has a number of advantages, not least being that because cron(8) runs these processes as the owner of the `crontab`, services may be started and maintained by non-`root` users.

This takes advantage of a feature of cron(8): the time specification may be replaced by `@reboot`, which will cause the job to be run when cron(8) is started shortly after system boot.

6.6 Virtual Hosts

A very common use of FreeBSD is virtual site hosting, where one server appears to the network as many servers. This is achieved by assigning multiple network addresses to a single interface.

A given network interface has one "real" address, and may have any number of "alias" addresses. These aliases are normally added by placing alias entries in `/etc/rc.conf`.

An alias entry for the interface `fxp0` looks like:

```
ifconfig_fxp0_alias0="inet xxx.xxx.xxx.xxx netmask xxx.xxx.xxx.xxx"
```

Note that alias entries must start with alias0 and proceed upwards in order, (for example, _alias1, _alias2, and so on). The configuration process will stop at the first missing number.

The calculation of alias netmasks is important, but fortunately quite simple. For a given interface, there must be one address which correctly represents the network's netmask. Any other addresses which fall within this network must have a netmask of all 1's.

For example, consider the case where the fxp0 interface is connected to two networks, the 10.1.1.0 network with a netmask of 255.255.255.0 and the 202.0.75.16 network with a netmask of 255.255.255.240. We want the system to appear at 10.1.1.1 through 10.1.1.5 and at 202.0.75.17 through 202.0.75.20.

The following entries configure the adapter correctly for this arrangement:

```
ifconfig_fxp0="inet 10.1.1.1 netmask 255.255.255.0"
ifconfig_fxp0_alias0="inet 10.1.1.2 netmask 255.255.255.255"
ifconfig_fxp0_alias1="inet 10.1.1.3 netmask 255.255.255.255"
ifconfig_fxp0_alias2="inet 10.1.1.4 netmask 255.255.255.255"
ifconfig_fxp0_alias3="inet 10.1.1.5 netmask 255.255.255.255"
ifconfig_fxp0_alias4="inet 202.0.75.17 netmask 255.255.255.240"
ifconfig_fxp0_alias5="inet 202.0.75.18 netmask 255.255.255.255"
ifconfig_fxp0_alias6="inet 202.0.75.19 netmask 255.255.255.255"
ifconfig_fxp0_alias7="inet 202.0.75.20 netmask 255.255.255.255"
```

6.7 Configuration Files

6.7.1 /etc Layout

There are a number of directories in which configuration information is kept. These include:

/etc	Generic system configuration information; data here is system-specific.
/etc/defaults	Default versions of system configuration files.
/etc/mail	Extra sendmail(8) configuration, other MTA configuration files.
/etc/ppp	Configuration for both user- and kernel-ppp programs.
/etc/namedb	Default location for named(8) data. Normally the boot file is located here, and contains a directive to refer to other data in /var/db.
/usr/local/etc	Configuration files for installed applications. May contain per-application subdirectories.
/usr/local/etc/rc.d	Start/stop scripts for installed applications.
/var/db	Persistent system-specific data files, such as named(8) zone files, database files, and so on.

6.7.2 Hostnames

`/etc/resolv.conf`

`/etc/resolv.conf` dictates how FreeBSD's resolver accesses the Internet Domain Name System (DNS).

The most common entries to `resolv.conf` are:

nameserver	The IP address of a name server the resolver should query. The servers are queried in the order listed with a maximum of three.
search	Search list for hostname lookup. This is normally determined by the domain of the local hostname.
domain	The local domain name.

A typical `resolv.conf`:

```
search example.com
nameserver 147.11.1.11
nameserver 147.11.100.30
```

If you are using DHCP, dhclient(8) usually rewrites `resolv.conf` with information received from the DHCP server.

`/etc/hosts`

`/etc/hosts` is a simple text database reminiscent of the old Internet. It works in conjunction with DNS and NIS providing name to IP address mappings. Local computers connected via a LAN can be placed in here for simplistic naming purposes instead of setting up a named(8) server. Additionally, `/etc/hosts` can be used to provide a local record of Internet names, reducing the need to query externally for commonly accessed names.

```
# $FreeBSD$
#
# Host Database
# This file should contain the addresses and aliases
# for local hosts that share this file.
# In the presence of the domain name service or NIS, this file may
# not be consulted at all; see /etc/nsswitch.conf for the resolution order.
#
#
::1                     localhost localhost.my.domain myname.my.domain
127.0.0.1               localhost localhost.my.domain myname.my.domain

#
# Imaginary network.
#10.0.0.2               myname.my.domain myname
#10.0.0.3               myfriend.my.domain myfriend
#
# According to RFC 1918, you can use the following IP networks for
```

```
# private nets which will never be connected to the Internet:
#
#       10.0.0.0        -    10.255.255.255
#       172.16.0.0      -    172.31.255.255
#       192.168.0.0     -    192.168.255.255
#
# In case you want to be able to connect to the Internet, you need
# real official assigned numbers.  PLEASE PLEASE PLEASE do not try
# to invent your own network numbers but instead get one from your
# network provider (if any) or from the Internet Registry (ftp to
# rs.internic.net, directory '/templates').
#
```

/etc/hosts takes on the simple format of:

```
[Internet address] [official hostname] [alias1] [alias2] ...
```

For example:

```
10.0.0.1 myRealHostname.example.com myRealHostname foobar1 foobar2
```

Consult hosts(5) for more information.

6.7.3 Log File Configuration

syslog.conf

syslog.conf is the configuration file for the syslogd(8) program. It indicates which types of syslog messages are logged to particular log files.

```
# $FreeBSD$
#
#       Spaces ARE valid field separators in this file. However,
#       other *nix-like systems still insist on using tabs as field
#       separators. If you are sharing this file between systems, you
#       may want to use only tabs as field separators here.
#       Consult the syslog.conf(5) manual page.
*.err;kern.debug;auth.notice;mail.crit          /dev/console
*.notice;kern.debug;lpr.info;mail.crit;news.err /var/log/messages
security.*                                      /var/log/security
mail.info                                       /var/log/maillog
lpr.info                                        /var/log/lpd-errs
cron.*                                          /var/log/cron
*.err                                           root
*.notice;news.err                               root
*.alert                                         root
*.emerg                                         *
# uncomment this to log all writes to /dev/console to /var/log/console.log
```

```
#console.info                              /var/log/console.log
# uncomment this to enable logging of all log messages to /var/log/all.log
#*.*                                       /var/log/all.log
# uncomment this to enable logging to a remote log host named loghost
#*.*                                       @loghost
# uncomment these if you're running inn
# news.crit                                /var/log/news/news.crit
# news.err                                 /var/log/news/news.err
# news.notice                              /var/log/news/news.notice
!startslip
*.*                                        /var/log/slip.log
!ppp
*.*                                        /var/log/ppp.log
```

Consult the syslog.conf(5) manual page for more information.

newsyslog.conf

newsyslog.conf is the configuration file for newsyslog(8), a program that is scheduled to run normally by cron(8). newsyslog(8) determines when log files require archiving or rearranging. logfile is moved to logfile.0, logfile.0 is moved to logfile.1, and so on. Additionally, the log files may be archived in gzip(1) format causing them to be named: logfile.0.gz, logfile.1.gz, and so on.

newsyslog.conf indicates which log files are to be managed, how many are to be kept, and when they are to be touched. Log files can be rearranged and/or archived when they have either reached a certain size, or at a certain periodic time/date.

```
# configuration file for newsyslog
# $FreeBSD$
#
# filename             [owner:group]    mode count size when [ZB] [/pid_file] [sig_num]
/var/log/cron                           600   3     100  *     Z
/var/log/amd.log                        644   7     100  *     Z
/var/log/kerberos.log                   644   7     100  *     Z
/var/log/lpd-errs                       644   7     100  *     Z
/var/log/maillog                        644   7     *    @T00  Z
/var/log/sendmail.st                    644   10    *    168   B
/var/log/messages                       644   5     100  *     Z
/var/log/all.log                        600   7     *    @T00  Z
/var/log/slip.log                       600   3     100  *     Z
/var/log/ppp.log                        600   3     100  *     Z
/var/log/security                       600   10    100  *     Z
/var/log/wtmp                           644   3     *    @01T05 B
/var/log/daily.log                      640   7     *    @T00  Z
/var/log/weekly.log                     640   5     1    $W6D0 Z
/var/log/monthly.log                    640   12    *    $M1D0 Z
/var/log/console.log                    640   5     100  *     Z
```

Consult the newsyslog(8) manual page for more information.

6.7.4 `sysctl.conf`

`sysctl.conf` looks much like `rc.conf`. Values are set in a `variable=value` form. The specified values are set after the system goes into multi-user mode. Not all variables are settable in this mode.

A sample `sysctl.conf` turning off logging of fatal signal exits and letting Linux programs know they are really running under FreeBSD.

```
kern.logsigexit=0          # Do not log fatal signal exits (e.g. sig 11)
compat.linux.osname=FreeBSD
compat.linux.osrelease=4.3-STABLE
```

6.8 Tuning with sysctl

sysctl(8) is an interface that allows you to make changes to a running FreeBSD system. This includes many advanced options of the TCP/IP stack and virtual memory system that can dramatically improve performance for an experienced system administrator. Over five hundred system variables can be read and set using sysctl(8).

At its core, sysctl(8) serves to do two functions: read and modify system settings.

To view all readable variables:

```
% sysctl -a
```

To read a particular variable, for example, `kern.maxproc`:

```
% sysctl kern.maxproc
kern.maxproc: 1044
```

To set a particular variable, use the intuitive `variable=value` syntax:

```
# sysctl kern.maxfiles=5000
kern.maxfiles: 2088 -> 5000
```

Settings of sysctl variables are usually either strings, numbers, or booleans. A boolean being 1 for yes or a 0 for no.

6.9 Tuning Disks

6.9.1 Sysctl Variables

`vfs.vmiodirenable`

The `vfs.vmiodirenable` sysctl variable defaults to 0 (off) (though soon it will default to 1) and may be set to 0 (off) or 1 (on). This parameter controls how directories are cached by the system. Most directories are small and use but a single fragment (typically 1K) in the filesystem and even less (typically 512 bytes) in the buffer cache. However, when operating in the default mode the buffer cache will only cache a fixed number of directories even if you have a huge amount of memory. Turning on this sysctl allows the buffer cache to use the VM Page Cache to cache the directories. The advantage is that all of memory is now available for caching directories. The disadvantage is that the minimum in-core memory used to cache a directory is the physical page size (typically 4K) rather than 512 bytes. We recommend turning this option on if you are running any services which manipulate large numbers of files. Such services can include web caches, large mail systems, and news systems. Turning on this option will generally not reduce performance even with the wasted memory but you should experiment to find out.

hw.ata.wc

FreeBSD 4.3 flirted with turning off IDE write caching. This reduced write bandwidth to IDE disks but was considered necessary due to serious data consistency issues introduced by hard drive vendors. Basically the problem is that IDE drives lie about when a write completes. With IDE write caching turned on, IDE hard drives will not only write data to disk out of order, they will sometimes delay some of the blocks indefinitely when under heavy disk loads. A crash or power failure can result in serious filesystem corruption. So our default was changed to be safe. Unfortunately, the result was such a huge loss in performance that we caved in and changed the default back to on after the release. You should check the default on your system by observing the `hw.ata.wc` sysctl variable. If IDE write caching is turned off, you can turn it back on by setting the kernel variable back to 1. This must be done from the boot loader at boot time. Attempting to do it after the kernel boots will have no effect.

For more information, please see ata(4).

6.9.2 Soft Updates

The tunefs(8) program can be used to fine-tune a filesystem. This program has many different options, but for now we are only concerned with toggling Soft Updates on and off, which is done by :

```
# tunefs -n enable /filesystem
# tunefs -n disable /filesystem
```

A filesystem cannot be modified with tunefs(8) while it is mounted. A good time to enable Soft Updates is before any partitions have been mounted, in single-user mode.

Soft Updates drastically improves meta-data performance, mainly file creation and deletion, through the use of a memory cache. We recommend turning Soft Updates on on all of your filesystems. There are two downsides to Soft Updates that you should be aware of: First, Soft Updates guarantees filesystem consistency in the case of a crash but could very easily be several seconds (even a minute!) behind updating the physical disk. If you crash you may lose more work than otherwise. Secondly, Soft Updates delays the freeing of filesystem blocks. If you have a filesystem (such as the root filesystem) which is close to full, doing a major update of it, e.g. `make installworld`, can run it out of space and cause the update to fail.

6.10 Tuning Kernel Limits

6.10.1 File/Process Limits

`kern.maxfiles`

`kern.maxfiles` can be raised or lowered based upon your system requirements. This variable indicates the maximum number of file descriptors on your system. When the file descriptor table is full, `file: table is full` will show up repeatedly in the system message buffer, which can be viewed with the `dmesg` command.

Each open file, socket, or fifo uses one file descriptor. A large-scale production server may easily require many thousands of file descriptors, depending on the kind and number of services running concurrently.

`kern.maxfile`'s default value is dictated by the `maxusers` option in your kernel configuration file. `kern.maxfiles` grows proportionally to the value of `maxusers`. When compiling a custom kernel, it is a good idea to set this kernel configuration option according to the uses of your system. From this number, the kernel is given most of its pre-defined limits. Even though a production machine may not actually have 256 users connected as once, the resources needed may be similar to a high-scale webserver.

6.10.2 Network Limits

The `NMBCLUSTERS` kernel configuration option dictate the amount of network mbufs available to the system. A heavily-trafficked server with a low number of MBUFs will hinder FreeBSD's ability. Each cluster represents approximately 2K of memory, so a value of 1024 represents 2 megabytes of kernel memory reserved for network buffers. A simple calculation can be done to figure out how many are needed. If you have a web server which maxes out at 1000 simultaneous connections, and each connection eats a 16K receive and 16K send buffer, you need approximately 32MB worth of network buffers to cover the webserver. A good rule of thumb is to multiply by 2, so 32MBx2 = 64MB/2K = 32768.

Chapter 7
The FreeBSD Booting Process

7.1 Synopsis

The process of starting a computer and loading the operating system is referred to as "the bootstrap process", or simply "booting". FreeBSD's boot process provides a great deal of flexibility in customizing what happens when you start the system, allowing you to select from different operating systems installed on the same computer, or even different versions of the same operating system or installed kernel.

This chapter details the configuration options you can set and how to customize the FreeBSD boot process. This includes everything that happens until the FreeBSD kernel has started, probed for devices, and started init(8). If you are not quite sure when this happens, it occurs when the text color changes from bright white to grey.

After reading this chapter, you will know:

- What the components of the FreeBSD bootstrap system are, and how they interact.
- The options you can give to the components in the FreeBSD bootstrap to control the boot process.

   x86 only: This chapter only describes the boot process for FreeBSD running on Intel x86 systems.

7.2 The Booting Problem

Turning on a computer and starting the operating system poses an interesting dilemma. By definition, the computer does not know how to do anything until the operating system is started. This includes running programs from the disk. So if the computer can not run a program from the disk without the operating system, and the operating system programs are on the disk, how is the operating system started?

This problem parallels one in the book *The Adventures of Baron Munchausen*. A character had fallen part way down a manhole, and pulled himself out by grabbing his bootstraps, and lifting. In the early days of computing the term *bootstrap* was applied to the mechanism used to load the operating system, which has become shortened to "booting".

On x86 hardware the Basic Input/Output System (BIOS) is responsible for loading the operating system. To do this, the BIOS looks on the hard disk for the Master Boot Record (MBR), which must be located on a specific place on the disk. The BIOS has enough knowledge to load and run the MBR, and assumes that the MBR can then carry out the rest of the tasks involved in loading the operating system.

If you only have one operating system installed on your disks then the standard MBR will suffice. This MBR searches for the first bootable slice on the disk, and then runs the code on that slice to load the remainder of the operating system.

If you have installed multiple operating systems on your disks then you can install a different MBR, one that can display a list of different operating systems, and allows you to choose the one to boot from. FreeBSD comes with one such MBR which can be installed, and other operating system vendors also provide alternative MBRs.

The remainder of the FreeBSD bootstrap system is divided into three stages. The first stage is run by the MBR, which knows just enough to get the computer into a specific state and run the second stage. The second stage can do a little bit more, before running the third stage. The third stage finishes the task of loading the operating system. The work is split into these three stages because the PC standards put limits on the size of the programs that can be run at stages one and two. Chaining the tasks together allows FreeBSD to provide a more flexible loader.

The kernel is then started and it begins to probe for devices and initialize them for use. Once the kernel boot process is finished, the kernel passes control to the user process init(8), which then makes sure the disks are in a usable state. init(8) then starts the user-level resource configuration which mounts filesystems, sets up network cards to communicate on the network, and generally starts all the processes that usually are run on a FreeBSD system at startup.

7.3 The MBR, and Boot Stages One, Two, and Three

7.3.1 MBR, /boot/boot0

The FreeBSD MBR is located in /boot/boot0. This is a *copy* of the MBR, as the real MBR must be placed on a special part of the disk, outside the FreeBSD area.

boot0 is very simple, since the program in the MBR can only be 512 bytes in size. If you have installed the FreeBSD MBR and have installed multiple operating systems on your hard disks then you will see a display similar to this one at boot time.

Example 7-1. boot0 **Screenshot**

```
F1 DOS
F2 FreeBSD
F3 Linux
F4 ??
F5 Drive 1

Default: F2
```

Other operating systems, in particular Windows 95, have been known to overwrite an existing MBR with their own. If this happens to you, or you want to replace your existing MBR with the FreeBSD MBR then use the following command.

```
# fdisk -B -b /boot/boot0 device
```

Where *device* is the device that you boot from, such as `ad0` for the first IDE disk, `ad2` for the first IDE disk on a second IDE controller, `da0` for the first SCSI disk, and so on.

7.3.2 Stage One, `/boot/boot1`, and Stage Two, `/boot/boot2`

Conceptually the first and second stages are part of the same program, on the same area of the disk. Because of space constraints they have been split into two, but you would always install them together.

They are found on the boot sector of the boot slice, which is where boot0 (Section 7.3.1), or any other program on the MBR expects to find the program to run to continue the boot process. The files in the `/boot` directory are copies of the real files, which are stored outside of the FreeBSD filesystem.

`boot1` is very simple, since it too can only be 512 bytes in size, and knows just enough about the FreeBSD *disklabel*, which stores information about the slice, to find and execute `boot2`.

`boot2` is slightly more sophisticated, and understands the FreeBSD filesystem enough to find files on it, and can provide a simple interface to choose the kernel or loader to run.

Since the loader (Section 7.3.3) is much more sophisticated, and provides a nice easy-to-use boot configuration, `boot2` usually runs it, but previously it was tasked to run the kernel directly.

Example 7-2. `boot2` **Screenshot**

```
>> FreeBSD/i386 BOOT
Default: 0:ad(0,a)/kernel
boot:
```

If you ever need to replace the installed `boot1` and `boot2` use disklabel(8).

```
# disklabel -B diskslice
```

Where *diskslice* is the disk and slice you boot from, such as `ad0s1` for the first slice on the first IDE disk.

> **Dangerously Dedicated Mode:** If you use just the disk name, such as `ad0`, in the disklabel(8) command you will create a dangerously dedicated disk, without slices. This is almost certainly not what you want to do, so make sure you double check the disklabel(8) command before you press **Return**.

7.3.3 Stage Three, `/boot/loader`

The loader is the final stage of the three-stage bootstrap, and is located on the filesystem, usually as `/boot/loader`.

The loader is intended as a user-friendly method for configuration, using an easy-to-use built-in command set, backed up by a more powerful interpreter, with a more complex command set.

Loader Program Flow

During initialization, the loader will probe for a console and for disks, and figure out what disk it is booting from. It will set variables accordingly, and an interpreter is started where user commands can be passed from a script or interactively.

The loader will then read `/boot/loader.rc`, which by default reads in `/boot/defaults/loader.conf` which sets reasonable defaults for variables and reads `/boot/loader.conf` for local changes to those variables. `loader.rc` then acts on these variables, loading whichever modules and kernel are selected.

Finally, by default, the loader issues a 10 second wait for key presses, and boots the kernel if it is not interrupted. If interrupted, the user is presented with a prompt which understands the easy-to-use command set, where the user may adjust variables, unload all modules, load modules, and then finally boot or reboot.

Loader Built-In Commands

These are the most commonly used loader commands. For a complete discussion of all available commands, please see loader(8)

autoboot *seconds*

> Proceeds to boot the kernel if not interrupted within the time span given, in seconds. It displays a countdown, and the default time span is 10 seconds.

boot [*-options*] [*kernelname*]

> Immediately proceeds to boot the kernel, with the given options, if any, and with the kernel name given, if it is.

boot-conf

> Goes through the same automatic configuration of modules based on variables as what happens at boot. This only makes sense if you use `unload` first, and change some variables, most commonly `kernel`.

help [*topic*]

> Shows help messages read from `/boot/loader.help`. If the topic given is `index`, then the list of available topics is given.

include *filename* ...

> Processes the file with the given filename. The file is read in, and interpreted line by line. An error immediately stops the include command.

load [-t *type*] *filename*

> Loads the kernel, kernel module, or file of the type given, with the filename given. Any arguments after filename are passed to the file.

ls [-l] [*path*]

> Displays a listing of files in the given path, or the root directory, if the path is not specified. If -l is specified, file sizes will be shown too.

lsdev [-v]

> Lists all of the devices from which it may be possible to load modules. If -v is specified, more details are printed.

lsmod [-v]

> Displays loaded modules. If -v is specified, more details are shown.

more *filename*

> Displays the files specified, with a pause at each LINES displayed.

reboot

> Immediately reboots the system.

set *variable*
set *variable*=*value*

> Sets the loader's environment variables.

unload

> Removes all loaded modules.

Loader Examples

Here are some practical examples of loader usage.

- To simply boot your usual kernel, but in single-user mode:

  ```
  boot -s
  ```

- To unload your usual kernel and modules, and then load just your old (or another) kernel:

  ```
  unload
  load kernel.old
  ```

  You can use kernel.GENERIC to refer to the generic kernel that comes on the install disk, or kernel.old to refer to your previously installed kernel (when you have upgraded or configured your own kernel, for example).

  > **Note:** Use the following to load your usual modules with another kernel:
  >
  > ```
  > unload
  > set kernel="kernel.old"
  > boot-conf
  > ```

- To load a kernel configuration script (an automated script which does the things you would normally do in the kernel boot-time configurator):

```
load -t userconfig_script /boot/kernel.conf
```

7.4 Kernel Interaction During Boot

Once the kernel is loaded by either loader (as usual) or boot2 (bypassing the loader), it examines its boot flags, if any, and adjusts its behavior as necessary.

7.4.1 Kernel Boot Flags

Here are the more common boot flags:

`-a`

during kernel initialization, ask for the device to mount as the root file system.

`-C`

boot from CDROM.

`-c`

run UserConfig, the boot-time kernel configurator

`-s`

boot into single-user mode

`-v`

be more verbose during kernel startup

Note: There are other boot flags, read boot(8) for more information on them.

7.5 Init: Process Control Initialization

Once the kernel has finished booting, it passes control to the user process `init`, which is located at `/sbin/init`, or the program path specified in the `init_path` variable in `loader`.

7.5.1 Automatic Reboot Sequence

The automatic reboot sequence makes sure that the filesystems available on the system are consistent. If they are not, and fsck cannot fix the inconsistencies, init drops the system into single-user mode (as described in the next section) for the system administrator to take care of the problems directly.

7.5.2 Single-User Mode

This mode can be reached through the automatic reboot sequence, or by the user booting with the -s option or setting the boot_single variable in loader.

It can also be reached by calling shutdown without the reboot (-r) or halt (-h) options, from multi-user mode.

If the system console is set to insecure in /etc/ttys, then the system prompts for the root password before initiating single-user mode.

Example 7-3. An Insecure Console in /etc/ttys

```
# name  getty                          type    status         comments
#
# This entry needed for asking password when init goes to single-user mode
# If you want to be asked for password, change "secure" to "insecure" here
console none                           unknown off insecure
```

Note: An insecure console means that you consider your physical security to the console to be insecure, and want to make sure only someone who knows the root password may use single-user mode, and it does not mean that you want to run your console insecurely. Thus, if you want security, choose insecure, not secure.

7.5.3 Multi-User Mode

If init finds your filesystems to be in order, or once the user has finished in single-user mode, the system enters multi-user mode, in which it starts the resource configuration of the system.

Resource Configuration (rc)

The resource configuration system reads in configuration defaults from /etc/defaults/rc.conf, and system-specific details from /etc/rc.conf, and then proceeds to mount the system filesystems mentioned in /etc/fstab, start up networking services, start up miscellaneous system daemons, and finally runs the startup scripts of locally installed packages.

The rc(8) manual page is a good reference to the resource configuration system, as is examining the scripts themselves.

7.6 Shutdown Sequence

Upon controlled shutdown, via `shutdown`, `init` will attempt to run the script `/etc/rc.shutdown`, and then proceed to send all processes the `TERM` signal, and subsequently the `KILL` signal to any that do not terminate timely.

Chapter 8

Users and Basic Account Management

8.1 Synopsis

FreeBSD allows multiple users to use the computer at the same time. Obviously, only one of those users can be sitting in front of the screen and keyboard at any one time [1], but any number of users can log in through the network to get their work done. To use the system every user must have an account.

After reading this chapter, you will know:

- The differences between the various user accounts on a FreeBSD system.
- How to add user accounts.
- How to remove user accounts.
- How to change account details, such as the user's full name, or preferred shell.
- How to set limits on a per-account basis, to control the resources such as memory and CPU time that accounts and groups of accounts are allowed to access.
- How to use groups to make account management easier.

Before reading this chapter, you should:

- Understand the basics of Unix and FreeBSD (Chapter 3).

8.2 Introduction

All access to the system is achieved via accounts, and all processes are run by users, so user and account management are of integral importance on FreeBSD systems.

Every account on a FreeBSD system has certain information associated with it to identify the account.

---

1. Well, unless you hook up multiple terminals, but we'll save that for Chapter 15

User name

The user name as it would be typed at the `login:` prompt. User names must be unique across the computer; you may not have two users with the same user name. There are a number of rules for creating valid user names, documented in passwd(5); you would typically use user names that consist of eight or fewer all lower case characters.

Password

Each account has a password associated with it. The password may be blank, in which case no password will be required to access the system. This is normally a very bad idea; every account should have a password.

User ID (UID)

The UID is a number from 0 to 65536 used to uniquely identify the user to the system. Internally, FreeBSD uses the UID to identify users—any FreeBSD commands that allow you to specify a user name will convert it to the UID before working with it. This means that you can have several accounts with different user names but the same UID. As far as FreeBSD is concerned these accounts are one user. It is unlikely you will ever need to do this.

Group ID (GID)

The GID is a number from 0 to 65536 used to uniquely identify the primary group that the user belongs to. Groups are a mechanism for controlling access to resources based on a user's GID rather than their UID. This can significantly reduce the size of some configuration files. A user may also be in more than one group.

Login class

Login classes are an extension to the group mechanism that provide additional flexibility when tailoring the system to different users.

Password change time

By default FreeBSD does not force users to change their passwords periodically. You can enforce this on a per-user basis, forcing some or all of your users to change their passwords after a certain amount of time has elapsed.

Account expiry time

By default FreeBSD does not expire accounts. If you are creating accounts that you know have a limited lifespan, for example, in a school where you have accounts for the students, then you can specify when the account expires. After the expiry time has elapsed the account cannot be used to log in to the system, although the account's directories and files will remain.

User's full name

The user name uniquely identifies the account to FreeBSD, but does not necessarily reflect the user's real name. This information can be associated with the account.

Home directory

The home directory is the full path to a directory on the system in which the user will start when logging on to the system. A common convention is to put all user home directories under `/home/username` or `/usr/home/username`.

The user would store their personal files in their home directory, and any directories they may create in there.

User shell

    The shell provides the default environment users use to interact with the system. There are many different kinds of shells, and experienced users will have their own preferences, which can be reflected in their account settings.

There are three main types of accounts; the Superuser, system users, and user accounts. The Superuser account, usually called `root`, is used to manage the system with no limitations on privileges. System users run services. Finally, user accounts are used by real people, who log on, read mail, and so forth.

8.3 The Superuser Account

The superuser account, usually called `root`, comes preconfigured to facilitate system administration, and should not be used for day-to-day tasks like sending and receiving mail, general exploration of the system, or programming.

This is because the superuser, unlike normal user accounts, can operate without limits, and misuse of the superuser account may result in spectacular disasters. User accounts are unable to destroy the system by mistake, so it is generally best to use normal user accounts whenever possible, unless you especially need the extra privilege.

You should always double and triple-check commands you issue as the superuser, since an extra space or missing character can mean irreparable data loss.

So, the first thing you should do after reading this chapter is to create an unprivileged user account for yourself for general usage if you have not already. This applies equally whether you are running a multi-user or single-user machine. Later in this chapter, we discuss how to create additional accounts, and how to change between the normal user and superuser.

8.4 System Accounts

System users are those used to run services such as DNS, mail, web servers, and so forth. The reason for this is security; if all services ran as the superuser, they could act without restriction.

Examples of system users are `daemon`, `operator`, `bind` (for the Domain Name Service), and `news`. Often sysadmins create `httpd` to run web servers they install.

`nobody` is the generic unprivileged system user. However, it is important to keep in mind that the more services that use `nobody`, the more files and processes that user will become associated with, and hence the more privileged that user becomes.

8.5 User Accounts

User accounts are the primary means of access for real people to the system, and these accounts insulate the user and the environment, preventing the users from damaging the system or other users, and allowing users to customize their environment without affecting others.

Every person accessing your system should have a unique user account. This allows you to find out who is doing what, prevent people from clobbering each others' settings or reading each others' mail, and so forth.

Each user can set up their own environment to accommodate their use of the system, by using alternate shells, editors, key bindings, and language.

8.6 Modifying Accounts

There are a variety of different commands available in the Unix environment to manipulate user accounts. The most common commands are summarized below, followed by more detailed examples of their usage.

Command	Summary
adduser	The recommended command-line application for adding new users.
rmuser	The recommended command-line application for removing users.
chpass	A flexible tool to change user database information.
passwd	The simple command-line tool to change user passwords.
pw	A powerful and flexible tool to modify all aspects of user accounts.

8.6.1 adduser

adduser is a simple program for adding new users. It creates entries in the system passwd and group files. It will also create a home directory for the new user, copy in the default configuration files ("dotfiles") from /usr/share/skel, and can optionally mail the new user a welcome message.

To create the initial configuration file, use adduser -s -config_create. [2] Next, we configure **adduser** defaults, and create our first user account, since using root for normal usage is evil and nasty.

Example 8-1. Configuring adduser

```
# adduser -v
Use option "-silent" if you don't want to see all warnings and questions.
Check /etc/shells
Check /etc/master.passwd
Check /etc/group
Enter your default shell: csh date no sh tcsh zsh [sh]: zsh
Your default shell is: zsh -> /usr/local/bin/zsh
Enter your default HOME partition: [/home]:
Copy dotfiles from: /usr/share/skel no [/usr/share/skel]:
Send message from file: /etc/adduser.message no
[/etc/adduser.message]: no
```

---

2.   The -s makes adduser default to quiet. We use -v later when we want to change defaults.

```
Do not send message
Use passwords (y/n) [y]: y

Write your changes to /etc/adduser.conf? (y/n) [n]: y

Ok, let's go.
Don't worry about mistakes. I will give you the chance later to correct any input.
Enter username [a-z0-9_-]: jru
Enter full name []: J. Random User
Enter shell csh date no sh tcsh zsh [zsh]:
Enter home directory (full path) [/home/jru]:
Uid [1001]:
Enter login class: default []:
Login group jru [jru]:
Login group is "jru". Invite jru into other groups: guest no
[no]: wheel
Enter password []:
Enter password again []:

Name:    jru
Password: ****
Fullname: J. Random User
Uid:    1001
Gid:    1001 (jru)
Class:
Groups:   jru wheel
HOME:     /home/jru
Shell:    /usr/local/bin/zsh
OK? (y/n) [y]: y
Added user "jru"
Copy files from /usr/share/skel to /home/jru
Add another user? (y/n) [y]: n
Goodbye!
#
```

In summary, we changed the default shell to **zsh** (an additional shell found in the Ports Collection), and turned off the sending of a welcome mail to added users. We then saved the configuration, created an account for jru, and made sure jru is in wheel group (so that she may assume the role of root with the su command.)

Note: The password you type in is not echoed, nor are asterisks displayed. Make sure you do not mistype the password twice.

Note: Just use adduser without arguments from now on, and you will not have to go through changing the defaults. If the program asks you to change the defaults, exit the program, and try the -s option.

8.6.2 rmuser

You can use rmuser to completely remove a user from the system. rmuser performs the following steps:

1. Removes the user's crontab(1) entry (if any).
2. Removes any at(1) jobs belonging to the user.
3. Kills all processes owned by the user.
4. Removes the user from the system's local password file.
5. Removes the user's home directory (if it is owned by the user).
6. Removes the incoming mail files belonging to the user from /var/mail.
7. Removes all files owned by the user from temporary file storage areas such as /tmp.
8. Finally, removes the username from all groups to which it belongs in /etc/group.

> **Note:** If a group becomes empty and the group name is the same as the username, the group is removed; this complements the per-user unique groups created by adduser(8).

rmuser cannot be used to remove superuser accounts, since that is almost always an indication of massive destruction.

By default, an interactive mode is used, which attempts to make sure you know what you are doing.

Example 8-2. rmuser Interactive Account Removal

```
# rmuser jru
Matching password entry:
jru:*:1001:1001::0:0:J. Random User:/home/jru:/usr/local/bin/tcsh
Is this the entry you wish to remove? y
Remove user's home directory (/home/jru)? y
Updating password file, updating databases, done.
Updating group file: trusted (removing group jru -- personal group is empty) done.
Removing user's incoming mail file /var/mail/jru: done.
Removing files belonging to jru from /tmp: done.
Removing files belonging to jru from /var/tmp: done.
Removing files belonging to jru from /var/tmp/vi.recover: done.
#
```

8.6.3 chpass

chpass changes user database information such as passwords, shells, and personal information.

Only system administrators, as the superuser, may change other users' information and passwords with chpass.

When passed no options, aside from an optional username, chpass displays an editor containing user information. When the user exists from the editor, the user database is updated with the new information.

Example 8-3. Interactive chpass by Superuser

```
#Changing user database information for jru.
Login: jru
Password: *
Uid [#]: 1000
Gid [# or name]: 1000
Change [month day year]:
Expire [month day year]:
Class:
Home directory: /home/jru
Shell: /usr/local/bin/tcsh
Full Name: J. Random User
Office Location:
Office Phone:
Home Phone:
Other information:
```

The normal user can change only a small subset of this information, and only for themselves.

Example 8-4. Interactive chpass by Normal User

```
#Changing user database information for jru.
Shell: /usr/local/bin/tcsh
Full Name: J. Random User
Office Location:
Office Phone:
Home Phone:
Other information:
```

Note: chfn and chsh are just links to chpass, as are ypchpass, ypchfn, and ypchsh. NIS support is automatic, so specifying the yp before the command is not necessary. If this is confusing to you, do not worry, NIS will be covered in Chapter 17

8.6.4 passwd

passwd is the usual way to change your own password as a user, or another user's password as the superuser.

Note: Users must type in their original password before changing their password, to prevent an unauthorized person from changing their password when the user is away from their console.

Example 8-5. Changing Your Password

```
% passwd
Changing local password for jru.
Old password:
New password:
Retype new password:
passwd: updating the database...
passwd: done
```

Example 8-6. Changing Another User's Password as the Superuser

```
# passwd jru
Changing local password for jru.
New password:
Retype new password:
passwd: updating the database...
passwd: done
```

Note: As with `chpass`, `yppasswd` is just a link to `passwd`, so NIS works with either command.

8.6.5 pw

pw(8) is a command line utility to create, remove, modify, and display users and groups. It functions as a front end to the system user and group files. `pw` has a very powerful set of command line options that make it suitable for use in shell scripts, but new users may find it more complicated than the other commands presented here.

8.7 Limiting Users

If you run a multi-user system, chances are that you do not trust all of your users not to damage your system. FreeBSD provides a number of ways a system administrator can limit the amount of system resources an individual user can use. These limits are generally divided into two sections: disk quotas, and other resource limits.

Disk quotas are a way for the system administrator to tell the filesystem the amount of disk space a user may use; moreover, they provide a way to quickly check on the disk usage of a user without having to calculate it every time. Quotas are discussed in Section 12.5.

The other resource limits include ways to limit the amount of CPU, memory, and other resources a user may consume. These are defined using login classes and are discussed here.

Login classes are defined in `/etc/login.conf`. The precise semantics are beyond the scope of this section, but are described in detail in the login.conf(5) manual page. It is sufficient to say that each user is assigned to a login class (`default` by default), and that each login class has a set of login capabilities associated with it. A login capability is a `name=value` pair, where `name` is a well-known identifier and `value` is an arbitrary string processed accordingly depending on the name. Setting up login classes and capabilities is rather straight-forward and is also described in login.conf(5).

Resource limits are different from plain vanilla login capabilities in two ways. First, for every limit, there is a soft (current) and hard limit. A soft limit may be adjusted by the user or application, but may be no higher than the hard limit. The latter may be lowered by the user, but never raised. Second, most resource limits apply per process to a specific user, not the user as a whole. Note, however, that these differences are mandated by the specific handling of the limits, not by the implementation of the login capability framework (i.e., they are not *really* a special case of login capabilities).

And so, without further ado, below are the most commonly used resource limits (the rest, along with all the other login capabilities, may be found in login.conf(5)).

`coredumpsize`

The limit on the size of a core file generated by a program is, for obvious reasons, subordinate to other limits on disk usage (e.g., `filesize`, or disk quotas). Nevertheless, it is often used as a less-severe method of controlling disk space consumption: since users do not generate core files themselves, and often do not delete them, setting this may save them from running out of disk space should a large program (e.g., **emacs**) crash.

`cputime`

This is the maximum amount of CPU time a user's process may consume. Offending processes will be killed by the kernel.

Note: This is a limit on CPU *time* consumed, not percentage of the CPU as displayed in some fields by top(1) and ps(1). A limit on the latter is, at the time of this writing, not possible, and would be rather useless: a compiler—probably a legitimate task—can easily use almost 100% of a CPU for some time.

`filesize`

This is the maximum size of a file the user may possess. Unlike disk quotas, this limit is enforced on individual files, not the set of all files a user owns.

`maxproc`

This is the maximum number of processes a user may be running. This includes foreground and background processes alike. For obvious reasons, this may not be larger than the system limit specified by the `kern.maxproc` `sysctl`. Also note that setting this too small may hinder a user's productivity: it is often useful to be logged in multiple times or execute pipelines. Some tasks, such as compiling a large program, also spawn multiple processes (e.g., make(1), cc(1), and other intermediate preprocessors).

`memorylocked`

This is the maximum amount a memory a process may have requested to be locked into main memory (e.g., see mlock(2)). Some system-critical programs, such as amd(8), lock into main memory such that in the event of being swapped out, they do not contribute to a system's trashing in time of trouble.

`memoryuse`

This is the maximum amount of memory a process may consume at any given time. It includes both core memory and swap usage. This is not a catch-all limit for restricting memory consumption, but it is a good start.

`openfiles`

This is the maximum amount of files a process may have open. In FreeBSD, files are also used to represent sockets and IPC channels; thus, be careful not to set this too low. The system-wide limit for this is defined by the `kern.maxfiles` `sysctl`.

`sbsize`

This is the limit on the amount of network memory, and thus mbufs, a user may consume. This originated as a response to an old DoS attack by creating a lot of sockets, but can be generally used to limit network communications.

`stacksize`

This is the maximum size a process' stack may grow to. This alone is not sufficient to limit the amount of memory a program may use; consequently, it should be used in conjunction with other limits.

There are a few other things to remember when setting resource limits. Following are some general tips, suggestions, and miscellaneous comments.

- Processes started at system startup by /etc/rc are assigned to the daemon login class.
- Although the /etc/login.conf that comes with the system is a good source of reasonable values for most limits, only you, the administrator, can know what is appropriate for your system. Setting a limit too high may open your system up to abuse, while setting it too low may put a strain on productivity.
- Users of the X Window System (X11) should probably be granted more resources than other users. X11 by itself takes a lot of resources, but it also encourages users to run more programs simultaneously.
- Remember that many limits apply to individual processes, not the user as a whole. For example, setting openfiles to 50 means that each process the user runs may open up to 50 files. Thus, the gross amount of files a user may open is the value of openfiles multiplied by the value of maxproc. This also applies to memory consumption.

For further information on resource limits and login classes and capabilities in general, please consult the relevant manual pages: cap_mkdb(1), getrlimit(2), login.conf(5).

8.8 Personalizing Users

Localization is an environment set up by the system administrator or user to accommodate different languages, character sets, date and time standards, and so on. This is discussed in Localization, Chapter 13.

8.9 Groups

A group is simply a list of users. Groups are identified by their group name and gid (group ID). In FreeBSD (and most other Unix systems), the two factors the kernel uses to decide whether a process is allowed to do something is its user ID and list of groups it belongs to. Unlike a user ID, a process has a list of groups associated with it. You may hear some things refer to the "group ID" of a user or process; most of the time, this just means the first group in the list.

The group name to group ID map is in /etc/group. This is a plain text file with four colon-delimited fields. The first field is the group name, the second is the encrypted password, the third the group ID, and the fourth the comma-delimited list of members. It can safely be edited by hand (assuming, of course, that you do not make any syntax errors!). For a more complete description of the syntax, see the group(5) manual page.

If you do not want to edit /etc/group manually, you can use the pw(8) command to add and edit groups. For example, to add a group called teamtwo and then confirm that it exists you can use:

Example 8-7. Adding a Group Using pw(8)

```
# pw groupadd teamtwo
# pw groupshow teamtwo
teamtwo:*:1100:
```

The number 1100 above is the group ID of the group teamtwo. Right now, teamtwo has no members, and is thus rather useless. Let's change that by inviting jru to the teamtwo group.

Example 8-8. Adding Somebody to a Group Using pw(8)

```
# pw groupmod teamtwo -M jru
# pw groupshow teamtwo
teamtwo:*:1100:jru
```

The argument to the -M option is a comma-delimited list of users who are members of the group. From the preceding sections, we know that the password file also contains a group for each user. The latter (the user) is automatically added to the group list by the system; the user will not show up as a member when using the groupshow command to pw(8), but will show up when the information is queried via id(1) or similar tool. In other words, pw(8) only manipulates the /etc/group file; it will never attempt to read additionally data from /etc/passwd.

Example 8-9. Using id(1) to Determine Group Membership

```
% id jru
uid=1001(jru) gid=1001(jru) groups=1001(jru), 1100(teamtwo)
```

As you can see, jru is a member of the groups jru and teamtwo.

For more information about pw(8), see its manual page, and for more information on the format of /etc/group, consult the group(5) manual page.

Chapter 9

Configuring the FreeBSD Kernel

9.1 Synopsis

The kernel is the core of the FreeBSD operating system. It is responsible for managing memory, enforcing security controls, networking, disk access, and much more. While more and more of FreeBSD becomes dynamically configurable it is still occasionally necessary to reconfigure and recompile your kernel.

After reading this chapter, you will know:

• Why you might need to build a custom kernel.

• How to write a kernel configuration file, or alter an existing configuration file.

• How to use the kernel configuration file to create and build a new kernel.

• How to install the new kernel.

• How to create any entries in /dev that may be required.

• How to troubleshoot if things go wrong.

9.2 Why Build a Custom Kernel?

Traditionally, FreeBSD has had what is called a "monolithic" kernel. This means that the kernel was one large program, supported a fixed list of devices, and if you wanted to change the kernel's behavior then you had to compile a new kernel, and then reboot your computer with the new kernel.

Today, FreeBSD is rapidly moving to a model where much of the kernel's functionality is contained in modules which can be dynamically loaded and unloaded from the kernel as necessary. This allows the kernel to adapt to new hardware suddenly becoming available (such as PCMCIA cards in a laptop), or for new functionality to be brought in to the kernel that was not necessary when the kernel was originally compiled. Colloquially these are called KLDs.

Despite this, it is still necessary to carry out some static kernel configuration. In some cases this is because the functionality is so tied to the kernel that it can not be made dynamically loadable. In others it may simply be because no one has yet taken the time to write a dynamic loadable kernel module for that functionality yet.

Building a custom kernel is one of the most important rites of passage nearly every Unix user must endure. This process, while time consuming, will provide many benefits to your FreeBSD system. Unlike the GENERIC kernel, which must support a wide range of hardware, a custom kernel only contains support for *your* PC's hardware. This has a number of benefits, such as:

- Faster boot time. Since the kernel will only probe the hardware you have on your system, the time it takes your system to boot will decrease dramatically.

- Less memory use. A custom kernel often uses less memory than the GENERIC kernel, which is important because the kernel is one process that must always be present in memory. For this reason, a custom kernel is especially useful on a system with a small amount of RAM.

- Additional hardware support. A custom kernel allows you to add in support for devices such as sound cards, which are not present in the GENERIC kernel.

9.3 Building and Installing a Custom Kernel

First, let us take a quick tour of the kernel build directory. All directories mentioned will be relative to the main /usr/src/sys directory, which is also accessible through /sys. There are a number of subdirectories here representing different parts of the kernel, but the most important, for our purposes, are arch/conf, where you will edit your custom kernel configuration, and compile, which is the staging area where your kernel will be built. *arch* represents either i386, alpha, or pc98 (an alternative development branch of PC hardware, popular in Japan). Everything inside a particular architecture's directory deals with that architecture only; the rest of the code is common to all platforms to which FreeBSD could potentially be ported. Notice the logical organization of the directory structure, with each supported device, filesystem, and option in its own subdirectory.

> **Note:** If there is *not* a /usr/src/sys directory on your system, then the kernel source has not been installed. The easiest way to do this is by running /stand/sysinstall as root, choosing Configure, then Distributions, then src, then sys.

Next, move to the arch/conf directory and copy the GENERIC configuration file to the name you want to give your kernel. For example:

```
# cd /usr/src/sys/i386/conf
# cp GENERIC MYKERNEL
```

Traditionally, this name is in all capital letters and, if you are maintaining multiple FreeBSD machines with different hardware, it is a good idea to name it after your machine's hostname. We will call it MYKERNEL for the purpose of this example.

> **Tip:** Storing your kernel config file directly under /usr/src can be a bad idea. If you are experiencing problems it can be tempting to just delete /usr/src and start again. Five seconds after you do that you realize that you have deleted your custom kernel config file.
>
> You might want to keep your kernel config file elsewhere, and then create a symbolic link to the file in the i386 directory.
>
> For example:
>
> ```
> # cd /usr/src/sys/i386/conf
> # mkdir /root/kernels
> # cp GENERIC /root/kernels/MYKERNEL
> # ln -s /root/kernels/MYKERNEL
> ```

Note: You must execute these and all of the following commands under the root account or you will get permission denied errors.

Now, edit MYKERNEL with your favorite text editor. If you are just starting out, the only editor available will probably be vi, which is too complex to explain here, but is covered well in many books in the bibliography. However, FreeBSD does offer an easier editor called "ee" which, if you are a beginner, should be your editor of choice. Feel free to change the comment lines at the top to reflect your configuration or the changes you have made to differentiate it from GENERIC.

If you have built a kernel under SunOS or some other BSD operating system, much of this file will be very familiar to you. If you are coming from some other operating system such as DOS, on the other hand, the GENERIC configuration file might seem overwhelming to you, so follow the descriptions in the Configuration File section slowly and carefully.

Note: Be sure to always check the file /usr/src/UPDATING, before you perform any update steps, in the case you sync your source-tree (explained in Chapter 19) with the latest sources of the FreeBSD project. In this file all important issues with updating FreeBSD are written down. /usr/src/UPDATING always fits to your version of the FreeBSD source, and is therefore more accurate for those information than the handbook.

You must now compile the source code for the kernel. There are two procedures you can use to do this, and the one you will use depends on why you are rebuilding the kernel, and the version of FreeBSD you are running.

- If you have installed *only* the kernel source code, use procedure 1.
- If you are running a FreeBSD version prior to 4.0, and you are *not* upgrading to FreeBSD 4.0 or higher using the "make world" procedure, use procedure 1.
- If you are building a new kernel without updating the source code (perhaps just to add a new option, such as IPFIREWALL) you can use either procedure.
- If you are rebuilding the kernel as part of a "make world" process, use procedure 2.

Procedure 1. Building a kernel the "traditional" way

1. Run config(8) to generate the kernel source code.

    ```
    # /usr/sbin/config MYKERNEL
    ```

2. Change in to the build directory.

    ```
    # cd ../../compile/MYKERNEL
    ```

3. Compile the kernel.

    ```
    # make depend
    # make
    ```

4. Install the new kernel.

```
# make install
```

Procedure 2. Building a kernel the "new" way

1. Change to the /usr/src directory

   ```
   # cd /usr/src
   ```

2. Compile the kernel.

   ```
   # make buildkernel KERNCONF=MYKERNEL
   ```

3. Install the new kernel.

   ```
   # make installkernel KERNCONF=MYKERNEL
   ```

> **Note:** In FreeBSD 4.2 and older you must replace KERNCONF= with KERNEL=. 4.2-STABLE that was fetched after Feb 2nd, 2001 does recognize KERNCONF=

If you have *not* upgraded your source tree in any way (you have not run **CVSup**, **CTM**, or used **anoncvs**), then you should use the config, make depend, make, make install sequence.

The new kernel will be copied to the root directory as /kernel and the old kernel will be moved to /kernel.old. Now, shutdown the system and reboot to use your kernel. In case something goes wrong, there are some troubleshooting instructions at the end of this chapter. Be sure to read the section which explains how to recover in case your new kernel does not boot section towards the end of this chapter.

> **Note:** If you have added any new devices (such as sound cards) you may have to add some device nodes to your /dev directory, as explained in the Making Device Nodes section, before you can use them. For more information, take a look at "Making Device Nodes" later on in this chapter.

9.4 The Configuration File

The general format of a configuration file is quite simple. Each line contains a keyword and one or more arguments. For simplicity, most lines only contain one argument. Anything following a # is considered a comment and ignored. The following sections describe each keyword, generally in the order they are listed in GENERIC, although some related keywords have been grouped together in a single section (such as Networking) even though they are actually scattered throughout the GENERIC file. An exhaustive list of options and more detailed explanations of the device lines is present in the LINT configuration file, located in the same directory as GENERIC. If you are in doubt as to the purpose or necessity of a line, check first in LINT.

> **Quoting numbers:** In all versions of FreeBSD up to and including 3.X, config(8) required that any strings in the configuration file that contained numbers used as text had to be enclosed in double quotes.

This requirement was removed in the 4.X branch, which this book covers, so if you are on a pre-4.X system, see the `/usr/src/sys/i386/conf/LINT` and `/usr/src/sys/i386/conf/GENERIC` files on your system for examples.

The following is an example GENERIC kernel configuration file with various additional comments where needed for clarity. This example should match your copy in `/usr/src/sys/i386/conf/GENERIC` fairly closely. For details of all the possible kernel options, see `/usr/src/sys/i386/conf/LINT`.

```
#
# GENERIC -- Generic kernel configuration file for FreeBSD/i386
#
# For more information on this file, please read the handbook section on
# Kernel Configuration Files:
#
#    http://www.freebsd.org/handbook/kernelconfig-config.html
#
# The handbook is also available locally in /usr/share/doc/handbook
# if you've installed the doc distribution, otherwise always see the
# FreeBSD World Wide Web server (http://www.FreeBSD.ORG/) for the
# latest information.
#
# An exhaustive list of options and more detailed explanations of the
# device lines is also present in the ./LINT configuration file. If you are
# in doubt as to the purpose or necessity of a line, check first in LINT.
#
# $FreeBSD: src/sys/i386/conf/GENERIC,v 1.246 2000/03/09 16:32:55 jlemon Exp $
```

The following are the mandatory keywords required in *every* kernel you build:

```
machine i386
```

This is the machine architecture. It must be either i386, alpha, or pc98.

```
cpu          I386_CPU
cpu          I486_CPU
cpu          I586_CPU
cpu          I686_CPU
```

The above specifies the type of CPU you have in your system. You may have multiple instances of the CPU line (i.e., you are not sure whether you should use I586_CPU or I686_CPU), however, for a custom kernel, it is best to specify only the CPU you have. If you are unsure of your CPU type, you can use the dmesg command to view your boot up messages.

The Alpha architecture has different values for cpu. They include:

```
cpu          EV4
cpu          EV5
```

If you are using an Alpha machine, you should be using one of the above CPU types.

```
ident          GENERIC
```

This is the identification of the kernel. You should change this to whatever you named your kernel, as in our previous example, MYKERNEL. The value you put in the ident string will print when you boot up the kernel, so it is useful to give the new kernel a different name if you want to keep it separate from your usual kernel (i.e., you want to build an experimental kernel).

```
maxusers          32
```

The maxusers option sets the size of a number of important system tables. This number is supposed to be roughly equal to the number of simultaneous users you expect to have on your machine. However, under normal circumstances, you will want to set maxusers to at least 4, especially if you are using the X Window System or compiling software. The reason is that the most important table set by maxusers is the maximum number of processes, which is set to 20 + 16 * maxusers, so if you set maxusers to 1, then you can only have 36 simultaneous processes, including the 18 or so that the system starts up at boot time, and the 15 or so you will probably create when you start the X Window System. Even a simple task like reading a manual page will start up nine processes to filter, decompress, and view it. Setting maxusers to 64 will allow you to have up to 1044 simultaneous processes, which should be enough for nearly all uses. If, however, you see the dreaded proc table full error when trying to start another program, or are running a server with a large number of simultaneous users (like ftp.FreeBSD.org), you can always increase the number and rebuild.

> **Note:** maxusers does *not* limit the number of users which can log into your machine. It simply sets various table sizes to reasonable values considering the maximum number of users you will likely have on your system and how many processes each of them will be running. One keyword which *does* limit the number of simultaneous *remote logins* is pseudo-device pty 16.

```
# Floating point support - do not disable.
device          npx0      at nexus? port IO_NPX irq 13
```

npx0 is the interface to the floating point math unit in FreeBSD, which is either the hardware co-processor or the software math emulator. This is *not* optional.

```
# Pseudo devices - the number indicates how many units to allocate.
pseudo-device  loop          # Network loopback
```

This is the generic loopback device for TCP/IP. If you telnet or FTP to localhost (a.k.a., 127.0.0.1) it will come back at you through this pseudo-device. This is *mandatory*.

Everything that follows is more or less optional. See the notes underneath or next to each option for more information.

```
#makeoptions    DEBUG=-g      #Build kernel with gdb(1) debug symbols
options         MATH_EMULATE  #Support for x87 emulation
```

This line allows the kernel to simulate a math co-processor if your computer does not have one (386 or 486SX). If you have a 486DX, or a 386 or 486SX (with a separate 387 or 487 chip), or higher (Pentium, Pentium II, etc.), you can comment this line out.

> **Note:** The normal math co-processor emulation routines that come with FreeBSD are *not* very accurate. If you do not have a math co-processor, and you need the best accuracy, it is recommended that you change this option to GPL_MATH_EMULATE to use the GNU math support, which is not included by default for licensing reasons.

```
options            INET          #InterNETworking
```

Networking support. Leave this in, even if you do not plan to be connected to a network. Most programs require at least loopback networking (i.e., making network connections within your PC), so this is essentially mandatory.

```
options            INET6         #IPv6 communications protocols
```

This enables the IPv6 communication protocols.

```
options            FFS           #Berkeley Fast Filesystem
options            FFS_ROOT      #FFS usable as root device [keep this!]
```

This is the basic hard drive filesystem. Leave it in if you boot from the hard disk.

```
options            MFS           #Memory Filesystem
options            MD_ROOT       #MD is a potential root device
```

This is the memory-mapped filesystem. This is basically a RAM disk for fast storage of temporary files, useful if you have a lot of swap space that you want to take advantage of. A perfect place to mount an MFS partition is on the `/tmp` directory, since many programs store temporary data here. To mount an MFS RAM disk on `/tmp`, add the following line to `/etc/fstab`:

```
/dev/ad1s2b /tmp mfs rw 0 0
```

Now you simply need to either reboot, or run the command `mount /tmp`.

```
options            NFS           #Network Filesystem
options            NFS_ROOT      #NFS usable as root device, NFS required
```

The network filesystem. Unless you plan to mount partitions from a Unix file server over TCP/IP, you can comment these out.

```
options            MSDOSFS       #MSDOS Filesystem
```

The MS-DOS filesystem. Unless you plan to mount a DOS formatted hard drive partition at boot time, you can safely comment this out. It will be automatically loaded the first time you mount a DOS partition, as described above. Also, the excellent **mtools** software (in the ports collection) allows you to access DOS floppies without having to mount and unmount them (and does not require `MSDOSFS` at all).

```
options            CD9660        #ISO 9660 Filesystem
options            CD9660_ROOT   #CD-ROM usable as root, CD9660 required
```

The ISO 9660 filesystem for CDROMs. Comment it out if you do not have a CDROM drive or only mount data CDs occasionally (since it will be dynamically loaded the first time you mount a data CD). Audio CDs do not need this filesystem.

```
options            PROCFS        #Process filesystem
```

The process filesystem. This is a "pretend" filesystem mounted on /proc which allows programs like ps(1) to give you more information on what processes are running.

```
options         COMPAT_43    #Compatible with BSD 4.3 [KEEP THIS!]
```

Compatibility with 4.3BSD. Leave this in; some programs will act strangely if you comment this out.

```
options         SCSI_DELAY=15000    #Delay (in ms) before probing SCSI
```

This causes the kernel to pause for 15 seconds before probing each SCSI device in your system. If you only have IDE hard drives, you can ignore this, otherwise you will probably want to lower this number, perhaps to 5 seconds, to speed up booting. Of course, if you do this, and FreeBSD has trouble recognizing your SCSI devices, you will have to raise it back up.

```
options         UCONSOLE            #Allow users to grab the console
```

Allow users to grab the console, which is useful for X users. For example, you can create a console xterm by typing xterm -C, which will display any write, talk, and any other messages you receive, as well as any console messages sent by the kernel.

```
options         USERCONFIG          #boot -c editor
```

This option allows you to boot the configuration editor from the boot menu.

```
options         VISUAL_USERCONFIG   #visual boot -c editor
```

This option allows you to boot the visual configuration editor from the boot menu.

```
options         KTRACE              #ktrace(1) support
```

This enables kernel process tracing, which is useful in debugging.

```
options         SYSVSHM             #SYSV-style shared memory
```

This option provides for System V shared memory. The most common use of this is the XSHM extension in X, which many graphics-intensive programs will automatically take advantage of for extra speed. If you use X, you will definitely want to include this.

```
options         SYSVSEM             #SYSV-style semaphores
```

Support for System V semaphores. Less commonly used but only adds a few hundred bytes to the kernel.

```
options         SYSVMSG             #SYSV-style message queues
```

Support for System V messages. Again, only adds a few hundred bytes to the kernel.

> **Note:** The ipcs(1) command will list any processes using each of these System V facilities.

```
options  P1003_1B #Posix P1003_1B real-time extensions
options  _KPOSIX_PRIORITY_SCHEDULING
```

Real-time extensions added in the 1993 POSIX. Certain applications in the ports collection use these (such as Star Office).

```
options   ICMP_BANDLIM #Rate limit bad replies
```

This option enables ICMP error response bandwidth limiting. You typically want this option as it will help protect the machine from denial of service packet attacks.

```
# To make an SMP kernel, the next two are needed
#options     SMP              # Symmetric MultiProcessor Kernel
#options     APIC_IO          # Symmetric (APIC) I/O
```

The above are both required for SMP support.

```
device      isa
```

All PCs supported by FreeBSD have one of these. If you have an IBM PS/2 (Micro Channel Architecture), you cannot run FreeBSD at this time (support is being worked on).

```
device      eisa
```

Include this if you have an EISA motherboard. This enables auto-detection and configuration support for all devices on the EISA bus.

```
device      pci
```

Include this if you have a PCI motherboard. This enables auto-detection of PCI cards and gatewaying from the PCI to ISA bus.

```
# Floppy drives
device      fdc0         at isa? port IO_FD1 irq 6 drq 2
device      fd0          at fdc0 drive 0
device      fd1          at fdc0 drive 1
```

This is the floppy drive controller. fd0 is the A: floppy drive, and fd1 is the B: drive.

```
device      ata
```

This driver supports all ATA and ATAPI devices. You only need one device ata line for the kernel to detect all PCI ATA/ATAPI devices on modern machines.

```
device      atadisk              # ATA disk drives
```

This is needed along with device ata for ATAPI disk drives.

```
device      atapicd              # ATAPI CDROM drives
```

This is needed along with device ata for ATAPI CDROM drives.

```
device      atapifd              # ATAPI floppy drives
```

This is needed along with `device ata` for ATAPI floppy drives.

```
device          atapist                 # ATAPI tape drives
```

This is needed along with `device ata` for ATAPI tape drives.

```
options         ATA_STATIC_ID           #Static device numbering
```

This makes the controller number static (like the old driver) or else the device numbers are dynamically allocated.

```
# ATA and ATAPI devices
device          ata0        at isa? port IO_WD1 irq 14
device          ata1        at isa? port IO_WD2 irq 15
```

Use the above for older, non-PCI systems.

```
# SCSI Controllers
device          ahb         # EISA AHA1742 family
device          ahc         # AHA2940 and onboard AIC7xxx devices
device          amd         # AMD 53C974 (Teckram DC-390(T))
device          dpt         # DPT Smartcache - See LINT for options!
device          isp         # Qlogic family
device          ncr         # NCR/Symbios Logic
device          sym         # NCR/Symbios Logic (newer chipsets)

device          adv0        at isa?
device          adw
device          bt0         at isa?
device          aha0        at isa?
device          aic0        at isa?
```

SCSI controllers. Comment out any you do not have in your system. If you have an IDE only system, you can remove these altogether.

```
# SCSI peripherals
device          scbus       # SCSI bus (required)
device          da          # Direct Access (disks)
device          sa          # Sequential Access (tape etc)
device          cd          # CD
device          pass        # Passthrough device (direct SCSI
access)
```

SCSI peripherals. Again, comment out any you do not have, or if you have only IDE hardware, you can remove them completely.

```
# RAID controllers
device          ida         # Compaq Smart RAID
device          amr         # AMI MegaRAID
device          mlx         # Mylex DAC960 family
```

Supported RAID controllers. If you do not have any of these, you can comment them out or remove them.

```
# atkbdc0 controls both the keyboard and the PS/2 mouse
device          atkbdc0    at isa? port IO_KBD
```

The keyboard controller (atkbdc) provides I/O services for the AT keyboard and PS/2 style pointing devices. This controller is required by the keyboard driver (atkbd) and the PS/2 pointing device driver (psm).

```
device          atkbd0     at atkbdc? irq 1
```

The atkbd driver, together with atkbdc controller, provides access to the AT 84 keyboard or the AT enhanced keyboard which is connected to the AT keyboard controller.

```
device          psm0       at atkbdc? irq 12
```

Use this device if your mouse plugs into the PS/2 mouse port.

```
device          vga0       at isa?
```

The video card driver.

```
# splash screen/screen saver
pseudo-device           splash
```

Splash screen at start up! Screen savers require this too.

```
# syscons is the default console driver, resembling an SCO console
device          sc0        at isa?
```

sc0 is the default console driver, which resembles a SCO console. Since most full-screen programs access the console through a terminal database library like termcap, it should not matter whether you use this or vt0, the VT220 compatible console driver. When you log in, set your TERM variable to scoansi if full-screen programs have trouble running under this console.

```
# Enable this and PCVT_FREEBSD for pcvt vt220 compatible console driver
#device         vt0     at isa?
#options        XSERVER          # support for X server on a vt console
#options        FAT_CURSOR       # start with block cursor
# If you have a ThinkPAD, uncomment this along with the rest of the PCVT lines
#options        PCVT_SCANSET=2   # IBM keyboards are non-std
```

This is a VT220-compatible console driver, backward compatible to VT100/102. It works well on some laptops which have hardware incompatibilities with sc0. Also set your TERM variable to vt100 or vt220 when you log in. This driver might also prove useful when connecting to a large number of different machines over the network, where termcap or terminfo entries for the sc0 device are often not available — vt100 should be available on virtually any platform.

```
# Power management support (see LINT for more options)
device          apm0       at nexus? disable flags 0x20  # Advanced Power Management
```

Advanced Power Management support. Useful for laptops.

```
# PCCARD (PCMCIA) support
```

```
device          card
device          pcic0    at isa? irq 10 port 0x3e0 iomem 0xd0000
device          pcic1    at isa? irq 11 port 0x3e2 iomem 0xd4000 disable
```

PCMCIA support. You want this if you are using a laptop.

```
# Serial (COM) ports
device          sio0     at isa? port IO_COM1 flags 0x10 irq 4
device          sio1     at isa? port IO_COM2 irq 3
device          sio2     at isa? disable port IO_COM3 irq 5
device          sio3     at isa? disable port IO_COM4 irq 9
```

These are the four serial ports referred to as COM1 through COM4 in the MS-DOS/Windows world.

> **Note:** If you have an internal modem on COM4 and a serial port at COM2, you will have to change the IRQ of the modem to 2 (for obscure technical reasons, IRQ2 = IRQ 9) in order to access it from FreeBSD. If you have a multiport serial card, check the manual page for sio(4) for more information on the proper values for these lines. Some video cards (notably those based on S3 chips) use IO addresses in the form of `0x*2e8`, and since many cheap serial cards do not fully decode the 16-bit IO address space, they clash with these cards making the COM4 port practically unavailable.

> Each serial port is required to have a unique IRQ (unless you are using one of the multiport cards where shared interrupts are supported), so the default IRQs for COM3 and COM4 cannot be used.

```
# Parallel port
device          ppc0     at isa? irq 7
```

This is the ISA-bus parallel port interface.

```
device          ppbus       # Parallel port bus (required)
```

Provides support for the parallel port bus.

```
device          lpt         # Printer
```

Support for parallel port printers.

> **Note:** All three of the above are required to enable parallel printer support.

```
device          plip        # TCP/IP over parallel
```

This is the driver for the parallel network interface.

```
device          ppi         # Parallel port interface device
```

The general-purpose I/O ("geek port") + IEEE1284 I/O.

```
#device         vpo         # Requires scbus and da
```

This is for an Iomega Zip drive. It requires `scbus` and `da` support. Best performance is achieved with ports in EPP 1.9 mode.

```
# PCI Ethernet NICs.
device          de          # DEC/Intel DC21x4x ("Tulip")
device          fxp         # Intel EtherExpress PRO/100B (82557, 82558)
device          tx          # SMC 9432TX (83c170 "EPIC")
device          vx          # 3Com 3c590, 3c595 ("Vortex")
device          wx          # Intel Gigabit Ethernet Card ("Wiseman")
```

Various PCI network card drivers. Comment out or remove any of these not present in your system.

```
# PCI Ethernet NICs that use the common MII bus controller code.
device          miibus      # MII bus support
```

MII bus support is required for some PCI 10/100 Ethernet NICs, namely those which use MII-compliant transceivers or implement transceiver control interfaces that operate like an MII. Adding `device miibus` to the kernel config pulls in support for the generic miibus API and all of the PHY drivers, including a generic one for PHYs that are not specifically handled by an individual driver

```
device          dc          # DEC/Intel 21143 and various workalikes
device          rl          # RealTek 8129/8139
device          sf          # Adaptec AIC-6915 ("Starfire")
device          sis         # Silicon Integrated Systems SiS 900/SiS 7016
device          ste         # Sundance ST201 (D-Link DFE-550TX)
device          tl          # Texas Instruments ThunderLAN
device          vr          # VIA Rhine, Rhine II
device          wb          # Winbond W89C840F
device          xl          # 3Com 3c90x ("Boomerang", "Cyclone")
```

Drivers that use the MII bus controller code.

```
# ISA Ethernet NICs.
device          ed0     at isa? port 0x280 irq 10 iomem 0xd8000
device          ex
device          ep
# WaveLAN/IEEE 802.11 wireless NICs. Note: the WaveLAN/IEEE really
# exists only as a PCMCIA device, so there is no ISA attachment needed
# and resources will always be dynamically assigned by the pccard code.
device          wi
# Aironet 4500/4800 802.11 wireless NICs. Note: the declaration below will
# work for PCMCIA and PCI cards, as well as ISA cards set to ISA PnP
# mode (the factory default). If you set the switches on your ISA
# card for a manually chosen I/O address and IRQ, you must specify
# those parameters here.
device          an
# The probe order of these is presently determined by i386/isa/isa_compat.c.
device          ie0     at isa? port 0x300 irq 10 iomem 0xd0000
device          fe0     at isa? port 0x300
device          le0     at isa? port 0x300 irq 5 iomem 0xd0000
device          lnc0    at isa? port 0x280 irq 10 drq 0
```

```
device          cs0     at isa? port 0x300
device          sn0     at isa? port 0x300 irq 10
# requires PCCARD (PCMCIA) support to be activated
#device         xe0     at isa?
```

ISA Ethernet drivers. See `/usr/src/sys/i386/conf/LINT` for which cards are supported by which driver.

```
pseudo-device   ether           # Ethernet support
```

`ether` is only needed if you have an Ethernet card. It includes generic Ethernet protocol code.

```
pseudo-device   sl      1       # Kernel SLIP
```

`sl` is for SLIP support. This has been almost entirely supplanted by PPP, which is easier to set up, better suited for modem-to-modem connection, and more powerful. The *number* after `sl` specifies how many simultaneous SLIP sessions to support.

```
pseudo-device   ppp     1       # Kernel PPP
```

This is for kernel PPP support for dial-up connections. There is also a version of PPP implemented as a userland application that uses `tun` and offers more flexibility and features such as demand dialing. The *number* after `ppp` specifies how many simultaneous PPP connections to support.

```
pseudo-device   tun             # Packet tunnel.
```

This is used by the userland PPP software. A *number* after `tun` specifies the number of simultaneous PPP sessions to support. See the PPP section of this book (Section 16.2) for more information.

```
pseudo-device   pty             # Pseudo-ttys (telnet etc)
```

This is a "pseudo-terminal" or simulated login port. It is used by incoming `telnet` and `rlogin` sessions, **xterm**, and some other applications such as **emacs**. A *number* after `pty` indicates the number of `pty`s to create. If you need more than the default of 16 simultaneous **xterm** windows and/or remote logins, be sure to increase this number accordingly, up to a maximum of 256.

```
pseudo-device   md              # Memory "disks"
```

Memory disk pseudo-devices.

```
pseudo-device   gif     4       # IPv6 and IPv4 tunneling
```

This implements IPv6 over IPv4 tunneling, IPv4 over IPv6 tunneling, IPv4 over IPv4 tunneling, and IPv6 over IPv6 tunneling.

```
pseudo-device   faith   1       # IPv6-to-IPv4 relaying (translation)
```

This pseudo-device captures packets that are sent to it and diverts them to the IPv4/IPv6 translation daemon.

```
# The 'bpf' pseudo-device enables the Berkeley Packet Filter.
# Be aware of the administrative consequences of enabling this!
```

```
pseudo-device    bpf            # Berkeley packet filter
```

This is the Berkeley Packet Filter. This pseudo-device allows network interfaces to be placed in promiscuous mode, capturing every packet on a broadcast network (e.g., an Ethernet). These packets can be captured to disk and or examined with the tcpdump(1) program.

> **Note:** The `bpf pseudo-device` is also used by dhclient(8) to obtain the IP address of the default router (gateway) and so on. If you use DHCP, leave this uncommented.

```
# USB support
#device         uhci           # UHCI PCI->USB interface
#device         ohci           # OHCI PCI->USB interface
#device         usb            # USB Bus (required)
#device         ugen           # Generic
#device         uhid           # "Human Interface Devices"
#device         ukbd           # Keyboard
#device         ulpt           # Printer
#device         umass          # Disks/Mass storage - Requires scbus and da
#device         ums            # Mouse
# USB Ethernet, requires mii
#device         aue            # ADMtek USB ethernet
#device         cue            # CATC USB ethernet
#device         kue            # Kawasaki LSI USB ethernet
```

Support for various USB devices.

For more information and additional devices supported by FreeBSD, see `/usr/src/sys/i386/conf/LINT`.

9.5 Making Device Nodes

Almost every device in the kernel has a corresponding "node" entry in the `/dev` directory. These nodes look like regular files, but are actually special entries into the kernel which programs use to access the device. The shell script `/dev/MAKEDEV`, which is executed when you first install the operating system, creates nearly all of the device nodes supported. However, it does not create *all* of them, so when you add support for a new device, it pays to make sure that the appropriate entries are in this directory, and if not, add them. Here is a simple example:

Suppose you add the IDE CD-ROM support to the kernel. The line to add is:

```
device acd0
```

This means that you should look for some entries that start with `acd0` in the `/dev` directory, possibly followed by a letter, such as `c`, or preceded by the letter `r`, which means a "raw" device. It turns out that those files are not there, so you must change to the `/dev` directory and type:

```
# sh MAKEDEV acd0
```

When this script finishes, you will find that there are now `acd0c` and `racd0c` entries in `/dev` so you know that it executed correctly.

For sound cards, the following command creates the appropriate entries:

```
# sh MAKEDEV snd0
```

Note: When creating device nodes for devices such as sound cards, if other people have access to your machine, it may be desirable to protect the devices from outside access by adding them to the `/etc/fbtab` file. See fbtab(5) for more information.

Follow this simple procedure for any other non-`GENERIC` devices which do not have entries.

Note: All SCSI controllers use the same set of `/dev` entries, so you do not need to create these. Also, network cards and SLIP/PPP pseudo-devices do not have entries in `/dev` at all, so you do not have to worry about these either.

9.6 If Something Goes Wrong

There are four categories of trouble that can occur when building a custom kernel. They are:

`config` fails:

If the `config` command fails when you give it your kernel description, you have probably made a simple error somewhere. Fortunately, `config` will print the line number that it had trouble with, so you can quickly skip to it with `vi`. For example, if you see:

```
config: line 17: syntax error
```

You can skip to the problem in `vi` by typing `17G` in command mode. Make sure the keyword is typed correctly, by comparing it to the `GENERIC` kernel or another reference.

`make` fails:

If the `make` command fails, it usually signals an error in your kernel description, but not severe enough for `config` to catch it. Again, look over your configuration, and if you still cannot resolve the problem, send mail to the FreeBSD general questions mailing list `<freebsd-questions@FreeBSD.org>` with your kernel configuration, and it should be diagnosed very quickly.

The kernel will not boot:

If your new kernel does not boot, or fails to recognize your devices, do not panic! Fortunately, BSD has an excellent mechanism for recovering from incompatible kernels. Simply choose the kernel you want to boot from at the FreeBSD boot loader. You can access this when the system counts down from 10. Hit any key except for the enter key, and type boot `kernel.old`, or the filename of any other kernel that will boot properly. When reconfiguring a kernel, it is always a good idea to keep a kernel that is known to work on hand.

After booting with a good kernel you can check over your configuration file and try to build it again. One helpful resource is the `/var/log/messages` file which records, among other things, all of the kernel messages from every successful boot. Also, the dmesg(8) command will print the kernel messages from the current boot.

> **Note:** If you are having trouble building a kernel, make sure to keep a GENERIC, or some other kernel that is known to work on hand as a different name that will not get erased on the next build. You cannot rely on `kernel.old` because when installing a new kernel, `kernel.old` is overwritten with the last installed kernel which may be non-functional. Also, as soon as possible, move the working kernel to the proper `kernel` location or commands such as ps(1) will not work properly. The proper command to "unlock" the kernel file that `make` installs (in order to move another kernel back permanently) is:
>
> # `chflags noschg /kernel`
>
> If you find you cannot do this, you are probably running at a securelevel(8) greater than zero. Edit `kern_securelevel` in `/etc/rc.conf` and set it to `-1`, then reboot. You can change it back to its previous setting when you are happy with your new kernel.
>
> And, if you want to "lock" your new kernel into place, or any file for that matter, so that it cannot be moved or tampered with:
>
> # `chflags schg /kernel`

The kernel works, but ps does not work any more!:

If you have installed a different version of the kernel from the one that the system utilities have been built with, for example, a 4.X kernel on a 3.X system, many system-status commands like ps(1) and vmstat(8) will not work any more. You must recompile the `libkvm` library as well as these utilities. This is one reason it is not normally a good idea to use a different version of the kernel from the rest of the operating system.

Chapter 10
Security

10.1 Synopsis

This chapter will provide a basic introduction to system security concepts, some general good rules of thumb, and some advanced topics under FreeBSD. A lot of the topics covered here can be applied to system and Internet security in general as well. The Internet is no longer a "friendly" place in which everyone wants to be your kind neighbor. Securing your system is imperative to protect your data, intellectual property, time, and much more from the hands of hackers and the like.

FreeBSD provides an array of utilities and mechanisms to ensure the integrity and security of your system and network.

After reading this chapter, you will know:

· Basic system security concepts, in respect to FreeBSD.

· About the various crypt mechanisms available in FreeBSD, such as DES and MD5.

· How to setup S/Key, an alternative, one-time password authentication system.

· How to setup Kerberos, another alternative authentication system.

· How to create firewalls using IPFW.

· How to configure IPSec.

· How to configure and use OpenSSH, FreeBSD's SSH implementation.

Before reading this chapter, you should:

· Understand basic FreeBSD and Internet concepts.

10.2 Introduction

Security is a function that begins and ends with the system administrator. While all BSD Unix multi-user systems have some inherent security, the job of building and maintaining additional security mechanisms to keep those users "honest" is probably one of the single largest undertakings of the sysadmin. Machines are only as secure as you make them, and security concerns are ever competing with the human necessity for convenience. Unix systems, in general, are capable of running a huge number of simultaneous processes and many of these processes operate as servers – meaning that external entities can connect and talk to them. As yesterday's mini-computers and mainframes become today's desktops, and as computers become networked and internetworked, security becomes an even bigger issue.

Security is best implemented through a layered "onion" approach. In a nutshell, what you want to do is to create as many layers of security as are convenient and then carefully monitor the system for intrusions. You do not want to overbuild your security or you will interfere with the detection side, and detection is one of the single most important aspects of any security mechanism. For example, it makes little sense to set the schg flags (see chflags(1)) on every system binary because while this may temporarily protect the binaries, it prevents an attacker who has broken in from making an easily detectable change that may result in your security mechanisms not detecting the attacker at all.

System security also pertains to dealing with various forms of attack, including attacks that attempt to crash, or otherwise make a system unusable, but do not attempt to break root. Security concerns can be split up into several categories:

1. Denial of service attacks.

2. User account compromises.

3. Root compromise through accessible servers.

4. Root compromise via user accounts.

5. Backdoor creation.

A denial of service attack is an action that deprives the machine of needed resources. Typically, DoS attacks are brute-force mechanisms that attempt to crash or otherwise make a machine unusable by overwhelming its servers or network stack. Some DoS attacks try to take advantage of bugs in the networking stack to crash a machine with a single packet. The latter can only be fixed by applying a bug fix to the kernel. Attacks on servers can often be fixed by properly specifying options to limit the load the servers incur on the system under adverse conditions. Brute-force network attacks are harder to deal with. A spoofed-packet attack, for example, is nearly impossible to stop, short of cutting your system off from the Internet. It may not be able to take your machine down, but it can saturate your Internet connection.

A user account compromise is even more common than a DoS attack. Many sysadmins still run standard **telnetd**, **rlogind**, **rshd**, and **ftpd** servers on their machines. These servers, by default, do not operate over encrypted connections. The result is that if you have any moderate-sized user base, one or more of your users logging into your system from a remote location (which is the most common and convenient way to login to a system) will have his or her password sniffed. The attentive system admin will analyze his remote access logs looking for suspicious source addresses even for successful logins.

One must always assume that once an attacker has access to a user account, the attacker can break root. However, the reality is that in a well secured and maintained system, access to a user account does not necessarily give the attacker access to root. The distinction is important because without access to root the attacker cannot generally hide his tracks and may, at best, be able to do nothing more than mess with the user's files, or crash the machine. User account compromises are very common because users tend not to take the precautions that sysadmins take.

System administrators must keep in mind that there are potentially many ways to break root on a machine. The attacker may know the root password, the attacker may find a bug in a root-run server and be able to break root over a network connection to that server, or the attacker may know of a bug in a suid-root program that allows the attacker to break root once he has broken into a user's account. If an attacker has found a way to break root on a machine, the attacker may not have a need to install a backdoor. Many of the root holes found and closed to date involve a considerable amount of work by the attacker to cleanup after himself, so most attackers install backdoors. A backdoor provides the attacker with a way to easily regain root access to the system, but it also gives the smart system administrator a convenient way to detect the intrusion. Making it impossible for an attacker to install a backdoor may actually be detrimental to your security, because it will not close off the hole the attacker found to break in the first place.

Security remedies should always be implemented with a multi-layered "onion peel" approach and can be categorized as follows:

1. Securing root and staff accounts.

2. Securing root – root-run servers and suid/sgid binaries.

3. Securing user accounts.

4. Securing the password file.

5. Securing the kernel core, raw devices, and filesystems.

6. Quick detection of inappropriate changes made to the system.

7. Paranoia.

The next section of this chapter will cover the above bullet items in greater depth.

10.3 Securing FreeBSD

> **Command vs. Protocol:** Throughout this document, we will use **bold** text to refer to a command or application. This is used for instances such as ssh, since it's a protocol as well as command.

The sections that follow will cover the methods of securing your FreeBSD system that were mentioned in the last section of this chapter.

10.3.1 Securing the `root` Account and Staff Accounts

First off, do not bother securing staff accounts if you have not secured the root account. Most systems have a password assigned to the root account. The first thing you do is assume that the password is *always* compromised. This does not mean that you should remove the password. The password is almost always necessary for console access to the machine. What it does mean is that you should not make it possible to use the password outside of the console or possibly even with the su(1) command. For example, make sure that your pty's are specified as being unsecure in the `/etc/ttys` file so that direct root logins via `telnet` or `rlogin` are disallowed. If using other login services such as **sshd**, make sure that direct root logins are disabled there as well. You can do this by editing your `/etc/ssh/sshd_config` file, and making sure that `PermitRootLogin` is set to `NO`. Consider every access method – services such as FTP often fall through the cracks. Direct root logins should only be allowed via the system console.

Of course, as a sysadmin you have to be able to get to root, so we open up a few holes. But we make sure these holes require additional password verification to operate. One way to make root accessible is to add appropriate staff accounts to the `wheel` group (in `/etc/group`). The staff members placed in the `wheel` group are allowed to `su` to root. You should never give staff members native wheel access by putting them in the `wheel` group in their password entry. Staff accounts should be placed in a `staff` group, and then added to the `wheel` group via the `/etc/group` file. Only those staff members who actually need to have root access should be placed in the `wheel` group. It is also possible, when using an authentication method such as kerberos, to use kerberos' `.k5login` file in the root account to allow a ksu(1) to root without having to place anyone at all in the `wheel` group. This may be the better solution since the `wheel` mechanism still allows an intruder to break root if the intruder has gotten hold of your password file and can break into a staff account. While having the `wheel` mechanism is better than having nothing at all, it is not necessarily the safest option.

An indirect way to secure staff accounts, and ultimately root access is to use an alternative login access method and do what is known as "starring" out the crypted password for the staff accounts. Using the vipw(8) command, one can replace each instance of a crypted password with a single "`*`" character. This command will update the `/etc/master.passwd` file and user/password database to disable password-authenticated logins.

A staff account entry such as:

```
foobar:R9DT/Fa1/LV9U:1000:1000::0:0:Foo Bar:/home/foobar:/usr/local/bin/tcsh
```

Should be changed to this :

```
foobar:*:1000:1000::0:0:Foo Bar:/home/foobar:/usr/local/bin/tcsh
```

This change will prevent normal logins from occurring, since the encrypted password will never match "`*`". With this done, staff members must use another mechanism to authenticate themselves such as kerberos(1) or ssh(1) using a public/private key pair. When using something like kerberos, one generally must secure the machines which run the kerberos servers and your desktop workstation. When using a public/private key pair with ssh, one must generally secure the machine used to login *from* (typically one's workstation). An additional layer of protection can be added to the key pair by password protecting the key pair when creating it with ssh-keygen(1). Being able to "star" out the passwords for staff accounts also guarantees that staff members can only login through secure access methods that you have setup. This forces all staff members to use secure, encrypted connections for all of their sessions, which closes an important hole used by many intruders: sniffing the network from an unrelated, less secure machine.

The more indirect security mechanisms also assume that you are logging in from a more restrictive server to a less restrictive server. For example, if your main box is running all sorts of servers, your workstation should not be running any. In order for your workstation to be reasonably secure you should run as few servers as possible, up to and including no servers at all, and you should run a password-protected screen blanker. Of course, given physical access to a workstation an attacker can break any sort of security you put on it. This is definitely a problem that you should consider, but you should also consider the fact that the vast majority of break-ins occur remotely, over a network, from people who do not have physical access to your workstation or servers.

Using something like kerberos also gives you the ability to disable or change the password for a staff account in one place, and have it immediately effect all the machines on which the staff member may have an account. If a staff member's account gets compromised, the ability to instantly change his password on all machines should not be underrated. With discrete passwords, changing a password on N machines can be a mess. You can also impose re-passwording restrictions with kerberos: not only can a kerberos ticket be made to timeout after a while, but the kerberos system can require that the user choose a new password after a certain period of time (say, once a month).

10.3.2 Securing Root-run Servers and SUID/SGID Binaries

The prudent sysadmin only runs the servers he needs to, no more, no less. Be aware that third party servers are often the most bug-prone. For example, running an old version of **imapd** or **popper** is like giving a universal root ticket out to the entire world. Never run a server that you have not checked out carefully. Many servers do not need to be run as root. For example, the **ntalk**, **comsat**, and **finger** daemons can be run in special user `sandboxes`. A sandbox is not perfect, unless you go through a large amount of trouble, but the onion approach to security still stands: If someone is able to break in through a server running in a sandbox, they still have to break out of the sandbox. The more layers the attacker must break through, the lower the likelihood of his success. Root holes have historically been found in virtually every server ever run as root, including basic system servers. If you are running a machine through which people only login via **sshd** and never login via **telnetd** or **rshd** or **rlogind**, then turn off those services!

FreeBSD now defaults to running **ntalkd**, **comsat**, and **finger** in a sandbox. Another program which may be a candidate for running in a sandbox is named(8). `/etc/defaults/rc.conf` includes the arguments necessary to run **named** in a sandbox in a commented-out form. Depending on whether you are installing a new system or upgrading an existing system, the special user accounts used by these sandboxes may not be installed. The prudent sysadmin would research and implement sandboxes for servers whenever possible.

There are a number of other servers that typically do not run in sandboxes: **sendmail**, **popper**, **imapd**, **ftpd**, and others. There are alternatives to some of these, but installing them may require more work than you are willing to perform (the convenience factor strikes again). You may have to run these servers as root and rely on other mechanisms to detect break-ins that might occur through them.

The other big potential root holes in a system are the suid-root and sgid binaries installed on the system. Most of these binaries, such as **rlogin**, reside in /bin, /sbin, /usr/bin, or /usr/sbin. While nothing is 100% safe, the system-default suid and sgid binaries can be considered reasonably safe. Still, root holes are occasionally found in these binaries. A root hole was found in Xlib in 1998 that made **xterm** (which is typically suid) vulnerable. It is better to be safe than sorry and the prudent sysadmin will restrict suid binaries, that only staff should run, to a special group that only staff can access, and get rid of (chmod 000) any suid binaries that nobody uses. A server with no display generally does not need an **xterm** binary. Sgid binaries can be almost as dangerous. If an intruder can break an sgid-kmem binary, the intruder might be able to read /dev/kmem and thus read the crypted password file, potentially compromising any passworded account. Alternatively an intruder who breaks group kmem can monitor keystrokes sent through pty's, including pty's used by users who login through secure methods. An intruder that breaks the tty group can write to almost any user's tty. If a user is running a terminal program or emulator with a keyboard-simulation feature, the intruder can potentially generate a data stream that causes the user's terminal to echo a command, which is then run as that user.

10.3.3 Securing User Accounts

User accounts are usually the most difficult to secure. While you can impose Draconian access restrictions on your staff and "star" out their passwords, you may not be able to do so with any general user accounts you might have. If you do have sufficient control, then you may win out and be able to secure the user accounts properly. If not, you simply have to be more vigilant in your monitoring of those accounts. Use of ssh and kerberos for user accounts is more problematic, due to the extra administration and technical support required, but still a very good solution compared to a crypted password file.

10.3.4 Securing the Password File

The only sure fire way is to * out as many passwords as you can and use ssh or kerberos for access to those accounts. Even though the crypted password file (/etc/spwd.db) can only be read by root, it may be possible for an intruder to obtain read access to that file even if the attacker cannot obtain root-write access.

Your security scripts should always check for and report changes to the password file (see the Checking file integrity section below).

10.3.5 Securing the Kernel Core, Raw Devices, and Filesystems

If an attacker breaks root he can do just about anything, but there are certain conveniences. For example, most modern kernels have a packet sniffing device driver built in. Under FreeBSD it is called the bpf device. An intruder will commonly attempt to run a packet sniffer on a compromised machine. You do not need to give the intruder the capability and most systems do not have the need for the bpf device compiled in.

But even if you turn off the bpf device, you still have /dev/mem and /dev/kmem to worry about. For that matter, the intruder can still write to raw disk devices. Also, there is another kernel feature called the module loader, kld-load(8). An enterprising intruder can use a KLD module to install his own bpf device, or other sniffing device, on a running kernel. To avoid these problems you have to run the kernel at a higher secure level, at least securelevel 1. The securelevel can be set with a sysctl on the **kern.securelevel** variable. Once you have set the securelevel to 1, write access to raw devices will be denied and special chflags flags, such as schg, will be enforced. You must also ensure that the schg flag is set on critical startup binaries, directories, and script files – everything that gets run up to the point where the securelevel is set. This might be overdoing it, and upgrading the system is much more difficult when you operate at a higher secure level. You may compromise and run the system at a higher secure level but not set the schg flag for every system file and directory under the sun. Another possibility is to simply mount / and /usr read-only. It should be noted that being too Draconian in what you attempt to protect may prevent the all-important detection of an intrusion.

10.3.6 Checking File Integrity: Binaries, Configuration Files, Etc.

When it comes right down to it, you can only protect your core system configuration and control files so much before the convenience factor rears its ugly head. For example, using chflags to set the schg bit on most of the files in / and /usr is probably counterproductive, because while it may protect the files, it also closes a detection window. The last layer of your security onion is perhaps the most important – detection. The rest of your security is pretty much useless (or, worse, presents you with a false sense of safety) if you cannot detect potential incursions. Half the job of the onion is to slow down the attacker, rather than stop him, in order to give the detection side of the equation a chance to catch him in the act.

The best way to detect an incursion is to look for modified, missing, or unexpected files. The best way to look for modified files is from another (often centralized) limited-access system. Writing your security scripts on the extra-secure limited-access system makes them mostly invisible to potential attackers, and this is important. In order to take maximum advantage you generally have to give the limited-access box significant access to the other machines in the business, usually either by doing a read-only NFS export of the other machines to the limited-access box, or by setting up ssh key-pairs to allow the limited-access box to ssh to the other machines. Except for its network traffic, NFS is the least visible method – allowing you to monitor the filesystems on each client box virtually undetected. If your limited-access server is connected to the client boxes through a switch, the NFS method is often the better choice. If your limited-access server is connected to the client boxes through a hub, or through several layers of routing, the NFS method may be too insecure (network-wise) and using ssh may be the better choice even with the audit-trail tracks that ssh lays.

Once you give a limited-access box, at least read access to the client systems it is supposed to monitor, you must write scripts to do the actual monitoring. Given an NFS mount, you can write scripts out of simple system utilities such as find(1) and md5(1). It is best to physically md5 the client-box files at least once a day, and to test control files such as those found in `/etc` and `/usr/local/etc` even more often. When mismatches are found, relative to the base md5 information the limited-access machine knows is valid, it should scream at a sysadmin to go check it out. A good security script will also check for inappropriate suid binaries and for new or deleted files on system partitions such as / and `/usr`.

When using ssh rather than NFS, writing the security script is much more difficult. You essentially have to `scp` the scripts to the client box in order to run them, making them visible, and for safety you also need to `scp` the binaries (such as find) that those scripts use. The **ssh** client on the client box may already be compromised. All in all, using ssh may be necessary when running over unsecure links, but it is also a lot harder to deal with.

A good security script will also check for changes to user and staff members access configuration files: `.rhosts`, `.shosts`, `.ssh/authorized_keys` and so forth... files that might fall outside the purview of the `MD5` check.

If you have a huge amount of user disk space, it may take too long to run through every file on those partitions. In this case, setting mount flags to disallow suid binaries and devices on those partitions is a good idea. The `nodev` and `nosuid` options (see mount(8)) are what you want to look into. You should probably scan them anyway, at least once a week, since the object of this layer is to detect a break-in whether or not the break-in is effective.

Process accounting (see accton(8)) is a relatively low-overhead feature of the operating system which might help as a post-break-in evaluation mechanism. It is especially useful in tracking down how an intruder has actually broken into a system, assuming the file is still intact after the break-in occurs.

Finally, security scripts should process the log files, and the logs themselves should be generated in as secure a manner as possible – remote syslog can be very useful. An intruder tries to cover his tracks, and log files are critical to the sysadmin trying to track down the time and method of the initial break-in. One way to keep a permanent record of the log files is to run the system console to a serial port and collect the information on a continuing basis through a secure machine monitoring the consoles.

10.3.7 Paranoia

A little paranoia never hurts. As a rule, a sysadmin can add any number of security features, as long as they do not effect convenience, and can add security features that *do* effect convenience with some added thought. Even more importantly, a security administrator should mix it up a bit – if you use recommendations such as those given by this document verbatim, you give away your methodologies to the prospective attacker who also has access to this document.

10.3.8 Denial of Service Attacks

This section covers Denial of Service attacks. A DoS attack is typically a packet attack. While there is not much you can do about modern spoofed packet attacks that saturate your network, you can generally limit the damage by ensuring that the attacks cannot take down your servers.

1. Limiting server forks.

2. Limiting springboard attacks (ICMP response attacks, ping broadcast, etc.).

3. Kernel Route Cache.

A common DoS attack is against a forking server that attempts to cause the server to eat processes, file descriptors, and memory, until the machine dies. **inetd** (see inetd(8)) has several options to limit this sort of attack. It should be noted that while it is possible to prevent a machine from going down, it is not generally possible to prevent a service from being disrupted by the attack. Read the **inetd** manual page carefully and pay specific attention to the -c, -C, and -R options. Note that spoofed-IP attacks will circumvent the -C option to **inetd**, so typically a combination of options must be used. Some standalone servers have self-fork-limitation parameters.

Sendmail has its -OMaxDaemonChildren option, which tends to work much better than trying to use sendmail's load limiting options due to the load lag. You should specify a MaxDaemonChildren parameter, when you start **sendmail**, high enough to handle your expected load, but not so high that the computer cannot handle that number of **sendmails** without falling on its face. It is also prudent to run sendmail in queued mode (-ODeliveryMode=queued) and to run the daemon (sendmail -bd) separate from the queue-runs (sendmail -q15m). If you still want real-time delivery you can run the queue at a much lower interval, such as -q1m, but be sure to specify a reasonable MaxDaemonChildren option for *that* sendmail to prevent cascade failures.

Syslogd can be attacked directly and it is strongly recommended that you use the -s option whenever possible, and the -a option otherwise.

You should also be fairly careful with connect-back services such as **tcpwrapper**'s reverse-identd, which can be attacked directly. You generally do not want to use the reverse-ident feature of **tcpwrappers** for this reason.

It is a very good idea to protect internal services from external access by firewalling them off at your border routers. The idea here is to prevent saturation attacks from outside your LAN, not so much to protect internal services from network-based root compromise. Always configure an exclusive firewall, i.e., "firewall everything *except* ports A, B, C, D, and M-Z". This way you can firewall off all of your low ports except for certain specific services such as **named** (if you are primary for a zone), **ntalkd**, **sendmail**, and other Internet-accessible services. If you try to configure the firewall the other way – as an inclusive or permissive firewall, there is a good chance that you will forget to "close" a couple of services, or that you will add a new internal service and forget to update the firewall. You can still open up the high-numbered port range on the firewall, to allow permissive-like operation, without compromising your low ports. Also take note that FreeBSD allows you to control the range of port numbers used for dynamic binding, via the various **net.inet.ip.portrange** sysctl's (sysctl -a | fgrep portrange), which can also ease the complexity of your firewall's configuration. For example, you might use a normal first/last range of 4000 to 5000, and a hiport range of 49152 to 65535, then block off everything under 4000 in your firewall (except for certain specific Internet-accessible ports, of course).

Another common DoS attack is called a springboard attack – to attack a server in a manner that causes the server to generate responses which overloads the server, the local network, or some other machine. The most common attack of this nature is the *ICMP ping broadcast attack*. The attacker spoofs ping packets sent to your LAN's broadcast address with the source IP address set to the actual machine they wish to attack. If your border routers are not configured to stomp on ping's to broadcast addresses, your LAN winds up generating sufficient responses to the spoofed source address to saturate the victim, especially when the attacker uses the same trick on several dozen broadcast addresses over several dozen different networks at once. Broadcast attacks of over a hundred and twenty megabits have been measured. A second common springboard attack is against the ICMP error reporting system. By constructing packets that generate ICMP error responses, an attacker can saturate a server's incoming network and cause the server to saturate its outgoing network with ICMP responses. This type of attack can also crash the server by running it out of mbuf's, especially if the server cannot drain the ICMP responses it generates fast enough. The FreeBSD kernel has a new kernel compile option called `ICMP_BANDLIM` which limits the effectiveness of these sorts of attacks. The last major class of springboard attacks is related to certain internal **inetd** services such as the udp echo service. An attacker simply spoofs a UDP packet with the source address being server A's echo port, and the destination address being server B's echo port, where server A and B are both on your LAN. The two servers then bounce this one packet back and forth between each other. The attacker can overload both servers and their LANs simply by injecting a few packets in this manner. Similar problems exist with the internal **chargen** port. A competent sysadmin will turn off all of these inetd-internal test services.

Spoofed packet attacks may also be used to overload the kernel route cache. Refer to the `net.inet.ip.rtexpire`, `rtminexpire`, and `rtmaxcache` `sysctl` parameters. A spoofed packet attack that uses a random source IP will cause the kernel to generate a temporary cached route in the route table, viewable with `netstat -rna | fgrep W3`. These routes typically timeout in 1600 seconds or so. If the kernel detects that the cached route table has gotten too big it will dynamically reduce the `rtexpire` but will never decrease it to less than `rtminexpire`. There are two problems:

1. The kernel does not react quickly enough when a lightly loaded server is suddenly attacked.

2. The `rtminexpire` is not low enough for the kernel to survive a sustained attack.

If your servers are connected to the Internet via a T3 or better, it may be prudent to manually override both `rtexpire` and `rtminexpire` via sysctl(8). Never set either parameter to zero (unless you want to crash the machine). Setting both parameters to 2 seconds should be sufficient to protect the route table from attack.

10.3.9 Access Issues with Kerberos and SSH

There are a few issues with both kerberos and ssh that need to be addressed if you intend to use them. Kerberos V is an excellent authentication protocol, but there are bugs in the kerberized **telnet** and **rlogin** applications that make them unsuitable for dealing with binary streams. Also, by default kerberos does not encrypt a session unless you use the `-x` option. **ssh** encrypts everything by default.

ssh works quite well in every respect except that it forwards encryption keys by default. What this means is that if you have a secure workstation holding keys that give you access to the rest of the system, and you ssh to an unsecure machine, your keys becomes exposed. The actual keys themselves are not exposed, but ssh installs a forwarding port for the duration of your login, and if an attacker has broken root on the unsecure machine he can utilize that port to use your keys to gain access to any other machine that your keys unlock.

We recommend that you use ssh in combination with kerberos whenever possible for staff logins. **ssh** can be compiled with kerberos support. This reduces your reliance on potentially exposable ssh keys while at the same time protecting passwords via kerberos. ssh keys should only be used for automated tasks from secure machines (something that kerberos is unsuited to do). We also recommend that you either turn off key-forwarding in the ssh configuration, or that you make use of the `from=IP/DOMAIN` option that ssh allows in its `authorized_keys` file to make the key only usable to entities logging in from specific machines.

10.4 DES, MD5, and Crypt

Every user on a Unix system has a password associated with their account. It seems obvious that these passwords need to be known only to the user and the actual operating system. In order to keep these passwords secret, they are encrypted with what is known as a "one-way hash", that is, they can only be easily encrypted but not decrypted. In other words, what we told you a moment ago was obvious is not even true: the operating system itself does not *really* know the password. It only knows the *encrypted* form of the password. The only way to get the "plain-text" password is by a brute force search of the space of possible passwords.

Unfortunately the only secure way to encrypt passwords when Unix came into being was based on DES, the Data Encryption Standard. This was not such a problem for users resident in the US, but since the source code for DES could not be exported outside the US, FreeBSD had to find a way to both comply with US law and retain compatibility with all the other Unix variants that still used DES.

The solution was to divide up the encryption libraries so that US users could install the DES libraries and use DES but international users still had an encryption method that could be exported abroad. This is how FreeBSD came to use MD5 as its default encryption method. MD5 is believed to be more secure than DES, so installing DES is offered primarily for compatibility reasons.

10.4.1 Recognizing Your Crypt Mechanism

It is pretty easy to identify which encryption method FreeBSD is set up to use. Examining the encrypted passwords in the /etc/master.passwd file is one way. Passwords encrypted with the MD5 hash are longer than those encrypted with the DES hash and also begin with the characters 1. DES password strings do not have any particular identifying characteristics, but they are shorter than MD5 passwords, and are coded in a 64-character alphabet which does not include the $ character, so a relatively short string which does not begin with a dollar sign is very likely a DES password.

The libraries can identify the passwords this way as well. As a result, the DES libraries are able to identify MD5 passwords, and use MD5 to check passwords that were encrypted that way, and DES for the rest. They are able to do this because the DES libraries also contain MD5. Unfortunately, the reverse is not true, so the MD5 libraries cannot authenticate passwords that were encrypted with DES.

Identifying which library is being used by the programs on your system is easy as well. Any program that uses crypt is linked against libcrypt, which for each type of library is a symbolic link to the appropriate implementation. For example, on a system using the DES versions:

```
% ls -l /usr/lib/libcrypt*
lrwxr-xr-x  1 root  wheel  13 Mar 19 06:56 libcrypt.a -> libdescrypt.a
lrwxr-xr-x  1 root  wheel  18 Mar 19 06:56 libcrypt.so.2.0 -> libdescrypt.so.2.0
lrwxr-xr-x  1 root  wheel  15 Mar 19 06:56 libcrypt_p.a -> libdescrypt_p.a
```

On a system using the MD5-based libraries, the same links will be present, but the target will be libscrypt rather than libdescrypt.

If you have installed the DES-capable crypt library libdescrypt (e.g. by installing the "crypto" distribution), then which password format will be used for new passwords is controlled by the "passwd_format" login capability in /etc/login.conf, which takes values of either "des" or "md5". See the login.conf(5) manual page for more information about login capabilities.

10.5 S/Key

S/Key is a one-time password scheme based on a one-way hash function. FreeBSD uses the MD4 hash for compatibility but other systems have used MD5 and DES-MAC. S/Key has been part of the FreeBSD base system since version 1.1.5 and is also used on a growing number of other operating systems. S/Key is a registered trademark of Bell Communications Research, Inc.

From version 5.0 of FreeBSD, S/Key has been replaced with the functionally equivalent OPIE (Onetime Passwords In Everything). OPIE uses the MD5 hash by default.

There are three different sorts of passwords which we will talk about in the discussion below. The first is your usual Unix-style or Kerberos password; we will call this a "Unix password". The second sort is the one-time password which is generated by the S/Key `key` program or the OPIE `opiekey` program and accepted by the `keyinit` or `opiepasswd` programs and the login prompt; we will call this a "one-time password". The final sort of password is the secret password which you give to the `key/opiekey` programs (and sometimes the `keyinit/opiepasswd` programs) which it uses to generate one-time passwords; we will call it a "secret password" or just unqualified "password".

The secret password does not have anything to do with your Unix password; they can be the same but this is not recommended. S/Key and OPIE secret passwords are not limited to 8 characters like Unix passwords, they can be as long as you like. Passwords of six or seven word long phrases are fairly common. For the most part, the S/Key or OPIE system operates completely independently of the Unix password system.

Besides the password, there are two other pieces of data that are important to S/Key and OPIE. One is what is known as the "seed" or "key", consisting of two letters and five digits. The other is what is called the "iteration count", a number between 1 and 100. S/Key creates the one-time password by concatenating the seed and the secret password, then applying the MD4/MD5 hash as many times as specified by the iteration count and turning the result into six short English words. These six English words are your one-time password. The authentication system (primarily PAM) keeps track of the last one-time password used, and the user is authenticated if the hash of the user-provided password is equal to the previous password. Because a one-way hash is used it is impossible to generate future one-time passwords if a successfully used password is captured; the iteration count is decremented after each successful login to keep the user and the login program in sync. When the iteration count gets down to 1, S/Key and OPIE must be reinitialized.

There are three programs involved in each system which we will discuss below. The `key` and `opiekey` programs accept an iteration count, a seed, and a secret password, and generate a one-time password or or a consecutive list of one-time passwords. The `keyinit` and `opiepasswd` programs are used to initialize S/Key and OPIE respectively, and to change passwords, iteration counts, or seeds; they take either a secret passphrase, or an iteration count, seed, and one-time password. The `keyinfo` and `opieinfo` programs examine the relevant credentials files (`/etc/skeykeys` or `/etc/opiekeys`) and print out the invoking user's current iteration count and seed.

There are four different sorts of operations we will cover. The first is using `keyinit` or `opiepasswd` over a secure connection to set up one-time-passwords for the first time, or to change your password or seed. The second operation is using `keyinit` or `opiepasswd` over an insecure connection, in conjunction with `key` or `opiekey` over a secure connection, to do the same. The third is using `key/opiekey` to log in over an insecure connection. The fourth is using `key` or `opiekey` to generate a number of keys which can be written down or printed out to carry with you when going to some location without secure connections to anywhere.

10.5.1 Secure Connection Initialization

To initialize S/Key for the first time, change your password, or change your seed while logged in over a secure connection (e.g., on the console of a machine or via ssh), use the `keyinit` command without any parameters while logged in as yourself:

```
% keyinit
Adding unfurl:
Reminder - Only use this method if you are directly connected.
If you are using telnet or rlogin exit with no password and use keyinit -s.
Enter secret password:
Again secret password:

ID unfurl s/key is 99 to17757
DEFY CLUB PRO NASH LACE SOFT
```

For OPIE, `opiepasswd` is used instead:

```
% opiepasswd -c
[grimreaper] ~ $ opiepasswd -f -c
Adding unfurl:
Only use this method from the console; NEVER from remote. If you are using
telnet, xterm, or a dial-in, type ^C now or exit with no password.
Then run opiepasswd without the -c parameter.
Using MD5 to compute responses.
Enter new secret pass phrase:
Again new secret pass phrase:
ID unfurl OTP key is 499 to4268
MOS MALL GOAT ARM AVID COED
```

At the `Enter new secret pass phrase:` or `Enter secret password:` prompts, you should enter a password or phrase. Remember, this is not the password that you will use to login with, this is used to generate your one-time login keys. The "ID" line gives the parameters of your particular instance; your login name, the iteration count, and seed. When logging in the system will remember these parameters and present them back to you so you do not have to remember them. The last line gives the particular one-time password which corresponds to those parameters and your secret password; if you were to re-login immediately, this one-time password is the one you would use.

10.5.2 Insecure Connection Initialization

To initialize change your secret password over an insecure connection, you will need to already have a secure connection to some place where you can run `key` or `opiekey`; this might be in the form of a desk accessory on a Macintosh, or a shell prompt on a machine you trust. You will also need to make up an iteration count (100 is probably a good value), and you may make up your own seed or use a randomly-generated one. Over on the insecure connection (to the machine you are initializing), use the `keyinit -s` command:

```
% keyinit -s
Updating unfurl:
Old key: to17758
Reminder you need the 6 English words from the key command.
```

```
Enter sequence count from 1 to 9999: 100
Enter new key [default to17759]:
s/key 100 to 17759
s/key access password:
s/key access password:CURE MIKE BANE HIM RACY GORE
```

For OPIE, you need to use `opiepasswd`:

```
% opiepasswd

Updating unfurl:
You need the response from an OTP generator.
Old secret pass phrase:
        otp-md5 498 to4268 ext
        Response: GAME GAG WELT OUT DOWN CHAT
New secret pass phrase:
        otp-md5 499 to4269
        Response: LINE PAP MILK NELL BUOY TROY

ID mark OTP key is 499 gr4269
LINE PAP MILK NELL BUOY TROY
```

To accept the default seed (which the `keyinit` program confusingly calls a `key`), press return. Then before entering an access password, move over to your secure connection or S/Key desk accessory, and give it the same parameters:

```
% key 100 to17759
Reminder - Do not use this program while logged in via telnet or rlogin.
Enter secret password: <secret password>
CURE MIKE BANE HIM RACY GORE
```

Or for OPIE:

```
% opiekey 498 to4268
Using the MD5 algorithm to compute response.
Reminder: Don't use opiekey from telnet or dial-in sessions.
Enter secret pass phrase:
GAME GAG WELT OUT DOWN CHAT
```

Now switch back over to the insecure connection, and copy the one-time password generated over to the relevant program.

10.5.3 Generating a Single one-time Password

Once you have initialized S/Key or OPIE, when you login you will be presented with a prompt like this:

```
% telnet example.com
Trying 10.0.0.1...
Connected to example.com
Escape character is '^]'.
```

```
FreeBSD/i386 (example.com) (ttypa)

login: <username>
s/key 97 fw13894
Password:
```

Or for OPIE:

```
% telnet example.com
Trying 10.0.0.1...
Connected to example.com
Escape character is '^]'.

FreeBSD/i386 (example.com) (ttypa)

login: <username>
otp-md5 498 gr4269 ext
Password:
```

As a side note, the S/Key and OPIE prompts have a useful feature (not shown here): if you press return at the password prompt, the prompter will turn echo on, so you can see what you are typing. This can be extremely useful if you are attempting to type in a password by hand, such as from a printout.

At this point you need to generate your one-time password to answer this login prompt. This must be done on a trusted system that you can run key or opiekey on. (There are versions of these for DOS, Windows and MacOS as well.) They need both the iteration count and the seed as command line options. You can cut-and-paste these right from the login prompt on the machine that you are logging in to.

On the trusted system:

```
% key 97 fw13894
Reminder - Do not use this program while logged in via telnet or rlogin.
Enter secret password:
WELD LIP ACTS ENDS ME HAAG
```

For OPIE:

```
% opiekey 498 to4268
Using the MD5 algorithm to compute response.
Reminder: Don't use opiekey from telnet or dial-in sessions.
Enter secret pass phrase:
GAME GAG WELT OUT DOWN CHAT
```

Now that you have your one-time password you can continue logging in:

```
login: <username>
s/key 97 fw13894
Password: <return to enable echo>
s/key 97 fw13894
Password [echo on]: WELD LIP ACTS ENDS ME HAAG
Last login: Tue Mar 21 11:56:41 from 10.0.0.2 ...
```

10.5.4 Generating Multiple one-time Passwords

Sometimes you have to go places where you do not have access to a trusted machine or secure connection. In this case, it is possible to use the `key` command to generate a number of one-time passwords before hand to be printed out and taken with you. For example:

```
% key -n 5 30 zz99999
Reminder - Do not use this program while logged in via telnet or rlogin.
Enter secret password: <secret password>
26: SODA RUDE LEA LIND BUDD SILT
27: JILT SPY DUTY GLOW COWL ROT
28: THEM OW COLA RUNT BONG SCOT
29: COT MASH BARR BRIM NAN FLAG
30: CAN KNEE CAST NAME FOLK BILK
```

The `-n 5` requests five keys in sequence, the `30` specifies what the last iteration number should be. Note that these are printed out in *reverse* order of eventual use. If you are really paranoid, you might want to write the results down by hand; otherwise you can cut-and-paste into `lpr`. Note that each line shows both the iteration count and the one-time password; you may still find it handy to scratch off passwords as you use them.

10.5.5 Restricting Use of Unix Passwords

Restrictions can be placed on the use of Unix passwords based on the host name, user name, terminal port, or IP address of a login session. These restrictions can be found in the configuration file `/etc/skey.access`. The skey.access(5) manual page has more info on the complete format of the file and also details some security cautions to be aware of before depending on this file for security.

If there is no `/etc/skey.access` file (this is the FreeBSD default), then all users will be allowed to use Unix passwords. If the file exists, however, then all users will be required to use S/Key unless explicitly permitted to do otherwise by configuration statements in the `skey.access` file. In all cases, Unix passwords are permitted on the console.

Here is a sample configuration file which illustrates the three most common sorts of configuration statements:

```
permit internet 192.168.0.0 255.255.0.0
permit user fnord
permit port ttyd0
```

The first line (`permit internet`) allows users whose IP source address (which is vulnerable to spoofing) matches the specified value and mask, to use Unix passwords. This should not be considered a security mechanism, but rather, a means to remind authorized users that they are using an insecure network and need to use S/Key for authentication.

The second line (`permit user`) allows the specified username, in this case `fnord`, to use Unix passwords at any time. Generally speaking, this should only be used for people who are either unable to use the `key` program, like those with dumb terminals, or those who are uneducable.

The third line (`permit port`) allows all users logging in on the specified terminal line to use Unix passwords; this would be used for dial-ups.

10.6 Kerberos

Kerberos is a network add-on system/protocol that allows users to authenticate themselves through the services of a secure server. Services such as remote login, remote copy, secure inter-system file copying and other high-risk tasks are made considerably safer and more controllable.

The following instructions can be used as a guide on how to set up Kerberos as distributed for FreeBSD. However, you should refer to the relevant manual pages for a complete description.

10.6.1 Installing Kerberos

Kerberos is an optional component of FreeBSD. The easiest way to install this software is by selecting the 'krb4' or 'krb5' distribution in **sysinstall** during the initial installation of FreeBSD. This will install the 'eBones' (KerberosIV) or 'Heimdal' (Kerberos5) implementation of Kerberos. These implementations are included because they are developed outside the USA/Canada and were thus available to system owners outside those countries during the era of restrictive export controls on cryptographic code from the USA.

Alternatively, the MIT implementation of Kerberos is available from the ports collection as `security/krb5`.

10.6.2 Creating the Initial Database

This is done on the Kerberos server only. First make sure that you do not have any old Kerberos databases around. You should change to the directory `/etc/kerberosIV` and check that only the following files are present:

```
# cd /etc/kerberosIV
# ls
README krb.conf      krb.realms
```

If any additional files (such as `principal.*` or `master_key`) exist, then use the `kdb_destroy` command to destroy the old Kerberos database, or if Kerberos is not running, simply delete the extra files.

You should now edit the `krb.conf` and `krb.realms` files to define your Kerberos realm. In this case the realm will be `EXAMPLE.COM` and the server is `grunt.example.com`. We edit or create the `krb.conf` file:

```
# cat krb.conf
EXAMPLE.COM
EXAMPLE.COM grunt.example.com admin server
CS.BERKELEY.EDU okeeffe.berkeley.edu
ATHENA.MIT.EDU kerberos.mit.edu
ATHENA.MIT.EDU kerberos-1.mit.edu
ATHENA.MIT.EDU kerberos-2.mit.edu
ATHENA.MIT.EDU kerberos-3.mit.edu
LCS.MIT.EDU kerberos.lcs.mit.edu
TELECOM.MIT.EDU bitsy.mit.edu
ARC.NASA.GOV trident.arc.nasa.gov
```

In this case, the other realms do not need to be there. They are here as an example of how a machine may be made aware of multiple realms. You may wish to not include them for simplicity.

The first line names the realm in which this system works. The other lines contain realm/host entries. The first item on a line is a realm, and the second is a host in that realm that is acting as a "key distribution center". The words `admin server` following a host's name means that host also provides an administrative database server. For further explanation of these terms, please consult the Kerberos manual pages.

Now we have to add `grunt.example.com` to the `EXAMPLE.COM` realm and also add an entry to put all hosts in the `.example.com` domain in the `EXAMPLE.COM` realm. The `krb.realms` file would be updated as follows:

```
# cat krb.realms
grunt.example.com EXAMPLE.COM
.example.com EXAMPLE.COM
.berkeley.edu CS.BERKELEY.EDU
.MIT.EDU ATHENA.MIT.EDU
.mit.edu ATHENA.MIT.EDU
```

Again, the other realms do not need to be there. They are here as an example of how a machine may be made aware of multiple realms. You may wish to remove them to simplify things.

The first line puts the *specific* system into the named realm. The rest of the lines show how to default systems of a particular subdomain to a named realm.

Now we are ready to create the database. This only needs to run on the Kerberos server (or Key Distribution Center). Issue the `kdb_init` command to do this:

```
# kdb_init
Realm name [default  ATHENA.MIT.EDU ]: EXAMPLE.COM
You will be prompted for the database Master Password.
It is important that you NOT FORGET this password.

Enter Kerberos master key:
```

Now we have to save the key so that servers on the local machine can pick it up. Use the `kstash` command to do this.

```
# kstash

Enter Kerberos master key:

Current Kerberos master key version is 1.

Master key entered. BEWARE!
```

This saves the encrypted master password in `/etc/kerberosIV/master_key`.

10.6.3 Making It All Run

Two principals need to be added to the database for *each* system that will be secured with Kerberos. Their names are `kpasswd` and `rcmd` These two principals are made for each system, with the instance being the name of the individual system.

These daemons, kpasswd and rcmd allow other systems to change Kerberos passwords and run commands like rcp, rlogin and rsh.

Now let us add these entries:

```
# kdb_edit
Opening database...

Enter Kerberos master key:

Current Kerberos master key version is 1.

Master key entered.  BEWARE!
Previous or default values are in [brackets] ,
enter return to leave the same, or new value.

Principal name: passwd
Instance: grunt

<Not found>, Create [y] ? y

Principal: passwd, Instance: grunt, kdc_key_ver: 1
New Password:                    <---- enter RANDOM here
Verifying password

New Password: <---- enter RANDOM here

Random password [y] ? y

Principal's new key version = 1
Expiration date (enter yyyy-mm-dd) [ 2000-01-01 ] ?
Max ticket lifetime (*5 minutes) [ 255 ] ?
Attributes [ 0 ] ?
Edit O.K.
Principal name: rcmd
Instance: grunt

<Not found>, Create [y] ?

Principal: rcmd, Instance: grunt, kdc_key_ver: 1
New Password: <---- enter RANDOM here
Verifying password

New Password:              <---- enter RANDOM here

Random password [y] ?

Principal's new key version = 1
Expiration date (enter yyyy-mm-dd) [ 2000-01-01 ] ?
Max ticket lifetime (*5 minutes) [ 255 ] ?
Attributes [ 0 ] ?
```

```
Edit O.K.
Principal name:          <---- null entry here will cause an exit
```

10.6.4 Creating the Server File

We now have to extract all the instances which define the services on each machine. For this we use the `ext_srvtab` command. This will create a file which must be copied or moved *by secure means* to each Kerberos client's `/etc/kerberosIV` directory. This file must be present on each server and client, and is crucial to the operation of Kerberos.

```
# ext_srvtab grunt
Enter Kerberos master key:

Current Kerberos master key version is 1.

Master key entered. BEWARE!
Generating 'grunt-new-srvtab'....
```

Now, this command only generates a temporary file which must be renamed to `srvtab` so that all the servers can pick it up. Use the `mv` command to move it into place on the original system:

```
# mv grunt-new-srvtab srvtab
```

If the file is for a client system, and the network is not deemed safe, then copy the `client-new-srvtab` to removable media and transport it by secure physical means. Be sure to rename it to `srvtab` in the client's `/etc/kerberosIV` directory, and make sure it is mode 600:

```
# mv grumble-new-srvtab srvtab
# chmod 600 srvtab
```

10.6.5 Populating the Database

We now have to add some user entries into the database. First let us create an entry for the user `jane`. Use the `kdb_edit` command to do this:

```
# kdb_edit
Opening database...

Enter Kerberos master key:

Current Kerberos master key version is 1.

Master key entered.  BEWARE!
Previous or default values are in [brackets] ,
enter return to leave the same, or new value.

Principal name: jane
Instance:
```

```
<Not found>, Create [y] ? y

Principal: jane, Instance: , kdc_key_ver: 1
New Password:                    <---- enter a secure password here
Verifying password

New Password:                    <---- re-enter the password here
Principal's new key version = 1
Expiration date (enter yyyy-mm-dd) [ 2000-01-01 ] ?
Max ticket lifetime (*5 minutes) [ 255 ] ?
Attributes [ 0 ] ?
Edit O.K.
Principal name:     <---- null entry here will cause an exit
```

10.6.6 Testing It All Out

First we have to start the Kerberos daemons. NOTE that if you have correctly edited your /etc/rc.conf then this will happen automatically when you reboot. This is only necessary on the Kerberos server. Kerberos clients will automagically get what they need from the /etc/kerberosIV directory.

```
# kerberos &
Kerberos server starting
Sleep forever on error
Log file is /var/log/kerberos.log
Current Kerberos master key version is 1.

Master key entered. BEWARE!

Current Kerberos master key version is 1
Local realm: EXAMPLE.COM
# kadmind -n &
KADM Server KADM0.0A initializing
Please do not use 'kill -9' to kill this job, use a
regular kill instead

Current Kerberos master key version is 1.

Master key entered.  BEWARE!
```

Now we can try using the kinit command to get a ticket for the id jane that we created above:

```
% kinit jane
MIT Project Athena (grunt.example.com)
Kerberos Initialization for "jane"
Password:
```

Try listing the tokens using klist to see if we really have them:

```
% klist
Ticket file:    /tmp/tkt245
Principal:      jane@EXAMPLE.COM

  Issued            Expires            Principal
Apr 30 11:23:22  Apr 30 19:23:22  krbtgt.EXAMPLE.COM@EXAMPLE.COM
```

Now try changing the password using `passwd` to check if the **kpasswd** daemon can get authorization to the Kerberos database:

```
% passwd
realm EXAMPLE.COM
Old password for jane:
New Password for jane:
Verifying password
New Password for jane:
Password changed.
```

10.6.7 Adding `su` Privileges

Kerberos allows us to give *each* user who needs root privileges their own *separate* su password. We could now add an id which is authorized to `su` to root. This is controlled by having an instance of `root` associated with a principal. Using `kdb_edit` we can create the entry `jane.root` in the Kerberos database:

```
# kdb_edit
Opening database...

Enter Kerberos master key:

Current Kerberos master key version is 1.

Master key entered.  BEWARE!
Previous or default values are in [brackets] ,
enter return to leave the same, or new value.

Principal name: jane
Instance: root

<Not found>, Create [y] ? y

Principal: jane, Instance: root, kdc_key_ver: 1
New Password:                   <---- enter a SECURE password here
Verifying password

New Password:        <---- re-enter the password here

Principal's new key version = 1
Expiration date (enter yyyy-mm-dd) [ 2000-01-01 ] ?
Max ticket lifetime (*5 minutes) [ 255 ] ? 12 <--- Keep this short!
```

```
Attributes [ 0 ] ?
Edit O.K.
Principal name:          <---- null entry here will cause an exit
```

Now try getting tokens for it to make sure it works:

```
# kinit jane.root
MIT Project Athena (grunt.example.com)
Kerberos Initialization for "jane.root"
Password:
```

Now we need to add the user to `root`'s `.klogin` file:

```
# cat /root/.klogin
jane.root@EXAMPLE.COM
```

Now try doing the su:

```
% su
Password:
```

and take a look at what tokens we have:

```
# klist
Ticket file: /tmp/tkt_root_245
Principal:      jane.root@EXAMPLE.COM

   Issued            Expires           Principal
May  2 20:43:12  May  3 04:43:12  krbtgt.EXAMPLE.COM@EXAMPLE.COM
```

10.6.8 Using Other Commands

In an earlier example, we created a principal called `jane` with an instance `root`. This was based on a user with the same name as the principal, and this is a Kerberos default; that a `<principal>.<instance>` of the form `<username>.root` will allow that `<username>` to su to root if the necessary entries are in the `.klogin` file in root's home directory:

```
# cat /root/.klogin
jane.root@EXAMPLE.COM
```

Likewise, if a user has in their own home directory lines of the form:

```
% cat ~/.klogin
jane@EXAMPLE.COM
jack@EXAMPLE.COM
```

This allows anyone in the `EXAMPLE.COM` realm who has authenticated themselves to `jane` or `jack` (via `kinit`, see above) access to `rlogin` to `jane`'s account or files on this system (`grunt`) via `rlogin`, `rsh` or `rcp`.

For example, `jane` now logs into another system using Kerberos:

```
% kinit
MIT Project Athena (grunt.example.com)
Password:
% rlogin grunt
Last login: Mon May  1 21:14:47 from grumble
Copyright (c) 1980, 1983, 1986, 1988, 1990, 1991, 1993, 1994
        The Regents of the University of California.   All rights reserved.

FreeBSD BUILT-19950429 (GR386) #0: Sat Apr 29 17:50:09 SAT 1995
```

Or Jack logs into Jane's account on the same machine (jane having set up the .klogin file as above, and the person in charge of Kerberos having set up principal *jack* with a null instance:

```
% kinit
% rlogin grunt -l jane
MIT Project Athena (grunt.example.com)
Password:
Last login: Mon May  1 21:16:55 from grumble
Copyright (c) 1980, 1983, 1986, 1988, 1990, 1991, 1993, 1994
        The Regents of the University of California.   All rights reserved.
FreeBSD BUILT-19950429 (GR386) #0: Sat Apr 29 17:50:09 SAT 1995
```

10.7 Firewalls

Firewalls are an area of increasing interest for people who are connected to the Internet, and are even finding applications on private networks to provide enhanced security. This section will hopefully explain what firewalls are, how to use them, and how to use the facilities provided in the FreeBSD kernel to implement them.

Note: People often think that having a firewall between your internal network and the "Big Bad Internet" will solve all your security problems. It may help, but a poorly setup firewall system is more of a security risk than not having one at all. A firewall can add another layer of security to your systems, but it cannot stop a really determined cracker from penetrating your internal network. If you let internal security lapse because you believe your firewall to be impenetrable, you have just made the crackers job that much easier.

10.7.1 What Is a Firewall?

There are currently two distinct types of firewalls in common use on the Internet today. The first type is more properly called a *packet filtering router*, where the kernel on a multi-homed machine chooses whether to forward or block packets based on a set of rules. The second type, known as a *proxy server*, relies on daemons to provide authentication and to forward packets, possibly on a multi-homed machine which has kernel packet forwarding disabled.

Sometimes sites combine the two types of firewalls, so that only a certain machine (known as a *bastion host*) is allowed to send packets through a packet filtering router onto an internal network. Proxy services are run on the bastion host, which are generally more secure than normal authentication mechanisms.

FreeBSD comes with a kernel packet filter (known as IPFW), which is what the rest of this section will concentrate on. Proxy servers can be built on FreeBSD from third party software, but there is such a variety of proxy servers available that it would be impossible to cover them in this section.

Packet Filtering Routers

A router is a machine which forwards packets between two or more networks. A packet filtering router has an extra piece of code in its kernel which compares each packet to a list of rules before deciding if it should be forwarded or not. Most modern IP routing software has packet filtering code within it that defaults to forwarding all packets. To enable the filters, you need to define a set of rules for the filtering code so it can decide if the packet should be allowed to pass or not.

To decide whether a packet should be passed on, the code looks through its set of rules for a rule which matches the contents of this packets headers. Once a match is found, the rule action is obeyed. The rule action could be to drop the packet, to forward the packet, or even to send an ICMP message back to the originator. Only the first match counts, as the rules are searched in order. Hence, the list of rules can be referred to as a "rule chain".

The packet matching criteria varies depending on the software used, but typically you can specify rules which depend on the source IP address of the packet, the destination IP address, the source port number, the destination port number (for protocols which support ports), or even the packet type (UDP, TCP, ICMP, etc).

Proxy Servers

Proxy servers are machines which have had the normal system daemons (**telnetd**, **ftpd**, etc) replaced with special servers. These servers are called *proxy servers* as they normally only allow onward connections to be made. This enables you to run (for example) a proxy telnet server on your firewall host, and people can telnet in to your firewall from the outside, go through some authentication mechanism, and then gain access to the internal network (alternatively, proxy servers can be used for signals coming from the internal network and heading out).

Proxy servers are normally more secure than normal servers, and often have a wider variety of authentication mechanisms available, including "one-shot" password systems so that even if someone manages to discover what password you used, they will not be able to use it to gain access to your systems as the password instantly expires. As they do not actually give users access to the host machine, it becomes a lot more difficult for someone to install backdoors around your security system.

Proxy servers often have ways of restricting access further, so that only certain hosts can gain access to the servers, and often they can be set up so that you can limit which users can talk to which destination machine. Again, what facilities are available depends largely on what proxy software you choose.

10.7.2 What Does IPFW Allow Me to Do?

IPFW, the software supplied with FreeBSD, is a packet filtering and accounting system which resides in the kernel, and has a user-land control utility, ipfw(8). Together, they allow you to define and query the rules currently used by the kernel in its routing decisions.

There are two related parts to IPFW. The firewall section allows you to perform packet filtering. There is also an IP accounting section which allows you to track usage of your router, based on similar rules to the firewall section. This allows you to see (for example) how much traffic your router is getting from a certain machine, or how much WWW (World Wide Web) traffic it is forwarding.

As a result of the way that IPFW is designed, you can use IPFW on non-router machines to perform packet filtering on incoming and outgoing connections. This is a special case of the more general use of IPFW, and the same commands and techniques should be used in this situation.

10.7.3 Enabling IPFW on FreeBSD

As the main part of the IPFW system lives in the kernel, you will need to add one or more options to your kernel configuration file, depending on what facilities you want, and recompile your kernel. See "Reconfiguring your Kernel" (Chapter 9) for more details on how to recompile your kernel.

There are currently three kernel configuration options relevant to IPFW:

`options IPFIREWALL`

> Compiles into the kernel the code for packet filtering.

`options IPFIREWALL_VERBOSE`

> Enables code to allow logging of packets through syslogd(8). Without this option, even if you specify that packets should be logged in the filter rules, nothing will happen.

`options IPFIREWALL_VERBOSE_LIMIT=10`

> Limits the number of packets logged through syslogd(8) on a per entry basis. You may wish to use this option in hostile environments in which you want to log firewall activity, but do not want to be open to a denial of service attack via syslog flooding.
>
> When a chain entry reaches the packet limit specified, logging is turned off for that particular entry. To resume logging, you will need to reset the associated counter using the ipfw(8) utility:
>
> > `# ipfw zero 4500`
>
> Where 4500 is the chain entry you wish to continue logging.

Note: Previous versions of FreeBSD contained an `IPFIREWALL_ACCT` option. This is now obsolete as the firewall code automatically includes accounting facilities.

10.7.4 Configuring IPFW

The configuration of the IPFW software is done through the ipfw(8) utility. The syntax for this command looks quite complicated, but it is relatively simple once you understand its structure.

There are currently four different command categories used by the utility: addition/deletion, listing, flushing, and clearing. Addition/deletion is used to build the rules that control how packets are accepted, rejected, and logged. Listing is used to examine the contents of your rule set (otherwise known as the chain) and packet counters (accounting). Flushing is used to remove all entries from the chain. Clearing is used to zero out one or more accounting entries.

Altering the IPFW Rules

The syntax for this form of the command is:

`ipfw` [-N] command [index] action [log] protocol addresses [options]

There is one valid flag when using this form of the command:

-N

Resolve addresses and service names in output.

The *command* given can be shortened to the shortest unique form. The valid *commands* are:

add

Add an entry to the firewall/accounting rule list

delete

Delete an entry from the firewall/accounting rule list

Previous versions of IPFW used separate firewall and accounting entries. The present version provides packet accounting with each firewall entry.

If an *index* value is supplied, it is used to place the entry at a specific point in the chain. Otherwise, the entry is placed at the end of the chain at an index 100 greater than the last chain entry (this does not include the default policy, rule 65535, deny).

The `log` option causes matching rules to be output to the system console if the kernel was compiled with `IPFIRE-WALL_VERBOSE`.

Valid *actions* are:

reject

Drop the packet, and send an ICMP host or port unreachable (as appropriate) packet to the source.

allow

Pass the packet on as normal. (aliases: `pass` and `accept`)

deny

Drop the packet. The source is not notified via an ICMP message (thus it appears that the packet never arrived at the destination).

count

> Update packet counters but do not allow/deny the packet based on this rule. The search continues with the next chain entry.

Each *action* will be recognized by the shortest unambiguous prefix.

The *protocols* which can be specified are:

all

> Matches any IP packet

icmp

> Matches ICMP packets

tcp

> Matches TCP packets

udp

> Matches UDP packets

The *address* specification is:

> from *address/mask* [*port*] to *address/mask* [*port*] [via *interface*]

You can only specify *port* in conjunction with *protocols* which support ports (UDP and TCP).

The *via* is optional and may specify the IP address or domain name of a local IP interface, or an interface name (e.g. ed0) to match only packets coming through this interface. Interface unit numbers can be specified with an optional wildcard. For example, ppp* would match all kernel PPP interfaces.

The syntax used to specify an *address/mask* is:

> *address*

or

> *address/mask-bits*

or

> *address:mask-pattern*

A valid hostname may be specified in place of the IP address. *mask-bits* is a decimal number representing how many bits in the address mask should be set. e.g. specifying 192.216.222.1/24 will create a mask which will allow any address in a class C subnet (in this case, 192.216.222) to be matched. *mask-pattern* is an IP address which will be logically AND'ed with the address given. The keyword any may be used to specify "any IP address".

The port numbers to be blocked are specified as:

port [,*port* [,*port* [...]]]

to specify either a single port or a list of ports, or

port-port

to specify a range of ports. You may also combine a single range with a list, but the range must always be specified first.

The *options* available are:

frag

> Matches if the packet is not the first fragment of the datagram.

in

> Matches if the packet is on the way in.

out

> Matches if the packet is on the way out.

ipoptions *spec*

> Matches if the IP header contains the comma separated list of options specified in *spec*. The supported list of IP options are: ssrr (strict source route), lsrr (loose source route), rr (record packet route), and ts (time stamp). The absence of a particular option may be denoted with a leading !.

established

> Matches if the packet is part of an already established TCP connection (i.e. it has the RST or ACK bits set). You can optimize the performance of the firewall by placing *established* rules early in the chain.

setup

> Matches if the packet is an attempt to establish a TCP connection (the SYN bit is set but the ACK bit is not).

tcpflags *flags*

> Matches if the TCP header contains the comma separated list of *flags*. The supported flags are fin, syn, rst, psh, ack, and urg. The absence of a particular flag may be indicated by a leading !.

icmptypes *types*

> Matches if the ICMP type is present in the list *types*. The list may be specified as any combination of ranges and/or individual types separated by commas. Commonly used ICMP types are: 0 echo reply (ping reply), 3 destination unreachable, 5 redirect, 8 echo request (ping request), and 11 time exceeded (used to indicate TTL expiration as with traceroute(8)).

Listing the IPFW Rules

The syntax for this form of the command is:

```
ipfw [-a] [-t] [-N] l
```

There are three valid flags when using this form of the command:

-a

While listing, show counter values. This option is the only way to see accounting counters.

-t

Display the last match times for each chain entry. The time listing is incompatible with the input syntax used by the ipfw(8) utility.

-N

Attempt to resolve given addresses and service names.

Flushing the IPFW Rules

The syntax for flushing the chain is:

```
ipfw flush
```

This causes all entries in the firewall chain to be removed except the fixed default policy enforced by the kernel (index 65535). Use caution when flushing rules, the default deny policy will leave your system cut off from the network until allow entries are added to the chain.

Clearing the IPFW Packet Counters

The syntax for clearing one or more packet counters is:

```
ipfw zero [index]
```

When used without an *index* argument, all packet counters are cleared. If an *index* is supplied, the clearing operation only affects a specific chain entry.

10.7.5 Example Commands for ipfw

This command will deny all packets from the host `evil.crackers.org` to the telnet port of the host `nice.people.org`:

```
# ipfw add deny tcp from evil.crackers.org to nice.people.org 23
```

The next example denies and logs any TCP traffic from the entire `crackers.org` network (a class C) to the `nice.people.org` machine (any port).

```
# ipfw add deny log tcp from evil.crackers.org/24 to nice.people.org
```

If you do not want people sending X sessions to your internal network (a subnet of a class C), the following command will do the necessary filtering:

```
# ipfw add deny tcp from any to my.org/28 6000 setup
```

To see the accounting records:

```
# ipfw -a list
```

or in the short form

```
# ipfw -a l
```

You can also see the last time a chain entry was matched with:

```
# ipfw -at l
```

10.7.6 Building a Packet Filtering Firewall

Note: The following suggestions are just that: suggestions. The requirements of each firewall are different and we cannot tell you how to build a firewall to meet your particular requirements.

When initially setting up your firewall, unless you have a test bench setup where you can configure your firewall host in a controlled environment, it is strongly recommend you use the logging version of the commands and enable logging in the kernel. This will allow you to quickly identify problem areas and cure them without too much disruption. Even after the initial setup phase is complete, I recommend using the logging for 'deny' as it allows tracing of possible attacks and also modification of the firewall rules if your requirements alter.

Note: If you use the logging versions of the `accept` command, it can generate *large* amounts of log data as one log line will be generated for every packet that passes through the firewall, so large FTP/http transfers, etc, will really slow the system down. It also increases the latencies on those packets as it requires more work to be done by the kernel before the packet can be passed on. **syslogd** will also start using up a lot more processor time as it logs all the extra data to disk, and it could quite easily fill the partition `/var/log` is located on.

You should enable your firewall from `/etc/rc.conf.local` or `/etc/rc.conf`. The associated manual page explains which knobs to fiddle and lists some preset firewall configurations. If you do not use a preset configuration, `ipfw list` will output the current ruleset into a file that you can pass to `rc.conf`. If you do not use `/etc/rc.conf.local` or `/etc/rc.conf` to enable your firewall, it is important to make sure your firewall is enabled before any IP interfaces are configured.

The next problem is what your firewall should actually *do*! This is largely dependent on what access to your network you want to allow from the outside, and how much access to the outside world you want to allow from the inside. Some general rules are:

· Block all incoming access to ports below 1024 for TCP. This is where most of the security sensitive services are, like finger, SMTP (mail) and telnet.

· Block *all* incoming UDP traffic. There are very few useful services that travel over UDP, and what useful traffic there is, is normally a security threat (e.g. Suns RPC and NFS protocols). This has its disadvantages also, since UDP is a connectionless protocol, denying incoming UDP traffic also blocks the replies to outgoing UDP traffic. This can cause a problem for people (on the inside) using external archie (prospero) servers. If you want to allow access to archie, you will have to allow packets coming from ports 191 and 1525 to any internal UDP port through the firewall. **ntp** is another service you may consider allowing through, which comes from port 123.

· Block traffic to port 6000 from the outside. Port 6000 is the port used for access to X11 servers, and can be a security threat (especially if people are in the habit of doing `xhost +` on their workstations). X11 can actually use a range of ports starting at 6000, the upper limit being how many X displays you can run on the machine. The upper limit as defined by RFC 1700 (Assigned Numbers) is 6063.

· Check what ports any internal servers use (e.g. SQL servers, etc). It is probably a good idea to block those as well, as they normally fall outside the 1-1024 range specified above.

Another checklist for firewall configuration is available from CERT at `http://www.cert.org/tech_tips/packet_filtering.html`

As stated above, these are only *guidelines*. You will have to decide what filter rules you want to use on your firewall yourself. We cannot accept ANY responsibility if someone breaks into your network, even if you follow the advice given above.

10.8 OpenSSL

As of FreeBSD 4.0, the OpenSSL toolkit is a part of the base system. OpenSSL[2] provides a general-purpose cryptography library, as well as the Secure Sockets Layer v2/v3 (SSLv2/SSLv3) and Transport Layer Security v1 (TLSv1) network security protocols.

However, one of the algorithms (specifically IDEA) included in OpenSSL is protected by patents in the USA and elsewhere, and is not available for unrestricted use. IDEA is included in the OpenSSL sources in FreeBSD, but it is not built by default. If you wish to use it, and you comply with the license terms, enable the MAKE_IDEA switch in /etc/make.conf and rebuild your sources using 'make world'.

Today, the RSA algorithm is free for use in USA and other countries. In the past it was protected by a patent.

2 http://www.openssl.org/

10.8.1 Source Code Installations

OpenSSL is part of the `src-crypto` and `src-secure` cvsup collections. See Obtaining FreeBSD, Appendix A for more information about obtaining and updating FreeBSD source code.

10.9 IPsec

Terminating Characters: Throughout examples in this section, and other sections, you will notice that there is a "^D" at the end of some examples. This means to hold down the **Control** key and hit the **D** key. Another commonly used character is "^C", which respectively means to hold down **Control** and press **C**.

Tip: For other HOWTOs detailing IPSec implementation in FreeBSD, take a look at `http://www.daemonnews.org/200101/ipsec-howto.html` and `http://www.freebsddiary.org/ipsec.php`.

The IPsec mechanism provides secure communication for IP layer and socket layer communication. This section should explain how to use them. For implementation details, please refer to The Developers' Handbook[5].

The current IPsec implementation supports both transport mode and tunnel mode. However, tunnel mode comes with some restrictions. `http://www.kame.net/newsletter/` has more comprehensive examples.

Please be aware that in order to use this functionality, you must have the following options compiled into your kernel:

```
options        IPSEC          #IP security
options        IPSEC_ESP      #IP security (crypto; define w/IPSEC)
```

10.9.1 Transport Mode Example with IPv4

Let us setup security association to deploy a secure channel between HOST A (10.2.3.4) and HOST B (10.6.7.8). Here we show a little complicated example. From HOST A to HOST B, only old AH is used. From HOST B to HOST A, new AH and new ESP are combined.

Now we should choose an algorithm to be used corresponding to "AH"/"new AH"/"ESP"/"new ESP". Please refer to the setkey(8) man page to know algorithm names. Our choice is MD5 for AH, new-HMAC-SHA1 for new AH, and new-DES-expIV with 8 byte IV for new ESP.

Key length highly depends on each algorithm. For example, key length must be equal to 16 bytes for MD5, 20 for new-HMAC-SHA1, and 8 for new-DES-expIV. Now we choose "MYSECRETMYSECRET", "KAMEKAMEKAMEKAMEKAME", "PASSWORD", respectively.

OK, let us assign SPI (Security Parameter Index) for each protocol. Please note that we need 3 SPIs for this secure channel since three security headers are produced (one for from HOST A to HOST B, two for from HOST B to HOST A). Please also note that SPI MUST be greater than or equal to 256. We choose, 1000, 2000, and 3000, respectively.

---

5 http://www.FreeBSD.org/doc/en_US.ISO8859-1/books/developers-handbook/ipv6.html

Host A   Host B

(1)PROTO=AH
ALG=MD5(RFC1826)
KEY=MYSECRETMYSECRET
SPI=1000

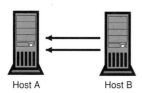

Host A   Host B

(2.1)
PROTO=AH
ALG=new-HMAC-SHA1(new AH)
KEY=KAMEKAMEKAMEKAMEKAME
SPI=2000

(2.2)
PROTO=ESP
ALG=new-DES-expIV(new ESP)
IV length = 8
KEY=PASSWORD
SPI=3000

Now, let us setup security association. Execute setkey(8) on both HOST A and B:

```
# setkey -c
add 10.2.3.4 10.6.7.8 ah-old  1000 -m transport -A keyed-md5 "MYSECRETMYSECRET" ;
add 10.6.7.8 10.2.3.4 ah  2000 -m transport -A hmac-sha1 "KAMEKAMEKAMEKAMEKAME" ;
add 10.6.7.8 10.2.3.4 esp 3000 -m transport -E des-cbc "PASSWORD" ;
^D
```

Actually, IPsec communication does not process until security policy entries are defined. In this case, you must setup each host.

```
At A:

# setkey -c
spdadd 10.2.3.4 10.6.7.8 any -P out ipsec
 ah/transport/10.2.3.4-10.6.7.8/require ;
^D

At B:

# setkey -c
spdadd 10.6.7.8 10.2.3.4 any -P out ipsec
 esp/transport/10.6.7.8-10.2.3.4/require ;
spdadd 10.6.7.8 10.2.3.4 any -P out ipsec
 ah/transport/10.6.7.8-10.2.3.4/require ;
^D
```

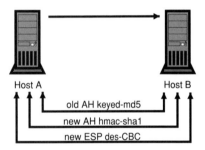

10.9.2 Transport Mode Example with IPv6

Another example using IPv6.

ESP transport mode is recommended for TCP port number 110 between Host-A and Host-B.

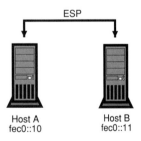

Encryption algorithm is blowfish-cbc whose key is "kamekame", and authentication algorithm is hmac-sha1 whose key is "this is the test key". Configuration at Host-A:

```
# setkey -c <<EOF
```

```
        spdadd fec0::10[any] fec0::11[110] tcp -P out ipsec
                esp/transport/fec0::10-fec0::11/use ;
        spdadd fec0::11[110] fec0::10[any] tcp -P in ipsec
                esp/transport/fec0::11-fec0::10/use ;
        add fec0::10 fec0::11 esp 0x10001
                -m transport
                -E blowfish-cbc "kamekame"
                -A hmac-sha1 "this is the test key" ;
        add fec0::11 fec0::10 esp 0x10002
                -m transport
                -E blowfish-cbc "kamekame"
                -A hmac-sha1 "this is the test key" ;
        EOF
```

and at Host-B:

```
# setkey -c <<EOF
        spdadd fec0::11[110] fec0::10[any] tcp -P out ipsec
                esp/transport/fec0::11-fec0::10/use ;
        spdadd fec0::10[any] fec0::11[110] tcp -P in ipsec
                esp/transport/fec0::10-fec0::11/use ;
        add fec0::10 fec0::11 esp 0x10001 -m transport
                -E blowfish-cbc "kamekame"
                -A hmac-sha1 "this is the test key" ;
        add fec0::11 fec0::10 esp 0x10002 -m transport
                -E blowfish-cbc "kamekame"
                -A hmac-sha1 "this is the test key" ;
        EOF
```

Note the direction of SP.

10.9.3 Tunnel Mode Example with IPv4

Tunnel mode between two security gateways

Security protocol is old AH tunnel mode, i.e. specified by RFC1826, with keyed-md5 whose key is "this is the test" as authentication algorithm.

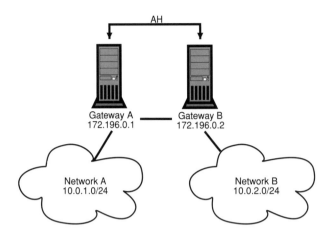

Configuration at Gateway-A:

```
# setkey -c <<EOF
spdadd 10.0.1.0/24 10.0.2.0/24 any -P out ipsec
        ah/tunnel/172.16.0.1-172.16.0.2/require ;
spdadd 10.0.2.0/24 10.0.1.0/24 any -P in ipsec
        ah/tunnel/172.16.0.2-172.16.0.1/require ;
add 172.16.0.1 172.16.0.2 ah-old 0x10003 -m any
        -A keyed-md5 "this is the test" ;
add 172.16.0.2 172.16.0.1 ah-old 0x10004 -m any
        -A keyed-md5 "this is the test" ;

EOF
```

If the port number field is omitted such as above then "[any]" is employed. '-m' specifies the mode of SA to be used. "-m any" means wild-card of mode of security protocol. You can use this SA for both tunnel and transport mode.

and at Gateway-B:

```
# setkey -c <<EOF
spdadd 10.0.2.0/24 10.0.1.0/24 any -P out ipsec
        ah/tunnel/172.16.0.2-172.16.0.1/require ;
spdadd 10.0.1.0/24 10.0.2.0/24 any -P in ipsec
        ah/tunnel/172.16.0.1-172.16.0.2/require ;
add 172.16.0.1 172.16.0.2 ah-old 0x10003 -m any
        -A keyed-md5 "this is the test" ;
add 172.16.0.2 172.16.0.1 ah-old 0x10004 -m any
        -A keyed-md5 "this is the test" ;

EOF
```

Making SA bundle between two security gateways

AH transport mode and ESP tunnel mode is required between Gateway-A and Gateway-B. In this case, ESP tunnel mode is applied first, and AH transport mode is next.

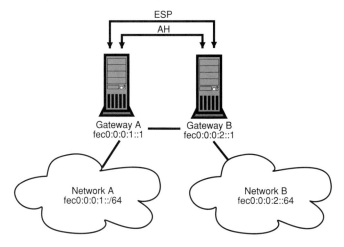

10.9.4 Tunnel Mode Example with IPv6

Encryption algorithm is 3des-cbc, and authentication algorithm for ESP is hmac-sha1. Authentication algorithm for AH is hmac-md5. Configuration at Gateway-A:

```
# setkey -c <<EOF
spdadd fec0:0:0:1::/64 fec0:0:0:2::/64 any -P out ipsec
        esp/tunnel/fec0:0:0:1::1-fec0:0:0:2::1/require
        ah/transport/fec0:0:0:1::1-fec0:0:0:2::1/require ;
spdadd fec0:0:0:2::/64 fec0:0:0:1::/64 any -P in ipsec
        esp/tunnel/fec0:0:0:2::1-fec0:0:0:1::1/require
        ah/transport/fec0:0:0:2::1-fec0:0:0:1::1/require ;
add fec0:0:0:1::1 fec0:0:0:2::1 esp 0x10001 -m tunnel
        -E 3des-cbc "kamekame12341234kame1234"
        -A hmac-sha1 "this is the test key" ;
add fec0:0:0:1::1 fec0:0:0:2::1 ah 0x10001 -m transport
        -A hmac-md5 "this is the test" ;
add fec0:0:0:2::1 fec0:0:0:1::1 esp 0x10001 -m tunnel
        -E 3des-cbc "kamekame12341234kame1234"
        -A hmac-sha1 "this is the test key" ;
add fec0:0:0:2::1 fec0:0:0:1::1 ah 0x10001 -m transport
        -A hmac-md5 "this is the test" ;

EOF
```

Making SAs with the different end

ESP tunnel mode is required between Host-A and Gateway-A. Encryption algorithm is cast128-cbc, and authentication algorithm for ESP is hmac-sha1. ESP transport mode is recommended between Host-A and Host-B. Encryption algorithm is rc5-cbc, and authentication algorithm for ESP is hmac-md5.

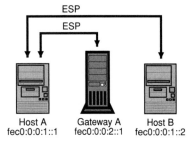

Host A	Gateway A	Host B
fec0:0:0:1::1	fec0:0:0:2::1	fec0:0:0:1::2

Configuration at Host-A:

```
# setkey -c <<EOF
spdadd fec0:0:0:1::1[any] fec0:0:0:2::2[80] tcp -P out ipsec
        esp/transport/fec0:0:0:1::1-fec0:0:0:2::2/use
        esp/tunnel/fec0:0:0:1::1-fec0:0:0:2::1/require ;
spdadd fec0:0:0:2::1[80] fec0:0:0:1::1[any] tcp -P in ipsec
        esp/transport/fec0:0:0:2::2-fec0:0:0:1::1/use
        esp/tunnel/fec0:0:0:2::1-fec0:0:0:1::1/require ;
add fec0:0:0:1::1 fec0:0:0:2::2 esp 0x10001
        -m transport
        -E cast128-cbc "12341234"
        -A hmac-sha1 "this is the test key" ;
add fec0:0:0:1::1 fec0:0:0:2::1 esp 0x10002
        -E rc5-cbc "kamekame"
        -A hmac-md5 "this is the test" ;
add fec0:0:0:2::2 fec0:0:0:1::1 esp 0x10003
        -m transport
        -E cast128-cbc "12341234"
        -A hmac-sha1 "this is the test key" ;
add fec0:0:0:2::1 fec0:0:0:1::1 esp 0x10004
        -E rc5-cbc "kamekame"
        -A hmac-md5 "this is the test" ;

EOF
```

10.10 OpenSSH

Secure shell is a set of network connectivity tools used to access remote machines securely. It can be used as a direct replacement for `rlogin`, `rsh`, `rcp`, and `telnet`. Additionally, any other TCP/IP connections can be tunneled/forwarded securely through ssh. ssh encrypts all traffic to effectively eliminate eavesdropping, connection hijacking, and other network-level attacks.

OpenSSH is maintained by the OpenBSD project, and is based upon SSH v1.2.12 with all the recent bug fixes and updates. It is compatible with both SSH protocols 1 and 2. OpenSSH has been in the base system since FreeBSD 4.0.

10.10.1 Advantages of Using OpenSSH

Normally, when using telnet(1) or rlogin(1), data is sent over the network in an clear, un-encrypted form. Network sniffers anywhere in between the client and server can steal your user/password information or data transferred in your session. OpenSSH offers a variety of authentication and encryption methods to prevent this from happening.

10.10.2 Enabling sshd

Be sure to make the following additions to your `rc.conf` file:

```
sshd_enable="YES"
```

This will load the **ssh** daemon the next time your system initializes. Alternatively, you can simply run the **sshd** daemon.

10.10.3 SSH Client

The ssh(1) utility works similarly to rlogin(1).

```
# ssh user@example.com
Host key not found from the list of known hosts.
Are you sure you want to continue connecting (yes/no)? yes
Host 'example.com' added to the list of known hosts.
user@example.com's password: *******
```

The login will continue just as it would have if a session was created using `rlogin` or telnet. SSH utilizes a key fingerprint system for verifying the authenticity of the server when the client connects. The user is prompted to enter 'yes' only when connecting for the first time. Future attempts to login are all verified against the saved fingerprint key. The SSH client will alert you if the saved fingerprint differs from the received fingerprint on future login attempts. The fingerprints are saved in ~/.ssh/known_hosts, or ~/.ssh/known_hosts2 for SSH v2 fingerprints.

By default, OpenSSH servers are configured to accept both SSH v1 and SSH v2 connections. The client, however, can choose between the two. Version 2 is known to be more robust and secure than its predecessor.

ssh can be forced to use either protocol by passing it the -1 or -2 argument for v1 and v2, respectively.

10.10.4 Secure Copy

The scp command works similarly to rcp; it copies a file to or from a remote machine, except in a secure fashion.

```
#  scp user@example.com:/COPYRIGHT COPYRIGHT
```

```
user@example.com's password:
COPYRIGHT                 100%  |****************************|  4735
00:00
#
```

Since the fingerprint was already saved for this host in the previous example, it is verified when using `scp` here.

The arguments passed to `scp` are similar to `cp`, with the file or files in the first argument, and the destination in the second. Since the file is fetched over the network, through SSH, one or more of the file arguments takes on the form `user@host:<path_to_remote_file>`.

10.10.5 Configuration

The system-wide configuration files for both the OpenSSH daemon and client reside within the `/etc/ssh` directory.

`ssh_config` configures the client settings, while `sshd_config` configures the daemon.

Additionally, the `sshd_program` (`/usr/sbin/sshd` by default), and `sshd_flags` `rc.conf` options can provide more levels of configuration.

10.10.6 ssh-keygen

Instead of using passwords, ssh-keygen(1) can be used to generate RSA keys to authenticate a user.

```
% ssh-keygen
Initializing random number generator...
Generating p:   .++ (distance 66)
Generating q:   ...........................++ (distance 498)
Computing the keys...
Key generation complete.
Enter file in which to save the key (/home/user/.ssh/identity):
Enter passphrase:
Enter the same passphrase again:
Your identification has been saved in /home/user/.ssh/identity.
...
```

ssh-keygen(1) will create a public and private key pair for use in authentication. The private key is stored in `~/.ssh/identity`, whereas the public key is stored in `~/.ssh/identity.pub`. The public key must be placed in `~/.ssh/authorized_keys` of the remote machine in order for the setup to work.

This will allow connection to the remote machine based upon RSA authentication instead of passwords.

If a passphrase is used in ssh-keygen(1), the user will be prompted for a password each time in order to use the private key.

A SSH v2 DSA key can be created for the same purpose by using the `ssh-keygen -d` command (or `ssh-keygen -t dsa` for FreeBSD FreeBSD-CURRENT). This will create a public/private DSA key for use in SSH v2 sessions only. The public key is stored in `~/.ssh/id_dsa.pub`, while the private key is in `~/.ssh/id_dsa`.

DSA public keys are placed in `~/.ssh/authorized_keys2` on the remote machine.

ssh-agent(1) and ssh-add(1) are utilities used in managing multiple passworded private keys.

10.10.7 SSH Tunneling

OpenSSH has the ability to create a tunnel to encapsulate another protocol in an encrypted session.

The following command tells ssh(1) to create a tunnel for telnet.

```
% ssh -2 -N -f -L 5023:localhost:23 user@foo.example.com
%
```

The ssh command is used with the following options:

-2

> Forces ssh to use version 2 of the protocol. (Do not use if you are working with older ssh servers)

-N

> Indicates no command, or tunnel only. If omitted, ssh would initiate a normal session.

-f

> Forces ssh to run in the background.

-L

> Indicates a local tunnel in *localport:remotehost:remoteport* fashion.

user@foo.example.com

> The remote SSH server.

An SSH tunnel works by creating a listen socket on localhost on the specified port. It then forwards any connection received on the local host/port via the SSH connection to the specified remote host and port.

In the example, port *5023* on localhost is being forwarded to port *23* on localhost of the remote machine. Since *23* is telnet, this would create a secure telnet session through an SSH tunnel.

This can be used to wrap any number of insecure TCP protocols such as smtp, pop3, ftp, etc.

A typical SSH Tunnel

```
% ssh -2 -N -f -L 5025:localhost:25 user@mailserver.example.com
user@mailserver.example.com's password: *****
% telnet localhost 5025
Trying 127.0.0.1...
Connected to localhost.
Escape character is '^]'.
220 mailserver.example.com ESMTP
```

This can be used in conjunction with an ssh-keygen(1) and additional user accounts to create a more seamless/hassle-free SSH tunneling environment. Keys can be used in place of typing a password, and the tunnels can be run as a separate user.

Practical SSH Tunneling Examples

Secure Access of a POP3 server

At work, there is an SSH server that accepts connections from the outside. On the same office network resides a mail server running a POP3 server. The network, or network path between your home and office may or may not be completely trustable. Because of this, you need to check your e-mail in a secure manner. The solution is to create an SSH connection to your office's SSH server, and tunnel through to the mail server.

```
% ssh -2 -N -f -L 2110:mail.example.com user@ssh-server.example.com
user@ssh-server.example.com's password: ******
```

When the tunnel is up and running, you can point your mail client to send POP3 requests to `localhost` port 2110. A connection here will be forwarded securely across the tunnel to `mail.example.com`.

Bypassing a Draconian Firewall

Some network administrators impose extremely Draconian firewall rules, filtering not only incoming connections, but outgoing connections. You may be only given access to contact remote machines on ports 22 and 80 for SSH and web surfing.

You may wish to access another (perhaps non-work related) service, such as an Ogg Vorbis server to stream music. If this Ogg Vorbis server is streaming on some other port than 22 or 80, you will not be able to access it.

The solution is to create an SSH connection to a machine outside of your network's firewall, and use it to tunnel to the Ogg Vorbis server.

```
% ssh -2 -N -f -L 8888:music.example.com:8000 user@unfirewalled.myserver.com
user@unfirewalled.myserver.com's password: *******
```

Your streaming client can now be pointed to `localhost` port 8888, which will be forwarded over to `music.example.com` port 8000, successfully evading the firewall.

10.10.8 Further Reading

OpenSSH[7]

ssh(1) scp(1) ssh-keygen(1) ssh-agent(1) ssh-add(1)

sshd(8) sftp-server(8)

---

7 http://www.openssh.com

Chapter 11

Printing

11.1 Synopsis

FreeBSD can be used to print to a wide variety of printers, from the oldest impact printer to the latest laser printers, and everything in between, allowing you to produce high quality printed output from the applications you run.

FreeBSD can also be configured to act as a print server on a network; in this capacity FreeBSD can receive print jobs from a variety of other computers, including other FreeBSD computers, Windows and MacOS hosts. FreeBSD will ensure that one job at a time is printed, and can keep statistics on which users and machines are doing the most printing, produce "banner" pages showing who's printout is who's, and more.

After reading this chapter, you will know:

- How to configure the FreeBSD print spooler.
- How to install print filters, to handle special print jobs differently, including converting incoming documents to print formats that your printers understand.
- How to enable header, or banner pages on your printout.
- How to print to printers connected to other computers.
- How to print to printers connected directly to the network.
- How to control printer restrictions, including limiting the size of print jobs, and preventing certain users from printing.
- How to keep printer statistics, and account for printer usage.
- How to troubleshoot printing problems.

Before reading this chapter, you should:

- Know how to configure and install a new kernel (Chapter 9).

11.2 Introduction

In order to use printers with FreeBSD, you will need to set them up to work with the Berkeley line printer spooling system, also known as the **LPD** spooling system. It is the standard printer control system in FreeBSD. This chapter introduces the **LPD** spooling system, often simply called **LPD**, and will guide you through its configuration.

If you are already familiar with **LPD** or another printer spooling system, you may wish to skip to section Setting up the spooling system.

LPD controls everything about a host's printers. It is responsible for a number of things:

- It controls access to attached printers and printers attached to other hosts on the network.
- It enables users to submit files to be printed; these submissions are known as *jobs*.
- It prevents multiple users from accessing a printer at the same time by maintaining a *queue* for each printer.
- It can print *header pages* (also known as *banner* or *burst* pages) so users can easily find jobs they have printed in a stack of printouts.
- It takes care of communications parameters for printers connected on serial ports.
- It can send jobs over the network to a **LPD** spooler on another host.
- It can run special filters to format jobs to be printed for various printer languages or printer capabilities.
- It can account for printer usage.

Through a configuration file (`/etc/printcap`), and by providing the special filter programs, you can enable the **LPD** system to do all or some subset of the above for a great variety of printer hardware.

11.2.1 Why You Should Use the Spooler

If you are the sole user of your system, you may be wondering why you should bother with the spooler when you do not need access control, header pages, or printer accounting. While it is possible to enable direct access to a printer, you should use the spooler anyway since:

- **LPD** prints jobs in the background; you do not have to wait for data to be copied to the printer.
- **LPD** can conveniently run a job to be printed through filters to add date/time headers or convert a special file format (such as a TeX DVI file) into a format the printer will understand. You will not have to do these steps manually.
- Many free and commercial programs that provide a print feature usually expect to talk to the spooler on your system. By setting up the spooling system, you will more easily support other software you may later add or already have.

11.3 Basic Setup

To use printers with the **LPD** spooling system, you will need to set up both your printer hardware and the **LPD** software. This document describes two levels of setup:

- See section Simple Printer Setup to learn how to connect a printer, tell **LPD** how to communicate with it, and print plain text files to the printer.
- See section Advanced Printer Setup to find out how to print a variety of special file formats, to print header pages, to print across a network, to control access to printers, and to do printer accounting.

11.3.1 Simple Printer Setup

This section tells how to configure printer hardware and the **LPD** software to use the printer. It teaches the basics:

- Section Hardware Setup gives some hints on connecting the printer to a port on your computer.
- Section Software Setup shows how to setup the **LPD** spooler configuration file (/etc/printcap).

If you are setting up a printer that uses a network protocol to accept data to print instead of a serial or parallel interface, see Printers With Networked Data Stream Interfaces.

Although this section is called "Simple Printer Setup", it is actually fairly complex. Getting the printer to work with your computer and the **LPD** spooler is the hardest part. The advanced options like header pages and accounting are fairly easy once you get the printer working.

Hardware Setup

This section tells about the various ways you can connect a printer to your PC. It talks about the kinds of ports and cables, and also the kernel configuration you may need to enable FreeBSD to speak to the printer.

If you have already connected your printer and have successfully printed with it under another operating system, you can probably skip to section Software Setup.

Ports and Cables

Nearly all printers you can get for a PC today support one or both of the following interfaces:

- *Serial* interfaces use a serial port on your computer to send data to the printer. Serial interfaces are common in the computer industry and cables are readily available and also easy to construct. Serial interfaces sometimes need special cables and might require you to configure somewhat complex communications options.

- *Parallel* interfaces use a parallel port on your computer to send data to the printer. Parallel interfaces are common in the PC market. Cables are readily available but more difficult to construct by hand. There are usually no communications options with parallel interfaces, making their configuration exceedingly simple.

  Parallel interfaces are sometimes known as "Centronics" interfaces, named after the connector type on the printer.

In general, serial interfaces are slower than parallel interfaces. Parallel interfaces usually offer just one-way communication (computer to printer) while serial gives you two-way. Many newer parallel ports and printers can communicate in both directions under FreeBSD when a IEEE1284 compliant cable is used.

Usually, the only time you need two-way communication with the printer is if the printer speaks PostScript. PostScript printers can be very verbose. In fact, PostScript jobs are actually programs sent to the printer; they need not produce paper at all and may return results directly to the computer. PostScript also uses two-way communication to tell the computer about problems, such as errors in the PostScript program or paper jams. Your users may be appreciative of such information. Furthermore, the best way to do effective accounting with a PostScript printer requires two-way communication: you ask the printer for its page count (how many pages it has printed in its lifetime), then send the user's job, then ask again for its page count. Subtract the two values and you know how much paper to charge the user.

Parallel Ports

To hook up a printer using a parallel interface, connect the Centronics cable between the printer and the computer. The instructions that came with the printer, the computer, or both should give you complete guidance.

Remember which parallel port you used on the computer. The first parallel port is /dev/lpt0 to FreeBSD; the second is /dev/lpt1, and so on.

Serial Ports

To hook up a printer using a serial interface, connect the proper serial cable between the printer and the computer. The instructions that came with the printer, the computer, or both should give you complete guidance.

If you are unsure what the "proper serial cable" is, you may wish to try one of the following alternatives:

• A *modem* cable connects each pin of the connector on one end of the cable straight through to its corresponding pin of the connector on the other end. This type of cable is also known as a "DTE-to-DCE" cable.

• A *null-modem* cable connects some pins straight through, swaps others (send data to receive data, for example), and shorts some internally in each connector hood. This type of cable is also known as a "DTE-to-DTE" cable.

• A *serial printer* cable, required for some unusual printers, is like the null-modem cable, but sends some signals to their counterparts instead of being internally shorted.

You should also set up the communications parameters for the printer, usually through front-panel controls or DIP switches on the printer. Choose the highest bps (bits per second, sometimes *baud rate*) rate that both your computer and the printer can support. Choose 7 or 8 data bits; none, even, or odd parity; and 1 or 2 stop bits. Also choose a flow control protocol: either none, or XON/XOFF (also known as "in-band" or "software") flow control. Remember these settings for the software configuration that follows.

Software Setup

This section describes the software setup necessary to print with the **LPD** spooling system in FreeBSD.

Here is an outline of the steps involved:

1. Configure your kernel, if necessary, for the port you are using for the printer; section Kernel Configuration tells you what you need to do.

2. Set the communications mode for the parallel port, if you are using a parallel port; section Setting the Communication Mode for the Parallel Port gives details.

3. Test if the operating system can send data to the printer. Section Checking Printer Communications gives some suggestions on how to do this.

4. Set up **LPD** for the printer by modifying the file /etc/printcap. You will find out how to do this later in this chapter.

Kernel Configuration

The operating system kernel is compiled to work with a specific set of devices. The serial or parallel interface for your printer is a part of that set. Therefore, it might be necessary to add support for an additional serial or parallel port if your kernel is not already configured for one.

To find out if the kernel you are currently using supports a serial interface, type:

```
# dmesg | grep sioN
```

Where N is the number of the serial port, starting from zero. If you see output similar to the following:

```
sio2 at 0x3e8-0x3ef irq 5 on isa
sio2: type 16550A
```

then the kernel supports the port.

To find out if the kernel supports a parallel interface, type:

```
# dmesg | grep lptN
```

Where N is the number of the parallel port, starting from zero. If you see output similar to the following

```
lpt0 at 0x378-0x37f on isa
```

then the kernel supports the port.

You might have to reconfigure your kernel in order for the operating system to recognize and use the parallel or serial port you are using for the printer.

To add support for a serial port, see the section on kernel configuration. To add support for a parallel port, see that section *and* the section that follows.

Adding /dev Entries for the Ports

Even though the kernel may support communication along a serial or parallel port, you will still need a software interface through which programs running on the system can send and receive data. That is what entries in the /dev directory are for.

To add a /dev entry for a port:

1. Become root with the su(1) command. Enter the root password when prompted.

2. Change to the /dev directory:

        # cd /dev

3. Type:

        # ./MAKEDEV port

   Where port is the device entry for the port you want to make. Use lpt0 for the first parallel port, lpt1 for the second, and so on; use ttyd0 for the first serial port, ttyd1 for the second, and so on.

4. Type:

    ```
    # ls -l port
    ```

    to make sure the device entry got created.

Setting the Communication Mode for the Parallel Port

When you are using the parallel interface, you can choose whether FreeBSD should use interrupt-driven or polled communication with the printer.

*   The *interrupt-driven* method is the default with the GENERIC kernel. With this method, the operating system uses an IRQ line to determine when the printer is ready for data.
*   The *polled* method directs the operating system to repeatedly ask the printer if it is ready for more data. When it responds ready, the kernel sends more data.

The interrupt-driven method is somewhat faster but uses up a precious IRQ line. You should use whichever one works.

You can set the communications mode in two ways: by configuring the kernel or by using the lptcontrol(8) program.

To set the communications mode by configuring the kernel:

1. Edit your kernel configuration file. Look for or add an `lpt0` entry. If you are setting up the second parallel port, use `lpt1` instead. Use `lpt2` for the third port, and so on.
    *   If you want interrupt-driven mode, add the `irq` specifier:

        ```
        device lpt0 at isa? port? tty irq N vector lptintr
        ```

        Where *N* is the IRQ number for your computer's parallel port.

    *   If you want polled mode, do not add the `irq` specifier:

        ```
        device lpt0 at isa? port? tty vector lptintr
        ```

2. Save the file. Then configure, build, and install the kernel, then reboot. See kernel configuration (Chapter 9) for more details.

To set the communications mode with lptcontrol(8):

1. Type:

    ```
    # lptcontrol -i -u N
    ```

    to set interrupt-driven mode for `lptN`.

2. Type:

    ```
    # lptcontrol -p -u N
    ```

    to set polled-mode for `lptN`.

You could put these commands in your `/etc/rc.local` file to set the mode each time your system boots. See lptcontrol(8) for more information.

Checking Printer Communications

Before proceeding to configure the spooling system, you should make sure the operating system can successfully send data to your printer. It is a lot easier to debug printer communication and the spooling system separately.

To test the printer, we will send some text to it. For printers that can immediately print characters sent to them, the program lptest(1) is perfect: it generates all 96 printable ASCII characters in 96 lines.

For a PostScript (or other language-based) printer, we will need a more sophisticated test. A small PostScript program, such as the following, will suffice:

```
%!PS
100 100 moveto 300 300 lineto stroke
310 310 moveto /Helvetica findfont 12 scalefont setfont
(Is this thing working?) show
showpage
```

The above PostScript code can be placed into a file and used as shown in the examples appearing in the following sections.

> **Note:** When this document refers to a printer language, it is assuming a language like PostScript, and not Hewlett Packard's PCL. Although PCL has great functionality, you can intermingle plain text with its escape sequences. PostScript cannot directly print plain text, and that is the kind of printer language for which we must make special accommodations.

Checking a Parallel Printer

This section tells you how to check if FreeBSD can communicate with a printer connected to a parallel port.

To test a printer on a parallel port:

1. Become root with su(1).

2. Send data to the printer.

   - If the printer can print plain text, then use lptest(1). Type:

     ```
     # lptest > /dev/lptN
     ```

     Where *N* is the number of the parallel port, starting from zero.

   - If the printer understands PostScript or other printer language, then send a small program to the printer. Type:

     ```
     # cat > /dev/lptN
     ```

     Then, line by line, type the program *carefully* as you cannot edit a line once you have pressed RETURN or ENTER. When you have finished entering the program, press CONTROL+D, or whatever your end of file key is.

Alternatively, you can put the program in a file and type:

```
# cat file > /dev/lptN
```

Where `file` is the name of the file containing the program you want to send to the printer.

You should see something print. Do not worry if the text does not look right; we will fix such things later.

Checking a Serial Printer

This section tells you how to check if FreeBSD can communicate with a printer on a serial port.

To test a printer on a serial port:

1. Become root with su(1).

2. Edit the file `/etc/remote`. Add the following entry:

   ```
   printer:dv=/dev/port:br#bps-rate:pa=parity
   ```

   Where `port` is the device entry for the serial port (`ttyd0`, `ttyd1`, etc.), `bps-rate` is the bits-per-second rate at which the printer communicates, and `parity` is the parity required by the printer (either `even`, `odd`, `none`, or `zero`).

   Here is a sample entry for a printer connected via a serial line to the third serial port at 19200 bps with no parity:

   ```
   printer:dv=/dev/ttyd2:br#19200:pa=none
   ```

3. Connect to the printer with tip(1). Type:

   ```
   # tip printer
   ```

   If this step does not work, edit the file `/etc/remote` again and try using `/dev/cuaaN` instead of `/dev/ttydN`.

4. Send data to the printer.

   - If the printer can print plain text, then use lptest(1). Type:

     ```
     % $lptest
     ```

   - If the printer understands PostScript or other printer language, then send a small program to the printer. Type the program, line by line, *very carefully* as backspacing or other editing keys may be significant to the printer. You may also need to type a special end-of-file key for the printer so it knows it received the whole program. For PostScript printers, press CONTROL+D.

     Alternatively, you can put the program in a file and type:

     ```
     % >file
     ```

     Where `file` is the name of the file containing the program. After tip(1) sends the file, press any required end-of-file key.

You should see something print. Do not worry if the text does not look right; we will fix that later.

Enabling the Spooler: The `/etc/printcap` File

At this point, your printer should be hooked up, your kernel configured to communicate with it (if necessary), and you have been able to send some simple data to the printer. Now, we are ready to configure **LPD** to control access to your printer.

You configure **LPD** by editing the file `/etc/printcap`. The **LPD** spooling system reads this file each time the spooler is used, so updates to the file take immediate effect.

The format of the printcap(5) file is straightforward. Use your favorite text editor to make changes to `/etc/printcap`. The format is identical to other capability files like `/usr/share/misc/termcap` and `/etc/remote`. For complete information about the format, see the cgetent(3).

The simple spooler configuration consists of the following steps:

1. Pick a name (and a few convenient aliases) for the printer, and put them in the `/etc/printcap` file; see the Naming the Printer section for more information on naming.

2. Turn off header pages (which are on by default) by inserting the `sh` capability; see the Suppressing Header Pages section for more information.

3. Make a spooling directory, and specify its location with the `sd` capability; see the Making the Spooling Directory section for more information.

4. Set the `/dev` entry to use for the printer, and note it in `/etc/printcap` with the `lp` capability; see the Identifying the Printer Device section for more information. Also, if the printer is on a serial port, set up the communication parameters with the `fs`, `fc`, `xs`, and `xc` capabilities; which is discussed in the Configuring Spooler Communications Parameters section.

5. Install a plain text input filter; see the Installing the Text Filter section for details.

6. Test the setup by printing something with the lpr(1) command. More details are available in the Trying It Out and Troubleshooting sections.

> **Note:** Language-based printers, such as PostScript printers, cannot directly print plain text. The simple setup outlined above and described in the following sections assumes that if you are installing such a printer you will print only files that the printer can understand.

Users often expect that they can print plain text to any of the printers installed on your system. Programs that interface to **LPD** to do their printing usually make the same assumption. If you are installing such a printer and want to be able to print jobs in the printer language *and* print plain text jobs, you are strongly urged to add an additional step to the simple setup outlined above: install an automatic plain-text-to-PostScript (or other printer language) conversion program. The section entitled Accommodating Plain Text Jobs on PostScript Printers tells how to do this.

Naming the Printer

The first (easy) step is to pick a name for your printer It really does not matter whether you choose functional or whimsical names since you can also provide a number of aliases for the printer.

At least one of the printers specified in the /etc/printcap should have the alias lp. This is the default printer's name. If users do not have the PRINTER environment variable nor specify a printer name on the command line of any of the **LPD** commands, then lp will be the default printer they get to use.

Also, it is common practice to make the last alias for a printer be a full description of the printer, including make and model.

Once you have picked a name and some common aliases, put them in the /etc/printcap file. The name of the printer should start in the leftmost column. Separate each alias with a vertical bar and put a colon after the last alias.

In the following example, we start with a skeletal /etc/printcap that defines two printers (a Diablo 630 line printer and a Panasonic KX-P4455 PostScript laser printer):

```
#
#  /etc/printcap for host rose
#
rattan|line|diablo|lp|Diablo 630 Line Printer:

bamboo|ps|PS|S|panasonic|Panasonic KX-P4455 PostScript v51.4:
```

In this example, the first printer is named rattan and has as aliases line, diablo, lp, and Diablo 630 Line Printer. Since it has the alias lp, it is also the default printer. The second is named bamboo, and has as aliases ps, PS, S, panasonic, and Panasonic KX-P4455 PostScript v51.4.

Suppressing Header Pages

The **LPD** spooling system will by default print a *header page* for each job. The header page contains the user name who requested the job, the host from which the job came, and the name of the job, in nice large letters. Unfortunately, all this extra text gets in the way of debugging the simple printer setup, so we will suppress header pages.

To suppress header pages, add the sh capability to the entry for the printer in /etc/printcap. Here is an example /etc/printcap with sh added:

```
#
#  /etc/printcap for host rose - no header pages anywhere
#
rattan|line|diablo|lp|Diablo 630 Line Printer:\
        :sh:

bamboo|ps|PS|S|panasonic|Panasonic KX-P4455 PostScript v51.4:\
        :sh:
```

Note how we used the correct format: the first line starts in the leftmost column, and subsequent lines are indented with a single TAB. Every line in an entry except the last ends in a backslash character.

Making the Spooling Directory

The next step in the simple spooler setup is to make a *spooling directory*, a directory where print jobs reside until they are printed, and where a number of other spooler support files live.

Because of the variable nature of spooling directories, it is customary to put these directories under /var/spool. It is not necessary to backup the contents of spooling directories, either. Recreating them is as simple as running mkdir(1).

It is also customary to make the directory with a name that is identical to the name of the printer, as shown below:

```
# mkdir /var/spool/printer-name
```

However, if you have a lot of printers on your network, you might want to put the spooling directories under a single directory that you reserve just for printing with **LPD**. We will do this for our two example printers rattan and bamboo:

```
# mkdir /var/spool/lpd
# mkdir /var/spool/lpd/rattan
# mkdir /var/spool/lpd/bamboo
```

Note: If you are concerned about the privacy of jobs that users print, you might want to protect the spooling directory so it is not publicly accessible. Spooling directories should be owned and be readable, writable, and searchable by user daemon and group daemon, and no one else. We will do this for our example printers:

```
# chown daemon:daemon /var/spool/lpd/rattan
# chown daemon:daemon /var/spool/lpd/bamboo
# chmod 770 /var/spool/lpd/rattan
# chmod 770 /var/spool/lpd/bamboo
```

Finally, you need to tell **LPD** about these directories using the /etc/printcap file. You specify the pathname of the spooling directory with the sd capability:

```
#
# /etc/printcap for host rose - added spooling directories
#
rattan|line|diablo|lp|Diablo 630 Line Printer:\
        :sh:sd=/var/spool/lpd/rattan:

bamboo|ps|PS|S|panasonic|Panasonic KX-P4455 PostScript v51.4:\
        :sh:sd=/var/spool/lpd/bamboo:
```

Note that the name of the printer starts in the first column but all other entries describing the printer should be indented with a tab and each line escaped with a backslash.

If you do not specify a spooling directory with sd, the spooling system will use /var/spool/lpd as a default.

Identifying the Printer Device

In the Adding /dev Entries for the Ports section, we identified which entry in the /dev directory FreeBSD will use to communicate with the printer. Now, we tell **LPD** that information. When the spooling system has a job to print, it will open the specified device on behalf of the filter program (which is responsible for passing data to the printer).

List the /dev entry pathname in the /etc/printcap file using the lp capability.

In our running example, let us assume that rattan is on the first parallel port, and bamboo is on a sixth serial port; here are the additions to /etc/printcap:

```
#
#  /etc/printcap for host rose - identified what devices to use
#
rattan|line|diablo|lp|Diablo 630 Line Printer:\
        :sh:sd=/var/spool/lpd/rattan:\
        :lp=/dev/lpt0:

bamboo|ps|PS|S|panasonic|Panasonic KX-P4455 PostScript v51.4:\
        :sh:sd=/var/spool/lpd/bamboo:\
        :lp=/dev/ttyd5:
```

If you do not specify the lp capability for a printer in your /etc/printcap file, **LPD** uses /dev/lp as a default. /dev/lp currently does not exist in FreeBSD.

If the printer you are installing is connected to a parallel port, skip to the section entitled, Installing the Text Filter. Otherwise, be sure to follow the instructions in the next section.

Configuring Spooler Communication Parameters

For printers on serial ports, **LPD** can set up the bps rate, parity, and other serial communication parameters on behalf of the filter program that sends data to the printer. This is advantageous since:

- It lets you try different communication parameters by simply editing the /etc/printcap file; you do not have to recompile the filter program.
- It enables the spooling system to use the same filter program for multiple printers which may have different serial communication settings.

The following /etc/printcap capabilities control serial communication parameters of the device listed in the lp capability:

br#*bps-rate*

> Sets the communications speed of the device to *bps-rate*, where *bps-rate* can be 50, 75, 110, 134, 150, 200, 300, 600, 1200, 1800, 2400, 4800, 9600, 19200, or 38400 bits-per-second.

fc#*clear-bits*

> Clears the flag bits *clear-bits* in the *sgttyb* structure after opening the device.

`fs#`*set-bits*

> Sets the flag bits *set-bits* in the *sgttyb* structure.

`xc#`*clear-bits*

> Clears local mode bits *clear-bits* after opening the device.

`xs#`*set-bits*

> Sets local mode bits *set-bits*.

For more information on the bits for the `fc`, `fs`, `xc`, and `xs` capabilities, see the file `/usr/include/sys/ioctl_compat.h`.

When **LPD** opens the device specified by the `lp` capability, it reads the flag bits in the `sgttyb` structure; it clears any bits in the `fc` capability, then sets bits in the `fs` capability, then applies the resultant setting. It does the same for the local mode bits as well.

Let us add to our example printer on the sixth serial port. We will set the bps rate to 38400. For the flag bits, we will set the `TANDEM`, `ANYP`, `LITOUT`, `FLUSHO`, and `PASS8` flags. For the local mode bits, we will set the `LITOUT` and `PASS8` flags:

```
bamboo|ps|PS|S|panasonic|Panasonic KX-P4455 PostScript v51.4:\
        :sh:sd=/var/spool/lpd/bamboo:\
        :lp=/dev/ttyd5:fs#0x82000c1:xs#0x820:
```

Installing the Text Filter

We are now ready to tell **LPD** what text filter to use to send jobs to the printer. A *text filter*, also known as an *input filter*, is a program that **LPD** runs when it has a job to print. When **LPD** runs the text filter for a printer, it sets the filter's standard input to the job to print, and its standard output to the printer device specified with the `lp` capability. The filter is expected to read the job from standard input, perform any necessary translation for the printer, and write the results to standard output, which will get printed. For more information on the text filter, see the Filters section.

For our simple printer setup, the text filter can be a small shell script that just executes `/bin/cat` to send the job to the printer. FreeBSD comes with another filter called `lpf` that handles backspacing and underlining for printers that might not deal with such character streams well. And, of course, you can use any other filter program you want. The filter `lpf` is described in detail in section entitled lpf: a Text Filter.

First, let us make the shell script `/usr/local/libexec/if-simple` be a simple text filter. Put the following text into that file with your favorite text editor:

```
#!/bin/sh
#
# if-simple - Simple text input filter for lpd
# Installed in /usr/local/libexec/if-simple
#
# Simply copies stdin to stdout.  Ignores all filter arguments.

/bin/cat && exit 0
exit 2
```

Make the file executable:

```
# chmod 555 /usr/local/libexec/if-simple
```

And then tell LPD to use it by specifying it with the `if` capability in `/etc/printcap`. We will add it to the two printers we have so far in the example `/etc/printcap`:

```
#
#  /etc/printcap for host rose - added text filter
#
rattan|line|diablo|lp|Diablo 630 Line Printer:\
        :sh:sd=/var/spool/lpd/rattan:\ :lp=/dev/lpt0:\
        :if=/usr/local/libexec/if-simple:

bamboo|ps|PS|S|panasonic|Panasonic KX-P4455 PostScript v51.4:\
        :sh:sd=/var/spool/lpd/bamboo:\
        :lp=/dev/ttyd5:fs#0x82000e1:xs#0x820:\
        :if=/usr/local/libexec/if-simple:
```

Turn on LPD

lpd(8) is run from `/etc/rc`, controlled by the `lpd_enable` variable. This variable defaults to NO. If you have not done so already, add the line:

```
lpd_enable="YES"
```

to `/etc/rc.conf`, and then either restart your machine, or just run lpd(8).

```
# lpd
```

Trying It Out

You have reached the end of the simple **LPD** setup. Unfortunately, congratulations are not quite yet in order, since we still have to test the setup and correct any problems. To test the setup, try printing something. To print with the **LPD** system, you use the command lpr(1), which submits a job for printing.

You can combine lpr(1) with the lptest(1) program, introduced in section Checking Printer Communications to generate some test text.

*To test the simple **LPD** setup:*

Type:

```
# lptest 20 5 | lpr -Pprinter-name
```

Where *printer-name* is a the name of a printer (or an alias) specified in `/etc/printcap`. To test the default printer, type lpr(1) without any -P argument. Again, if you are testing a printer that expects PostScript, send a PostScript program in that language instead of using lptest(1). You can do so by putting the program in a file and typing `lpr` *file*.

For a PostScript printer, you should get the results of the program. If you are using lptest(1), then your results should look like the following:

```
!"#$%&'()*+,-./01234
"#$%&'()*+,-./012345
#$%&'()*+,-./0123456
$%&'()*+,-./01234567
%&'()*+,-./012345678
```

To further test the printer, try downloading larger programs (for language-based printers) or running lptest(1) with different arguments. For example, `lptest 80 60` will produce 60 lines of 80 characters each.

If the printer did not work, see the Troubleshooting section.

11.4 Advanced Printer Setup

This section describes filters for printing specially formatted files, header pages, printing across networks, and restricting and accounting for printer usage.

11.4.1 Filters

Although **LPD** handles network protocols, queuing, access control, and other aspects of printing, most of the *real* work happens in the *filters*. Filters are programs that communicate with the printer and handle its device dependencies and special requirements. In the simple printer setup, we installed a plain text filter—an extremely simple one that should work with most printers (section Installing the Text Filter).

However, in order to take advantage of format conversion, printer accounting, specific printer quirks, and so on, you should understand how filters work. It will ultimately be the filter's responsibility to handle these aspects. And the bad news is that most of the time *you* have to provide filters yourself. The good news is that many are generally available; when they are not, they are usually easy to write.

Also, FreeBSD comes with one, `/usr/libexec/lpr/lpf`, that works with many printers that can print plain text. (It handles backspacing and tabs in the file, and does accounting, but that is about all it does.) There are also several filters and filter components in the FreeBSD Ports Collection.

Here is what you will find in this section:

* Section How Filters Work, tries to give an overview of a filter's role in the printing process. You should read this section to get an understanding of what is happening "under the hood" when **LPD** uses filters. This knowledge could help you anticipate and debug problems you might encounter as you install more and more filters on each of your printers.

* **LPD** expects every printer to be able to print plain text by default. This presents a problem for PostScript (or other language-based printers) which cannot directly print plain text. Section Accommodating Plain Text Jobs on

PostScript Printers tells you what you should do to overcome this problem. You should read this section if you have a PostScript printer.

• PostScript is a popular output format for many programs. Even some people (myself included) write PostScript code directly. But PostScript printers are expensive. Section Simulating PostScript on Non-PostScript Printers tells how you can further modify a printer's text filter to accept and print PostScript data on a *non-PostScript* printer. You should read this section if you do not have a PostScript printer.

• Section Conversion Filters tells about a way you can automate the conversion of specific file formats, such as graphic or typesetting data, into formats your printer can understand. After reading this section, you should be able to set up your printers such that users can type `lpr -t` to print troff data, or `lpr -d` to print TeX DVI data, or `lpr -v` to print raster image data, and so forth. I recommend reading this section.

• Section Output Filters tells all about a not often used feature of **LPD**: output filters. Unless you are printing header pages (see Header Pages), you can probably skip that section altogether.

• Section lpf: a Text Filter describes `lpf`, a fairly complete if simple text filter for line printers (and laser printers that act like line printers) that comes with FreeBSD. If you need a quick way to get printer accounting working for plain text, or if you have a printer which emits smoke when it sees backspace characters, you should definitely consider `lpf`.

How Filters Work

As mentioned before, a filter is an executable program started by **LPD** to handle the device-dependent part of communicating with the printer.

When **LPD** wants to print a file in a job, it starts a filter program. It sets the filter's standard input to the file to print, its standard output to the printer, and its standard error to the error logging file (specified in the `lf` capability in `/etc/printcap`, or `/dev/console` by default).

Which filter **LPD** starts and the filter's arguments depend on what is listed in the `/etc/printcap` file and what arguments the user specified for the job on the lpr(1) command line. For example, if the user typed `lpr -t`, **LPD** would start the troff filter, listed in the `tf` capability for the destination printer. If the user wanted to print plain text, it would start the `if` filter (this is mostly true: see the Output Filters section for details).

There are three kinds of filters you can specify in `/etc/printcap`:

• The *text filter*, confusingly called the *input filter* in **LPD** documentation, handles regular text printing. Think of it as the default filter. **LPD** expects every printer to be able to print plain text by default, and it is the text filter's job to make sure backspaces, tabs, or other special characters do not confuse the printer. If you are in an environment where you have to account for printer usage, the text filter must also account for pages printed, usually by counting the number of lines printed and comparing that to the number of lines per page the printer supports. The text filter is started with the following argument list:

```
filter-name [-c] -wwidth -llength -iindent -n login -h host acct-file
```

where

`-c`

> appears if the job is submitted with `lpr -l`

width

> is the value from the `pw` (page width) capability specified in `/etc/printcap`, default 132

length

> is the value from the `pl` (page length) capability, default 66

indent

> is the amount of the indentation from `lpr -i`, default 0

login

> is the account name of the user printing the file

host

> is the host name from which the job was submitted

acct-file

> is the name of the accounting file from the `af` capability.

- A *conversion filter* converts a specific file format into one the printer can render onto paper. For example, ditroff typesetting data cannot be directly printed, but you can install a conversion filter for ditroff files to convert the ditroff data into a form the printer can digest and print. Section Conversion Filters tells all about them. Conversion filters also need to do accounting, if you need printer accounting. Conversion filters are started with the following arguments:

`filter-name -x`*pixel-width* `-y`*pixel-height* `-n` *login* `-h` *host* *acct-file*

> where *pixel-width* is the value from the `px` capability (default 0) and *pixel-height* is the value from the `py` capability (default 0).

- The *output filter* is used only if there is no text filter, or if header pages are enabled. In my experience, output filters are rarely used. Section Output Filters describe them. There are only two arguments to an output filter:

`filter-name -w`*width* `-l`*length*

> which are identical to the text filters `-w` and `-l` arguments.

Filters should also *exit* with the following exit status:

exit 0

> If the filter printed the file successfully.

exit 1

If the filter failed to print the file but wants **LPD** to try to print the file again. **LPD** will restart a filter if it exits with this status.

exit 2

If the filter failed to print the file and does not want **LPD** to try again. **LPD** will throw out the file.

The text filter that comes with the FreeBSD release, `/usr/libexec/lpr/lpf`, takes advantage of the page width and length arguments to determine when to send a form feed and how to account for printer usage. It uses the login, host, and accounting file arguments to make the accounting entries.

If you are shopping for filters, see if they are LPD-compatible. If they are, they must support the argument lists described above. If you plan on writing filters for general use, then have them support the same argument lists and exit codes.

Accommodating Plain Text Jobs on PostScript Printers

If you are the only user of your computer and PostScript (or other language-based) printer, and you promise to never send plain text to your printer and to never use features of various programs that will want to send plain text to your printer, then you do not need to worry about this section at all.

But, if you would like to send both PostScript and plain text jobs to the printer, then you are urged to augment your printer setup. To do so, we have the text filter detect if the arriving job is plain text or PostScript. All PostScript jobs must start with `%!` (for other printer languages, see your printer documentation). If those are the first two characters in the job, we have PostScript, and can pass the rest of the job directly. If those are not the first two characters in the file, then the filter will convert the text into PostScript and print the result.

How do we do this?

If you have got a serial printer, a great way to do it is to install `lprps`. `lprps` is a PostScript printer filter which performs two-way communication with the printer. It updates the printer's status file with verbose information from the printer, so users and administrators can see exactly what the state of the printer is (such as `toner low` or `paper jam`). But more importantly, it includes a program called `psif` which detects whether the incoming job is plain text and calls `textps` (another program that comes with `lprps`) to convert it to PostScript. It then uses `lprps` to send the job to the printer.

`lprps` is part of the FreeBSD Ports Collection. You can fetch, build and install it yourself, of course. After installing `lprps`, just specify the pathname to the `psif` program that is part of `lprps`. If you installed `lprps` from the ports collection, use the following in the serial PostScript printer's entry in `/etc/printcap`:

```
:if=/usr/local/libexec/psif:
```

You should also specify the `rw` capability; that tells **LPD** to open the printer in read-write mode.

If you have a parallel PostScript printer (and therefore cannot use two-way communication with the printer, which `lprps` needs), you can use the following shell script as the text filter:

```
#!/bin/sh
#
#  psif - Print PostScript or plain text on a PostScript printer
```

```
#   Script version; NOT the version that comes with lprps
#   Installed in /usr/local/libexec/psif
#

read first_line
first_two_chars=`expr "$first_line" : '\(..\)'`

if [ "$first_two_chars" = "%!" ]; then
    #
    #   PostScript job, print it.
    #
    echo "$first_line" && cat && printf "\004" && exit 0
    exit 2
else
    #
    #   Plain text, convert it, then print it.
    #
    ( echo "$first_line"; cat ) | /usr/local/bin/textps && printf "\004" && exit 0
    exit 2
fi
```

In the above script, `textps` is a program we installed separately to convert plain text to PostScript. You can use any text-to-PostScript program you wish. The FreeBSD Ports Collection (Chapter 4) includes a full featured text-to-PostScript program called `a2ps` that you might want to investigate.

Simulating PostScript on Non-PostScript Printers

PostScript is the *de facto* standard for high quality typesetting and printing. PostScript is, however, an *expensive* standard. Thankfully, Alladin Enterprises has a free PostScript work-alike called **Ghostscript** that runs with FreeBSD. Ghostscript can read most PostScript files and can render their pages onto a variety of devices, including many brands of non-PostScript printers. By installing Ghostscript and using a special text filter for your printer, you can make your non-PostScript printer act like a real PostScript printer.

Ghostscript is in the FreeBSD Ports Collection, if you would like to install it from there. You can fetch, build, and install it quite easily yourself, as well.

To simulate PostScript, we have the text filter detect if it is printing a PostScript file. If it is not, then the filter will pass the file directly to the printer; otherwise, it will use Ghostscript to first convert the file into a format the printer will understand.

Here is an example: the following script is a text filter for Hewlett Packard DeskJet 500 printers. For other printers, substitute the `-sDEVICE` argument to the `gs` (Ghostscript) command. (Type `gs  -h` to get a list of devices the current installation of Ghostscript supports.)

```
#!/bin/sh
#
#   ifhp - Print Ghostscript-simulated PostScript on a DeskJet 500
#   Installed in /usr/local/libexec/hpif

#
```

```
#   Treat LF as CR+LF:
#
printf "\033&k2G" || exit 2


#
#  Read first two characters of the file
#
read first_line
first_two_chars=`expr "$first_line" : '\(..\)'`

if [ "$first_two_chars" = "%!" ]; then
    #
    #  It is PostScript; use Ghostscript to scan-convert and print it.
    #
    #  Note that PostScript files are actually interpreted programs,
    #  and those programs are allowed to write to stdout, which will
    #  mess up the printed output.  So, we redirect stdout to stderr
    #  and then make descriptor 3 go to stdout, and have Ghostscript
    #  write its output there.  Exercise for the clever reader:
    #  capture the stderr output from Ghostscript and mail it back to
    #  the user originating the print job.
    #
    exec 3>&1 1>&2
    /usr/local/bin/gs -dSAFER -dNOPAUSE -q -sDEVICE=djet500 \
        -sOutputFile=/dev/fd/3 - && exit 0

    #
    /usr/local/bin/gs -dSAFER -dNOPAUSE -q -sDEVICE=djet500 -sOutputFile=- - \
        && exit 0
else
    #
    #  Plain text or HP/PCL, so just print it directly; print a form feed
    #  at the end to eject the last page.
    #
    echo $first_line && cat && printf "\033&l0H" &&
exit 0
fi

exit 2
```

Finally, you need to notify **LPD** of the filter via the `if` capability:

```
:if=/usr/local/libexec/hpif:
```

That is it. You can type `lpr plain.text` and **lprwhatever.ps** and both should print successfully.

Conversion Filters

After completing the simple setup described in Simple Printer Setup, the first thing you will probably want to do is install conversion filters for your favorite file formats (besides plain ASCII text).

Why Install Conversion Filters?

Conversion filters make printing various kinds of files easy. As an example, suppose we do a lot of work with the TeX typesetting system, and we have a PostScript printer. Every time we generate a DVI file from TeX, we cannot print it directly until we convert the DVI file into PostScript. The command sequence goes like this:

```
% dvips seaweed-analysis.dvi
% lpr seaweed-analysis.ps
```

By installing a conversion filter for DVI files, we can skip the hand conversion step each time by having **LPD** do it for us. Now, each time we get a DVI file, we are just one step away from printing it:

```
% lpr -d seaweed-analysis.dvi
```

We got **LPD** to do the DVI file conversion for us by specifying the -d option. Section Formatting and Conversion Options lists the conversion options.

For each of the conversion options you want a printer to support, install a *conversion filter* and specify its pathname in /etc/printcap. A conversion filter is like the text filter for the simple printer setup (see section Installing the Text Filter) except that instead of printing plain text, the filter converts the file into a format the printer can understand.

Which Conversions Filters Should I Install?

You should install the conversion filters you expect to use. If you print a lot of DVI data, then a DVI conversion filter is in order. If you have got plenty of troff to print out, then you probably want a troff filter.

The following table summarizes the filters that **LPD** works with, their capability entries for the /etc/printcap file, and how to invoke them with the lpr command:

File type	/etc/printcap **capability**	lpr **option**
cifplot	cf	-c
DVI	df	-d
plot	gf	-g
ditroff	nf	-n
FORTRAN text	rf	-f
troff	rf	-f
raster	vf	-v
plain text	if	none, -p, or -l

In our example, using lpr -d means the printer needs a df capability in its entry in /etc/printcap.

Despite what others might contend, formats like FORTRAN text and plot are probably obsolete. At your site, you can give new meanings to these or any of the formatting options just by installing custom filters. For example, suppose you would like to directly print Printerleaf files (files from the Interleaf desktop publishing program), but will never print plot files. You could install a Printerleaf conversion filter under the gf capability and then educate your users that lpr -g mean "print Printerleaf files."

Installing Conversion Filters

Since conversion filters are programs you install outside of the base FreeBSD installation, they should probably go under /usr/local. The directory /usr/local/libexec is a popular location, since they are specialized programs that only **LPD** will run; regular users should not ever need to run them.

To enable a conversion filter, specify its pathname under the appropriate capability for the destination printer in /etc/printcap.

In our example, we will add the DVI conversion filter to the entry for the printer named bamboo. Here is the example /etc/printcap file again, with the new df capability for the printer bamboo.

```
#
#  /etc/printcap for host rose - added df filter for bamboo
#
rattan|line|diablo|lp|Diablo 630 Line Printer:\
        :sh:sd=/var/spool/lpd/rattan:\
        :lp=/dev/lpt0:\
        :if=/usr/local/libexec/if-simple:

bamboo|ps|PS|S|panasonic|Panasonic KX-P4455 PostScript v51.4:\
        :sh:sd=/var/spool/lpd/bamboo:\
        :lp=/dev/ttyd5:fs#0x82000e1:xs#0x820:rw:\
        :if=/usr/local/libexec/psif:\
        :df=/usr/local/libexec/psdf:
```

The DVI filter is a shell script named /usr/local/libexec/psdf. Here is that script:

```
#!/bin/sh
#
#  psdf - DVI to PostScript printer filter
#  Installed in /usr/local/libexec/psdf
#
#  Invoked by lpd when user runs lpr -d
#
exec /usr/local/bin/dvips -f | /usr/local/libexec/lprps "$@"
```

This script runs dvips in filter mode (the -f argument) on standard input, which is the job to print. It then starts the PostScript printer filter lprps (see section Accommodating Plain Text Jobs on PostScript Printers) with the arguments **LPD** passed to this script. lprps will use those arguments to account for the pages printed.

More Conversion Filter Examples

Since there is no fixed set of steps to install conversion filters, let me instead provide more examples. Use these as guidance to making your own filters. Use them directly, if appropriate.

This example script is a raster (well, GIF file, actually) conversion filter for a Hewlett Packard LaserJet III-Si printer:

```
#!/bin/sh
#
#  hpvf - Convert GIF files into HP/PCL, then print
#  Installed in /usr/local/libexec/hpvf

PATH=/usr/X11R6/bin:$PATH; export PATH
giftopnm | ppmtopgm | pgmtopbm | pbmtolj -resolution 300 \
    && exit 0 \
    || exit 2
```

It works by converting the GIF file into a portable anymap, converting that into a portable graymap, converting that into a portable bitmap, and converting that into LaserJet/PCL-compatible data.

Here is the /etc/printcap file with an entry for a printer using the above filter:

```
#
#  /etc/printcap for host orchid
#
teak|hp|laserjet|Hewlett Packard LaserJet 3Si:\
        :lp=/dev/lpt0:sh:sd=/var/spool/lpd/teak:mx#0:\
        :if=/usr/local/libexec/hpif:\
        :vf=/usr/local/libexec/hpvf:
```

The following script is a conversion filter for troff data from the groff typesetting system for the PostScript printer named bamboo:

```
#!/bin/sh
#
#  pstf - Convert groff's troff data into PS, then print.
#  Installed in /usr/local/libexec/pstf
#
exec grops | /usr/local/libexec/lprps "$@"
```

The above script makes use of lprps again to handle the communication with the printer. If the printer were on a parallel port, we would use this script instead:

```
#!/bin/sh
#
#  pstf - Convert groff's troff data into PS, then print.
#  Installed in /usr/local/libexec/pstf
#
exec grops
```

That is it. Here is the entry we need to add to /etc/printcap to enable the filter:

```
:tf=/usr/local/libexec/pstf:
```

Here is an example that might make old hands at FORTRAN blush. It is a FORTRAN-text filter for any printer that can directly print plain text. We will install it for the printer teak:

```
#!/bin/sh
#
# hprf - FORTRAN text filter for LaserJet 3si:
# Installed in /usr/local/libexec/hprf
#

printf "\033&k2G" && fpr && printf "\033&l0H" &&
 exit 0
exit 2
```

And we will add this line to the `/etc/printcap` for the printer `teak` to enable this filter:

```
:rf=/usr/local/libexec/hprf:
```

Here is one final, somewhat complex example. We will add a DVI filter to the LaserJet printer `teak` introduced earlier. First, the easy part: updating `/etc/printcap` with the location of the DVI filter:

```
:df=/usr/local/libexec/hpdf:
```

Now, for the hard part: making the filter. For that, we need a DVI-to-LaserJet/PCL conversion program. The FreeBSD Ports Collection (see The Ports Collection) has one: `dvi2xx` is the name of the package. Installing this package gives us the program we need, `dvilj2p`, which converts DVI into LaserJet IIp, LaserJet III, and LaserJet 2000 compatible codes.

`dvilj2p` makes the filter `hpdf` quite complex since `dvilj2p` cannot read from standard input. It wants to work with a filename. What is worse, the filename has to end in `.dvi` so using `/dev/fd/0` for standard input is problematic. We can get around that problem by linking (symbolically) a temporary file name (one that ends in `.dvi`) to `/dev/fd/0`, thereby forcing `dvilj2p` to read from standard input.

The only other fly in the ointment is the fact that we cannot use `/tmp` for the temporary link. Symbolic links are owned by user and group `bin`. The filter runs as user `daemon`. And the `/tmp` directory has the sticky bit set. The filter can create the link, but it will not be able clean up when done and remove it since the link will belong to a different user.

Instead, the filter will make the symbolic link in the current working directory, which is the spooling directory (specified by the `sd` capability in `/etc/printcap`). This is a perfect place for filters to do their work, especially since there is (sometimes) more free disk space in the spooling directory than under `/tmp`.

Here, finally, is the filter:

```
#!/bin/sh
#
#  hpdf - Print DVI data on HP/PCL printer
#  Installed in /usr/local/libexec/hpdf

PATH=/usr/local/bin:$PATH; export PATH

#
#  Define a function to clean up our temporary files.  These exist
#  in the current directory, which will be the spooling directory
#  for the printer.
#
cleanup() {
```

```
    rm -f hpdf$$.dvi
}

#
# Define a function to handle fatal errors: print the given message
# and exit 2.  Exiting with 2 tells LPD to do not try to reprint the
# job.
#
fatal() {
    echo "$@" 1>&2
    cleanup
    exit 2
}

#
# If user removes the job, LPD will send SIGINT, so trap SIGINT
# (and a few other signals) to clean up after ourselves.
#
trap cleanup 1 2 15

#
# Make sure we are not colliding with any existing files.
#
cleanup

#
# Link the DVI input file to standard input (the file to print).
#
ln -s /dev/fd/0 hpdf$$.dvi || fatal "Cannot symlink /dev/fd/0"

#
# Make LF = CR+LF
#
printf "\033&k2G" || fatal "Cannot initialize printer"

#
# Convert and print.  Return value from dvilj2p does not seem to be
# reliable, so we ignore it.
#
dvilj2p -M1 -q -e- dfhp$$.dvi

#
# Clean up and exit
#
cleanup
exit 0
```

Automated Conversion: An Alternative To Conversion Filters

All these conversion filters accomplish a lot for your printing environment, but at the cost forcing the user to specify (on the lpr(1) command line) which one to use. If your users are not particularly computer literate, having to specify a filter option will become annoying. What is worse, though, is that an incorrectly specified filter option may run a filter on the wrong type of file and cause your printer to spew out hundreds of sheets of paper.

Rather than install conversion filters at all, you might want to try having the text filter (since it is the default filter) detect the type of file it has been asked to print and then automatically run the right conversion filter. Tools such as `file` can be of help here. Of course, it will be hard to determine the differences between *some* file types—and, of course, you can still provide conversion filters just for them.

The FreeBSD Ports Collection has a text filter that performs automatic conversion called `apsfilter`. It can detect plain text, PostScript, and DVI files, run the proper conversions, and print.

Output Filters

The **LPD** spooling system supports one other type of filter that we have not yet explored: an output filter. An output filter is intended for printing plain text only, like the text filter, but with many simplifications. If you are using an output filter but no text filter, then:

- **LPD** starts an output filter once for the entire job instead of once for each file in the job.

- **LPD** does not make any provision to identify the start or the end of files within the job for the output filter.

- **LPD** does not pass the user's login or host to the filter, so it is not intended to do accounting. In fact, it gets only two arguments:

  ```
  filter-name -wwidth -llength
  ```

  Where `width` is from the `pw` capability and `length` is from the `pl` capability for the printer in question.

Do not be seduced by an output filter's simplicity. If you would like each file in a job to start on a different page an output filter *will not work*. Use a text filter (also known as an input filter); see section Installing the Text Filter. Furthermore, an output filter is actually *more complex* in that it has to examine the byte stream being sent to it for special flag characters and must send signals to itself on behalf of **LPD**.

However, an output filter is *necessary* if you want header pages and need to send escape sequences or other initialization strings to be able to print the header page. (But it is also *futile* if you want to charge header pages to the requesting user's account, since **LPD** does not give any user or host information to the output filter.)

On a single printer, **LPD** allows both an output filter and text or other filters. In such cases, **LPD** will start the output filter to print the header page (see section Header Pages) only. **LPD** then expects the output filter to *stop itself* by sending two bytes to the filter: ASCII 031 followed by ASCII 001. When an output filter sees these two bytes (031, 001), it should stop by sending `SIGSTOP` to itself. When **LPD**'s done running other filters, it will restart the output filter by sending `SIGCONT` to it.

If there is an output filter but *no* text filter and **LPD** is working on a plain text job, **LPD** uses the output filter to do the job. As stated before, the output filter will print each file of the job in sequence with no intervening form feeds or other paper advancement, and this is probably *not* what you want. In almost all cases, you need a text filter.

The program `lpf`, which we introduced earlier as a text filter, can also run as an output filter. If you need a quick-and-dirty output filter but do not want to write the byte detection and signal sending code, try `lpf`. You can also wrap `lpf` in a shell script to handle any initialization codes the printer might require.

`lpf`: a Text Filter

The program `/usr/libexec/lpr/lpf` that comes with FreeBSD binary distribution is a text filter (input filter) that can indent output (job submitted with `lpr -i`), allow literal characters to pass (job submitted with `lpr -l`), adjust the printing position for backspaces and tabs in the job, and account for pages printed. It can also act like an output filter.

`lpf` is suitable for many printing environments. And although it has no capability to send initialization sequences to a printer, it is easy to write a shell script to do the needed initialization and then execute `lpf`.

In order for `lpf` to do page accounting correctly, it needs correct values filled in for the `pw` and `pl` capabilities in the `/etc/printcap` file. It uses these values to determine how much text can fit on a page and how many pages were in a user's job. For more information on printer accounting, see Accounting for Printer Usage.

11.4.2 Header Pages

If you have *lots* of users, all of them using various printers, then you probably want to consider *header pages* as a necessary evil.

Header pages, also known as *banner* or *burst pages* identify to whom jobs belong after they are printed. They are usually printed in large, bold letters, perhaps with decorative borders, so that in a stack of printouts they stand out from the real documents that comprise users' jobs. They enable users to locate their jobs quickly. The obvious drawback to a header page is that it is yet one more sheet that has to be printed for every job, their ephemeral usefulness lasting not more than a few minutes, ultimately finding themselves in a recycling bin or rubbish heap. (Note that header pages go with each job, not each file in a job, so the paper waste might not be that bad.)

The **LPD** system can provide header pages automatically for your printouts *if* your printer can directly print plain text. If you have a PostScript printer, you will need an external program to generate the header page; see Header Pages on PostScript Printers.

Enabling Header Pages

In the Simple Printer Setup section, we turned off header pages by specifying `sh` (meaning "suppress header") in the `/etc/printcap` file. To enable header pages for a printer, just remove the `sh` capability.

Sounds too easy, right?

You are right. You *might* have to provide an output filter to send initialization strings to the printer. Here is an example output filter for Hewlett Packard PCL-compatible printers:

```
#!/bin/sh
```

```
#
#  hpof - Output filter for Hewlett Packard PCL-compatible printers
#  Installed in /usr/local/libexec/hpof

printf "\033&k2G" || exit 2
exec /usr/libexec/lpr/lpf
```

Specify the path to the output filter in the `of` capability. See the Output Filters section for more information.

Here is an example `/etc/printcap` file for the printer `teak` that we introduced earlier; we enabled header pages and added the above output filter:

```
#
#  /etc/printcap for host orchid
#
teak|hp|laserjet|Hewlett Packard LaserJet 3Si:\
        :lp=/dev/lpt0:sd=/var/spool/lpd/teak:mx#0:\
        :if=/usr/local/libexec/hpif:\
        :vf=/usr/local/libexec/hpvf:\
        :of=/usr/local/libexec/hpof:
```

Now, when users print jobs to `teak`, they get a header page with each job. If users want to spend time searching for their printouts, they can suppress header pages by submitting the job with `lpr -h`; see the Header Page Options section for more lpr(1) options.

> **Note: LPD** prints a form feed character after the header page. If your printer uses a different character or sequence of characters to eject a page, specify them with the `ff` capability in `/etc/printcap`.

Controlling Header Pages

By enabling header pages, **LPD** will produce a *long header*, a full page of large letters identifying the user, host, and job. Here is an example (kelly printed the job named outline from host `rose`):

```
k                      ll      ll
k                       l       l
k                       l       l
k   k      eeee         l       l      y     y
k  k     e    e         l       l      y     y
k k      eeeeee         l       l      y     y
kk k     e              l       l      y     y
k   k    e    e         l       l      y    yy
k    k    eeee         111     111      yyy y
                                           y
                                        y    y
                                        yyyy


                        11
```

```
                          t          l          i
                          t          l
          oooo    u    u  ttttt      l          ii     n nnn      eeee
           o   o  u    u    t        l          i      nn  n     e    e
           o   o  u    u    t        l          i      n    n    eeeeee
           o   o  u    u    t        l          i      n    n    e
           o   o  u   uu    t  t      l          i      n    n    e    e
          oooo    uuu  u      tt    lll        iii    n    n      eeee
```

```
     r rrr      oooo      ssss      eeee
     rr   r    o    o    s    s    e    e
     r         o    o     ss       eeeeee
     r         o    o       ss     e
     r         o    o    s    s    e    e
     r          oooo      ssss      eeee
```

```
                              Job:   outline
                              Date:  Sun Sep 17 11:04:58 1995
```

LPD appends a form feed after this text so the job starts on a new page (unless you have `sf` (suppress form feeds) in the destination printer's entry in `/etc/printcap`).

If you prefer, **LPD** can make a *short header*; specify `sb` (short banner) in the `/etc/printcap` file. The header page will look like this:

```
     rose:kelly  Job: outline  Date: Sun Sep 17 11:07:51 1995
```

Also by default, **LPD** prints the header page first, then the job. To reverse that, specify `hl` (header last) in `/etc/printcap`.

Accounting for Header Pages

Using **LPD**'s built-in header pages enforces a particular paradigm when it comes to printer accounting: header pages must be *free of charge*.

Why?

Because the output filter is the only external program that will have control when the header page is printed that could do accounting, and it is not provided with any *user or host* information or an accounting file, so it has no idea whom to charge for printer use. It is also not enough to just "add one page" to the text filter or any of the conversion filters (which do have user and host information) since users can suppress header pages with `lpr -h`. They could still be charged for header pages they did not print. Basically, `lpr -h` will be the preferred option of environmentally-minded users, but you cannot offer any incentive to use it.

It is *still not enough* to have each of the filters generate their own header pages (thereby being able to charge for them). If users wanted the option of suppressing the header pages with `lpr -h`, they will still get them and be charged for them since **LPD** does not pass any knowledge of the `-h` option to any of the filters.

So, what are your options?

You can:

- Accept **LPD**'s paradigm and make header pages free.
- Install an alternative to **LPD**, such as **LPRng**. Section Alternatives to the Standard Spooler tells more about other spooling software you can substitute for **LPD**.
- Write a *smart* output filter. Normally, an output filter is not meant to do anything more than initialize a printer or do some simple character conversion. It is suited for header pages and plain text jobs (when there is no text (input) filter). But, if there is a text filter for the plain text jobs, then **LPD** will start the output filter only for the header pages. And the output filter can parse the header page text that **LPD** generates to determine what user and host to charge for the header page. The only other problem with this method is that the output filter still does not know what accounting file to use (it is not passed the name of the file from the `af` capability), but if you have a well-known accounting file, you can hard-code that into the output filter. To facilitate the parsing step, use the `sh` (short header) capability in `/etc/printcap`. Then again, all that might be too much trouble, and users will certainly appreciate the more generous system administrator who makes header pages free.

Header Pages on PostScript Printers

As described above, **LPD** can generate a plain text header page suitable for many printers. Of course, PostScript cannot directly print plain text, so the header page feature of **LPD** is useless—or mostly so.

One obvious way to get header pages is to have every conversion filter and the text filter generate the header page. The filters should use the user and host arguments to generate a suitable header page. The drawback of this method is that users will always get a header page, even if they submit jobs with `lpr -h`.

Let us explore this method. The following script takes three arguments (user login name, host name, and job name) and makes a simple PostScript header page:

```
#!/bin/sh
#
#   make-ps-header - make a PostScript header page on stdout
#   Installed in /usr/local/libexec/make-ps-header
#

#
#   These are PostScript units (72 to the inch).  Modify for A4 or
```

```
#   whatever size paper you are using:
#
page_width=612
page_height=792
border=72


#
#   Check arguments
#
if [ $# -ne 3 ]; then
    echo "Usage: `basename $0` <user> <host> <job>" 1>&2
    exit 1
fi


#
#   Save these, mostly for readability in the PostScript, below.
#
user=$1
host=$2
job=$3
date=`date`


#
#   Send the PostScript code to stdout.
#
exec cat <<EOF
%!PS


%
%   Make sure we do not interfere with user's job that will follow
%
save


%
%   Make a thick, unpleasant border around the edge of the paper.
%
$border $border moveto
$page_width $border 2 mul sub 0 rlineto
0 $page_height $border 2 mul sub rlineto
currentscreen 3 -1 roll pop 100 3 1 roll setscreen
$border 2 mul $page_width sub 0 rlineto closepath
0.8 setgray 10 setlinewidth stroke 0 setgray


%
%   Display user's login name, nice and large and prominent
%
/Helvetica-Bold findfont 64 scalefont setfont
$page_width ($user) stringwidth pop sub 2 div $page_height 200 sub moveto
($user) show


%
```

```
%  Now show the boring particulars
%
/Helvetica findfont 14 scalefont setfont
/y 200 def
[ (Job:) (Host:) (Date:) ] {
200 y moveto show /y y 18 sub def }
forall

/Helvetica-Bold findfont 14 scalefont setfont
/y 200 def
[ ($job) ($host) ($date) ] {
        270 y moveto show /y y 18 sub def
} forall

%
% That is it
%
restore
showpage
EOF
```

Now, each of the conversion filters and the text filter can call this script to first generate the header page, and then print the user's job. Here is the DVI conversion filter from earlier in this document, modified to make a header page:

```
#!/bin/sh
#
#  psdf - DVI to PostScript printer filter
#  Installed in /usr/local/libexec/psdf
#
#  Invoked by lpd when user runs lpr -d
#

orig_args="$@"

fail() {
    echo "$@" 1>&2
    exit 2
}

while getopts "x:y:n:h:" option; do
    case $option in
        x|y)  ;; # Ignore
        n)    login=$OPTARG ;;
        h)    host=$OPTARG ;;
        *)    echo "LPD started `basename $0` wrong." 1>&2
              exit 2
              ;;
    esac
done

[ "$login" ] || fail "No login name"
```

```
[ "$host" ] || fail "No host name"

( /usr/local/libexec/make-ps-header $login $host "DVI File"
  /usr/local/bin/dvips -f ) | eval /usr/local/libexec/lprps $orig_args
```

Notice how the filter has to parse the argument list in order to determine the user and host name. The parsing for the other conversion filters is identical. The text filter takes a slightly different set of arguments, though (see section How Filters Work).

As we have mentioned before, the above scheme, though fairly simple, disables the "suppress header page" option (the -h option) to lpr. If users wanted to save a tree (or a few pennies, if you charge for header pages), they would not be able to do so, since every filter's going to print a header page with every job.

To allow users to shut off header pages on a per-job basis, you will need to use the trick introduced in section Accounting for Header Pages: write an output filter that parses the LPD-generated header page and produces a PostScript version. If the user submits the job with lpr -h, then **LPD** will not generate a header page, and neither will your output filter. Otherwise, your output filter will read the text from **LPD** and send the appropriate header page PostScript code to the printer.

If you have a PostScript printer on a serial line, you can make use of lprps, which comes with an output filter, psof, which does the above. Note that psof does not charge for header pages.

11.4.3 Networked Printing

FreeBSD supports networked printing: sending jobs to remote printers. Networked printing generally refers to two different things:

- Accessing a printer attached to a remote host. You install a printer that has a conventional serial or parallel interface on one host. Then, you set up **LPD** to enable access to the printer from other hosts on the network. Section Printers Installed on Remote Hosts tells how to do this.

- Accessing a printer attached directly to a network. The printer has a network interface in addition (or in place of) a more conventional serial or parallel interface. Such a printer might work as follows:

  - It might understand the **LPD** protocol and can even queue jobs from remote hosts. In this case, it acts just like a regular host running **LPD**. Follow the same procedure in section Printers Installed on Remote Hosts to set up such a printer.

  - It might support a data stream network connection. In this case, you "attach" the printer to one host on the network by making that host responsible for spooling jobs and sending them to the printer. Section Printers with Networked Data Stream Interfaces gives some suggestions on installing such printers.

Printers Installed on Remote Hosts

The **LPD** spooling system has built-in support for sending jobs to other hosts also running **LPD** (or are compatible with **LPD**). This feature enables you to install a printer on one host and make it accessible from other hosts. It also works with printers that have network interfaces that understand the **LPD** protocol.

To enable this kind of remote printing, first install a printer on one host, the *printer host*, using the simple printer setup described in the Simple Printer Setup section. Do any advanced setup in Advanced Printer Setup that you need. Make sure to test the printer and see if it works with the features of **LPD** you have enabled. Also ensure that the *local host* has authorization to use the **LPD** service in the *remote host* (see Restricting Jobs from Remote Printers).

If you are using a printer with a network interface that is compatible with **LPD**, then the *printer host* in the discussion below is the printer itself, and the *printer name* is the name you configured for the printer. See the documentation that accompanied your printer and/or printer-network interface.

> **Tip:** If you are using a Hewlett Packard Laserjet then the printer name `text` will automatically perform the LF to CRLF conversion for you, so you will not require the `hpif` script.

Then, on the other hosts you want to have access to the printer, make an entry in their `/etc/printcap` files with the following:

1. Name the entry anything you want. For simplicity, though, you probably want to use the same name and aliases as on the printer host.

2. Leave the `lp` capability blank, explicitly (`:lp=:`).

3. Make a spooling directory and specify its location in the `sd` capability. **LPD** will store jobs here before they get sent to the printer host.

4. Place the name of the printer host in the `rm` capability.

5. Place the printer name on the *printer host* in the `rp` capability.

That is it. You do not need to list conversion filters, page dimensions, or anything else in the `/etc/printcap` file.

Here is an example. The host `rose` has two printers, `bamboo` and `rattan`. We will enable users on the host `orchid` to print to those printers. Here is the `/etc/printcap` file for `orchid` (back from section Enabling Header Pages). It already had the entry for the printer `teak`; we have added entries for the two printers on the host `rose`:

```
#
#  /etc/printcap for host orchid - added (remote) printers on rose
#

#
#  teak is local; it is connected directly to orchid:
#
teak|hp|laserjet|Hewlett Packard LaserJet 3Si:\
        :lp=/dev/lpt0:sd=/var/spool/lpd/teak:mx#0:\
        :if=/usr/local/libexec/ifhp:\
        :vf=/usr/local/libexec/vfhp:\
        :of=/usr/local/libexec/ofhp:

#
#  rattan is connected to rose; send jobs for rattan to rose:
#
```

```
rattan|line|diablo|lp|Diablo 630 Line Printer:\
        :lp=:rm=rose:rp=rattan:sd=/var/spool/lpd/rattan:

#
#  bamboo is connected to rose as well:
#
bamboo|ps|PS|S|panasonic|Panasonic KX-P4455 PostScript v51.4:\
        :lp=:rm=rose:rp=bamboo:sd=/var/spool/lpd/bamboo:
```

Then, we just need to make spooling directories on `orchid`:

```
# mkdir -p /var/spool/lpd/rattan /var/spool/lpd/bamboo
# chmod 770 /var/spool/lpd/rattan /var/spool/lpd/bamboo
# chown daemon:daemon /var/spool/lpd/rattan /var/spool/lpd/bamboo
```

Now, users on `orchid` can print to `rattan` and `bamboo`. If, for example, a user on `orchid` typed

```
% lpr -P bamboo -d sushi-review.dvi
```

the **LPD** system on `orchid` would copy the job to the spooling directory `/var/spool/lpd/bamboo` and note that it was a DVI job. As soon as the host `rose` has room in its `bamboo` spooling directory, the two **LPDs** would transfer the file to `rose`. The file would wait in `rose`'s queue until it was finally printed. It would be converted from DVI to PostScript (since `bamboo` is a PostScript printer) on `rose`.

Printers with Networked Data Stream Interfaces

Often, when you buy a network interface card for a printer, you can get two versions: one which emulates a spooler (the more expensive version), or one which just lets you send data to it as if you were using a serial or parallel port (the cheaper version). This section tells how to use the cheaper version. For the more expensive one, see the previous section Printers Installed on Remote Hosts.

The format of the `/etc/printcap` file lets you specify what serial or parallel interface to use, and (if you are using a serial interface), what baud rate, whether to use flow control, delays for tabs, conversion of newlines, and more. But there is no way to specify a connection to a printer that is listening on a TCP/IP or other network port.

To send data to a networked printer, you need to develop a communications program that can be called by the text and conversion filters. Here is one such example: the script `netprint` takes all data on standard input and sends it to a network-attached printer. We specify the hostname of the printer as the first argument and the port number to which to connect as the second argument to `netprint`. Note that this supports one-way communication only (FreeBSD to printer); many network printers support two-way communication, and you might want to take advantage of that (to get printer status, perform accounting, etc.).

```
#!/usr/bin/perl
#
#  netprint - Text filter for printer attached to network
#  Installed in /usr/local/libexec/netprint
#
$#ARGV eq 1 || die "Usage: $0 <printer-hostname> <port-number>";

$printer_host = $ARGV[0];
```

```
$printer_port = $ARGV[1];

require 'sys/socket.ph';

($ignore, $ignore, $protocol) = getprotobyname('tcp');
($ignore, $ignore, $ignore, $ignore, $address)
    = gethostbyname($printer_host);

$sockaddr = pack('S n a4 x8', &AF_INET, $printer_port, $address);

socket(PRINTER, &PF_INET, &SOCK_STREAM, $protocol)
    || die "Can't create TCP/IP stream socket: $!";
connect(PRINTER, $sockaddr) || die "Can't contact $printer_host: $!";
while (<STDIN>) { print PRINTER; }
exit 0;
```

We can then use this script in various filters. Suppose we had a Diablo 750-N line printer connected to the network. The printer accepts data to print on port number 5100. The host name of the printer is scrivener. Here is the text filter for the printer:

```
#!/bin/sh
#
#  diablo-if-net - Text filter for Diablo printer 'scrivener' listening
#  on port 5100.  Installed in /usr/local/libexec/diablo-if-net
#
exec /usr/libexec/lpr/lpf "$@" | /usr/local/libexec/netprint scrivener 5100
```

11.4.4 Restricting Printer Usage

This section gives information on restricting printer usage. The **LPD** system lets you control who can access a printer, both locally or remotely, whether they can print multiple copies, how large their jobs can be, and how large the printer queues can get.

Restricting Multiple Copies

The **LPD** system makes it easy for users to print multiple copies of a file. Users can print jobs with lpr -#5 (for example) and get five copies of each file in the job. Whether this is a good thing is up to you.

If you feel multiple copies cause unnecessary wear and tear on your printers, you can disable the -# option to lpr(1) by adding the sc capability to the /etc/printcap file. When users submit jobs with the -# option, they will see:

```
lpr: multiple copies are not allowed
```

Note that if you have set up access to a printer remotely (see section Printers Installed on Remote Hosts), you need the sc capability on the remote /etc/printcap files as well, or else users will still be able to submit multiple-copy jobs by using another host.

Here is an example. This is the `/etc/printcap` file for the host `rose`. The printer `rattan` is quite hearty, so we will allow multiple copies, but the laser printer `bamboo` is a bit more delicate, so we will disable multiple copies by adding the `sc` capability:

```
#
#   /etc/printcap for host rose - restrict multiple copies on bamboo
#
rattan|line|diablo|lp|Diablo 630 Line Printer:\
        :sh:sd=/var/spool/lpd/rattan:\
        :lp=/dev/lpt0:\
        :if=/usr/local/libexec/if-simple:

bamboo|ps|PS|S|panasonic|Panasonic KX-P4455 PostScript v51.4:\
        :sh:sd=/var/spool/lpd/bamboo:sc:\
        :lp=/dev/ttyd5:fs#0x82000e1:xs#0x820:rw:\
        :if=/usr/local/libexec/psif:\
        :df=/usr/local/libexec/psdf:
```

Now, we also need to add the `sc` capability on the host `orchid`'s `/etc/printcap` (and while we are at it, let us disable multiple copies for the printer `teak`):

```
#
#   /etc/printcap for host orchid - no multiple copies for local
#   printer teak or remote printer bamboo
teak|hp|laserjet|Hewlett Packard LaserJet 3Si:\
        :lp=/dev/lpt0:sd=/var/spool/lpd/teak:mx#0:sc:\
        :if=/usr/local/libexec/ifhp:\
        :vf=/usr/local/libexec/vfhp:\
        :of=/usr/local/libexec/ofhp:

rattan|line|diablo|lp|Diablo 630 Line Printer:\
        :lp=:rm=rose:rp=rattan:sd=/var/spool/lpd/rattan:

bamboo|ps|PS|S|panasonic|Panasonic KX-P4455 PostScript v51.4:\
        :lp=:rm=rose:rp=bamboo:sd=/var/spool/lpd/bamboo:sc:
```

By using the `sc` capability, we prevent the use of `lpr -#`, but that still does not prevent users from running lpr(1) multiple times, or from submitting the same file multiple times in one job like this:

```
% lpr forsale.sign forsale.sign forsale.sign forsale.sign forsale.sign
```

There are many ways to prevent this abuse (including ignoring it) which you are free to explore.

Restricting Access To Printers

You can control who can print to what printers by using the Unix group mechanism and the `rg` capability in `/etc/printcap`. Just place the users you want to have access to a printer in a certain group, and then name that group in the `rg` capability.

Users outside the group (including root) will be greeted with `lpr: Not a member of the restricted group` if they try to print to the controlled printer.

As with the `sc` (suppress multiple copies) capability, you need to specify `rg` on remote hosts that also have access to your printers, if you feel it is appropriate (see section Printers Installed on Remote Hosts).

For example, we will let anyone access the printer `rattan`, but only those in group `artists` can use `bamboo`. Here is the familiar `/etc/printcap` for host `rose`:

```
#
#   /etc/printcap for host rose - restricted group for bamboo
#
rattan|line|diablo|lp|Diablo 630 Line Printer:\
        :sh:sd=/var/spool/lpd/rattan:\
        :lp=/dev/lpt0:\
        :if=/usr/local/libexec/if-simple:

bamboo|ps|PS|S|panasonic|Panasonic KX-P4455 PostScript v51.4:\
        :sh:sd=/var/spool/lpd/bamboo:sc:rg=artists:\
        :lp=/dev/ttyd5:fs#0x82000e1:xs#0x820:rw:\
        :if=/usr/local/libexec/psif:\
        :df=/usr/local/libexec/psdf:
```

Let us leave the other example `/etc/printcap` file (for the host `orchid`) alone. Of course, anyone on `orchid` can print to `bamboo`. It might be the case that we only allow certain logins on `orchid` anyway, and want them to have access to the printer. Or not.

Note: There can be only one restricted group per printer.

Controlling Sizes of Jobs Submitted

If you have many users accessing the printers, you probably need to put an upper limit on the sizes of the files users can submit to print. After all, there is only so much free space on the filesystem that houses the spooling directories, and you also need to make sure there is room for the jobs of other users.

LPD enables you to limit the maximum byte size a file in a job can be with the `mx` capability. The units are in BUFSIZ blocks, which are 1024 bytes. If you put a zero for this capability, there will be no limit on file size; however, if no `mx` capability is specified, then a default limit of 1000 blocks will be used.

Note: The limit applies to *files* in a job, and *not* the total job size.

LPD will not refuse a file that is larger than the limit you place on a printer. Instead, it will queue as much of the file up to the limit, which will then get printed. The rest will be discarded. Whether this is correct behavior is up for debate.

Let us add limits to our example printers `rattan` and `bamboo`. Since those artists' PostScript files tend to be large, we will limit them to five megabytes. We will put no limit on the plain text line printer:

```
#
#  /etc/printcap for host rose
#

#
#  No limit on job size:
#
rattan|line|diablo|lp|Diablo 630 Line Printer:\
        :sh:mx#0:sd=/var/spool/lpd/rattan:\
        :lp=/dev/lpt0:\
        :if=/usr/local/libexec/if-simple:

#
#  Limit of five megabytes:
#
bamboo|ps|PS|S|panasonic|Panasonic KX-P4455 PostScript v51.4:\
        :sh:sd=/var/spool/lpd/bamboo:sc:rg=artists:mx#5000:\
        :lp=/dev/ttyd5:fs#0x82000e1:xs#0x820:rw:\
        :if=/usr/local/libexec/psif:\
        :df=/usr/local/libexec/psdf:
```

Again, the limits apply to the local users only. If you have set up access to your printers remotely, remote users will not get those limits. You will need to specify the `mx` capability in the remote `/etc/printcap` files as well. See section Printers Installed on Remote Hosts for more information on remote printing.

There is another specialized way to limit job sizes from remote printers; see section Restricting Jobs from Remote Printers.

Restricting Jobs from Remote Printers

The **LPD** spooling system provides several ways to restrict print jobs submitted from remote hosts:

Host restrictions

> You can control from which remote hosts a local **LPD** accepts requests with the files `/etc/hosts.equiv` and `/etc/hosts.lpd`. **LPD** checks to see if an incoming request is from a host listed in either one of these files. If not, **LPD** refuses the request.
>
> The format of these files is simple: one host name per line. Note that the file `/etc/hosts.equiv` is also used by the ruserok(3) protocol, and affects programs like rsh(1) and rcp(1), so be careful.
>
> For example, here is the `/etc/hosts.lpd` file on the host `rose`:
>
> ```
> orchid
> violet
> madrigal.fishbaum.de
> ```

This means `rose` will accept requests from the hosts `orchid`, `violet`, and `madrigal.fishbaum.de`. If any other host tries to access `rose`'s **LPD**, the job will be refused.

Size restrictions

You can control how much free space there needs to remain on the filesystem where a spooling directory resides. Make a file called `minfree` in the spooling directory for the local printer. Insert in that file a number representing how many disk blocks (512 bytes) of free space there has to be for a remote job to be accepted.

This lets you insure that remote users will not fill your filesystem. You can also use it to give a certain priority to local users: they will be able to queue jobs long after the free disk space has fallen below the amount specified in the `minfree` file.

For example, let us add a `minfree` file for the printer `bamboo`. We examine `/etc/printcap` to find the spooling directory for this printer; here is `bamboo`'s entry:

```
bamboo|ps|PS|S|panasonic|Panasonic KX-P4455 PostScript v51.4:\
        :sh:sd=/var/spool/lpd/bamboo:sc:rg=artists:mx#5000:\
        :lp=/dev/ttyd5:fs#0x82000e1:xs#0x820:rw:mx#5000:\
        :if=/usr/local/libexec/psif:\
        :df=/usr/local/libexec/psdf:
```

The spooling directory is given in the `sd` capability. We will make three megabytes (which is 6144 disk blocks) the amount of free disk space that must exist on the filesystem for **LPD** to accept remote jobs:

```
# echo 6144 > /var/spool/lpd/bamboo/minfree
```

User restrictions

You can control which remote users can print to local printers by specifying the `rs` capability in `/etc/printcap`. When `rs` appears in the entry for a locally-attached printer, **LPD** will accept jobs from remote hosts *if* the user submitting the job also has an account of the same login name on the local host. Otherwise, **LPD** refuses the job.

This capability is particularly useful in an environment where there are (for example) different departments sharing a network, and some users transcend departmental boundaries. By giving them accounts on your systems, they can use your printers from their own departmental systems. If you would rather allow them to use *only* your printers and not your computer resources, you can give them "token" accounts, with no home directory and a useless shell like `/usr/bin/false`.

11.4.5 Accounting for Printer Usage

So, you need to charge for printouts. And why not? Paper and ink cost money. And then there are maintenance costs—printers are loaded with moving parts and tend to break down. You have examined your printers, usage patterns, and maintenance fees and have come up with a per-page (or per-foot, per-meter, or per-whatever) cost. Now, how do you actually start accounting for printouts?

Well, the bad news is the **LPD** spooling system does not provide much help in this department. Accounting is highly dependent on the kind of printer in use, the formats being printed, and *your* requirements in charging for printer usage.

To implement accounting, you have to modify a printer's text filter (to charge for plain text jobs) and the conversion filters (to charge for other file formats), to count pages or query the printer for pages printed. You cannot get away with using the simple output filter, since it cannot do accounting. See section Filters.

Generally, there are two ways to do accounting:

- *Periodic accounting* is the more common way, possibly because it is easier. Whenever someone prints a job, the filter logs the user, host, and number of pages to an accounting file. Every month, semester, year, or whatever time period you prefer, you collect the accounting files for the various printers, tally up the pages printed by users, and charge for usage. Then you truncate all the logging files, starting with a clean slate for the next period.

- *Timely accounting* is less common, probably because it is more difficult. This method has the filters charge users for printouts as soon as they use the printers. Like disk quotas, the accounting is immediate. You can prevent users from printing when their account goes in the red, and might provide a way for users to check and adjust their "print quotas." But this method requires some database code to track users and their quotas.

The **LPD** spooling system supports both methods easily: since you have to provide the filters (well, most of the time), you also have to provide the accounting code. But there is a bright side: you have enormous flexibility in your accounting methods. For example, you choose whether to use periodic or timely accounting. You choose what information to log: user names, host names, job types, pages printed, square footage of paper used, how long the job took to print, and so forth. And you do so by modifying the filters to save this information.

Quick and Dirty Printer Accounting

FreeBSD comes with two programs that can get you set up with simple periodic accounting right away. They are the text filter `lpf`, described in section lpf: a Text Filter, and pac(8), a program to gather and total entries from printer accounting files.

As mentioned in the section on filters (Filters), **LPD** starts the text and the conversion filters with the name of the accounting file to use on the filter command line. The filters can use this argument to know where to write an accounting file entry. The name of this file comes from the `af` capability in `/etc/printcap`, and if not specified as an absolute path, is relative to the spooling directory.

LPD starts `lpf` with page width and length arguments (from the `pw` and `pl` capabilities). `lpf` uses these arguments to determine how much paper will be used. After sending the file to the printer, it then writes an accounting entry in the accounting file. The entries look like this:

```
2.00  rose:andy
3.00  rose:kelly
3.00  orchid:mary
5.00  orchid:mary
2.00  orchid:zhang
```

You should use a separate accounting file for each printer, as `lpf` has no file locking logic built into it, and two `lpfs` might corrupt each other's entries if they were to write to the same file at the same time. An easy way to insure a separate accounting file for each printer is to use `af=acct` in `/etc/printcap`. Then, each accounting file will be in the spooling directory for a printer, in a file named `acct`.

When you are ready to charge users for printouts, run the pac(8) program. Just change to the spooling directory for the printer you want to collect on and type `pac`. You will get a dollar-centric summary like the following:

```
    Login           pages/feet    runs      price
orchid:kelly              5.00      1     $   0.10
orchid:mary             31.00      3     $   0.62
orchid:zhang             9.00      1     $   0.18
rose:andy                2.00      1     $   0.04
rose:kelly             177.00    104     $   3.54
rose:mary              87.00      32     $   1.74
rose:root              26.00      12     $   0.52

total                  337.00    154     $   6.74
```

These are the arguments pac(8) expects:

`-Pprinter`

> Which `printer` to summarize. This option works only if there is an absolute path in the `af` capability in `/etc/printcap`.

`-c`

> Sort the output by cost instead of alphabetically by user name.

`-m`

> Ignore host name in the accounting files. With this option, user `smith` on host `alpha` is the same user `smith` on host `gamma`. Without, they are different users.

`-pprice`

> Compute charges with `price` dollars per page or per foot instead of the price from the `pc` capability in `/etc/printcap`, or two cents (the default). You can specify `price` as a floating point number.

`-r`

> Reverse the sort order.

`-s`

> Make an accounting summary file and truncate the accounting file.

`name ...`

> Print accounting information for the given user `names` only.

In the default summary that pac(8) produces, you see the number of pages printed by each user from various hosts. If, at your site, host does not matter (because users can use any host), run pac -m, to produce the following summary:

```
    Login           pages/feet    runs      price
andy                     2.00      1     $   0.04
kelly                  182.00    105     $   3.64
mary                   118.00     35     $   2.36
```

```
root                       26.00   12   $   0.52
zhang                       9.00    1   $   0.18

total                     337.00  154   $   6.74
```

To compute the dollar amount due, pac(8) uses the `pc` capability in the `/etc/printcap` file (default of 200, or 2 cents per page). Specify, in hundredths of cents, the price per page or per foot you want to charge for printouts in this capability. You can override this value when you run pac(8) with the `-p` option. The units for the `-p` option are in dollars, though, not hundredths of cents. For example,

```
# pac -p1.50
```

makes each page cost one dollar and fifty cents. You can really rake in the profits by using this option.

Finally, running `pac -s` will save the summary information in a summary accounting file, which is named the same as the printer's accounting file, but with `_sum` appended to the name. It then truncates the accounting file. When you run pac(8) again, it rereads the summary file to get starting totals, then adds information from the regular accounting file.

How Can You Count Pages Printed?

In order to perform even remotely accurate accounting, you need to be able to determine how much paper a job uses. This is the essential problem of printer accounting.

For plain text jobs, the problem is not that hard to solve: you count how many lines are in a job and compare it to how many lines per page your printer supports. Do not forget to take into account backspaces in the file which overprint lines, or long logical lines that wrap onto one or more additional physical lines.

The text filter `lpf` (introduced in lpf: a Text Filter) takes into account these things when it does accounting. If you are writing a text filter which needs to do accounting, you might want to examine `lpf`'s source code.

How do you handle other file formats, though?

Well, for DVI-to-LaserJet or DVI-to-PostScript conversion, you can have your filter parse the diagnostic output of `dvilj` or `dvips` and look to see how many pages were converted. You might be able to do similar things with other file formats and conversion programs.

But these methods suffer from the fact that the printer may not actually print all those pages. For example, it could jam, run out of toner, or explode—and the user would still get charged.

So, what can you do?

There is only one *sure* way to do *accurate* accounting. Get a printer that can tell you how much paper it uses, and attach it via a serial line or a network connection. Nearly all PostScript printers support this notion. Other makes and models do as well (networked Imagen laser printers, for example). Modify the filters for these printers to get the page usage after they print each job and have them log accounting information based on that value *only*. There is no line counting nor error-prone file examination required.

Of course, you can always be generous and make all printouts free.

11.5 Using Printers

This section tells you how to use printers you have setup with FreeBSD. Here is an overview of the user-level commands:

lpr(1)

> Print jobs

lpq(1)

> Check printer queues

lprm(1)

> Remove jobs from a printer's queue

There is also an administrative command, lpc(8), described in the section Administrating the **LPD** Spooler, used to control printers and their queues.

All three of the commands lpr(1), lprm(1), and lpq(1) accept an option `-P printer-name` to specify on which printer/queue to operate, as listed in the `/etc/printcap` file. This enables you to submit, remove, and check on jobs for various printers. If you do not use the `-P` option, then these commands use the printer specified in the `PRINTER` environment variable. Finally, if you do not have a `PRINTER` environment variable, these commands default to the printer named `lp`.

Hereafter, the terminology *default printer* means the printer named in the `PRINTER` environment variable, or the printer named `lp` when there is no `PRINTER` environment variable.

11.5.1 Printing Jobs

To print files, type:

```
% lpr filename ...
```

This prints each of the listed files to the default printer. If you list no files, lpr(1) reads data to print from standard input. For example, this command prints some important system files:

```
% lpr /etc/host.conf /etc/hosts.equiv
```

To select a specific printer, type:

```
% lpr -P printer-name filename ...
```

This example prints a long listing of the current directory to the printer named `rattan`:

```
% ls -l | lpr -P rattan
```

Because no files were listed for the lpr(1) command, `lpr` read the data to print from standard input, which was the output of the `ls -l` command.

The lpr(1) command can also accept a wide variety of options to control formatting, apply file conversions, generate multiple copies, and so forth. For more information, see the section Printing Options.

11.5.2 Checking Jobs

When you print with lpr(1), the data you wish to print is put together in a package called a "print job", which is sent to the **LPD** spooling system. Each printer has a queue of jobs, and your job waits in that queue along with other jobs from yourself and from other users. The printer prints those jobs in a first-come, first-served order.

To display the queue for the default printer, type lpq(1). For a specific printer, use the -P option. For example, the command

```
% lpq -P bamboo
```

shows the queue for the printer named bamboo. Here is an example of the output of the lpq command:

```
bamboo is ready and printing
Rank   Owner   Job  Files                          Total Size
active kelly   9    /etc/host.conf, /etc/hosts.equiv  88 bytes
2nd    kelly   10   (standard input)               1635 bytes
3rd    mary    11   ...                            78519 bytes
```

This shows three jobs in the queue for bamboo. The first job, submitted by user kelly, got assigned "job number" 9. Every job for a printer gets a unique job number. Most of the time you can ignore the job number, but you will need it if you want to cancel the job; see section Removing Jobs for details.

Job number nine consists of two files; multiple files given on the lpr(1) command line are treated as part of a single job. It is the currently active job (note the word active under the "Rank" column), which means the printer should be currently printing that job. The second job consists of data passed as the standard input to the lpr(1) command. The third job came from user mary; it is a much larger job. The pathname of the file she is trying to print is too long to fit, so the lpq(1) command just shows three dots.

The very first line of the output from lpq(1) is also useful: it tells what the printer is currently doing (or at least what **LPD** thinks the printer is doing).

The lpq(1) command also support a -l option to generate a detailed long listing. Here is an example of lpq -l:

```
waiting for bamboo to become ready (offline ?)
kelly: 1st  [job 009rose]
       /etc/host.conf                73 bytes
       /etc/hosts.equiv              15 bytes

kelly: 2nd  [job 010rose]
       (standard input)              1635 bytes

mary: 3rd                           [job 011rose]
      /home/orchid/mary/research/venus/alpha-regio/mapping 78519 bytes
```

11.5.3 Removing Jobs

If you change your mind about printing a job, you can remove the job from the queue with the lprm(1) command. Often, you can even use lprm(1) to remove an active job, but some or all of the job might still get printed.

To remove a job from the default printer, first use lpq(1) to find the job number. Then type:

```
% lprm job-number
```

To remove the job from a specific printer, add the -P option. The following command removes job number 10 from the queue for the printer bamboo:

```
% lprm -P bamboo 10
```

The lprm(1) command has a few shortcuts:

lprm -

> Removes all jobs (for the default printer) belonging to you.

lprm *user*

> Removes all jobs (for the default printer) belonging to *user*. The superuser can remove other users' jobs; you can remove only your own jobs.

lprm

> With no job number, user name, or - appearing on the command line, lprm(1) removes the currently active job on the default printer, if it belongs to you. The superuser can remove any active job.

Just use the -P option with the above shortcuts to operate on a specific printer instead of the default. For example, the following command removes all jobs for the current user in the queue for the printer named rattan:

```
% lprm -P rattan -
```

Note: If you are working in a networked environment, lprm(1) will let you remove jobs only from the host from which the jobs were submitted, even if the same printer is available from other hosts. The following command sequence demonstrates this:

```
% lpr -P rattan myfile
% rlogin orchid
% lpq -P rattan
Rank    Owner    Job  Files                    Total Size
active  seeyan   12 ...                        49123 bytes
2nd     kelly     13   myfile                      12 bytes
% lprm -P rattan 13
rose: Permission denied
% logout
% lprm -P rattan 13
dfA013rose dequeued
cfA013rose dequeued
```

11.5.4 Beyond Plain Text: Printing Options

The lpr(1) command supports a number of options that control formatting text, converting graphic and other file formats, producing multiple copies, handling of the job, and more. This section describes the options.

Formatting and Conversion Options

The following lpr(1) options control formatting of the files in the job. Use these options if the job does not contain plain text or if you want plain text formatted through the pr(1) utility.

For example, the following command prints a DVI file (from the TeX typesetting system) named `fish-report.dvi` to the printer named `bamboo`:

```
% lpr -P bamboo -d fish-report.dvi
```

These options apply to every file in the job, so you cannot mix (say) DVI and ditroff files together in a job. Instead, submit the files as separate jobs, using a different conversion option for each job.

> **Note:** All of these options except `-p` and `-T` require conversion filters installed for the destination printer. For example, the `-d` option requires the DVI conversion filter. Section Conversion Filters gives details.

`-c`

Print cifplot files.

`-d`

Print DVI files.

`-f`

Print FORTRAN text files.

`-g`

Print plot data.

`-i` *number*

Indent the output by *number* columns; if you omit *number*, indent by 8 columns. This option works only with certain conversion filters.

> **Note:** Do not put any space between the `-i` and the number.

`-l`

Print literal text data, including control characters.

`-n`

> Print ditroff (device independent troff) data.

`-p`

> Format plain text with pr(1) before printing. See pr(1) for more information.

`-T` *title*

> Use *title* on the pr(1) header instead of the file name. This option has effect only when used with the `-p` option.

`-t`

> Print troff data.

`-v`

> Print raster data.

Here is an example: this command prints a nicely formatted version of the ls(1) manual page on the default printer:

```
% zcat /usr/share/man/man1/ls.1.gz | troff -t -man | lpr -t
```

The zcat(1) command uncompresses the source of the ls(1) manual page and passes it to the troff(1) command, which formats that source and makes GNU troff output and passes it to lpr(1), which submits the job to the **LPD** spooler. Because we used the `-t` option to lpr(1), the spooler will convert the GNU troff output into a format the default printer can understand when it prints the job.

Job Handling Options

The following options to lpr(1) tell **LPD** to handle the job specially:

`-#` *copies*

> Produce a number of *copies* of each file in the job instead of just one copy. An administrator may disable this option to reduce printer wear-and-tear and encourage photocopier usage. See section Restricting Multiple Copies.
>
> This example prints three copies of `parser.c` followed by three copies of `parser.h` to the default printer:
>
> ```
> % lpr -#3 parser.c parser.h
> ```

`-m`

> Send mail after completing the print job. With this option, the **LPD** system will send mail to your account when it finishes handling your job. In its message, it will tell you if the job completed successfully or if there was an error, and (often) what the error was.

-s

Do not copy the files to the spooling directory, but make symbolic links to them instead.

If you are printing a large job, you probably want to use this option. It saves space in the spooling directory (your job might overflow the free space on the filesystem where the spooling directory resides). It saves time as well since **LPD** will not have to copy each and every byte of your job to the spooling directory.

There is a drawback, though: since **LPD** will refer to the original files directly, you cannot modify or remove them until they have been printed.

> **Note:** If you are printing to a remote printer, **LPD** will eventually have to copy files from the local host to the remote host, so the -s option will save space only on the local spooling directory, not the remote. It is still useful, though.

-r

Remove the files in the job after copying them to the spooling directory, or after printing them with the -s option. Be careful with this option!

Header Page Options

These options to lpr(1) adjust the text that normally appears on a job's header page. If header pages are suppressed for the destination printer, these options have no effect. See section Header Pages for information about setting up header pages.

-C *text*

Replace the hostname on the header page with *text*. The hostname is normally the name of the host from which the job was submitted.

-J *text*

Replace the job name on the header page with *text*. The job name is normally the name of the first file of the job, or stdin if you are printing standard input.

-h

Do not print any header page.

> **Note:** At some sites, this option may have no effect due to the way header pages are generated. See Header Pages for details.

11.5.5 Administrating Printers

As an administrator for your printers, you have had to install, set up, and test them. Using the lpc(8) command, you can interact with your printers in yet more ways. With lpc(8), you can

- Start and stop the printers
- Enable and disable their queues
- Rearrange the order of the jobs in each queue.

First, a note about terminology: if a printer is *stopped*, it will not print anything in its queue. Users can still submit jobs, which will wait in the queue until the printer is *started* or the queue is cleared.

If a queue is *disabled*, no user (except root) can submit jobs for the printer. An *enabled* queue allows jobs to be submitted. A printer can be *started* for a disabled queue, in which case it will continue to print jobs in the queue until the queue is empty.

In general, you have to have root privileges to use the lpc(8) command. Ordinary users can use the lpc(8) command to get printer status and to restart a hung printer only.

Here is a summary of the lpc(8) commands. Most of the commands take a `printer-name` argument to tell on which printer to operate. You can use `all` for the `printer-name` to mean all printers listed in `/etc/printcap`.

`abort printer-name`

> Cancel the current job and stop the printer. Users can still submit jobs if the queue is enabled.

`clean printer-name`

> Remove old files from the printer's spooling directory. Occasionally, the files that make up a job are not properly removed by **LPD**, particularly if there have been errors during printing or a lot of administrative activity. This command finds files that do not belong in the spooling directory and removes them.

`disable printer-name`

> Disable queuing of new jobs. If the printer is running, it will continue to print any jobs remaining in the queue. The superuser (root) can always submit jobs, even to a disabled queue.
>
> This command is useful while you are testing a new printer or filter installation: disable the queue and submit jobs as root. Other users will not be able to submit jobs until you complete your testing and re-enable the queue with the `enable` command.

`down printer-name message`

> Take a printer down. Equivalent to `disable` followed by `stop`. The `message` appears as the printer's status whenever a user checks the printer's queue with lpq(1) or status with `lpc status`.

`enable printer-name`

> Enable the queue for a printer. Users can submit jobs but the printer will not print anything until it is started.

`help` `command-name`

> Print help on the command `command-name`. With no `command-name`, print a summary of the commands available.

`restart` `printer-name`

> Start the printer. Ordinary users can use this command if some extraordinary circumstance hangs **LPD**, but they cannot start a printer stopped with either the `stop` or `down` commands. The `restart` command is equivalent to `abort` followed by `start`.

`start` `printer-name`

> Start the printer. The printer will print jobs in its queue.

`stop` `printer-name`

> Stop the printer. The printer will finish the current job and will not print anything else in its queue. Even though the printer is stopped, users can still submit jobs to an enabled queue.

`topq` `printer-name job-or-username`

> Rearrange the queue for `printer-name` by placing the jobs with the listed `job` numbers or the jobs belonging to `username` at the top of the queue. For this command, you cannot use `all` as the `printer-name`.

`up` `printer-name`

> Bring a printer up; the opposite of the `down` command. Equivalent to `start` followed by `enable`.

lpc(8) accepts the above commands on the command line. If you do not enter any commands, lpc(8) enters an interactive mode, where you can enter commands until you type `exit`, `quit`, or end-of-file.

11.6 Alternatives to the Standard Spooler

If you have been reading straight through this manual, by now you have learned just about everything there is to know about the **LPD** spooling system that comes with FreeBSD. You can probably appreciate many of its shortcomings, which naturally leads to the question: "What other spooling systems are out there (and work with FreeBSD)?"

LPRng

> **LPRng**, which purportedly means "LPR: the Next Generation" is a complete rewrite of PLP. Patrick Powell and Justin Mason (the principal maintainer of PLP) collaborated to make **LPRng**. The main site for **LPRng** is `http://www.astart.com/lprng/LPRng.html`.

11.7 Troubleshooting

After performing the simple test with lptest(1), you might have gotten one of the following results instead of the correct printout:

It worked, after awhile; or, it did not eject a full sheet.

The printer printed the above, but it sat for awhile and did nothing. In fact, you might have needed to press a PRINT REMAINING or FORM FEED button on the printer to get any results to appear.

If this is the case, the printer was probably waiting to see if there was any more data for your job before it printed anything. To fix this problem, you can have the text filter send a FORM FEED character (or whatever is necessary) to the printer. This is usually sufficient to have the printer immediately print any text remaining in its internal buffer. It is also useful to make sure each print job ends on a full sheet, so the next job does not start somewhere on the middle of the last page of the previous job.

The following replacement for the shell script `/usr/local/libexec/if-simple` prints a form feed after it sends the job to the printer:

```
#!/bin/sh
#
# if-simple - Simple text input filter for lpd
# Installed in /usr/local/libexec/if-simple
#
# Simply copies stdin to stdout.  Ignores all filter arguments.
# Writes a form feed character (\f) after printing job.

/bin/cat && printf "\f" && exit 0
exit 2
```

It produced the "staircase effect."

You got the following on paper:

```
!"#$%&'()*+,-./01234
         "#$%&'()*+,-./012345
                  #$%&'()*+,-./0123456
```

You have become another victim of the *staircase effect*, caused by conflicting interpretations of what characters should indicate a new line. Unix-style operating systems use a single character: ASCII code 10, the line feed (LF). MS-DOS, OS/2, and others uses a pair of characters, ASCII code 10 *and* ASCII code 13 (the carriage return or CR). Many printers use the MS-DOS convention for representing new-lines.

When you print with FreeBSD, your text used just the line feed character. The printer, upon seeing a line feed character, advanced the paper one line, but maintained the same horizontal position on the page for the next character to print. That is what the carriage return is for: to move the location of the next character to print to the left edge of the paper.

Here is what FreeBSD wants your printer to do:

Printer received CR	Printer prints CR
Printer received LF	Printer prints CR + LF

Here are some ways to achieve this:

- Use the printer's configuration switches or control panel to alter its interpretation of these characters. Check your printer's manual to find out how to do this.

> **Note:** If you boot your system into other operating systems besides FreeBSD, you may have to *reconfigure* the printer to use a an interpretation for CR and LF characters that those other operating systems use. You might prefer one of the other solutions, below.

- Have FreeBSD's serial line driver automatically convert LF to CR+LF. Of course, this works with printers on serial ports *only*. To enable this feature, set the CRMOD bit in fs capability in the /etc/printcap file for the printer.

- Send an *escape code* to the printer to have it temporarily treat LF characters differently. Consult your printer's manual for escape codes that your printer might support. When you find the proper escape code, modify the text filter to send the code first, then send the print job.

  Here is an example text filter for printers that understand the Hewlett-Packard PCL escape codes. This filter makes the printer treat LF characters as a LF and CR; then it sends the job; then it sends a form feed to eject the last page of the job. It should work with nearly all Hewlett Packard printers.

```
#!/bin/sh
#
# hpif - Simple text input filter for lpd for HP-PCL based printers
# Installed in /usr/local/libexec/hpif
#
# Simply copies stdin to stdout.  Ignores all filter arguments.
# Tells printer to treat LF as CR+LF.  Ejects the page when done.

printf "\033&k2G" && cat && printf "\033&l0H" && exit 0
exit 2
```

  Here is an example /etc/printcap from a host called orchid. It has a single printer attached to its first parallel port, a Hewlett Packard LaserJet 3Si named teak. It is using the above script as its text filter:

```
#
#  /etc/printcap for host orchid
#
teak|hp|laserjet|Hewlett Packard LaserJet 3Si:\
        :lp=/dev/lpt0:sh:sd=/var/spool/lpd/teak:mx#0:\
        :if=/usr/local/libexec/hpif:
```

It overprinted each line.

The printer never advanced a line. All of the lines of text were printed on top of each other on one line.

This problem is the "opposite" of the staircase effect, described above, and is much rarer. Somewhere, the LF characters that FreeBSD uses to end a line are being treated as CR characters to return the print location to the left edge of the paper, but not also down a line.

Use the printer's configuration switches or control panel to enforce the following interpretation of LF and CR characters:

Printer receives	Printer prints
CR	CR
LF	CR + LF

The printer lost characters.

While printing, the printer did not print a few characters in each line. The problem might have gotten worse as the printer ran, losing more and more characters.

The problem is that the printer cannot keep up with the speed at which the computer sends data over a serial line (this problem should not occur with printers on parallel ports). There are two ways to overcome the problem:

- If the printer supports XON/XOFF flow control, have FreeBSD use it by specifying the TANDEM bit in the `fs` capability.

- If the printer supports carrier flow control, specify the MDMBUF bit in the `fs` capability. Make sure the cable connecting the printer to the computer is correctly wired for carrier flow control.

- If the printer does not support any flow control, use some combination of the NLDELAY, TBDELAY, CRDELAY, VTDELAY, and BSDELAY bits in the `fs` capability to add appropriate delays to the stream of data sent to the printer.

It printed garbage.

The printer printed what appeared to be random garbage, but not the desired text.

This is usually another symptom of incorrect communications parameters with a serial printer. Double-check the bps rate in the `br` capability, and the parity bits in the `fs` and `fc` capabilities; make sure the printer is using the same settings as specified in the `/etc/printcap` file.

Nothing happened.

If nothing happened, the problem is probably within FreeBSD and not the hardware. Add the log file (`lf`) capability to the entry for the printer you are debugging in the `/etc/printcap` file. For example, here is the entry for `rattan`, with the `lf` capability:

```
rattan|line|diablo|lp|Diablo 630 Line Printer:\
        :sh:sd=/var/spool/lpd/rattan:\
        :lp=/dev/lpt0:\
        :if=/usr/local/libexec/if-simple:\
        :lf=/var/log/rattan.log
```

Then, try printing again. Check the log file (in our example, `/var/log/rattan.log`) to see any error messages that might appear. Based on the messages you see, try to correct the problem.

If you do not specify a `lf` capability, **LPD** uses `/dev/console` as a default.

Chapter 12
Storage

12.1 Synopsis

This chapter covers the use of disks in FreeBSD. This includes memory-backed disks, network-attached disks, and standard SCSI/IDE storage devices.

After reading this chapter, you will know:

- The terminology FreeBSD uses to describe the organization of data on a physical disk (partitions and slices).
- How to mount and unmount filesystems.
- How to add additional hard disks to your system.
- How to setup virtual filesystems, such as memory disks.
- How to use quotas to limit disk space usage.
- How to create and burn CDs and DVDs on FreeBSD.
- The various storage media options for backups.
- How to use backup programs available under FreeBSD.
- How to backup to floppy disks.

12.2 Device Names

The following is a list of physical storage devices supported in FreeBSD, and the device names associated with them.

Table 12-1. Physical Disk Naming Conventions

Drive type	Drive device name
IDE hard drives	`ad`
IDE CDROM drives	`acd`
SCSI hard drives and USB Mass storage devices	`da`
SCSI CDROM drives	`cd`
Assorted non-standard CDROM drives	`mcd` for Mitsumi CD-ROM, `scd` for Sony CD-ROM, `matcd` for Matsushita/Panasonic CD-ROM

Drive type	Drive device name
Floppy drives	`fd`
SCSI tape drives	`sa`
IDE tape drives	`ast`
Flash drives	`fla` for DiskOnChip Flash device
RAID drives	`myxd` for Mylex, and `amrd` for AMI MegaRAID, `idad` for Compaq Smart RAID.

12.3 Adding Disks

Lets say we want to add a new SCSI disk to a machine that currently only has a single drive. First turn off the computer and install the drive in the computer following the instructions of the computer, controller, and drive manufacturer. Due to the wide variations of procedures to do this, the details are beyond the scope of this document.

Login as user `root`. After you have installed the drive, inspect `/var/run/dmesg.boot` to ensure the new disk was found. Continuing with our example, the newly added drive will be `da1` and we want to mount it on `/1` (if you are adding an IDE drive, the device name will be `wd1` in pre-4.0 systems, or `ad1` in most 4.X systems).

Because FreeBSD runs on IBM-PC compatible computers, it must take into account the PC BIOS partitions. These are different from the traditional BSD partitions. A PC disk has up to four BIOS partition entries. If the disk is going to be truly dedicated to FreeBSD, you can use the *dedicated* mode. Otherwise, FreeBSD will have to live within one of the PC BIOS partitions. FreeBSD calls the PC BIOS partitions *slices* so as not to confuse them with traditional BSD partitions. You may also use slices on a disk that is dedicated to FreeBSD, but used in a computer that also has another operating system installed. This is to not confuse the `fdisk` utility of the other operating system.

In the slice case the drive will be added as `/dev/da1s1e`. This is read as: SCSI disk, unit number 1 (second SCSI disk), slice 1 (PC BIOS partition 1), and `e` BSD partition. In the dedicated case, the drive will be added simply as `/dev/da1e`.

12.3.1 Using sysinstall(8)

1. Navigating **Sysinstall**

   You may use `/stand/sysinstall` to partition and label a new disk using its easy to use menus. Either login as user `root` or use the `su` command. Run `/stand/sysinstall` and enter the `Configure` menu. Within the `FreeBSD Configuration Menu`, scroll down and select the `Partition` item. Next you should be presented with a list of hard drives installed in your system. If you do not see `da1` listed, you need to recheck your physical installation and `dmesg` output in the file `/var/run/dmesg.boot`.

2. FDISK Partition Editor

   Select `da1` to enter the `FDISK Partition Editor`. Type **A** to use the entire disk for FreeBSD. When asked if you want to "remain cooperative with any future possible operating systems", answer `YES`. Write the changes to the disk using **W**. Now exit the FDISK editor by typing **q**. Next you will be asked about the Master Boot Record. Since you are adding a disk to an already running system, choose `None`.

3. Disk Label Editor

Next, **Sysinstall** will enter the `Disk Label Editor`. This is where you will create the traditional BSD partitions. A disk can have up to eight partitions, labeled `a-h`. A few of the partition labels have special uses. The `a` partition is used for the root partition (`/`). Thus only your system disk (e.g, the disk you boot from) should have an `a` partition. The `b` partition is used for swap partitions, and you may have many disks with swap partitions. The `c` partition addresses the entire disk in dedicated mode, or the entire FreeBSD slice in slice mode. The other partitions are for general use.

Sysinstall's Label editor favors the `e` partition for non-root, non-swap partitions. Within the Label editor, create a single file system by typing **C**. When prompted if this will be a FS (file system) or swap, choose `FS` and type in a mount point (e.g, `/mnt`). When adding a disk in post-install mode, **Sysinstall** will not create entries in `/etc/fstab` for you, so the mount point you specify is not important.

You are now ready to write the new label to the disk and create a file system on it. Do this by typing **W**. Ignore any errors from **Sysinstall** that it could not mount the new partition. Exit the Label Editor and **Sysinstall** completely.

4. Finish

The last step is to edit `/etc/fstab` to add an entry for your new disk.

12.3.2 Using Command Line Utilities

Using Slices

This setup will allow your disk to work correctly with other operating systems that might be installed on your computer and will not confuse other operating systems' `fdisk` utilities. It is recommended to use this method for new disk installs. Only use `dedicated` mode if you have a good reason to do so!

```
# dd if=/dev/zero of=/dev/rda1 bs=1k count=1
# fdisk -BI da1 #Initialize your new disk
# disklabel -B -w -r da1s1 auto #Label it.
# disklabel -e da1s1 # Edit the disklabel just created and add any partitions.
# mkdir -p /1
# newfs /dev/da1s1e # Repeat this for every partition you created.
# mount -t ufs /dev/da1s1e /1 # Mount the partition(s)
# vi /etc/fstab # Add the appropriate entry/entries to your /etc/fstab.
```

If you have an IDE disk, substitute `ad` for `da`. On pre-4.X systems use `wd`.

Dedicated

If you will not be sharing the new drive with another operating system, you may use the `dedicated` mode. Remember this mode can confuse Microsoft operating systems; however, no damage will be done by them. IBM's OS/2 however, will "appropriate" any partition it finds which it doesn't understand.

```
# dd if=/dev/zero of=/dev/rda1 bs=1k count=1
# disklabel -Brw da1 auto
# disklabel -e da1 # create the 'e' partition
```

```
# newfs -d0 /dev/rda1e
# mkdir -p /1
# vi /etc/fstab # add an entry for /dev/da1e
# mount /1
```

An alternate method is:

```
# dd if=/dev/zero of=/dev/rda1 count=2
# disklabel /dev/rda1 | disklabel -BrR da1 /dev/stdin
# newfs /dev/rda1e
# mkdir -p /1
# vi /etc/fstab # add an entry for /dev/da1e
# mount /1
```

12.4 Network, Memory, and File-Based Filesystems

Aside from the disks you physically insert into your computer: floppies, CDs, hard drives, and so forth; other forms of disks are understood by FreeBSD - the *virtual disks*.

These include network filesystems such as the Network Filesystem and Coda, memory-based filesystems such as md and file-backed filesystems created by vnconfig or `mdconfig`.

12.4.1 vnconfig: File-Backed Filesystem

vnconfig(8) configures and enables vnode pseudo-disk devices. A *vnode* is a representation of a file, and is the focus of file activity. This means that vnconfig(8) uses files to create and operate a filesystem. One possible use is the mounting of floppy or CD images kept in files.

To mount an existing filesystem image:

Example 12-1. Using vnconfig to mount an Existing Filesystem Image

```
# vnconfig vn0 diskimage
# mount /dev/vn0c /mnt
```

To create a new filesystem image with vnconfig:

Example 12-2. Creating a New File-Backed Disk with vnconfig

```
# dd if=/dev/zero of=newimage bs=1k count=5k
5120+0 records in
5120+0 records out
# vnconfig -s labels -c vn0 newimage
# disklabel -r -w vn0 auto
# newfs vn0c
```

```
Warning: 2048 sector(s) in last cylinder unallocated
/dev/rvn0c:    10240 sectors in 3 cylinders of 1 tracks, 4096 sectors
        5.0MB in 1 cyl groups (16 c/g, 32.00MB/g, 1280 i/g)
super-block backups (for fsck -b #) at:
 32
# mount /dev/vn0c /mnt
# df /mnt
Filesystem  1K-blocks     Used    Avail Capacity  Mounted on
/dev/vn0c        4927        1     4532      0%   /mnt
```

12.4.2 md: Memory Filesystem

md is a simple, efficient means to create memory filesystems.

Simply take a filesystem you have prepared with, for example, vnconfig(8), and:

Example 12-3. md Memory Disk

```
# dd if=newimage of=/dev/md0
5120+0 records in
5120+0 records out
# mount /dev/md0c /mnt
# df /mnt
Filesystem  1K-blocks     Used    Avail Capacity  Mounted on
/dev/md0c        4927        1     4532      0%   /mnt
```

12.5 File System Quotas

Quotas are an optional feature of the operating system that allow you to limit the amount of disk space and/or the number of files a user or members of a group may allocate on a per-file system basis. This is used most often on timesharing systems where it is desirable to limit the amount of resources any one user or group of users may allocate. This will prevent one user or group of users from consuming all of the available disk space.

12.5.1 Configuring Your System to Enable Disk Quotas

Before attempting to use disk quotas, it is necessary to make sure that quotas are configured in your kernel. This is done by adding the following line to your kernel configuration file:

```
options QUOTA
```

The stock GENERIC kernel does not have this enabled by default, so you will have to configure, build and install a custom kernel in order to use disk quotas. Please refer to Chapter 9 for more information on kernel configuration.

Next you will need to enable disk quotas in /etc/rc.conf. This is done by adding the line:

```
enable_quotas="YES"
```

For finer control over your quota startup, there is an additional configuration variable available. Normally on bootup, the quota integrity of each file system is checked by the `quotacheck` program. The `quotacheck` facility insures that the data in the quota database properly reflects the data on the file system. This is a very time consuming process that will significantly affect the time your system takes to boot. If you would like to skip this step, a variable in `/etc/rc.conf` is made available for the purpose:

```
check_quotas="NO"
```

If you are running FreeBSD prior to 3.2-RELEASE, the configuration is simpler, and consists of only one variable. Set the following in your `/etc/rc.conf`:

```
check_quotas="YES"
```

Finally you will need to edit `/etc/fstab` to enable disk quotas on a per-file system basis. This is where you can either enable user or group quotas or both for all of your file systems.

To enable per-user quotas on a file system, add the `userquota` option to the options field in the `/etc/fstab` entry for the file system you want to enable quotas on. For example:

```
/dev/da1s2g   /home    ufs rw,userquota 1 2
```

Similarly, to enable group quotas, use the `groupquota` option instead of `userquota`. To enable both user and group quotas, change the entry as follows:

```
/dev/da1s2g   /home    ufs rw,userquota,groupquota 1 2
```

By default, the quota files are stored in the root directory of the file system with the names `quota.user` and `quota.group` for user and group quotas respectively. See fstab(5) for more information. Even though the fstab(5) manual page says that you can specify an alternate location for the quota files, this is not recommended because the various quota utilities do not seem to handle this properly.

At this point you should reboot your system with your new kernel. `/etc/rc` will automatically run the appropriate commands to create the initial quota files for all of the quotas you enabled in `/etc/fstab`, so there is no need to manually create any zero length quota files.

In the normal course of operations you should not be required to run the `quotacheck`, `quotaon`, or `quotaoff` commands manually. However, you may want to read their manual pages just to be familiar with their operation.

12.5.2 Setting Quota Limits

Once you have configured your system to enable quotas, verify that they really are enabled. An easy way to do this is to run:

```
# quota -v
```

You should see a one line summary of disk usage and current quota limits for each file system that quotas are enabled on.

You are now ready to start assigning quota limits with the `edquota` command.

You have several options on how to enforce limits on the amount of disk space a user or group may allocate, and how many files they may create. You may limit allocations based on disk space (block quotas) or number of files (inode quotas) or a combination of both. Each of these limits are further broken down into two categories: hard and soft limits.

A hard limit may not be exceeded. Once a user reaches his hard limit he may not make any further allocations on the file system in question. For example, if the user has a hard limit of 500 blocks on a file system and is currently using 490 blocks, the user can only allocate an additional 10 blocks. Attempting to allocate an additional 11 blocks will fail.

Soft limits, on the other hand, can be exceeded for a limited amount of time. This period of time is known as the grace period, which is one week by default. If a user stays over his or her soft limit longer than the grace period, the soft limit will turn into a hard limit and no further allocations will be allowed. When the user drops back below the soft limit, the grace period will be reset.

The following is an example of what you might see when you run the `edquota` command. When the `edquota` command is invoked, you are placed into the editor specified by the EDITOR environment variable, or in the `vi` editor if the EDITOR variable is not set, to allow you to edit the quota limits.

```
# edquota -u test

Quotas for user test:
/usr: blocks in use: 65, limits (soft = 50, hard = 75)
        inodes in use: 7, limits (soft = 50, hard = 60)
/usr/var: blocks in use: 0, limits (soft = 50, hard = 75)
        inodes in use: 0, limits (soft = 50, hard = 60)
```

You will normally see two lines for each file system that has quotas enabled. One line for the block limits, and one line for inode limits. Simply change the value you want updated to modify the quota limit. For example, to raise this user's block limit from a soft limit of 50 and a hard limit of 75 to a soft limit of 500 and a hard limit of 600, change:

```
/usr: blocks in use: 65, limits (soft = 50, hard = 75)
```

to:

```
 /usr: blocks in use: 65, limits (soft = 500, hard = 600)
```

The new quota limits will be in place when you exit the editor.

Sometimes it is desirable to set quota limits on a range of uids. This can be done by use of the `-p` option on the `edquota` command. First, assign the desired quota limit to a user, and then run `edquota -p protouser startuid-enduid`. For example, if user `test` has the desired quota limits, the following command can be used to duplicate those quota limits for uids 10,000 through 19,999:

```
# edquota -p test 10000-19999
```

For more information see edquota(8).

12.5.3 Checking Quota Limits and Disk Usage

You can use either the `quota` or the `repquota` commands to check quota limits and disk usage. The `quota` command can be used to check individual user or group quotas and disk usage. A user may only examine his own quota, and the quota of a group he is a member of. Only the super-user may view all user and group quotas. The `repquota` command can be used to get a summary of all quotas and disk usage for file systems with quotas enabled.

The following is some sample output from the `quota -v` command for a user that has quota limits on two file systems.

```
Disk quotas for user test (uid 1002):
    Filesystem blocks   quota   limit   grace   files   quota   limit   grace
          /usr    65*      50      75   5days       7      50      60
      /usr/var      0      50      75               0      50      60
```

On the `/usr` file system in the above example, this user is currently 15 blocks over the soft limit of 50 blocks and has 5 days of the grace period left. Note the asterisk * which indicates that the user is currently over his quota limit.

Normally file systems that the user is not using any disk space on will not show up in the output from the `quota` command, even if he has a quota limit assigned for that file system. The `-v` option will display those file systems, such as the `/usr/var` file system in the above example.

12.5.4 Quotas over NFS

Quotas are enforced by the quota subsystem on the NFS server. The rpc.rquotad(8) daemon makes quota information available to the quota(1) command on NFS clients, allowing users on those machines to see their quota statistics.

Enable `rpc.rquotad` in `/etc/inetd.conf` like so:

```
rquotad/1      dgram rpc/udp wait root /usr/libexec/rpc.rquotad rpc.rquotad
```

Now restart `inetd`:

```
# kill -HUP `cat /var/run/inetd.pid`
```

12.6 Creating and Using Optical Media (CDs & DVDs)

12.6.1 Introduction

CDs have a number of features that differentiate them from conventional disks. Initially, they were not writable by the user. They are designed so that they can be read continuously without delays to move the head between tracks. They are also much easier to transport between systems than similarly sized media were at the time.

CDs do have tracks, but this refers to a section of data to be read continuously and not a physical property of the disk. To produce a CD on FreeBSD, you prepare the data files that are going to make up the tracks on the CD, then write the tracks to the CD.

The ISO 9660 file system was designed to deal with these differences. It unfortunately codifies file system limits that were common then. Fortunately, it provides an extension mechanism that allows properly written CDs to exceed those limits while still working with systems that do not support those extensions.

The mkisofs program is used to produce a data file containing an ISO 9660 file system. It has options that support various extensions, and is described below. You can install it with the sysutils/mkisofs port.

Which tool to use to burn the CD depends on whether your CD burner is ATAPI or something else. ATAPI CD burners use the burncd program that is part of the base system. SCSI and USB CD burners should use cdrecord from the sysutils/cdrtools port.

burncd has a limited number of supported drives. To find out if a drive is supported, see CD-R/RW supported drives[1].

12.6.2 mkisofs

mkisofs produces an ISO 9660 file system that is an image of a directory tree in the Unix file system name space. The simplest usage is:

```
# mkisofs -o imagefile.iso /path/to/tree
```

This command will create an *imagefile* containing an ISO 9660 file system that is a copy of the tree at */path/to/tree*. In the process, it will map the file names to names that fit the limitations of the standard ISO 9660 file system, and will exclude files that have names uncharacteristic of ISO file systems.

A number of options are available to overcome those restrictions. In particular, -R enables the Rock Ridge extensions common to Unix systems, -J enables Joliet extensions used by Microsoft systems, and -hfs can be used to create HFS file systems used by MacOS.

For CDs that are going to be used only on FreeBSD systems, -U can be used to disable all filename restrictions. When used with -R, it produces a file system image that is identical to the FreeBSD tree you started from, though it may violate the ISO 9660 standard in a number of ways.

The last option of general use is -b. This is used to specify the location of the boot image for use in producing an "El Torito" bootable CD. This option takes an argument which is the path to a boot image from the top of the tree being written to the CD. So, given that /tmp/myboot holds a bootable FreeBSD system with the boot image in /tmp/myboot/boot/cdboot, you could produce the image of an ISO 9660 file system in /tmp/bootable.iso like so:

```
# mkisofs -U -R -b boot/cdboot -o /tmp/bootable.iso /tmp/myboot
```

Having done that, if you have vn configured in your kernel, you can mount the file system with:

```
# vnconfig -e vn0c /tmp/bootable.iso
# mount -t cd9660 /dev/vn0c /mnt
```

At which point you can verify that /mnt and /tmp/myboot are identical.

There are many other options you can use with mkisofs to fine-tune its behavior. In particular: modifications to an ISO 9660 layout and the creation of Joilet and HFS discs. See the mkisofs(8) manual page for details.

---

1 http://freebsd.dk/ata/

12.6.3 burncd

If you have an ATAPI CD burner, you can use the `burncd` command to burn an ISO image onto a CD. `burncd` is part of the base system, installed as `/usr/sbin/burncd`. Usage is very simple, as it has few options:

```
# burncd -f cddevice data imagefile.iso fixate
```

Will burn a copy of *imagefile.iso* on *cddevice*. The default device is `/dev/acd0c`. See burncd(8) for options to set the write speed, eject the CD after burning, and write audio data.

12.6.4 cdrecord

If you do not have an ATAPI CD burner, you will have to use `cdrecord` to burn your CDs. `cdrecord` is not part of the base system; you must install it from either the port at `sysutils/cdrtools` or the appropriate package. Changes to the base system can cause binary versions of this program to fail, possibly resulting in a "coaster". You should therefore either upgrade the port when you upgrade your system, or if you are tracking -STABLE, upgrade the port when a new version becomes available.

While `cdrecord` has many options, basic usage is even simpler than `burncd`. Burning an ISO 9660 image is done with:

```
# cdrecord dev=device imagefile.iso
```

The tricky part of using `cdrecord` is finding the `dev` to use. To find the proper setting, use the `-scanbus` flag of `cdrecord`, which might produce results like this:

```
# cdrecord -scanbus
Cdrecord 1.9 (i386-unknown-freebsd4.2) Copyright (C) 1995-2000 Jörg Schilling
Using libscg version 'schily-0.1'
scsibus0:
        0,0,0     0) 'SEAGATE ' 'ST39236LW       ' '0004' Disk
        0,1,0     1) 'SEAGATE ' 'ST39173W        ' '5958' Disk
        0,2,0     2) *
        0,3,0     3) 'iomega  ' 'jaz 1GB         ' 'J.86' Removable Disk
        0,4,0     4) 'NEC     ' 'CD-ROM DRIVE:466' '1.26' Removable CD-ROM
        0,5,0     5) *
        0,6,0     6) *
        0,7,0     7) *
scsibus1:
        1,0,0   100) *
        1,1,0   101) *
        1,2,0   102) *
        1,3,0   103) *
        1,4,0   104) *
        1,5,0   105) 'YAMAHA  ' 'CRW4260         ' '1.0q' Removable CD-ROM
        1,6,0   106) 'ARTEC   ' 'AM12S           ' '1.06' Scanner
        1,7,0   107) *
```

This lists the appropriate `dev` value for the devices on the list. Locate your CD burner, and use the three numbers separated by commas as the value for `dev`. In this case, the CRW device is 1,5,0, so the appropriate input would be **dev=1,5,0**. There are easier ways to specify this value; see cdrecord(1) for details. That is also the place to look for information on writing audio tracks, controlling the speed, and other things.

12.7 ccd (Concatenated Disk Configuration)

It seems like today everyone has a collection of multimedia files. Everything from mp3's to video clips. I've converted most of my audio CDROM collection to mp3's so I can have all of my music in one centralized location, and not have to hunt down the audio CD with that one song I got stuck in my head. The problem I was faced with is where to store all these files?

When choosing a mass storage solution, the most important factors to consider are speed, reliability, and cost. It is very rare to have all three in favor, normally a fast, reliable mass storage device is expensive, and to cut back on cost either speed or reliability must be sacrificed. In designing my system, I ranked the requirements by most favorable to least favorable. In this situation, cost was the biggest factor. I needed a lot of storage for a reasonable price. The next factor, speed, is not quite as important, since most of the usage would be over a one hundred megabit switched Ethernet, and that would most likely be the bottleneck. The ability to spread the file input/output operations out over several disks would be more than enough speed for this network. Finally, the consideration of reliability was an easy one to answer. All of the data being put on this mass storage device was already backed up on CD-R's. This drive was primarily here for online live storage for easy access, so if a drive went bad, I could just replace it, rebuild the filesystem, and copy back the data from CD-R's.

To sum it up, I need something that will give me the most amount of storage space for my money. The cost of large IDE disks are cheap these days. I found a place that was selling Western Digital 30.7gb 5400 RPM IDE disks for about one-hundred and thirty US dollars. I bought three of them, giving me approximately ninety gigabytes of online storage.

12.7.1 Installing the Hardware

I installed the hard drives in a system that already had one IDE disk in as the system disk. The ideal solution would be for each IDE disk to have its own IDE controller and cable, but without fronting more costs to acquire a dual IDE controller this wouldn't be a possibility. So, I jumpered two disks as slaves, and one as master. One went on the first IDE controller as a slave to the system disk, and the other two where slave/master on the secondary IDE controller.

Upon reboot, the system BIOS was configured to automatically detect the disks attached. More importantly, FreeBSD detected them on reboot:

```
ad0: 19574MB <WDC WD205BA> [39770/16/63] at ata0-master UDMA33
ad1: 29333MB <WDC WD307AA> [59598/16/63] at ata0-slave UDMA33
ad2: 29333MB <WDC WD307AA> [59598/16/63] at ata1-master UDMA33
ad3: 29333MB <WDC WD307AA> [59598/16/63] at ata1-slave UDMA33
```

At this point, if FreeBSD doesn't detect the disks, be sure that you have jumpered them correctly. I have heard numerous reports with problems using cable select instead of true slave/master configuration.

The next consideration was how to attach them as part of the filesystem. I did a little research on vinum(8)[2] and FreeBSD's ccd(4). In this particular configuration, ccd(4) appeared to be a better choice mainly because it has fewer parts. Less parts tends to indicate less chance of breakage. Vinum appears to be a bit of an overkill for my needs.

12.7.2 Setting up the CCD

CCD allows me to take several identical disks and concatenate them into one logical filesystem. In order to use **ccd**, I need a kernel with **ccd** support built into it. I added this line to my kernel configuration file and rebuilt the kernel:

```
pseudo-device   ccd     4
```

ccd support can also be loaded as a kernel loadable module in FreeBSD 4.0 or later.

To set up **ccd**, first I need to disklabel the disks. Here's how I disklabeled them:

```
disklabel -r -w ad1 auto
disklabel -r -w ad2 auto
disklabel -r -w ad3 auto
```

This created a disklabel ad1c, ad2c and ad3c that spans the entire disk.

The next step is to change the disklabel type. To do that I had to edit the disklabel:

```
disklabel -e ad1
disklabel -e ad2
disklabel -e ad3
```

This opened up the current disklabel on each disk respectively in whatever editor the EDITOR environment variable was set to, in my case, vi(1). Inside the editor I had a section like this:

```
8 partitions:
#        size   offset    fstype   [fsize bsize bps/cpg]
  c: 60074784       0    unused        0     0     0   # (Cyl.    0 - 59597)
```

I needed to add a new "e" partition for ccd(4) to use. This usually can be copied of the "c" partition, but the fstype must be **4.2BSD**. Once I was done, my disklabel should look like this:

```
8 partitions:
#        size   offset    fstype   [fsize bsize bps/cpg]
  c: 60074784       0    unused        0     0     0   # (Cyl.    0 - 59597)
  e: 60074784       0    4.2BSD        0     0     0   # (Cyl.    0 - 59597)
```

12.7.3 Building the Filesystem

Now that I have all of the disks labeled, I needed to build the **ccd**. To do that, I used a utility called ccdconfig(8). ccdconfig takes several arguments, the first argument being the device to configure, in this case, /dev/ccd0c. The device node for ccd0c may not exist yet, so to create it, perform the following commands:

---

2 http://www.vinumvm.org

```
cd /dev
sh MAKEDEV ccd0
```

The next argument `ccdconfig` expects is the interleave for the filesystem. The interleave defines the size of a stripe in disk blocks, normally five hundred and twelve bytes. So, an interleave of thirty-two would be sixteen thousand three hundred and eighty-four bytes.

After the interleave comes the flags for `ccdconfig`. If you want to enable drive mirroring, you can specify a flag here. In this configuration, I am not mirroring the **ccd**, so I left it as zero.

The final arguments to `ccdconfig` are the devices to place into the array. Putting it all together I get this command:

```
ccdconfig ccd0 32 0 /dev/ad1e /dev/ad2e /dev/ad3e
```

This configures the **ccd**. I can now newfs(8) the filesystem.

```
newfs /dev/ccd0c
```

12.7.4 Making It All Automagic

Finally, if I want to be able to mount the **ccd**, I need to configure it first. I write out my current configuration to `/etc/ccd.conf` using the following command:

```
ccdconfig -g > /etc/ccd.conf
```

When I reboot, the script `/etc/rc` runs `ccdconfig -C` if /etc/ccd.conf exists. This automatically configures the **ccd** so it can be mounted.

If you are booting into single user mode, before you can mount the **ccd**, you need to issue the following command to configure the array:

```
ccdconfig -C
```

Then, we need an entry for the **ccd** in `/etc/fstab` so it will be mounted at boot time.

```
/dev/ccd0c              /media      ufs     rw     2      2
```

12.8 Bootstrapping Vinum: A Foundation for Reliable Servers

In the most abstract sense, these instructions show how to build a pair of disk drives where either one is adequate to keep your server running if the other fails. Life is better if they are both working, but your server will never die unless both disk drives die at once. If you choose ATAPI drives and use a fairly generic kernel, you can be confident that either of these drives can be plugged into most any main board to produce a working server in a pinch. The drives need not be identical. These techniques work equally well with SCSI drives as they do with ATAPI, but I will focus on

ATAPI here because main boards with this interface are ubiquitous. After building the foundation of a reliable server as shown here, you can expand to as many disk drives as necessary to build the failure-resilient server of your dreams.

12.8.1 Introduction

Any machine that is going to provide reliable service needs to have either redundant components on-line or a pool of off-line spares that can be promptly swapped in. Commodity PC hardware makes it affordable for even small organizations to have some spare parts available that could be pressed into service following the failure of production equipment. In many organizations, a failed power supply, NIC, memory, or main board could easily be swapped with a standby in a matter of minutes and be ready to return to production work.

If a disk drive fails, however, it often has to be restored from a tape backup. This may take many hours. With disk drive capacities rising faster than tape drive capacities, the time needed to restore a failed disk drive seems to increase as technology progresses.

Vinum is a volume manager for FreeBSD that provides a standard block I/O layer interface to the file system code just as any hardware device driver would. It works by managing partitions of type `vinum` and allows you to subdivide and group the space in such partitions into logical devices called *volumes* that can be used in the same way as disk partitions. Volumes can be configured for resilience, performance, or both. Experienced system administrators will immediately recognize the benefits of being able to configure each file system to match the way it is most often used.

In some ways, **Vinum** is similar to ccd(4), but it is far more flexible and robust in the face of failures. It is only slightly more difficult to set up than ccd(4). ccd(4) may meet your needs if you are only interested in concatenation.

Terminology

Discussion of storage management can get very tricky simply because of the terminology involved. As we will see below, the terms *disk*, *slice*, *partition*, *subdisk*, and *volume* each refer to different things that present the same interface to a kernel function like swapping. The potential for confusion is compounded because the objects that these terms represent can be nested inside each other.

I will refer to a physical disk drive as a *spindle*. A *partition* here means a BSD partition as maintained by `disklabel`. It does not refer to *slices* or *BIOS partitions* as maintained by `fdisk`.

Vinum Objects

Vinum defines a hierarchy of four objects that it uses to manage storage (see Figure 12-1). Different combinations of these objects are used to achieve failure resilience, performance, and/or extra capacity. I will give a whirlwind tour of the objects here--see the Vinum web site[3] for a more thorough description.

---

3 http://www.vinumvm.org/

Figure 12-1. Vinum Objects and Architecture

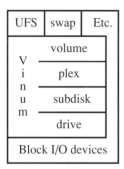

The top object, a vinum *volume*, implements a virtual disk that provides a standard block I/O layer interface to other parts of the kernel. The bottom object, a vinum *drive*, uses this same interface to request I/O from physical devices below it.

In between these two (from top to bottom) we have objects called a vinum *plex* and a vinum *subdisk*. As you can probably guess from the name, a vinum subdisk is a contiguous subset of the space available on a vinum drive. It lets you subdivide a vinum drive in much the same way that a disk BSD partition lets you subdivide a BIOS slice.

A plex allows subdisks to be grouped together making the space of all subdisks available as a single object.

A plex can be organized with its constituent subdisks concatenated or striped. Both organizations are useful for spreading I/O requests across spindles since plexes reside on distinct spindles. A striped plex will switch spindles each time a multiple of the strip size is reached. A concatenated plex will switch spindles only when the end of a subdisk is reached.

An important characteristic of a **Vinum** volume is that it can be made up of more than one plex. In this case, writes go to all plexes and a read may be satisfied by any plex. Configuring two or more plexes on distinct spindles yields a volume that is resilient to failure.

Vinum maintains a *configuration* that defines instances of the above objects and the way they are related to each other. This configuration is automatically written to all spindles under **Vinum** management whenever it changes.

Vinum Volume/Plex Organization

Although **Vinum** can manage any number of spindles, I will only cover scenarios with two spindles here for simplification. See Table 12-2 to see how two spindles organized with **Vinum** compare to two spindles without **Vinum**.

Table 12-2. Characteristics of Two Spindles Organized with Vinum

Organization	Total Capacity	Failure Resilient	Peak Read Performance	Peak Write Performance

Organization	Total Capacity	Failure Resilient	Peak Read Performance	Peak Write Performance
Concatenated Plexes	Unchanged, but appears as a single drive	No	Unchanged	Unchanged
Striped Plexes (RAID-0)	Unchanged, but appears as a single drive	No	2x	2x
Mirrored Volumes (RAID-1)	1/2, appearing as a single drive	Yes	2x	Unchanged

Table 12-2 shows that striping yields the same capacity and lack of failure resilience as concatenation, but it has better peak read and write performance. Hence we will not be using concatenation in any of the examples here. Mirrored volumes provide the benefits of improved peak read performance and failure resilience--but this comes at a loss in capacity.

Note: Both concatenation and striping bring their benefits over a single spindle at the cost of increased likelihood of failure since more than one spindle is now involved.

When three or more spindles are present, **Vinum** also supports rotated, block-interleaved parity (also called *RAID-5*) that provides better capacity than mirroring (but not quite as good as striping), better read performance than both mirroring and striping, and good failure resilience. There is, however, a substantial decrease in write performance with RAID-5. Most of the benefits become more pronounced with five or more spindles.

The organizations described above may be combined to provide benefits that no single organization can match. For example, mirroring and striping can be combined to provide failure-resilience with very fast read performance.

Vinum History

Vinum is a standard part of even a "minimum" FreeBSD distribution and it has been standard since 3.0-RELEASE. The official pronunciation of the name is *VEE-noom*.

Vinum was inspired by the Veritas Volume Manager, but was not derived from it. The name is a play on that history and the Latin adage *In Vino Veritas* (*Vino* is the accusative form of *Vinum*). Literally translated, that is "Truth lies in wine" hinting that drunkards have a hard time lying.

I have been using it in production on six different servers for over two years with no data loss. Like the rest of FreeBSD, **Vinum** provides "rock-stable performance." (On a personal note, I have seen **Vinum** panic when I misconfigured something, but I have never had any trouble in normal operation.) Greg Lehey wrote **Vinum** for FreeBSD, but he is seeking help in porting it to NetBSD and OpenBSD.

Warning: Just like the rest of FreeBSD, **Vinum** is undergoing continuous development. Several subtle, but significant bugs have been fixed in recent releases. It is always best to use the most recent code base that meets your stability requirements.

Vinum Deployment Strategy

Vinum, coupled with prudent partition management, lets you keep "warm-spare" spindles on-line so that failures are transparent to users. Failed spindles can be replaced during regular maintenance periods or whenever it is convenient. When all spindles are working, the server benefits from increased performance and capacity.

Having redundant copies of your home directory does not help you if the spindle holding root, /usr, or swap fails on your server. Hence I focus here on building a simple foundation for a failure-resilient server covering the root, /usr, /home, and swap partitions.

> **Warning: Vinum** mirroring does not remove the need for making backups! Mirroring cannot help you recover from site disasters or the dreaded `rm -r -f /` command.

Why Bootstrap Vinum?

It is possible to add **Vinum** to a server configuration after it is already in production use, but this is much harder than designing for it from the start. Ironically, **Vinum** is not supported by /stand/sysinstall and hence you cannot install /usr right onto a **Vinum** volume.

> **Note: Vinum** currently does not support the root file system (this feature is in development).

Hence it is a bit tricky to get started using **Vinum**, but these instructions take you though the process of planning for **Vinum**, installing FreeBSD without it, and then beginning to use it.

I have come to call this whole process "bootstrapping Vinum." That is, the process of getting **Vinum** initially installed and operating to the point where you have met your resilience or performance goals. My purpose here is to document a **Vinum** bootstrapping method that I have found that works well for me.

Vinum Benefits

The server foundation scenario I have chosen here allows me to show you examples of configuring for resilience on /usr and /home. Yet **Vinum** provides benefits other than resilience--namely performance, capacity, and manageability. It can significantly improve disk performance (especially under multi-user loads). **Vinum** can easily concatenate many smaller disks to produce the illusion of a single larger disk (but my server foundation scenario does not allow me to illustrate these benefits here).

For servers with many spindles, **Vinum** provides substantial benefits in volume management, particularly when coupled with hot-pluggable hardware. Data can be moved from spindle to spindle while the system is running without loss of production time. Again, details of this will not be given here, but once you get your feet wet with **Vinum**, other documentation will help you do things like this. See "The Vinum Volume Manager[4]" for a technical introduction to **Vinum**, vinum(8) for a description of the `vinum` command, and vinum(4) for a description of the vinum device driver and the way **Vinum** objects are named.

> **Note:** Breaking up your disk space into smaller and smaller partitions has the benefit of allowing you to "tune" for the most common type of access and tends to keep disk hogs "within their pens." However it also causes some loss in total available disk space due to fragmentation.

Server Operation in Degraded Mode

Some disk failures in this two-spindle scenario will result in **Vinum** automatically routing all disk I/O to the remaining good spindle. Others will require brief manual intervention on the console to configure the server for degraded mode operation and a quick reboot. Other than actual hardware repairs, most recovery work can be done while the server is running in multi-user degraded mode so there is as little production impact from failures as possible.

I give the instructions in Section 12.8.7 needed to configure the server for degraded mode operation in those cases where **Vinum** cannot do it automatically. I also give the instructions needed to return to normal operation once the failed hardware is repaired. You might call these instructions **Vinum** failure recovery techniques.

I recommend practicing using these instructions by recovering from simulated failures. For each failure scenario, I also give tips below for simulating a failure even when your hardware is working well. Even a minimum **Vinum** system as described in Section 12.8.1.10 below can be a good place to experiment with recovery techniques without impacting production equipment.

Hardware RAID vs. Vinum (Software RAID)

Manual intervention is sometimes required to configure a server for degraded mode because **Vinum** is implemented in software that runs after the FreeBSD kernel is loaded. One disadvantage of such *software RAID* solutions is that there is nothing that can be done to hide spindle failures from the BIOS or the FreeBSD boot sequence. Hence the manual reconfiguration of the server for degraded operation mentioned above just informs the BIOS and boot sequence of failed spindles. *Hardware RAID* solutions generally have an advantage in that they require no such reconfiguration since spindle failures are hidden from the BIOS and boot sequence.

Hardware RAID, however, may have some disadvantages that can be significant in some cases:

• The hardware RAID controller itself may become a single point of failure for the system.

• The data is usually kept in a proprietary format so that a disk drive cannot be simply plugged into another main board and booted.

• You often cannot mix and match drives with different sizes and interfaces.

• You are often limited to the number of drives supported by the hardware RAID controller (often only four or eight).

In other words, **Vinum** may offers advantages in that there is no single point of failure, the drives can boot on most any main board, and you are free to mix and match as many drives using whatever interface you choose.

---

4 http://www.vinumvm.org/vinum/vinum.ps

Tip: Keep your kernel fairly generic (or at least keep /kernel.GENERIC around). This will improve the chances that you can come back up on "foreign" hardware more quickly.

The pros and cons discussed above suggest that the root file system and swap partition are good candidates for hardware RAID if available. This is especially true for servers where it is difficult for administrators to get console access (recall that this is sometimes required to configure a server for degraded mode operation). A server with only software RAID is well suited to office and home environments where an administrator can be close at hand.

Note: A common myth is that hardware RAID is always faster than software RAID. Since it runs on the host CPU, **Vinum** often has more CPU power and memory available than a dedicated RAID controller would have. If performance is a prime concern, it is best to benchmark your application running bon your CPU with your spindles using both hardware and software RAID systems before making a decision.

Hardware for Vinum

These instructions may be timely since commodity PC hardware can now easily host several hundred megabytes of reasonably high-performance disk space at a low price. Many disk drive manufactures now sell 7,200 RPM disk drives with quite low seek times and high transfer rates through ATA-100 interfaces, all at very attractive prices. Four such drives, attached to a suitable main board and configured with **Vinum** and prudent partitioning, yields a failure-resilient, high performance disk server at a very reasonable cost.

However, you can indeed get started with **Vinum** very simply. A minimum system can be as simple as an old CPU (even a 486 is fine) and a pair of drives that are 500 MB or more. They need not be the same size or even use the same interface (i.e., it is fine to mix ATAPI and SCSI). So get busy and give this a try today! You will have the foundation of a failure-resilient server running in an hour or so!

12.8.2 Bootstrapping Phases

Greg Lehey suggested this bootstrapping method. It uses knowledge of how **Vinum** internally allocates disk space to avoid copying data. Instead, **Vinum** objects are configured so that they occupy the same disk space where /stand/ sysinstall built file systems. The file systems are thus embedded within **Vinum** objects without copying.

There are several distinct phases to the **Vinum** bootstrapping procedure. Each of these phases is presented in a separate section below. The section starts with a general overview of the phase and its goals. It then gives example steps for the two-spindle scenario presented here and advice on how to adapt them for your server. (If you are reading for a general understanding of **Vinum** bootstrapping, the example sections for each phase can safely be skipped.) The remainder of this section gives an overview of the entire bootstrapping process.

Phase 1 involves planning and preparation. We will balance requirements for the server against available resources and make design tradeoffs. We will plan the transition from no **Vinum** to **Vinum** on just one spindle, to **Vinum** on two spindles.

In phase 2, we will install a minimum FreeBSD system on a single spindle using partitions of type 4.2BSD (regular UFS file systems).

Phase 3 will embed the non-root file systems from phase 2 in **Vinum** objects. Note that **Vinum** will be up and running at this point, but it cannot yet provide any resilience since it only has one spindle on which to store data.

Finally in phase 4, we configure **Vinum** on a second spindle and make a backup copy of the root file system. This will give us resilience on all file systems.

Bootstrapping Phase 1: Planning and Preparation

Our goal in this phase is to define the different partitions we will need and examine their requirements. We will also look at available disk drives and controllers and allocate partitions to them. Finally, we will determine the size of each partition and its use during the bootstrapping process. After this planning is complete, we can optionally prepare to use some tools that will make bootstrapping **Vinum** easier.

Several key questions must be answered in this planning phase:

- What file system and partitions will be needed?
- How will they be used?
- How will we name each spindle?
- How will the partitions be ordered for each spindle?
- How will partitions be assigned to the spindles?
- How will partitions be configured? Resilience or performance?
- What technique will be used to achieve resilience?
- What spindles will be used?
- How will they be configured on the available controllers?
- How much space is required for each partition?

Phase 1 Example

In this example, I will assume a scenario where we are building a minimal foundation for a failure-resilient server. Hence we will need at least root, /usr, /home, and swap partitions. The root, /usr, and /home file systems all need resilience since the server will not be much good without them. The swap partition needs performance first and generally does not need resilience since nothing it holds needs to be retained across a reboot.

Spindle Naming

The kernel would refer to the master spindle on the primary and secondary ATA controllers as /dev/ad0 and /dev/ad2 respectively. [1] But **Vinum** also needs to have a name for each spindle that will stay the same name regardless of how it is attached to the CPU (i.e., if the drive moves, the **Vinum** name moves with the drive).

---

1.   This assumes that you have not removed the line options ATA_STATIC_ID from your kernel configuration.

Some recovery techniques documented below suggest moving a spindle from the secondary ATA controller to the primary ATA controller. (Indeed, the flexibility of making such moves is a key benefit of **Vinum** especially if you are managing a large number of spindles.) After such a drive/controller swap, the kernel will see what used to be /dev/ad2 as /dev/ad0 but **Vinum** will still call it by whatever name it had when it was attached to /dev/ad2 (i.e., when it was "created" or first made known to **Vinum**).

Since connections can change, it is best to give each spindle a unique, abstract name that gives no hint of how it is attached. Avoid names that suggest a manufacturer, model number, physical location, or membership in a sequence (e.g. avoid names like upper, lower, etc., alpha, beta, etc., SCSI1, SCSI2, etc., or Seagate1, Seagate2 etc.). Such names are likely to lose their uniqueness or get out of sequence someday even if they seem like great names today.

> **Tip:** Once you have picked names for your spindles, label them with a permanent marker. If you have hot-swappable hardware, write the names on the sleds in which the spindles are mounted. This will significantly reduce the likelihood of error when you are moving spindles around later as part of failure recovery or routine system management procedures.

In the instructions that follow, **Vinum** will name the root spindle YouCrazy and the rootback spindle UpWindow. I will only use /dev/ad0 when I want to refer to whichever of the two spindles is currently attached as /dev/ad0.

Partition Ordering

Modern disk drives operate with fairly uniform areal density across the surface of the disk. That implies that more data is available under the heads without seeking on the outer cylinders than on the inner cylinders. We will allocate partitions most critical to system performance from these outer cylinders as /stand/sysinstall generally does.

The root file system is traditionally the outermost, even though it generally is not as critical to system performance as others. (However root can have a larger impact on performance if it contains /tmp and /var as it does in this example.) The FreeBSD boot loaders assume that the root file system lives in the a partition. There is no requirement that the a partition start on the outermost cylinders, but this convention makes it easier to manage disk labels.

Swap performance is critical so it comes next on our way toward the center. I/O operations here tend to be large and contiguous. Having as much data under the heads as possible avoids seeking while swapping.

With all the smaller partitions out of the way, we finish up the disk with /home and /usr. Access patterns here tend not to be as intense as for other file systems (especially if there is an abundant supply of RAM and read cache hit rates are high).

If the pair of spindles you have are large enough to allow for more than /home and /usr, it is fine to plan for additional file systems here.

Assigning Partitions to Spindles

We will want to assign partitions to these spindles so that either can fail without loss of data on file systems configured for resilience.

Reliability on /usr and /home is best achieved using **Vinum** mirroring. Resilience will have to come differently, however, for the root file system since **Vinum** is not a part of the FreeBSD boot sequence. Here we will have to settle for two identical partitions with a periodic copy from the primary to the backup secondary.

The kernel already has support for interleaved swap across all available partitions so there is no need for help from **Vinum** here. /stand/sysinstall will automatically configure /etc/fstab for all swap partitions given.

The **Vinum** bootstrapping method given below requires a pair of spindles that I will call the *root spindle* and the *rootback spindle*.

> **Important:** The rootback spindle must be the same size or larger than the root spindle.

These instructions first allocate all space on the root spindle and then allocate exactly that amount of space on a rootback spindle. (After **Vinum** is bootstrapped, there is nothing special about either of these spindles--they are interchangeable.) You can later use the remaining space on the rootback spindle for other file systems.

If you have more than two spindles, the bootvinum Perl script and the procedure below will help you initialize them for use with **Vinum**. However you will have to figure out how to assign partitions to them on your own.

Assigning Space to Partitions

For this example, I will use two spindles: one with 4,124,673 blocks (about 2 GB) on /dev/ad0 and one with 8,420,769 blocks (about 4 GB) on /dev/ad2.

It is best to configure your two spindles on separate controllers so that both can operate in parallel and so that you will have failure resilience in case a controller dies. Note that mirrored volume write performance will be halved in cases where both spindles share a controller that requires they operate serially (as is often the case with ATA controllers). One spindle will be the master on the primary ATA controller and the other will be the master on the secondary ATA controller.

Recall that we will be allocating space on the smaller spindle first and the larger spindle second.

Assigning Partitions on the Root Spindle

We will allocate 200,000 blocks (about 93 MB) for a root file system on each spindle (/dev/ad0s1a and /dev/ad2s1a). We will initially allocate 200,265 blocks for a swap partition on each spindle, giving a total of about 186 MB of swap space (/dev/ad0s1b and /dev/ad2s1b).

> **Note:** We will lose 265 blocks from each swap partition as part of the bootstrapping process. This is the size of the space used by **Vinum** to store configuration information. The space will be taken from swap and given to a vinum partition but will be unavailable for **Vinum** subdisks.

> **Note:** I have done the partition allocation in nice round numbers of blocks just to emphasize where the 265 blocks go. There is nothing wrong with allocating space in MB if that is more convenient for you.

This leaves 4,124,673 - 200,000 - 200,265 = 3,724,408 blocks (about 1,818 MB) on the root spindle for **Vinum** partitions (/dev/ad0s1e and /dev/ad2s1f). From this, allocate the 265 blocks for **Vinum** configuration information, 1,000,000 blocks (about 488 MB) for /home, and the remaining 2,724,408 blocks (about 1,330 MB) for /usr. See Figure 12-2 below to see this graphically.

The left-hand side of Figure 12-2 below shows what spindle ad0 will look like at the end of phase 2. The right-hand side shows what it will look like at the end of phase 3.

Figure 12-2. Spindle ad0 Before and After Vinum

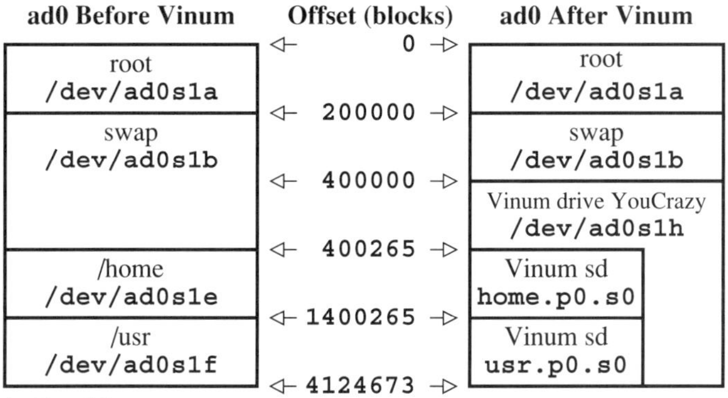

ad0 Before Vinum	Offset (blocks)	ad0 After Vinum
	← 0 →	
root `/dev/ad0s1a`		root `/dev/ad0s1a`
	← 200000 →	
swap `/dev/ad0s1b`		swap `/dev/ad0s1b`
	← 400000 →	
		Vinum drive YouCrazy `/dev/ad0s1h`
	← 400265 →	
/home `/dev/ad0s1e`		Vinum sd `home.p0.s0`
	← 1400265 →	
/usr `/dev/ad0s1f`		Vinum sd `usr.p0.s0`
	← 4124673 →	

(not to scale)

Assigning Partitions on the Rootback Spindle

The /rootback and swap partition sizes on the rootback spindle must match the root and swap partition sizes on the root spindle. That leaves 8,420,769 - 200,000 - 200,265 = 8,020,504 blocks for the **Vinum** partition. Mirrors of /home and /usr receive the same allocation as on the root spindle. That will leave an extra 2 GB or so that we can deal with later. See Figure 12-3 below to see this graphically.

The left-hand side of Figure 12-3 below shows what spindle ad2 will look like at the beginning of phase 4. The right-hand side shows what it will look like at the end.

Figure 12-3. Spindle ad2 Before and After Vinum

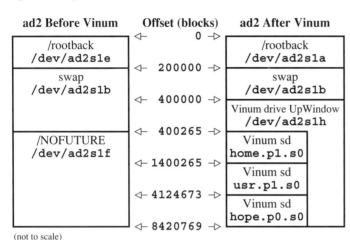

(not to scale)

Preparation of Tools

The `bootvinum` Perl script given below in Section 12.8.8.1 will make the **Vinum** bootstrapping process much easier if you can run it on the machine being bootstrapped. It is over 200 lines and you would not want to type it in. At this point, I recommend that you copy it to a floppy or arrange some alternative method of making it readily available so that it can be available later when needed. For example:

```
# fdformat -f 1440 /dev/fd0
# newfs_msdos -f 1440 /dev/fd0
# mount /dev/fd0 /mnt
# cp /usr/share/examples/vinum/bootvinum /mnt
```

12.8.3 Bootstrapping Phase 2: Minimal OS Installation

Our goal in this phase is to complete the smallest possible FreeBSD installation in such a way that we can later install **Vinum**. We will use only partitions of type `4.2BSD` (i.e., regular UFS file systems) since that is the only type supported by `/stand/sysinstall`.

Phase 2 Example

1. Start up the FreeBSD installation process by running `/stand/sysinstall` from installation media as you normally would.

2. Fdisk partition all spindles as needed.

    Important: Make sure to select BootMgr for all spindles.

3. Partition the root spindle with appropriate block allocations as described above in Section 12.8.2.1.1.5. For this example on a 2 GB spindle, I will use 200,000 blocks for root, 200,265 blocks for swap, 1,000,000 blocks for /home, and the rest of the spindle (2,724,408 blocks) for /usr. (/stand/sysinstall should automatically assign these to /dev/ad0s1a, /dev/ad0s1b, /dev/ad0s1e, and /dev/ad0s1f by default.)

    Note: If you prefer soft updates as I do and you are using 4.4-RELEASE or better, this is a good time to enable them.

4. Partition the rootback spindle with the appropriate block allocations as described above in Section 12.8.2.1.1.6. For this example on a 4 GB spindle, I will use 200,000 blocks for /rootback, 200,265 blocks for swap, and the rest of the spindle (8,020,504 blocks) for /NOFUTURE. (/stand/sysinstall should automatically assign these to /dev/ad2s1e, /dev/ad2s1b, and /dev/ad2s1f by default.)

    Note: We do not really want to have a /NOFUTURE UFS file system (we want a vinum partition instead), but that is the best choice we have for the space given the limitations of /stand/sysinstall. Mount point names beginning with NOFUTURE and rootback serve as sentinels to the bootstrapping script presented in Section 12.8.8.1 below.

5. Partition any other spindles with swap if desired and a single /NOFUTURExx file system.

6. Select a minimum system install for now even if you want to end up with more distributions loaded later.

    Tip: Do not worry about system configuration options at this point--get **Vinum** set up and get the partitions in the right places first.

7. Exit /stand/sysinstall and reboot. Do a quick test to verify that the minimum installation was successful.

The left-hand side of Figure 12-2 above and the left-hand side of Figure 12-3 above show how the disks will look at this point.

12.8.4 Bootstrapping Phase 3: Root Spindle Setup

Our goal in this phase is get **Vinum** set up and running on the root spindle. We will embed the existing /usr and /home file systems in a **Vinum** partition. Note that the **Vinum** volumes created will not yet be failure-resilient since we have only one underlying **Vinum** drive to hold them. The resulting system will automatically start **Vinum** as it boots to multi-user mode.

Phase 3 Example

1. Login as root.

2. We will need a directory in the root file system in which to keep a few files that will be used in the **Vinum** bootstrapping process.

   ```
   # mkdir /bootvinum
   # cd /bootvinum
   ```

3. Several files need to be prepared for use in bootstrapping. I have written a Perl script that makes all the required files for you. Copy this script to /bootvinum by floppy disk, tape, network, or any convenient means and then run it. (If you cannot get this script copied onto the machine being bootstrapped, then see Section 12.8.8.2 below for a manual alternative.)

   ```
   # cp /mnt/bootvinum .
   # ./bootvinum
   ```

   Note: bootvinum produces no output when run successfully. If you get any errors, something may have gone wrong when you were creating partitions with /stand/sysinstall above.

   Running bootvinum will:

   • Create /etc/fstab.vinum based on what it finds in your existing /etc/fstab

   • Create new disk labels for each spindle mentioned in /etc/fstab and keep copies of the current disk labels

   • Create files needed as input to vinum create for building **Vinum** objects on each spindle

   • Create many alternates to /etc/fstab.vinum that might come in handy should a spindle fail

   You may want to take a look at these files to learn more about the disk partitioning required for **Vinum** or to learn more about the commands needed to create **Vinum** objects.

4. We now need to install new spindle partitioning for /dev/ad0. This requires that /dev/ad0s1b not be in use for swapping so we have to reboot in single-user mode.

   a. First, reboot the system.

      ```
      # reboot
      ```

   b. Next, enter single-user mode.

      ```
      Hit [Enter] to boot immediately, or any other key for command prompt.
      Booting [kernel] in 8 seconds...

      Type '?' for a list of commands, 'help' for more detailed help.
      ok boot -s
      ```

5. In single-user mode, install the new partitioning created above.

   ```
   # cd /bootvinum
   # disklabel -R ad0s1 disklabel.ad0s1
   # disklabel -R ad2s1 disklabel.ad2s1
   ```

Note: If you have additional spindles, repeat the above commands as appropriate for them.

6. We are about to start **Vinum** for the first time. It is going to want to create several device nodes under /dev/vinum so we will need to mount the root file system for read/write access.

    ```
    # fsck -p /
    # mount /
    ```

7. Now it is time to create the **Vinum** objects that will embed the existing non-root file systems on the root spindle in a **Vinum** partition. This will load the **Vinum** kernel module and start **Vinum** as a side effect.

    ```
    # vinum create create.YouCrazy
    ```

    You should see a list of **Vinum** objects created that looks like the following:

    ```
    1 drives:
    D YouCrazy              State: up Device /dev/ad0s1h Avail: 0/1818 MB (0%)

    2 volumes:
    V home                State: up Plexes:       1 Size:        488 MB
    V usr                 State: up Plexes:       1 Size:       1330 MB

    2 plexes:
    P home.p0          C State: up Subdisks:    1 Size:        488 MB
    P usr.p0           C State: up Subdisks:    1 Size:       1330 MB

    2 subdisks:
    S home.p0.s0          State: up PO:       0  B Size:        488 MB
    S usr.p0.s0           State: up PO:       0  B Size:       1330 MB
    ```

    You should also see several kernel messages which state that the **Vinum** objects you have created are now up.

8. Our non-root file systems should now be embedded in a **Vinum** partition and hence available through **Vinum** volumes. It is important to test that this embedding worked.

    ```
    # fsck -n /dev/vinum/home
    # fsck -n /dev/vinum/usr
    ```

    This should produce no errors. If it does produce errors *do not fix them*. Instead, go back and examine the root spindle partition tables before and after **Vinum** to see if you can spot the error. You can back out the partition table changes by using disklabel -R with the disklabel.*.b4vinum files.

9. While we have the root file system mounted read/write, this is a good time to install /etc/fstab.

    ```
    # mv /etc/fstab /etc/fstab.b4vinum
    # cp /etc/fstab.vinum /etc/fstab
    ```

10. We are now done with tasks requiring single-user mode, so it is safe to go multi-user from here on.

    ```
    # ^D
    ```

11. Login as root.

12. Edit /etc/rc.conf and add this line:

    ```
    start_vinum="YES"
    ```

12.8.5 Bootstrapping Phase 4: Rootback Spindle Setup

Our goal in this phase is to get redundant copies of all data from the root spindle to the rootback spindle. We will first create the necessary **Vinum** objects on the rootback spindle. Then we will ask **Vinum** to copy the data from the root spindle to the rootback spindle. Finally, we use dump and restore to copy the root file system.

Phase 4 Example

1. Now that **Vinum** is running on the root spindle, we can bring it up on the rootback spindle so that our **Vinum** volumes can become failure-resilient.

    ```
    # cd /bootvinum
    # vinum create create.UpWindow
    ```

    You should see a list of **Vinum** objects created that looks like the following:

    ```
    2 drives:
    D YouCrazy            State: up        Device /dev/ad0s1h  Avail: 0/1818 MB (0%)
    D UpWindow            State: up        Device /dev/ad2s1h  Avail: 2096/3915 MB (53%)

    2 volumes:
    V home                State: up        Plexes:      2 Size:      488 MB
    V usr                 State: up        Plexes:      2 Size:     1330 MB

    4 plexes:
    P home.p0         C State: up          Subdisks:    1 Size:      488 MB
    P usr.p0          C State: up          Subdisks:    1 Size:     1330 MB
    P home.p1         C State: faulty      Subdisks:    1 Size:      488 MB
    P usr.p1          C State: faulty      Subdisks:    1 Size:     1330 MB

    4 subdisks:
    S home.p0.s0          State: up        PO:      0   B Size:      488 MB
    S usr.p0.s0           State: up        PO:      0   B Size:     1330 MB
    S home.p1.s0          State: stale     PO:      0   B Size:      488 MB
    S usr.p1.s0           State: stale     PO:      0   B Size:     1330 MB
    ```

    You should also see several kernel messages which state that some of the **Vinum** objects you have created are now up while others are faulty or stale.

2. Now we ask **Vinum** to copy each of the subdisks on drive YouCrazy to drive UpWindow. This will change the state of the newly created **Vinum** subdisks from stale to up. It will also change the state of the newly created **Vinum** plexes from faulty to up.

    First, we do the new subdisk we added to /home.

    ```
    # vinum start -w home.p1.s0
    reviving home.p1.s0
    ```

```
(time passes . . . )
home.p1.s0 is up by force
home.p1 is up
home.p1.s0 is up
```

Note: My 5,400 RPM EIDE spindles copied at about 3.5 MBytes/sec. Your mileage may vary.

3. Next we do the new subdisk we added to /usr.

```
# vinum -w start usr.p1.s0
reviving usr.p1.s0
(time passes . . . )
usr.p1.s0 is up by force
usr.p1 is up
usr.p1.s0 is up
```

All **Vinum** objects should be in state up at this point. The output of vinum list should look like the following:

```
2 drives:
D YouCrazy              State: up Device /dev/ad0s1h Avail: 0/1818 MB (0%)
D UpWindow              State: up Device /dev/ad2s1h Avail: 2096/3915 MB (53%)

2 volumes:
V home                  State: up Plexes:      2 Size:      488 MB
V usr                   State: up Plexes:      2 Size:     1330 MB

4 plexes:
P home.p0       C State: up Subdisks:      1 Size:      488 MB
P usr.p0        C State: up Subdisks:      1 Size:     1330 MB
P home.p1       C State: up Subdisks:      1 Size:      488 MB
P usr.p1        C State: up Subdisks:      1 Size:     1330 MB

4 subdisks:
S home.p0.s0            State: up PO:        0 B Size:      488 MB
S usr.p0.s0             State: up PO:        0 B Size:     1330 MB
S home.p1.s0           State: up PO:        0 B Size:      488 MB
S usr.p1.s0            State: up PO:        0 B Size:     1330 MB
```

4. Copy the root file system so that you will have a backup.

```
# cd /rootback
# dump 0f - / | restore rf -
# rm restoresymtable
# cd /
```

Note: You may see errors like this:

```
./tmp/rstdir1001216411: (inode 558) not found on tape
cannot find directory inode 265
abort? [yn] n
expected next file 492, got 491
```

They seem to cause no harm. I suspect they are a consequence of dumping the file system containing /tmp and/or the pipe connecting `dump` and `restore`.

5. Make a directory on which we can mount a damaged root file system during the recovery process.

    ```
    # mkdir /rootbad
    ```

6. Remove sentinel mount points that are now unused.

    ```
    # rmdir /NOFUTURE*
    ```

7. Create empty **Vinum** drives on remaining spindles.

    ```
    # vinum create create.ThruBank
    # ...
    ```

At this point, the reliable server foundation is complete. The right-hand side of Figure 12-2 above and the right-hand side of Figure 12-3 above show how the disks will look.

You may want to do a quick reboot to multi-user and give it a quick test drive. This is also a good point to complete installation of other distributions beyond the minimal install. Add packages, ports, and users as required. Configure /etc/rc.conf as required.

Tip: After you have completed your server configuration, remember to do one more copy of root to /rootback as shown above before placing the server into production.

Tip: Make a schedule to refresh /rootback periodically.

Tip: It may be a good idea to mount /rootback read-only for normal operation of the server. This does, however, complicate the periodic refresh a bit.

Tip: Do not forget to watch /var/log/messages carefully for errors. **Vinum** may automatically avoid failed hardware in a way that users do not notice. You must watch for such failures and get them repaired before a second failure results in data loss. You may see **Vinum** noting damaged objects at server boot time.

12.8.6 Where to Go from Here?

Now that you have established the foundation of a reliable server, there are several things you might want to try next.

Make a Vinum Volume with Remaining Space

Following are the steps to create another **Vinum** volume with space remaining on the rootback spindle.

> **Note:** This volume will not be resilient to spindle failure since it has only one plex on a single spindle.

1. Create a file with the following contents:

   ```
   volume hope
     plex name hope.p0 org concat volume hope
       sd name hope.p0.s0 drive UpWindow plex hope.p0 len 0
   ```

   > **Note:** Specifying a length of 0 for the `hope.p0.s0` subdisk asks **Vinum** to use whatever space is left available on the underlying drive.

2. Feed these commands into `vinum create`.

   ```
   # vinum create filename
   ```

3. Now we `newfs` the volume and `mount` it.

   ```
   # newfs -v /dev/vinum/hope
   # mkdir /hope
   # mount /dev/vinum/hope /hope
   ```

4. Edit `/etc/fstab` if you want `/hope` mounted at boot time.

Try Out More Vinum Commands

You might already be familiar with `vinum list` to get a list of all **Vinum** objects. Try `-v` following it to see more detail.

If you have more spindles and you want to bring them up as concatenated, mirrored, or striped volumes, then give `vinum concat` *drivelist*, `vinum mirror` *drivelist*, or `vinum stripe` *drivelist* a try.

See vinum(8) for sample configurations and important performance considerations before settling on a final organization for your additional spindles.

The failure recovery instructions below will also give you some experience using more **Vinum** commands.

12.8.7 Failure Scenarios

This section contains descriptions of various failure scenarios. For each scenario, there is a subsection on how to configure your server for degraded mode operation, how to recover from the failure, how to exit degraded mode, and how to simulate the failure.

Tip: Make a hard copy of these instructions and leave them inside the CPU case, being careful not to interfere with ventilation.

Root file system on ad0 unusable, rest of drive ok

Note: We assume here that the boot blocks and disk label on `/dev/ad0` are ok. If your BIOS can boot from a drive other than `c:`, you may be able to get around this limitation.

Configure Server for Degraded Mode

1. Use BootMgr to load kernel from `/dev/ad2s1a`.

    a. Hit **F5** in BootMgr to select `Drive 1`.

    b. Hit **F1** to select `FreeBSD`.

2. After the kernel is loaded, hit any key but enter to interrupt the boot sequence. Boot into single-user mode and allow explicit entry of a root file system.

    ```
    Hit [Enter] to boot immediately, or any other key for command prompt.
    Booting [kernel] in 8 seconds...

    Type '?' for a list of commands, 'help' for more detailed help.
    ok boot -as
    ```

3. Select `/rootback` as your root file system.

    ```
    Manual root file system specification:
        <fstype>:<device>  Mount <device> using filesystem <fstype>
      e.g. ufs:/dev/da0s1a
        ?                  List valid disk boot devices
        <empty line>       Abort manual input

    mountroot> ufs:/dev/ad2s1a
    ```

4. Now that you are in single-user mode, change `/etc/fstab` to avoid the bad root file system.

    Tip: If you used the `bootvinum` Perl script from Section 12.8.8.1 below, then these commands should configure your server for degraded mode.

    ```
    # fsck -p /
    # mount /
    # cd /etc
    # mv fstab fstab.bak
    # cp fstab_ad0s1_root_bad fstab
    # cd /
    # mount -o ro /
    # vinum start
    # fsck -p
    ```

```
# ^D
```

Recovery

1. Restore `/dev/ad0s1a` from backups or copy `/rootback` to it with these commands:

```
# umount /rootbad
# newfs /dev/ad0s1a
# tunefs -n enable /dev/ad0s1a
# mount /rootbad
# cd /rootbad
# dump 0f - / | restore rf -
# rm restoresymtable
```

Exiting Degraded Mode

1. Enter single-user mode.

```
# shutdown now
```

2. Put `/etc/fstab` back to normal and reboot.

```
# cd /rootbad/etc
# rm fstab
# mv fstab.bak fstab
# reboot
```

3. Reboot and hit **F1** to boot from `/dev/ad0` when prompted by BootMgr.

Simulation

This kind of failure can be simulated by shutting down to single-user mode and then booting as shown above in Section 12.8.7.1.1.

Drive ad2 Fails

This section deals with the total failure of `/dev/ad2`.

Configure Server for Degraded Mode

1. After the kernel is loaded, hit any key but **Enter** to interrupt the boot sequence. Boot into single-user mode.

```
Hit [Enter] to boot immediately, or any other key for command prompt.
```

```
Booting [kernel] in 8 seconds...

Type '?' for a list of commands, 'help' for more detailed help.
ok boot -s
```

2. Change /etc/fstab to avoid the bad drive. If you used the bootvinum Perl script from Section 12.8.8.1 below, then these commands should configure your server for degraded mode.

```
# fsck -p /
# mount /
# cd /etc
# mv fstab fstab.bak
# cp fstab_only_have_ad0s1 fstab
# cd /
# mount -o ro /
# vinum start
# fsck -p
# ^D
```

If you do not have modified versions of /etc/fstab that are ready for use, then you can use ed to make one. Alternatively, you can fsck and mount /usr and then use your favorite editor.

Recovery

We assume here that your server is up and running multi-user in degraded mode on just /dev/ad0 and that you have a new spindle now on /dev/ad2 ready to go.

You will need a new spindle with enough room to hold root and swap partitions plus a **Vinum** partition large enough to hold /home and /usr.

1. Create a BIOS partition (slice) on the new spindle.

    ```
    # /stand/sysinstall
    ```

    a. Select Custom.

    b. Select Partition.

    c. Select ad2.

    d. Create a FreeBSD (type 165) slice large enough to hold everything mentioned above.

    e. Write changes.

    f. Yes, you are absolutely sure.

    g. Select BootMgr.

    h. Quit Partitioning.

    i. Exit /stand/sysinstall.

2. Create disk label partitioning based on current /dev/ad0 partitioning.

    ```
    # disklabel ad0 > /tmp/ad0
    ```

```
# disklabel -e ad2
```
This will drop you into your favorite editor.

    a.   Copy the lines for the a and b partitions from /tmp/ad0 to the ad2 disklabel.

    b.   Add the size of the a and b partitions to find the proper offset for the h partition.

    c.   Subtract this offset from the size of the c partition to find the proper size for the h partition.

    d.   Define an h partition with the size and offset calculated above.

    e.   Set the fstype column to vinum.

    f.   Save the file and quit your editor.

3.   Tell **Vinum** about the new drive.

    a.   Ask **Vinum** to start an editor with a copy of the current configuration.

```
# vinum create
```

    b.   Uncomment the drive line referring to drive UpWindow and set device to /dev/ad2s1h.

    c.   Save the file and quit your editor.

4.   Now that **Vinum** has two spindles again, revive the mirrors.

```
# vinum start -w usr.p1.s0
# vinum start -w home.p1.s0
```

5.   Now we need to restore /rootback to a current copy of the root file system. These commands will accomplish this.

```
# newfs /dev/ad2s1a
# tunefs -n enable /dev/ad2s1a
# mount /dev/ad2s1a /mnt
# cd /mnt
# dump 0f - / | restore rf -
# rm restoresymtable
# cd /
# umount /mnt
```

Exiting Degraded Mode

1.   Enter single-user mode.

```
# shutdown now
```

2.   Return /etc/fstab to its normal state and reboot.

```
# cd /etc
# rm fstab
# mv fstab.bak fstab
# reboot
```

Simulation

You can simulate this kind of failure by unplugging /dev/ad2, write-protecting it, or by this procedure:

1. Shutdown to single-user mode.

2. Unmount all non-root file systems.

3. Clobber any existing **Vinum** configuration and partitioning on /dev/ad2.

```
# vinum stop
# dd if=/dev/zero of=/dev/ad2s1h count=512
# dd if=/dev/zero of=/dev/ad2 count=512
```

Drive ad0 Fails

Some BIOSes can boot from drive 1 or drive 2 (often called C: or D:), while others can boot only from drive 1. If your BIOS can boot from either, the fastest road to recovery might be to boot directly from /dev/ad2 in single-user mode and install /etc/fsatb_only_have_ad2s1 as /etc/fstab. You would then have to adapt the /dev/ad2 failure recovery instructions from Section 12.8.7.2.2 above.

If your BIOS can only boot from drive one, then you will have to unplug drive YouCrazy from the controller for /dev/ad2 and plug it into the controller for /dev/ad0. Then continue with the instructions for /dev/ad2 failure recovery in Section 12.8.7.2.2 above.

12.8.8 Vinum Appendix

bootvinum Perl Script

The bootvinum Perl script below reads /etc/fstab and current drive partitioning. It then writes several files in the current directory and several variants of /etc/fstab in /etc. These files significantly simplify the installation of **Vinum** and recovery from spindle failures.

```
#!/usr/bin/perl -w
use strict;
use FileHandle;

my $config_tag1 = '$Id: VinumBootstrap.sgml,v 1.28 2001/10/14 14:08:39 bob Exp bob $';
# Copyright (C) 2001 Robert A. Van Valzah
#
# Bootstrap Vinum
#
# Read /etc/fstab and current partitioning for all spindles mentioned there.
# Generate files needed to mirror all file systems on root spindle.
#  A new partition table for each spindle
#  Input for the vinum create command to create Vinum objects on each spindle
```

```
#  A copy of fstab mounting Vinum volumes instead of BSD partitions
#  Copies of fstab altered for server's degraded modes of operation
# See handbook for instructions on how to use the the files generated.
# N.B. This bootstrapping method shrinks size of swap partition by the size
# of Vinum's on-disk configuration (265 sectors).  It embeds existing file
# systems on the root spindle in Vinum objects without having to copy them.
# Thanks to Greg Lehey for suggesting this bootstrapping method.
# Expectations:
#  The root spindle must contain at least root, swap, and /usr partitions
#  The rootback spindle must have matching /rootback and swap partitions
#  Other spindles should only have a /NOFUTURE* file system and maybe swap
#  File systems named /NOFUTURE* will be replaced with Vinum drives

# Change configuration variables below to suit your taste
my $vip = 'h'; # VInum Partition
my @drv = ('YouCrazy', 'UpWindow', 'ThruBank', # Vinum DRiVe names
  'OutSnakes', 'MeWild', 'InMovie', 'HomeJames', 'DownPrices', 'WhileBlind');
# No configuration variables beyond this point

my %vols; # One entry per Vinum volume to be created
my @spndl; # One entry per SPiNDLe
my $rsp; # Root SPindle (as in /dev/$rsp)
my $rbsp; # RootBack SPindle (as in /dev/$rbsp)
my $cfgsiz = 265; # Size of Vinum on-disk configuration info in sectors
my $nxtpas = 2; # Next fsck pass number for non-root file systems

# Parse fstab, generating the version we'll need for Vinum and noting
# spindles in use.
my $fsin = "/etc/fstab";
#my $fsin = "simu/fstab";
open(FSIN, "$fsin") || die("Couldn't open $fsin: $!\n");

my $fsout = "/etc/fstab.vinum";
open(FSOUT, ">$fsout") || die("Couldn't open $fsout for writing: $!\n");

while (<FSIN>) {
  my ($dev, $mnt, $fstyp, $opt, $dump, $pass) = split;
  next if $dev =~ /^#/;
  if ($mnt eq '/' || $mnt eq '/rootback' || $mnt =~ /^\/NOFUTURE/) {
    my $dn = substr($dev, 5, length($dev)-6); # Device Name without /dev/
    push(@spndl, $dn) unless grep($_ eq $dn, @spndl);
    $rsp = $dn if $mnt eq '/';
    next if $mnt =~ /^\/NOFUTURE/;
  }
  # Move /rootback from partition e to a
  if ($mnt =~ /^\/rootback/) {
    $dev =~ s/e$/a/;
    $pass = 1;
    $rbsp = substr($dev, 5, length($dev)-6);
    print FSOUT "$dev\t\t$mnt\t$fstyp\t$opt\t\t$dump\t$pass\n";
    next;
```

```
    }
    # Move non-root file systems on smallest spindle into Vinum
    if (defined($rsp) && $dev =~ /^\/dev\/$rsp/ && $dev =~ /[d-h]$/) {
      $pass = $nxtpas++;
      print FSOUT "/dev/vinum$mnt\t\t$mnt\t\t$fstyp\t$opt\t\t$dump\t$pass\n";
      $vols{$dev}->{mnt} = substr($mnt, 1);
      next;
    }
    print FSOUT $_;
}
close(FSOUT);
die("Found more spindles than we have abstract names\n") if $#spndl > $#drv;
die("Didn't find a root partition!\n") if !defined($rsp);
die("Didn't find a /rootback partition!\n") if !defined($rbsp);

# Table of server's Degraded Modes
# One row per mode with hash keys
#    fn FileName
#    xpr eXPRession needed to convert fstab lines for this mode
#    cm1 CoMment 1 describing this mode
#    cm2 CoMment 2 describing this mode
#    FH  FileHandle (dynamically initialized below)
my @DM = (
  { cm1 => "When we only have $rsp, comment out lines using $rbsp",
    fn  => "/etc/fstab_only_have_$rsp",
    xpr => "s:^/dev/$rbsp:#\$&:",
  },
  { cm1 => "When we only have $rbsp, comment out lines using $rsp and",
    cm2 => "rootback becomes root",
    fn  => "/etc/fstab_only_have_$rbsp",
    xpr => "s:^/dev/$rsp:#\$&: || s:/rootback:/\t:",
  },
  { cm1 => "When only $rsp root is bad, /rootback becomes root and",
    cm2 => "root becomes /rootbad",
    fn  => "/etc/fstab_${rsp}_root_bad",
    xpr => "s:\t/\t:\t/rootbad: || s:/rootback:/\t:",
  },
);

# Initialize output FileHandles and write comments
foreach my $dm (@DM) {
  my $fh = new FileHandle;
  $fh->open(">$dm->{fn}") || die("Can't write $dm->{fn}: $!\n");
  print $fh "# $dm->{cm1}\n" if $dm->{cm1};
  print $fh "# $dm->{cm2}\n" if $dm->{cm2};
  $dm->{FH} = $fh;
}

# Parse the Vinum version of fstab written above and write versions needed
# for server's degraded modes.
open(FSOUT, "$fsout") || die("Couldn't open $fsout: $!\n");
```

```
while (<FSOUT>) {
  my $line = $_;
  foreach my $dm (@DM) {
    $_ = $line;
    eval $dm->{xpr};
    print {$dm->{FH}} $_;
  }
}

# Parse partition table for each spindle and write versions needed for Vinum
my $rootsiz; # ROOT partition SIZe
my $swapsiz; # SWAP partition SIZe
my $rspminoff; # Root SPindle MINimum OFFset of non-root, non-swap, non-c parts
my $rspsiz; # Root SPindle SIZe
my $rbspsiz; # RootBack SPindle SIZe
foreach my $i (0..$#spndl) {
  my $dlin = "disklabel $spndl[$i] |";
#   my $dlin = "simu/disklabel.$spndl[$i]";
  open(DLIN, "$dlin") || die("Couldn't open $dlin: $!\n");

  my $dlout = "disklabel.$spndl[$i]";
  open(DLOUT, ">$dlout") || die("Couldn't open $dlout for writing: $!\n");

  my $dlb4 = "$dlout.b4vinum";
  open(DLB4, ">$dlb4") || die("Couldn't open $dlb4 for writing: $!\n");

  my $minoff; # MINimum OFFset of non-root, non-swap, non-c partitions
  my $totsiz = 0; # TOTal SIZe of all non-root, non-swap, non-c partitions
  my $swapspndl = 0; # True if SWAP partition on this SPiNDLe
  while (<DLIN>) {
    print DLB4 $_;
    my ($part, $siz, $off, $fstyp, $fsiz, $bsiz, $bps) = split;

    if ($part && $part eq 'a:' && $spndl[$i] eq $rsp) {
$rootsiz = $siz;
    }
    if ($part && $part eq 'e:' && $spndl[$i] eq $rbsp) {
      if ($rootsiz != $siz) {
die("Rootback size ($siz) != root size ($rootsiz)\n");
      }
    }
    if ($part && $part eq 'c:') {
      $rspsiz  = $siz if $spndl[$i] eq $rsp;
      $rbspsiz = $siz if $spndl[$i] eq $rbsp;
    }
    # Make swap partition $cfgsiz sectors smaller
    if ($part && $part eq 'b:') {
      if ($spndl[$i] eq $rsp) {
$swapsiz = $siz;
      } else {
if ($swapsiz != $siz) {
```

```
     die("Swap partition sizes unequal across spindles\n");
 }
         }
         printf DLOUT "%4s%9d%9d%10s\n", $part, $siz-$cfgsiz, $off, $fstyp;
         $swapspndl = 1;
         next;
       }
       # Move rootback spindle e partitions to a
       if ($part && $part eq 'e:' && $spndl[$i] eq $rbsp) {
         printf DLOUT "%4s%9d%9d%10s%9d%6d%6d\n", 'a:', $siz, $off, $fstyp,
$fsiz, $bsiz, $bps;
         next;
       }
       # Delete non-root, non-swap, non-c partitions but note their minimum
       # offset and total size that're needed below.
       if ($part && $part =~ /^[d-h]:$/) {
         $minoff = $off unless $minoff;
         $minoff = $off if $off < $minoff;
         $totsiz += $siz;
         if ($spndl[$i] eq $rsp) { # If doing spindle containing root
my $dev = "/dev/$spndl[$i]" . substr($part, 0, 1);
$vols{$dev}->{siz} = $siz;
$vols{$dev}->{off} = $off;
$rspminoff = $minoff;
         }
         next;
       }
       print DLOUT $_;
   }
   if ($swapspndl) { # If there was a swap partition on this spindle
     # Make a Vinum partition the size of all non-root, non-swap,
     # non-c partitions + the size of Vinum's on-disk configuration.
     # Set its offset so that the start of the first subdisk it contains
     # coincides with the first file system we're embedding in Vinum.
     printf DLOUT "%4s%9d%9d%10s\n", "$vip:", $totsiz+$cfgsiz, $minoff-$cfgsiz,
       'vinum';
   } else {
     # No need to mess with size size and offset if there was no swap
     printf DLOUT "%4s%9d%9d%10s\n", "$vip:", $totsiz, $minoff,
       'vinum';
   }
 }
die("Swap partition not found\n") unless $swapsiz;
die("Swap partition not larger than $cfgsiz blocks\n") unless $swapsiz>$cfgsiz;
die("Rootback spindle size not >= root spindle size\n") unless $rbspsiz>=$rspsiz;

# Generate input to vinum create command needed for each spindle.
foreach my $i (0..$#spndl) {
  my $cfn = "create.$drv[$i]"; # Create File Name
  open(CF, ">$cfn") || die("Can't open $cfn for writing: $!\n");
  print CF "drive $drv[$i] device /dev/$spndl[$i]$vip\n";
```

```
    next unless $spndl[$i] eq $rsp || $spndl[$i] eq $rbsp;
    foreach my $dev (keys(%vols)) {
      my $mnt = $vols{$dev}->{mnt};
      my $siz = $vols{$dev}->{siz};
      my $off = $vols{$dev}->{off}-$rspminoff+$cfgsiz;
      print CF "volume $mnt\n" if $spndl[$i] eq $rsp;
      print CF <<EOF;
    plex name $mnt.p$i org concat volume $mnt
      sd name $mnt.p$i.s0 drive $drv[$i] plex $mnt.p$i len ${siz}s driveoffset ${off}s
EOF
    }
}
```

Manual Vinum Bootstrapping

The `bootvinum` Perl script in Section 12.8.8.1 makes life easier, but it may be necessary to manually perform some or all of the steps that it automates. This appendix describes how you would manually mimic the script.

1. Make a copy of `/etc/fstab` to be customized.

   ```
   # cp /etc/fstab /etc/fstab.vinum
   ```

2. Edit `/etc/fstab.vinum`.

   a. Change the `device` column of non-root partitions on the root spindle to `/dev/vinum/mnt`.

   b. Change the `pass` column of non-root partitions on the root spindle to **2**, **3**, etc.

   c. Delete any lines with mountpoint matching `/NOFUTURE*`.

   d. Change the `device` column of `/rootback` from e to a.

   e. Change the `pass` column of `/rootback` to **1**.

3. Prepare disklabels for editing:

   ```
   # cd /bootvinum
   # disklabel ad0s1 > disklabel.ad0s1
   # cp disklabel.ad0s1 disklabel.ad0s1.b4vinum
   # disklabel ad2s1 > disklabel.ad2s1
   # cp disklabel.ad2s1 disklabel.ad2s1.b4vinum
   ```

4. Edit `/etc/disklabel.ad?s1`.

   a. On the root spindle:

      i. Decrease the `size` of the b partition by 265 blocks.

      ii. Note the `size` and `offset` of the a and b partitions.

      iii. Note the smallest `offset` for partitions d-h.

      iv. Note the `size` and `offset` for all non-root, non-swap partitions (`/home` was probably on e and `/usr` was probably on f).

      v.   Delete partitions d-h.

     vi.   Create a new h partition with `offset` 265 blocks less than the smallest `offset` for partitions d-h noted above. Set its `size` to the `size` of the c partition less the smallest `offset` for partitions d-h noted above + 265 blocks.

> **Note: Vinum** can use any partition other than c. It is not strictly necessary to use h for all your **Vinum** partitions, but it is good practice to be consistent across all spindles.

    vii.   Set the `fstype` of this new partition to **vinum**.

  b.   On the rootback spindle:

      i.   Move the e partition to a.

     ii.   Verify that the `size` of the a and b partitions matches the root spindle.

    iii.   Note the smallest `offset` for partitions d-h.

    iv.   Delete partitions d-h.

     v.   Create a new h partition with `offset` 265 blocks less than the smallest `offset` noted above for partitions d-h. Set its `size` to the `size` of the c partition less the smallest `offset` for partitions d-h noted above + 265 blocks.

     vi.   Set the `fstype` of this new partition to **vinum**.

5.   Create a file named `create.YouCrazy` that contains:

```
drive YouCrazy device /dev/ad0s1h
volume home
  plex name home.p0 org concat volume home
    sd name home.p0.s0 drive YouCrazy plex home.p0 len $hl driveoffset $ho
volume usr
  plex name usr.p0 org concat volume usr
    sd name usr.p0.s0 drive YouCrazy plex usr.p0 len $ul driveoffset $uo
```

Where:

- $hl is the length noted above for /home.
- $ho is the offset noted above for /home less the smallest offset noted above + 265 blocks.
- $ul is the length noted above for /usr.
- $uo is the offset noted above for /usr less the smallest offset noted above + 265 blocks.

6.   Create a file named `create.UpWindow` containing:

```
drive UpWindow device /dev/ad2s1h
  plex name home.p1 org concat volume home
    sd name home.p1.s0 drive UpWindow plex home.p1 len $hl driveoffset $ho
  plex name usr.p1 org concat volume usr
    sd name usr.p1.s0 drive UpWindow plex usr.p1 len $ul driveoffset $uo
```

Where $hl, $ho, $ul, and $uo are set as above.

Acknowledgements

I would like to thank Greg Lehey for writing **Vinum** and for providing very helpful comments on early drafts. Several others made helpful suggestions after reviewing later drafts including Dag-Erling Smørgrav, Michael Splendoria, Chern Lee, Stefan Aeschbacher, Fleming Froekjaer, Bernd Walter, Aleksey Baranov, and Doug Swarin.

12.9 Hardware RAID

FreeBSD supports a wide variety of hardware RAID controllers from many popular manufacturers such as Adaptec, 3Ware, Mylex, DPT, AMI, Dell, HP, IBM, and more. The list of supported adapters is growing all the time, so make sure to check the release notes for complete information.

12.10 Tape Backup Media

The major tape media are the 4mm, 8mm, QIC, mini-cartridge and DLT.

12.10.1 4mm (DDS: Digital Data Storage)

4mm tapes are replacing QIC as the workstation backup media of choice. This trend accelerated greatly when Conner purchased Archive, a leading manufacturer of QIC drives, and then stopped production of QIC drives. 4mm drives are small and quiet but do not have the reputation for reliability that is enjoyed by 8mm drives. The cartridges are less expensive and smaller (3 x 2 x 0.5 inches, 76 x 51 x 12 mm) than 8mm cartridges. 4mm, like 8mm, has comparatively short head life for the same reason, both use helical scan.

Data throughput on these drives starts ~150kB/s, peaking at ~500kB/s. Data capacity starts at 1.3 GB and ends at 2.0 GB. Hardware compression, available with most of these drives, approximately doubles the capacity. Multi-drive tape library units can have 6 drives in a single cabinet with automatic tape changing. Library capacities reach 240 GB.

The DDS-3 standard now supports tape capacities up to 12 GB (or 24 GB compressed).

4mm drives, like 8mm drives, use helical-scan. All the benefits and drawbacks of helical-scan apply to both 4mm and 8mm drives.

Tapes should be retired from use after 2,000 passes or 100 full backups.

12.10.2 8mm (Exabyte)

8mm tapes are the most common SCSI tape drives; they are the best choice of exchanging tapes. Nearly every site has an Exabyte 2 GB 8mm tape drive. 8mm drives are reliable, convenient and quiet. Cartridges are inexpensive and small (4.8 x 3.3 x 0.6 inches; 122 x 84 x 15 mm). One downside of 8mm tape is relatively short head and tape life due to the high rate of relative motion of the tape across the heads.

Data throughput ranges from ~250kB/s to ~500kB/s. Data sizes start at 300 MB and go up to 7 GB. Hardware compression, available with most of these drives, approximately doubles the capacity. These drives are available as single units or multi-drive tape libraries with 6 drives and 120 tapes in a single cabinet. Tapes are changed automatically by the unit. Library capacities reach 840+ GB.

The Exabyte "Mammoth" model supports 12 GB on one tape (24 GB with compression) and costs approximately twice as much as conventional tape drives.

Data is recorded onto the tape using helical-scan, the heads are positioned at an angle to the media (approximately 6 degrees). The tape wraps around 270 degrees of the spool that holds the heads. The spool spins while the tape slides over the spool. The result is a high density of data and closely packed tracks that angle across the tape from one edge to the other.

12.10.3 QIC

QIC-150 tapes and drives are, perhaps, the most common tape drive and media around. QIC tape drives are the least expensive "serious" backup drives. The downside is the cost of media. QIC tapes are expensive compared to 8mm or 4mm tapes, up to 5 times the price per GB data storage. But, if your needs can be satisfied with a half-dozen tapes, QIC may be the correct choice. QIC is the *most* common tape drive. Every site has a QIC drive of some density or another. Therein lies the rub, QIC has a large number of densities on physically similar (sometimes identical) tapes. QIC drives are not quiet. These drives audibly seek before they begin to record data and are clearly audible whenever reading, writing or seeking. QIC tapes measure (6 x 4 x 0.7 inches; 15.2 x 10.2 x 1.7 mm). Mini-cartridges, which also use 1/4" wide tape are discussed separately. Tape libraries and changers are not available.

Data throughput ranges from ~150kB/s to ~500kB/s. Data capacity ranges from 40 MB to 15 GB. Hardware compression is available on many of the newer QIC drives. QIC drives are less frequently installed; they are being supplanted by DAT drives.

Data is recorded onto the tape in tracks. The tracks run along the long axis of the tape media from one end to the other. The number of tracks, and therefore the width of a track, varies with the tape's capacity. Most if not all newer drives provide backward-compatibility at least for reading (but often also for writing). QIC has a good reputation regarding the safety of the data (the mechanics are simpler and more robust than for helical scan drives).

Tapes should be retired from use after 5,000 backups.

12.10.4 DLT

DLT has the fastest data transfer rate of all the drive types listed here. The 1/2" (12.5mm) tape is contained in a single spool cartridge (4 x 4 x 1 inches; 100 x 100 x 25 mm). The cartridge has a swinging gate along one entire side of the cartridge. The drive mechanism opens this gate to extract the tape leader. The tape leader has an oval hole in it which the drive uses to "hook" the tape. The take-up spool is located inside the tape drive. All the other tape cartridges listed here (9 track tapes are the only exception) have both the supply and take-up spools located inside the tape cartridge itself.

Data throughput is approximately 1.5MB/s, three times the throughput of 4mm, 8mm, or QIC tape drives. Data capacities range from 10 GB to 20 GB for a single drive. Drives are available in both multi-tape changers and multi-tape, multi-drive tape libraries containing from 5 to 900 tapes over 1 to 20 drives, providing from 50 GB to 9 TB of storage.

With compression, DLT Type IV format supports up to 70 GB capacity.

Data is recorded onto the tape in tracks parallel to the direction of travel (just like QIC tapes). Two tracks are written at once. Read/write head lifetimes are relatively long; once the tape stops moving, there is no relative motion between the heads and the tape.

12.10.5 AIT

AIT is a new format from Sony, and can hold up to 50 GB (with compression) per tape. The tapes contain memory chips which retain an index of the tape's contents. This index can be rapidly read by the tape drive to determine the position of files on the tape, instead of the several minutes that would be required for other tapes. Software such as SAMS:Alexandria can operate forty or more AIT tape libraries, communicating directly with the tape's memory chip to display the contents on screen, determine what files were backed up to which tape, locate the correct tape, load it, and restore the data from the tape.

Libraries like this cost in the region of $20,000, pricing them a little out of the hobbyist market.

12.10.6 Using a New Tape for the First Time

The first time that you try to read or write a new, completely blank tape, the operation will fail. The console messages should be similar to:

```
sa0(ncr1:4:0): NOT READY asc:4,1
sa0(ncr1:4:0):  Logical unit is in process of becoming ready
```

The tape does not contain an Identifier Block (block number 0). All QIC tape drives since the adoption of QIC-525 standard write an Identifier Block to the tape. There are two solutions:

mt fsf 1 causes the tape drive to write an Identifier Block to the tape.

Use the front panel button to eject the tape.

Re-insert the tape and dump data to the tape.

dump will report DUMP: End of tape detected and the console will show: HARDWARE FAILURE info:280 asc:80,96.

rewind the tape using: mt rewind.

Subsequent tape operations are successful.

12.11 Backup Programs

The three major programs are dump(8), tar(1), and cpio(1).

12.11.1 Dump and Restore

The traditional Unix backup programs are `dump` and `restore`. They operate on the drive as a collection of disk blocks, below the abstractions of files, links and directories that are created by the filesystems. `dump` backs up an entire filesystem on a device. It is unable to backup only part of a filesystem or a directory tree that spans more than one filesystem. `dump` does not write files and directories to tape, but rather writes the raw data blocks that comprise files and directories.

> **Note:** If you use `dump` on your root directory, you would not back up `/home`, `/usr` or many other directories since these are typically mount points for other filesystems or symbolic links into those filesystems.

`dump` has quirks that remain from its early days in Version 6 of AT&T Unix (circa 1975). The default parameters are suitable for 9-track tapes (6250 bpi), not the high-density media available today (up to 62,182 ftpi). These defaults must be overridden on the command line to utilize the capacity of current tape drives.

It is also possible to backup data across the network to a tape drive attached to another computer with `rdump` and `rrestore`. Both programs rely upon `rcmd` and `ruserok` to access the remote tape drive. Therefore, the user performing the backup must have `rhosts` access to the remote computer. The arguments to `rdump` and `rrestore` must be suitable to use on the remote computer. (e.g. When rdumping from a FreeBSD computer to an Exabyte tape drive connected to a Sun called `komodo`, use: `/sbin/rdump 0dsbfu 54000 13000 126 komodo:/dev/nrsa8 /dev/rda0a 2>&1`) Beware: there are security implications to allowing `rhosts` commands. Evaluate your situation carefully.

It is also possible to use `rdump` and `rrestore` in a more secure fashion over `ssh`.

Example 12-4. Using `rdump` over ssh

```
# /sbin/dump -0uan -f - /usr | gzip -2 | ssh1 -c blowfish \
        targetuser@targetmachine.example.com dd of=/mybigfiles/dump-usr-10.gz
```

12.11.2 `tar`

tar(1) also dates back to Version 6 of AT&T Unix (circa 1975). `tar` operates in cooperation with the filesystem; `tar` writes files and directories to tape. `tar` does not support the full range of options that are available from cpio(1), but `tar` does not require the unusual command pipeline that `cpio` uses.

Most versions of `tar` do not support backups across the network. The GNU version of `tar`, which FreeBSD utilizes, supports remote devices using the same syntax as `rdump`. To `tar` to an Exabyte tape drive connected to a Sun called `komodo`, use: `/usr/bin/tar cf komodo:/dev/nrsa8 . 2>&1`. For versions without remote device support, you can use a pipeline and `rsh` to send the data to a remote tape drive.

```
# tar cf - . | rsh hostname dd of=tape-device obs=20b
```

If you are worried about the security of backing up over a network you should use the ssh command instead of rsh.

12.11.3 cpio

cpio(1) is the original Unix file interchange tape program for magnetic media. cpio has options (among many others) to perform byte-swapping, write a number of different archive formats, and pipe the data to other programs. This last feature makes cpio and excellent choice for installation media. cpio does not know how to walk the directory tree and a list of files must be provided through stdin.

cpio does not support backups across the network. You can use a pipeline and rsh to send the data to a remote tape drive.

```
# for f in directory_list; do
find $f >> backup.list
done
# cpio -v -o --format=newc < backup.list | ssh user@host "cat > backup_device
```

Where *directory_list* is the list of directories you want to back up, *user@host* is the user/hostname combination that will be performing the backups, and *backup_device* is where the backups should be written to (e.g., /dev/nrsa0).

12.11.4 pax

pax(1) is IEEE/POSIX's answer to tar and cpio. Over the years the various versions of tar and cpio have gotten slightly incompatible. So rather than fight it out to fully standardize them, POSIX created a new archive utility. pax attempts to read and write many of the various cpio and tar formats, plus new formats of its own. Its command set more resembles cpio than tar.

12.11.5 Amanda

Amanda (Advanced Maryland Network Disk Archiver) is a client/server backup system, rather than a single program. An Amanda server will backup to a single tape drive any number of computers that have Amanda clients and a network connection to the Amanda server. A common problem at sites with a number of large disks is that the length of time required to backup to data directly to tape exceeds the amount of time available for the task. Amanda solves this problem. Amanda can use a "holding disk" to backup several filesystems at the same time. Amanda creates "archive sets": a group of tapes used over a period of time to create full backups of all the filesystems listed in Amanda's configuration file. The "archive set" also contains nightly incremental (or differential) backups of all the filesystems. Restoring a damaged filesystem requires the most recent full backup and the incremental backups.

The configuration file provides fine control of backups and the network traffic that Amanda generates. Amanda will use any of the above backup programs to write the data to tape. Amanda is available as either a port or a package, it is not installed by default.

12.11.6 Do Nothing

"Do nothing" is not a computer program, but it is the most widely used backup strategy. There are no initial costs. There is no backup schedule to follow. Just say no. If something happens to your data, grin and bear it!

If your time and your data is worth little to nothing, then "Do nothing" is the most suitable backup program for your computer. But beware, Unix is a useful tool, you may find that within six months you have a collection of files that are valuable to you.

"Do nothing" is the correct backup method for /usr/obj and other directory trees that can be exactly recreated by your computer. An example is the files that comprise the HTML or Postscript version of this Handbook. These document formats have been created from SGML input files. Creating backups of the HTML or PostScript files is not necessary. The SGML files are backed up regularly.

12.11.7 Which Backup Program Is Best?

dump(8) *Period*. Elizabeth D. Zwicky torture tested all the backup programs discussed here. The clear choice for preserving all your data and all the peculiarities of Unix filesystems is dump. Elizabeth created filesystems containing a large variety of unusual conditions (and some not so unusual ones) and tested each program by doing a backup and restore of those filesystems. The peculiarities included: files with holes, files with holes and a block of nulls, files with funny characters in their names, unreadable and unwritable files, devices, files that change size during the backup, files that are created/deleted during the backup and more. She presented the results at LISA V in Oct. 1991. See torture-testing Backup and Archive Programs[5].

12.11.8 Emergency Restore Procedure

Before the Disaster

There are only four steps that you need to perform in preparation for any disaster that may occur.

First, print the disklabel from each of your disks (e.g. disklabel da0 | lpr), your filesystem table (/etc/ fstab) and all boot messages, two copies of each.

Second, determine that the boot and fix-it floppies (boot.flp and fixit.flp) have all your devices. The easiest way to check is to reboot your machine with the boot floppy in the floppy drive and check the boot messages. If all your devices are listed and functional, skip on to step three.

Otherwise, you have to create two custom bootable floppies which have a kernel that can mount all of your disks and access your tape drive. These floppies must contain: fdisk, disklabel, newfs, mount, and whichever backup program you use. These programs must be statically linked. If you use dump, the floppy must contain restore.

Third, create backup tapes regularly. Any changes that you make after your last backup may be irretrievably lost. Write-protect the backup tapes.

Fourth, test the floppies (either boot.flp and fixit.flp or the two custom bootable floppies you made in step two.) and backup tapes. Make notes of the procedure. Store these notes with the bootable floppy, the printouts and the

---

5 http://reality.sgi.com/zwicky_neu/testdump.doc.html

backup tapes. You will be so distraught when restoring that the notes may prevent you from destroying your backup tapes (How? In place of `tar xvf /dev/rsa0`, you might accidently type `tar cvf /dev/rsa0` and over-write your backup tape).

For an added measure of security, make bootable floppies and two backup tapes each time. Store one of each at a remote location. A remote location is NOT the basement of the same office building. A number of firms in the World Trade Center learned this lesson the hard way. A remote location should be physically separated from your computers and disk drives by a significant distance.

Example 12-5. A Script for Creating a Bootable Floppy

```
#!/bin/sh
#
# create a restore floppy
#
# format the floppy
#
PATH=/bin:/sbin:/usr/sbin:/usr/bin

fdformat -q fd0
if [ $? -ne 0 ]
then
  echo "Bad floppy, please use a new one"
  exit 1
fi

# place boot blocks on the floppy
#
disklabel -w -B /dev/fd0c fd1440

#
# newfs the one and only partition
#
newfs -t 2 -u 18 -l 1 -c 40 -i 5120 -m 5 -o space /dev/fd0a

#
# mount the new floppy
#
mount /dev/fd0a /mnt

#
# create required directories
#
mkdir /mnt/dev
mkdir /mnt/bin
mkdir /mnt/sbin
mkdir /mnt/etc
mkdir /mnt/root
mkdir /mnt/mnt # for the root partition
mkdir /mnt/tmp
```

```
mkdir /mnt/var

#
# populate the directories
#
if [ ! -x /sys/compile/MINI/kernel ]
then
  cat << EOM
The MINI kernel does not exist, please create one.
Here is an example config file:
#
# MINI -- A kernel to get FreeBSD onto a disk.
#
machine        "i386"
cpu            "I486_CPU"
ident          MINI
maxusers       5

options        INET               # needed for _tcp _icmpstat _ipstat
                                  #            _udpstat _tcpstat _udb
options        FFS                #Berkeley Fast File System
options        FAT_CURSOR         #block cursor in syscons or pccons
options        SCSI_DELAY=15      #Be pessimistic about Joe SCSI device
options        NCONS=2            #1 virtual consoles
options        USERCONFIG         #Allow user configuration with -c XXX

config         kernel root on da0 swap on da0 and da1 dumps on da0

device         isa0
device         pci0

device         fdc0 at isa? port "IO_FD1" bio irq 6 drq 2 vector fdintr
device         fd0 at fdc0 drive 0

device         ncr0

device         scbus0

device         sc0 at isa? port "IO_KBD" tty irq 1 vector scintr
device         npx0 at isa? port "IO_NPX" irq 13 vector npxintr

device         da0
device         da1
device         da2

device         sa0

pseudo-device  loop          # required by INET
pseudo-device  gzip          # Exec gzipped a.out's
EOM
  exit 1
```

```
fi

cp -f /sys/compile/MINI/kernel /mnt

gzip -c -best /sbin/init > /mnt/sbin/init
gzip -c -best /sbin/fsck > /mnt/sbin/fsck
gzip -c -best /sbin/mount > /mnt/sbin/mount
gzip -c -best /sbin/halt > /mnt/sbin/halt
gzip -c -best /sbin/restore > /mnt/sbin/restore

gzip -c -best /bin/sh > /mnt/bin/sh
gzip -c -best /bin/sync > /mnt/bin/sync

cp /root/.profile /mnt/root

cp -f /dev/MAKEDEV /mnt/dev
chmod 755 /mnt/dev/MAKEDEV

chmod 500 /mnt/sbin/init
chmod 555 /mnt/sbin/fsck /mnt/sbin/mount /mnt/sbin/halt
chmod 555 /mnt/bin/sh /mnt/bin/sync
chmod 6555 /mnt/sbin/restore

#
# create the devices nodes
#
cd /mnt/dev
./MAKEDEV std
./MAKEDEV da0
./MAKEDEV da1
./MAKEDEV da2
./MAKEDEV sa0
./MAKEDEV pty0
cd /

#
# create minimum filesystem table
#
cat > /mnt/etc/fstab <<EOM
/dev/fd0a    /    ufs    rw 1 1
EOM

#
# create minimum passwd file
#
cat > /mnt/etc/passwd <<EOM
root:*:0:0:Charlie &:/root:/bin/sh
EOM

cat > /mnt/etc/master.passwd <<EOM
root::0:0::0:0:Charlie &:/root:/bin/sh
```

```
EOM

chmod 600 /mnt/etc/master.passwd
chmod 644 /mnt/etc/passwd
/usr/sbin/pwd_mkdb -d/mnt/etc /mnt/etc/master.passwd

#
# umount the floppy and inform the user
#
/sbin/umount /mnt
echo "The floppy has been unmounted and is now ready."
```

After the Disaster

The key question is: did your hardware survive? You have been doing regular backups so there is no need to worry about the software.

If the hardware has been damaged. First, replace those parts that have been damaged.

If your hardware is okay, check your floppies. If you are using a custom boot floppy, boot single-user (type -s at the boot: prompt). Skip the following paragraph.

If you are using the boot.flp and fixit.flp floppies, keep reading. Insert the boot.flp floppy in the first floppy drive and boot the computer. The original install menu will be displayed on the screen. Select the Fixit--Repair mode with CDROM or floppy. option. Insert the fixit.flp when prompted. restore and the other programs that you need are located in /mnt2/stand.

Recover each filesystem separately.

Try to mount (e.g. mount /dev/da0a /mnt) the root partition of your first disk. If the disklabel was damaged, use disklabel to re-partition and label the disk to match the label that you printed and saved. Use newfs to re-create the filesystems. Re-mount the root partition of the floppy read-write (mount -u -o rw /mnt). Use your backup program and backup tapes to recover the data for this filesystem (e.g. restore vrf /dev/sa0). Unmount the filesystem (e.g. umount /mnt) Repeat for each filesystem that was damaged.

Once your system is running, backup your data onto new tapes. Whatever caused the crash or data loss may strike again. Another hour spent now may save you from further distress later.

12.12 Backups to Floppies

12.12.1 Can I Use floppies for Backing Up My Data?

Floppy disks are not really a suitable media for making backups as:

• The media is unreliable, especially over long periods of time

- Backing up and restoring is very slow
- They have a very limited capacity (the days of backing up an entire hard disk onto a dozen or so floppies has long since passed).

However, if you have no other method of backing up your data then floppy disks are better than no backup at all.

If you do have to use floppy disks then ensure that you use good quality ones. Floppies that have been lying around the office for a couple of years are a bad choice. Ideally use new ones from a reputable manufacturer.

12.12.2 So How Do I Backup My Data to Floppies?

The best way to backup to floppy disk is to use `tar` with the `-M` (multi volume) option, which allows backups to span multiple floppies.

To backup all the files in the current directory and sub-directory use this (as root):

```
# tar Mcvf /dev/fd0 *
```

When the first floppy is full `tar` will prompt you to insert the next volume (because `tar` is media independent it refers to volumes. In this context it means floppy disk)

```
Prepare volume #2 for /dev/fd0 and hit return:
```

This is repeated (with the volume number incrementing) until all the specified files have been archived.

12.12.3 Can I Compress My Backups?

Unfortunately, `tar` will not allow the `-z` option to be used for multi-volume archives. You could, of course, `gzip` all the files, `tar` them to the floppies, then `gunzip` the files again!

12.12.4 How Do I Restore My Backups?

To restore the entire archive use:

```
# tar Mxvf /dev/fd0
```

There are two ways that you can use to restore only specific files. First, you can start with the first floppy and use:

```
# tar Mxvf /dev/fd0 filename
```

`tar` will prompt you to insert subsequent floppies until it finds the required file.

Alternatively, if you know which floppy the file is on then you can simply insert that floppy and use the same command as above. Note that if the first file on the floppy is a continuation from the previous one then `tar` will warn you that it cannot restore it, even if you have not asked it to!

Chapter 13

Localization - I18N/L10N Usage and Setup

13.1 Synopsis

FreeBSD is a very distributed project with users and contributors located all over the world. This chapter discusses the internationalization and localization features of FreeBSD that allow non-English speaking users to get real work done. There are many aspects of the i18n implementation in both the system and application levels, so where applicable we refer the reader to more specific sources of documentation.

After reading this chapter, you will know:

- How different languages and locales are encoded on modern operating systems.
- How to set the locale for your login shell.
- How to configure your console for non-English languages.
- How to use X Windows effectively with different languages.
- Where to find more information about writing i18n-compliant applications.

Before reading this chapter, you should:

- Know how to install additional third-party applications (Chapter 4).

13.2 The Basics

13.2.1 What is I18N/L10N?

Developers shortened internationalization into the term I18N, counting the number of letters between the first and the last letters of internationalization. L10N uses the same naming scheme, coming from "localization". Combined together, I18N/L10N methods, protocols, and applications allow users to use languages of their choice.

I18N applications are programmed using I18N kits under libraries. It allows for developers to write a simple file and translate displayed menus and texts to each language. We strongly encourage programmers to follow this convention.

13.2.2 Why Should I Use I18N/L10N?

I18N/L10N is used whenever you wish to either view, input, or process data in non-English languages.

13.2.3 What Languages Are Supported in the I18N Effort?

I18N and L10N are not FreeBSD specific. Currently, one can choose from most of the major languages of the World, including but not limited to: Chinese, German, Japanese, Korean, French, Russian, Vietnamese and others.

13.3 Using Localization

In all its splendor, I18N is not FreeBSD-specific and is a convention. We encourage you to help FreeBSD in following this convention.

Localization settings are based on three main terms: Language Code, Country Code, and Encoding. Locale names are constructed from these parts as follows:

```
LanguageCode_CountryCode.Encoding
```

13.3.1 Language and Country Codes

In order to localize a FreeBSD system to a specific language (or any other I18N-supporting Unixes), the user needs to find out the codes for the specify country and language (country codes tell applications what variation of given language to use). In addition, web browsers, SMTP/POP servers, web servers, etc. make decisions based on them. The following are examples of language/country codes:

Language/Country Code	Description
en_US	English - United States
ru_RU	Russian for Russia
zh_TW	Traditional Chinese for Taiwan

13.3.2 Encodings

Some languages use non-ASCII encodings that are 8-bit, wide or multibyte characters, see multibyte(3) for more details. Older applications do not recognize them and mistake them for control characters. Newer applications usually do recognize 8-bit characters. Depending on the implementation, users may be required to compile an application with wide or multibyte characters support, or configure it correctly. To be able to input and process wide or multibyte characters, the FreeBSD Ports collection[1] has provided each language with different programs. Refer to the I18N documentation in the respective FreeBSD Port.

---

1 /ports/

Specifically, the user needs to look at the application documentation to decide on how to configure it correctly or to pass correct values into the configure/Makefile/compiler.

Some things to keep in mind are:

- Language specific single C chars character sets (see multibyte(3)), i.e., ISO-8859-1, ISO-8859-15, KOI8-R, CP437.
- Wide or multibyte encodings, f.e. EUC, Big5.

You can check the active list of character sets at the IANA Registry[2].

> **Note:** FreeBSD versions 5.0 and up use X11-compatible locale encodings instead.

13.3.3 I18N Applications

In the FreeBSD Ports and Package system, I18N applications have been named with `I18N` in their names for easy identification. However, they do not always support the language needed.

13.3.4 Setting Locale

Theoretically, one only needs to export the value of his/her locale name as `LANG` in the login shell and is usually done through the user's `~/.login_conf` or the user login shell configuration (`~/.profile`, `~/.bashrc`, `~/.cshrc`). This should set all of the locale subsets (such as `LC_CTYPE`, `LC_CTIME`, etc.). Please refer to language-specific FreeBSD documentation for more information.

You should set the following two values in your configuration files:

- `LANG` for POSIX setlocale(3) family functions
- `MM_CHARSET` for applications' MIME character set

This includes the user shell config, the specific application config, and the X11 config.

Setting Locale Methods

There are two methods for setting locale, and both are described below. The first (recommended one) is by assigning the environment variables in login class, and the second is by adding the environment variable assignments to the system's shell startup file.

Login Classes Method

This method allows environment variables needed for locale name and MIME character sets to be assigned once for every possible shell instead of adding specific shell assignments to each shell's startup file. User Level Setup can be done by an user himself and Administrator Level Setup require superuser privileges.

---

2 ftp://ftp.isi.edu/in-notes/iana/assignments/character-sets

User Level Setup

Here is a minimal example of a `.login_conf` file in user's home directory which has both variables set for Latin-1 encoding:

```
german:German User:\
 :charset=ISO-8859-1:\
 :lang=de_DE.ISO_8859-1:
```

Note: `de_DE.ISO8859-1` for FreeBSD versions 5.0 and up.

Here is an example of a `.login_conf` that sets the variables for Traditional Chinese in BIG-5 encoding. Notice the many more variables set because some software does not respect locale variables correctly for Chinese, Japanese, and Korean.

```
#Users who do not wish to use monetary units or time formats
#of Taiwan can manually change each variable
taiwan:Taiwanese User:\
 lang=zh_TW.Big5:\
 lc_all=zh_TW.Big:\
 lc_collate=zh_TW.Big5:\
 lc_ctype=zh_TW.Big5:\
 lc_messages=zh_TW.Big5:\
 lc_monetary=zh_TW.Big5:\
 lc_numeric=zh_TW.Big5:\
 lc_time=zh_TW.Big5:\
 charset=big5:\
 xmodifiers="@im=xcin": #Setting the XIM Input Server
```

See the next section, and login.conf(5) for more details.

Administrator Level Setup

Check that `/etc/login.conf` have the correct language user's class. Make sure these settings appear in `/etc/login.conf`:

```
language_name:accounts_title:\
 :charset=MIME_charset:\
 :lang=locale_name:\
 :tc=default:
```

So sticking with our previous example using Latin-1, it would look like this:

```
german:German Users Accounts:\
 :charset=ISO-8859-1:\
 :lang=de_DE.ISO_8859-1:\
 :tc=default:
```

Note: `de_DE.ISO8859-1` for FreeBSD versions 5.0 and up.

Changing Login Classes with vipw(8)

Use `vipw` to add new users, and make the entry look like this:

```
user:password:1111:11:language:0:0:User Name:/home/user:/bin/sh
```

Changing Login Classes with adduser(8)

Use `adduser` to add new users, and do the following:

- Set `defaultclass` = *language* in `/etc/adduser.conf`. Keep in mind you must enter a `default` class for all users of other languages in this case.
- An alternative variant is answering the specified language each time that

  ```
  Enter login class: default []:
  ```

  appears from adduser(8)

- Another alternative is to use the following for each user of a different language that you wish to add:

  ```
  # adduser -class language
  ```

Changing Login Classes with pw(8)

If you use pw(8) for adding new users, call it in this form:

```
# pw useradd user_name -L language
```

Shell Startup File Method

Note: This method is not recommended because it requires a different setup for each possible login program chosen. Use the Login Class Method (explained earlier in this chapter) instead.

To add the locale name and MIME character set, just set the two environment variables shown below in the `/etc/profile` and/or `/etc/csh.login` shell startup files. We will use the German language as an example below:

In `/etc/profile`:

```
LANG=de_DE.ISO_8859-1; export LANG
MM_CHARSET=ISO-8859-1; export MM_CHARSET
```

Or in `/etc/csh.login`:

```
setenv LANG de_DE.ISO_8859-1
setenv MM_CHARSET ISO-8859-1
```

Note: `de_DE.ISO8859-1` for FreeBSD versions 5.0 and up.

Alternatively, you can add the above instructions to `/usr/share/skel/dot.profile` (similar to what was used in `/etc/profile` above), or `/usr/share/skel/dot.login` (similar to what was used in `/etc/csh.login` above).

For X11:

In `$HOME/.xinitrc`:

```
LANG=de_DE.ISO_8859-1; export LANG
```

Or:

```
setenv LANG de_DE.ISO_8859-1
```

Depending on your shell (see above).

Note: `de_DE.ISO8859-1` for FreeBSD versions 5.0 and up.

13.3.5 Console Setup

For all single C chars character sets, set the correct console fonts in `/etc/rc.conf` for the language in question with:

```
font8x16=font_name
font8x14=font_name
font8x8=font_name
```

The *font_name* here is taken from the `/usr/share/syscons/fonts` directory, without the `.fnt` suffix.

Also be sure to set the correct keymap and screenmap for your single C chars character set through `/stand/sysinstall`. Once inside sysinstall, choose `Configure`, then `Console`. Alternatively, you can add the following to `/etc/rc.conf`:

```
scrnmap=screenmap_name
keymap=keymap_name
keychange="fkey_number sequence"
```

The *screenmap_name* here is taken from the `/usr/share/syscons/scrnmaps` directory, without the `.scm` suffix. A screenmap with a corresponding mapped font is usually needed as a workaround for expanding bit 8 to bit 9 on a VGA adapter's font character matrix in pseudographics area, i.e., to move letters out of that area if screen font uses a bit 8 column.

If you have the **moused daemon** enabled by setting the following in your `/etc/rc.conf`:

```
moused_enable="YES"
```

then examine the mouse cursor information in the next paragraph.

By default the mouse cursor of the syscons driver occupies the 0xd0-0xd3 range in the character set. If your language uses this range, you need to move the cursor's range outside of it. To enable the workaround for FreeBSD versions before 5.0, insert the following line into your kernel config:

```
options SC_MOUSE_CHAR=0x03
```

For the FreeBSD versions 5.0 and up insert the following line into /etc/rc.conf:

```
mousechar_start=3
```

The *keymap_name* here is taken from the /usr/share/syscons/keymaps directory, without the .kbd suffix.

The keychange is usually needed to program function keys to match the selected terminal type because function key sequences cannot be defined in the key map.

Also be sure to set the correct console terminal type in /etc/ttys for all ttyv* entries. Current pre-defined correspondences are:

Character Set	Terminal Type
ISO-8859-1 or ISO-8859-15	cons25l1
ISO-8859-2	cons25l2
KOI8-R	cons25r
KOI8-U	cons25u
CP437 (hardware default) or US-ASCII	cons25

For wide or multibyte characters languages, use the correct FreeBSD port in your /usr/ports/language directory. Some ports appear as console while the system sees it as serial vtty's, hence you must reserve enough vtty's for both X11 and the pseudo-serial console. Here is a partial list of applications for using other languages in console:

Language	Location
Traditional Chinese (BIG-5)	chinese/big5con
Japanese	japanese/ja-kon2-* or japanese/Mule_Wnn
Korean	korean/ko-han

13.3.6 X11 Setup

Although X11 is not part of the FreeBSD Project, we have included some information here for FreeBSD users. For more details, refer to the XFree86 web site[3] or whichever X11 Server you use.

In ~/.Xresources, you can additionally tune application specific I18N settings (e.g., fonts, menus, etc.).

Displaying Fonts

Install the X11 True Type-Common server (XTT-common) and install the language truetype fonts. Setting the correct

---

3 http://www.xfree86.org/

locale should allow you to view your selected language in menus and such.

Inputting Non-English Characters

The X11 Input Method (XIM) Protocol is a new standard for all X11 clients. All X11 applications should be written as XIM clients that take input from XIM Input servers. There are several XIM servers available for different languages.

13.3.7 Printer Setup

Some single C chars character sets are usually hardware coded into printers. Wide or multibyte character sets require special setup and we recommend using **apsfilter**. You may also convert the document to PostScript or PDF formats using language specific converters.

13.3.8 Kernel and File Systems

The FreeBSD FFS filesystem is 8-bit clean, so it can be used with any single C chars character set (see multibyte(3)), but there is no character set name stored in the filesystem; i.e., it is raw 8-bit and does not know anything about encoding order. Officially, FFS does not support any form of wide or multibyte character sets yet. However, some wide or multibyte character sets have independent patches for FFS enabling such support. They are only temporary unportable solutions or hacks and we have decided to not include them in the source tree. Refer to respective languages' web sites for more informations and the patch files.

The FreeBSD MS-DOS filesystem has the configurable ability to convert between MS-DOS, Unicode character sets and chosen FreeBSD filesystem character sets. See mount_msdos(8) for details.

13.4 Compiling I18N Programs

Many FreeBSD Ports have been ported with I18N support. Some of them are marked with -I18N in the port name. These and many other programs have built in support for I18N and need no special consideration.

However, some applications such as **MySQL** need to be have the `Makefile` configured with the specific charset. This is usually done in the `Makefile` or done by passing a value to configure in the source.

13.5 Localizing FreeBSD to Specific Languages

13.5.1 Russian Language (KOI8-R encoding)

For more information about KOI8-R encoding, see the KOI8-R References (Russian Net Character Set)[4].

Locale Setup

Put the following lines into your ~/.login_conf file:

```
me:My Account:\
  :charset=KOI8-R:\
  :lang=ru_RU.KOI8-R:
```

See earlier in this chapter for examples of setting up the locale.

Console Setup

- For the FreeBSD versions before 5.0 add the following line to your kernel configuration file:

    ```
    options SC_MOUSE_CHAR=0x03
    ```

    For the FreeBSD versions 5.0 and up insert the following line into /etc/rc.conf:

    ```
    mousechar_start=3
    ```

- Use following settings in /etc/rc.conf:

    ```
    keymap="ru.koi8-r"
    scrnmap="koi8-r2cp866"
    font8x16="cp866b-8x16"
    font8x14="cp866-8x14"
    font8x8="cp866-8x8"
    ```

- For each ttyv* entry in /etc/ttys, use cons25r as the terminal type.

See earlier in this chapter for examples of setting up the console.

Printer Setup

Since most printers with Russian characters come with hardware code page CP866, a special output filter is needed for KOI8-R -> CP866 conversion. Such a filter is installed by default as /usr/libexec/lpr/ru/koi2alt. A Russian printer /etc/printcap entry should look like:

---

4 http://koi8.pp.ru/

```
lp|Russian local line printer:\
 :sh:of=/usr/libexec/lpr/ru/koi2alt:\
 :lp=/dev/lpt0:sd=/var/spool/output/lpd:lf=/var/log/lpd-errs:
```

See printcap(5) for a detailed description.

MS-DOS FS and Russian Filenames

The following example fstab(5) entry enables support for Russian filenames in mounted MS-DOS filesystems:

```
/dev/ad0s2      /dos/c  msdos   rw,-Wkoi2dos,-Lru_RU.KOI8-R 0 0
```

See mount_msdos(8) for a detailed description of the -W and -L options.

X11 Setup

1. Do non-X locale setup first as described.

   Note: The Russian KOI8-R locale may not work with old XFree86 releases (lower than 3.3). The XFree86 port from x11/XFree86 already is the most recent XFree86 version, so it will work if you install XFree86 from the port. This should not be an issue unless you are using an old version of FreeBSD.

2. Go to the russian/X.language directory and issue the following command:

   ```
   # make install
   ```

   The above port installs the latest version of the KOI8-R fonts. XFree86 3.3 already has some KOI8-R fonts, but these are scaled better.

   Check the "Files" section in your /etc/XF86Config file. The following lines must be added *before* any other FontPath entries:

   ```
   FontPath    "/usr/X11R6/lib/X11/fonts/cyrillic/misc"
   FontPath    "/usr/X11R6/lib/X11/fonts/cyrillic/75dpi"
   FontPath    "/usr/X11R6/lib/X11/fonts/cyrillic/100dpi"
   ```

   If you use a high resolution video mode, swap the 75 dpi and 100 dpi lines.

3. To activate a Russian keyboard, add the following to the "Keyboard" section of your XF86Config file.

   For XFree86 v3.*:

   ```
   XkbLayout   "ru"
   XkbOptions "grp:caps_toggle"
   ```

   For XFree86 v4.*:

   ```
   Option "XkbLayout"    "ru"
   ```

```
Option "XkbOptions"  "grp:caps_toggle"
```

Also make sure that `XkbDisable` is turned off (commented out) there.

The RUS/LAT switch will be `CapsLock`. The old `CapsLock` function is still available via `Shift+CapsLock` (in LAT mode only).

If you have "Windows" keys on your keyboard, and notice that some non-alphabetical keys are mapped incorrectly in RUS mode, add the following line in your `XF86Config` file.

For XFree86 v3.*:

```
XkbVariant "winkeys"
```

For XFree86 v4.*:

```
Option "XkbVariant" "winkeys"
```

Note: The Russian XKB keyboard may not work with old XFree86 versions, see the note above for more information. The Russian XKB keyboard may also not work with non-localized applications as well. Minimally localized applications should call a `XtSetLanguageProc (NULL, NULL, NULL);` function early in the program. See KOI8-R for X-Window[5] for more instructions on localizing X11 applications.

13.5.2 Traditional Chinese Localization for Taiwan

The FreeBSD-Taiwan Project has an I18N/L10N tutorial for FreeBSD at `http://freebsd.sinica.edu.tw/~ncvs/zh-l10n-tut/index.html` using many `chinese/*` applications. The editor for the `zh-L10N-tut` is Clive Lin `<Clive@CirX.org>`. You can also cvsup the following collections at `freebsd.sinica.edu.tw`:

Collection	Description
outta-port tag=.	Beta-quality ports collection for Chinese
zh-L10N-tut tag=.	Localizing FreeBSD Tutorial in BIG-5 Traditional Chinese
zh-doc tag=.	FreeBSD Documentation Translation to BIG-5 Traditional Chinese

Chuan-Hsing Shen `<s874070@mail.yzu.edu.tw>` has created the Chinese FreeBSD Collection (CFC)[7] using FreeBSD-Taiwan's `zh-L10N-tut`. The packages and the script files are available at `ftp://ftp.csie.ncu.edu.tw/OS/FreeBSD/taiwan/CFC/`.

13.5.3 German Language Localization (For All ISO 8859-1

---

5 http://koi8.pp.ru/xwin.html
7 http://cnpa.yzu.edu.tw/~cfc/

Languages)

Slaven Rezic <eserte@cs.tu-berlin.de> wrote a tutorial how to use umlauts on a FreeBSD machine. The tutorial is written in German and available at `http://www.de.FreeBSD.org/de/umlaute/`.

13.5.4 Japanese and Korean Language Localization

For Japanese, refer to `http://www.jp.FreeBSD.org/`, and for Korean, refer to `http://www.kr.FreeBSD.org/`.

13.5.5 Non-English FreeBSD Documentation

Some FreeBSD contributors have translated parts of FreeBSD to other languages. They are available through links on the main site or in `/usr/share/doc`.

Chapter 14

Sound

14.1 Synopsis

FreeBSD supports a wide variety of sound cards, allowing you to enjoy high fidelity output from your computer. This includes the ability to record and playback audio in the MPEG Audio Layer 3 (MP3), WAV, and Ogg Vorbis formats as well as many other formats. The FreeBSD Ports Collection also contains applications allowing you to edit your recorded audio, add sound effects, and control attached MIDI devices.

After reading this chapter, you will know:

- How to locate your sound card.
- How to configure your system so that your sound card is recognized.
- Methods to test that your card is working using sample applications.
- How to troubleshoot your sound setup.
- How to playback and encode MP3s.
- How to rip CD audio tracks into data files.

Before reading this chapter, you should:

- Know how to configure and install a new kernel (Chapter 9).

14.2 Locating the Correct Device

Before you begin, you should know the model of the card you have, the chip it uses, and whether it is a PCI or ISA card. FreeBSD supports a wide variety of both PCI and ISA cards. If you do not see your card in the following list, check the pcm(4) manual page. This is not a complete list; however, it does list some of the most common cards.

- Crystal 4237, 4236, 4232, 4231
- Yamaha OPL-SAx
- OPTi931
- Ensoniq AudioPCI 1370/1371
- ESS Solo-1/1E

- NeoMagic 256AV/ZX

- Sound Blaster Pro, 16, 32, AWE64, AWE128, Live

- Creative ViBRA16

- Advanced Asound 100, 110, and Logic ALS120

- ES 1868, 1869, 1879, 1888

- Gravis UltraSound

- Aureal Vortex 1 or 2

The driver you use in your kernel depends on the kind of card you have. The sections below provide more information and what you will need to add to your kernel configuration (Chapter 9).

14.2.1 Creative, Advance, and ESS Sound Cards

If you have one of the above cards, you will need to add:

```
device pcm
```

to your kernel configuration file. If you have a PnP ISA card, you will also need to add:

```
device sbc
```

For a non-PnP ISA card, add:

```
device pcm
device sbc0 at isa? port 0x220 irq 5 drq 1 flags 0x15
```

to your kernel configuration file. The settings shown above are the defaults. You may need to change the IRQ or the other settings to match your card. See the sbc(4) manual page for more information.

> **Note:** The Sound Blaster Live is not supported under FreeBSD 4.0 without a patch, which this section will not cover. It is recommended that you update to the latest -STABLE before trying to use this card.

14.2.2 Gravis UltraSound Cards

For a PnP ISA card, you will need to add:

```
device pcm
device gusc
```

to your kernel configuration file. If you have a non-PnP ISA card, you will need to add:

```
device pcm
device gus0 at isa? port 0x220 irq 5 drq 1 flags 0x13
```

to your kernel configuration file. You may need to change the IRQ or the other settings to match your card. See the gusc(4) manual page for more information.

14.2.3 Crystal Sound Cards

For Crystal cards, you will need to add:

```
device pcm
device csa
```

to your kernel configuration file.

14.2.4 Generic Support

For PnP ISA or PCI cards, you will need to add:

```
device pcm
```

to your kernel configuration file. If you have a non-PnP ISA sound card that does not have a bridge driver, you will need to add:

```
device pcm0 at isa? irq 10 drq 1 flags 0x0
```

to your kernel configuration file. You may need to change the IRQ or the other settings to match your card.

14.2.5 Onboard Sound

Some systems with built-in motherboard sound devices may require the following option in your kernel configuration:

```
options PNPBIOS
```

14.3 Recompiling the Kernel

After adding the requisite driver(s) to your kernel configuration file, you will need to recompile your kernel. Please see Section 9.3 of the handbook for more information.

14.4 Creating and Testing the Device Nodes

After you reboot, log in and run dmesg | grep pcm as shown below:

```
# dmesg | grep pcm
```

```
pcm0: <SB16 DSP 4.11> on sbc0
```

The output from your system may look different. If no pcm devices show up, something went wrong earlier. If that happens, go through your kernel configuration file again and make sure you chose the correct device. Consult the troubleshooting section for additional options.

If the previous command returned pcm0, you will have to run the following as root:

```
# cd /dev
# sh MAKEDEV snd0
```

If the command returned pcm1, follow the same steps as shown above, replacing snd0 with snd1.

> **Note:** The above commands will *not* create a /dev/snd device!

MAKEDEV will create a group of device nodes, including:

Device	Description
/dev/audio	SPARC-compatible audio device
/dev/dsp	Digitized voice device
/dev/dspW	Like /dev/dsp, but 16 bits per sample
/dev/midi	Raw midi access device
/dev/mixer	Control port mixer device
/dev/music	Level 2 sequencer interface
/dev/sequencer	Sequencer device
/dev/pss	Programmable device interface

If all goes well, you should now have a functioning sound card. If you do not, read the next section.

14.5 Common Problems

1. I get an unsupported subdevice XX error!

One or more of the device nodes was not created correctly. Repeat the steps above.

2. I get a sb_dspwr(XX) timed out error!

The I/O port is not set correctly.

3. I get a bad irq XX error!

The IRQ is set incorrectly. Make sure that the set IRQ and the sound IRQ are the same.

4. I get a xxx: gus pcm not attached, out of memory error. What causes that?

If this happens, it is because there is not enough available memory to use the device.

14.6 MP3 Audio

MP3 (MPEG Layer 3 Audio) accomplishes near CD-quality sound, leaving no reason to let your FreeBSD workstation fall short of its offerings.

14.6.1 MP3 Players

By far, the most popular XFree86 MP3 player is **XMMS** (X Multimedia System). **WinAmp** skins can be used with **XMMS** since the GUI is almost identical to that of Nullsoft **Winamp**'s. **XMMS** also has native plug-in support.

XMMS can be installed from the `audio/xmms` port or package.

XMMS' interface is intuitive, with a playlist, graphic equalizer, and more. Those familiar with WinAmp will find **XMMS** simple to use.

The `audio/mpg123` port is an alternative, command-line MP3 player.

mpg123 can be run by specifying the sound device and the MP3 file on the command line, as shown below:

```
# mpg123 -a /dev/dsp1.0 Foobar-GreatestHits.mp3
High Performance MPEG 1.0/2.0/2.5 Audio Player for Layer 1, 2 and 3.
Version 0.59r (1999/Jun/15). Written and copyrights by Michael Hipp.
Uses code from various people. See 'README' for more!
THIS SOFTWARE COMES WITH ABSOLUTELY NO WARRANTY! USE AT YOUR OWN RISK!




Playing MPEG stream from BT - Foobar-GreastHits.mp3 ...
MPEG 1.0 layer III, 128 kbit/s, 44100 Hz joint-stereo
```

`/dev/dsp1.0` should be replaced with the `dsp` device entry on your system.

14.6.2 Ripping CD Audio Tracks

Before encoding a CD or CD track to MP3, the audio data on the CD must be ripped onto the hard drive. This is done by copying the raw CDDA (CD Digital Audio) data to WAV files.

The `cdda2wav` tool, which is a part of the `sysutils/cdrtools` suite, is used for ripping audio information of CDs and the information associated with it.

With the audio CD in the drive, the following command can be issued (as `root`) to rip an entire CD into individual (per track) WAV files:

```
# cdda2wav -D 0,1,0 -B
```

The `-D 0,1,0` indicates the SCSI device `0,1,0`, which corresponds to the output of `cdrecord -scanbus`.

To rip individual tracks, make use of the `-t` option as shown:

```
# cdda2wav -D 0,1,0 -t 7
```

This example rips track seven of the audio CDROM. To rip a range of tracks, for example, track one to seven, specify a range:

```
# cdda2wav -D 0,1,0 -t 1+7
```

cdda2wav only supports SCSI CDROM drives. For IDE drives, try out `audio/cdd` or some of the various other utilities in the audio ports collection.

14.6.3 Encoding MP3s

Nowadays, the mp3 encoder of choice is **lame**. **Lame** can be found at `audio/lame` in the ports tree.

Using the ripped WAV files, the following command will convert `audio01.wav` to `audio01.mp3`:

```
# lame -h -b 128 \
--tt "Foo Song Title" \
--ta "FooBar Artist" \
--tl "FooBar Album" \
--ty "2001" \
--tc "Ripped and encoded by Foo" \
--tg "Genre" \
audio01.wav audio01.mp3
```

128 kbits seems to be the standard MP3 bitrate in use. Many enjoy the higher quality 160, or 192. The higher the bitrate, the more disk space the resulting MP3 will consume--but the quality will be higher. The `-h` option turns on the "higher quality but a little slower" mode. The options beginning with `--t` indicate ID3 tags, which usually contain song information, to be embedded within the MP3 file. Additional encoding options can be found by consulting the lame man page.

14.6.4 Decoding MP3s

In order to burn an audio CD from MP3s, they must be converted to a non-compressed WAV format. Both **XMMS** and **mpg123** support the output of MP3 to an uncompressed file format.

Writing to Disk in **XMMS**:

1. Launch **XMMS**.

2. Right-click on the window to bring up the **XMMS** menu.

3. Select `Preference` under `Options`.

4. Change the Output Plugin to "Disk Writer Plugin".

5. Press `Configure`.

6. Enter (or choose browse) a directory to write the uncompressed files to.

7. Load the MP3 file into **XMMS** as usual, with volume at 100% and EQ settings turned off.

8. Press `Play` — **XMMS** will appear as if it is playing the MP3, but no music will be heard. It is actually playing the MP3 to a file.

9. Be sure to set the default Output Plugin back to what it was before in order to listen to MP3s again.

Writing to stdout in **mpg123**:

1. Run mpg123 -s *audio01.mp3* > audio01.pcm

XMMS writes a file in the WAV format, while **mpg123** converts the MP3 into raw PCM audio data. Both of these formats can be used with **cdrecord** or **burncd** to create audio CDROMs.

Read Section 12.6 for more information on using a CD burner in FreeBSD.

Chapter 15
Serial Communications

15.1 Synopsis

Unix has always had support for serial communications. In fact, the very first Unix machines relied on serial lines for user input and output. Things have changed a lot from the days when the average "terminal" consisted of a 10-character-per-second serial printer and a keyboard. This chapter will cover some of the ways in which FreeBSD uses serial communications.

After reading this chapter, you will know:

- How to connect terminals to your FreeBSD system.
- How to use a modem to dial out to remote hosts.
- How to allow remote users to login to your system with a modem.
- How to boot your system from a serial console.

Before reading this chapter, you should:

- Know how to configure and install a new kernel (Chapter 9).
- Understand Unix permissions and processes (Chapter 3).
- Have access to the technical manual for the serial hardware (modem or multi-port card) that you would like to use with FreeBSD.

15.2 Introduction

15.2.1 Terminology

bps

> Bits per Second — the rate at which data is transmitted

DTE

> Data Terminal Equipment — for example, your computer

DCE

> Data Communications Equipment — your modem

RS-232

> EIA standard for hardware serial communications

When talking about communications data rates, this section does not use the term "baud". Baud refers to the number of electrical state transitions that may be made in a period of time, while "bps" (bits per second) is the *correct* term to use (at least it does not seem to bother the curmudgeons quite a much).

15.2.2 Cables and Ports

To connect a modem or terminal to your FreeBSD system, you will need a serial port on your computer and the proper cable to connect to your serial device. If you are already familiar with your hardware and the cable it requires, you can safely skip this section.

Cables

There are several different kinds of serial cables. The two most common types for our purposes are null-modem cables and standard ("straight") RS-232 cables. The documentation for your hardware should describe the type of cable required.

Null-modem Cables

A null-modem cable passes some signals straight through, like "signal ground," but switches other signals. For example, the "send data" pin on one end goes to the "receive data" pin on the other end.

If you like making your own cables, you can construct a null-modem cable for use with terminals. This table shows the RS-232C signal names and the pin numbers on a DB-25 connector.

Signal	Pin #		Pin #	Signal
TxD	2	connects to	3	RxD
RxD	3	connects to	2	TxD
DTR	20	connects to	6	DSR
DSR	6	connects to	20	DTR
SG	7	connects to	7	SG
DCD	8	connects to	4	RTS
RTS	4		5	CTS
CTS	5	connects to	8	DCD

Note: For DCD to RTS, connect pins 4 to 5 internally in the connector hood, and then to pin 8 in the remote hood.

Standard RS-232C Cables

A standard serial cable passes all the RS-232C signals straight-through. That is, the "send data" pin on one end of the cable goes to the "send data" pin on the other end. This is the type of cable to connect a modem to your FreeBSD system, and the type of cable needed for some terminals.

Ports

Serial ports are the devices through which data is transferred between the FreeBSD host computer and the terminal. This section describes the kinds of ports that exist and how they are addressed in FreeBSD.

Kinds of Ports

Several kinds of serial ports exist. Before you purchase or construct a cable, you need to make sure it will fit the ports on your terminal and on the FreeBSD system.

Most terminals will have DB25 ports. Personal computers, including PCs running FreeBSD, will have DB25 or DB9 ports. If you have a multiport serial card for your PC, you may have RJ-12 or RJ-45 ports.

See the documentation that accompanied the hardware for specifications on the kind of port in use. A visual inspection of the port often works too.

Port Names

In FreeBSD, you access each serial port through an entry in the `/dev` directory. There are two different kinds of entries:

* Call-in ports are named `/dev/ttydN` where *N* is the port number, starting from zero. Generally, you use the call-in port for terminals. Call-in ports require that the serial line assert the data carrier detect (DCD) signal to work.
* Call-out ports are named `/dev/cuaaN`. You usually do not use the call-out port for terminals, just for modems. You may use the call-out port if the serial cable or the terminal does not support the carrier detect signal.

If you have connected a terminal to the first serial port (`COM1` in MS-DOS), then you want to use `/dev/ttyd0` to refer to the terminal. If it is on the second serial port (also known as `COM2`), it is `/dev/ttyd1`, and so forth.

15.2.3 Kernel Configuration

FreeBSD supports four serial ports by default. In the MS-DOS world, these are known as `COM1:`, `COM2:`, `COM3:`, and `COM4:`. FreeBSD currently supports "dumb" multiport serial interface cards, such as the BocaBoard 1008 and 2016, as well as more intelligent multi-port cards such as those made by Digiboard and Stallion Technologies. However, the default kernel only looks for the standard COM ports.

To see if your kernel recognizes any of your serial ports, watch for messages while the kernel is booting, or use the `/sbin/dmesg` command to replay the kernel's boot messages. In particular, look for messages that start with the characters `sio`.

Tip: To view just the messages that have the word `sio`, use the command:

```
# /sbin/dmesg | grep 'sio'
```

For example, on a system with four serial ports, these are the serial-port specific kernel boot messages:

```
sio0 at 0x3f8-0x3ff irq 4 on isa
sio0: type 16550A
sio1 at 0x2f8-0x2ff irq 3 on isa
sio1: type 16550A
sio2 at 0x3e8-0x3ef irq 5 on isa
sio2: type 16550A
sio3 at 0x2e8-0x2ef irq 9 on isa
sio3: type 16550A
```

If your kernel does not recognize all of your serial ports, you will probably need to configure a custom FreeBSD kernel for your system. For detailed information on configuring your kernel, please see Chapter 9.

The relevant device lines for your kernel configuration file would look like this:

```
device sio0 at isa? port "IO_COM1" tty irq 4 vector siointr
device sio1 at isa? port "IO_COM2" tty irq 3 vector siointr
device sio2 at isa? port "IO_COM3" tty irq 5 vector siointr
device sio3 at isa? port "IO_COM4" tty irq 9 vector siointr
```

You can comment-out or completely remove lines for devices you do not have. Please see the sio(4) manual page for complete information on how to write configuration lines for multiport boards. Be careful if you are using a configuration file that was previously used for a different version of FreeBSD because the device flags have changed between versions.

Note: port `"IO_COM1"` is a substitution for port `0x3f8`, `IO_COM2` is `0x2f8`, `IO_COM3` is `0x3e8`, and `IO_COM4` is `0x2e8`, which are fairly common port addresses for their respective serial ports; interrupts 4, 3, 5, and 9 are fairly common interrupt request lines. Also note that regular serial ports *cannot* share interrupts on ISA-bus PCs (multiport boards have on-board electronics that allow all the 16550A's on the board to share one or two interrupt request lines).

15.2.4 Device Special Files

Most devices in the kernel are accessed through "device special files", which are located in the /dev directory. The sio devices are accessed through the /dev/ttydN (dial-in) and /dev/cuaaN (call-out) devices. FreeBSD also provides initialization devices (/dev/ttyidN and /dev/cuai0N) and locking devices (/dev/ttyldN and /dev/cual0N). The initialization devices are used to initialize communications port parameters each time a port is opened, such as crtscts for modems which use CTS/RTS signaling for flow control. The locking devices are used to lock flags on ports to prevent users or programs changing certain parameters; see the manual pages termios(4), sio(4), and stty(1) for information on the terminal settings, locking and initializing devices, and setting terminal options, respectively.

Making Device Special Files

Note: FreeBSD 5.0 includes the `devfs` filesystem which automatically creates device nodes as needed. If you are running a version of FreeBSD with `devfs` enabled then you can safely skip this section.

A shell script called MAKEDEV in the `/dev` directory manages the device special files. To use MAKEDEV to make dial-up device special files for COM1: (port 0), `cd` to `/dev` and issue the command MAKEDEV `ttyd0`. Likewise, to make dial-up device special files for COM2: (port 1), use MAKEDEV `ttyd1`.

MAKEDEV not only creates the `/dev/ttyd`N device special files, but also the `/dev/cuaa`N, `/dev/cuaia`N, `/dev/cuala`N, `/dev/ttyld`N, and `/dev/ttyid`N nodes.

After making new device special files, be sure to check the permissions on the files (especially the `/dev/cua*` files) to make sure that only users who should have access to those device special files can read and write on them — you probably do not want to allow your average user to use your modems to dial-out. The default permissions on the `/dev/cua*` files should be sufficient:

```
crw-rw----   1 uucp     dialer    28, 129 Feb 15 14:38 /dev/cuaa1
crw-rw----   1 uucp     dialer    28, 161 Feb 15 14:38 /dev/cuaia1
crw-rw----   1 uucp     dialer    28, 193 Feb 15 14:38 /dev/cuala1
```

These permissions allow the user `uucp` and users in the group `dialer` to use the call-out devices.

15.2.5 Serial Port Configuration

The `ttyd`N (or `cuaa`N) device is the regular device you will want to open for your applications. When a process opens the device, it will have a default set of terminal I/O settings. You can see these settings with the command

```
# stty -a -f /dev/ttyd1
```

When you change the settings to this device, the settings are in effect until the device is closed. When it is reopened, it goes back to the default set. To make changes to the default set, you can open and adjust the settings of the "initial state" device. For example, to turn on CLOCAL mode, 8 bit communication, and XON/XOFF flow control by default for `ttyd5`, type:

```
# stty -f /dev/ttyid5 clocal cs8 ixon ixoff
```

System-wide initialization of the serial devices is controlled in `/etc/rc.serial`. This file affects the default settings of serial devices.

To prevent certain settings from being changed by an application, make adjustments to the "lock state" device. For example, to lock the speed of `ttyd5` to 57600 bps, type:

```
# stty -f /dev/ttyld5 57600
```

Now, an application that opens `ttyd5` and tries to change the speed of the port will be stuck with 57600 bps.

Naturally, you should make the initial state and lock state devices writable only by the `root` account.

15.3 Terminals

Terminals provide a convenient and low-cost way to access your FreeBSD system when you are not at the computer's console or on a connected network. This section describes how to use terminals with FreeBSD.

15.3.1 Uses and Types of Terminals

The original Unix systems did not have consoles. Instead, people logged in and ran programs through terminals that were connected to the computer's serial ports. It is quite similar to using a modem and terminal software to dial into a remote system to do text-only work.

Today's PCs have consoles capable of high quality graphics, but the ability to establish a login session on a serial port still exists in nearly every Unix-style operating system today; FreeBSD is no exception. By using a terminal attached to an unused serial port, you can log in and run any text program that you would normally run on the console or in an xterm window in the X Window System.

For the business user, you can attach many terminals to a FreeBSD system and place them on your employees' desktops. For a home user, a spare computer such as an older IBM PC or a Macintosh can be a terminal wired into a more powerful computer running FreeBSD. You can turn what might otherwise be a single-user computer into a powerful multiple user system.

For FreeBSD, there are three kinds of terminals:

- Dumb terminals
- PCs acting as terminals
- X terminals

The remaining subsections describe each kind.

Dumb Terminals

Dumb terminals are specialized pieces of hardware that let you connect to computers over serial lines. They are called "dumb" because they have only enough computational power to display, send, and receive text. You cannot run any programs on them. It is the computer to which you connect them that has all the power to run text editors, compilers, email, games, and so forth.

There are hundreds of kinds of dumb terminals made by many manufacturers, including Digital Equipment Corporation's VT-100 and Wyse's WY-75. Just about any kind will work with FreeBSD. Some high-end terminals can even display graphics, but only certain software packages can take advantage of these advanced features.

Dumb terminals are popular in work environments where workers do not need access to graphic applications such as those provided by the X Window System.

PCs Acting As Terminals

If a dumb terminal has just enough ability to display, send, and receive text, then certainly any spare personal computer can be a dumb terminal. All you need is the proper cable and some *terminal emulation* software to run on the computer.

Such a configuration is popular in homes. For example, if your spouse is busy working on your FreeBSD system's console, you can do some text-only work at the same time from a less powerful personal computer hooked up as a terminal to the FreeBSD system.

X Terminals

X terminals are the most sophisticated kind of terminal available. Instead of connecting to a serial port, they usually connect to a network like Ethernet. Instead of being relegated to text-only applications, they can display any X application.

We introduce X terminals just for the sake of completeness. However, this chapter does *not* cover setup, configuration, or use of X terminals.

15.3.2 Configuration

This section describes what you need to configure on your FreeBSD system to enable a login session on a terminal. It assumes you have already configured your kernel to support the serial port to which the terminal is connected—and that you have connected it.

Recall from Chapter 7 that the `init` process is responsible for all process control and initialization at system startup. One of the tasks performed by `init` is to read the `/etc/ttys` file and start a `getty` process on the available terminals. The `getty` process is responsible for reading a login name and starting the `login` program.

Thus, to configure terminals for your FreeBSD system the following steps should be taken as `root` :

1. Add a line to `/etc/ttys` for the entry in the `/dev` directory for the serial port if it is not already there.
2. Specify that `/usr/libexec/getty` be run on the port, and specify the appropriate *getty* type from the `/etc/gettytab` file.
3. Specify the default terminal type.
4. Set the port to "on."
5. Specify whether the port should be "secure."
6. Force `init` to reread the `/etc/ttys` file.

As an optional step, you may wish to create a custom *getty* type for use in step 2 by making an entry in `/etc/gettytab`. This chapter does not explain how to do so; you are encouraged to see the gettytab(5) and the getty(8) manual pages for more information.

Adding an Entry to `/etc/ttys`

The `/etc/ttys` file lists all of the ports on your FreeBSD system where you want to allow logins. For example, the first virtual console `ttyv0` has an entry in this file. You can log in on the console using this entry. This file also contains entries for the other virtual consoles, serial ports, and pseudo-ttys. For a hardwired terminal, just list the serial port's `/dev` entry without the `/dev` part (for example, `/dev/ttyv0` would be listed as `ttyv0`).

A default FreeBSD install includes an `/etc/ttys` file with support for the first four serial ports: `ttyd0` through `ttyd3`. If you are attaching a terminal to one of those ports, you do not need to add another entry.

Example 15-1. Adding Terminal Entries to `/etc/ttys`

Suppose we would like to connect two terminals to the system: a Wyse-50 and an old 286 IBM PC running **Procomm** terminal software emulating a VT-100 terminal. We connect the Wyse to the second serial port and the 286 to the sixth serial port (a port on a multiport serial card). The corresponding entries in the `/etc/ttys` file would look like this:

```
ttyd1❶  "/usr/libexec/getty std.38400"❷  wy50❸  on❹  insecure❺
ttyd5  "/usr/libexec/getty std.19200"  vt100  on  insecure
```

❶   The first field normally specifies the name of the terminal special file as it is found in `/dev`.

❷   The second field is the command to execute for this line, which is usually getty(8). `getty` initializes and opens the line, sets the speed, prompts for a user name and then executes the login(1) program.

The `getty` program accepts one (optional) parameter on its command line, the *getty* type. A *getty* type tells about characteristics on the terminal line, like bps rate and parity. The `getty` program reads these characteristics from the file `/etc/gettytab`.

The file `/etc/gettytab` contains lots of entries for terminal lines both old and new. In almost all cases, the entries that start with the text `std` will work for hardwired terminals. These entries ignore parity. There is a `std` entry for each bps rate from 110 to 115200. Of course, you can add your own entries to this file. The gettytab(5) manual page provides more information.

When setting the *getty* type in the `/etc/ttys` file, make sure that the communications settings on the terminal match.

For our example, the Wyse-50 uses no parity and connects at 38400 bps. The 286 PC uses no parity and connects at 19200 bps.

❸   The third field is the type of terminal usually connected to that tty line. For dial-up ports, `unknown` or `dialup` is typically used in this field since users may dial up with practically any type of terminal or software. For hardwired terminals, the terminal type does not change, so you can put a real terminal type from the termcap(5) database file in this field.

For our example, the Wyse-50 uses the real terminal type while the 286 PC running **Procomm** will be set to emulate at VT-100.

❹   The fourth field specifies if the port should be enabled. Putting `on` here will have the `init` process start the program in the second field, `getty`. If you put `off` in this field, there will be no `getty`, and hence no logins on the port.

❺   The final field is used to specify whether the port is secure. Marking a port as secure means that you trust it enough to allow the `root` account (or any account with a user ID of 0) to login from that port. Insecure ports do not allow `root` logins. On an insecure port, users must login from unprivileged accounts and then use su(1) or a similar mechanism to gain superuser privileges.

It is highly recommended that you use "insecure" even for terminals that are behind locked doors. It is quite easy to login and use `su` if you need superuser privileges.

Force `init` to Reread `/etc/ttys`

After making the necessary changes to the `/etc/ttys` file you should send a SIGHUP (hangup) signal to the `init` process to force it to re-read its configuration file. For example :

```
# kill -HUP 1
```

Note: `init` is always the first process run on a system, therefore it will always have PID 1.

If everything is set up correctly, all cables are in place, and the terminals are powered up, then a `getty` process should be running on each terminal and you should see login prompts on your terminals at this point.

15.3.3 Troubleshooting Your Connection

Even with the most meticulous attention to detail, something could still go wrong while setting up a terminal. Here is a list of symptoms and some suggested fixes.

1. No login prompt appears

Make sure the terminal is plugged in and powered up. If it is a personal computer acting as a terminal, make sure it is running terminal emulation software on the correct serial port.

Make sure the cable is connected firmly to both the terminal and the FreeBSD computer. Make sure it is the right kind of cable.

Make sure the terminal and FreeBSD agree on the bps rate and parity settings. If you have a video display terminal, make sure the contrast and brightness controls are turned up. If it is a printing terminal, make sure paper and ink are in good supply.

Make sure that a `getty` process is running and serving the terminal. For example, to get a list of running `getty` processes with `ps`, type:

```
# ps -axww|grep getty
```

You should see an entry for the terminal. For example, the following display shows that a `getty` is running on the second serial port `ttyd1` and is using the `std.38400` entry in `/etc/gettytab`:

```
22189  d1  Is+    0:00.03 /usr/libexec/getty std.38400 ttyd1
```

If no `getty` process is running, make sure you have enabled the port in `/etc/ttys`. Also remember to run `kill -HUP 1` after modifying the `ttys` file.

2. Garbage appears instead of a login prompt

Make sure the terminal and FreeBSD agree on the bps rate and parity settings. Check the `getty` processes to make sure the correct *getty* type is in use. If not, edit `/etc/ttys` and run `kill -HUP 1`.

3. Characters appear doubled; the password appears when typed

Switch the terminal (or the terminal emulation software) from "half duplex" or "local echo" to "full duplex."

15.4 Dial-in Service

Configuring your FreeBSD system for dial-in service is very similar to connecting terminals except that you are dealing with modems instead of terminals.

15.4.1 External vs. Internal Modems

External modems seem to be more convenient for dial-up, because external modems often can be semi-permanently configured via parameters stored in non-volatile RAM and they usually provide lighted indicators that display the state of important RS-232 signals. Blinking lights impress visitors, but lights are also very useful to see whether a modem is operating properly.

Internal modems usually lack non-volatile RAM, so their configuration may be limited only to setting DIP switches. If your internal modem has any signal indicator lights, it is probably difficult to view the lights when the system's cover is in place.

Modems and Cables

If you are using an external modem, then you will of course need the proper cable. A standard RS-232C serial cable should suffice as long as all of the normal signals are wired :

- Transmitted Data (SD)
- Received Data (RD)
- Request to Send (RTS)
- Clear to Send (CTS)
- Data Set Ready (DSR)
- Data Terminal Ready (DTR)
- Carrier Detect (CD)
- Signal Ground (SG)

FreeBSD needs the RTS and CTS signals for flow-control at speeds above 2400bps, the CD signal to detect when a call has been answered or the line has been hung up, and the DTR signal to reset the modem after a session is complete. Some cables are wired without all of the needed signals, so if you have problems, such as a login session not going away when the line hangs up, you may have a problem with your cable.

Like other Unix-like operating systems, FreeBSD uses the hardware signals to find out when a call has been answered or a line has been hung up and to hangup and reset the modem after a call. FreeBSD avoids sending commands to the modem or watching for status reports from the modem. If you are familiar with connecting modems to PC-based bulletin board systems, this may seem awkward.

15.4.2 Serial Interface Considerations

FreeBSD supports NS8250-, NS16450-, NS16550-, and NS16550A-based EIA RS-232C (CCITT V.24) communications interfaces. The 8250 and 16450 devices have single-character buffers. The 16550 device provides a 16-character buffer, which allows for better system performance. (Bugs in plain 16550's prevent the use of the 16-character buffer, so use 16550A's if possible). Because single-character-buffer devices require more work by the operating system than the 16-character-buffer devices, 16550A-based serial interface cards are much preferred. If the system has many active serial ports or will have a heavy load, 16550A-based cards are better for low-error-rate communications.

15.4.3 Quick Overview

As with terminals, `init` spawns a `getty` process for each configured serial port for dial-in connections. For example, if a modem is attached to `/dev/ttyd0`, the command `ps ax` might show this:

```
4850 ??  I      0:00.09 /usr/libexec/getty V19200 ttyd0
```

When a user dials the modem's line and the modems connect, the CD (Carrier Detect) line is reported by the modem. The kernel notices that carrier has been detected and completes `getty`'s open of the port. `getty` sends a `login:` prompt at the specified initial line speed. `getty` watches to see if legitimate characters are received, and, in a typical configuration, if it finds junk (probably due to the modem's connection speed being different than `getty`'s speed), `getty` tries adjusting the line speeds until it receives reasonable characters.

After the user enters his/her login name, `getty` executes `/usr/bin/login`, which completes the login by asking for the user's password and then starting the user's shell.

15.4.4 Configuration Files

There are three system configuration files in the `/etc` directory that you will probably need to edit to allow dial-up access to your FreeBSD system. The first, `/etc/gettytab`, contains configuration information for the `/usr/libexec/getty` daemon. Second, `/etc/ttys` holds information that tells `/sbin/init` what tty devices should have `getty` processes running on them. Lastly, you can place port initialization commands in the `/etc/rc.serial` script.

There are two schools of thought regarding dial-up modems on Unix. One group likes to configure their modems and systems so that no matter at what speed a remote user dials in, the local computer-to-modem RS-232 interface runs at a locked speed. The benefit of this configuration is that the remote user always sees a system login prompt immediately. The downside is that the system does not know what a user's true data rate is, so full-screen programs like Emacs will not adjust their screen-painting methods to make their response better for slower connections.

The other school configures their modems' RS-232 interface to vary its speed based on the remote user's connection speed. For example, V.32bis (14.4 Kbps) connections to the modem might make the modem run its RS-232 interface at 19.2 Kbps, while 2400 bps connections make the modem's RS-232 interface run at 2400 bps. Because `getty` does not understand any particular modem's connection speed reporting, getty gives a login: message at an initial speed and watches the characters that come back in response. If the user sees junk, it is assumed that they know they should press the Enter key until they see a recognizable prompt. If the data rates do not match, getty sees anything the user types as "junk", tries going to the next speed and gives the login: prompt again. This procedure can continue ad nauseam, but normally only takes a keystroke or two before the user sees a good prompt. Obviously, this login sequence does not look as clean as the former "locked-speed" method, but a user on a low-speed connection should receive better interactive response from full-screen programs.

This section will try to give balanced configuration information, but is biased towards having the modem's data rate follow the connection rate.

/etc/gettytab

/etc/gettytab is a termcap(5)-style file of configuration information for getty(8). Please see the gettytab(5) manual page for complete information on the format of the file and the list of capabilities.

Locked-Speed Config

If you are locking your modem's data communications rate at a particular speed, you probably will not need to make any changes to /etc/gettytab.

Matching-Speed Config

You will need to setup an entry in /etc/gettytab to give getty information about the speeds you wish to use for your modem. If you have a 2400 bps modem, you can probably use the existing D2400 entry.

```
#
# Fast dialup terminals, 2400/1200/300 rotary (can start either way)
#
D2400|d2400|Fast-Dial-2400:\
        :nx=D1200:tc=2400-baud:
3|D1200|Fast-Dial-1200:\
        :nx=D300:tc=1200-baud:
5|D300|Fast-Dial-300:\
        :nx=D2400:tc=300-baud:
```

If you have a higher speed modem, you will probably need to add an entry in /etc/gettytab; here is an entry you could use for a 14.4 Kbps modem with a top interface speed of 19.2 Kbps:

```
#
# Additions for a V.32bis Modem
#
um|V300|High Speed Modem at 300,8-bit:\
        :nx=V19200:tc=std.300:
un|V1200|High Speed Modem at 1200,8-bit:\
        :nx=V300:tc=std.1200:
uo|V2400|High Speed Modem at 2400,8-bit:\
        :nx=V1200:tc=std.2400:
up|V9600|High Speed Modem at 9600,8-bit:\
```

```
           :nx=V2400:tc=std.9600:
   uq|V19200|High Speed Modem at 19200,8-bit:\
           :nx=V9600:tc=std.19200:
```

This will result in 8-bit, no parity connections.

The example above starts the communications rate at 19.2 Kbps (for a V.32bis connection), then cycles through 9600 bps (for V.32), 2400 bps, 1200 bps, 300 bps, and back to 19.2 Kbps. Communications rate cycling is implemented with the nx= ("next table") capability. Each of the lines uses a tc= ("table continuation") entry to pick up the rest of the "standard" settings for a particular data rate.

If you have a 28.8 Kbps modem and/or you want to take advantage of compression on a 14.4 Kbps modem, you need to use a higher communications rate than 19.2 Kbps. Here is an example of a gettytab entry starting a 57.6 Kbps:

```
   #
   # Additions for a V.32bis or V.34 Modem
   # Starting at 57.6 Kbps
   #
   vm|VH300|Very High Speed Modem at 300,8-bit:\
           :nx=VH57600:tc=std.300:
   vn|VH1200|Very High Speed Modem at 1200,8-bit:\
           :nx=VH300:tc=std.1200:
   vo|VH2400|Very High Speed Modem at 2400,8-bit:\
           :nx=VH1200:tc=std.2400:
   vp|VH9600|Very High Speed Modem at 9600,8-bit:\
           :nx=VH2400:tc=std.9600:
   vq|VH57600|Very High Speed Modem at 57600,8-bit:\
           :nx=VH9600:tc=std.57600:
```

If you have a slow CPU or a heavily loaded system and do not have 16550A-based serial ports, you may receive sio "silo" errors at 57.6 Kbps.

/etc/ttys

Configuration of the /etc/ttys file was covered in Example 15-1. Configuration for modems is similar but we must pass a different argument to getty and specify a different terminal type. The general format for both locked-speed and matching-speed configurations is:

```
   ttyd0    "/usr/libexec/getty xxx"    dialup on
```

The first item in the above line is the device special file for this entry — ttyd0 means /dev/ttyd0 is the file that this getty will be watching. The second item, "/usr/libexec/getty *xxx*" (*xxx* will be replaced by the initial gettytab capability) is the process init will run on the device. The third item, dialup, is the default terminal type. The fourth parameter, on, indicates to init that the line is operational. There can be a fifth parameter, secure, but it should only be used for terminals which are physically secure (such as the system console).

The default terminal type (dialup in the example above) may depend on local preferences. dialup is the traditional default terminal type on dial-up lines so that users may customize their login scripts to notice when the terminal is dialup and automatically adjust their terminal type. However, the author finds it easier at his site to specify vt102 as the default terminal type, since the users just use VT102 emulation on their remote systems.

After you have made changes to /etc/ttys, you may send the init process a HUP signal to re-read the file. You can use the command

```
# kill -HUP 1
```

to send the signal. If this is your first time setting up the system, you may want to wait until your modem(s) are properly configured and connected before signaling init.

Locked-Speed Config

For a locked-speed configuration, your ttys entry needs to have a fixed-speed entry provided to getty. For a modem whose port speed is locked at 19.2 Kbps, the ttys entry might look like this:

```
ttyd0    "/usr/libexec/getty std.19200"    dialup on
```

If your modem is locked at a different data rate, substitute the appropriate value for std.*speed* instead of std.19200. Make sure that you use a valid type listed in /etc/gettytab.

Matching-Speed Config

In a matching-speed configuration, your ttys entry needs to reference the appropriate beginning "auto-baud" (sic) entry in /etc/gettytab. For example, if you added the above suggested entry for a matching-speed modem that starts at 19.2 Kbps (the gettytab entry containing the V19200 starting point), your ttys entry might look like this:

```
ttyd0    "/usr/libexec/getty V19200"    dialup on
```

/etc/rc.serial

High-speed modems, like V.32, V.32bis, and V.34 modems, need to use hardware (RTS/CTS) flow control. You can add stty commands to /etc/rc.serial to set the hardware flow control flag in the FreeBSD kernel for the modem ports.

For example to set the termios flag crtscts on serial port #1's (COM2:) dial-in and dial-out initialization devices, the following lines could be added to /etc/rc.serial :

```
# Serial port initial configuration
stty -f /dev/ttyid1 crtscts
stty -f /dev/cuai01 crtscts
```

15.4.5 Modem Settings

If you have a modem whose parameters may be permanently set in non-volatile RAM, you will need to use a terminal program (such as Telix under MS-DOS or tip under FreeBSD) to set the parameters. Connect to the modem using the same communications speed as the initial speed `getty` will use and configure the modem's non-volatile RAM to match these requirements:

- CD asserted when connected
- DTR asserted for operation; dropping DTR hangs up line and resets modem
- CTS transmitted data flow control
- Disable XON/XOFF flow control
- RTS received data flow control
- Quiet mode (no result codes)
- No command echo

Please read the documentation for your modem to find out what commands and/or DIP switch settings you need to give it.

For example, to set the above parameters on a USRobotics Sportster 14,400 external modem, one could give these commands to the modem:

```
ATZ
AT&C1&D2&H1&I0&R2&W
```

You might also want to take this opportunity to adjust other settings in the modem, such as whether it will use V.42bis and/or MNP5 compression.

The USR Sportster 14,400 external modem also has some DIP switches that need to be set; for other modems, perhaps you can use these settings as an example:

- Switch 1: UP — DTR Normal
- Switch 2: N/A (Verbal Result Codes/Numeric Result Codes)
- Switch 3: UP — Suppress Result Codes
- Switch 4: DOWN — No echo, offline commands
- Switch 5: UP — Auto Answer
- Switch 6: UP — Carrier Detect Normal
- Switch 7: UP — Load NVRAM Defaults
- Switch 8: N/A (Smart Mode/Dumb Mode)

Result codes should be disabled/suppressed for dial-up modems to avoid problems that can occur if `getty` mistakenly gives a `login:` prompt to a modem that is in command mode and the modem echoes the command or returns a result code. This sequence can result in a extended, silly conversation between `getty` and the modem.

Locked-speed Config

For a locked-speed configuration, you will need to configure the modem to maintain a constant modem-to-computer data rate independent of the communications rate. On a USR Sportster 14,400 external modem, these commands will lock the modem-to-computer data rate at the speed used to issue the commands:

```
ATZ
AT&B1&W
```

Matching-speed Config

For a variable-speed configuration, you will need to configure your modem to adjust its serial port data rate to match the incoming call rate. On a USR Sportster 14,400 external modem, these commands will lock the modem's error-corrected data rate to the speed used to issue the commands, but allow the serial port rate to vary for non-error-corrected connections:

```
ATZ
AT&B2&W
```

Checking the Modem's Configuration

Most high-speed modems provide commands to view the modem's current operating parameters in a somewhat human-readable fashion. On the USR Sportster 14,400 external modems, the command ATI5 displays the settings that are stored in the non-volatile RAM. To see the true operating parameters of the modem (as influenced by the USR's DIP switch settings), use the commands ATZ and then ATI4.

If you have a different brand of modem, check your modem's manual to see how to double-check your modem's configuration parameters.

15.4.6 Troubleshooting

Here are a few steps you can follow to check out the dial-up modem on your system.

Checking out the FreeBSD System

Hook up your modem to your FreeBSD system, boot the system, and, if your modem has status indication lights, watch to see whether the modem's DTR indicator lights when the login: prompt appears on the system's console — if it lights up, that should mean that FreeBSD has started a getty process on the appropriate communications port and is waiting for the modem to accept a call.

If the DTR indicator does not light, login to the FreeBSD system through the console and issue a ps ax to see if FreeBSD is trying to run a getty process on the correct port. You should see a lines like this among the processes displayed:

```
    114 ??  I      0:00.10 /usr/libexec/getty V19200 ttyd0
```

```
115 ??  I      0:00.10 /usr/libexec/getty V19200 ttyd1
```

If you see something different, like this:

```
114 d0  I      0:00.10 /usr/libexec/getty V19200 ttyd0
```

and the modem has not accepted a call yet, this means that `getty` has completed its open on the communications port. This could indicate a problem with the cabling or a mis-configured modem, because `getty` should not be able to open the communications port until CD (carrier detect) has been asserted by the modem.

If you do not see any `getty` processes waiting to open the desired `ttydN` port, double-check your entries in `/etc/ttys` to see if there are any mistakes there. Also, check the log file `/var/log/messages` to see if there are any log messages from `init` or `getty` regarding any problems. If there are any messages, triple-check the configuration files `/etc/ttys` and `/etc/gettytab`, as well as the appropriate device special files `/dev/ttydN`, for any mistakes, missing entries, or missing device special files.

Try Dialing In

Try dialing into the system; be sure to use 8 bits, no parity, and 1 stop bit on the remote system. If you do not get a prompt right away, or get garbage, try pressing Enter about once per second. If you still do not see a `login:` prompt after a while, try sending a BREAK. If you are using a high-speed modem to do the dialing, try dialing again after locking the dialing modem's interface speed (via AT&B1 on a USR Sportster, for example).

If you still cannot get a `login:` prompt, check `/etc/gettytab` again and double-check that

- The initial capability name specified in `/etc/ttys` for the line matches a name of a capability in `/etc/gettytab`
- Each `nx=` entry matches another `gettytab` capability name
- Each `tc=` entry matches another `gettytab` capability name

If you dial but the modem on the FreeBSD system will not answer, make sure that the modem is configured to answer the phone when DTR is asserted. If the modem seems to be configured correctly, verify that the DTR line is asserted by checking the modem's indicator lights (if it has any).

If you have gone over everything several times and it still does not work, take a break and come back to it later. If it still does not work, perhaps you can send an electronic mail message to the FreeBSD general questions mailing list `<freebsd-questions@FreeBSD.org>`describing your modem and your problem, and the good folks on the list will try to help.

15.5 Dial-out Service

The following are tips to getting your host to be able to connect over the modem to another computer. This is appropriate for establishing a terminal session with a remote host.

This is useful to log onto a BBS.

This kind of connection can be extremely helpful to get a file on the Internet if you have problems with PPP. If you need to FTP something and PPP is broken, use the terminal session to FTP it. Then use zmodem to transfer it to your machine.

15.5.1 My Stock Hayes Modem Is Not Supported, What Can I Do?

Actually, the manual page for `tip` is out of date. There is a generic Hayes dialer already built in. Just use `at=hayes` in your `/etc/remote` file.

The Hayes driver is not smart enough to recognize some of the advanced features of newer modems—messages like BUSY, NO DIALTONE, or CONNECT 115200 will just confuse it. You should turn those messages off when you use `tip` (using ATX0&W).

Also, the dial timeout for `tip` is 60 seconds. Your modem should use something less, or else tip will think there is a communication problem. Try ATS7=45&W.

> **Note:** As shipped, `tip` does not yet support Hayes modems fully. The solution is to edit the file `tipconf.h` in the directory `/usr/src/usr.bin/tip/tip`. Obviously you need the source distribution to do this.
>
> Edit the line `#define HAYES 0` to `#define HAYES 1`. Then `make` and `make install`. Everything works nicely after that.

15.5.2 How Am I Expected to Enter These AT Commands?

Make what is called a "direct" entry in your `/etc/remote` file. For example, if your modem is hooked up to the first serial port, `/dev/cuaa0`, then put in the following line:

```
cuaa0:dv=/dev/cuaa0:br#19200:pa=none
```

Use the highest bps rate your modem supports in the br capability. Then, type `tip cuaa0` and you will be connected to your modem.

If there is no `/dev/cuaa0` on your system, do this:

```
# cd /dev
# sh MAKEDEV cuaa0
```

Or use `cu` as root with the following command:

```
# cu -lline -sspeed
```

line is the serial port (e.g. `/dev/cuaa0`) and *speed* is the speed (e.g. `57600`). When you are done entering the AT commands hit `~.` to exit.

15.5.3 The @ Sign for the pn Capability Does Not Work!

The @ sign in the phone number capability tells tip to look in `/etc/phones` for a phone number. But the @ sign is also a special character in capability files like `/etc/remote`. Escape it with a backslash:

```
pn=\@
```

15.5.4 How Can I Dial a Phone Number on the Command Line?

Put what is called a "generic" entry in your `/etc/remote` file. For example:

```
tip115200|Dial any phone number at 115200 bps:\
        :dv=/dev/cuaa0:br#115200:at=hayes:pa=none:du:
tip57600|Dial any phone number at 57600 bps:\
        :dv=/dev/cuaa0:br#57600:at=hayes:pa=none:du:
```

Then you can things like:

```
# tip -115200 5551234
```

If you prefer cu over tip, use a generic cu entry:

```
cu115200|Use cu to dial any number at 115200bps:\
        :dv=/dev/cuaa1:br#57600:at=hayes:pa=none:du:
```

and type:

```
# cu 5551234 -s 115200
```

15.5.5 Do I Have to Type in the bps Rate Every Time I Do That?

Put in an entry for `tip1200` or `cu1200`, but go ahead and use whatever bps rate is appropriate with the br capability. tip thinks a good default is 1200 bps which is why it looks for a `tip1200` entry. You do not have to use 1200 bps, though.

15.5.6 I Access a Number of Hosts through a Terminal Server.

Rather than waiting until you are connected and typing CONNECT <host> each time, use tip's cm capability. For example, these entries in `/etc/remote`:

```
pain|pain.deep13.com|Forrester's machine:\
        :cm=CONNECT pain\n:tc=deep13:
muffin|muffin.deep13.com|Frank's machine:\
        :cm=CONNECT muffin\n:tc=deep13:
deep13:Gizmonics Institute terminal server:\
        :dv=/dev/cuaa2:br#38400:at=hayes:du:pa=none:pn=5551234:
```

will let you type `tip pain` or `tip muffin` to connect to the hosts pain or muffin, and `tip deep13` to get to the terminal server.

15.5.7 Can Tip Try More Than one Line for each Site?

This is often a problem where a university has several modem lines and several thousand students trying to use them...

Make an entry for your university in `/etc/remote` and use @ for the `pn` capability:

```
big-university:\
        :pn=\@:tc=dialout
dialout:\
        :dv=/dev/cuaa3:br#9600:at=courier:du:pa=none:
```

Then, list the phone numbers for the university in `/etc/phones`:

```
big-university 5551111
big-university 5551112
big-university 5551113
big-university 5551114
```

`tip` will try each one in the listed order, then give up. If you want to keep retrying, run `tip` in a while loop.

15.5.8 Why Do I Have to Hit Ctrl+P Twice to Send Ctrl+P Once?

Ctrl+P is the default "force" character, used to tell `tip` that the next character is literal data. You can set the force character to any other character with the ~s escape, which means "set a variable."

Type ~s`force=`*single-char* followed by a newline. *single-char* is any single character. If you leave out *single-char*, then the force character is the nul character, which you can get by typing **Ctrl+2** or **Ctrl+Space**. A pretty good value for *single-char* is **Shift+Ctrl+6**, which is only used on some terminal servers.

You can have the force character be whatever you want by specifying the following in your $HOME/.tiprc file:

```
force=<single-char>
```

15.5.9 Suddenly Everything I Type Is in UPPER CASE??

You must have pressed **Ctrl+A**, `tip`'s "raise character," specially designed for people with broken caps-lock keys. Use ~s as above and set the variable `raisechar` to something reasonable. In fact, you can set it to the same as the force character, if you never expect to use either of these features.

Here is a sample .tiprc file perfect for **Emacs** users who need to type **Ctrl+2** and **Ctrl+A** a lot:

```
force=^^
raisechar=^^
```

The ^^ is **Shift+Ctrl+6**.

15.5.10 How Can I Do File Transfers with `tip`?

If you are talking to another Unix system, you can send and receive files with ~p (put) and ~t (take). These commands run `cat` and `echo` on the remote system to accept and send files. The syntax is:

~p local-file [remote-file]

~t remote-file [local-file]

There is no error checking, so you probably should use another protocol, like zmodem.

15.5.11 How Can I Run zmodem with `tip`?

To receive files, start the sending program on the remote end. Then, type ~C rz to begin receiving them locally.

To send files, start the receiving program on the remote end. Then, type ~C sz *files* to send them to the remote system.

15.6 Setting Up the Serial Console

15.6.1 Introduction

FreeBSD has the ability to boot on a system with only a dumb terminal on a serial port as a console. Such a configuration should be useful for two classes of people: system administrators who wish to install FreeBSD on machines that have no keyboard or monitor attached, and developers who want to debug the kernel or device drivers.

As described in Chapter 7, FreeBSD employs a three stage bootstrap. The first two stages are in the boot block code which is stored at the beginning of the FreeBSD slice on the boot disk. The boot block will then load and run the boot loader (/boot/loader) as the third stage code.

In order to set up the serial console you must configure the boot block code, the boot loader code and the kernel.

15.6.2 Serial Console Configuration

1. Prepare a serial cable.

   You will need either a null-modem cable or a standard serial cable and a null-modem adapter. See Section 15.2.2 for a discussion on serial cables.

2. Unplug your keyboard.

   Most PC systems probe for the keyboard during the Power-On Self-Test (POST) and will generate an error if the keyboard is not detected. Some machines complain loudly about the lack of a keyboard and will not continue to boot until it is plugged in.

   If your computer complains about the error, but boots anyway, then you do not have to do anything special. (Some machines with Phoenix BIOS installed merely say `Keyboard failed` and continue to boot normally.)

   If your computer refuses to boot without a keyboard attached then you will have to configure the BIOS so that it ignores this error (if it can). Consult your motherboard's manual for details on how to do this.

   > **Tip:** Setting the keyboard to "Not installed" in the BIOS setup does *not* mean that you will not be able to use your keyboard. All this does is tell the BIOS not to probe for a keyboard at power-on, so it will not complain if the keyboard is not plugged in. You can leave the keyboard plugged in even with this flag set to "Not installed" and the keyboard will still work.

   > **Note:** If your system has a PS/2 mouse, chances are very good that you may have to unplug your mouse as well as your keyboard. This is because PS/2 mice share some hardware with the keyboard and leaving the mouse plugged in can fool the keyboard probe into thinking the keyboard is still there. It is said that a Gateway 2000 Pentium 90MHz system with an AMI BIOS that behaves this way. In general, this is not a problem since the mouse is not much good without the keyboard anyway.

3. Plug a dumb terminal into COM1: (sio0).

   If you do not have a dumb terminal, you can use an old PC/XT with a modem program, or the serial port on another Unix box. If you do not have a COM1: (sio0), get one. At this time, there is no way to select a port other than COM1: for the boot blocks without recompiling the boot blocks. If you are already using COM1: for another device, you will have to temporarily remove that device and install a new boot block and kernel once you get FreeBSD up and running. (It is assumed that COM1: will be available on a file/compute/terminal server anyway; if you really need COM1: for something else (and you cannot switch that something else to COM2: (sio1)), then you probably should not even be bothering with all this in the first place.)

4. Make sure the configuration file of your kernel has appropriate flags set for COM1: (sio0).

   Relevant flags are:

0x10

   Enables console support for this unit. The other console flags are ignored unless this is set. Currently, at most one unit can have console support; the first one (in config file order) with this flag set is preferred. This option alone will not make the serial port the console. Set the following flag or use the -h option described below, together with this flag.

0x20

   Forces this unit to be the console (unless there is another higher priority console), regardless of the -h option discussed below. This flag replaces the COMCONSOLE option in FreeBSD versions 2.*X*. The flag 0x20 must be used together with the `0x10` flag.

`0x40`

Reserves this unit (in conjunction with `0x10`) and makes the unit unavailable for normal access. You should not set this flag to the serial port unit which you want to use as the serial console. The only use of this flag is to designate the unit for kernel remote debugging. See The Developer's Handbook[1] for more information on remote debugging.

> **Note:** In FreeBSD 4.0 or later the semantics of the flag `0x40` are slightly different and there is another flag to specify a serial port for remote debugging.

Example:

```
device sio0 at isa? port "IO_COM1" tty flags 0x10 irq 4
```

See the sio(4) manual page for more details.

If the flags were not set, you need to run UserConfig (on a different console) or recompile the kernel.

5. Create `boot.config` in the root directory of the a partition on the boot drive.

This file will instruct the boot block code how you would like to boot the system. In order to activate the serial console, you need one or more of the following options—if you want multiple options, include them all on the same line:

`-h`

Toggles internal and serial consoles. You can use this to switch console devices. For instance, if you boot from the internal (video) console, you can use `-h` to direct the boot loader and the kernel to use the serial port as its console device. Alternatively, if you boot from the serial port, you can use the `-h` to tell the boot loader and the kernel to use the video display as the console instead.

`-D`

Toggles single and dual console configurations. In the single configuration the console will be either the internal console (video display) or the serial port, depending on the state of the `-h` option above. In the dual console configuration, both the video display and the serial port will become the console at the same time, regardless of the state of the `-h` option. However, that the dual console configuration takes effect only during the boot block is running. Once the boot loader gets control, the console specified by the `-h` option becomes the only console.

`-P`

Makes the boot block probe the keyboard. If no keyboard is found, the `-D` and `-h` options are automatically set.

---

1 http://www.FreeBSD.org/doc/en_US.ISO8859-1/books/developers-handbook/

> **Note:** Due to space constraints in the current version of the boot blocks, the -P option is capable of detecting extended keyboards only. Keyboards with less than 101 keys (and without F11 and F12 keys) may not be detected. Keyboards on some laptop computers may not be properly found because of this limitation. If this is the case with your system, you have to abandon using the -P option. Unfortunately there is no workaround for this problem.

Use either the -P option to select the console automatically, or the -h option to activate the serial console.

You may include other options described in boot(8) as well.

The options, except for -P, will be passed to the boot loader (/boot/loader). The boot loader will determine which of the internal video or the serial port should become the console by examining the state of the -h option alone. This means that if you specify the -D option but not the -h option in /boot.config, you can use the serial port as the console only during the boot block; the boot loader will use the internal video display as the console.

6. Boot the machine.

    When you start your FreeBSD box, the boot blocks will echo the contents of /boot.config to the console. For example;

    ```
    /boot.config: -P
    Keyboard: no
    ```

    The second line appears only if you put -P in /boot.config and indicates presence/absence of the keyboard. These messages go to either serial or internal console, or both, depending on the option in /boot.config.

Options	Message goes to
none	internal console
-h	serial console
-D	serial and internal consoles
-Dh	serial and internal consoles
-P, keyboard present	internal console
-P, keyboard absent	serial console

After the above messages, there will be a small pause before the boot blocks continue loading the boot loader and before any further messages printed to the console. Under normal circumstances, you do not need to interrupt the boot blocks, but you may want to do so in order to make sure things are set up correctly.

Hit any key, other than Enter, at the console to interrupt the boot process. The boot blocks will then prompt you for further action. You should now see something like:

```
>> FreeBSD/i386 BOOT
Default: 0:wd(0,a)/boot/loader
boot:
```

Verify the above message appears on either the serial or internal console or both, according to the options you put in /boot.config. If the message appears in the correct console, hit Enter to continue the boot process.

If you want the serial console but you do not see the prompt on the serial terminal, something is wrong with your settings. In the meantime, you enter -h and hit Enter/Return (if possible) to tell the boot block (and then the boot loader and the kernel) to choose the serial port for the console. Once the system is up, go back and check what went wrong.

After the boot loader is loaded and you are in the third stage of the boot process you can still switch between the internal console and the serial console by setting appropriate environment variables in the boot loader. See Section 15.6.5.

15.6.3 Summary

Here is the summary of various settings discussed in this section and the console eventually selected.

Case 1: You Set the flags to 0x10 for `sio0`

```
device sio0 at isa? port "IO_COM1" tty flags 0x10 irq 4
```

Options in /boot.config	Console during boot blocks	Console during boot loader	Console in kernel
nothing	internal	internal	internal
-h	serial	serial	serial
-D	serial and internal	internal	internal
-Dh	serial and internal	serial	serial
-P, keyboard present	internal	internal	internal
-P, keyboard absent	serial and internal	serial	serial

Case 2: You Set the flags to 0x30 for sio0

```
device sio0 at isa? port "IO_COM1" tty flags 0x30 irq 4
```

Options in /boot.config	Console during boot blocks	Console during boot loader	Console in kernel
nothing	internal	internal	serial
-h	serial	serial	serial
-D	serial and internal	internal	serial
-Dh	serial and internal	serial	serial
-P, keyboard present	internal	internal	serial
-P, keyboard absent	serial and internal	serial	serial

15.6.4 Tips for the Serial Console

Setting a Faster Serial Port Speed

By default, the serial port settings are: 9600 baud, 8 bits, no parity, and 1 stop bit. If you wish to change the speed, you need to recompile at least the boot blocks. Add the following line to `/etc/make.conf` and compile new boot blocks:

```
BOOT_COMCONSOLE_SPEED=19200
```

If the serial console is configured in some other way than by booting with -h, or if the serial console used by the kernel is different from the one used by the boot blocks, then you must also add the following option to the kernel configuration file and compile a new kernel:

```
options CONSPEED=19200
```

Using Serial Port Other Than `sio0` for the Console

Using a port other than `sio0` as the console requires some recompiling. If you want to use another serial port for whatever reasons, recompile the boot blocks, the boot loader and the kernel as follows.

1. Get the kernel source. (See Chapter 19)

2. Edit `/etc/make.conf` and set `BOOT_COMCONSOLE_PORT` to the address of the port you want to use (0x3F8, 0x2F8, 0x3E8 or 0x2E8). Only `sio0` through `sio3` (`COM1:` through `COM4:`) can be used; multiport serial cards will not work. No interrupt setting is needed.

3. Create a custom kernel configuration file and add appropriate flags for the serial port you want to use. For example, if you want to make `sio1` (`COM2:`) the console:

    ```
    device sio1 at isa? port "IO_COM2" tty flags 0x10 irq 3
    ```

   or

    ```
    device sio1 at isa? port "IO_COM2" tty flags 0x30 irq 3
    ```

    The console flags for the other serial ports should not be set.

4. Recompile and install the boot blocks:

    ```
    # cd /sys/boot/i386/boot2
    # make
    # make install
    ```

5. Recompile and install the boot loader:

    ```
    # cd /sys/boot/i386/loader
    # make
    # make install
    ```

6. Rebuild and install the kernel.

7. Write the boot blocks to the boot disk with disklabel(8) and boot from the new kernel.

Entering the DDB Debugger from the Serial Line

If you wish to drop into the kernel debugger from the serial console (useful for remote diagnostics, but also dangerous if you generate a spurious BREAK on the serial port!) then you should compile your kernel with the following options:

```
options BREAK_TO_DEBUGGER
options DDB
```

Getting a Login Prompt on the Serial Console

While this is not required, you may wish to get a *login* prompt over the serial line, now that you can see boot messages and can enter the kernel debugging session through the serial console. Here is how to do it.

Open the file /etc/ttys with an editor and locate the lines:

```
ttyd0 "/usr/libexec/getty std.9600" unknown off secure
ttyd1 "/usr/libexec/getty std.9600" unknown off secure
ttyd2 "/usr/libexec/getty std.9600" unknown off secure
ttyd3 "/usr/libexec/getty std.9600" unknown off secure
```

ttyd0 through ttyd3 corresponds to COM1 through COM4. Change off to on for the desired port. If you have changed the speed of the serial port, you need to change std.9600 to match the current setting, e.g. std.19200.

You may also want to change the terminal type from unknown to the actual type of your serial terminal.

After editing the file, you must kill -HUP 1 to make this change take effect.

15.6.5 Changing Console from the Boot Loader

Previous sections described how to set up the serial console by tweaking the boot block. This section shows that you can specify the console by entering some commands and environment variables in the boot loader. As the boot loader is invoked at the third stage of the boot process, after the boot block, the settings in the boot loader will override the settings in the boot block.

Setting up the Serial Console

You can easily specify the boot loader and the kernel to use the serial console by writing just one line in /boot/loader.rc:

```
set console=comconsole
```

This will take effect regardless of the settings in the boot block discussed in the previous section.

You had better put the above line as the first line of /boot/loader.rc so as to see boot messages on the serial console as early as possible.

Likewise, you can specify the internal console as:

```
set console=vidconsole
```

If you do not set the boot loader environment variable console, the boot loader, and subsequently the kernel, will use whichever console indicated by the -h option in the boot block.

In versions 3.2 or later, you may specify the console in /boot/loader.conf.local or /boot/loader.conf, rather than in /boot/loader.rc. In this method your /boot/loader.rc should look like:

```
include /boot/loader.4th
start
```

Then, create /boot/loader.conf.local and put the following line there.

```
console=comconsole
```

or

```
console=vidconsole
```

See loader.conf(5) for more information.

> **Note:** At the moment, the boot loader has no option equivalent to the -P option in the boot block, and there is no provision to automatically select the internal console and the serial console based on the presence of the keyboard.

Using Serial Port Other than sio0 for the Console

You need to recompile the boot loader to use a serial port other than sio0 for the serial console. Follow the procedure described in Section 15.6.4.2.

15.6.6 Caveats

The idea here is to allow people to set up dedicated servers that require no graphics hardware or attached keyboards. Unfortunately, while most systems will let you boot without a keyboard, there are quite a few that will not let you boot without a graphics adapter. Machines with AMI BIOSes can be configured to boot with no graphics adapter installed simply by changing the 'graphics adapter' setting in the CMOS configuration to 'Not installed.'

However, many machines do not support this option and will refuse to boot if you have no display hardware in the system. With these machines, you will have to leave some kind of graphics card plugged in, (even if it is just a junky mono board) although you will not have to attach a monitor into it. You might also try installing an AMI BIOS.

Chapter 16

PPP and SLIP

16.1 Synopsis

FreeBSD has a number of ways to link one computer to another. To establish a network or Internet connection through a dial-up modem, or to allow others to do so through you, requires the use of PPP or SLIP. This chapter describes setting up these modem-based communication services in detail.

After reading this chapter, you will know:

- How to setup User PPP.
- How to setup Kernel PPP.
- How to setup PPPoE (PPP over Ethernet).
- How to setup PPPoA (PPP over ATM).
- How to configure and setup a SLIP client and server.

Before reading this chapter, you should:

- be familiar with basic network terminology.
- understand the basics and purpose of a dialup connection and PPP and/or SLIP.

You may be wondering what the main difference is between User PPP and kernel PPP. The answer is simple; user PPP processes the inbound and outbound data in userland rather than in the kernel. This is expensive in terms of copying the data between the kernel and userland, but allows a far more feature-rich ppp implementation. User PPP uses the `tun` device to communicate with the outside world whereas kernel-ppp uses the `ppp` device.

> **Note:** Throughout in this chapter, user ppp will simply be referred to as ppp unless a distinction needs to be made between it and any other PPP software such as `pppd`. Unless otherwise stated, all of the commands explained in this section should be executed as `root`.

16.2 Using User PPP

16.2.1 User PPP

Assumptions

This document assumes you have the following:

- An account with an Internet Service Provider (ISP) which you connect to using PPP.
- Further, you have a modem or other device connected to your system and configured correctly, which allows you to connect to your ISP.
- The dial-up number(s) of your ISP.
- Your login name and password. (Either a regular Unix-style login and password pair, or a PAP or CHAP login and password pair.)
- The IP address of one or more name servers. Normally, you will be given two IP addresses by your ISP to use for this. If they have not given you at least one, then you can use the `enable dns` command in your `ppp.conf` file to tell **ppp** to set the name servers for you. This feature depends on your ISPs PPP implementation supporting DNS negotiation.

The following information may be supplied by your ISP, but is not completely necessary:

- The IP address of your ISP's gateway. The gateway is the machine to which you will connect and will be set up as your *default route*. If you do not have this information, we can make one up and your ISP's PPP server will tell us the correct value when we connect.

    This IP number is referred to as `HISADDR` by **ppp**.

- The netmask you should use. If your ISP has not provided you with one, you can safely use `255.255.255.255`.
- If your ISP provides you with a static IP address and hostname, you can enter it. Otherwise, we simply let the peer assign whatever IP address it sees fit.

If you do not have any of the required information, contact your ISP.

> **Note:** Throughout this section, many of the examples showing the contents of configuration files are numbered by line. These numbers serve to aid in the presentation and discussion only and are not meant to be placed in the actual file. Proper indentation with tab and space characters is also important.

Preparing the Kernel

As previously mentioned, **ppp** uses the `tun` device. If this device has not been compiled into your kernel, **ppp** will load it on demand as a module. The tunnel driver is dynamic, so any number of devices may be created (you are not limited by any kernel configuration values).

> **Note:** It should be noted that the tunnel driver creates devices on demand, so `ifconfig -a` will not necessarily show any `tun` devices.

Check the `tun` Device

Under normal circumstances, most users will only use one `tun` device (`/dev/tun0`). References to `tun0` below may be changed to `tunN` where `N` is any unit number corresponding to your system.

For FreeBSD installations that do not have DEVFS enabled, the existence of the `tun0` device should be verified (this is not necessary if DEVFS is enabled as device nodes will be created on demand).

The easiest way to make sure that the `tun0` device is configured correctly is to remake the device. To remake the device, do the following:

```
# cd /dev
# sh MAKEDEV tun0
```

If you need 16 tunnel devices in your kernel, you will need to create them. This can be done by executing the following commands:

```
# cd /dev
# sh MAKEDEV tun15
```

Name Resolution Configuration

The resolver is the part of the system that looks up IP addresses into hostnames and vice versa. It can be configured to look for maps that describe IP to hostname mappings in one of two places. The first is a file called `/etc/hosts`. Read hosts(5) for more information. The second is the Internet Domain Name Service (DNS), a distributed data base. For more information on DNS and DNS services, refer to Section 17.9.

The resolver is a set of system calls that perform the name mappings, but you have to tell it where to find the information. For versions of FreeBSD prior to 5.0. This is done by editing the file `/etc/host.conf`. FreeBSD 5.0 uses the `/etc/nsswitch.conf` file.

Edit `/etc/host.conf`

For versions of FreeBSD prior to 5.0, this file should contain the following two lines (in this order):

```
hosts
bind
```

This instructs the resolver to first look in the file /etc/hosts, and to then consult the DNS if the name was not found.

Edit /etc/nsswitch.conf

For FreeBSD version 5.0 or above, this file should contain at least the following line:

```
hosts: files, dns
```

This instructs the resolver to first look in the file /etc/hosts, and to then consult DNS if the name was not found.

Edit /etc/hosts

This file may contain the IP addresses and names of machines on your local network. At a bare minimum it should contain entries for the machine which will be running ppp. Assuming that your machine is called foo.example.com with the IP address 10.0.0.1, /etc/hosts should contain:

```
127.0.0.1 localhost.example.com localhost
::1 localhost.example.com localhost
10.0.0.1 foo.example.com foo
```

The first two lines define the alias localhost as a synonym for the current machine. Regardless of your own IP address, the IP addresses for these lines should always be 127.0.0.1 and ::1. The last line maps the name foo.example.com (and the shorthand foo) to the IP address 10.0.0.1.

Note: 127.0.0.1 and localhost are known as loopback addresses, which loopback to the local machine.

If your provider allocates you a static IP address and name, and you are not using that as your host name, add this to the /etc/hosts too.

Edit /etc/resolv.conf

The /etc/resolv.conf file tells the resolver how to behave. Normally, you will need to enter the following line(s):

```
domain example.com
nameserver x.x.x.x
nameserver y.y.y.y
```

The x.x.x.x and y.y.y.y addresses are those given to you by your ISP. Add as many nameserver lines as your ISP provides. The domain line is set to your hosts domain name. Refer to the resolv.conf(5) manual page for details of other possible entries in this file.

If you are running a local name server, replace the above nameserver lines with:

```
nameserver 0.0.0.0
```

The `enable dns` command (entered in the `/etc/ppp/ppp.conf` file - see below) will tell PPP to request that your ISP confirms the nameserver values. If your ISP supplies different addresses (or if there are no nameserver lines in `/etc/resolv.conf`), PPP will rewrite the file with the ISP-supplied values.

PPP Configuration

Both `ppp` and `pppd` (the kernel level implementation of PPP) use the configuration files located in the `/etc/ppp` directory. Examples for user ppp can be found in `/usr/share/examples/ppp/`.

Configuring `ppp` requires that you edit a number of files, depending on your requirements. What you put in them depends to some extent on whether your ISP allocates IP addresses statically (i.e., you get given one IP address, and always use that one) or dynamically (i.e., your IP address changes each time you connect to your ISP).

PPP and Static IP Addresses

You will need to edit the `/etc/ppp/ppp.conf` configuration file. It should look similar to the example below.

Note: Lines that end in a : start in the first column (beginning of the line)— all other lines should be indented as shown using spaces or tabs.

```
1    default:
2       set log Phase Chat LCP IPCP CCP tun command
3       ident user-ppp VERSION (built COMPILATIONDATE)
4       set device /dev/cuaa0
5       set speed 115200
6       set dial "ABORT BUSY ABORT NO\\sCARRIER TIMEOUT 5 \
7                \"\" AT OK-AT-OK ATE1Q0 OK \\dATDT\\TTIMEOUT 40 CONNECT"
8       set timeout 180
9       enable dns
10
11   provider:
12       set phone "(123) 456 7890"
13       set authname foo
14       set authkey bar
15       set login "TIMEOUT 10 \"\" \"\" gin:--gin: \\U word: \\P col: ppp"
16       set timeout 300
17       set ifaddr x.x.x.x y.y.y.y 255.255.255.255 0.0.0.0
18       add default HISADDR
```

Line 1:

Identifies the default entry. Commands in this entry are executed automatically when ppp is run.

Line 2:

Enables logging parameters. When the configuration is working satisfactorily, this line should be reduced to saying

```
set log phase tun
```

in order to avoid excessive log file sizes.

Line 3:

Tells PPP how to identify itself to the peer. PPP identifies itself to the peer if it has any trouble negotiating and setting up the link, providing information that the peers administrator may find useful when investigating such problems.

Line 4:

Identifies the device to which the modem is connected. COM1 is /dev/cuaa0 and COM2 is /dev/cuaa1.

Line 5:

Sets the speed you want to connect at. If 115200 does not work (it should with any reasonably new modem), try 38400 instead.

Line 6 & 7:

The dial string. User PPP uses an expect-send syntax similar to the chat(8) program. Refer to the manual page for information on the features of this language.

Note that this command continues onto the next line for readability. Any command in ppp.conf may do this if the last character on the line is a "\" character.

Line 8:

Sets the idle timeout for the link. 180 seconds is the default, so this line is purely cosmetic.

Line 9:

Tells PPP to ask the peer to confirm the local resolver settings. If you run a local name server, this line should be commented out or removed.

Line 10:

A blank line for readability. Blank lines are ignored by PPP.

Line 11:

Identifies an entry for a provider called "provider".

Line 12:

Sets the phone number for this provider. Multiple phone numbers may be specified using the colon (:) or pipe character (|)as a separator. The difference between the two separators is described in ppp(8). To summarize, if you want to rotate through the numbers, use a colon. If you want to always attempt to dial the first number first and only use the other numbers if the first number fails, use the pipe character. Always quote the entire set of phone numbers as shown.

Line 13 & 14:

Identifies the user name and password. When connecting using a Unix-style login prompt, these values are referred to by the `set login` command using the \U and \P variables. When connecting using PAP or CHAP, these values are used at authentication time.

Line 15:

If you are using PAP or CHAP, there will be no login at this point, and this line should be commented out or removed. See PAP and CHAP authentication for further details.

The login string is of the same chat-like syntax as the dial string. In this example, the string works for a service whose login session looks like this:

```
J. Random Provider
login: foo
password: bar
protocol: ppp
```

You will need to alter this script to suit your own needs. When you write this script for the first time, you should ensure that you have enabled "chat" logging so you can determine if the conversation is going as expected.

Line 16:

Sets the default idle timeout (in seconds) for the connection. Here, the connection will be closed automatically after 300 seconds of inactivity. If you never want to timeout, set this value to zero or use the `-ddial` command line switch.

Line 17:

Sets the interface addresses. The string $x.x.x.x$ should be replaced by the IP address that your provider has allocated to you. The string $y.y.y.y$ should be replaced by the IP address that your ISP indicated for their gateway (the machine to which you connect). If your ISP has not given you a gateway address, use 10.0.0.2/0. If you need to use a "guessed" address, make sure that you create an entry in /etc/ppp/ppp.linkup as per the instructions for PPP and Dynamic IP addresses. If this line is omitted, ppp cannot run in `-auto` mode.

Line 18:

Adds a default route to your ISP's gateway. The special word HISADDR is replaced with the gateway address specified on line 9. It is important that this line appears after line 9, otherwise HISADDR will not yet be initialized.

If you do not wish to run ppp in `-auto`, this line should be moved to the ppp.linkup file.

It is not necessary to add an entry to ppp.linkup when you have a static IP address and are running ppp in `-auto` mode as your routing table entries are already correct before you connect. You may however wish to create an entry to invoke programs after connection. This is explained later with the sendmail example.

Example configuration files can be found in the `/usr/share/examples/ppp/` directory.

PPP and Dynamic IP Addresses

If your service provider does not assign static IP addresses, ppp can be configured to negotiate the local and remote addresses. This is done by "guessing" an IP address and allowing ppp to set it up correctly using the IP Configuration Protocol (IPCP) after connecting. The `ppp.conf` configuration is the same as PPP and Static IP Addresses, with the following change:

```
17      set ifaddr 10.0.0.1/0 10.0.0.2/0 255.255.255.255
```

Again, do not include the line number, it is just for reference. Indentation of at least one space is required.

Line 17:

> The number after the / character is the number of bits of the address that ppp will insist on. You may wish to use IP numbers more appropriate to your circumstances, but the above example will always work.

> The last argument (`0.0.0.0`) tells PPP to start negotiations using address `0.0.0.0` rather than `10.0.0.1` and is necessary for some ISPs. Do not use `0.0.0.0` as the first argument to `set ifaddr` as it prevents PPP from setting up an initial route in `-auto` mode.

If you are not running in `-auto` mode, you will need to create an entry in `/etc/ppp/ppp.linkup`. `ppp.linkup` is used after a connection has been established. At this point, ppp will have assigned the interface addresses and it will now be possible to add the routing table entries:

```
1       provider:
2         add default HISADDR
```

Line 1:

> On establishing a connection, ppp will look for an entry in `ppp.linkup` according to the following rules: First, try to match the same label as we used in `ppp.conf`. If that fails, look for an entry for the IP address of our gateway. This entry is a four-octet IP style label. If we still have not found an entry, look for the MYADDR entry.

Line 2:

> This line tells ppp to add a default route that points to HISADDR. HISADDR will be replaced with the IP number of the gateway as negotiated by the IPCP.

See the pmdemand entry in the files `/usr/share/examples/ppp/ppp.conf.sample` and `/usr/share/examples/ppp/ppp.linkup.sample` for a detailed example.

Receiving Incoming Calls

When you configure **ppp** to receive incoming calls on a machine connected to a LAN, you must decide if you wish to forward packets to the LAN. If you do, you should allocate the peer an IP number from your LAN's subnet, and use the command `enable proxy` in your `/etc/ppp/ppp.conf` file. You should also confirm that the `/etc/rc.conf` file contains the following:

```
gateway_enable="YES"
```

Which getty?

Configuring FreeBSD for Dial-up Services provides a good description on enabling dial-up services using getty(8).

An alternative to `getty` is mgetty[1], a smarter version of `getty` designed with dial-up lines in mind.

The advantages of using `mgetty` is that it actively *talks* to modems, meaning if port is turned off in `/etc/ttys` then your modem will not answer the phone.

Later versions of `mgetty` (from 0.99beta onwards) also support the automatic detection of PPP streams, allowing your clients script-less access to your server.

Refer to the Mgetty and AutoPPP section for more information on `mgetty`.

PPP Permissions

The `ppp` command must normally be run as the `root` user. If however, you wish to allow `ppp` to run in server mode as a normal user by executing `ppp` as described below, that user must be given permission to run `ppp` by adding them to the `network` group in `/etc/group`.

You will also need to give them access to one or more sections of the configuration file using the `allow` command:

```
allow users fred mary
```

If this command is used in the `default` section, it gives the specified users access to everything.

PPP Shells for Dynamic-IP Users

Create a file called `/etc/ppp/ppp-shell` containing the following:

```
#!/bin/sh
IDENT=`echo $0 | sed -e 's/^.*-\(.*\)$/\1/'`
CALLEDAS="$IDENT"
TTY=`tty`

if [ x$IDENT = xdialup ]; then
        IDENT=`basename $TTY`
fi

echo "PPP for $CALLEDAS on $TTY"
echo "Starting PPP for $IDENT"

exec /usr/sbin/ppp -direct $IDENT
```

---

1 http://www.leo.org/~doering/mgetty/index.html

This script should be executable. Now make a symbolic link called `ppp-dialup` to this script using the following commands:

```
# ln -s ppp-shell /etc/ppp/ppp-dialup
```

You should use this script as the *shell* for all of your dialup users. This is an example from `/etc/password` for a dialup PPP user with username `pchilds` (remember do not directly edit the password file, use `vipw`).

```
pchilds:*:1011:300:Peter Childs PPP:/home/ppp:/etc/ppp/ppp-dialup
```

Create a `/home/ppp` directory that is world readable containing the following 0 byte files:

```
-r--r--r--   1 root     wheel           0 May 27 02:23 .hushlogin
-r--r--r--   1 root     wheel           0 May 27 02:22 .rhosts
```

which prevents `/etc/motd` from being displayed.

PPP Shells for Static-IP Users

Create the `ppp-shell` file as above, and for each account with statically assigned IPs create a symbolic link to `ppp-shell`.

For example, if you have three dialup customers, `fred`, `sam`, and `mary`, that you route class C networks for, you would type the following:

```
# ln -s /etc/ppp/ppp-shell /etc/ppp/ppp-fred
# ln -s /etc/ppp/ppp-shell /etc/ppp/ppp-sam
# ln -s /etc/ppp/ppp-shell /etc/ppp/ppp-mary
```

Each of these users dialup accounts should have their shell set to the symbolic link created above (for example, `mary`'s shell should be `/etc/ppp/ppp-mary`).

Setting up ppp.conf for Dynamic-IP Users

The `/etc/ppp/ppp.conf` file should contain something along the lines of:

```
default:
  set debug phase lcp chat
  set timeout 0

ttyd0:
  set ifaddr 203.14.100.1 203.14.100.20 255.255.255.255
  enable proxy

ttyd1:
  set ifaddr 203.14.100.1 203.14.100.21 255.255.255.255
  enable proxy
```

Note: The indenting is important.

The `default:` section is loaded for each session. For each dialup line enabled in `/etc/ttys` create an entry similar to the one for `ttyd0:` above. Each line should get a unique IP address from your pool of IP addresses for dynamic users.

Setting up *ppp.conf* for Static-IP Users

Along with the contents of the sample `/usr/share/examples/ppp/ppp.conf` above you should add a section for each of the statically assigned dialup users. We will continue with our `fred`, `sam`, and `mary` example.

```
fred:
  set ifaddr 203.14.100.1 203.14.101.1 255.255.255.255

sam:
  set ifaddr 203.14.100.1 203.14.102.1 255.255.255.255

mary:
  set ifaddr 203.14.100.1 203.14.103.1 255.255.255.255
```

The file `/etc/ppp/ppp.linkup` should also contain routing information for each static IP user if required. The line below would add a route for the `203.14.101.0` class C via the client's ppp link.

```
fred:
  add 203.14.101.0 netmask 255.255.255.0 HISADDR

sam:
  add 203.14.102.0 netmask 255.255.255.0 HISADDR

mary:
  add 203.14.103.0 netmask 255.255.255.0 HISADDR
```

More on `mgetty`, AutoPPP, and MS Extensions

mgetty and AutoPPP

Configuring and compiling `mgetty` with the `AUTO_PPP` option enabled allows `mgetty` to detect the LCP phase of PPP connections and automatically spawn off a ppp shell. However, since the default login/password sequence does not occur it is necessary to authenticate users using either PAP or CHAP.

This section assumes the user has successfully configured, compiled, and installed a version of `mgetty` with the `AUTO_PPP` option (v0.99beta or later).

Make sure your `/usr/local/etc/mgetty+sendfax/login.config` file has the following in it:

```
/AutoPPP/ -       -       /etc/ppp/ppp-pap-dialup
```

This will tell `mgetty` to run the `ppp-pap-dialup` script for detected PPP connections.

Create a file called `/etc/ppp/ppp-pap-dialup` containing the following (the file should be executable):

```
#!/bin/sh
exec /usr/sbin/ppp -direct pap$IDENT
```

For each dialup line enabled in `/etc/ttys`, create a corresponding entry in `/etc/ppp/ppp.conf`. This will happily co-exist with the definitions we created above.

```
pap:
  enable pap
  set ifaddr 203.14.100.1 203.14.100.20-203.14.100.40
  enable proxy
```

Each user logging in with this method will need to have a username/password in `/etc/ppp/ppp.secret` file, or alternatively add the following option to authenticate users via PAP from `/etc/password` file.

```
enable passwdauth
```

If you wish to assign some users a static IP number, you can specify the number as the third argument in `/etc/ppp/ppp.secret`. See `/usr/share/examples/ppp/ppp.secret.sample` for examples.

MS Extensions

It is possible to configure PPP to supply DNS and NetBIOS nameserver addresses on demand.

To enable these extensions with PPP version 1.x, the following lines might be added to the relevant section of `/etc/ppp/ppp.conf`.

```
enable msext
set ns 203.14.100.1 203.14.100.2
set nbns 203.14.100.5
```

And for PPP version 2 and above:

```
accept dns
set dns 203.14.100.1 203.14.100.2
set nbns 203.14.100.5
```

This will tell the clients the primary and secondary name server addresses, and a NetBIOS nameserver host.

In version 2 and above, if the `set dns` line is omitted, PPP will use the values found in `/etc/resolv.conf`.

PAP and CHAP Authentication

Some ISPs set their system up so that the authentication part of your connection is done using either of the PAP or CHAP authentication mechanisms. If this is the case, your ISP will not give a `login:` prompt when you connect, but will start talking PPP immediately.

PAP is less secure than CHAP, but security is not normally an issue here as passwords, although being sent as plain text with PAP, are being transmitted down a serial line only. There's not much room for crackers to "eavesdrop".

Referring back to the PPP and Static IP addresses or PPP and Dynamic IP addresses sections, the following alterations must be made:

```
7          set login
...
12         set authname MyUserName
13         set authkey MyPassword
```

Line 7:

Your ISP will not normally require that you log into the server if you are using PAP or CHAP. You must therefore disable your "set login" string.

Line 12:

This line specifies your PAP/CHAP user name. You will need to insert the correct value for *MyUserName*.

Line 13:

This line specifies your PAP/CHAP password. You will need to insert the correct value for *MyPassword*. You may want to add an additional line, such as:

```
15         accept PAP
```

or

```
15         accept CHAP
```

to make it obvious that this is the intention, but PAP and CHAP are both accepted by default.

Changing Your ppp Configuration on the Fly

It is possible to talk to the ppp program while it is running in the background, but only if a suitable diagnostic port has been set up. To do this, add the following line to your configuration:

```
set server /var/run/ppp-tun%d DiagnosticPassword 0177
```

This will tell PPP to listen to the specified Unix-domain socket, asking clients for the specified password before allowing access. The %d in the name is replaced with the tun device number that is in use.

Once a socket has been set up, the pppctl(8) program may be used in scripts that wish to manipulate the running program.

Final System Configuration

You now have ppp configured, but there are a few more things to do before it is ready to work. They all involve editing the /etc/rc.conf file.

Working from the top down in this file, make sure the hostname= line is set, e.g.:

```
hostname="foo.example.com"
```

If your ISP has supplied you with a static IP address and name, it is probably best that you use this name as your host name.

Look for the `network_interfaces` variable. If you want to configure your system to dial your ISP on demand, make sure the `tun0` device is added to the list, otherwise remove it.

```
network_interfaces="lo0 tun0" ifconfig_tun0=
```

> **Note:** The `ifconfig_tun0` variable should be empty, and a file called `/etc/start_if.tun0` should be created. This file should contain the line:
>
> ```
> ppp -auto mysystem
> ```
>
> This script is executed at network configuration time, starting your ppp daemon in automatic mode. If you have a LAN for which this machine is a gateway, you may also wish to use the `-alias` switch. Refer to the manual page for further details.

Set the router program to `NO` with following line in your `/etc/rc.conf`:

```
router_enable="NO"
```

It is important that the `routed` daemon is not started (it is started by default), as `routed` tends to delete the default routing table entries created by `ppp`.

It is probably worth your while ensuring that the `sendmail_flags` line does not include the `-q` option, otherwise `sendmail` will attempt to do a network lookup every now and then, possibly causing your machine to dial out. You may try:

```
sendmail_flags="-bd"
```

The downside of this is that you must force `sendmail` to re-examine the mail queue whenever the ppp link is up by typing:

```
# /usr/sbin/sendmail -q
```

You may wish to use the `!bg` command in `ppp.linkup` to do this automatically:

```
1       provider:
2          delete ALL
3          add 0 0 HISADDR
4          !bg sendmail -bd -q30m
```

If you do not like this, it is possible to set up a "dfilter" to block SMTP traffic. Refer to the sample files for further details.

Now the only thing left to do is reboot the machine.

All that is left is to reboot the machine. After rebooting, you can now either type:

```
# ppp
```

and then `dial provider` to start the PPP session, or, if you want ppp to establish sessions automatically when there is outbound traffic (and you have not created the `start_if.tun0` script), type:

```
# ppp -auto provider
```

Summary

To recap, the following steps are necessary when setting up ppp for the first time:

Client side:

1. Ensure that the `tun` device is built into your kernel.

2. Ensure that the `tunX` device file is available in the `/dev` directory.

3. Create an entry in `/etc/ppp/ppp.conf`. The `pmdemand` example should suffice for most ISPs.

4. If you have a dynamic IP address, create an entry in `/etc/ppp/ppp.linkup`.

5. Update your `/etc/rc.conf` file.

6. Create a `start_if.tun0` script if you require demand dialing.

Server side:

1. Ensure that the `tun` device is built into your kernel.

2. Ensure that the `tunX` device file is available in the `/dev` directory.

3. Create an entry in `/etc/passwd` (using the vipw(8) program).

4. Create a profile in this users home directory that runs `ppp -direct direct-server` or similar.

5. Create an entry in `/etc/ppp/ppp.conf`. The `direct-server` example should suffice.

6. Create an entry in `/etc/ppp/ppp.linkup`.

7. Update your `/etc/rc.conf` file.

16.3 Using Kernel PPP

16.3.1 Setting up Kernel PPP

Before you start setting up PPP on your machine make sure that `pppd` is located in `/usr/sbin` and the directory `/etc/ppp` exists.

`pppd` can work in two modes:

1. As a "client" — you want to connect your machine to the outside world via a PPP serial connection or modem line.

2. as a "server" — your machine is located on the network and used to connect other computers using PPP.

In both cases you will need to set up an options file (`/etc/ppp/options` or `~/.ppprc` if you have more than one user on your machine that uses PPP).

You also will need some modem/serial software (preferably kermit) so you can dial and establish a connection with the remote host.

16.3.2 Using `pppd` as a Client

The following `/etc/ppp/options` might be used to connect to a CISCO terminal server PPP line.

```
crtscts          # enable hardware flow control
modem            # modem control line
noipdefault      # remote PPP server must supply your IP address.
                 # if the remote host doesn't send your IP during IPCP
                 # negotiation , remove this option
passive          # wait for LCP packets
domain ppp.foo.com      # put your domain name here

:<remote_ip>     # put the IP of remote PPP host here
                 # it will be used to route packets via PPP link
                 # if you didn't specified the noipdefault option
                 # change this line to <local_ip>:<remote_ip>

defaultroute     # put this if you want that PPP server will be your
                 # default router
```

To connect:

1. Dial to the remote host using kermit (or some other modem program), and enter your user name and password (or whatever is needed to enable PPP on the remote host).

2. Exit kermit (without hanging up the line).

3. Enter the following:

    ```
    # /usr/src/usr.sbin/pppd.new/pppd /dev/tty01 19200
    ```

    Be sure to use the appropriate speed and device name.

Now your computer is connected with PPP. If the connection fails, you can add the `debug` option to the `/etc/ppp/` `options` file and check messages on the console to track the problem.

Following `/etc/ppp/pppup` script will make all 3 stages automatically:

```
#!/bin/sh
ps ax |grep pppd |grep -v grep
pid=`ps ax |grep pppd |grep -v grep|awk '{print $1;}'`
```

```
if [ "X${pid}" != "X" ] ; then
        echo 'killing pppd, PID=' ${pid}
        kill ${pid}
fi
ps ax |grep kermit |grep -v grep
pid='ps ax |grep kermit |grep -v grep|awk '{print $1;}''
if [ "X${pid}" != "X" ] ; then
        echo 'killing kermit, PID=' ${pid}
        kill -9 ${pid}
fi

ifconfig ppp0 down
ifconfig ppp0 delete

kermit -y /etc/ppp/kermit.dial
pppd /dev/tty01 19200
```

`/etc/ppp/kermit.dial` is a kermit script that dials and makes all necessary authorization on the remote host (an example of such a script is attached to the end of this document).

Use the following `/etc/ppp/pppdown` script to disconnect the PPP line:

```
#!/bin/sh
pid='ps ax |grep pppd |grep -v grep|awk '{print $1;}''
if [ X${pid} != "X" ] ; then
        echo 'killing pppd, PID=' ${pid}
        kill -TERM ${pid}
fi

ps ax |grep kermit |grep -v grep
pid='ps ax |grep kermit |grep -v grep|awk '{print $1;}''
if [ "X${pid}" != "X" ] ; then
        echo 'killing kermit, PID=' ${pid}
        kill -9 ${pid}
fi

/sbin/ifconfig ppp0 down
/sbin/ifconfig ppp0 delete
kermit -y /etc/ppp/kermit.hup
/etc/ppp/ppptest
```

Check to see if PPP is still running by executing `/usr/etc/ppp/ppptest`, which should look like this:

```
#!/bin/sh
pid='ps ax| grep pppd |grep -v grep|awk '{print $1;}''
if [ X${pid} != "X" ] ; then
        echo 'pppd running: PID=' ${pid-NONE}
else
        echo 'No pppd running.'
fi
set -x
```

```
netstat -n -I ppp0
ifconfig ppp0
```

To hang up the modem, execute /etc/ppp/kermit.hup, which should contain:

```
set line /dev/tty01 ; put your modem device here
set speed 19200
set file type binary
set file names literal
set win 8
set rec pack 1024
set send pack 1024
set block 3
set term bytesize 8
set command bytesize 8
set flow none

pau 1
out +++
inp 5 OK
out ATH0\13
echo \13
exit
```

Here is an alternate method using chat instead of kermit.

The following two files are sufficient to accomplish a pppd connection.

/etc/ppp/options:

```
/dev/cuaa1 115200

crtscts # enable hardware flow control
modem # modem control line
connect "/usr/bin/chat -f /etc/ppp/login.chat.script"
noipdefault # remote PPP serve must supply your IP address.
        # if the remote host doesn't send your IP during
            # IPCP negotiation, remove this option
passive        # wait for LCP packets
domain <your.domain> # put your domain name here

: # put the IP of remote PPP host here
        # it will be used to route packets via PPP link
            # if you didn't specified the noipdefault option
            # change this line to <local_ip>:<remote_ip>

defaultroute # put this if you want that PPP server will be
        # your default router
```

/etc/ppp/login.chat.script:

Note: The following should go on a single line.

```
ABORT BUSY ABORT 'NO CARRIER' "" AT OK ATDT<phone.number>
  CONNECT "" TIMEOUT 10 ogin:-\\r-ogin: <login-id>
  TIMEOUT 5 sword: <password>
```

Once these are installed and modified correctly, all you need to do is run pppd, like so:

```
# pppd
```

16.3.3 Using pppd as a Server

/etc/ppp/options should contain something similar to the following:

```
crtscts                          # Hardware flow control
netmask 255.255.255.0            # netmask ( not required )
192.114.208.20:192.114.208.165  # ip's of local and remote hosts
                                 # local ip must be different from one
                                 # you assigned to the ethernet ( or other )
                                 # interface on your machine.
                                 # remote IP is ip address that will be
                                 # assigned to the remote machine
domain ppp.foo.com               # your domain
passive                          # wait for LCP
modem                            # modem line
```

The following /etc/ppp/pppserv script will enable tell **pppd** to behave as a server:

```
#!/bin/sh
ps ax |grep pppd |grep -v grep
pid=`ps ax |grep pppd |grep -v grep|awk '{print $1;}'`
if [ "X${pid}" != "X" ] ; then
        echo 'killing pppd, PID=' ${pid}
        kill ${pid}
fi
ps ax |grep kermit |grep -v grep
pid=`ps ax |grep kermit |grep -v grep|awk '{print $1;}'`
if [ "X${pid}" != "X" ] ; then
        echo 'killing kermit, PID=' ${pid}
        kill -9 ${pid}
fi

# reset ppp interface
ifconfig ppp0 down
ifconfig ppp0 delete

# enable autoanswer mode
kermit -y /etc/ppp/kermit.ans
```

```
# run ppp
pppd /dev/tty01 19200
```

Use this /etc/ppp/pppservdown script to stop the server:

```
#!/bin/sh
ps ax |grep pppd |grep -v grep
pid='ps ax |grep pppd |grep -v grep|awk '{print $1;}''
if [ "X${pid}" != "X" ] ; then
        echo 'killing pppd, PID=' ${pid}
        kill ${pid}
fi
ps ax |grep kermit |grep -v grep
pid='ps ax |grep kermit |grep -v grep|awk '{print $1;}''
if [ "X${pid}" != "X" ] ; then
        echo 'killing kermit, PID=' ${pid}
        kill -9 ${pid}
fi
ifconfig ppp0 down
ifconfig ppp0 delete

kermit -y /etc/ppp/kermit.noans
```

The following kermit script (/etc/ppp/kermit.ans) will enable/disable autoanswer mode on your modem. It should look like this:

```
set line /dev/tty01
set speed 19200
set file type binary
set file names literal
set win 8
set rec pack 1024
set send pack 1024
set block 3
set term bytesize 8
set command bytesize 8
set flow none

pau 1
out +++
inp 5 OK
out ATH0\13
inp 5 OK
echo \13
out ATS0=1\13    ; change this to out ATS0=0\13 if you want to disable
                 ; autoanswer mod
inp 5 OK
echo \13
exit
```

A script named `/etc/ppp/kermit.dial` is used for dialing and authenticating on the remote host. You will need to customize it for your needs. Put your login and password in this script; you will also need to change the input statement depending on responses from your modem and remote host.

```
;
; put the com line attached to the modem here:
;
set line /dev/tty01
;
; put the modem speed here:
;
set speed 19200
set file type binary            ; full 8 bit file xfer
set file names literal
set win 8
set rec pack 1024
set send pack 1024
set block 3
set term bytesize 8
set command bytesize 8
set flow none
set modem hayes
set dial hangup off
set carrier auto                ; Then SET CARRIER if necessary,
set dial display on             ; Then SET DIAL if necessary,
set input echo on
set input timeout proceed
set input case ignore
def \%x 0                       ; login prompt counter
goto slhup

:slcmd                          ; put the modem in command mode
echo Put the modem in command mode.
clear                           ; Clear unread characters from input buffer
pause 1
output +++                      ; hayes escape sequence
input 1 OK\13\10                ; wait for OK
if success goto slhup
output \13
pause 1
output at\13
input 1 OK\13\10
if fail goto slcmd              ; if modem doesn't answer OK, try again

:slhup                          ; hang up the phone
clear                           ; Clear unread characters from input buffer
pause 1
echo Hanging up the phone.
output ath0\13                  ; hayes command for on hook
input 2 OK\13\10
if fail goto slcmd              ; if no OK answer, put modem in command mode
```

```
:sldial                              ; dial the number
pause 1
echo Dialing.
output atdt9,550311\13\10               ; put phone number here
assign \%x 0                         ; zero the time counter

:look
clear                                ; Clear unread characters from input buffer
increment \%x                        ; Count the seconds
input 1 {CONNECT }
if success goto sllogin
reinput 1 {NO CARRIER\13\10}
if success goto sldial
reinput 1 {NO DIALTONE\13\10}
if success goto slnodial
reinput 1 {\255}
if success goto slhup
reinput 1 {\127}
if success goto slhup
if < \%x 60 goto look
else goto slhup

:sllogin                             ; login
assign \%x 0                         ; zero the time counter
pause 1
echo Looking for login prompt.

:slloop
increment \%x                        ; Count the seconds
clear                                ; Clear unread characters from input buffer
output \13
;
; put your expected login prompt here:
;
input 1 {Username: }
if success goto sluid
reinput 1 {\255}
if success goto slhup
reinput 1 {\127}
if success goto slhup
if < \%x 10 goto slloop              ; try 10 times to get a login prompt
else goto slhup                      ; hang up and start again if 10 failures

:sluid
;
; put your userid here:
;
output ppp-login\13
input 1 {Password: }
;
```

```
; put your password here:
;
output ppp-password\13
input 1 {Entering SLIP mode.}
echo
quit

:slnodial
echo \7No dialtone.  Check the telephone line!\7
exit 1

; local variables:
; mode: csh
; comment-start: "; "
; comment-start-skip: "; "
; end:
```

16.4 Using PPP over Ethernet (PPPoE)

This section describes how to set up PPP over Ethernet (PPPoE).

16.4.1 Configuring the kernel

No kernel configuration is necessary for PPPoE any longer. If the necessary netgraph support is not built into the kernel, it will be dynamically loaded by **ppp**.

16.4.2 Setting up ppp.conf

Here is an example of a working ppp.conf:

```
default:
  set log Phase tun command # you can add more detailed logging if you wish
  set ifaddr 10.0.0.1/0 10.0.0.2/0

name_of_service_provider:
  set device PPPoE:xl1 # replace xl1 with your ethernet device
  set authname YOURLOGINNAME
  set authkey YOURPASSWORD
  set dial
  set login
  add default HISADDR
```

16.4.3 Running PPP

As root, you can run:

```
# ppp -ddial name_of_service_provider
```

16.4.4 Starting PPP at Boot

Add the following to your /etc/rc.conf file:

```
ppp_enable="YES"
ppp_mode="ddial"
ppp_nat="YES" # if you want to enable nat for your local network, otherwise NO
ppp_profile="name_of_service_provider"
```

16.4.5 Using a PPPoE Service tag

Sometimes it will be necessary to use a service tag to establish your connection. Service tags are used to distinguish between different PPPoE servers attached to a given network.

You should have been given any required service tag information in the documentation provided by your ISP. If you cannot locate it there, ask your ISP's tech support personnel.

As a last resort, you could try the method suggested by the Roaring Penguin PPPoE[2] program which can be found in the ports collection (Chapter 4). Bear in mind however, this may de-program your modem and render it useless, so think twice before doing it. Simply install the program shipped with the modem by your provider. Then, access the System menu from the program. The name of your profile should be listed there. It is usually *ISP*.

The profile name (service tag) will be used in the PPPoE configuration entry in ppp.conf as the provider part of the set device command (see the ppp(8) manual page for full details). It should look like this:

```
set device PPPoE:xl1:ISP
```

Do not forget to change *xl1* to the proper device for your Ethernet card.

Do not forget to change *ISP* to the profile you have just found above.

For additional information, see:

* *Cheaper Broadband with FreeBSD on DSL* by Renaud Waldura in Daemon News[3].

---

2 http://www.roaringpenguin.com/pppoe/
3 http://www.daemonnews.org/200101/pppoe.html

16.4.6 PPPoE with a 3Com HomeConnect ADSL Modem Dual Link

This modem does not follow RFC 2516[4] (*A Method for transmitting PPP over Ethernet (PPPoE)*, written by L. Mamakos, K. Lidl, J. Evarts, D. Carrel, D. Simone, and R. Wheeler). Instead, different packet type codes have been used for the Ethernet frames. Please complain to 3Com[5] if you think it should comply with the PPPoE specification.

In order to make FreeBSD capable of communicating with this device, a sysctl must be set. This can be done automatically at boot time by updating `/etc/sysctl.conf`:

```
net.graph.nonstandard_pppoe=1
```

or can be done for immediate effect with the command `sysctl -w net.graph.nonstandard_pppoe=1`.

Unfortunately, because this is a system-wide setting, it is not possible to talk to a normal PPPoE client or server and a 3Com HomeConnect ADSL Modem at the same time.

16.5 Using PPP over ATM (PPPoA)

The following describes how to set up PPP over ATM, a.k.a, PPPoA. Currently, the only hardware supported is the Alcatel Speedtouch USB ADSL modem

16.5.1 Installing PPPoA

PPPoA is supplied as a port in FreeBSD because the firmware is not distributable under Alcatel's license agreement[6].

To install the port, simply use the ports collection (Chapter 4) to install the `net/pppoa` port and follow the instructions provided there.

16.6 Using SLIP

16.6.1 Setting up a SLIP Client

The following is one way to set up a FreeBSD machine for SLIP on a static host network. For dynamic hostname assignments (your address changes each time you dial up), you probably need to have a more complex setup.

First, determine which serial port your modem is connected to. Many people setup a symbolic link, such as `/dev/modem`, to point to the real device name, `/dev/cuaaN`. This allows you to abstract the actual device name should you ever need to move the modem to a different port. It can become quite cumbersome when you need to fix a bunch of files in `/etc` and `.kermrc` files all over the system!

---

4 http://www.faqs.org/rfcs/rfc2516.html
5 http://www.3com.com/
6 http://www.alcatel.com/consumer/dsl/disclaimer_lx.htm

Note: `/dev/cuaa0` is COM1, `cuaa1` is COM2, etc.

Make sure you have the following in your kernel configuration file:

```
pseudo-device    sl       1
```

It is included in the GENERIC kernel, so this should not be a problem unless you have deleted it.

Things You Have to Do Only Once

1. Add your home machine, the gateway and nameservers to your `/etc/hosts` file. Mine looks like this:

```
127.0.0.1               localhost loghost
136.152.64.181          water.CS.Example.EDU water.CS water
136.152.64.1            inr-3.CS.Example.EDU inr-3 slip-gateway
128.32.136.9            ns1.Example.EDU ns1
128.32.136.12           ns2.Example.EDU ns2
```

2. Make sure you have `hosts` before `bind` in your `/etc/host.conf`. Otherwise, funny things may happen.

3. Edit the `/etc/rc.conf` file.

   1. Set your hostname by editing the line that says:

      ```
      hostname="myname.my.domain"
      ```

      Your machine's full Internet hostname should be placed here.

   2. Add `sl0` to the list of network interfaces by changing the line that says:

      ```
      network_interfaces="lo0"
      ```

      to:

      ```
      network_interfaces="lo0 sl0"
      ```

   3. Set the startup flags of sl0 by adding a line:

      ```
      ifconfig_sl0="inet ${hostname} slip-gateway netmask 0xffffff00 up"
      ```

   4. Designate the default router by changing the line:

      ```
      defaultrouter="NO"
      ```

      to:

      ```
      defaultrouter="slip-gateway"
      ```

4. Make a file `/etc/resolv.conf` which contains:

   ```
   domain CS.Example.EDU
   ```

```
nameserver 128.32.136.9
nameserver 128.32.136.12
```

As you can see, these set up the nameserver hosts. Of course, the actual domain names and addresses depend on your environment.

5. Set the password for `root` and `toor` (and any other accounts that do not have a password).

6. Reboot your machine and make sure it comes up with the correct hostname.

Making a SLIP Connection

1. Dial up, type `slip` at the prompt, enter your machine name and password. What is required to be entered depends on your environment. If you use kermit, you can try a script like this:

```
# kermit setup
set modem hayes
set line /dev/modem
set speed 115200
set parity none
set flow rts/cts
set terminal bytesize 8
set file type binary
# The next macro will dial up and login
define slip dial 643-9600, input 10 =>, if failure stop, -
output slip\x0d, input 10 Username:, if failure stop, -
output silvia\x0d, input 10 Password:, if failure stop, -
output ***\x0d, echo \x0aCONNECTED\x0a
```

Of course, you have to change the hostname and password to fit yours. After doing so, you can just type `slip` from the kermit prompt to connect.

Note: Leaving your password in plain text anywhere in the filesystem is generally a *bad* idea. Do it at your own risk.

2. Leave the kermit there (you can suspend it by **Ctrl-z**) and as root, type:

```
# slattach -h -c -s 115200 /dev/modem
```

If you are able to `ping` hosts on the other side of the router, you are connected! If it does not work, you might want to try `-a` instead of `-c` as an argument to `slattach`.

How to Shutdown the Connection

Do the following:

```
# kill -INT `cat /var/run/slattach.modem.pid`
```

to kill `slattach`. Keep in mind you must be `root` to do the above. Then go back to kermit (by running `fg` if you suspended it) and exit from it (q).

The `slattach` manual page says you have to use `ifconfig sl0 down` to mark the interface down, but this does not seem to make any difference for me. (`ifconfig sl0` reports the same thing.)

Some times, your modem might refuse to drop the carrier (mine often does). In that case, simply start kermit and quit it again. It usually goes out on the second try.

Troubleshooting

If it does not work, feel free to ask me. The things that people tripped over so far:

• Not using `-c` or `-a` in `slattach` (This shouldn't be fatal, but some users have reported that this solves their problems.)

• Using `sl0` instead of `sl0` (might be hard to see the difference on some fonts).

• Try `ifconfig sl0` to see your interface status. For example, you might get:

```
# ifconfig sl0
sl0: flags=10<POINTOPOINT>
        inet 136.152.64.181 --> 136.152.64.1 netmask ffffff00
```

• Also, `netstat -r` will give the routing table, in case you get the "no route to host" messages from ping. An example shown here:

```
# netstat -r
Routing tables
Destination      Gateway         Flags   Refs   Use  IfaceMTU  Rtt  Netmasks:

(root node)
(root node)

Route Tree for Protocol Family inet:
(root node) =>
default          inr-3.Example.EDU  UG       8   224515  sl0 -      -
localhost.Exampl localhost.Example. UH       5    42127  lo0 -      0.438
inr-3.Example.ED water.CS.Example.E UH       1        0  sl0 -      -
water.CS.Example localhost.Example. UGH     34 47641234  lo0 -      0.438
(root node)
```

This is after the link has been up for a while, the numbers on your system will vary.

16.6.2 Setting up a SLIP Server

This document provides suggestions for setting up SLIP Server services on a FreeBSD system, which typically means configuring your system to automatically startup connections upon login for remote SLIP clients.

Prerequisites

This section is very technical in nature, so background knowledge is required. It is assumed that you are familiar with the TCP/IP network protocol, and in particular, network and node addressing, network address masks, subnetting, routing, and routing protocols, such as RIP. Configuring SLIP services on a dial-up server requires a knowledge of these concepts, and if you are not familiar with them, please read a copy of either Craig Hunt's *TCP/IP Network Administration* published by O'Reilly & Associates, Inc. (ISBN Number 0-937175-82-X), or Douglas Comer's books on the TCP/IP protocol.

It is further assumed that you have already setup your modem(s) and configured the appropriate system files to allow logins through your modems. If you have not prepared your system for this yet, please see the tutorial for configuring dialup services; if you have a World-Wide Web browser available, browse the list of tutorials at `http://www.FreeBSD.org/`. You may also want to check the manual pages for sio(4) for information on the serial port device driver and ttys(5), gettytab(5), getty(8), & init(8) for information relevant to configuring the system to accept logins on modems, and perhaps stty(1) for information on setting serial port parameters (such as `clocal` for directly-connected serial interfaces).

Quick Overview

In its typical configuration, using FreeBSD as a SLIP server works as follows: a SLIP user dials up your FreeBSD SLIP Server system and logs in with a special SLIP login ID that uses `/usr/sbin/sliplogin` as the special user's shell. The `sliplogin` program browses the file `/etc/sliphome/slip.hosts` to find a matching line for the special user, and if it finds a match, connects the serial line to an available SLIP interface and then runs the shell script `/etc/sliphome/slip.login` to configure the SLIP interface.

An Example of a SLIP Server Login

For example, if a SLIP user ID were `Shelmerg`, `Shelmerg`'s entry in `/etc/master.passwd` would look something like this:

```
Shelmerg:password:1964:89::0:0:Guy - SLIP:/usr/users/Shelmerg:/usr/sbin/sliplogin
```

When `Shelmerg` logs in, `sliplogin` will search `/etc/sliphome/slip.hosts` for a line that had a matching user ID; for example, there may be a line in `/etc/sliphome/slip.hosts` that reads:

```
Shelmerg        dc-slip sl-helmer       0xfffffc00   autocomp
```

`sliplogin` will find that matching line, hook the serial line into the next available SLIP interface, and then execute `/etc/sliphome/slip.login` like this:

```
/etc/sliphome/slip.login 0 19200 Shelmerg dc-slip sl-helmer 0xfffffc00 autocomp
```

If all goes well, /etc/sliphome/slip.login will issue an ifconfig for the SLIP interface to which sliplogin attached itself (slip interface 0, in the above example, which was the first parameter in the list given to slip.login) to set the local IP address (dc-slip), remote IP address (sl-helmer), network mask for the SLIP interface (0xfffffc00), and any additional flags (autocomp). If something goes wrong, sliplogin usually logs good informational messages via the daemon syslog facility, which usually logs to /var/log/messages (see the manual pages for syslogd(8) and syslog.conf(5) and perhaps check /etc/syslog.conf to see to what syslogd is logging and where it is logging to.

OK, enough of the examples — let us dive into setting up the system.

Kernel Configuration

FreeBSD's default kernels usually come with two SLIP interfaces defined (sl0 and sl1); you can use netstat -i to see whether these interfaces are defined in your kernel.

Sample output from netstat -i:

Name	Mtu	Network	Address	Ipkts	Ierrs	Opkts	Oerrs	Coll
ed0	1500	<Link>0.0.c0.2c.5f.4a		291311	0	174209	0	133
ed0	1500	138.247.224	ivory	291311	0	174209	0	133
lo0	65535	<Link>		79	0	79	0	0
lo0	65535	loop	localhost	79	0	79	0	0
sl0*	296	<Link>		0	0	0	0	0
sl1*	296	<Link>		0	0	0	0	0

The sl0 and sl1 interfaces shown from netstat -i indicate that there are two SLIP interfaces built into the kernel. (The asterisks after the sl0 and sl1 indicate that the interfaces are "down".)

However, FreeBSD's default kernel does not come configured to forward packets (by default, your FreeBSD machine will not act as a router) due to Internet RFC requirements for Internet hosts (see RFCs 1009 [Requirements for Internet Gateways], 1122 [Requirements for Internet Hosts — Communication Layers], and perhaps 1127 [A Perspective on the Host Requirements RFCs]). If you want your FreeBSD SLIP Server to act as a router, you will have to edit the /etc/rc.conf file and change the setting of the gateway_enable variable to YES.

You will then need to reboot for the new settings to take effect.

You will notice that near the end of the default kernel configuration file (/sys/i386/conf/GENERIC) is a line that reads:

```
pseudo-device sl 2
```

This is the line that defines the number of SLIP devices available in the kernel; the number at the end of the line is the maximum number of SLIP connections that may be operating simultaneously.

Please refer to Chapter 9 on Configuring the FreeBSD Kernel for help in reconfiguring your kernel.

Sliplogin Configuration

As mentioned earlier, there are three files in the /etc/sliphome directory that are part of the configuration for /usr/sbin/sliplogin (see sliplogin(8) for the actual manual page for sliplogin): slip.hosts, which defines the SLIP users & their associated IP addresses; `slip.login`, which usually just configures the SLIP interface; and (optionally) `slip.logout`, which undoes `slip.login`'s effects when the serial connection is terminated.

`slip.hosts` **Configuration**

`/etc/sliphome/slip.hosts` contains lines which have at least four items separated by whitespace:

- SLIP user's login ID
- Local address (local to the SLIP server) of the SLIP link
- Remote address of the SLIP link
- Network mask

The local and remote addresses may be host names (resolved to IP addresses by `/etc/hosts` or by the domain name service, depending on your specifications in `/etc/host.conf`), and the network mask may be a name that can be resolved by a lookup into `/etc/networks`. On a sample system, `/etc/sliphome/slip.hosts` looks like this:

```
#
# login local-addr     remote-addr     mask              opt1      opt2
#                                                  (normal,compress,noicmp)
#
Shelmerg   dc-slip      sl-helmerg      0xfffffc00        autocomp
```

At the end of the line is one or more of the options.

- `normal` — no header compression
- `compress` — compress headers
- `autocomp` — compress headers if the remote end allows it
- `noicmp` — disable ICMP packets (so any "ping" packets will be dropped instead of using up your bandwidth)

Your choice of local and remote addresses for your SLIP links depends on whether you are going to dedicate a TCP/IP subnet or if you are going to use "proxy ARP" on your SLIP server (it is not "true" proxy ARP, but that is the terminology used in this section to describe it). If you are not sure which method to select or how to assign IP addresses, please refer to the TCP/IP books referenced in the SLIP Prerequisites (Section 16.6.2.1) and/or consult your IP network manager.

If you are going to use a separate subnet for your SLIP clients, you will need to allocate the subnet number out of your assigned IP network number and assign each of your SLIP client's IP numbers out of that subnet. Then, you will probably either need to configure a static route to the SLIP subnet via your SLIP server on your nearest IP router, or install `gated` on your FreeBSD SLIP server and configure it to talk the appropriate routing protocols to your other routers to inform them about your SLIP server's route to the SLIP subnet.

Otherwise, if you will use the "proxy ARP" method, you will need to assign your SLIP client's IP addresses out of your SLIP server's Ethernet subnet, and you will also need to adjust your `/etc/sliphome/slip.login` and `/etc/sliphome/slip.logout` scripts to use arp(8) to manage the proxy-ARP entries in the SLIP server's ARP table.

slip.login **Configuration**

The typical `/etc/sliphome/slip.login` file looks like this:

```
#!/bin/sh -
#
#       @(#)slip.login  5.1 (Berkeley) 7/1/90
#
# generic login file for a slip line.  sliplogin invokes this with
# the parameters:
#     1       2       3       4        5         6     7-n
#   slipunit ttyspeed loginname local-addr remote-addr mask opt-args
#
/sbin/ifconfig sl$1 inet $4 $5 netmask $6
```

This `slip.login` file merely runs `ifconfig` for the appropriate SLIP interface with the local and remote addresses and network mask of the SLIP interface.

If you have decided to use the "proxy ARP" method (instead of using a separate subnet for your SLIP clients), your `/etc/sliphome/slip.login` file will need to look something like this:

```
#!/bin/sh -
#
#       @(#)slip.login  5.1 (Berkeley) 7/1/90
#
# generic login file for a slip line.  sliplogin invokes this with
# the parameters:
#     1       2       3       4        5         6     7-n
#   slipunit ttyspeed loginname local-addr remote-addr mask opt-args
#
/sbin/ifconfig sl$1 inet $4 $5 netmask $6
# Answer ARP requests for the SLIP client with our Ethernet addr
/usr/sbin/arp -s $5 00:11:22:33:44:55 pub
```

The additional line in this `slip.login`, `arp -s $5 00:11:22:33:44:55 pub`, creates an ARP entry in the SLIP server's ARP table. This ARP entry causes the SLIP server to respond with the SLIP server's Ethernet MAC address whenever another IP node on the Ethernet asks to speak to the SLIP client's IP address.

When using the example above, be sure to replace the Ethernet MAC address (`00:11:22:33:44:55`) with the MAC address of your system's Ethernet card, or your "proxy ARP" will definitely not work! You can discover your SLIP server's Ethernet MAC address by looking at the results of running `netstat -i`; the second line of the output should look something like:

```
ed0   1500   <Link>0.2.c1.28.5f.4a         191923 0   129457    0   116
```

This indicates that this particular system's Ethernet MAC address is `00:02:c1:28:5f:4a` — the periods in the Ethernet MAC address given by `netstat -i` must be changed to colons and leading zeros should be added to each single-digit hexadecimal number to convert the address into the form that arp(8) desires; see the manual page on arp(8) for complete information on usage.

Note: When you create /etc/sliphome/slip.login and /etc/sliphome/slip.logout, the "execute" bit (chmod 755 /etc/sliphome/slip.login /etc/sliphome/slip.logout) must be set, or sliplogin will be unable to execute it.

slip.logout **Configuration**

/etc/sliphome/slip.logout is not strictly needed (unless you are implementing "proxy ARP"), but if you decide to create it, this is an example of a basic slip.logout script:

```
#!/bin/sh -
#
#       slip.logout

#
# logout file for a slip line.  sliplogin invokes this with
# the parameters:
#     1         2         3          4          5          6     7-n
#   slipunit ttyspeed loginname local-addr remote-addr mask opt-args
#
/sbin/ifconfig sl$1 down
```

If you are using "proxy ARP", you will want to have /etc/sliphome/slip.logout remove the ARP entry for the SLIP client:

```
#!/bin/sh -
#
#       @(#)slip.logout

#
# logout file for a slip line.  sliplogin invokes this with
# the parameters:
#     1         2         3          4          5          6     7-n
#   slipunit ttyspeed loginname local-addr remote-addr mask opt-args
#
/sbin/ifconfig sl$1 down
# Quit answering ARP requests for the SLIP client
/usr/sbin/arp -d $5
```

The arp -d $5 removes the ARP entry that the "proxy ARP" slip.login added when the SLIP client logged in.

It bears repeating: make sure /etc/sliphome/slip.logout has the execute bit set after you create it (ie, chmod 755 /etc/sliphome/slip.logout).

Routing Considerations

If you are not using the "proxy ARP" method for routing packets between your SLIP clients and the rest of your network (and perhaps the Internet), you will probably either have to add static routes to your closest default router(s) to route your SLIP client subnet via your SLIP server, or you will probably need to install and configure gated on your FreeBSD SLIP server so that it will tell your routers via appropriate routing protocols about your SLIP subnet.

Static Routes

Adding static routes to your nearest default routers can be troublesome (or impossible if you do not have authority to do so...). If you have a multiple-router network in your organization, some routers, such as those made by Cisco and Proteon, may not only need to be configured with the static route to the SLIP subnet, but also need to be told which static routes to tell other routers about, so some expertise and troubleshooting/tweaking may be necessary to get static-route-based routing to work.

Running gated

An alternative to the headaches of static routes is to install gated on your FreeBSD SLIP server and configure it to use the appropriate routing protocols (RIP/OSPF/BGP/EGP) to tell other routers about your SLIP subnet. You can use gated from the ports collection or retrieve and build it yourself from the GateD anonymous FTP site[8]; the current version as of this writing is gated-R3_5Alpha_8.tar.Z, which includes support for FreeBSD "out-of-the-box". Complete information and documentation on gated is available on the Web starting at the Merit GateD Consortium[9]. Compile and install it, and then write a /etc/gated.conf file to configure your gated; here is a sample, similar to what the author used on a FreeBSD SLIP server:

```
#
# gated configuration file for dc.dsu.edu; for gated version 3.5alpha5
# Only broadcast RIP information for xxx.xxx.yy out the ed Ethernet interface
#
#
# tracing options
#
traceoptions "/var/tmp/gated.output" replace size 100k files 2 general ;

rip yes {
  interface sl noripout noripin ;
  interface ed ripin ripout version 1 ;
  traceoptions route ;
} ;

#
# Turn on a bunch of tracing info for the interface to the kernel:
kernel {
  traceoptions remnants request routes info interface ;
} ;
```

---

8 ftp://ftp.gated.merit.edu/research.and.development/gated/
9 http://www.gated.merit.edu/

```
#
# Propagate the route to xxx.xxx.yy out the Ethernet interface via RIP
#

export proto rip interface ed {
  proto direct {
      xxx.xxx.yy mask 255.255.252.0 metric 1; # SLIP connections
  } ;
} ;

#
# Accept routes from RIP via ed Ethernet interfaces

import proto rip interface ed {
  all ;
} ;
```

The above sample `gated.conf` file broadcasts routing information regarding the SLIP subnet *xxx.xxx.yy* via RIP onto the Ethernet; if you are using a different Ethernet driver than the `ed` driver, you will need to change the references to the `ed` interface appropriately. This sample file also sets up tracing to `/var/tmp/gated.output` for debugging `gated`'s activity; you can certainly turn off the tracing options if `gated` works OK for you. You will need to change the *xxx.xxx.yy*'s into the network address of your own SLIP subnet (be sure to change the net mask in the `proto direct` clause as well).

Once you have installed and configured `gated` on your system, you will need to tell the FreeBSD startup scripts to run `gated` in place of `routed`. The easiest way to accomplish this is to set the `router` and `router_flags` variables in `/etc/rc.conf`. Please see the manual page for `gated` for information on command-line parameters.

Chapter 17

Advanced Networking

17.1 Synopsis

This chapter will cover some of the more frequently used network services on Unix systems. We will cover how to define, setup, test and maintain all of the network services that FreeBSD utilizes. In addition, there have been example configuration files included throughout this chapter for you to benefit from.

After reading this chapter, you will know:

- The basics of gateways and routes.
- How to make FreeBSD act as a bridge.
- How to setup a network file system.
- How to setup network booting on a diskless machine.
- How to setup a network information server for sharing user accounts.
- How to setup automatic network settings using DHCP.
- How to setup a domain name server.
- How to synchronize the time and date, and setup a time server, with the NTP protocol.
- How to setup network address translation.
- How to manage the `inetd` daemon.

Before reading this chapter, you should:

- Understand the basics of the `/etc/rc` scripts.
- Be familiar with basic network terminology.

17.2 Gateways and Routes

For one machine to be able to find another over a network, there must be a mechanism in place to describe how to get from one to the other. This is called *routing*. A "route" is a defined pair of addresses: a "destination" and a "gateway". The pair indicates that if you are trying to get to this *destination*, communicate through this *gateway*. There are three types of destinations: individual hosts, subnets, and "default". The "default route" is used if none of the other routes apply. We will talk a little bit more about default routes later on. There are also three types of gateways: individual hosts, interfaces (also called "links"), and Ethernet hardware addresses (MAC addresses).

17.2.1 An Example

To illustrate different aspects of routing, we will use the following example from netstat:

```
% netstat -r
Routing tables
```

Destination	Gateway	Flags	Refs	Use	Netif	Expire
default	outside-gw	UGSc	37	418	ppp0	
localhost	localhost	UH	0	181	lo0	
test0	0:e0:b5:36:cf:4f	UHLW	5	63288	ed0	77
10.20.30.255	link#1	UHLW	1	2421		
example.com	link#1	UC	0	0		
host1	0:e0:a8:37:8:1e	UHLW	3	4601	lo0	
host2	0:e0:a8:37:8:1e	UHLW	0	5	lo0 =>	
host2.example.com	link#1	UC	0	0		
224	link#1	UC	0	0		

The first two lines specify the default route (which we will cover in the next section, Section 17.2.2) and the localhost route.

The interface (Netif column) that it specifies to use for localhost is lo0, also known as the loopback device. This says to keep all traffic for this destination internal, rather than sending it out over the LAN, since it will only end up back where it started.

The next thing that stands out are the addresses beginning with 0:e0:. These are Ethernet hardware addresses, which are also known as MAC addresses. FreeBSD will automatically identify any hosts (test0 in the example) on the local Ethernet and add a route for that host, directly to it over the Ethernet interface, ed0. There is also a timeout (Expire column) associated with this type of route, which is used if we fail to hear from the host in a specific amount of time. In this case the route will be automatically deleted. These hosts are identified using a mechanism known as RIP (Routing Information Protocol), which figures out routes to local hosts based upon a shortest path determination.

FreeBSD will also add subnet routes for the local subnet (10.20.30.255 is the broadcast address for the subnet 10.20.30, and example.com is the domain name associated with that subnet). The designation link#1 refers to the first Ethernet card in the machine. You will notice no additional interface is specified for those.

Both of these groups (local network hosts and local subnets) have their routes automatically configured by a daemon called **routed**. If this is not run, then only routes which are statically defined (ie. entered explicitly) will exist.

The host1 line refers to our host, which it knows by Ethernet address. Since we are the sending host, FreeBSD knows to use the loopback interface (lo0) rather than sending it out over the Ethernet interface.

The two host2 lines are an example of what happens when we use an ifconfig(8) alias (see the section of Ethernet for reasons why we would do this). The => symbol after the lo0 interface says that not only are we using the loopback (since this is address also refers to the local host), but specifically it is an alias. Such routes only show up on the host that supports the alias; all other hosts on the local network will simply have a link#1 line for such.

The final line (destination subnet `224`) deals with MultiCasting, which will be covered in a another section.

The other column that we should talk about are the `Flags`. Each route has different attributes that are described in the column. Below is a short table of some of these flags and their meanings:

U	Up: The route is active.
H	Host: The route destination is a single host.
G	Gateway: Send anything for this destination on to this remote system, which will figure out from there where to send it.
S	Static: This route was configured manually, not automatically generated by the system.
C	Clone: Generates a new route based upon this route for machines we connect to. This type of route is normally used for local networks.
W	WasCloned: Indicated a route that was auto-configured based upon a local area network (Clone) route.
L	Link: Route involves references to Ethernet hardware.

17.2.2 Default Routes

When the local system needs to make a connection to remote host, it checks the routing table to determine if a known path exists. If the remote host falls into a subnet that we know how to reach (Cloned routes), then the system checks to see if it can connect along that interface.

If all known paths fail, the system has one last option: the "default" route. This route is a special type of gateway route (usually the only one present in the system), and is always marked with a `c` in the flags field. For hosts on a local area network, this gateway is set to whatever machine has a direct connection to the outside world (whether via PPP link, DSL, cable modem, T1, or another network interface).

If you are configuring the default route for a machine which itself is functioning as the gateway to the outside world, then the default route will be the gateway machine at your Internet Service Provider's (ISP) site.

Let us look at an example of default routes. This is a common configuration:

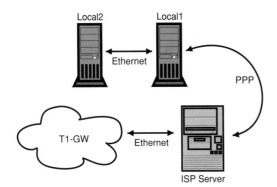

The hosts Local1 and Local2 are at your site. Local1 is connected to an ISP via a dial up PPP connection. This PPP server computer is connected through a local area network to another gateway computer with an external interface to the ISPs Internet feed.

The default routes for each of your machines will be:

Host	Default Gateway	Interface
Local2	Local1	Ethernet
Local1	T1-GW	PPP

A common question is "Why (or how) would we set the T1-GW to be the default gateway for Local1, rather than the ISP server it is connected to?".

Remember, since the PPP interface is using an address on the ISP's local network for your side of the connection, routes for any other machines on the ISP's local network will be automatically generated. Hence, you will already know how to reach the T1-GW machine, so there is no need for the intermediate step of sending traffic to the ISP server.

As a final note, it is common to use the address X.X.X.1 as the gateway address for your local network. So (using the same example), if your local class-C address space was 10.20.30 and your ISP was using 10.9.9 then the default routes would be:

Host	Default Route
Local2 (10.20.3.2)	Local1 (10.20.30.1)
Local1 (10.20.30.1, 10.9.9.30)	T1-GW (10.9.9.1)

17.2.3 Dual Homed Hosts

There is one other type of configuration that we should cover, and that is a host that sits on two different networks. Technically, any machine functioning as a gateway (in the example above, using a PPP connection) counts as a dual-homed host. But the term is really only used to refer to a machine that sits on two local-area networks.

In one case, the machine has two Ethernet cards, each having an address on the separate subnets. Alternately, the machine may only have one Ethernet card, and be using ifconfig(8) aliasing. The former is used if two physically separate Ethernet networks are in use, the latter if there is one physical network segment, but two logically separate subnets.

Either way, routing tables are set up so that each subnet knows that this machine is the defined gateway (inbound route) to the other subnet. This configuration, with the machine acting as a Bridge between the two subnets, is often used when we need to implement packet filtering or firewall security in either or both directions.

17.2.4 Routing Propagation

We have already talked about how we define our routes to the outside world, but not about how the outside world finds us.

We already know that routing tables can be set up so that all traffic for a particular address space (in our examples, a class-C subnet) can be sent to a particular host on that network, which will forward the packets inbound.

When you get an address space assigned to your site, your service provider will set up their routing tables so that all traffic for your subnet will be sent down your PPP link to your site. But how do sites across the country know to send to your ISP?

There is a system (much like the distributed DNS information) that keeps track of all assigned address-spaces, and defines their point of connection to the Internet Backbone. The "Backbone" are the main trunk lines that carry Internet traffic across the country, and around the world. Each backbone machine has a copy of a master set of tables, which direct traffic for a particular network to a specific backbone carrier, and from there down the chain of service providers until it reaches your network.

It is the task of your service provider to advertise to the backbone sites that they are the point of connection (and thus the path inward) for your site. This is known as route propagation.

17.2.5 Troubleshooting

Sometimes, there is a problem with routing propagation, and some sites are unable to connect to you. Perhaps the most useful command for trying to figure out where a routing is breaking down is the traceroute(8) command. It is equally useful if you cannot seem to make a connection to a remote machine (i.e. ping(8) fails).

The traceroute(8) command is run with the name of the remote host you are trying to connect to. It will show the gateway hosts along the path of the attempt, eventually either reaching the target host, or terminating because of a lack of connection.

For more information, see the manual page for traceroute(8).

17.3 Bridging

17.3.1 Introduction

It is sometimes useful to divide one physical network (such as an Ethernet segment) into two separate network segments without having to create IP subnets and use a router to connect the segments together. A device that connects two networks together in this fashion is called a bridge. A FreeBSD system with two network interface cards can act as a bridge.

The bridge works by learning the MAC layer addresses (Ethernet addresses) of the devices on each of its network interfaces. It forwards traffic between two networks only when its source and destination are on different networks.

In many respects, a bridge is like an Ethernet switch with very few ports.

17.3.2 Situations Where Bridging Is Appropriate

There are two common situations in which a bridge is used today.

High Traffic on a Segment

Situation one is where your physical network segment is overloaded with traffic, but you do not want for whatever reason to subnet the network and interconnect the subnets with a router.

Let us consider an example of a newspaper where the Editorial and Production departments are on the same subnetwork. The Editorial users all use server A for file service, and the Production users are on server B. An Ethernet is used to connect all users together, and high loads on the network are slowing things down.

If the Editorial users could be segregated on one network segment and the Production users on another, the two network segments could be connected with a bridge. Only the network traffic destined for interfaces on the "other" side of the bridge would be sent to the other network, reducing congestion on each network segment.

Filtering/Traffic Shaping Firewall

The second common situation is where firewall functionality is needed without IP Masquerading (NAT).

An example is a small company that is connected via DSL or ISDN to their ISP. They have a 13 globally-accessible IP addresses from their ISP and have 10 PCs on their network. In this situation, using a router-based firewall is difficult because of subnetting issues.

A bridge-based firewall can be configured and dropped into the path just downstream of their DSL/ISDN router without any IP numbering issues.

17.3.3 Configuring a Bridge

Network Interface Card Selection

A bridge requires at least two network cards to function. Unfortunately, not all network interface cards as of FreeBSD 4.0 support bridging. Read bridge(4) for details on the cards that are supported.

Install and test the two network cards before continuing.

Kernel Configuration Changes

To enable kernel support for bridging, add the:

```
options BRIDGE
```

statement to your kernel configuration file, and rebuild your kernel.

Firewall Support

If you are planning to use the bridge as a firewall, you will need to add the IPFIREWALL option as well. Read Section 10.7 for general information on configuring the bridge as a firewall.

If you need to allow non-IP packets (such as ARP) to flow through the bridge, there is an undocumented firewall option that must be set. This option is IPFIREWALL_DEFAULT_TO_ACCEPT. Note that this changes the default rule for the firewall to accept any packet. Make sure you know how this changes the meaning of your ruleset before you set it.

Traffic Shaping Support

If you want to use the bridge as a traffic shaper, you will need to add the DUMMYNET option to your kernel configuration. Read dummynet(4) for further information.

17.3.4 Enabling the Bridge

Add the line:

```
net.link.ether.bridge=1
```

to /etc/sysctl.conf to enable the bridge at runtime. If you want the bridged packets to be filtered by ipfw(8), you should also add:

```
net.link.ether.bridge_ipfw=1
```

as well.

17.3.5 Performance

My bridge/firewall is a Pentium 90 with one 3Com 3C900B and one 3C905B. The protected side of the network runs at 10mbps half duplex and the connection between the bridge and my router (a Cisco 675) runs at 100mbps full duplex. With no filtering enabled, I have found that the bridge adds about 0.4 milliseconds of latency to pings from the protected 10mbps network to the Cisco 675.

17.3.6 Other Information

If you want to be able to telnet into the bridge from the network, it is OK to assign one of the network cards an IP address. The consensus is that assigning both cards an address is a bad idea.

If you have multiple bridges on your network, there cannot be more than one path between any two workstations. Technically, this means that there is no support for spanning tree link management.

17.4 NFS

Among the many different file systems that FreeBSD supports is the Network File System or NFS. NFS allows you to share directories and files on one machine with others via the network they are attached to. Using NFS, users and programs can access files on remote systems as if they were local files.

NFS has several benefits:

- Local workstations do not need as much disk space because commonly used data can be stored on a single machine and still remain accessible to everyone on the network.

- There is no need for users to have unique home directories on every machine on your network. Once they have an established directory that is available via NFS it can be accessed from anywhere.

- Storage devices such as floppies and CDROM drives can be used by other machines on the network eliminating the need for extra hardware.

17.4.1 How It Works

NFS is composed of two sides – a client side and a server side. Think of it as a want/have relationship. The client *wants* the data that the server side *has*. The server shares its data with the client. In order for this system to function properly a few processes have to be configured and running.

The server has to be running the following daemons:

Daemon	Description
nfsd	The NFS Daemon which services requests from NFS clients.
mountd	The NFS Mount Daemon which actually carries out requests that nfsd(8) passes on to it.

Daemon	Description
portmap	The `portmapper` daemon which allows NFS clients to find out which port the NFS server is using.

The client side only needs to run a single daemon:

nfsiod	The NFS async I/O Daemon which services requests from its NFS server.

17.4.2 Configuring NFS

Luckily for us, on a FreeBSD system this setup is a snap. The processes that need to be running can all be run at boot time with a few modifications to your `/etc/rc.conf` file.

On the NFS server make sure you have:

```
portmap_enable="YES"
nfs_server_enable="YES"
nfs_server_flags="-u -t -n 4"
mountd_flags="-r"
```

`mountd` is automatically run whenever the NFS server is enabled. The `-u` and `-t` flags to `nfsd` tell it to serve UDP and TCP clients. The `-n 4` flag tells `nfsd` to start 4 copies of itself.

On the client, make sure you have:

```
nfs_client_enable="YES"
nfs_client_flags="-n 4"
```

Like `nfsd`, the `-n 4` tells `nfsiod` to start 4 copies of itself.

The last configuration step requires that you create a file called `/etc/exports`. The exports file specifies which file systems on your server will be shared (a.k.a., "exported") and with what clients they will be shared. Each line in the file specifies a file system to be shared. There are a handful of options that can be used in this file but only a few will be mentioned here. You can find out about the rest in the exports(5) manual page.

Here are a few example `/etc/exports` entries:

The following line exports `/cdrom` to three silly machines that have the same domain name as the server (hence the lack of a domain name for each) or have entries in your `/etc/hosts` file. The `-ro` flag makes the shared file system read-only. With this flag, the remote system will not be able to make any changes to the shared file system.

```
/cdrom -ro moe larry curly
```

The following line exports `/home` to three hosts by IP address. This is a useful setup if you have a private network but do not have DNS running. The `-alldirs` flag allows all the directories below the specified file system to be exported as well.

```
/home   -alldirs  10.0.0.2 10.0.0.3 10.0.0.4
```

The following line exports /a to two machines that have different domain names than the server. The -maproot=0 flag allows the root user on the remote system to write to the shared file system as root. Without the -maproot=0 flag even if someone has root access on the remote system they will not be able to modify files on the shared file system.

```
/a  -maproot=0  host.domain.com box.example.com
```

In order for a client to access- an exported file system it must have permission to do so. Make sure your client is listed in your /etc/exports file.

It is important to remember that you must restart mountd whenever you modify /etc/exports so that your changes take effect. This can be accomplished by sending the hangup signal to the mountd process :

```
# kill -HUP `cat /var/run/mountd.pid`
```

Now that you have made all these changes you can just reboot and let FreeBSD start everything for you at boot time or you can run the following commands as root:

On the NFS server:

```
# portmap
# nfsd -u -t -n 4
# mountd -r
```

On the NFS client:

```
# nfsiod -n 4
```

Now you should be ready to actually mount a remote file system. This can be done one of two ways. In these examples the server's name will be server and the client's name will be client. If you just want to temporarily mount a remote file system or just want to test out your configuration you can run a command like this as root on the client:

```
# mount server:/home /mnt
```

This will mount the /home directory on the server at /mnt on the client. If everything is setup correctly you should be able to go into /mnt on the client and see all the files that are on the server.

If you want to permanently (each time you reboot) mount a remote file system you need to add it to your /etc/fstab file. Here is an example line:

```
server:/home /mnt nfs rw 0 0
```

Read the fstab(5) manual page for more options.

17.4.3 Practical Uses

There are many very cool uses for NFS. Some of the more common ones are listed below.

- Have several machines on a network and share a CDROM or floppy drive among them. This is cheaper and often more convenient.

- With so many machines on a network, it gets old having your personal files strewn all over the place. You can have a central NFS server that houses all user home directories and shares them with the rest of the machines on the LAN, so no matter where you log in you will have the same home directory.

- When you get to reinstalling FreeBSD on one of your machines, NFS is the way to go! Just pop your distribution CDROM into your file server and away you go!

- Have a common `/usr/ports/distfiles` directory that all your machines share. That way, when you go to install a port that you have already installed on a different machine, you do not have to download the source all over again!

17.4.4 amd

amd(8), which is also known as the automatic mounter daemon, is a useful utility used for automatically mounting a remote filesystem whenever a file or directory within that filesystem is accessed. Filesystems that are inactive for a period of time will also be automatically unmounted by **amd**. Using **amd** provides a simplistic alternative to static mounts.

amd operates by attaching itself as an NFS server to the `/host` and `/net` directories. When a file is accessed within one of these directories, **amd** looks up the corresponding remote mount and automatically mounts it. `/net` is used to mount an exported filesystem from an IP address, while `/host` is used to mount an export from a remote hostname.

An access to a file within `/host/foobar/usr` would tell **amd** to attempt to mount the `/usr` export on the host `foobar`.

Example 17-1. Mounting an Export with amd

```
% showmount -e foobar
Exports list on foobar:
/usr                         10.10.10.0
/a                           10.10.10.0
% cd /host/foobar/usr
```

As seen in the example, the `showmount` shows `/usr` as an export. When changing directories to `/host/foobar/usr`, **amd** attempts to resolve the hostname `foobar` and automatically mount the desired export.

amd can be started through the `rc.conf` system by placing the following lines in `/etc/rc.conf`:

```
amd_enable="YES"
```

Additionally, custom flags can be passed to **amd** from the `amd_flags` option. By default, `amd_flags` is set to:

```
amd_flags="-a /.amd_mnt -l syslog /host /etc/amd.map /net /etc/amd.map"
```

The `/etc/amd.map` file defines the default options that exports are mounted with. The `/etc/amd.conf` file defines some of the more advanced features of **amd**.

Consult the amd(8) and amd.conf(5) man pages for more information.

17.4.5 Problems Integrating with Other Systems

Certain Ethernet adapters for ISA PC systems have limitations which can lead to serious network problems, particularly with NFS. This difficulty is not specific to FreeBSD, but FreeBSD systems are affected by it.

The problem nearly always occurs when (FreeBSD) PC systems are networked with high-performance workstations, such as those made by Silicon Graphics, Inc., and Sun Microsystems, Inc. The NFS mount will work fine, and some operations may succeed, but suddenly the server will seem to become unresponsive to the client, even though requests to and from other systems continue to be processed. This happens to the client system, whether the client is the FreeBSD system or the workstation. On many systems, there is no way to shut down the client gracefully once this problem has manifested itself. The only solution is often to reset the client, because the NFS situation cannot be resolved.

Though the "correct" solution is to get a higher performance and capacity Ethernet adapter for the FreeBSD system, there is a simple workaround that will allow satisfactory operation. If the FreeBSD system is the *server*, include the option -w=1024 on the mount from the client. If the FreeBSD system is the *client*, then mount the NFS file system with the option -r=1024. These options may be specified using the fourth field of the fstab entry on the client for automatic mounts, or by using the -o parameter of the mount command for manual mounts.

It should be noted that there is a different problem, sometimes mistaken for this one, when the NFS servers and clients are on different networks. If that is the case, make *certain* that your routers are routing the necessary UDP information, or you will not get anywhere, no matter what else you are doing.

In the following examples, fastws is the host (interface) name of a high-performance workstation, and freebox is the host (interface) name of a FreeBSD system with a lower-performance Ethernet adapter. Also, /sharedfs will be the exported NFS filesystem (see exports(5)), and /project will be the mount point on the client for the exported file system. In all cases, note that additional options, such as hard or soft and bg may be desirable in your application.

Examples for the FreeBSD system (freebox) as the client: in /etc/fstab on freebox:

```
fastws:/sharedfs /project nfs rw,-r=1024 0 0
```

As a manual mount command on freebox:

```
# mount -t nfs -o -r=1024 fastws:/sharedfs /project
```

Examples for the FreeBSD system as the server: in /etc/fstab on fastws:

```
freebox:/sharedfs /project nfs rw,-w=1024 0 0
```

As a manual mount command on fastws:

```
# mount -t nfs -o -w=1024 freebox:/sharedfs /project
```

Nearly any 16-bit Ethernet adapter will allow operation without the above restrictions on the read or write size.

For anyone who cares, here is what happens when the failure occurs, which also explains why it is unrecoverable. NFS typically works with a "block" size of 8k (though it may do fragments of smaller sizes). Since the maximum Ethernet packet is around 1500 bytes, the NFS "block" gets split into multiple Ethernet packets, even though it is still a single unit to the upper-level code, and must be received, assembled, and *acknowledged* as a unit. The high-performance workstations can pump out the packets which comprise the NFS unit one right after the other, just as close together as the standard allows. On the smaller, lower capacity cards, the later packets overrun the earlier packets of the same unit before they can be transferred to the host and the unit as a whole cannot be reconstructed or acknowledged. As a result, the workstation will time out and try again, but it will try again with the entire 8K unit, and the process will be repeated, ad infinitum.

By keeping the unit size below the Ethernet packet size limitation, we ensure that any complete Ethernet packet received can be acknowledged individually, avoiding the deadlock situation.

Overruns may still occur when a high-performance workstations is slamming data out to a PC system, but with the better cards, such overruns are not guaranteed on NFS "units". When an overrun occurs, the units affected will be retransmitted, and there will be a fair chance that they will be received, assembled, and acknowledged.

17.5 Diskless Operation

A FreeBSD machine can boot over the network and operate without a local disk, using file systems mounted from an NFS server. No system modification is necessary, beyond standard configuration files. Such a system is easy to set up because all the necessary elements are readily available:

- There are at least two possible methods to load the kernel over the network:
  - *PXE*: Intel's Preboot Execution Environment system is a form of smart boot ROM built into some networking cards or motherboards. See pxeboot(8) for more details.
  - *The **etherboot** port* (`/usr/ports/net/etherboot`) produces ROM-able code to boot kernels over the network. The code can be either burnt into a boot PROM on a network card, or loaded from a local floppy (or hard) disk drive, or from a running MS-DOS system. Many network cards are supported.

- A sample script (`/usr/local/share/examples/clone_root`) eases the creation and maintenance of the workstation's root filesystem on the server. The script will probably require a little customization but it will get you started very quickly

- Standard system startup files exist in `/etc` to detect and support a diskless system startup.

- Swapping, if needed, can be done either to an NFS file or to a local disk

There are many ways to set up diskless workstations. Many elements are involved, and most can be customized to suit local taste. The following will describe the setup of a complete system, emphasizing simplicity and compatibility with the standard FreeBSD startup scripts. The system described has the following characteristics:

- The diskless workstations use a shared read-only `root` filesystem, and a shared read-only /usr.

  The `root` file system is a copy of a standard FreeBSD root (typically the server's), with some configuration files overridden by ones specific to diskless operation or, possibly, to the workstation they belong to.

  The parts of the `root` which have to be writable are overlaid with mfs(8) filesystems. Any changes will be lost when the system reboots.

- The kernel is loaded by **etherboot** , using DHCP (or BOOTP) and TFTP.

Caution: As described, this system is insecure. It should live in a protected area of a network, and be untrusted by other hosts.

17.5.1 Setup Instructions

Configuring DHCP/BOOTP

There are two protocols that are commonly used to boot a workstation that retrieves its configuration over the network: BOOTP and DHCP. They are used at several points in the workstation bootstrap:

- **etherboot** uses DHCP (by default) or BOOTP (needs a configuration option) to find the kernel. (PXE uses DHCP).
- The kernel uses BOOTP to locate the NFS root.

It is possible to configure a system to use only BOOTP. The bootpd(8) server program is included in the base FreeBSD system.

However, DHCP has a number of advantages over BOOTP (nicer configuration files, possibility of using PXE, plus many others not directly related to diskless operation), and we shall describe both a pure BOOTP, and a BOOTP+DHCP configuration, with an emphasis on the latter, which will use the ISC DHCP software package.

Configuration Using ISC DHCP

The **isc-dhcp** server can answer both BOOTP and DHCP requests.

As of release 4.4, **isc-dhcp** is not part of the base system. You will first need to install the `/usr/ports/net/isc-dhcp3` port or the corresponding package. Please refer to Chapter 4 for general information about ports and packages.

Once **isc-dhcp** is installed, it needs a configuration file to run, (normally named `/usr/local/etc/dhcpd.conf`). Here follows a commented example:

```
default-lease-time 600;
max-lease-time 7200;
authoritative;

option domain-name "example.com";
option domain-name-servers 192.168.4.1;
option routers 192.168.4.1;

subnet 192.168.4.0 netmask 255.255.255.0 {
  use-host-decl-names on; ❶
  option subnet-mask 255.255.255.0;
  option broadcast-address 192.168.4.255;

  host margaux {
    hardware ethernet 01:23:45:67:89:ab;
    fixed-address margaux.example.com;
    next-server 192.168.4.4;❷
```

```
        filename "/tftpboot/kernel.diskless";❸
        option root-path "192.168.4.4:/data/misc/diskless";❹
    }
}
```

❶ This option tells `dhcpd` to send the value in the `host` declarations as the hostname for the diskless host. An alternate way would be to add an `option host-name` *margaux* inside the host declarations.

❷ The `next-server` directive designates the TFTP server (the default is to use the same host as the DHCP server).

❸ The `filename` directive defines the file that **etherboot** will load as a kernel.

Note: PXE appears to prefer a relative file name, and it loads `pxeboot`, not the kernel (`option filename "pxe-boot"`).

❹ The `root-path` option defines the path to the root filesystem, in usual NFS notation

Configuration Using BOOTP

Here follows an equivalent `bootpd` configuration. This would be found in `/etc/bootptab`.

Please note that **etherboot** must be compiled with the non-default option `NO_DHCP_SUPPORT` in order to use BOOTP, and that PXE *needs* DHCP. The only obvious advantage of **bootpd** is that it exists in the base system.

```
.def100:\
  :hn:ht=1:sa=192.168.4.4:vm=rfc1048:\
  :sm=255.255.255.0:\
  :ds=192.168.4.1:\
  :gw=192.168.4.1:\
  :hd="/tftpboot":\
  :bf="/kernel.diskless":\
  :rp="192.168.4.4:/data/misc/diskless":

margaux:ha=0123456789ab:tc=.def100
```

Preparing a Boot Program with Etherboot

Etherboot's Web site[1] contains extensive documentation[2] mainly intended for Linux systems, but nonetheless containing useful information. The following will just outline how you would use **etherboot** on a FreeBSD system.

1 http://etherboot.sourceforge.net
2 http://etherboot.sourceforge.net/doc/html/userman.html

You must first install - and possibly compile - the **etherboot** package. The **etherboot** port can normally be found in /usr/ports/net/etherboot. If the ports tree is installed on your system, just typing make in this directory should take care of everything. Else refer to Chapter 4 for information about ports and packages.

For our setup, we shall use a boot floppy. For other methods (PROM, or dos program), please refer to the **etherboot** documentation.

To make a boot floppy, insert a floppy in the drive on the machine where you installed **etherboot**, then change your current directory to the src directory in the **etherboot** tree and type:

```
# gmake bin32/devicetype.fd0
```

devicetype depends on the type of the Ethernet card in the diskless workstation. Refer to the NIC file in the same directory to determine the right *devicetype*.

Configuring the TFTP and NFS Servers

You need to enable tftpd on the TFTP server:

1. Create a directory from which tftpd will serve the files, ie: /tftpboot

2. Add this line to your /etc/inetd.conf:

```
tftp    dgram   udp     wait    nobody  /usr/libexec/tftpd    tftpd /tftpboot
```

> **Note:** It appears that at least some PXE versions wants the TCP version of TFTP. In this case, add a second line, replacing dgram udp with stream tcp

3. Tell inetd to reread its configuration file:

```
# kill -HUP `cat /var/run/inetd.pid`
```

You can place the tftpboot directory anywhere on the server, but, of course, the actual location, the value in inetd.conf, and the value in dhcpd.conf must be consistent !

You also need to enable NFS service and export the appropriate filesystem on the NFS server

1. Add this to /etc/rc.conf:

```
nfs_server_enable="YES"
```

2. Export the filesystem where the diskless root directory is located by adding the following to /etc/exports (adjust the volume mount point and workstation name!):

```
/data/misc -alldirs -ro margaux
```

3. Tell mountd to reread its configuration file. If you actually needed to configure NFS service at step 1, you probably want to reboot instead.

```
# kill -HUP `cat /var/run/mountd.pid`
```

Building a Diskless Kernel

Create a kernel configuration file for the diskless client with the following options (in addition to the usual ones):

```
options     BOOTP           # Use BOOTP to obtain IP address/hostname
options     BOOTP_NFSROOT   # NFS mount root filesystem using BOOTP info
options     BOOTP_COMPAT    # Workaround for broken bootp daemons.
```

You may also want to use BOOTP_NFSV3 and BOOTP_WIRED_TO (refer to LINT).

Build the kernel (See Chapter 9), and copy it to the tftp directory, under the name listed in dhcpd.conf

Preparing the root Filesystem

You need to create a root filesystem for the diskless workstations, in the location listed as root-path in dhcpd.conf.

The easiest way to do this is to use the /usr/share/examples/diskless/clone_root shell script. This script needs customization, at least to adjust the place where the filesystem will be created (the DEST variable).

Refer to the comments at the top of the script for instructions. They explain how the base filesystem is built, and how files may be selectively overridden by versions specific to diskless operation, to a subnetwork, or to an individual workstation. They also give examples for the diskless /etc/fstab and /etc/rc.conf

The README files in /usr/share/examples/diskless contain a lot of interesting background information, but, together with the other examples in the diskless directory, they actually document a configuration method which is distinct from the one used by clone_root and /etc/rc.diskless[12], which is a little confusing. Use them for reference only, except if you prefer the method that they describe, in which case you will need customized rc scripts

As of FreeBSD version 4.4-RELEASE, there is a small incompatibility between the clone_root script and the /etc/rc.diskless1 script. Please refer to PR conf/31200[3] for the small adjustment needed in clone_root. Also see PR conf/29870[4] about a small adjustment needed in /etc/rc.diskless2.

Configuring Swap

If needed, it is possible to do swapping over NFS, to a file on the server. The exact bootptab or dhcpd.conf options are a little mysterious and poorly documented. Anyway, here is what worked for me, using isc-dhcp 3.0rc11.

1. Add the following lines to dhcpd.conf:

```
# Global section
option swap-path code 128 = string;
option swap-size code 129 = integer 32;

host margaux {
  ... # Standard lines, see above
  option swap-path "192.168.4.4:/netswapvolume/netswap";
  option swap-size 64000;
```

---

3 http://www.freebsd.org/cgi/query-pr.cgi?pr=31200
4 http://www.freebsd.org/cgi/query-pr.cgi?pr=29870

```
    }
```

The idea is that, at least for a FreeBSD client, DHCP/BOOTP option code 128 is the path to the NFS swap file, and option code 129 is the swap size in kilobytes. Older versions of dhcpd allowed a syntax of option option-128 "..., which does not seem to work any more.

/etc/bootptab would use the following syntax instead:

```
T128="192.168.4.4:/netswapvolume/netswap":T129=64000
```

2. On the NFS swap file server, create the swap file(s)

```
# mkdir /netswapvolume/netswap
# cd /netswapvolume/netswap
# dd if=/dev/zero bs=1024 count=64000 of=swap.192.168.4.6
# chmod 0600 swap.192.168.4.6
```

192.168.4.6 is the IP address for the diskless client

3. On the NFS swap file server, add the following line to /etc/exports

```
/netswapvolume  -maproot=0:10 -alldirs margaux
```

Then tell **mountd** to reread the exports file, as above.

Miscellaneous Issues

Running with a read-only /usr

If the diskless workstation is configured to run X, you will have to adjust the xdm configuration file, which puts the error log on /usr by default.

Using a non-FreeBSD Server

When the server for the root filesystem is not running FreeBSD, you will have to create the root file system on a FreeBSD machine, then copy it to its destination, using tar or cpio.

In this situation, it seems that there are sometimes problems with the special files in /dev, because of differing minor/major number integer sizes. It seems that a solution to this problem is to run MAKEDEV on a FreeBSD machine, in a directory mounted through NFS from the final server.

17.6 ISDN

A good resource for information on ISDN technology and hardware is Dan Kegel's ISDN Page[5].

A quick simple road map to ISDN follows:

- If you live in Europe you might want to investigate the ISDN card section.

- If you are planning to use ISDN primarily to connect to the Internet with an Internet Provider on a dial-up non-dedicated basis, you might look into Terminal Adapters. This will give you the most flexibility, with the fewest problems, if you change providers.

- If you are connecting two LANs together, or connecting to the Internet with a dedicated ISDN connection, you might consider the stand alone router/bridge option.

Cost is a significant factor in determining what solution you will choose. The following options are listed from least expensive to most expensive.

17.6.1 ISDN Cards

FreeBSD's ISDN implementation supports only the DSS1/Q.931 (or Euro-ISDN) standard using passive cards. Starting with FreeBSD 4.4, some active cards are supported where the firmware also supports other signaling protocols; this also includes the first supported Primary Rate (PRI) ISDN card.

Isdn4bsd allows you to connect to other ISDN routers using either IP over raw HDLC or by using synchronous PPP: either by using kernel PPP with isppp, a modified sppp driver, or by using userland ppp(8). By using userland ppp(8), channel bonding of two or more ISDN B-channels is possible. A telephone answering machine application is also available as well as many utilities such as a software 300 Baud modem.

Some growing number of PC ISDN cards are supported under FreeBSD and the reports show that it is successfully used all over Europe and in many other parts of the world.

The passive ISDN cards supported are mostly the ones with the Infineon (formerly Siemens) ISAC/HSCX/IPAC ISDN chipsets, but also ISDN cards with chips from Cologne Chip (ISA bus only), PCI cards with Winbond W6692 chips, some cards with the Tiger300/320/ISAC chipset combinations and some vendor specific chipset based cards such as the AVM Fritz!Card PCI V.1.0 and the AVM Fritz!Card PnP.

Currently the active supported ISDN cards are the AVM B1 (ISA and PCI) BRI cards and the AVM T1 PCI PRI cards.

For documentation on **isdn4bsd**, have a look at `/usr/share/examples/isdn/` directory on your FreeBSD system or at the homepage of isdn4bsd[6] which also has pointers to hints, erratas and much more documentation such as the isdn4bsd handbook[7].

In case you are interested in adding support for a different ISDN protocol, a currently unsupported ISDN PC card or otherwise enhancing **isdn4bsd**, please get in touch with <hm@freebsd.org>.

For questions regarding the installation, configuration and troubleshooting **isdn4bsd**, a majordomo maintained mailing list is available. To join, send mail to <majordomo@FreeBSD.org> and specify:

---

5 http://alumni.caltech.edu/~dank/isdn/
6 http://www.freebsd-support.de/i4b/
7 http://people.freebsd.org/~hm/

```
subscribe freebsd-isdn
```

in the body of your message.

17.6.2 ISDN Terminal Adapters

Terminal adapters(TA), are to ISDN what modems are to regular phone lines.

Most TA's use the standard hayes modem AT command set, and can be used as a drop in replacement for a modem.

A TA will operate basically the same as a modem except connection and throughput speeds will be much faster than your old modem. You will need to configure PPP (Section 16.3) exactly the same as for a modem setup. Make sure you set your serial speed as high as possible.

The main advantage of using a TA to connect to an Internet Provider is that you can do Dynamic PPP. As IP address space becomes more and more scarce, most providers are not willing to provide you with a static IP anymore. Most stand-alone routers are not able to accommodate dynamic IP allocation.

TA's completely rely on the PPP daemon that you are running for their features and stability of connection. This allows you to upgrade easily from using a modem to ISDN on a FreeBSD machine, if you already have PPP setup. However, at the same time any problems you experienced with the PPP program and are going to persist.

If you want maximum stability, use the kernel PPP (Section 16.3) option, not the user-land iijPPP (Section 16.2).

The following TA's are know to work with FreeBSD.

- Motorola BitSurfer and Bitsurfer Pro
- Adtran

Most other TA's will probably work as well, TA vendors try to make sure their product can accept most of the standard modem AT command set.

The real problem with external TA's is like modems you need a good serial card in your computer.

You should read the FreeBSD Serial Hardware[8] tutorial for a detailed understanding of serial devices, and the differences between asynchronous and synchronous serial ports.

A TA running off a standard PC serial port (asynchronous) limits you to 115.2Kbs, even though you have a 128Kbs connection. To fully utilize the 128Kbs that ISDN is capable of, you must move the TA to a synchronous serial card.

Do not be fooled into buying an internal TA and thinking you have avoided the synchronous/asynchronous issue. Internal TA's simply have a standard PC serial port chip built into them. All this will do, is save you having to buy another serial cable, and find another empty electrical socket.

A synchronous card with a TA is at least as fast as a stand-alone router, and with a simple 386 FreeBSD box driving it, probably more flexible.

The choice of sync/TA v.s. stand-alone router is largely a religious issue. There has been some discussion of this in the mailing lists. I suggest you search the archives[9] for the complete discussion.

---

8 http://www.FreeBSD.org/tutorials
9 http://www.FreeBSD.org/search.html

17.6.3 Stand-alone ISDN Bridges/Routers

ISDN bridges or routers are not at all specific to FreeBSD or any other operating system. For a more complete description of routing and bridging technology, please refer to a Networking reference book.

In the context of this page, the terms router and bridge will be used interchangeably.

As the cost of low end ISDN routers/bridges comes down, it will likely become a more and more popular choice. An ISDN router is a small box that plugs directly into your local Ethernet network, and manages its own connection to the other bridge/router. It has built in software to communicate via PPP and other popular protocols.

A router will allow you much faster throughput that a standard TA, since it will be using a full synchronous ISDN connection.

The main problem with ISDN routers and bridges is that interoperability between manufacturers can still be a problem. If you are planning to connect to an Internet provider, you should discuss your needs with them.

If you are planning to connect two LAN segments together, such as your home LAN to the office LAN, this is the simplest lowest maintenance solution. Since you are buying the equipment for both sides of the connection you can be assured that the link will work.

For example to connect a home computer or branch office network to a head office network the following setup could be used.

Example 17-2. Branch Office or Home Network

Network uses a bus based topology with 10 base 2 Ethernet ("thinnet"). Connect router to network cable with AUI/10BT transceiver, if necessary.

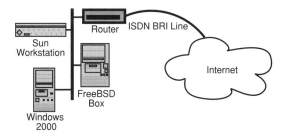

If your home/branch office is only one computer you can use a twisted pair crossover cable to connect to the stand-alone router directly.

Example 17-3. Head Office or Other LAN

Network uses a star topology with 10 base T Ethernet ("Twisted Pair").

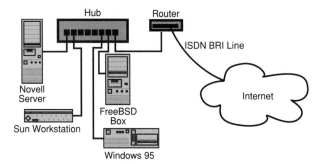

One large advantage of most routers/bridges is that they allow you to have 2 *separate independent* PPP connections to 2 separate sites at the *same* time. This is not supported on most TA's, except for specific (usually expensive) models that have two serial ports. Do not confuse this with channel bonding, MPP, etc.

This can be very useful feature if, for example, you have an dedicated ISDN connection at your office and would like to tap into it, but do not want to get another ISDN line at work. A router at the office location can manage a dedicated B channel connection (64Kbps) to the Internet and use the other B channel for a separate data connection. The second B channel can be used for dial-in, dial-out or dynamically bonding (MPP, etc.) with the first B channel for more bandwidth.

An Ethernet bridge will also allow you to transmit more than just IP traffic. You can also send IPX/SPX or whatever other protocols you use.

17.7 NIS/YP

17.7.1 What Is It?

NIS, which stands for Network Information Services, was developed by Sun Microsystems to centralize administration of Unix (originally SunOS) systems. It has now essentially become an industry standard; all major Unix systems (Solaris, HP-UX, AIX, Linux, NetBSD, OpenBSD, FreeBSD, etc) support NIS.

NIS was formerly known as Yellow Pages, but because of trademark issues, Sun changed the name. The old term (and yp) is still often seen and used.

It is a RPC-based client/server system that allows a group of machines within an NIS domain to share a common set of configuration files. This permits a system administrator to set up NIS client systems with only minimal configuration data and add, remove or modify configuration data from a single location.

It is similar to Windows NT's domain system; although the internal implementation of the two are not at all similar, the basic functionality can be compared.

17.7.2 Terms/Processes You Should Know

There are several terms and several important user processes that you will come across when attempting to implement NIS on FreeBSD, whether you are trying to create an NIS server or act an NIS client:

Term	Description
NIS domainname	An NIS master server and all of its clients (including its slave servers) have a NIS domainname. Similar to an NT domain name, the NIS domainname does not have anything to do with DNS.
portmap	Must be running in order to enable RPC (Remote Procedure Call, a network protocol used by NIS). If `portmap` is not running, it will be impossible to run an NIS server, or to act as an NIS client.
ypbind	"binds" an NIS client to its NIS server. It will take the NIS domainname from the system, and using RPC, connect to the server. `ypbind` is the core of client-server communication in an NIS environment; if `ypbind` dies on a client machine, it will not be able to access the NIS server.
ypserv	Should only be running on NIS servers, is the NIS server process itself. If ypserv(8) dies, then the server will no longer be able to respond to NIS requests (hopefully, there is a slave server to take over for it). There are some implementations of NIS (but not the FreeBSD one), that do not try to reconnect to another server if the server it used before dies. Often, the only thing that helps in this case is to restart the server process (or even the whole server) or the `ypbind` process on the client.
rpc.yppasswdd	Another process that should only be running on NIS master servers, is a daemon that will allow NIS clients to change their NIS passwords. If this daemon is not running, users will have to login to the NIS master server and change their passwords there.

17.7.3 How Does It Work?

There are three types of hosts in an NIS environment: master servers, slave servers, and clients. Servers act as a central repository for host configuration information. Master servers hold the authoritative copy of this information, while slave servers mirror this information for redundancy. Clients rely on the servers to provide this information to them.

Information in many files can be shared in this manner. The `master.passwd`, `group`, and `hosts` files are commonly shared via NIS. Whenever a process on a client needs information that would normally be found in these files locally, it makes a query to the NIS server that it is bound to instead.

Machine Types

- A *NIS master server*. This server, analogous to a Windows NT primary domain controller, maintains the files used by all of the NIS clients. The `passwd`, `group`, and other various files used by the NIS clients live on the master server.

> **Note:** It is possible for one machine to be an NIS master server for more than one NIS domain. However, this will not be covered in this introduction, which assumes a relatively small-scale NIS environment.

- *NIS slave servers*. Similar to NT's backup domain controllers, NIS slave servers maintain copies of the NIS master's data files. NIS slave servers provide the redundancy, which is needed in important environments. They also help to balance the load of the master server: NIS Clients always attach to the NIS server whose response they get first, and this includes slave-server-replies.

- *NIS clients*. NIS clients, like most NT workstations, authenticate against the NIS server (or the NT domain controller in the NT Workstation case) to log on.

17.7.4 Using NIS/YP

This section will deal with setting up a sample NIS environment.

> **Note:** This section assumes that you are running FreeBSD 3.3 or later. The instructions given here will *probably* work for any version of FreeBSD greater than 3.0, but there are no guarantees that this is true.

Planning

Let us assume that you are the administrator of a small university lab. This lab, which consists of 15 FreeBSD machines, currently has no centralized point of administration; each machine has its own /etc/passwd and /etc/master.passwd. These files are kept in sync with each other only through manual intervention; currently, when you add a user to the lab, you must run adduser on all 15 machines. Clearly, this has to change, so you have decided to convert the lab to use NIS, using two of the machines as servers.

Therefore, the configuration of the lab now looks something like:

Machine name	IP address	Machine role
ellington	10.0.0.2	NIS master
coltrane	10.0.0.3	NIS slave
basie	10.0.0.4	Faculty workstation
bird	10.0.0.5	Client machine
cli[1-11]	10.0.0.[6-17]	Other client machines

If you are setting up a NIS scheme for the first time, it is a good idea to think through how you want to go about it. No matter what the size of your network, there are a few decisions that need to be made.

Choosing a NIS Domain Name

This might not be the "domainname" that you are used to. It is more accurately called the "NIS domainname". When a client broadcasts its requests for info, it includes the name of the NIS domain that it is part of. This is how multiple servers on one network can tell which server should answer which request. Think of the NIS domainname as the name for a group of hosts that are related in some way.

Some organizations choose to use their Internet domainname for their NIS domainname. This is not recommended as it can cause confusion when trying to debug network problems. The NIS domainname should be unique within your network and it is helpful if it describes the group of machines it represents. For example, the Art department at Acme Inc. might be in the "acme-art" NIS domain. For this example, assume you have chosen the name *test-domain*.

However, some operating systems (notably SunOS) use their NIS domain name as their Internet domain name. If one or more machines on your network have this restriction, you *must* use the Internet domain name as your NIS domain name.

Physical Server Requirements

There are several things to keep in mind when choosing a machine to use as a NIS server. One of the unfortunate things about NIS is the level of dependency the clients have on the server. If a client cannot contact the server for its NIS domain, very often the machine becomes unusable. The lack of user and group information causes most systems to temporarily freeze up. With this in mind you should make sure to choose a machine that will not be prone to being rebooted regularly, or one that might be used for development. The NIS server should ideally be a stand alone machine whose sole purpose in life is to be an NIS server. If you have a network that is not very heavily used, it is acceptable to put the NIS server on a machine running other services, just keep in mind that if the NIS server becomes unavailable, it will affect *all* of your NIS clients adversely.

NIS Servers

The canonical copies of all NIS information are stored on a single machine called the NIS master server. The databases used to store the information are called NIS maps. In FreeBSD, these maps are stored in /var/yp/[domainname] where [domainname] is the name of the NIS domain being served. A single NIS server can support several domains at once, therefore it is possible to have several such directories, one for each supported domain. Each domain will have its own independent set of maps.

NIS master and slave servers handle all NIS requests with the ypserv daemon. ypserv is responsible for receiving incoming requests from NIS clients, translating the requested domain and map name to a path to the corresponding database file and transmitting data from the database back to the client.

Setting Up a NIS Master Server

Setting up a master NIS server can be relatively straight forward, depending on your needs. FreeBSD comes with support for NIS out-of-the-box. All you need is to add the following lines to /etc/rc.conf, and FreeBSD will do the rest for you.

1.

```
nisdomainname="test-domain"
```

This line will set the NIS domainname to *test-domain* upon network setup (e.g. after reboot).

2.

```
nis_server_enable="YES"
```

This will tell FreeBSD to start up the NIS server processes when the networking is next brought up.

3.

```
nis_yppasswdd_enable="YES"
```

This will enable the `rpc.yppasswdd` daemon, which, as mentioned above, will allow users to change their NIS password from a client machine.

> **Note:** Depending on your NIS setup, you may need to add further entries. See the section about NIS servers that are also NIS clients (Section 17.7.10), below, for details.

Now, all you have to do is to run the command `/etc/netstart` as superuser. It will setup everything for you, using the values you defined in `/etc/rc.conf`.

Initializing the NIS Maps

The *NIS maps* are database files, that are kept in the `/var/yp` directory. They are generated from configuration files in the `/etc` directory of the NIS master, with one exception: the `/etc/master.passwd` file. This is for a good reason; you do not want to propagate passwords to your root and other administrative accounts to all the servers in the NIS domain. Therefore, before we initialize the NIS maps, you should:

```
# cp /etc/master.passwd /var/yp/master.passwd
# cd /var/yp
# vi master.passwd
```

You should remove all entries regarding system accounts (`bin`, `tty`, `kmem`, `games`, etc), as well as any accounts that you do not want to be propagated to the NIS clients (for example root and any other UID 0 (superuser) accounts).

> **Note:** Make sure the `/var/yp/master.passwd` is neither group nor world readable (mode 600)! Use the `chmod` command, if appropriate.

When you have finished, it is time to initialize the NIS maps! FreeBSD includes a script named `ypinit` to do this for you (see its manual page for more information). Note that this script is available on most Unix Operating Systems, but not on all. On Digital Unix/Compaq Tru64 Unix it is called `ypsetup`. Because we are generating maps for an NIS master, we are going to pass the `-m` option to `ypinit`. To generate the NIS maps, assuming you already performed the steps above, run:

```
ellington# ypinit -m test-domain
Server Type: MASTER Domain: test-domain
Creating an YP server will require that you answer a few questions.
Questions will all be asked at the beginning of the procedure.
Do you want this procedure to quit on non-fatal errors? [y/n: n] n
Ok, please remember to go back and redo manually whatever fails.
```

```
If you don't, something might not work.
At this point, we have to construct a list of this domains YP servers.
rod.darktech.org is already known as master server.
Please continue to add any slave servers, one per line. When you are
done with the list, type a <control D>.
master server   :  ellington
next host to add: coltrane
next host to add:  ^D
The current list of NIS servers looks like this:
ellington
coltrane
Is this correct?  [y/n: y] y

[..output from map generation..]

NIS Map update completed.
ellington has been setup as an YP master server without any errors.
```

ypinit should have created /var/yp/Makefile from /var/yp/Makefile.dist. When created, this file assumes that you are operating in a single server NIS environment with only FreeBSD machines. Since *test-domain* has a slave server as well, you must edit /var/yp/Makefile:

```
ellington# vi /var/yp/Makefile
```

You should comment out the line that says 'NOPUSH = "True"' (if it is not commented out already).

Setting up a NIS Slave Server

Setting up an NIS slave server is even more simple than setting up the master. Log on to the slave server and edit the file /etc/rc.conf as you did before. The only difference is that we now must use the -s option when running ypinit. The -s option requires the name of the NIS master be passed to it as well, so our command line looks like:

```
coltrane# ypinit -s ellington test-domain

Server Type: SLAVE Domain: test-domain Master: ellington

Creating an YP server will require that you answer a few questions.
Questions will all be asked at the beginning of the procedure.

Do you want this procedure to quit on non-fatal errors? [y/n: n]  n

Ok, please remember to go back and redo manually whatever fails.
If you don't, something might not work.
There will be no further questions. The remainder of the procedure
should take a few minutes, to copy the databases from ellington.
Transferring netgroup...
ypxfr: Exiting: Map successfully transferred
Transferring netgroup.byuser...
ypxfr: Exiting: Map successfully transferred
Transferring netgroup.byhost...
```

```
ypxfr: Exiting: Map successfully transferred
Transferring master.passwd.byuid...
ypxfr: Exiting: Map successfully transferred
Transferring passwd.byuid...
ypxfr: Exiting: Map successfully transferred
Transferring passwd.byname...
ypxfr: Exiting: Map successfully transferred
Transferring group.bygid...
ypxfr: Exiting: Map successfully transferred
Transferring group.byname...
ypxfr: Exiting: Map successfully transferred
Transferring services.byname...
ypxfr: Exiting: Map successfully transferred
Transferring rpc.bynumber...
ypxfr: Exiting: Map successfully transferred
Transferring rpc.byname...
ypxfr: Exiting: Map successfully transferred
Transferring protocols.byname...
ypxfr: Exiting: Map successfully transferred
Transferring master.passwd.byname...
ypxfr: Exiting: Map successfully transferred
Transferring networks.byname...
ypxfr: Exiting: Map successfully transferred
Transferring networks.byaddr...
ypxfr: Exiting: Map successfully transferred
Transferring netid.byname...
ypxfr: Exiting: Map successfully transferred
Transferring hosts.byaddr...
ypxfr: Exiting: Map successfully transferred
Transferring protocols.bynumber...
ypxfr: Exiting: Map successfully transferred
Transferring ypservers...
ypxfr: Exiting: Map successfully transferred
Transferring hosts.byname...
ypxfr: Exiting: Map successfully transferred

coltrane has been setup as an YP slave server without any errors.
Don't forget to update map ypservers on ellington.
```

You should now have a directory called /var/yp/test-domain. Copies of the NIS master server's maps should be in this directory. You will need to make sure that these stay updated. The following /etc/crontab entries on your slave servers should do the job:

```
20      *       *       *       *       root    /usr/libexec/ypxfr passwd.byname
21      *       *       *       *       root    /usr/libexec/ypxfr passwd.byuid
```

These two lines force the slave to sync its maps with the maps on the master server. Although these entries are not mandatory, since the master server attempts to ensure any changes to its NIS maps are communicated to its slaves and because password information is vital to systems depending on the server, it is a good idea to force the updates. This is more important on busy networks where map updates might not always complete.

Now, run the command `/etc/netstart` on the slave server as well, which again starts the NIS server.

NIS Clients

An NIS client establishes what is called a binding to a particular NIS server using the `ypbind` daemon. `ypbind` checks the system's default domain (as set by the `domainname` command), and begins broadcasting RPC requests on the local network. These requests specify the name of the domain for which `ypbind` is attempting to establish a binding. If a server that has been configured to serve the requested domain receives one of the broadcasts, it will respond to `ypbind`, which will record the server's address. If there are several servers available (a master and several slaves, for example), `ypbind` will use the address of the first one to respond. From that point on, the client system will direct all of its NIS requests to that server. `ypbind` will occasionally "ping" the server to make sure it is still up and running. If it fails to receive a reply to one of its pings within a reasonable amount of time, `ypbind` will mark the domain as unbound and begin broadcasting again in the hopes of locating another server.

Setting Up an NIS Client

Setting up a FreeBSD machine to be a NIS client is fairly straightforward.

1. Edit the file `/etc/rc.conf` and add the following lines in order to set the NIS domainname and start `ypbind` upon network startup:

    ```
    nisdomainname="test-domain"
    nis_client_enable="YES"
    ```

2. To import all possible password entries from the NIS server, remove all user accounts from your `/etc/master.passwd` file and use `vipw` to add the following line to the end of the file:

    ```
    +:::::::::::
    ```

    Note: This line will afford anyone with a valid account in the NIS server's password maps an account. There are many ways to configure your NIS client by changing this line. See the netgroups section (Section 17.7.7) below for more information. For more detailed reading see O'Reilly's book on `Managing NFS and NIS`.

    Note: You should keep at least one local account (i.e. not imported via NIS) in your `/etc/master.passwd` and this account should also be a member of the group `wheel`. If there is something wrong with NIS, this account can be used to log in remotely, become root, and fix things.

3. To import all possible group entries from the NIS server, add this line to your `/etc/group` file:

    ```
    +:*::
    ```

After completing these steps, you should be able to run `ypcat passwd` and see the NIS server's passwd map.

17.7.5 NIS Security

In general, any remote user can issue an RPC to ypserv(8) and retrieve the contents of your NIS maps, provided the remote user knows your domainname. To prevent such unauthorized transactions, ypserv(8) supports a feature called securenets which can be used to restrict access to a given set of hosts. At startup, ypserv(8) will attempt to load the securenets information from a file called `/var/yp/securenets`.

> **Note:** This path varies depending on the path specified with the `-p` option. This file contains entries that consist of a network specification and a network mask separated by white space. Lines starting with "#" are considered to be comments. A sample securenets file might look like this:

```
# allow connections from local host -- mandatory
127.0.0.1      255.255.255.255
# allow connections from any host
# on the 192.168.128.0 network
192.168.128.0 255.255.255.0
# allow connections from any host
# between 10.0.0.0 to 10.0.15.255
# this includes the machines in the testlab
10.0.0.0       255.255.240.0
```

If ypserv(8) receives a request from an address that matches one of these rules, it will process the request normally. If the address fails to match a rule, the request will be ignored and a warning message will be logged. If the `/var/yp/securenets` file does not exist, `ypserv` will allow connections from any host.

The `ypserv` program also has support for Wietse Venema's **tcpwrapper** package. This allows the administrator to use the **tcpwrapper** configuration files for access control instead of `/var/yp/securenets`.

> **Note:** While both of these access control mechanisms provide some security, they, like the privileged port test, are vulnerable to "IP spoofing" attacks. All NIS-related traffic should be blocked at your firewall.
>
> Servers using `/var/yp/securenets` may fail to serve legitimate NIS clients with archaic TCP/IP implementations. Some of these implementations set all host bits to zero when doing broadcasts and/or fail to observe the subnet mask when calculating the broadcast address. While some of these problems can be fixed by changing the client configuration, other problems may force the retirement of the client systems in question or the abandonment of `/var/yp/securenets`.
>
> Using `/var/yp/securenets` on a server with such an archaic implementation of TCP/IP is a really bad idea and will lead to loss of NIS functionality for large parts of your network.
>
> The use of the **tcpwrapper** package increases the latency of your NIS server. The additional delay may be long enough to cause timeouts in client programs, especially in busy networks or with slow NIS servers. If one or more of your client systems suffers from these symptoms, you should convert the client systems in question into NIS slave servers and force them to bind to themselves.

17.7.6 Barring Some Users from Logging On

In our lab, there is a machine `basie` that is supposed to be a faculty only workstation. We do not want to take this machine out of the NIS domain, yet the `passwd` file on the master NIS server contains accounts for both faculty and students. What can we do?

There is a way to bar specific users from logging on to a machine, even if they are present in the NIS database. To do this, all you must do is add -*username* to the end of the `/etc/master.passwd` file on the client machine, where *username* is the username of the user you wish to bar from logging in. This should preferably be done using `vipw`, since `vipw` will sanity check your changes to `/etc/master.passwd`, as well as automatically rebuild the password database when you finish editing. For example, if we wanted to bar user *bill* from logging on to `basie` we would:

```
basie# vipw
[add -bill to the end, exit]
vipw: rebuilding the database...
vipw: done

basie# cat /etc/master.passwd

root:[password]:0:0::0:0:The super-user:/root:/bin/csh
toor:[password]:0:0::0:0:The other super-user:/root:/bin/sh
daemon:*:1:1::0:0:Owner of many system processes:/root:/sbin/nologin
operator:*:2:5::0:0:System &:/:/sbin/nologin
bin:*:3:7::0:0:Binaries Commands and Source,,:/:/sbin/nologin
tty:*:4:65533::0:0:Tty Sandbox:/:/sbin/nologin
kmem:*:5:65533::0:0:KMem Sandbox:/:/sbin/nologin
games:*:7:13::0:0:Games pseudo-user:/usr/games:/sbin/nologin
news:*:8:8::0:0:News Subsystem:/:/sbin/nologin
man:*:9:9::0:0:Mister Man Pages:/usr/share/man:/sbin/nologin
bind:*:53:53::0:0:Bind Sandbox:/:/sbin/nologin
uucp:*:66:66::0:0:UUCP pseudo-user:/var/spool/uucppublic:/usr/libexec/uucp/uucico
xten:*:67:67::0:0:X-10 daemon:/usr/local/xten:/sbin/nologin
pop:*:68:6::0:0:Post Office Owner:/nonexistent:/sbin/nologin
nobody:*:65534:65534::0:0:Unprivileged user:/nonexistent:/sbin/nologin
+:::::::::
-bill

basie#
```

17.7.7 Using Netgroups

The method shown in the previous section works reasonably well if you need special rules for a very small number of users and/or machines. On larger networks, you *will* forget to bar some users from logging onto sensitive machines, or you may even have to modify each machine separately, thus losing the main benefit of NIS, *centralized* administration.

The NIS developers' solution for this problem is called *netgroups*. Their purpose and semantics can be compared to the normal groups used by Unix file systems. The main differences are the lack of a numeric id and the ability to define a netgroup by including both user accounts and other netgroups.

Netgroups were developed to handle large, complex networks with hundreds of users and machines. On one hand, this is a Good Thing if you are forced to deal with such a situation. On the other hand, this complexity makes it almost impossible to explain netgroups with really simple examples. The example used in the remainder of this section demonstrates this problem.

Let us assume that your successful introduction of NIS in your laboratory caught your superiors' interest. Your next job is to extend your NIS domain to cover some of the other machines on campus. The two tables contain the names of the new users and new machines as well as brief descriptions of them.

User Name(s)	Description
alpha, beta	Normal employees of the IT department
charlie, delta	The new apprentices of the IT department
echo, foxtrott, golf, ...	Ordinary employees
able, baker, ...	The current interns

Machine Name(s)	Description
war, death, famine, pollution	Your most important servers. Only the IT employees are allowed to log onto these machines.
pride, greed, envy, wrath, lust, sloth	Less important servers. All members of the IT department are allowed to login onto these machines.
one, two, three, four, ...	Ordinary workstations. Only the *real* employees are allowed to use these machines.
trashcan	A very old machine without any critical data. Even the intern is allowed to use this box.

If you tried to implement these restrictions by separately blocking each user, you would have to add one -`user` line to each system's `passwd` for each user who is not allowed to login onto that system. If you forget just one entry, you could be in trouble. It may be feasible to do this correctly during the initial setup, however you *will* eventually forget to add the lines for new users during day-to-day operations. After all, Murphy was an optimist.

Handling this situation with netgroups offers several advantages. Each user need not be handled separately; you assign a user to one or more netgroups and allow or forbid logins for all members of the netgroup. If you add a new machine, you will only have to define login restrictions for netgroups. If a new user is added, you will only have to add the user to one or more netgroups. Those changes are independent of each other; no more "for each combination of user and machine do..." If your NIS setup is planned carefully, you will only have to modify exactly one central configuration file to grant or deny access to machines.

The first step is the initialization of the NIS map netgroup. FreeBSD's ypinit(8) does not create this map by default, but its NIS implementation will support it once it has been created. To create an empty map, simply type

```
ellington# vi /var/yp/netgroup
```

and start adding content. For our example, we need at least four netgroups: IT employees, IT apprentices, normal employees and interns.

```
IT_EMP  (,alpha,test-domain)   (,beta,test-domain)
```

```
IT_APP   (,charlie,test-domain)   (,delta,test-domain)
USERS    (,echo,test-domain)      (,foxtrott,test-domain) \
         (,golf,test-domain)
INTERNS  (,able,test-domain)      (,baker,test-domain)
```

IT_EMP, IT_APP etc. are the names of the netgroups. Each bracketed group adds one or more user accounts to it. The three fields inside a group are:

1. The name of the host(s) where the following items are valid. If you do not specify a hostname, the entry is valid on all hosts. If you do specify a hostname, you will enter a realm of darkness, horror and utter confusion.

2. The name of the account that belongs to this netgroup.

3. The NIS domain for the account. You can import accounts from other NIS domains into your netgroup if you are one of unlucky fellows with more than one NIS domain.

Each of these fields can contain wildcards. See netgroup(5) for details.

> **Note:** Netgroup names longer than 8 characters should not be used, especially if you have machines running other operating systems within your NIS domain. The names are case sensitive; using capital letters for your netgroup names is an easy way to distinguish between user, machine and netgroup names.
>
> Some NIS clients (other than FreeBSD) cannot handle netgroups with a large number of entries. For example, some older versions of SunOS start to cause trouble if a netgroup contains more than 15 *entries*. You can circumvent this limit by creating several sub-netgroups with 15 users or less and a real netgroup that consists of the sub-netgroups:
>
> ```
> BIGGRP1   (,joe1,domain)    (,joe2,domain)    (,joe3,domain) [...]
> BIGGRP2   (,joe16,domain)   (,joe17,domain) [...]
> BIGGRP3   (,joe31,domain)   (,joe32,domain)
> BIGGROUP  BIGGRP1 BIGGRP2 BIGGRP3
> ```
>
> You can repeat this process if you need more than 225 users within a single netgroup.

Activating and distributing your new NIS map is easy:

```
ellington# cd /var/yp
ellington# make
```

This will generate the three NIS maps netgroup, netgroup.byhost and netgroup.byuser. Use ypcat(1) to check if your new NIS maps are available:

```
ellington% ypcat -k netgroup
ellington% ypcat -k netgroup.byhost
ellington% ypcat -k netgroup.byuser
```

The output of the first command should resemble the contents of /var/yp/netgroup. The second command will not produce output if you have not specified host-specific netgroups. The third command can be used to get the list of netgroups for a user.

The client setup is quite simple. To configure the server *war*, you only have to start vipw(8) and replace the line

```
+::::::::::
```

with

```
+@IT_EMP::::::::::
```

Now, only the data for the users defined in the netgroup *IT_EMP* is imported into *war*'s password database and only these users are allowed to login.

Unfortunately, this limitation also applies to the ~ function of the shell and all routines converting between user names and numerical user ids. In other words, `cd ~user` will not work, `ls -l` will show the numerical id instead of the username and `find . -user joe -print` will fail with `No such user`. To fix this, you will have to import all user entries *without allowing them to login onto your servers*.

This can be achieved by adding another line to `/etc/master.passwd`. This line should contain:

`+:::::::::/sbin/nologin`, meaning "Import all entries but replace the shell with `/sbin/nologin` in the imported entries". You can replace any field in the passwd entry by placing a default value in your `/etc/master.passwd`.

> **Warning:** Make sure that the line `+:::::::::/sbin/nologin` is placed after `+@IT_EMP:::::::::.` Otherwise, all user accounts imported from NIS will have /sbin/nologin as their login shell.

After this change, you will only have to change one NIS map if a new employee joins the IT department. You could use a similar approach for the less important servers by replacing the old `+:::::::::` in their local version of `/etc/master.passwd` with something like this:

```
+@IT_EMP::::::::::
+@IT_APP::::::::::
+:::::::::/sbin/nologin
```

The corresponding lines for the normal workstations could be:

```
+@IT_EMP::::::::::
+@USERS::::::::::
+:::::::::/sbin/nologin
```

And everything would be fine until there is a policy change a few weeks later: The IT department starts hiring interns. The IT interns are allowed to use the normal workstations and the less important servers; and the IT apprentices are allowed to login onto the main servers. You add a new netgroup IT_INTERN, add the new IT interns to this netgroup and start to change the config on each and every machine... As the old saying goes: "Errors in centralized planning lead to global mess".

NIS' ability to create netgroups from other netgroups can be used to prevent situations like these. One possibility is the creation of role-based netgroups. For example, you could create a netgroup called *BIGSRV* to define the login restrictions for the important servers, another netgroup called *SMALLSRV* for the less important servers and a third netgroup called *USERBOX* for the normal workstations. Each of these netgroups contains the netgroups that are allowed to login onto these machines. The new entries for your NIS map netgroup should look like this:

```
BIGSRV    IT_EMP   IT_APP
SMALLSRV  IT_EMP   IT_APP   ITINTERN
```

```
USERBOX    IT_EMP   ITINTERN USERS
```

This method of defining login restrictions works reasonably well if you can define groups of machines with identical restrictions. Unfortunately, this is the exception and not the rule. Most of the time, you will need the ability to define login restrictions on a per-machine basis.

Machine-specific netgroup definitions are the other possibility to deal with the policy change outlined above. In this scenario, the `/etc/master.passwd` of each box contains two lines starting with "+". The first of them adds a netgroup with the accounts allowed to login onto this machine, the second one adds all other accounts with `/sbin/nologin` as shell. It is a good idea to use the ALL-CAPS version of the machine name as the name of the netgroup. In other words, the lines should look like this:

```
+@BOXNAME:::::::::
+:::::::::/sbin/nologin
```

Once you have completed this task for all your machines, you will not have to modify the local versions of `/etc/master.passwd` ever again. All further changes can be handled by modifying the NIS map. Here is an example of a possible netgroup map for this scenario with some additional goodies.

```
# Define groups of users first
IT_EMP    (,alpha,test-domain)    (,beta,test-domain)
IT_APP    (,charlie,test-domain)  (,delta,test-domain)
DEPT1     (,echo,test-domain)     (,foxtrott,test-domain)
DEPT2     (,golf,test-domain)     (,hotel,test-domain)
DEPT3     (,india,test-domain)    (,juliet,test-domain)
ITINTERN  (,kilo,test-domain)     (,lima,test-domain)
D_INTERNS (,able,test-domain)     (,baker,test-domain)
#
# Now, define some groups based on roles
USERS     DEPT1   DEPT2     DEPT3
BIGSRV    IT_EMP  IT_APP
SMALLSRV  IT_EMP  IT_APP    ITINTERN
USERBOX   IT_EMP  ITINTERN  USERS
#
# And a groups for a special tasks
# Allow echo and golf to access our anti-virus-machine
SECURITY  IT_EMP  (,echo,test-domain)  (,golf,test-domain)
#
# machine-based netgroups
# Our main servers
WAR       BIGSRV
FAMINE    BIGSRV
# User india needs access to this server
POLLUTION BIGSRV  (,india,test-domain)
#
# This one is really important and needs more access restrictions
DEATH     IT_EMP
#
# The anti-virus-machine mentioned above
ONE       SECURITY
#
```

```
# Restrict a machine to a single user
TWO        (,hotel,test-domain)
# [...more groups to follow]
```

If you are using some kind of database to manage your user accounts, you should be able to create the first part of the map with your database's report tools. This way, new users will automatically have access to the boxes.

One last word of caution: It may not always be advisable to use machine-based netgroups. If you are deploying a couple dozen or even hundreds of identical machines for student labs, you should use role-based netgroups instead of machine-based netgroups to keep the size of the NIS map within reasonable limits.

17.7.8 Important Things to Remember

There are still a couple of things that you will need to do differently now that you are in an NIS environment.

- Every time you wish to add a user to the lab, you must add it to the master NIS server *only*, and *you must remember to rebuild the NIS maps*. If you forget to do this, the new user will not be able to login anywhere except on the NIS master. For example, if we needed to add a new user "jsmith" to the lab, we would:

  ```
  # pw useradd jsmith
  # cd /var/yp
  # make test-domain
  ```

  You could also run adduser jsmith instead of pw useradd jsmith.

- *Keep the administration accounts out of the NIS maps.* You do not want to be propagating administrative accounts and passwords to machines that will have users that should not have access to those accounts.

- *Keep the NIS master and slave secure, and minimize their downtime.* If somebody either hacks or simply turns off these machines, they have effectively rendered many people without the ability to login to the lab.

  This is the chief weakness of any centralized administration system, and it is probably the most important weakness. If you do not protect your NIS servers, you will have a lot of angry users!

17.7.9 NIS v1 Compatibility

FreeBSD's **ypserv** has some support for serving NIS v1 clients. FreeBSD's NIS implementation only uses the NIS v2 protocol, however other implementations include support for the v1 protocol for backwards compatibility with older systems. The **ypbind** daemons supplied with these systems will try to establish a binding to an NIS v1 server even though they may never actually need it (and they may persist in broadcasting in search of one even after they receive a response from a v2 server). Note that while support for normal client calls is provided, this version of ypserv does not handle v1 map transfer requests; consequently, it cannot be used as a master or slave in conjunction with older NIS servers that only support the v1 protocol. Fortunately, there probably are not any such servers still in use today.

17.7.10 NIS Servers that are also NIS Clients

Care must be taken when running ypserv in a multi-server domain where the server machines are also NIS clients. It is generally a good idea to force the servers to bind to themselves rather than allowing them to broadcast bind requests and possibly become bound to each other. Strange failure modes can result if one server goes down and others are dependent upon on it. Eventually all the clients will time out and attempt to bind to other servers, but the delay involved can be considerable and the failure mode is still present since the servers might bind to each other all over again.

You can force a host to bind to a particular server by running ypbind with the -S flag. If you do not want to do this manually each time you reboot your NIS server, you can add the following lines to your /etc/rc.conf:

```
nis_client_enable="YES" # run client stuff as well
nis_client_flags="-S NIS domain,server"
```

See ypbind(8) for further information.

17.7.11 libscrypt v.s. libdescrypt

One of the most common issues that people run into when trying to implement NIS is crypt library compatibility. If your NIS server is using the DES crypt libraries, it will only support clients that are using DES as well. To check which one your server and clients are using look at the symlinks in /usr/lib. If the machine is configured to use the DES libraries, it will look something like this:

```
% ls -l /usr/lib/*crypt*
lrwxrwxrwx  1 root   wheel        13 Jul 15 08:55 libcrypt.a@ -> libdescrypt.a
lrwxrwxrwx  1 root   wheel        14 Jul 15 08:55 libcrypt.so@ -> libdescrypt.so
lrwxrwxrwx  1 root   wheel        16 Jul 15 08:55 libcrypt.so.2@ -> libdescrypt.so.2
lrwxrwxrwx  1 root   wheel        15 Jul 15 08:55 libcrypt_p.a@ -> libdescrypt_p.a
-r--r--r--  1 root   wheel     13018 Nov  8 14:27 libdescrypt.a
lrwxr-xr-x  1 root   wheel        16 Nov  8 14:27 libdescrypt.so@ -> libdescrypt.so.2
-r--r--r--  1 root   wheel     12965 Nov  8 14:27 libdescrypt.so.2
-r--r--r--  1 root   wheel     14750 Nov  8 14:27 libdescrypt_p.a
```

If the machine is configured to use the standard FreeBSD MD5 crypt libraries they will look something like this:

```
% ls -l /usr/lib/*crypt*
lrwxrwxrwx  1 root   wheel        13 Jul 15 08:55 libcrypt.a@ -> libscrypt.a
lrwxrwxrwx  1 root   wheel        14 Jul 15 08:55 libcrypt.so@ -> libscrypt.so
lrwxrwxrwx  1 root   wheel        16 Jul 15 08:55 libcrypt.so.2@ -> libscrypt.so.2
lrwxrwxrwx  1 root   wheel        15 Jul 15 08:55 libcrypt_p.a@ -> libscrypt_p.a
-r--r--r--  1 root   wheel      6194 Nov  8 14:27 libscrypt.a
lrwxr-xr-x  1 root   wheel        14 Nov  8 14:27 libscrypt.so@ -> libscrypt.so.2
-r--r--r--  1 root   wheel      7579 Nov  8 14:27 libscrypt.so.2
-r--r--r--  1 root   wheel      6684 Nov  8 14:27 libscrypt_p.a
```

If you have trouble authenticating on an NIS client, this is a pretty good place to start looking for possible problems. If you want to deploy an NIS server for a heterogenous network, you will probably have to use DES on all systems because it is the lowest common standard.

17.8 DHCP

17.8.1 What Is DHCP?

DHCP, the Dynamic Host Configuration Protocol, describes the means by which a system can connect to a network and obtain the necessary information for communication upon that network. FreeBSD uses the ISC (Internet Software Consortium) DHCP implementation, so all implementation-specific information here is for use with the ISC distribution.

17.8.2 What this Section Covers

This section attempts to describe only the parts of the DHCP system that are integrated with FreeBSD; consequently, the server portions are not described. The DHCP manual pages, in addition to the references below, are useful resources.

17.8.3 How It Works

When `dhclient`, the DHCP client, is executed on the client machine, it begins broadcasting requests for configuration information. By default, these requests are on UDP port 68. The server replies on UDP 67, giving the client an IP address and other relevant network information such as netmask, router, and DNS servers. All of this information comes in the form of a DHCP "lease" and is only valid for a certain time (configured by the DHCP server maintainer). In this manner, stale IP addresses for clients no longer connected to the network can be automatically reclaimed.

DHCP clients can obtain a great deal of information from the server. An exhaustive list may be found in dhcp-options(5).

17.8.4 FreeBSD Integration

FreeBSD fully integrates the ISC DHCP client, `dhclient`. DHCP client support is provided within both the installer and the base system, obviating the need for detailed knowledge of network configurations on any network that runs a DHCP server. `dhclient` has been included in all FreeBSD distributions since 3.2.

DHCP is supported by **sysinstall**. When configuring a network interface within sysinstall, the first question asked is, "Do you want to try DHCP configuration of this interface?" Answering affirmatively will execute `dhclient`, and if successful, will fill in the network configuration information automatically.

There are two things you must do to have your system use DHCP upon startup:

- Make sure that the `bpf` device is compiled into your kernel. To do this, add `pseudo-device bpf` to your kernel configuration file, and rebuild the kernel. For more information about building kernels, see Chapter 9.

  The `bpf` device is already part of the `GENERIC` kernel that is supplied with FreeBSD, so if you do not have a custom kernel, you should not need to create one in order to get DHCP working.

Note: For those who are particularly security conscious, you should be warned that `bpf` is also the device that allows packet sniffers to work correctly (although they still have to be run as root). `bpf` *is* required to use DHCP, but if you are very sensitive about security, you probably should not add `bpf` to your kernel in the expectation that at some point in the future you will be using DHCP.

- Edit your `/etc/rc.conf` to include the following:

  ```
  ifconfig_fxp0="DHCP"
  ```

  Note: Be sure to replace `fxp0` with the designation for the interface that you wish to dynamically configure.

If you are using a different location for `dhclient`, or if you wish to pass additional flags to `dhclient`, also include the following (editing as necessary):

```
dhcp_program="/sbin/dhclient"
dhcp_flags=""
```

The DHCP server, `dhcpd`, is included as part of the `isc-dhcp2` port in the ports collection. This port contains the full ISC DHCP distribution, consisting of client, server, relay agent and documentation.

17.8.5 Files

- `/etc/dhclient.conf`

  `dhclient` requires a configuration file, `/etc/dhclient.conf`. Typically the file contains only comments, the defaults being reasonably sane. This configuration file is described by the dhclient.conf(5) manual page.

- `/sbin/dhclient`

  `dhclient` is statically linked and resides in `/sbin`. The dhclient(8) manual page gives more information about `dhclient`.

- `/sbin/dhclient-script`

  `dhclient-script` is the FreeBSD-specific DHCP client configuration script. It is described in dhclient-script(8), but should not need any user modification to function properly.

- `/var/db/dhclient.leases`

  The DHCP client keeps a database of valid leases in this file, which is written as a log. dhclient.leases(5) gives a slightly longer description.

17.8.6 Further Reading

The DHCP protocol is fully described in RFC 2131[10]. An informational resource has also been set up at dhcp.org[11].

17.9 DNS

17.9.1 Overview

FreeBSD utilizes, by default, a version of BIND (Berkeley Internet Name Domain), which is the most common implementation of the DNS protocol. DNS is the protocol through which names are mapped to IP addresses, and vice versa. For example, a query for `www.FreeBSD.org` will receive a reply with the IP address of The FreeBSD Project's web server, whereas, a query for `ftp.FreeBSD.org` will return the IP address of the corresponding FTP machine. Likewise, the opposite can happen. A query for an IP address can resolve its hostname. It is not necessary to run a name server to perform DNS lookups on a system.

DNS is coordinated across the Internet through a somewhat complex system of authoritative root name servers, and other smaller-scale name servers who host and cache individual domain information.

This document refers to BIND 8.x, as it is the stable version used in FreeBSD. BIND 9.x in FreeBSD can be installed through the `net/bind9` port.

RFC1034 and RFC1035 dictates the DNS protocol.

Currently, BIND is maintained by the Internet Software Consortium (www.isc.org)[12]

17.9.2 Terminology

To understand this document, some terms related to DNS must be understood.

Term	Definition
forward DNS	mapping of hostnames to IP addresses
origin	refers to the domain covered for the particular zone file
named, bind, name server	common names for the BIND name server package within FreeBSD
resolver	a system process through which a machine queries a name server for zone information
reverse DNS	the opposite of forward DNS, mapping of IP addresses to hostnames

---

10 http://www.freesoft.org/CIE/RFC/2131/
11 http://www.dhcp.org/
12 http://www.isc.org

Term	Definition
root zone	literally, a ".", refers to the root, or beginning zone. All zones fall under this, as do all files in fall under the root directory. It is the beginning of the Internet zone hierarchy.
zone	Each individual domain, subdomain, or area dictated by DNS

Examples of zones:

- `.` is the root zone
- `org.` is a zone under the root zone
- `example.org` is a zone under the org. zone
- `foo.example.org.` is a subdomain, a zone under the `example.org.` zone
- `1.2.3.in-addr.arpa` is a zone referencing all IP addresses which fall under the 3.2.1.* IP space.

As one can see, the more specific part of a hostname appears to its left. For example, `example.org.` is more specific than `org.`, as `org.` is more specific than the root zone. The layout of each part of a hostname is much like a filesystem: the `/dev` directory falls within the root, and so on.

17.9.3 Reasons to Run a Name Server

Name servers usually come in two forms: an authoritative name server, and a caching name server.

An authoritative name server is needed when:

- one wants to serve DNS information to the world, replying authoritatively to queries.
- a domain, such as `example.org`, is registered and IP addresses need to be assigned to hostnames under it.
- an IP address block requires reverse DNS entries (IP to hostname).
- a backup name server, called a slave, must reply to queries when the primary is down or inaccessible.

A caching name server is needed when:

- a local DNS server may cache and respond more quickly then querying an outside name server.
- a reduction in overall network traffic is desired. (DNS traffic has been measured to account for 5% or more of total Internet traffic)

When one queries for `www.FreeBSD.org`, the resolver usually queries the uplink ISP's name server, and retrieves the reply. With a local, caching DNS server, the query only has to be made once to the outside world by the caching DNS server. Every additional query will not have to look to the outside of the local network, since the information is cached locally.

17.9.4 How It Works

In FreeBSD, the BIND daemon is called **named** for obvious reasons.

File	Description
named	the BIND daemon
ndc	name daemon control program
/etc/namedb	directory where BIND zone information resides
/etc/namedb/named.conf	daemon configuration file

Zone files are usually contained within the /etc/namedb directory, and contain the DNS zone information served by the name server.

17.9.5 Starting BIND

Since BIND is installed by default, configuring it all is relatively simple.

To ensure the named daemon is started at boot, put the following modifications in /etc/rc.conf:

```
named_enable="YES"
```

To start the daemon manually (after configuring it)

```
# ndc start
```

17.9.6 Configuration Files

make-localhost

Be sure to:

```
# cd /etc/namedb
# sh make-localhost
```

to properly create the local reverse DNS zone file in /etc/namedb/localhost.rev.

/etc/namedb/named.conf

```
// $FreeBSD$
//
// Refer to the named(8) manual page for details.  If you are ever going
// to setup a primary server, make sure you've understood the hairy
// details of how DNS is working.  Even with simple mistakes, you can
// break connectivity for affected parties, or cause huge amount of
```

```
// useless Internet traffic.

options {
        directory "/etc/namedb";

// In addition to the "forwarders" clause, you can force your name
// server to never initiate queries of its own, but always ask its
// forwarders only, by enabling the following line:
//
//      forward only;

// If you've got a DNS server around at your upstream provider, enter
// its IP address here, and enable the line below.  This will make you
// benefit from its cache, thus reduce overall DNS traffic in the
Internet.
/*
        forwarders {
                127.0.0.1;
        };
*/
```

Just as the comment says, to benefit from an uplink's cache, `forwarders` can be enabled here. Under normal circumstances, a name server will recursively query the Internet looking at certain name servers until it finds the answer it is looking for. Having this enabled will have it query the uplink's name server (or name server provided) first, taking advantage of its cache. If the uplink name server in question is a heavily trafficked, fast name server, enabling this may be worthwhile.

Warning: 127.0.0.1 will *not* work here. Change this IP address to a name server at your uplink.

```
        /*
         * If there is a firewall between you and name servers you want
         * to talk to, you might need to uncomment the query-source
         * directive below.  Previous versions of BIND always asked
         * questions using port 53, but BIND 8.1 uses an unprivileged
         * port by default.
         */
        // query-source address * port 53;

        /*
         * If running in a sandbox, you may have to specify a different
         * location for the dumpfile.
         */
        // dump-file "s/named_dump.db";
};

// Note: the following will be supported in a future release.
/*
host { any; } {
        topology {
```

```
                      127.0.0.0/8;
          };
};
*/

// Setting up secondaries is way easier and the rough picture for this
// is explained below.
//
// If you enable a local name server, don't forget to enter 127.0.0.1
// into your /etc/resolv.conf so this server will be queried first.
// Also, make sure to enable it in /etc/rc.conf.

zone "." {
        type hint;
        file "named.root";
};

zone "0.0.127.IN-ADDR.ARPA" {
        type master;
        file "localhost.rev";
};

zone
"0.0.0.0.0.0.0.0.0.0.0.0.0.0.0.0.0.0.0.0.0.0.0.0.0.0.0.0.0.0.0.0.IP6.INT" {
        type master;
        file "localhost.rev";
};

// NB: Do not use the IP addresses below, they are faked, and only
// serve demonstration/documentation purposes!
//
// Example secondary config entries.  It can be convenient to become
// a secondary at least for the zone where your own domain is in.  Ask
// your network administrator for the IP address of the responsible
// primary.
//
// Never forget to include the reverse lookup (IN-ADDR.ARPA) zone!
// (This is the first bytes of the respective IP address, in reverse
// order, with ".IN-ADDR.ARPA" appended.)
//
// Before starting to setup a primary zone, better make sure you fully
// understand how DNS and BIND works, however.  There are sometimes
// unobvious pitfalls.  Setting up a secondary is comparably simpler.
//
// NB: Don't blindly enable the examples below. :-)  Use actual names
// and addresses instead.
//
// NOTE!!! FreeBSD runs bind in a sandbox (see named_flags in rc.conf).
// The directory containing the secondary zones must be write accessible
// to bind.  The following sequence is suggested:
//
```

```
//        mkdir /etc/namedb/s
//        chown bind:bind /etc/namedb/s
//        chmod 750 /etc/namedb/s
```

For more information on running BIND in a sandbox, see the unning named in a sandbox section (Section 17.9.8).

```
/*
zone "domain.com" {
        type slave;
        file "s/domain.com.bak";
        masters {
                192.168.1.1;
        };
};

zone "0.168.192.in-addr.arpa" {
        type slave;
        file "s/0.168.192.in-addr.arpa.bak";
        masters {
                192.168.1.1;
        };
};
*/
```

In `named.conf`, these are examples of slave entries for a forward and reverse zone.

For each new zone served, a new zone entry must be added to `named.conf`

For example, the simplest zone entry for example.org can look like:

```
zone "example.org" {
 type master;
 file "example.org";
};
```

The zone is a master, as indicated by the `type` statement, holding its zone information in `/etc/namedb/example.org` indicated by the `file` statement.

```
zone "example.org" {
 type slave;
 file "example.org";
};
```

In the slave case, the zone information is transferred from the master name server for the particular zone, and saved in the file specified. If and when the master server dies or is unreachable, the slave name server will have the transferred zone information and will be able to serve it.

Zone Files

An example master zone file for `example.org` (existing within /etc/namedb/example.org) is as follows:

```
$TTL 3600

example.org. IN SOA ns1.example.org. admin.example.org. (
                            5              ; Serial
                            10800          ; Refresh
                            3600           ; Retry
                            604800         ; Expire
                            86400 )        ; Minimum TTL

; DNS Servers
@       IN NS           ns1.example.org.
@       IN NS           ns2.example.org.

; Machine Names
localhost       IN A    127.0.0.1
ns1             IN A    3.2.1.2
ns2             IN A    3.2.1.3
mail            IN A    3.2.1.10
@               IN A    3.2.1.30

; Aliases
www             IN CNAME        @

; MX Record
@               IN MX   10      mail.example.org.
```

Note that every hostname ending in a "." is an exact hostname, whereas everything without a trailing "." is referenced to the origin. For example, www is translated into www + origin. In our fictitious zone file, our origin is example. org., so www would translate to www.example.org.

The format of a zone file follows:

```
recordname      IN recordtype   value
```

The most commonly used DNS records:

SOA

   start of zone authority

NS

   an authoritative name server

A

   A host address

CNAME

the canonical name for an alias

MX

mail exchange

PTR

a domain name pointer (used in reverse DNS)

```
example.org. IN SOA ns1.example.org. admin.example.org. (
                      5                 ; Serial
                      10800             ; Refresh after 3 hours
                      3600              ; Retry after 1 hour
                      604800            ; Expire after 1 week
                      86400 )           ; Minimum TTL of 1 day
```

example.org.

the domain name, also the origin for this zone file.

ns1.example.org.

the primary/authoritative name server for this zone

admin.example.org.

the responsible person for this zone, email address with @ replaced. (`<admin@example.org>` becomes `admin.example.org`)

5

the serial number of the file. this must be incremented each time the zone file is modified. Nowadays, many admins prefer a `yyyymmddrr` format for the serial number. 2001041002 would mean last modified 04/10/2001, the latter 02 being the second time the zone file has been modified this day. The serial number is important as it alerts slave name servers for a zone when it is updated.

```
@       IN NS         ns1.example.org.
```

This is an NS entry. Every name server that is going to reply authoritatively for the zone must have one of these entries. The @ as seen here could have been `example.org`. The @ translates to the origin.

```
localhost       IN A    127.0.0.1
ns1             IN A    3.2.1.2
ns2             IN A    3.2.1.3
mail            IN A    3.2.1.10
@               IN A    3.2.1.30
```

The A record indicates machine names. As seen above, `ns1.example.org` would resolve to 3.2.1.2. Again, the origin symbol, @, is used here, thus meaning `example.org` would resolve to 3.2.1.30.

```
www               IN CNAME       @
```

The canonical name record is usually used for giving aliases to a machine. In the example, www is aliased to the machine addressed to the origin, or example.org (3.2.1.30). CNAMEs can be used to provide alias hostnames, or round robin one hostname among multiple machines.

```
@                 IN MX   10     mail.example.org.
```

The MX record indicates which mail servers are responsible for handling incoming mail for the zone. mail.example.org is the hostname of the mail server, and 10 being the priority of that mail server.

One can have several mail servers, with priorities of 3, 2, 1. A mail server attempting to deliver to example.org would first try the highest priority MX, then the second highest, etc, until the mail can be properly delivered.

For in-addr.arpa zone files (reverse DNS), the same format is used, except with PTR entries instead of A or CNAME.

```
$TTL 3600

1.2.3.in-addr.arpa. IN SOA ns1.example.org. admin.example.org. (
                        5                 ; Serial
                        10800             ; Refresh
                        3600              ; Retry
                        604800            ; Expire
                        3600 )            ; Minimum

@        IN NS    ns1.example.org.
@        IN NS    ns2.example.org.

2        IN PTR   ns1.example.org.
3        IN PTR   ns2.example.org.
10       IN PTR   mail.example.org.
30       IN PTR   example.org.
```

This file gives the proper IP address to hostname mappings of our above fictitious domain.

17.9.7 Caching Name Server

A caching name server is a name server that is not authoritative for any zones. It simply asks queries of its own, and remembers them for later use. To set one up, just configure the name server as usual, omitting any inclusions of zones.

17.9.8 Running named in a Sandbox

For added security you may want to run named(8) in a sandbox. This will reduce the potential damage should it be compromised. If you include a sandbox directory in its command line, named will chroot(8) into that directory immediately upon finishing processing its command line. It is also a good idea to have named run as a non-privileged user in the sandbox. The default FreeBSD install contains a user bind with group bind. If we wanted the sandbox in the /etc/namedb/sandbox directory the command line for named would look like this:

```
# /usr/sbin/named -u bind -g bind -t /etc/namedb/sandbox <path_to_named.conf>
```

The following steps should be taken in order to successfully run named in a sandbox. Throughout the following discussion we will assume the path to your sandbox is `/etc/namedb/sandbox`

- Create the sandbox directory: `/etc/namedb/sandbox`
- Create other necessary directories off of the sandbox directory: `etc` and `var/run`
- copy `/etc/localtime` to `sandbox/etc`
- make bind:bind the owner of all files and directories in the sandbox:

```
# chown -R bind:bind /etc/namedb/sandbox
# chmod -R 750 /etc/namedb/sandbox
```

There are some issues you need to be aware of when running named in a sandbox.

- Your named.conf(5) file and all your zone files must be in the sandbox
- `sandbox/etc/localtime` is needed in order to have the correct time for your time zone in log messages.
- named(8) will write its process id to a file in `sandbox/var/run`
- The Unix socket used for communication by the ndc(8) utility will be created in `sandbox/var/run`
- When using the ndc(8) utility you need to specify the location of the Unix socket created in the sandbox, by named(8), by using the -c switch: `# ndc -c /etc/namedb/sandbox/var/run/ndc`
- If you enable logging to file, the log files must be in the sandbox

named(8) can be started in a sandbox properly, if the following is in `/etc/rc.conf`:

```
named_flags="-u bind -g bind -t /etc/namedb/sandbox <path_to_named.conf>"
```

17.9.9 How to Use the Name Server

If setup properly, the name server should be accessible through the network and locally. `/etc/resolv.conf` must contain a name server entry with the local IP address so it will query the local name server first.

To access it over the network, the machine must have the name server's IP address set properly in its own name server configuration options.

17.9.10 Security

Although BIND is the most common implementation of DNS, there is always the issue of security. Possible and exploitable security holes are sometimes found.

It is a good idea to subscribe to CERT[13] and freebsd-announce[14] to stay up to date with the current Internet and FreeBSD security issues.

> **Tip:** If a problem arises, keeping sources up to date and having a fresh build of named would not hurt.

17.9.11 Further Reading

BIND/named manual pages: ndc(8) named(8) named.conf(5)

- Official ISC Bind Page (`http://www.isc.org/products/BIND/`)
- BIND FAQ (`http://www.nominum.com/resources/faqs/bind-faqs.html`)
- O'Reilly DNS and BIND 4th Edition (`http://www.oreilly.com/catalog/dns4/`)
- RFC1034 - Domain Names - Concepts and Facilities (`ftp://ftp.isi.edu/in-notes/rfc1034.txt`)
- RFC1035 - Domain Names - Implementation and Specification (`ftp://ftp.isi.edu/in-notes/rfc1035.txt`)

17.10 NTP

17.10.1 Overview

Over time, a computer's clock is prone to drift. As time passes, the computer's clock becomes less accurate. NTP (Network Time Protocol) is one way to ensure your clock is right.

Many Internet services rely on, or greatly benefit from, computers' clocks being accurate. For example, a Web server may receive requests to send a file if it has modified since a certain time. Services such as cron(8) run commands at a given time. If the clock is inaccurate, these commands may not run when expected.

FreeBSD ships with the ntpd(8) NTP server which can be used to query other NTP servers to set the clock on your machine or provide time services to others.

17.10.2 Choosing Appropriate NTP Servers

In order to synchronize your clock, you will need to find one or more NTP servers to use. Your network administrator or ISP may have setup an NTP server for this purpose—check their documentation to see if this is the case. There is a list of publicly accessible NTP servers[15] which you can use to find an NTP server near to you. Make sure you are aware of the policy for any servers you choose, and ask for permission if required.

---

13 http://www.cert.org
14 http://www.FreeBSD.org/handbook/eresources.html#ERESOURCES-MAIL
15 http://www.eecis.udel.edu/~mills/ntp/servers.htm

Choosing several unconnected NTP servers is a good idea in case one of the servers you are using becomes unreachable or its clock is unreliable. ntpd(8) uses the responses it receives from other servers intelligently—it will favor unreliable servers less than reliable ones.

17.10.3 Configuring Your Machine

Basic Configuration

If you only wish to synchronize your clock when the machine boots up, you can use ntpdate(8). This may be appropriate for some desktop machines which are frequently rebooted and only require infrequent synchronization, but most machines should run ntpd(8).

Using ntpdate(8) at boot time is also a good idea for machines that run ntpd(8). ntpd(8) changes the clock gradually, whereas ntpdate(8) sets the clock, no matter how great the difference between a machine's current clock setting and the correct time.

To enable ntpdate(8) at boot time, add

```
ntpdate_enable="YES"
```

to /etc/rc.conf. You will also need to specify all servers you wish to synchronize with and any flags to be passed to ntpdate(8) in `ntpdate_flags`.

General Configuration

NTP is configured by the `/etc/ntp.conf` file in the format described in ntp.conf(5). Here is a simple example:

```
server ntplocal.example.com prefer
server timeserver.example.org
server ntp2a.example.net

driftfile /var/db/ntp.drift
```

The `server` option specifies which servers are to be used, with one server listed on each line. If a server is specified with the `prefer` argument, as with `ntplocal.example.com`, that server is preferred over other servers. A response from a preferred server will be discarded if it differs significantly from other servers' responses, otherwise it will be used without any consideration to other responses. The `prefer` argument is normally used for NTP servers that are known to be highly accurate, such as those with special time monitoring hardware.

The `driftfile` option specifies which file is used to store the system clock's frequency offset. ntpd(8) uses this to automatically compensate for the clock's natural drift, allowing it to maintain a reasonably correct setting even if it is cut off from all external time sources for a period of time.

The `driftfile` option specifies which file is used to store information about previous responses from the NTP servers you are using. This file contains internal information for NTP. It should not be modified by any other process.

Controlling Access to Your Server

By default, your NTP server will be accessible to all hosts on the Internet. The `restrict` option in ntp.conf(5) allows you to control which machines can access your server.

If you want to deny all machines from accessing your NTP server, add the line

```
restrict default ignore
```

to `/etc/ntp.conf`. If you only want to allow machines within your own network to synchronize their clocks with your server, but ensure they are not allowed to configure the server or used as peers to synchronize against, add

```
restrict 192.168.1.0 mask 255.255.255.0 notrust nomodify notrap
```

instead, where `192.168.1.0` in an IP address on your network and `255.255.255.0` is your network's netmask.

`/etc/ntp.conf` can contain multiple `restrict` options. For more details, see the `Access Control Support` sub-section of ntp.conf(5).

17.10.4 Running the NTP Server

To ensure the NTP server is started at boot time, add the line

```
xntpd_enable="YES"
```

to `/etc/rc.conf`. If you wish to pass additional flags to ntpd(8) edit the `xntpd_flags` parameter in `/etc/rc.conf`.

To start the server without rebooting your machine, run `ntpd` being sure to specify any additional parameters from `xntpd_flags` in `/etc/rc.conf`. For example:

```
# ntpd -p /var/run/ntpd.pid
```

17.10.5 Using ntpd(8) with a temporary Internet connection

`ntpd` does not need a permanent connection to the Internet to function properly. However, if you have a temporary connection that is configured to dial out on demand, it is a good idea to prevent NTP traffic from triggering a dial out or keeping the connection alive. If you are using user PPP, you can use `filter` directives in `/etc/ppp/ppp.conf`. For example:

```
set filter dial 0 deny udp src eq 123
# Prevent NTP traffic from initiating dial out
set filter dial 1 permit 0 0
set filter alive 0 deny udp src eq 123
# Prevent incoming NTP traffic from keeping the connection open
set filter alive 1 deny udp dst eq 123
# Prevent outgoing NTP traffic from keeping the connection open
set filter alive 2 permit 0/0 0/0
```

For more details see the PACKET FILTERING section in ppp(8) and the examples in `/usr/share/examples/ppp/`.

> **Note:** Some Internet access providers block low-numbered ports, preventing NTP from from functioning since replies never reach your machine.

17.10.6 Further Information

Documentation for the NTP server can be found in `/usr/share/doc/ntp/` in HTML format.

17.11 Network Address Translation

17.11.1 Overview

FreeBSD's Network Address Translation daemon, commonly known as natd(8) is a daemon that accepts incoming raw IP packets, changes the source to the local machine and re-injects these packets back into the outgoing IP packet stream. natd does this by changing the source IP address and port such that when data is received back, it is able to determine the original location of the data and forward it back to its original requester.

The most common use of NAT is to perform what is commonly known as Internet Connection Sharing.

17.11.2 Setup

Due to the diminishing IP space in IPv4, and the increased number of users on high-speed consumer lines such as cable or DSL, people are in more and more need of an Internet Connection Sharing solution. The ability to connect several computers online through one connection and IP address makes natd(8) a reasonable choice.

Most commonly, a user has a machine connected to a cable or DSL line with one IP address and wishes to use this one connected computer to provide Internet access to several more over a LAN.

To do this, the FreeBSD machine on the Internet must act as a gateway. This gateway machine must have two NICs-- one for connecting to the Internet router, the other connecting to a LAN. All the machines on the LAN are connected through a hub or switch.

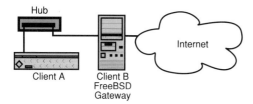

With this setup, the machine without Internet access can use the machine with access as a gateway to access the outside world.

17.11.3 Configuration

The following options must be in the kernel configuration file:

```
options IPFIREWALL
options IPDIVERT
```

Additionally, at choice, the following may also be suitable:

```
options IPFIREWALL_DEFAULT_TO_ACCEPT
options IPFIREWALL_VERBOSE
```

The following must be in `/etc/rc.conf`:

```
gateway_enable="YES"
firewall_enable="YES"
firewall_type="OPEN"
natd_enable="YES"
natd_interface="fxp0"
natd_flags=""
```

gateway_enable="YES"	Sets up the machine to act as a gateway. Running `sysctl -w net.inet.ip.forwarding=1` would have the same effect.
firewall_enable="YES"	Enables the firewall rules in `/etc/rc.firewall` at boot.
firewall_type="OPEN"	This specifies a predefined firewall ruleset that allows anything in. See `/etc/rc.firewall` for additional types.
natd_interface="fxp0"	Indicates which interface to forward packets through. (the interface connected to the Internet)
natd_flags=""	Any additional configuration options passed to natd(8) on boot.

Having the previous options defined in `/etc/rc.conf` would run `natd -interface fxp0` at boot. This can also be run manually.

Each machine and interface behind the LAN should be assigned IP address numbers in the private network space as defined by RFC 1918[16] and have a default gateway of the natd machine's internal IP address.

For example, client a and b behind the LAN have IP addresses of 192.168.0.2 and 192.168.0.3, while the natd machine's LAN interface has an IP address of 192.168.0.1. Client a and b's default gateway must be set to that of the natd machine, 192.168.0.1. The natd machine's external, or Internet interface does not require any special modification for natd to work.

---

16 ftp://ftp.isi.edu/in-notes/rfc1918.txt

17.11.4 Port Redirection

The drawback with natd is that the LAN clients are not accessible from the Internet. Clients on the LAN can make outgoing connections to the world but cannot receive incoming ones. This presents a problem if trying to run Internet services on one of the LAN client machines. A simple way around this is to redirect selected Internet ports on the natd machine to a LAN client.

For example, an IRC server runs on Client A, and a web server runs on Client B. For this to work properly, connections received on ports 6667 (irc) and 80 (web) must be redirected to the respective machines.

The `-redirect_port` must be passed to natd(8) with the proper options. The syntax is as follows:

```
-redirect_port proto targetIP:targetPORT[-targetPORT]
        [aliasIP:]aliasPORT[-aliasPORT]
        [remoteIP[:remotePORT[-remotePORT]]]
```

In the above example, the argument should be:

```
-redirect_port tcp 192.168.0.2:6667 6667
-redirect_port tcp 192.168.0.3:80 80
```

This will redirect the proper *tcp* ports to the LAN client machines.

The -redirect_port argument can be used to indicate port ranges over individual ports. For example, `tcp 192.168.0.2:2000-3000 2000-3000` would redirect all connections received on ports 2000 to 3000 to ports 2000 to 3000 on Client A.

These options can be used when directly running natd(8) or placed within the

```
natd_flags=""
```

option in /etc/rc.conf.

For further configuration options, consult natd(8)

17.11.5 Address Redirection

Address redirection is useful if several IP addresses are available, yet they must be on one machine. With this, natd(8) can assign each LAN client its own external IP address. natd(8) then rewrites outgoing packets from the LAN clients with the proper external IP address and redirects all traffic incoming on that particular IP address back to the specific LAN client. This is also known as static NAT. For example, the IP addresses 128.1.1.1, 128.1.1.2, and 128.1.1.3 belong to the natd gateway machine. 128.1.1.1 can be used as the natd gateway machine's external IP address, while 128.1.1.2 and 128.1.1.3 are forwarded back to LAN clients A and B.

The -redirect_address syntax is as follows:

```
-redirect_address localIP publicIP
```

localIP   The internal IP address of the LAN client.

publicIP   The external IP address corresponding to the LAN client.

In the example, this argument would read:

`-redirect_address 192.168.0.2 128.1.1.2 -redirect_address 192.168.0.3 128.1.1.3`

Like -redirect_port, these arguments are also placed within natd_flags of `/etc/rc.conf`. With address redirection, there is no need for port redirection since all data received on a particular IP address is redirected.

The external IP addresses on the natd machine must be active and aliased to the external interface. Look at rc.conf(5) to do so.

17.12 inetd "Super-Server"

17.12.1 Overview

inetd(8) is referred to as the "Internet Super-Server" because it manages connections for several daemons. Programs that provide network service are commonly known as daemons. **inetd** serves as a managing server for other daemons. When a connection is received by **inetd**, it determines which daemon the connection is destined for, spawns the particular daemon and delegates the socket to it. Running one instance of **inetd** reduces the overall system load as compared to running each daemon individually in stand-alone mode.

Primarily, **inetd** is used to spawn other daemons, but several trivial protocols are handled directly, such as **chargen**, **auth**, and **daytime**.

This section will cover the basics in configuring **inetd** through its command-line options and its configuration file, `/etc/inetd.conf`.

17.12.2 Settings

inetd is initialized through the `/etc/rc.conf` system. The `inetd_enable` option is set to "NO" by default, but is often times turned on by **sysinstall** with the medium security profile. Placing:

```
inetd_enable="YES"
```

or

```
inetd_enable="NO"
```

into `/etc/rc.conf` can enable or disable **inetd** starting at boot time.

Additionally, different command-line options can be passed to **inetd** via the `inetd_flags` option.

17.12.3 Command-Line Options

inetd sypnosis:

```
inetd [-d] [-l] [-w] [-W] [-c maximum] [-C rate] [-a address | hostname] [-p filename] [-R rate] [configuration file]
```

-d

> Turn on debugging.

-l

> Turn on logging of successful connections.

-w

> Turn on TCP Wrapping for external services. (on by default)

-W

> Turn on TCP Wrapping for internal services which are built in to **inetd**. (on by default)

-c maximum

> Specify the default maximum number of simultaneous invocations of each service; the default is unlimited. May be overridden on a per-service basis with the `max-child` parameter.

-C rate

> Specify the default maximum number of times a service can be invoked from a single IP address in one minute; the default is unlimited. May be overridden on a per-service basis with the `max-connections-per-ip-per-minute` parameter.

-R rate

> Specify the maximum number of times a service can be invoked in one minute; the default is 256. A rate of 0 allows an unlimited number of invocations.

-a

> Specify one specific IP address to bind to. Alternatively, a hostname can be specified, in which case the IPv4 or IPv6 address which corresponds to that hostname is used. Usually a hostname is specified when **inetd** is run inside a jail(8), in which case the hostname corresponds to the jail(8) environment.

> When hostname specification is used and both IPv4 and IPv6 bindings are desired, one entry with the appropriate protocol type for each binding is required for each service in `/etc/inetd.conf`. For example, a TCP-based service would need two entries, one using "tcp4" for the protocol and the other using "tcp6".

-p

> Specify an alternate file in which to store the process ID.

These options can be passed to **inetd** using the `inetd_flags` option in `/etc/rc.conf`. By default, `inetd_flags` is set to "-wW", which turns on TCP wrapping for **inetd**'s internal and external services. For novice users, these parameters usually do not need to be modified or even entered in `/etc/rc.conf`

> **Note:** An external service is a daemon outside of **inetd**, which is invoked when a connection is received for it. On the other hand, an internal service is one that **inetd** has the facility of offering within itself.

17.12.4 `inetd.conf`

Configuration of **inetd** is controlled through the `/etc/inetd.conf` file.

When a modification is made to `/etc/inetd.conf`, **inetd** can be forced to re-read its configuration file by sending a HangUP signal to the **inetd** process as shown:

Example 17-4. Sending inetd a HangUP Signal

```
# kill -HUP `cat /var/run/inetd.pid`
```

Each line of the configuration file specifies an individual daemon. Comments in the file are preceded by a "#". The format of `/etc/inetd.conf` is as follows:

```
service-name
socket-type
protocol
{wait|nowait}[/max-child[/max-connections-per-ip-per-minute]]
user[:group][/login-class]
server-program
server-program-arguments
```

An example entry for the **ftpd** daemon using IPv4:

```
ftp      stream tcp    nowait root    /usr/libexec/ftpd      ftpd -l
```

service-name

This is the service name of the particular daemon. It must correspond to a service listed in `/etc/services`. This determines which port **inetd** must listen to. If a new service is being created, it must be placed in `/etc/services` first.

socket-type

Either `stream`, `dgram`, `raw`, or `seqpacket`. `stream` must be used for connection-based, TCP daemons, while `dgram` is used for daemons utilizing the UDP transport protocol.

protocol

One of the following:

Protocol	Explanation
tcp, tcp4	TCP IPv4
udp, udp4	UDP IPv4
tcp6	TCP IPv6
udp6	UDP IPv6
tcp46	Both TCP IPv4 and v6
udp46	Both UDP IPv4 and v6

{wait|nowait}[/max-child[/max-connections-per-ip-per-minute]]

wait|nowait indicates whether the daemon invoked from **inetd** is able to handle its own socket or not. dgram socket types must use the wait option, while stream socket daemons, which are usually multi-threaded, should use nowait. wait usually hands off multiple sockets to a single daemon, while nowait spawns a child daemon for each new socket.

The maximum number of child daemons **inetd** may spawn can be set using the max-child option. If a limit of ten instances of a particular daemon is needed, a /10 would be placed after nowait.

In addition to max-child another option limiting the maximum connections from a single place to a particular daemon can be enabled. max-connections-per-ip-per-minute does just this. A value of ten here would limit any particular IP address connecting to a particular service to ten attempts per minute. This is useful to prevent intentional or unintentional resource consumption and Denial of Service (DoS) attacks to a machine.

In this field, wait or nowait is mandatory. max-child and max-connections-per-ip-per-minute are optional.

A stream-type multi-threaded daemon without any max-child or max-connections-per-ip-per-minute limits would simply be: nowait

The same daemon with a maximum limit of ten daemons would read: nowait/10

Additionally, the same setup with a limit of twenty connections per IP address per minute and a maximum total limit of ten child daemons would read: nowait/10/20

These options are all utilized by the default settings of the **fingerd** daemon, as seen here:

```
finger stream  tcp     nowait/3/10 nobody /usr/libexec/fingerd fingerd -s
```

user

The user is the username that the particular daemon should run as. Most commonly, daemons run as the root user. For security purposes, it is common to find some servers running as the daemon user, or the least privileged nobody user.

server-program

> The full path of the daemon to be executed when a connection is received. If the daemon is a service provided by **inetd** internally, then `internal` should be used.

server-program-arguments

> This works in conjunction with `server-program` by specifying the arguments, starting with argv[0], passed to the daemon on invocation. If **mydaemon -d** is the command line, `mydaemon -d` would be the value of `server program arguments`. Again, if the daemon is an internal service, use `internal` here.

17.12.5 Security

Depending on the security profile chosen at install, many of **inetd**'s daemons may be enabled by default. If there is no apparent need for a particular daemon, disable it! Place a "#" in front of the daemon in question, and send a hangup signal to inetd as shown in the previous example. Some daemons, such as **fingerd**, may not be desired at all because they provide an attacker with too much information.

Some daemons are not security-conscious and have long, or non-existent timeouts for connection attempts. This allows an attacker to slowly send connections to a particular daemon, thus saturating available resources. It may be a good idea to place `ip-per-minute` and `max-child` limitations on certain daemons.

By default, TCP wrapping is turned on. Consult the hosts_access(5) manual page for more information on placing TCP restrictions on various **inetd** invoked daemons.

17.12.6 Miscellaneous

daytime, **time**, **echo**, **discard**, **chargen**, and **auth** are all internally provided services of **inetd**.

The **auth** service provides identity (ident, identd) network services, and is configurable to a certain degree.

Consult the inetd(8) manual page for more in-depth information.

Chapter 18

Electronic Mail

18.1 Synopsis

Electronic Mail, better known as email, is one of the most widely used forms of communication today. This chapter provides a basic introduction to running a mail server on FreeBSD. However, it is not a complete reference and in fact many important considerations are omitted. For more complete coverage of the subject, the reader is referred to the many excellent books listed in Appendix B.

After reading this chapter, you will know:

- What software components are involved in sending and receiving electronic mail.
- Where basic **sendmail** configuration files are located in FreeBSD.
- How to block spammers from illegally using your mail server as a relay.
- How to troubleshoot common mail server problems.

Before reading this chapter, you should:

- Properly setup your network connection (Chapter 17).
- Properly setup the DNS information for your mail host (Chapter 17).
- Know how to install additional third-party software (Chapter 4).

18.2 Using Electronic Mail

There are five major parts involved in an email exchange. They are: the user program, the server daemon, DNS, a POP or IMAP daemon, and of course, the mailhost itself.

18.2.1 The User Program

This includes command line programs such as **mutt**, **pine**, **elm**, and **mail**, and GUI programs such as **balsa**, **xfmail** to name a few, and something more "sophisticated" like a WWW browser. These programs simply pass off the email transactions to the local "mailhost", either by calling one of the server daemons available or delivering it over TCP.

18.2.2 Mailhost Server Daemon

This is usually **sendmail** (by default with FreeBSD) or one of the other mail server daemons such as **qmail**, **postfix**, or **exim**. There are others, but those are the most widely used.

The server daemon usually has two functions—it looks after receiving incoming mail and delivers outgoing mail. It does not allow you to connect to it via POP or IMAP to read your mail. You need an additional daemon for that.

Be aware that some older versions of **sendmail** have some serious security problems, however as long as you run a current version of it you should not have any problems. As always, it is a good idea to stay up-to-date with any software you run.

18.2.3 Email and DNS

The Domain Name System (DNS) and its daemon `named` play a large role in the delivery of email. In order to deliver mail from your site to another, the server daemon will look up the site in the DNS to determine the host that will receive mail for the destination.

It works the same way when you have mail sent to you. The DNS contains the database mapping hostname to an IP address, and a hostname to mailhost. The IP address is specified in an A record. The MX (Mail eXchanger) record specifies the mailhost that will receive mail for you. If you do not have an MX record for your hostname, the mail will be delivered directly to your host.

18.2.4 Receiving Mail

Receiving mail for your domain is done by the mail host. It will collect mail sent to you and store it for reading or pickup. In order to pick the stored mail up, you will need to connect to the mail host. This is done by either using POP or IMAP. If you want to read mail directly on the mail host, then a POP or IMAP server is not needed.

If you want to run a POP or IMAP server, there are two things you need to do:

1. Get a POP or IMAP daemon from the ports collection[1] and install it on your system.
2. Modify `/etc/inetd.conf` to load the POP or IMAP server.

18.2.5 The Mail Host

The mail host is the name given to a server that is responsible for delivering and receiving mail for your host, and possibly your network.

---

1 http://www.FreeBSD.org/ports/mail.html

18.3 sendmail Configuration

sendmail(8) is the default Mail Transfer Agent (MTA) in FreeBSD. **sendmail**'s job is to accept mail from Mail User Agents (MUA) and deliver it to the appropriate mailer as defined by its configuration file. **sendmail** can also accept network connections and deliver mail to local mailboxes or deliver it to another program.

sendmail uses the following configuration files:

Filename	Function
`/etc/mail/access`	**sendmail** access database file
`/etc/mail/aliases`	Mailbox aliases
`/etc/mail/local-host-names`	Lists of hosts **sendmail** accepts mail for
`/etc/mail/mailer.conf`	Mailer program configuration
`/etc/mail/mailertable`	Mailer delivery table
`/etc/mail/sendmail.cf`	**sendmail** master configuration file
`/etc/mail/virtusertable`	Virtual users and domain tables

18.3.1 `/etc/mail/access`

The access database defines what host(s) or IP addresses have access to the local mail server and what kind of access they have. Hosts can be listed as `OK`, `REJECT`, `RELAY` or simply passed to **sendmail**'s error handling routine with a given mailer error. Hosts that are listed as `OK`, which is the default, are allowed to send mail to this host as long as the mail's final destination is the local machine. Hosts that are listed as `REJECT` are rejected for all mail connections. Hosts that have the `RELAY` option for their hostname are allowed to send mail for any destination through this mail server.

Example 18-1. Configuring the sendmail Access Database

```
cyberspammer.com              550 We don't accept mail from spammers
FREE.STEALTH.MAILER@          550 We don't accept mail from spammers
another.source.of.spam        REJECT
okay.cyberspammer.com         OK
128.32                        RELAY
```

In this example we have five entries. Mail senders that match the left hand side of the table are affected by the action on the right side of the table. The first two examples give an error code to **sendmail**'s error handling routine. The message is printed to the remote host when a mail matches the left hand side of the table. The next entry rejects mail from a specific host on the Internet, `another.source.of.spam`. The next entry accepts mail connections from a host `okay.cyberspammer.com`, which is more exact than the `cyberspammer.com` line above. More specific matches override less exact matches. The last entry allows relaying of electronic mail from hosts with an IP address that begins with `128.32`. These hosts would be able to send mail through this mail server that are destined for other mail servers.

When this file is updated, you need to run `make` in `/etc/mail/` to update the database.

18.3.2 /etc/mail/aliases

The aliases database contains a list of virtual mailboxes that are expanded to other user(s), files, programs or other aliases. Here are a few examples that can be used in /etc/mail/aliases:

Example 18-2. Mail Aliases

```
root: localuser
ftp-bugs: joe,eric,paul
bit.bucket:  /dev/null
procmail: "|/usr/local/bin/procmail"
```

The aliases update matches the mailbox name on the left of the colon, and will expand it to the target(s) on the right. The first example simply expands the mailbox root to the mailbox localuser , which is then looked up again in the aliases database. If no match is found, then the message is delivered to the local user localuser. The next example shows a mail list. Mail to the mailbox ftp-bugs is expanded to the three local mailboxes joe, eric, and paul. Note that a remote mailbox could be specified as user@domain.com. The next example shows writing mail to a file, in this case /dev/null. The last example shows sending mail to a program, in this case the mail message is written to the standard input of /usr/local/bin/procmail through a Unix pipe.

When this file is updated, you need to run make in /etc/mail/ to update the database.

18.3.3 /etc/mail/local-host-names

This is a list of hostnames sendmail(8) is to accept as the local host name. Place any domains or hosts that **sendmail** is to be receiving mail for. For example, if this mail server was to accept mail for the domain example.com and the host mail.example.com, its local-host-names might look something like this:

```
example.com
mail.example.com
```

When this file is updated, sendmail(8) needs to be restarted for it to read the changes.

18.3.4 /etc/mail/mailer.conf

The mailer.conf configuration file holds a table containing the real mailer that is used for the given action. Very old software programs would hard-code in the name and path to the mailer, /usr/sbin/sendmail, which meant they where incompatible with other mailers such as postfix. Today, /usr/sbin/sendmail is a wrapper that looks at /etc/mail/ mailer.conf and executes the correct binary. When another mail transfer agent is installed on the system, mailer.conf should be updated to reflect the correct programs to execute.

18.3.5 /etc/mail/sendmail.cf

sendmail's master configuration file, sendmail.cf controls the overall behavior of **sendmail**, including everything from rewriting e-mail addresses to printing reject messages for remote mail servers. Naturally, with such a diverse role, this configuration file is quite complex and its details are a bit out of the scope of this section. Fortunately, this file rarely needs to be changed for standard mail servers.

The master **sendmail** configuration file can be built from m4(1) macros that define features and behavior of sendmail. Please see `/usr/src/contrib/sendmail/cf/README` for some of the details.

When changes to this file are made, **sendmail** needs to be restarted for the changes to take effect.

18.3.6 `/etc/mail/virtusertable`

The `virtualusertable` maps mail for virtual domains and mailboxes to real mailboxes. These mailboxes can be local, remote, an alias defined in `/etc/mail/aliases` or a file.

Example 18-3. Example Virtual Domain Mail Map

```
root@example.com                 root
postmaster@example.com           postmaster@noc.example.net
@example.com                     joe
```

In the above example, we have a mapping for a domain `example.com`. This file is processed in a first match order down the file. The first item maps root@example.com to the local mailbox root. The next entry maps postmaster@example.com to the mailbox postmaster on the host noc.example.net. Finally, if nothing from example.com has matched so far, it will match the last mapping, which matches every other mail message addressed to someone at `example.com`. This will be mapped to the local mail box joe.

18.4 Troubleshooting

1. Why do I have to use the FQDN for hosts on my site?

You will probably find that the host is actually in a different domain; for example, if you are in `foo.bar.edu` and you wish to reach a host called `mumble` in the `bar.edu` domain, you will have to refer to it by the fully-qualified domain name, `mumble.bar.edu`, instead of just `mumble`.

Traditionally, this was allowed by BSD BIND resolvers. However the current version of **BIND** that ships with FreeBSD no longer provides default abbreviations for non-fully qualified domain names other than the domain you are in. So an unqualified host `mumble` must either be found as `mumble.foo.bar.edu`, or it will be searched for in the root domain.

This is different from the previous behavior, where the search continued across `mumble.bar.edu`, and `mumble.edu`. Have a look at RFC 1535 for why this was considered bad practice, or even a security hole.

As a good workaround, you can place the line:

```
search foo.bar.edu bar.edu
```

instead of the previous:

```
domain foo.bar.edu
```

into your `/etc/resolv.conf`. However, make sure that the search order does not go beyond the "boundary between local and public administration", as RFC 1535 calls it.

2. sendmail says `mail loops back to myself`

This is answered in the **sendmail** FAQ as follows:

```
* I am getting "Local configuration error" messages, such as:

553 relay.domain.net config error: mail loops back to myself
554 <user@domain.net>... Local configuration error

How can I solve this problem?

You have asked mail to the domain (e.g., domain.net) to be
forwarded to a specific host (in this case, relay.domain.net)
by using an MX record, but the relay machine does not recognize
itself as domain.net. Add domain.net to /etc/sendmail.cw
(if you are using FEATURE(use_cw_file)) or add "Cw domain.net"
to /etc/sendmail.cf.
```

The **sendmail** FAQ is in `/usr/src/usr.sbin/sendmail` and is recommended reading if you want to do any "tweaking" of your mail setup.

3. How can I run a mail server on a dial-up PPP host?

You want to connect a FreeBSD box on a LAN to the Internet. The FreeBSD box will be a mail gateway for the LAN. The PPP connection is non-dedicated.

There are at least two ways to do this, an alternative being UUCP.

The key is to get a Internet site to provide secondary MX service for your domain. For example:

```
bigco.com.              MX       10       bigco.com.
                        MX       20       smalliap.com.
```

Only one host should be specified as the final recipient (add `Cw bigco.com` in `/etc/sendmail.cf` on bigco.com).

When the senders' `sendmail` is trying to deliver the mail it will try to connect to you over the modem link. It will most likely time out because you are not online. `sendmail` will automatically deliver it to the secondary MX site, i.e., your Internet provider. The secondary MX site will try every (`sendmail_flags = -bd -q15m` in `/etc/rc.conf`) 15 minutes to connect to your host to deliver the mail to the primary MX site.

You might want to use something like this as a login script.

```
#!/bin/sh
# Put me in /usr/local/bin/pppbigco
( sleep 60 ; /usr/sbin/sendmail -q ) &
```

```
/usr/sbin/ppp -direct pppbigco
```

If you are going to create a separate login script for a user you could use `sendmail -qRbigco.com` instead in the script above. This will force all mail in your queue for bigco.com to be processed immediately.

A further refinement of the situation is as follows.

Message stolen from the FreeBSD Internet service provider's mailing list `<freebsd-isp@FreeBSD.org>`.

```
> we provide the secondary MX for a customer. The customer connects to
> our services several times a day automatically to get the mails to
> his primary MX (We do not call his site when a mail for his domains
> arrived). Our sendmail sends the mailqueue every 30 minutes. At the
> moment he has to stay 30 minutes online to be sure that all mail is
> gone to the primary MX.
>
> Is there a command that would initiate sendmail to send all the mails
> now? The user has not root-privileges on our machine of course.

In the "privacy flags" section of sendmail.cf, there is a
definition Opgoaway,restrictqrun

Remove restrictqrun to allow non-root users to start the queue processing.
You might also like to rearrange the MXs. We are the 1st MX for our
customers like this, and we have defined:

# If we are the best MX for a host, try directly instead of generating
# local config error.
OwTrue

That way a remote site will deliver straight to you, without trying
the customer connection.  You then send to your customer.  Only works for
"hosts", so you need to get your customer to name their mail
machine "customer.com" as well as
"hostname.customer.com" in the DNS.  Just put an A record in
the DNS for "customer.com".
```

18.5 Advanced Topics

The following section covers more involved topics such as mail configuration and setting up mail for your entire domain.

18.5.1 Basic Configuration

Out of the box, you should be able to send email to external hosts as long as you have set up `/etc/resolv.conf` or are running your own name server. If you would like to have mail for your host delivered to that specific host, there are two methods:

- Run your own name server and have your own domain. For example, `FreeBSD.org`

- Get mail delivered directly to your host. This is done by delivering mail directly to the current DNS name for your machine. For example, `example.FreeBSD.org`.

Regardless of which of the above you choose, in order to have mail delivered directly to your host, you must have a permanent (static) IP address (no dynamic PPP dial-up). If you are behind a firewall, it must pass SMTP traffic on to you. If you want to receive mail at your host itself, you need to be sure of one of two things:

- Make sure that the MX record in your DNS points to your host's IP address.
- Make sure there is no MX entry in your DNS for your host.

Either of the above will allow you to receive mail directly at your host.

Try this:

```
# hostname
example.FreeBSD.org
# host example.FreeBSD.org
example.FreeBSD.org has address 204.216.27.XX
```

If that is what you see, mail directly to <`yourlogin@example.FreeBSD.org`> should work without problems.

If instead you see something like this:

```
# host example.FreeBSD.org
example.FreeBSD.org has address 204.216.27.XX
example.FreeBSD.org mail is handled (pri=10) by hub.FreeBSD.org
```

All mail sent to your host (`example.FreeBSD.org`) will end up being collected on `hub` under the same username instead of being sent directly to your host.

The above information is handled by your DNS server. The DNS record that carries mail routing information is the *M*ail e*X*change entry. If no MX record exists, mail will be delivered directly to the host by way of its IP address.

The MX entry for `freefall.FreeBSD.org` at one time looked like this:

```
freefall MX 30 mail.crl.net
freefall MX 40 agora.rdrop.com
freefall MX 10 freefall.FreeBSD.org
freefall MX 20 who.cdrom.com
```

As you can see, `freefall` had many MX entries. The lowest MX number is the host that ends up receiving the mail in the end while the others will queue mail temporarily if `freefall` is busy or down.

Alternate MX sites should have separate Internet connections from your own in order to be the most useful. Your ISP or other friendly site should have no problem providing this service for you.

18.5.2 Mail for Your Domain

In order to set up a "mailhost" (a.k.a., mail server) you need to have any mail sent to various workstations directed to it. Basically, you want to "hijack" any mail for your domain (in this case `*.FreeBSD.org`) and divert it to your mail server so your users can check their mail via POP or directly on the server.

To make life easiest, a user account with the same *username* should exist on both machines. Use `adduser` to do this.

The mailhost you will be using must be the designated mail exchange for each workstation on the network. This is done in your DNS configuration like so:

```
example.FreeBSD.org A 204.216.27.XX ; Workstation
    MX 10 hub.FreeBSD.org ; Mailhost
```

This will redirect mail for the workstation to the mailhost no matter where the A record points. The mail is sent to the MX host.

You cannot do this yourself unless you are running a DNS server. If you are not, or cannot, run your own DNS server, talk to your ISP or whoever does your DNS for you.

If you are doing virtual email hosting, the following information will come in handy. For the sake of an example, we will assume you have a customer with their own domain, in this case `customer1.org` and you want all the mail for `customer1.org` sent to your mailhost, which is named `mail.myhost.com`. The entry in your DNS should look like this:

```
customer1.org MX 10 mail.myhost.com
```

You do *not* need an A record if you only want to handle email for the domain.

> **Note:** Be aware that this means pinging `customer1.org` will not work unless an A record exists for it.

The last thing that you must do is tell **sendmail** on your mailhost what domains and/or hostnames it should be accepting mail for. There are a few different ways this can be done. Either of the following will work:

- Add the hosts to your `/etc/sendmail.cw` file if you are using the `FEATURE(use_cw_file)`. If you are using sendmail 8.10 or higher, the file is `/etc/mail/local-host-names`.

- Add a `Cwyour.host.com` line to your `/etc/sendmail.cf` or `/etc/mail/sendmail.cf` if you are using sendmail 8.10 or higher.

Chapter 19

The Cutting Edge

19.1 Synopsis

FreeBSD is under constant development between releases. For people who want to be on the cutting edge, there are several easy mechanisms for keeping your system in sync with the latest developments. Be warned—the cutting edge is not for everyone! This chapter will help you decide if you want to track the development system, or stick with one of the released versions.

After reading this chapter, you will know:

- The difference between the two development branches; FreeBSD-STABLE and FreeBSD-CURRENT.
- How to keep your system up to date with **CVSup**, **CVS**, or **CTM**.
- How to rebuild and reinstall the entire base system with `make world`.

Before reading this chapter, you should:

- Properly setup your network connection (Chapter 17).
- Know how to install additional third-party software (Chapter 4).

19.2 FreeBSD-CURRENT vs. FreeBSD-STABLE

There are two development branches to FreeBSD; FreeBSD-CURRENT and FreeBSD-STABLE. This section will explain a bit about each and describe how to keep your system up-to-date with each respective tree. FreeBSD-CURRENT will be discussed first, then FreeBSD-STABLE.

19.2.1 Staying Current with FreeBSD

As you are reading this, keep in mind that FreeBSD-CURRENT is the "bleeding edge" of FreeBSD development and that if you are new to FreeBSD, you are most likely going to want to think twice about running it.

What Is FreeBSD-CURRENT?

FreeBSD-CURRENT is, quite literally, nothing more than a daily snapshot of the working sources for FreeBSD. These include work in progress, experimental changes and transitional mechanisms that may or may not be present in the next official release of the software. While many of us compile almost daily from FreeBSD-CURRENT sources, there are periods of time when the sources are literally un-compilable. These problems are generally resolved as expeditiously as possible, but whether or not FreeBSD-CURRENT sources bring disaster or greatly desired functionality can literally be a matter of which part of any given 24 hour period you grabbed them in!

Who Needs FreeBSD-CURRENT?

FreeBSD-CURRENT is made generally available for 3 primary interest groups:

1. Members of the FreeBSD group who are actively working on some part of the source tree and for whom keeping "current" is an absolute requirement.

2. Members of the FreeBSD group who are active testers, willing to spend time working through problems in order to ensure that FreeBSD-CURRENT remains as sane as possible. These are also people who wish to make topical suggestions on changes and the general direction of FreeBSD.

3. Peripheral members of the FreeBSD (or some other) group who merely wish to keep an eye on things and use the current sources for reference purposes (e.g. for *reading*, not running). These people also make the occasional comment or contribute code.

What Is FreeBSD-CURRENT *Not*?

1. A fast-track to getting pre-release bits because you heard there is some cool new feature in there and you want to be the first on your block to have it.

2. A quick way of getting bug fixes.

3. In any way "officially supported" by us. We do our best to help people genuinely in one of the 3 "legitimate" FreeBSD-CURRENT categories, but we simply *do not have the time* to provide tech support for it. This is not because we are mean and nasty people who do not like helping people out (we would not even be doing FreeBSD if we were), it is literally because we cannot answer 400 messages a day *and* actually work on FreeBSD! Given the choice between improving FreeBSD and answering lots of questions, most developers, and users, would probably opt for the former.

Using FreeBSD-CURRENT

1. Join the FreeBSD-current mailing list `<freebsd-current@FreeBSD.org>` and the FreeBSD CVS commit message mailing list `<cvs-all@FreeBSD.org>` . This is not just a good idea, it is *essential*. If you are not on the *FreeBSD-current mailing list* `<freebsd-current@FreeBSD.org>`, you will not see the comments that people are making about the current state of the system and thus will probably end up stumbling over a lot of problems that others have already found and solved. Even more importantly, you will miss out on important bulletins which may be critical to your system's continued health.

   The FreeBSD CVS commit message mailing list `<cvs-all@FreeBSD.org>` mailing list will allow you to see the commit log entry for each change as it is made along with any pertinent information on possible side-effects.

To join these lists, send mail to <majordomo@FreeBSD.org> and specify the following in the body of your message:

```
subscribe freebsd-current
subscribe cvs-all
```

Optionally, you can also say help and Majordomo will send you full help on how to subscribe and unsubscribe to the various other mailing lists we support.

2. Grab the sources from ftp.FreeBSD.org. You can do this in one of three ways:

   a. Use the cvsup program (explained in Section A.6) with this supfile[1]. This is the second most recommended method, since it allows you to grab the entire collection once and then only what has changed from then on. Many people run cvsup from cron and keep their sources up-to-date automatically. For a fairly easy interface to this, simply type:

   ```
   # pkg_add -f ftp://ftp.FreeBSD.org/pub/FreeBSD/development/CVSup/cvsupit.tgz
   ```

   b. Use ftp. The source tree for FreeBSD-CURRENT is always "exported" on: ftp://ftp.FreeBSD.org/pub/FreeBSD/FreeBSD-current/. Our FTP server also allows compressed/tarred grabbing of whole trees. e.g. you see:

   ```
   usr.bin/lex
   ```

   You can do the following to get the whole directory as a tar file:

   ```
   ftp> cd usr.bin
   ftp> get lex.tar
   ```

   c. Use the **CTM** facility (Section A.5). If you have very bad connectivity (high price connections or only email access) **CTM** is an option. However, it is a lot of hassle and can give you broken files. This leads to it being rarely used, which again increases the chance of it not working for fairly long periods of time. We recommend using **CVSup** (Section A.6) for anybody with a 9600bps modem or faster connection.

3. If you are grabbing the sources to run, and not just look at, then grab *all* of FreeBSD-CURRENT, not just selected portions. The reason for this is that various parts of the source depend on updates elsewhere, and trying to compile just a subset is almost guaranteed to get you into trouble.

   Before compiling FreeBSD-CURRENT, read the Makefile in /usr/src carefully. You should at least run a make world (Section 19.4) the first time through as part of the upgrading process. Reading the FreeBSD-current mailing list <freebsd-current@FreeBSD.org> will keep you up-to-date on other bootstrapping procedures that sometimes become necessary as we move towards the next release.

4. Be active! If you are running FreeBSD-CURRENT, we want to know what you have to say about it, especially if you have suggestions for enhancements or bug fixes. Suggestions with accompanying code are received most enthusiastically!

---

1 ftp://ftp.FreeBSD.org/pub/FreeBSD/FreeBSD-current/src/share/examples/cvsup/standard-supfile

19.2.2 Staying Stable with FreeBSD

What Is FreeBSD-STABLE?

FreeBSD-STABLE is our development branch from which major releases are made. Changes go into this branch at a different pace, and with the general assumption that they have first gone into FreeBSD-CURRENT first for testing. This is *still* a development branch, however, and this means that at any given time, the sources for FreeBSD-STABLE may or may not be suitable for any particular purpose. It is simply another engineering development track, not a resource for end-users.

Who Needs FreeBSD-STABLE?

If you are interested in tracking or contributing to the FreeBSD development process, especially as it relates to the next "point" release of FreeBSD, then you should consider following FreeBSD-STABLE.

While it is true that security fixes also go into the FreeBSD-STABLE branch, you do not *need* to track FreeBSD-STABLE to do this. Every security advisory for FreeBSD explains how to fix the problem for the releases it affects [1], and tracking an entire development branch just for security reasons is likely to bring in a lot of unwanted changes as well.

Although we endeavor to ensure that the FreeBSD-STABLE branch compiles and runs at all times, this cannot be guaranteed. In addition, while code is developed in FreeBSD-CURRENT before including it in FreeBSD-STABLE, more people run FreeBSD-STABLE than FreeBSD-CURRENT, so it is inevitable that bugs and corner cases will sometimes be found in FreeBSD-STABLE that were not apparent in FreeBSD-CURRENT.

For these reasons, we do *not* recommend that you blindly track FreeBSD-STABLE, and it is particularly important that you do not update any production servers to FreeBSD-STABLE without first thoroughly testing the code in your development environment.

If you do not have the resources to do this then we recommend that you run the most recent release of FreeBSD, and use the binary update mechanism to move from release to release.

Using FreeBSD-STABLE

1. Join the FreeBSD-stable mailing list `<freebsd-stable@FreeBSD.org>`. This will keep you informed of build-dependencies that may appear in FreeBSD-STABLE or any other issues requiring special attention. Developers will also make announcements in this mailing list when they are contemplating some controversial fix or update, giving the users a chance to respond if they have any issues to raise concerning the proposed change.

   The FreeBSD CVS commit message mailing list `<cvs-all@FreeBSD.org>` mailing list will allow you to see the commit log entry for each change as it is made along with any pertinent information on possible side-effects.

   To join these lists, send mail to `<majordomo@FreeBSD.org>` and specify the following in the body of your message:

---

1. That's not quite true. We can't continue to support old releases of FreeBSD forever, although we do support them for many years. For a complete description of the current security policy for old releases of FreeBSD, please see `http://www.FreeBSD.org/security`

```
subscribe freebsd-stable
subscribe cvs-all
```

Optionally, you can also say `help` and Majordomo will send you full help on how to subscribe and unsubscribe to the various other mailing lists we support.

2. If you are installing a new system and want it to be as stable as possible, you can simply grab the latest dated branch snapshot from `ftp://releng4.FreeBSD.org/pub/FreeBSD/` and install it like any other release.

   If you are already running a previous release of FreeBSD and wish to upgrade via sources then you can easily do so from `ftp.FreeBSD.org`. This can be done in one of three ways:

   a. Use the **CTM** facility (Section A.5). Unless you have a good TCP/IP connection at a flat rate, this is the way to do it.

   b. Use the cvsup program (Section A.6) with this supfile[5]. This is the second most recommended method, since it allows you to grab the entire collection once and then only what has changed from then on. Many people run `cvsup` from `cron` to keep their sources up-to-date automatically. For a fairly easy interface to this, simply type:

      ```
      # pkg_add -f ftp://ftp.FreeBSD.org/pub/FreeBSD/development/CVSup/cvsupit.tgz
      ```

   c. Use `ftp`. The source tree for FreeBSD-STABLE is always "exported" on: `ftp://ftp.FreeBSD.org/pub/FreeBSD/FreeBSD-stable/`

      Our FTP server also allows compressed/tarred grabbing of whole trees. e.g. you see:

      ```
      usr.bin/lex
      ```

      You can do the following to get the whole directory for you as a tar file:

      ```
      ftp> cd usr.bin
      ftp> get lex.tar
      ```

3. Essentially, if you need rapid on-demand access to the source and communications bandwidth is not a consideration, use `cvsup` or `ftp`. Otherwise, use **CTM**.

4. Before compiling FreeBSD-STABLE, read the `Makefile` in `/usr/src` carefully. You should at least run a make world (Section 19.4) the first time through as part of the upgrading process. Reading the FreeBSD-stable mailing list <freebsd-stable@FreeBSD.org> will keep you up-to-date on other bootstrapping procedures that sometimes become necessary as we move towards the next release.

---

5 ftp://ftp.FreeBSD.org/pub/FreeBSD/FreeBSD-current/src/share/examples/cvsup/stable-supfile

19.3 Synchronizing Your Source

There are various ways of using an Internet (or email) connection to stay up-to-date with any given area of the FreeBSD project sources, or all areas, depending on what interests you. The primary services we offer are Anonymous CVS (Section A.4), CVSup (Section A.6), and CTM (Section A.5).

> **Warning:** While it is possible to update only parts of your source tree, the only supported update procedure is to update the entire tree and recompile both userland (i.e., all the programs that run in user space, such as those in /bin and /sbin) and kernel sources. Updating only part of your source tree, only the kernel, or only userland will often result in problems. These problems may range from compile errors to kernel panics or data corruption.

Anonymous CVS and **CVSup** use the *pull* model of updating sources. In the case of **CVSup** the user (or a cron script) invokes the cvsup program, and it interacts with a cvsupd server somewhere to bring your files up-to-date. The updates you receive are up-to-the-minute and you get them when, and only when, you want them. You can easily restrict your updates to the specific files or directories that are of interest to you. Updates are generated on the fly by the server, according to what you have and what you want to have. **Anonymous CVS** is quite a bit more simplistic than CVSup in that it is just an extension to **CVS** which allows it to pull changes directly from a remote CVS repository. **CVSup** can do this far more efficiently, but **Anonymous CVS** is easier to use.

CTM, on the other hand, does not interactively compare the sources you have with those on the master archive or otherwise pull them across.. Instead, a script which identifies changes in files since its previous run is executed several times a day on the master CTM machine, any detected changes being compressed, stamped with a sequence-number and encoded for transmission over email (in printable ASCII only). Once received, these "CTM deltas" can then be handed to the ctm.rmail(1) utility which will automatically decode, verify and apply the changes to the user's copy of the sources. This process is far more efficient than **CVSup**, and places less strain on our server resources since it is a *push* rather than a *pull* model.

There are other trade-offs, of course. If you inadvertently wipe out portions of your archive, **CVSup** will detect and rebuild the damaged portions for you. **CTM** will not do this, and if you wipe some portion of your source tree out (and do not have it backed up) then you will have to start from scratch (from the most recent CVS "base delta") and rebuild it all with CTM or, with anoncvs, simply delete the bad bits and resync.

More information about **Anonymous CVS**, **CTM**, and **CVSup** is available further down in this section.

19.4 Using make world

Once you have synchronized your local source tree against a particular version of FreeBSD (FreeBSD-STABLE, FreeBSD-CURRENT, and so on) you can then use the source tree to rebuild the system.

> **Take a Backup:** It cannot be stressed enough how important it is to take a backup of your system *before* you do this. While rebuilding the world is (as long as you follow these instructions) an easy task to do, there will inevitably be times when you make mistakes, or when mistakes made by others in the source tree render your system unbootable.
>
> Make sure you have taken a backup. And have a fix-it floppy to hand. You will probably never have to use it, but it is better to be safe than sorry!

Subscribe to the Right Mailing List: The FreeBSD-STABLE and FreeBSD-CURRENT branches are, by their nature, *in development*. People that contribute to FreeBSD are human, and mistakes occasionally happen.

Sometimes these mistakes can be quite harmless, just causing your system to print a new diagnostic warning. Or the change may be catastrophic, and render your system unbootable or destroy your filesystems (or worse).

If problems like these occur, a "heads up" is posted to the appropriate mailing list, explaining the nature of the problem and which systems it affects. And an "all clear" announcement is posted when the problem has been solved.

If you try to track FreeBSD-STABLE or FreeBSD-CURRENT and do not read the FreeBSD-stable mailing list `<freebsd-stable@FreeBSD.org>` or the FreeBSD-current mailing list `<freebsd-current@FreeBSD.org>` respectively, then you are asking for trouble.

19.4.1 Read `/usr/src/UPDATING`

Before you do anything else, read `/usr/src/UPDATING` (or the equivalent file wherever you have a copy of the source code). This file should contain important information about problems you might encounter, or specify the order in which you might have to run certain commands. If UPDATING contradicts something you read here, UPDATING takes precedence.

Important: Reading UPDATING is not an acceptable substitute for subscribing to the correct mailing list, as described previously. The two requirements are complementary, not exclusive.

19.4.2 Check `/etc/make.conf`

Examine the files `/etc/defaults/make.conf` and `/etc/make.conf`. The first contains some default defines – most of which are commented out. To make use of them when you rebuild your system from source, add them to `/etc/make.conf`. Keep in mind that anything you add to `/etc/make.conf` is also used every time you run make, so it is a good idea to set them to something sensible for your system.

A typical user will probably want to copy the CFLAGS and NOPROFILE lines found in `/etc/defaults/make.conf` to `/etc/make.conf` and uncomment them.

Examine the other definitions (COPTFLAGS, NOPORTDOCS and so on) and decide if they are relevant to you.

19.4.3 Update `/etc/group`

The `/etc` directory contains a large part of your system's configuration information, as well as scripts that are run at system startup. Some of these scripts change from version to version of FreeBSD.

Some of the configuration files are also used in the day to day running of the system. In particular, `/etc/group`.

There have been occasions when the installation part of "make world" has expected certain usernames or groups to exist. When performing an upgrade it is likely that these groups did not exist. This caused problems when upgrading.

The most recent example of this is when the "ppp" group (later renamed "network") was added. Users had the installation process fail for them when parts of the ppp subsystem were installed using a non-existent (for them) group name.

The solution is to examine /usr/src/etc/group and compare its list of groups with your own. If there are any groups in the new file that are not in your file then copy them over. Similarly, you should rename any groups in /etc/group which have the same GID but a different name to those in /usr/src/etc/group.

> **Tip:** If you are feeling particularly paranoid, you can check your system to see which files are owned by the group you are renaming or deleting.
>
> ```
> # find / -group GID -print
> ```
>
> will show all files owned by group *GID* (which can be either a group name or a numeric group ID).

19.4.4 Drop to Single User Mode

You may want to compile the system in single user mode. Apart from the obvious benefit of making things go slightly faster, reinstalling the system will touch a lot of important system files, all the standard system binaries, libraries, include files and so on. Changing these on a running system (particularly if you have active users on the system at the time) is asking for trouble.

Another method is to compile the system in multi-user mode, and then drop into single user mode for the installation. If you would like to do it this way, simply hold off on the following steps until the build has completed.

As the superuser, you can execute

```
# shutdown now
```

from a running system, which will drop it to single user mode.

Alternatively, reboot the system, and at the boot prompt, enter the -s flag. The system will then boot single user. At the shell prompt you should then run:

```
# fsck -p
# mount -u /
# mount -a -t ufs
# swapon -a
```

This checks the filesystems, remounts / read/write, mounts all the other UFS filesystems referenced in /etc/fstab and then turns swapping on.

19.4.5 Remove /usr/obj

As parts of the system are rebuilt they are placed in directories which (by default) go under /usr/obj. The directories shadow those under /usr/src.

You can speed up the "make world" process, and possibly save yourself some dependency headaches by removing this directory as well.

Some files below /usr/obj may have the immutable flag set (see chflags(1) for more information) which must be removed first.

```
# cd /usr/obj
# chflags -R noschg *
# rm -rf *
```

19.4.6 Recompile the Source

Saving the Output

It is a good idea to save the output you get from running make(1) to another file. If something goes wrong you will have a copy of the error message. While this might not help you in diagnosing what has gone wrong, it can help others if you post your problem to one of the FreeBSD mailing lists.

The easiest way to do this is to use the script(1) command, with a parameter that specifies the name of the file to save all output to. You would do this immediately before rebuilding the world, and then type **exit** when the process has finished.

```
# script /var/tmp/mw.out
Script started, output file is /var/tmp/mw.out
# make TARGET
... compile, compile, compile ...
# exit
Script done, ...
```

If you do this, *do not* save the output in /tmp. This directory may be cleared next time you reboot. A better place to store it is in /var/tmp (as in the previous example) or in root's home directory.

Compile and Install the Base System

You must be in the /usr/src directory...

```
# cd /usr/src
```

(unless, of course, your source code is elsewhere, in which case change to that directory instead).

To rebuild the world you use the make(1) command. This command reads instructions from the Makefile, which describes how the programs that comprise FreeBSD should be rebuilt, the order in which they should be built, and so on.

The general format of the command line you will type is as follows:

```
# make -x -DVARIABLE target
```

In this example, -*x* is an option that you would pass to make(1). See the make(1) manual page for an example of the options you can pass.

-*DVARIABLE* passes a variable to the Makefile. The behavior of the Makefile is controlled by these variables. These are the same variables as are set in /etc/make.conf, and this provides another way of setting them.

```
# make -DNOPROFILE=true target
```

is another way of specifying that profiled libraries should not be built, and corresponds with the

```
NOPROFILE=    true
#    Avoid compiling profiled libraries
```

lines in /etc/make.conf.

target tells make(1) what you want to do. Each Makefile defines a number of different "targets", and your choice of target determines what happens.

Some targets are listed in the Makefile, but are not meant for you to run. Instead, they are used by the build process to break out the steps necessary to rebuild the system into a number of sub-steps.

Most of the time you will not need to pass any parameters to make(1), and so your command like will look like this:

```
# make target
```

Beginning with version 2.2.5 of FreeBSD (actually, it was first created on the FreeBSD-CURRENT branch, and then retrofitted to FreeBSD-STABLE midway between 2.2.2 and 2.2.5) the world target has been split in two. buildworld and installworld.

As the names imply, buildworld builds a complete new tree under /usr/obj, and installworld installs this tree on the current machine.

This is very useful for 2 reasons. First, it allows you to do the build safe in the knowledge that no components of your running system will be affected. The build is "self hosted". Because of this, you can safely run buildworld on a machine running in multi-user mode with no fear of ill-effects. It is still recommended that you run the installworld part in single user mode, though.

Secondly, it allows you to use NFS mounts to upgrade multiple machines on your network. If you have three machines, A, B and C that you want to upgrade, run make buildworld and make installworld on A. B and C should then NFS mount /usr/src and /usr/obj from A, and you can then run make installworld to install the results of the build on B and C.

Although the world target still exists, you are strongly encouraged not to use it.

Run

```
# make buildworld
```

It is now possible to specify a -j option to make which will cause it to spawn several simultaneous processes. This is most useful on multi-CPU machines. However, since much of the compiling process is IO bound rather than CPU bound it is also useful on single CPU machines.

On a typical single-CPU machine you would run:

```
# make -j4 buildworld
```

make(1) will then have up to 4 processes running at any one time. Empirical evidence posted to the mailing lists shows this generally gives the best performance benefit.

If you have a multi-CPU machine and you are using an SMP configured kernel try values between 6 and 10 and see how they speed things up.

Be aware that this is still somewhat experimental, and commits to the source tree may occasionally break this feature. If the world fails to compile using this parameter try again without it before you report any problems.

Timings

Many factors influence the build time, but currently a 500 MHz Pentium 3 with 128 MB of RAM takes about 2 hours to build the FreeBSD-STABLE tree, with no tricks or shortcuts used during the process. A FreeBSD-CURRENT tree will take somewhat longer.

19.4.7 Compile and Install a New Kernel

To take full advantage of your new system you should recompile the kernel. This is practically a necessity, as certain memory structures may have changed, and programs like ps(1) and top(1) will fail to work until the kernel and source code versions are the same.

The simplest, safest way to do this is to build and install a kernel based on GENERIC. While GENERIC may not have all the necessary devices for your system, it should contain everything necessary to boot your system back to single user mode. This is a good test that the new system works properly. After booting from GENERIC and verifying that your system works you can then build a new kernel based on your normal kernel configuration file.

If you are upgrading to FreeBSD 4.0 or above then the standard kernel build procedure (as described in Chapter 9) is deprecated. Instead, you should run these commands.

```
# cd /usr/src
# make buildkernel
# make installkernel
```

If you are upgrading to a version of FreeBSD below 4.0 you should use the standard kernel build procedure. However, it is recommended that you use the new version of config(8), using a command line like this.

```
# /usr/obj/usr/src/usr.sbin/config/config KERNELNAME
```

19.4.8 Reboot into Single User Mode

You should reboot in to single user mode to test the new kernel works. Do this by following the instructions in Section 19.4.4.

19.4.9 Install the New System Binaries

If you were building a version of FreeBSD recent enough to have used `make buildworld` then you should now use the `installworld` to install the new system binaries.

Run

```
# make installworld
```

> **Note:** If you specified variables on the `make buildworld` command line, you must specify the same variables in the `make installworld` command line. This does not necessarily hold true for other options; for example, `-j` must never be used with `installworld`.
>
> For example, if you ran:
>
> ```
> # make -DNOPROFILE=true buildworld
> ```
>
> you must install the results with:
>
> ```
> # make -DNOPROFILE=true installworld
> ```
>
> otherwise it would try and install profiled libraries that had not been built during the `make buildworld` phase.

19.4.10 Update Files Not Updated by `make world`

Remaking the world will not update certain directories (in particular, /etc, /var and /usr) with new or changed configuration files.

The simplest way to update these files is to use mergemaster(8), though it is possible to do it manually if you would prefer to do that. We strongly recommend you use mergemaster(8), however, and if you do then you can skip forward to the next section, since mergemaster(8) is very simple to use. You should read the manual page first, and make a backup of /etc in case anything goes wrong.

If you wish to do the update manually, you cannot just copy over the files from /usr/src/etc to /etc and have it work. Some of these files must be "installed" first. This is because the /usr/src/etc directory *is not* a copy of what your /etc directory should look like. In addition, there are files that should be in /etc that are not in /usr/src/etc.

The simplest way to do this by hand is to install the files into a new directory, and then work through them looking for differences.

> **Backup Your Existing** /etc: Although, in theory, nothing is going to touch this directory automatically, it is always better to be sure. So copy your existing /etc directory somewhere safe. Something like:

```
# cp -Rp /etc /etc.old
```

-R does a recursive copy, -p preserves times, ownerships on files and suchlike.

You need to build a dummy set of directories to install the new /etc and other files into. /var/tmp/root is a reasonable choice, and there are a number of subdirectories required under this as well.

```
# mkdir /var/tmp/root
# cd /usr/src/etc
# make DESTDIR=/var/tmp/root distrib-dirs distribution
```

This will build the necessary directory structure and install the files. A lot of the subdirectories that have been created under /var/tmp/root are empty and should be deleted. The simplest way to do this is to:

```
# cd /var/tmp/root
# find -d . -type d | xargs rmdir 2>/dev/null
```

This will remove all empty directories. (Standard error is redirected to /dev/null to prevent the warnings about the directories that are not empty.)

/var/tmp/root now contains all the files that should be placed in appropriate locations below /. You now have to go through each of these files, determining how they differ with your existing files.

Note that some of the files that will have been installed in /var/tmp/root have a leading ".". At the time of writing the only files like this are shell startup files in /var/tmp/root/ and /var/tmp/root/root/, although there may be others (depending on when you are reading this. Make sure you use ls -a to catch them.

The simplest way to do this is to use diff(1) to compare the two files.

```
# diff /etc/shells /var/tmp/root/etc/shells
```

This will show you the differences between your /etc/shells file and the new /etc/shells file. Use these to decide whether to merge in changes that you have made or whether to copy over your old file.

Name the New Root Directory (/var/tmp/root) **with a Time Stamp, So You Can Easily Compare Differences Between Versions:** Frequently rebuilding the world means that you have to update /etc frequently as well, which can be a bit of a chore.

You can speed this process up by keeping a copy of the last set of changed files that you merged into /etc. The following procedure gives one idea of how to do this.

1. Make the world as normal. When you want to update /etc and the other directories, give the target directory a name based on the current date. If you were doing this on the 14th of February 1998 you could do the following.

   ```
   # mkdir /var/tmp/root-19980214
   # cd /usr/src/etc
   # make DESTDIR=/var/tmp/root-19980214 \
   distrib-dirs distribution
   ```

2. Merge in the changes from this directory as outlined above.

Do not remove the `/var/tmp/root-19980214` directory when you have finished.

3. When you have downloaded the latest version of the source and remade it, follow step 1. This will give you a new directory, which might be called `/var/tmp/root-19980221` (if you wait a week between doing updates).

4. You can now see the differences that have been made in the intervening week using diff(1) to create a recursive diff between the two directories.

   ```
   # cd /var/tmp
   # diff -r root-19980214 root-19980221
   ```

   Typically, this will be a much smaller set of differences than those between `/var/tmp/root-19980221/etc` and `/etc`. Because the set of differences is smaller, it is easier to migrate those changes across into your `/etc` directory.

5. You can now remove the older of the two `/var/tmp/root-*` directories.

   ```
   # rm -rf /var/tmp/root-19980214
   ```

6. Repeat this process every time you need to merge in changes to `/etc`.

You can use date(1) to automate the generation of the directory names.

```
# mkdir /var/tmp/root-`date "+%Y%m%d"`
```

19.4.11 Update `/dev`

DEVFS: If you are using DEVFS this is unnecessary.

In most cases, the mergemaster(8) tool will realize when it is necessary to update the devices, and offer to complete it automatically. These instructions tell how to update the devices manually.

For safety's sake, this is a multi-step process.

1. Copy `/var/tmp/root/dev/MAKEDEV` to `/dev`.

   ```
   # cp /var/tmp/root/dev/MAKEDEV /dev
   ```

   If you used mergemaster(8) to update `/etc`, then your MAKEDEV script should have been updated already, though it cannot hurt to check (with diff(1)) and copy it manually if necessary.

2. Now, take a snapshot of your current `/dev`. This snapshot needs to contain the permissions, ownerships, major and minor numbers of each filename, but it should not contain the time stamps. The easiest way to do this is to use awk(1) to strip out some of the information.

   ```
   # cd /dev
   # ls -l | awk '{print $1, $2, $3, $4, $5, $6, $NF}' > /var/tmp/dev.out
   ```

3. Remake all the devices.

   ```
   # sh MAKEDEV all
   ```

4. Write another snapshot of the directory, this time to `/var/tmp/dev2.out`. Now look through these two files for any devices that you missed creating. There should not be any, but it is better to be safe than sorry.

   ```
   # diff /var/tmp/dev.out /var/tmp/dev2.out
   ```

   You are most likely to notice disk slice discrepancies which will involve commands such as

   ```
   # sh MAKEDEV sd0s1
   ```

   to recreate the slice entries. Your precise circumstances may vary.

19.4.12 Update `/stand`

Note: This step is included only for completeness. It can safely be omitted.

For the sake of completeness, you may want to update the files in `/stand` as well. These files consist of hard links to the `/stand/sysinstall` binary. This binary should be statically linked, so that it can work when no other filesystems (and in particular `/usr`) have been mounted.

```
# cd /usr/src/release/sysinstall
# make all install
```

19.4.13 Rebooting

You are now done. After you have verified that everything appears to be in the right place you can reboot the system. A simple fastboot(8) should do it.

```
# fastboot
```

19.4.14 Finished

You should now have successfully upgraded your FreeBSD system. Congratulations.

If things went slightly wrong, it is easy to rebuild a particular piece of the system. For example, if you accidently deleted `/etc/magic` as part of the upgrade or merge of `/etc`, the file(1) command will stop working. In this case, the fix would be to run:

```
# cd /usr/src/usr.bin/file
# make all install
```

19.4.15 Questions

1. Do I need to re-make the world for every change?

There is no easy answer to this one, as it depends on the nature of the change. For example, if you just ran CVSup, and it has shown the following files as being updated,

```
src/games/cribbage/instr.c
src/games/sail/pl_main.c
src/release/sysinstall/config.c
src/release/sysinstall/media.c
src/share/mk/bsd.port.mk
```

it probably is not worth rebuilding the entire world. You could just go to the appropriate sub-directories and `make all install`, and that's about it. But if something major changed, for example `src/lib/libc/stdlib` then you should either re-make the world, or at least those parts of it that are statically linked (as well as anything else you might have added that is statically linked).

At the end of the day, it is your call. You might be happy re-making the world every fortnight say, and let changes accumulate over that fortnight. Or you might want to re-make just those things that have changed, and are confident you can spot all the dependencies.

And, of course, this all depends on how often you want to upgrade, and whether you are tracking FreeBSD-STABLE or FreeBSD-CURRENT.

2. My compile failed with lots of signal 11 (or other signal number) errors. What has happened?

This is normally indicative of hardware problems. (Re)making the world is an effective way to stress test your hardware, and will frequently throw up memory problems. These normally manifest themselves as the compiler mysteriously dying on receipt of strange signals.

A sure indicator of this is if you can restart the make and it dies at a different point in the process.

In this instance there is little you can do except start swapping around the components in your machine to determine which one is failing.

3. Can I remove `/usr/obj` when I have finished?

The short answer is yes.

`/usr/obj` contains all the object files that were produced during the compilation phase. Normally, one of the first steps in the "make world" process is to remove this directory and start afresh. In this case, keeping `/usr/obj` around after you have finished makes little sense, and will free up a large chunk of disk space (currently about 340MB).

However, if you know what you are doing you can have "make world" skip this step. This will make subsequent builds run much faster, since most of sources will not need to be recompiled. The flip side of this is that subtle dependency problems can creep in, causing your build to fail in odd ways. This frequently generates noise on the FreeBSD mailing lists, when one person complains that their build has failed, not realising that it is because they have tried to cut corners.

If you want to live dangerously then make the world, passing the NOCLEAN definition to make, like this:

```
# make -DNOCLEAN world
```

4. Can interrupted builds be resumed?

This depends on how far through the process you got before you found a problem.

In general (and this is not a hard and fast rule) the "make world" process builds new copies of essential tools (such as gcc(1), and make(1)) and the system libraries. These tools and libraries are then installed. The new tools and libraries are then used to rebuild themselves, and are installed again. The entire system (now including regular user programs, such as ls(1) or grep(1)) is then rebuilt with the new system files.

If you are at the last stage, and you know it (because you have looked through the output that you were storing) then you can (fairly safely) do

```
... fix the problem ...
# cd /usr/src
# make -DNOCLEAN all
```

This will not undo the work of the previous "make world".

If you see the message

```
------------------------------------------------------------
Building everything..
------------------------------------------------------------
```

in the "make world" output then it is probably fairly safe to do so.

If you do not see that message, or you are not sure, then it is always better to be safe than sorry, and restart the build from scratch.

5. Can I use one machine as a *master* to upgrade lots of machines (NFS)?

This is a fairly easy task, and can save hours of compile time for many machines. Simply run the `buildworld` on a central machine, and then NFS mount /usr/src and /usr/obj on the remote machine and `installworld` there.

6. How can I speed up making the world?

· Run in single user mode.

· Put the /usr/src and /usr/obj directories on separate filesystems held on separate disks. If possible, put these disks on separate disk controllers.

· Better still, put these filesystems across multiple disks using the ccd(4) (concatenated disk driver) device.

· Turn off profiling (set "NOPROFILE=true" in /etc/make.conf). You almost certainly do not need it.

· Also in /etc/make.conf, set CFLAGS to something like "-O -pipe". The optimization "-O2" is much slower, and the optimization difference between "-O" and "-O2" is normally negligible. "-pipe" lets the compiler use pipes rather than temporary files for communication, which saves disk access (at the expense of memory).

- Pass the -j<n> option to make to run multiple processes in parallel. This usually helps regardless of whether you have a single or a multi processor machine.

- The filesystem holding /usr/src can be mounted (or remounted) with the noatime option. This prevents the filesystem from recording the file access time. You probably do not need this information anyway.

```
# mount -u -o noatime /usr/src
```

> **Warning:** The example assumes /usr/src is on its own filesystem. If it is not (if it is a part of /usr for example) then you will need to use that filesystem mount point, and not /usr/src.

- The filesystem holding /usr/obj can be mounted (or remounted) with the "async" option. This causes disk writes to happen asynchronously. In other words, the write completes immediately, and the data is written to the disk a few seconds later. This allows writes to be clustered together, and can be a dramatic performance boost.

> **Warning:** Keep in mind that this option makes your filesystem more fragile. With this option there is an increased chance that, should power fail, the filesystem will be in an unrecoverable state when the machine restarts.
>
> If /usr/obj is the only thing on this filesystem then it is not a problem. If you have other, valuable data on the same filesystem then ensure your backups are fresh before you enable this option.

```
# mount -u -o async /usr/obj
```

> **Warning:** As above, if /usr/obj is not on its own filesystem, replace it in the example with the name of the appropriate mount point.

Chapter 20
Linux Binary Compatibility

20.1 Synopsis

FreeBSD provides binary compatibility with several other Unix-like operating systems, including Linux. At this point, you may be asking yourself why exactly, does FreeBSD need to be able to run Linux binaries? The answer to that question is quite simple. Many companies and developers develop only for Linux, since it is the latest "hot thing" in the computing world. That leaves the rest of us FreeBSD users bugging these same companies and developers to put out native FreeBSD versions of their applications. The problem is, that most of these companies do not really realize how many people would use their product if there were FreeBSD versions too, and most continue to only develop for Linux. So what is a FreeBSD user to do? This is where the Linux binary compatibility of FreeBSD comes into play.

In a nutshell, the compatibility allows FreeBSD users to run about 90% of all Linux applications without modification. This includes applications such as **Star Office**, the Linux version of **Netscape**, **Adobe Acrobat**, **RealPlayer** 5 and 7, **VMWare**, **Oracle**, **WordPerfect**, **Doom**, **Quake**, and more. It is also reported that in some situations, Linux binaries perform better on FreeBSD than they do under Linux.

There are, however, some Linux-specific operating system features that are not supported under FreeBSD. Linux binaries will not work on FreeBSD if they overly use the Linux /proc filesystem (which is different from FreeBSD's /proc filesystem), or i386-specific calls, such as enabling virtual 8086 mode.

After reading this chapter, you will know:

- How to enable Linux binary compatibility on your system.

- How to install additional Linux shared libraries.

- How to install Linux applications on your FreeBSD system.

- The implementation details of Linux compatibility in FreeBSD.

Before reading this chapter, you should:

- Know how to install additional third-party software (Chapter 4).

20.2 Installation

Linux binary compatibility is not turned on by default. The easiest way to enable this functionality is to load the linux KLD object ("Kernel LoaDable object"). You can load this module by simply typing linux at the command prompt.

If you would like Linux compatibility to always be enabled, then you should add the following line to /etc/rc.conf:

```
linux_enable="YES"
```

This, in turn, triggers the following action in /etc/rc.i386:

```
# Start the Linux binary compatibility if requested.
#
case ${linux_enable} in
[Yy][Ee][Ss])
 echo -n ' linux'; linux > /dev/null 2>&1
 ;;
esac
```

The kldstat(8) command can be used to verify that the KLD is loaded:

```
% kldstat
Id Refs Address    Size    Name
 1    2 0xc0100000 16bdb8  kernel
 7    1 0xc24db000 d000    linux.ko
```

If for some reason you do not want to or cannot load the KLD, then you may statically link Linux binary compatibility into the kernel by adding options LINUX to your kernel configuration file. Then install your new kernel as described in Chapter 9.

20.2.1 Installing Linux Runtime Libraries

This can be done one of two ways, either by using the linux_base port, or by installing them manually.

Installing Using the linux_base Port

This is by far the easiest method to use when installing the runtime libraries. It is just like installing any other port from the ports collection[1]. Simply do the following:

```
# cd /usr/ports/emulators/linux_base
# make install distclean
```

You should now have working Linux binary compatibility. Some programs may complain about incorrect minor versions of the system libraries. In general, however, this does not seem to be a problem.

Installing Libraries Manually

If you do not have the "ports" collection installed, you can install the libraries by hand instead. You will need the Linux shared libraries that the program depends on and the runtime linker. Also, you will need to create a "shadow root" directory, /compat/linux, for Linux libraries on your FreeBSD system. Any shared libraries opened by Linux programs run under FreeBSD will look in this tree first. So, if a Linux program loads, for example, /lib/libc.so,

---

1 /usr/ports/

FreeBSD will first try to open `/compat/linux/lib/libc.so`, and if that does not exist, it will then try `/lib/libc.so`. Shared libraries should be installed in the shadow tree `/compat/linux/lib` rather than the paths that the Linux `ld.so` reports.

Generally, you will need to look for the shared libraries that Linux binaries depend on only the first few times that you install a Linux program on your FreeBSD system. After a while, you will have a sufficient set of Linux shared libraries on your system to be able to run newly imported Linux binaries without any extra work.

How to Install Additional Shared Libraries

What if you install the `linux_base` port and your application still complains about missing shared libraries? How do you know which shared libraries Linux binaries need, and where to get them? Basically, there are 2 possibilities (when following these instructions you will need to be root on your FreeBSD system).

If you have access to a Linux system, see what shared libraries the application needs, and copy them to your FreeBSD system. Look at the following example:

Let us assume you used FTP to get the Linux binary of Doom, and put it on a Linux system you have access to. You then can check which shared libraries it needs by running `ldd linuxdoom`, like so:

```
% ldd linuxdoom
libXt.so.3 (DLL Jump 3.1) => /usr/X11/lib/libXt.so.3.1.0
libX11.so.3 (DLL Jump 3.1) => /usr/X11/lib/libX11.so.3.1.0
libc.so.4 (DLL Jump 4.5pl26) => /lib/libc.so.4.6.29
```

You would need to get all the files from the last column, and put them under `/compat/linux`, with the names in the first column as symbolic links pointing to them. This means you eventually have these files on your FreeBSD system:

```
/compat/linux/usr/X11/lib/libXt.so.3.1.0
/compat/linux/usr/X11/lib/libXt.so.3 -> libXt.so.3.1.0
/compat/linux/usr/X11/lib/libX11.so.3.1.0
/compat/linux/usr/X11/lib/libX11.so.3 -> libX11.so.3.1.0
/compat/linux/lib/libc.so.4.6.29 /compat/linux/lib/libc.so.4 -> libc.so.4.6.29
```

> **Note:** Note that if you already have a Linux shared library with a matching major revision number to the first column of the `ldd` output, you will not need to copy the file named in the last column to your system, the one you already have should work. It is advisable to copy the shared library anyway if it is a newer version, though. You can remove the old one, as long as you make the symbolic link point to the new one. So, if you have these libraries on your system:
>
> ```
> /compat/linux/lib/libc.so.4.6.27
> /compat/linux/lib/libc.so.4 -> libc.so.4.6.27
> ```
>
> and you find a new binary that claims to require a later version according to the output of `ldd`:
>
> ```
> libc.so.4 (DLL Jump 4.5pl26) -> libc.so.4.6.29
> ```
>
> If it is only one or two versions out of date in the in the trailing digit then do not worry about copying `/lib/libc.so.4.6.29` too, because the program should work fine with the slightly older version. However, if you like, you can decide to replace the `libc.so` anyway, and that should leave you with:
>
> ```
> /compat/linux/lib/libc.so.4.6.29
> /compat/linux/lib/libc.so.4 -> libc.so.4.6.29
> ```

> **Note:** The symbolic link mechanism is *only* needed for Linux binaries. The FreeBSD runtime linker takes care of looking for matching major revision numbers itself and you do not need to worry about it.

20.2.2 Installing Linux ELF Binaries

ELF binaries sometimes require an extra step of "branding". If you attempt to run an unbranded ELF binary, you will get an error message like the following;

```
% ./my-linux-elf-binary
ELF binary type not known
Abort
```

To help the FreeBSD kernel distinguish between a FreeBSD ELF binary from a Linux binary, use the brandelf(1) utility.

```
% brandelf -t Linux my-linux-elf-binary
```

The GNU toolchain now places the appropriate branding information into ELF binaries automatically, so you this step should become increasingly more rare in the future.

20.2.3 Configuring the Hostname Resolver

If DNS does not work or you get this message:

```
resolv+: "bind" is an invalid keyword resolv+:
"hosts" is an invalid keyword
```

You will need to configure a `/compat/linux/etc/host.conf` file containing:

```
order hosts, bind
multi on
```

The order here specifies that `/etc/hosts` is searched first and DNS is searched second. When `/compat/linux/etc/host.conf` is not installed, Linux applications find FreeBSD's `/etc/host.conf` and complain about the incompatible FreeBSD syntax. You should remove `bind` if you have not configured a name server using the `/etc/resolv.conf` file.

20.3 Installing Mathematica

This document describes the process of installing the Linux version of **Mathematica 4.X** onto a FreeBSD system.

The Linux version of **Mathematica** runs perfectly under FreeBSD however the binaries shipped by Wolfram need to be branded so that FreeBSD knows to use the Linux ABI to execute them.

The Linux version of **Mathematica** or **Mathematica for Students** can be ordered directly from Wolfram at http://www.wolfram.com/.

20.3.1 Branding the Linux Binaries

The Linux binaries are located in the Unix directory of the **Mathematica** CDROM distributed by Wolfram. You need to copy this directory tree to your local hard drive so that you can brand the Linux binaries with brandelf(1) before running the installer:

```
# mount /cdrom
# cp -rp /cdrom/Unix/ /localdir/
# brandelf -t Linux /localdir/Files/SystemFiles/Kernel/Binaries/Linux/*
# brandelf -t Linux /localdir/Files/SystemFiles/FrontEnd/Binaries/Linux/*
# brandelf -t Linux /localdir/Files/SystemFiles/Installation/Binaries/Linux/*
# brandelf -t Linux /localdir/Files/SystemFiles/Graphics/Binaries/Linux/*
# brandelf -t Linux /localdir/Files/SystemFiles/Converters/Binaries/Linux/*
# brandelf -t Linux /localdir/Files/SystemFiles/LicenseManager/Binaries/Linux/mathlm
# cd /localdir/Installers/Linux/
# ./MathInstaller
```

Alternatively, you can simply set the default ELF brand to Linux for all unbranded binaries with the command:

```
# sysctl -w kern.fallback_elf_brand=3
```

This will make FreeBSD assume that unbranded ELF binaries use the Linux ABI and so you should be able to run the installer straight from the CDROM.

20.3.2 Obtaining Your Mathematica Password

Before you can run **Mathematica** you will have to obtain a password from Wolfram that corresponds to your "machine ID".

Once you have installed the Linux compatibility runtime libraries and unpacked **Mathematica** you can obtain the "machine ID" by running the program mathinfo in the Install directory. This machine ID is based solely on the MAC address of your first Ethernet card.

```
# cd /localdir/Files/SystemFiles/Installation/Binaries/Linux
# mathinfo
disco.example.com 7115-70839-20412
```

When you register with Wolfram, either by email, phone or fax, you will give them the "machine ID" and they will respond with a corresponding password consisting of groups of numbers. You can then enter this information when you attempt to run **Mathematica** for the first time exactly as you would for any other **Mathematica** platform.

20.3.3 Running the Mathematica Frontend over a Network

Mathematica uses some special fonts to display characters not present in any of the standard font sets (integrals, sums, Greek letters, etc.). The X protocol requires these fonts to be install *locally*. This means you will have to copy these fonts from the CDROM or from a host with **Mathematica** installed to your local machine. These fonts are normally stored in `/cdrom/Unix/Files/SystemFiles/Fonts` on the CDROM, or `/usr/local/mathematica/SystemFiles/Fonts` on your hard drive. The actual fonts are in the subdirectories `Type1` and `X`. There are several ways to use them, as described below.

The first way is to copy them into one of the existing font directories in `/usr/X11R6/lib/X11/fonts`. This will require editing the `fonts.dir` file, adding the font names to it, and changing the number of fonts on the first line. Alternatively, you should also just be able to run `mkfontdir` in the directory you have copied them to.

The second way to do this is to copy the directories to `/usr/X11R6/lib/X11/fonts`:

```
# cd /usr/X11R6/lib/X11/fonts
# mkdir X
# mkdir MathType1
# cd /cdrom/Unix/Files/SystemFiles/Fonts
# cp X/* /usr/X11R6/lib/X11/fonts/X
# cp Type1/* /usr/X11R6/lib/X11/fonts/MathType1
# cd /usr/X11R6/lib/X11/fonts/X
# mkfontdir
# cd ../MathType1
# mkfontdir
```

Now add the new font directories to your font path:

```
# xset fp+ /usr/X11R6/lib/X11/fonts/X
# xset fp+ /usr/X11R6/lib/X11/fonts/MathType1
# xset fp rehash
```

If you are using the XFree86 server, you can have these font directories loaded automatically by adding them to your `XF86Config` file.

If you *do not* already have a directory called `/usr/X11R6/lib/X11/fonts/Type1`, you can change the name of the `MathType1` directory in the example above to `Type1`.

20.4 Installing Maple

Maple is a commercial mathematics program similar to Mathematica. You must purchase this software from `http://www.maplesoft.com/` and then register there for a license file. To install this software on FreeBSD, please follow these simple steps.

1. Execute the INSTALL shell script from the product distribution. Choose the "RedHat" option when prompted by the installation program. A typical installation directory might be /usr/local/maple

2. If you have not done so, order a license for Maple from Maple Waterloo Software (http://register.maplesoft.com) and copy it to /usr/local/maple/license/license.dat

3. Install the **FLEXlm** license manager by running the INSTALL_LIC install shell script that comes with **Maple**. Specify the primary hostname for your machine for the license server.

4. Patch the usr/local/maple/bin/maple.system.type file with the following :

```
----- snip -----------------
*** maple.system.type.orig      Sun Jul  8 16:35:33 2001
--- maple.system.type   Sun Jul  8 16:35:51 2001
***************
*** 72,77 ****
--- 72,78 ----
          # the IBM RS/6000 AIX case
          MAPLE_BIN="bin.IBM_RISC_UNIX"
          ;;
+     "FreeBSD"|\
      "Linux")
          # the Linux/x86 case
        # We have two Linux implementations, one for Red Hat and
----- snip end of patch -----
```

Please note that after the "FreeBSD"|\ no other whitespace should be present.

This patch instructs **Maple** to recognize "FreeBSD" as a type of Linux system. The bin/maple shell script calls the bin/maple.system.type shell script which in turn calls uname -a to find out the operating system name. Depending on the OS name it will find out which binaries to use.

5. Start the license server.

The following script, installed as /usr/local/etc/rc.d/lmgrd.sh is a convenient way to start up lmgrd:

```
----- snip -----------

#! /bin/sh
PATH=/usr/local/sbin:/usr/local/bin:/sbin:/bin:/usr/sbin:/usr/bin:/usr/X11R6/bin
PATH=${PATH}:/usr/local/maple/bin:/usr/local/maple/FLEXlm/UNIX/LINUX
export PATH

LICENSE_FILE=/usr/local/maple/license/license.dat
LOG=/var/log/lmgrd.log

case "$1" in
start)
 lmgrd -c ${LICENSE_FILE} 2>> ${LOG} 1>&2
 echo -n " lmgrd"
 ;;
stop)
```

```
      lmgrd -c ${LICENSE_FILE} -x lmdown 2>> ${LOG} 1>&2
      ;;
*)
      echo "Usage: `basename $0` {start|stop}" 1>&2
      exit 64
      ;;
esac

exit 0
      ----- snip ------------
```

6. Test-start maple:

```
% cd /usr/local/maple/bin
% ./xmaple
```

You should be up and running. Make sure to write Maplesoft to let them know you would like a native FreeBSD version!

20.4.1 Common Pitfalls

- The FLEXlm license manager can be a difficult tool to work with. Additional documentation on the subject can be found at http://www.globetrotter.com/.

- lmgrd is known to be very picky about the license file and to core dump if there are any problems. A correct license file should look like this :

```
# =========================================================
# License File for UNIX Installations ("Pointer File")
# =========================================================
SERVER chillig ANY
#USE_SERVER
VENDOR maplelmg

FEATURE Maple maplelmg 2000.0831 permanent 1 XXXXXXXXXXXX \
        PLATFORMS=i86_r ISSUER="Waterloo Maple Inc." \
        ISSUED=11-may-2000 NOTICE=" Technische Universitat Wien" \
        SN=XXXXXXXXX
```

Note: Serial number and key 'X"ed out. "chillig" is a hostname.

Editing the license file works as long as you don't touch the "FEATURE" line (which is protected by the license key).

20.5 Installing Oracle

20.5.1 Preface

This document describes the process of installing Oracle 8.0.5 and Oracle 8.0.5.1 Enterprise Edition for Linux onto a FreeBSD machine

20.5.2 Installing the Linux Environment

Make sure you have both `linux_base` and `linux_devtools` from the ports collection installed. These ports are added to the collection after the release of FreeBSD 3.2. If you are using FreeBSD 3.2 or an older version for that matter, update your ports collection. You may want to consider updating your FreeBSD version too. If you run into difficulties with `linux_base-6.1` or `linux_devtools-6.1` you may have to use version 5.2 of these packages.

If you want to run the intelligent agent, you will also need to install the Red Hat Tcl package: `tcl-8.0.3-20.i386.rpm`. The general command for installing packages with the official RPM port is :

```
# rpm -i --ignoreos --root /compat/linux --dbpath /var/lib/rpm package
```

Installation of the package should not generate any errors.

20.5.3 Creating the Oracle Environment

Before you can install Oracle, you need to set up a proper environment. This document only describes what to do *specially* to run Oracle for Linux on FreeBSD, not what has been described in the Oracle installation guide.

Kernel Tuning

As described in the Oracle installation guide, you need to set the maximum size of shared memory. Do not use `SHMMAX` under FreeBSD. `SHMMAX` is merely calculated out of `SHMMAXPGS` and `PGSIZE`. Therefore define `SHMMAXPGS`. All other options can be used as described in the guide. For example:

```
options SHMMAXPGS=10000
options SHMMNI=100
options SHMSEG=10
options SEMMNS=200
options SEMMNI=70
options SEMMSL=61
```

Set these options to suit your intended use of Oracle.

Also, make sure you have the following options in your kernel config-file:

```
options SYSVSHM #SysV shared memory
options SYSVSEM #SysV semaphores
options SYSVMSG #SysV interprocess communication
```

Oracle Account

Create an Oracle account just as you would create any other account. The Oracle account is special only that you need to give it a Linux shell. Add `/compat/linux/bin/bash` to `/etc/shells` and set the shell for the Oracle account to `/compat/linux/bin/bash`.

Environment

Besides the normal Oracle variables, such as `ORACLE_HOME` and `ORACLE_SID` you must set the following environment variables:

Variable	Value
LD_LIBRARY_PATH	$ORACLE_HOME/lib
CLASSPATH	$ORACLE_HOME/jdbc/lib/classes111.zip
PATH	/compat/linux/bin /compat/linux/sbin /compat/linux/usr/bin /compat/linux/usr/sbin /bin /sbin /usr/bin /usr/sbin /usr/local/bin $ORACLE_HOME/bin

It is advised to set all the environment variables in `.profile`. A complete example is:

```
ORACLE_BASE=/oracle; export ORACLE_BASE
ORACLE_HOME=/oracle; export ORACLE_HOME
LD_LIBRARY_PATH=$ORACLE_HOME/lib
export LD_LIBRARY_PATH
ORACLE_SID=ORCL; export ORACLE_SID
ORACLE_TERM=386x; export ORACLE_TERM
CLASSPATH=$ORACLE_HOME/jdbc/lib/classes111.zip
export CLASSPATH
PATH=/compat/linux/bin:/compat/linux/sbin:/compat/linux/usr/bin
PATH=$PATH:/compat/linux/usr/sbin:/bin:/sbin:/usr/bin:/usr/sbin
PATH=$PATH:/usr/local/bin:$ORACLE_HOME/bin
export PATH
```

20.5.4 Installing Oracle

Due to a slight inconsistency in the Linux emulator, you need to create a directory named `.oracle` in `/var/tmp` before you start the installer. Either make it world writable or let it be owner by the oracle user. You should be able to install Oracle without any problems. If you have problems, check your Oracle distribution and/or configuration first! After you have installed Oracle, apply the patches described in the next two subsections.

A frequent problem is that the TCP protocol adapter is not installed right. As a consequence, you cannot start any TCP listeners. The following actions help solve this problem:

```
# cd $ORACLE_HOME/network/lib
# make -f ins_network.mk ntcontab.o
```

```
# cd $ORACLE_HOME/lib
# ar r libnetwork.a ntcontab.o
# cd $ORACLE_HOME/network/lib
# make -f ins_network.mk install
```

Do not forget to run `root.sh` again!

Patching root.sh

When installing Oracle, some actions, which need to be performed as `root`, are recorded in a shell script called `root.sh`. `root.sh` is written in the `orainst` directory. Apply the following patch to root.sh, to have it use to proper location of `chown` or alternatively run the script under a Linux native shell.

```
*** orainst/root.sh.orig Tue Oct 6 21:57:33 1998
--- orainst/root.sh Mon Dec 28 15:58:53 1998
***************
*** 31,37 ****
# This is the default value for CHOWN
# It will redefined later in this script for those ports
# which have it conditionally defined in ss_install.h
! CHOWN=/bin/chown
#
# Define variables to be used in this script
--- 31,37 ----
# This is the default value for CHOWN
# It will redefined later in this script for those ports
# which have it conditionally defined in ss_install.h
! CHOWN=/usr/sbin/chown
#
# Define variables to be used in this script
```

When you do not install Oracle from CD, you can patch the source for `root.sh`. It is called `rthd.sh` and is located in the `orainst` directory in the source tree.

Patching genclntsh

The script `genclntsh` is used to create a single shared client library. It is used when building the demos. Apply the following patch to comment out the definition of PATH:

```
*** bin/genclntsh.orig Wed Sep 30 07:37:19 1998
--- bin/genclntsh Tue Dec 22 15:36:49 1998
***************
*** 32,38 ****
#
# Explicit path to ensure that we're using the correct commands
#PATH=/usr/bin:/usr/ccs/bin export PATH
! PATH=/usr/local/bin:/bin:/usr/bin:/usr/X11R6/bin export PATH
#
# each product MUST provide a $PRODUCT/admin/shrept.lst
```

```
--- 32,38 ----
  #
  # Explicit path to ensure that we're using the correct commands
  #PATH=/usr/bin:/usr/ccs/bin export PATH
  ! #PATH=/usr/local/bin:/bin:/usr/bin:/usr/X11R6/bin export PATH
  #
  # each product MUST provide a $PRODUCT/admin/shrept.lst
```

20.5.5 Running Oracle

When you have followed the instructions, you should be able to run **Oracle** as if it was run on Linux itself.

20.6 Installing SAP R/3 (4.6B - IDES)

Installations of SAP Systems using FreeBSD will not be supported by the SAP support team — they only offer support for certified platforms.

20.6.1 Preface

This document describes a possible way of installing a **SAP R/3 4.6B IDES-System** with **Oracle 8.0.5** for Linux onto a FreeBSD 4.3 machine, including the installation of FreeBSD 4.3-STABLE and **Oracle 8.0.5**.

Even though this document tries to describe all important steps in a greater detail, it is not intended as a replacement for the **Oracle** and **SAP R/3** installation guides.

Please see the documentation that comes with the **SAP R/3** Linux edition for **SAP-** and **Oracle**-specific questions, as well as resources from **Oracle** and **SAP OSS**.

20.6.2 Software

The following CDROMs have been used for SAP-installation:

Name	Number	Description
KERNEL	51009113	SAP Kernel Oracle / Installation / AIX, Linux, Solaris
RDBMS	51007558	Oracle / RDBMS 8.0.5.X / Linux
EXPORT1	51010208	IDES / DB-Export / Disc 1 of 6
EXPORT2	51010209	IDES / DB-Export / Disc 2 of 6
EXPORT3	51010210	IDES / DB-Export / Disc3 of 6
EXPORT4	51010211	IDES / DB-Export / Disc4 of 6

Name	Number	Description
EXPORT5	51010212	IDES / DB-Export / Disc5 of 6
EXPORT6	51010213	IDES / DB-Export / Disc6 of 6

Additionally, I used the **Oracle 8 Server** (Pre-production version 8.0.5 for Linux, Kernel Version 2.0.33) CD which is not really necessary, and of course FreeBSD 4.3 stable (it was only a few days past 4.3 RELEASE).

20.6.3 SAP-Notes

The following notes should be read before installing **SAP R/3** or proved to be useful during installation:

Number	Title
0171356	SAP Software auf Linux: grundlegenden Anmerkungen
0201147	INST: 4.6C R/3 Inst. on UNIX - Oracle
0373203	Update / Migration Oracle 8.0.5 --> 8.0.6/8.1.6 LINUX
0072984	Release of Digital UNIX 4.0B for Oracle
0130581	R3SETUP step DIPGNTAB terminates
0144978	Your system has not been installed correctly
0162266	Questions and tips for R3SETUP on Windows NT / W2K

20.6.4 Hardware-Requirements

The following equipment is sufficient for a **SAP R/3 System** (4.6B):

Component	4.6B	4.6C
Processor	2 x 800MHz Pentium III	2 x 800MHz Pentium III
Memory	1GB ECC	2GB ECC
Hard Disc Space	50-60GB (IDES)	50-60GB (IDES)

For use in production, Xeon-Processors with large cache, high-speed disc access (SCSI, RAID hardware controller), USV and ECC-RAM is recommended. The large amount of Hard disc space is due to the preconfigured IDES System, which creates 27 GB of database files during installation. Usually after installation it is then necessary to extend some tablespaces.

I used a dual processor board with 2 800MHz Pentium III processors, Adaptec 29160 Ultra160 SCSI adapter (for accessing a 40/80 GB DLT tape drive and CDROM), Mylex AcelleRAID (2 channels, firmware 6.00-1-00 with 32MB RAM). To the Mylex Raid-controller are attached two 17GB hard discs (mirrored) and four 36GB hard discs (RAID level 5).

20.6.5 Installation of FreeBSD 4.3-STABLE

First I installed FreeBSD 4.3 stable. I did the default-installation via FTP.

Installation via FTP

Get the diskimages kern.flp and mfsroot.flp and put them on floppy disks (I got mine from ftp7.de.freebsd.org. Please choose the appropriate mirror).

```
# dd if=kern.flp of=/dev/fd0
# dd if=mfsroot.flp of=/dev/fd0
```

Do not forget to use different disks for the two images, then boot from the floppy with the kern.flp-image on it and follow instructions. I used the following disk layout:

Filesystem	Size (1k-blocks)	Size (GB)	Mounted on
/dev/da0s1a	1.016.303	1	/
/dev/da0s1b		6	<swap>
/dev/da0s1e	2.032.623	2	/var
/dev/da0s1f	8.205.339	8	/usr
/dev/da1s1e	45.734.361	45	/compat/linux/oracle
/dev/da1s1f	2.032.623	2	/compat/linux/sapmnt
/dev/da1s1g	2.032.623	2	/compat/linux/usr/sap

I had to configure and initialize the two logical drives with the Mylex software beforehand. It is located on the board itself and can be started during the boot phase of the PC.

Please note that this disk layout differs slightly from the SAP recommendations, as SAP suggests mounting the oracle-subdirectories (and some others) separately - I decided to just create them as real subdirectories for simplicity.

Get the Latest STABLE Sources

For FreeBSD 4.3 stable onwards, it is quite easy to get the latest stable sources. With the older versions of FreeBSD, I had my own script located in /etc/cvsup. Setting up **CVSup** for FreeBSD 4.3 is quite easy. As user root do the following:

```
# cp /etc/defaults/make.conf /etc/make.conf
# vi /etc/make.conf
```

The file /etc/make.conf requires the following entries to be active:

```
SUP_UPDATE=     yes
SUP=            /usr/local/bin/cvsup
SUPFLAGS=       -g -L 2
SUPHOST=        cvsup8.FreeBSD.org
SUPFILE=        /usr/share/examples/cvsup/stable-supfile
PORTSSUPFILE=   /usr/share/examples/cvsup/ports-supfile
```

```
DOCSUPFILE=    /usr/share/examples/cvsup/doc-supfile
```

Change the *SUPHOST*-value appropriately. The supfiles in `/usr/share/examples/cvsup` should be fine. If you do not want to load all the docfiles, leave the corresponding *DOCSUPFILE*-entry inactive. Starting **cvsup** to get the latest stable-sources is then very easy:

```
# cd /usr/src
# make update
```

`make world` and a New Kernel

The first thing to do is to install the sources. As user root, do the following:

```
# cd /usr/src
# make world
```

If this goes through, one can then continue creating and configuring the new kernel. Usually this is where to customize the kernel configuration file. As the computer is named `troubadix`, the natural name for the config file also is `troubadix`:

```
# cd /usr/src/sys/i386/conf
# cp GENERIC TROUBADIX
# vi TROUBADIX
```

At this stage one can define the drivers to use and not to use, etc. See the appropriate documentation or have a look at file `LINT` for some additional explanations.

One can then also include the parameters as described below Creating the new kernel then requires:

```
# cd /usr/src/sys/i386/conf
# config TROUBADIX
# cd /usr/src/sys/compile/TROUBADIX
# make depend
# make
# make install
```

After `make install` finished successfully, one should reboot the computer to have the new kernel available.

20.6.6 Installing the Linux Environment

I had some trouble downloading the required RPM-files (for 4.3 stable, 2nd May 2001), so you might try one of the following locations (if all the others fail and the following are not out of date):

- ftp7.de.freebsd.org/pub/FreeBSD/distfiles/rpm
- ftp.redhat.com/pub/redhat/linux/6.1/en/os/i386/RedHat/RPMS

Installing Linux Base-system

First the Linux base-system needs to be installed (as root):

```
# cd /usr/ports/emulators/linux_base
# make package
```

Installing Linux Development

Next, the Linux development is needed:

```
# cd /usr/ports/devel/linux_devtools
# make package
```

Installing Necessary RPMs

To start the R3SETUP-Program, pam support is needed. As this also requires some other packages, I ended up installing several packages. After that, pam still complained about a missing package, so I forced the installation and it worked. I wonder if the other packages are really needed or if it would have been sufficient to install the pam-package.

Anyway, here is the list of packages I installed:

- cracklib-2.7-5.i386.rpm
- cracklib-dicts-2.7-5.i386.rpm
- pwdb-0.60-1.i386.rpm
- pam-0.68-7.i386.rpm

I installed these packages with the following command:

```
# rpm -i --ignoreos --root /compat/linux --dbpath /var/lib/rpm <package_name>
```

except for the pam package, which I forced with

```
# rpm -i --ignoreos --nodeps --root /compat/linux --dbpath /var/lib/rpm \
  pam-0.68-7.i386.rpm
```

For **Oracle** to run the intelligent agent, I also had to install the following RedHat Tcl package (as is stated in the FreeBSD Handbook): `tcl-8.0.5-30.i386.rpm` (otherwise the relinking during **Oracle** install will not work). There are some other issues regarding relinking of **Oracle**, but that is a Oracle-Linux issue, not FreeBSD specific as far as I understand it.

20.6.7 Creating the SAP/R3 Environment

Creating the Necessary Filesystems and Mountpoints

For a simple installation, it is sufficient to create the following filesystems:

mountpoint	size in GB
/compat/linux/oracle	45 GB
/compat/linux/sapmnt	2 GB
/compat/linux/usr/sap	2 GB

I also created some links, so FreeBSD will also find the correct path:

```
# ln -s /compat/linux/oracle /oracle
# ln -s /compat/linux/sapmnt /sapmnt
# ln -s /compat/linux/usr/sap /usr/sap
```

Creating Users and Directories

SAP R/3 needs two users and three groups. The usernames depend on the **SAP** system id (SID) which consists of three letters. Some of these SIDs are reserved by **SAP** (for example *SAP* and *NIX*. For a complete list please see the SAP documentation). For the IDES installation I used *IDS*. We have therefore the following groups (group ids might differ, these are just the values I used with my installation):

group id	group name	description
100	dba	Data Base Administrator
101	sapsys	SAP System
102	oper	Data Base Operator

For a default Oracle-Installation, only group `dba` is used. As `oper`-group, one also uses group `dba` (see Oracle- and SAP-documentation for further information).

We also need the following users:

user id	username	generic name	group	additional groups	description
1000	idsadm	\<sid\>adm	sapsys	oper	SAP Administrator
1002	oraids	ora\<sid\>	dba	oper	DB Administrator

Adding the users with `adduser` requires the following (please note shell and home directory) entries for SAP-Administrator:

```
Name: idsadm        <sid>adm
Password: ******
```

```
Fullname: SAP IDES Administrator
Uid: 1000
Gid: 101 (sapsys)
Class:
Groups: sapsys dba
HOME: /home/idsadm      /home/<sid>adm
Shell: /bin/sh
```

and for Database-Administrator:

```
Name: oraids          ora<sid>
Password: ******
Fullname: Oracle IDES Administrator
Uid: 1002
Gid: 100 (dba)
Class:
Groups: dba
HOME: /oracle/IDS     /oracle/<sid>
Shell: /bin/sh
```

This should also include group oper in case you are using both groups dba and oper.

Creating Directories

These directories are usually created as separate filesystems. This depends entirely on your requirements. I choose to create them as simple directories, as they are all located on the same RAID 5 anyway:

First we will set owners and right of some directories (as user root):

```
# chmod 775 /oracle
# chmod 777 /sapmnt
# chown root:dba /oracle
# chown idsadm:sapsys /compat/linux/usr/sap
# chmow 775 /compat/linux/usr/sap
```

Second we will create directories as user ora<sid>. These will all be subdirectories of /oracle/IDS:

```
# su - oraids
# mkdir mirrlogA mirrlogB origlogA origlogB
# mkdir sapdata1 sapdata2 sapdata3 sapdata4 sapdata5 sapdata6
# mkdir saparch sapreorg
# exit
```

In the third step we create directories as user idsadm (<sid>adm):

```
# su - idsadm
# cd /usr/sap
# mkdir IDS
# mkdir trans
# exit
```

Entries in /etc/services

SAP R/3 requires some entries in file /etc/services , which will not be set correctly during installation under FreeBSD. Please add the following entries (you need at least those entries corresponding to the instance number - in this case, *00*. It'll do no harm adding all entries from *00* to *99* for *dp*, *gw*, *sp* and *ms*);

```
sapdp00 3200/tcp # SAP Dispatcher.       3200 + Instance-Number
sapgw00 3300/tcp # SAP Gateway.          3300 + Instance-Number
sapsp00 3400/tcp #                       3400 + Instance-Number
sapms00 3500/tcp #                       3500 + Instance-Number
sapmsIDS 3600/tcp # SAP Message Server.  3600 + Instance-Number
```

Necessary Locales

SAP requires at least two locales that are not part of the default RedHat installation. SAP offers the required RPMs as download from their FTP-server (which is only accessible if you are a customer with OSS-access). See note 0171356 for a list of RPMs you need.

It is also possible to just create appropriate links (for example from *de_DE* and *en_US*), but I would not recommend this for a production system (so far it worked with the IDES system without any problems, though). The following locales are needed:

```
de_DE.ISO-8859-1
en_US.ISO-8859-1
```

If they are not present, there will be some problems during the installation. If these are then subsequently ignored (eg by setting the status of the offending steps to OK in file CENTRDB.R3S), it will be impossible to log onto the SAP-system without some additional effort.

Kernel Tuning

SAP R/3 Systems need a lot of resources. I therefore added the following parameters to my kernel config-file:

```
# Set these for memory pigs (SAP and Oracle):
options MAXDSIZ="(1024*1024*1024)"
options DFLDSIZ="(1024*1024*1024)" # System V options needed.
options SYSVSHM #SYSV-style shared memory
options SHMMAXPGS=262144 #max amount of shared mem. pages
options SHMMNI=256 #max number of shared memory ident if.
options SHMSEG=100 #max shared mem.segs per process
options SYSVMSG #SYSV-style message queues
options MSGSEG=32767 #max num. of mes.segments in system
options MSGSSZ=32 #size of msg-seg. MUST be power of 2
options MSGMNB=65535 #max char. per message queue
options MSGTQL=2046 #max amount of msgs in system
options SYSVSEM #SYSV-style semaphores
options SEMMNU=256 #number of semaphore UNDO structures
options SEMMNS=1024 #number of semaphores in system
```

```
options SEMMNI=520 #number of semaphore indentifiers
options SEMUME=100 #number of UNDO keys
```

The minimum values are specified in the documentation that comes from SAP. As there is no description for Linux, see the HP-UX-section (32-bit) for further information.

20.6.8 Installing SAP R/3

Preparing SAP CDROMs

There are lots of CDROMs to mount and unmount during installation. Assuming you have enough CDROM-drives, you can just mount them all. I decided to copy the CDROM contents to corresponding directories:

```
/oracle/IDS/sapreorg/<cd-name>
```

where <cd-name> was one of KERNEL, RDBMS, EXPORT1, EXPORT2, EXPORT3, EXPORT4, EXPORT5 and EXPORT6. All the filenames should be in capital letters, otherwise use the -g option for mounting. So use the following commands:

```
# mount_cd9660 -g /dev/cd0a /mnt
# cp -R /mnt/* /oracle/IDS/sapreorg/<cd-name>
# umount /mnt
```

Running the install-script

First we need to prepare an install-directory:

```
# cd /oracle/IDS/sapreorg
# mkdir install
# cd install
```

Then the install-script is started, which will copy nearly all the relevant files into the install-directory:

```
/oracle/IDS/sapreorg/KERNEL/UNIX/INSTTOOL.SH
```

As this is an IDES-Installation with a fully customized SAP R/3 Demo-System, we have six instead of just three EXPORT-CDs. At this point the installation template CENTRDB.R3S is for installing a standard central instance (R/3 and Database), not an IDES central instance, so copy the corresponding CENTRDB.R3S from the EXPORT1 directory, otherwise R3SETUP will only ask for three EXPORT-CDs.

Start R3SETUP

Make sure LD_LIBRARY_PATH is set correctly:

```
# export LD_LIBRARY_PATH=/oracle/IDS/lib:/sapmnt/IDS/exe:/oracle/805_32/lib
```

Start R3SETUP as user root from installation directory:

```
# cd /oracle/IDS/sapreorg/install
# ./R3SETUP -f CENTRDB.R3S
```

The script then asks some questions (defaults in brackets, followed by actual input):

Question	Default	Input
Enter SAP System ID	[C11]	IDS<ret>
Enter SAP Instance Number	[00]	<ret>
Enter SAPMOUNT Directory	[/sapmnt]	<ret>
Enter name of SAP central host	[troubadix.domain.de]	<ret>
Enter name of SAP db host	[troubadix]	<ret>
Select character set	[1] (WE8DEC)	<ret>
Enter Oracle server version (1) Oracle 8.0.5, (2) Oracle 8.0.6, (3) Oracle 8.1.5, (4) Oracle 8.1.6		1<ret>
Extract Oracle Client archive	[1] (Yes, extract)	<ret>
Enter path to KERNEL CD	[/sapcd]	/oracle/IDS/sapreorg/KERNEL
Enter path to RDBMS CD	[/sapcd]	/oracle/IDS/sapreorg/RDBMS
Enter path to EXPORT1 CD	[/sapcd]	/oracle/IDS/sapreorg/EXPORT1
Directory to copy EXPORT1 CD	[/oracle/IDS/sapreorg/CD4_DIR]	<ret>
Enter path to EXPORT2 CD	[/sapcd]	/oracle/IDS/sapreorg/EXPORT2
Directory to copy EXPORT2 CD	[/oracle/IDS/sapreorg/CD5_DIR]	<ret>
Enter path to EXPORT3 CD	[/sapcd]	/oracle/IDS/sapreorg/EXPORT3
Directory to copy EXPORT3 CD	[/oracle/IDS/sapreorg/CD6_DIR]	<ret>
Enter path to EXPORT4 CD	[/sapcd]	/oracle/IDS/sapreorg/EXPORT4
Directory to copy EXPORT4 CD	[/oracle/IDS/sapreorg/CD7_DIR]	<ret>
Enter path to EXPORT5 CD	[/sapcd]	/oracle/IDS/sapreorg/EXPORT5
Directory to copy EXPORT5 CD	[/oracle/IDS/sapreorg/CD8_DIR]	<ret>
Enter path to EXPORT6 CD	[/sapcd]	/oracle/IDS/sapreorg/EXPORT6
Directory to copy EXPORT6 CD	[/oracle/IDS/sapreorg/CD9_DIR]	<ret>
Enter amount of RAM for SAP + DB		850<ret> (in Megabytes)
Service Entry Message Server	[3600]	<ret>
Enter Group-ID of sapsys	[101]	<ret>
Enter Group-ID of oper	[102]	<ret>
Enter Group-ID of dba	[100]	<ret>
Enter User-ID of <sid>adm	[1000]	<ret>
Enter User-ID of ora<sid>	[1002]	<ret>
Number of parallel procs	[2]	<ret>

If I had not copied the CDs to the different locations, then the SAP-Installer cannot find the CD needed (identified by the `LABEL.ASC`-File on CD) and would then ask you to insert / mount the CD and confirm or enter the mount path.

The `CENTRDB.R3S` might not be error-free. In my case, it requested EXPORT4 again (but indicated the correct key (6_LOCATI ON, then 7_LOCATION etc.), so one can just continue with entering the correct values. Do not get irritated.

Apart from some problems mentioned below, everything should go straight through up to the point where the Oracle database software needs to be installed.

20.6.9 Installing Oracle 8.0.5

Please see the corresponding SAP-Notes and Oracle Readmes regarding Linux and Oracle DB for possible problems. Most if not all problems stem from incompatible libraries

For more information on installing Oracle, refer to the Installing Oracle chapter.

Installing the Oracle 8.0.5 with orainst

If **Oracle 8.0.5** is to be used, some additional libraries are needed for successfully relinking, as Oracle 8.0.5 was linked with an old glibc (RedHat 6.0), but RedHat 6.1 already uses a new glibc. So you have to install the following additional packages to ensure that linking will work:

```
compat-libs-5.2-2.i386.rpm
```

```
compat-glibc-5.2-2.0.7.2.i386.rpm
```

```
compat-egcs-5.2-1.0.3a.1.i386.rpm
```

```
compat-egcs-c++-5.2-1.0.3a.1.i386.rpm
```

```
compat-binutils-5.2-2.9.1.0.23.1.i386.rpm
```

See the corresponding SAP-Notes or Oracle Readmes for further information. If this is no option (at the time of installation I did not have enough time to check this), one could use the original binaries, or use the relinked binaries from an original RedHat System.

For compiling the intelligent agent, the RedHat Tcl package must be installed. If you cannot get `tcl-8.0.3-20.i386.rpm`, a newer one like `tcl-8.0.5-30.i386.rpm` for RedHat 6.1 should also do.

Apart from relinking, the installation is straightforward:

```
# su - oraids
# export TERM=xterm
# export ORACLE_TERM=xterm
# export ORACLE_HOME=/oracle/IDS
# cd /ORACLE_HOME/orainst_sap
# ./orainst
```

Confirm all Screens with Enter until the software is installed, except that one has to deselect the *Oracle On-Line Text Viewer* , as this is not currently available for Linux. Oracle then wants to relink with `i386-glibc20-linux-gcc` instead of the available `gcc`, `egcs` or `i386-redhat-linux-gcc` .

Due to time constrains I decided to use the binaries from an **Oracle 8.0.5 PreProduction** release, after the first attempt at getting the version from the RDBMS-CD working, failed, and finding / accessing the correct RPMs was a nightmare at that time.

Installing the Oracle 8.0.5 Pre-Production release for Linux (Kernel 2.0.33)

This installation is quite easy. Mount the CD, start the installer. It will then ask for the location of the Oracle home directory, and copy all binaries there. I did not delete the remains of my previous RDBMS-installation tries, though.

Afterwards, Oracle Database could be started with no problems.

20.6.10 Continue with SAP R/3 Installation

First check the environment settings of users `idsamd` (<sid>adm) and `oraids` (ora<sid>). They should now both have the files `.profile`, `.login` and `.cshrc` which are all using `hostname`. In case the system's hostname is the fully qualified name, you need to change `hostname` to `hostname -s` within all three files.

Database Load

Afterwards, R3SETUP can either be restarted or continued (depending on whether exit was chosen or not). R3SETUP then creates the tablespaces and loads the data from EXPORT1 to EXPORT6 (remember, it is an IDES system, otherwise it would only be EXPORT1 to EXPORT3) with R3load into the database.

When the database load is finished (might take a few hours), some passwords are requested. For test installations, one can use the well known default passwords (use different ones if security is an issue!):

Question	Input
Enter Password for sapr3	sap<ret>
Confirum Password for sapr3	sap<ret>
Enter Password for sys	change_on_install<ret>
Confirm Password for sys	change_on_install<ret>
Enter Password for system	manager<ret>
Confirm Password for system	manager<ret>

At this point I had a few problems with `dipgntab`.

Listener

Start the Oracle-Listener as user `oraids` (ora<sid>) as follows:

```
umask 0; lsnrctl start
```

Otherwise you might get ORA-12546 as the sockets will not have the correct permissions. See SAP note 072984.

20.6.11 Post-installation Steps

Request SAP R/3 License Key

This is needed, as the temporary license is only valid for four weeks. Do not forget to enter the correct Operating System: (X) Other: *FreeBSD 4.3 Stable*. First get the hardware key. Log on as user `idsadm` and call `saplicense`:

```
# /sapmnt/IDS/exe/saplicense -get
```

Calling `saplicense` without options gives a list of options. Upon receiving the license key, it can be installed using

```
# /sapmnt/IDS/exe/saplicense -install
```

You are then required to enter the following values:

```
SAP SYSTEM ID    = <SID, 3 chars>
CUSTOMER KEY     = <hardware key, 11 chars>
INSTALLATION NO = <installation, 10 digits>
EXPIRATION DATE = <yyyymmdd, usually "99991231">
LICENSE KEY      = <license key, 24 chars>
```

Creating Users

Create a user within client 000 (for some tasks required to be done within client 000, but with a user different from users `sap*` and `ddic`). As a username, I usually choose *wartung* (or *service* in English). Profiles required are *sap_new* and *sap_all*. For additional safety the passwords of default users within all clients should be changed (this includes users `sap*` and `ddic`).

Configure Transport System, Profile, Operation Modes, Etc.

Within client 000, user different from `ddic` and sap*, do at least the following:

Task	Transaction
Configure Transport System, eg as *Stand-Alone Transport Domain Entity*	STMS
Create / Edit Profile for System	RZ10
Maintain Operation Modes and Instances	RZ04

These and all the other post-installation steps are thoroughly described in SAP installation guides.

Edit init<sid>.sap (initIDS.sap)

The file `/oracle/IDS/dbs/initIDS.sap` contains the SAP backup profile. Here the size of the tape to be used, type of compression and so on need to be defined. To get this running with `sapdba` / `brbackup`, I changed the following values:

```
compress = hardware
archive_function = copy_delete_save
cpio_flags = "-ov --format=newc --block-size=128 --quiet"
cpio_in_flags = "-iuv --block-size=128 --quiet"
tape_size = 38000M
tape_address = /dev/nsa0
tape_address_rew = /dev/sa0
```

Explanations:

compress The tape I use is a HP DLT1 which does hardware compression.

archive_function This defines the default behavior for saving Oracle archive logs: New logfiles are saved to tape, already saved logfiles are saved again and are then deleted. This prevents lots of trouble if one needs to recover the database, and one of the archive-tapes has gone bad.

cpio_flags Default is to use -B which sets blocksize to 5120 Bytes. For DLT-Tapes, HP recommends at least 32K blocksize, so I used --block-size=128 for 64K. --format=newc is needed I have inode numbers greater than 65535. The last option --quiet is needed as otherwise brbackup complains as soon as cpio outputs the numbers of blocks saved.

cpio_in_flags Flags needed for loading data back from tape. Format is recognized automagically.

tape_size This usually gives the raw storage capability of the tape. For security reason (we use hardware compression), the

value is slightly lower than the actual value.

tape_address The non-rewindable device to be used with cpio.

tape_address_rew The rewindable device to be used with cpio.

Configuration Issues after Installation

The following SAP-parameters should be tuned after installation:

Name	Value
ztta/roll_extension	250000000
abap/heap_area_dia	300000000
abap/heap_area_nondia	400000000
em/initial_size_MB	256
em/blocksize_kB	1024
ipc/shm_psize_40	70000000

SAP-Note 0013026:

Name	Value
ztta/dynpro_area	2500000

SAP-Note 0157246:

Name	Value
rdisp/ROLL_MAXFS	16000
rdisp/PG_MAXFS	30000

Note: With the above parameters, on a system with 1 gigabyte of memory, one may find memory consumption similar to:

```
Mem: 547M Active, 305M Inact, 109M Wired, 40M Cache, 112M Buf, 3492K Free
```

20.6.12 Problems During Installation

OSUSERSIDADM_IND_ORA During R3SETUP

If R3SETUP complains at this stage, edit file CENTRDB.R3S. Locate [OSUSERSIDADM_IND_ORA] and edit the following values:

```
HOME=/home/idsadm (was empty)
STATUS=OK (had status ERROR)
```

Then you can restart R3SETUP with:

```
# ./R3SETUP -f CENTRDB.R3S
```

OSUSERDBSID_IND_ORA During R3SETUP

Possibly R3SETUP also complains at this stage. Just edit CENTRDB.R3S. Locate [OSUSERDBSID_IND_ORA] and edit the following value in that section:

```
STATUS=OK
```

Then just restart R3SETUP again:

```
# ./R3SETUP -f CENTRDB.R3S
```

oraview.vrf FILE NOT FOUND During Oracle Installation

You have not deselected *Oracle On-Line Text Viewer* before starting the installation. This is marked for installation even though this option is currently not available for Linux. Deselect this product inside the Oracle installation menu and restart installation.

TEXTENV_INVALID During R3SETUP, RFC or SAPGUI Start

If this error is encountered, the correct locale is missing. SAP note 0171356 lists the necessary RPMs that need be installed (eg *saplocales-1.0-3*, *saposcheck-1.0-1* for RedHat 6.1). In case you ignored all the related errors and set the corresponding status from ERROR to OK (in CENTRDB.R3S) every time R3SETUP complained and just restarted R3SETUP, the SAP-System will not be properly configured and you will then not be able to connect to the system with a `sapgui`, even though the system can be started. Trying to connect with the old Linux `sapgui` gave the following messages:

```
Sat May 5 14:23:14 2001
*** ERROR => no valid userarea given [trgmsgo. 0401]
Sat May 5 14:23:22 2001
*** ERROR => ERROR NR 24 occured [trgmsgi. 0410]
*** ERROR => Error when generating text environment. [trgmsgi. 0435]
*** ERROR => function failed [trgmsgi. 0447]
*** ERROR => no socket operation allowed [trxio.c 3363]
Speicherzugriffsfehler
```

This behavior is due to SAP R/3 being unable to correctly assign a locale and also not being properly configured itself (missing entries in some database tables). To be able to connect to SAP, add the following entries to file DEFAULT.PFL (see note 0043288):

```
abap/set_etct_env_at_new_mode =0
install/collate/active =0
rscp/TCP0B =TCP0B
```

Restart the SAP system. Now one can connect to the system, even though country-specific language settings might not work as expected. After correcting country-settings (and providing the correct locales), these entries can be removed from DEFAULT.PFL and the SAP system can be restarted.

ORA-12546. Start Listener with Correct Permissions

Start the Oracle Listener as user `oraids` with the following commands:

```
# umask 0; lsnrctl start
```

Otherwise one might get ORA-12546 as the sockets will not have the correct permissions. See SAP note 0072984.

[DIPGNTAB_IND_IND] During R3SETUP

In general, see SAP note 0130581 (R3SETUP step `DIPGNTAB` terminates). During this specific installation, for some reasons the installation process was not using the proper SAP system name "IDS", but the empty string "" instead. This lead to some minor problems with accessing directories, as the paths are generated dynamically using <sid> (in this case IDS). So instead of accessing:

```
/usr/sap/IDS/SYS/...
/usr/sap/IDS/DVMGS00
```

the following path were used:

```
/usr/sap//SYS/...
/usr/sap/D00i
```

To continue with the installation, I created a link and an additional directory:

```
# pwd
/compat/linux/usr/sap
# ls -l
total 4
drwxr-xr-x 3  idsadm sapsys 512 May 5 11:20 D00
drwxr-x--x 5  idsadm sapsys 512 May 5 11:35 IDS
lrwxr-xr-x 1  root   sapsys 7 May 5 11:35 SYS -> IDS/SYS
drwxrwxr-x 2  idsadm sapsys 512 May 5 13:00 tmp
drwxrwxr-x 11 idsadm sapsys 512 May 4 14:20 trans
```

I also found SAP notes (0029227 and 0008401) describing this behavior.

[RFCRSWBOINI_IND_IND] During R3SETUP

Set STATUS of the offending step from ERROR to OK (file `CENTRDB.R3S`) and restart R3SETUP. After installation, you have to execute the report `RSWBOINS` from transaction SE38. See SAP note 0162266 for additional information about phase `RFCRSWBOINI` and `RFCRADDBDIF`.

[RFCRADDBDIF_IND_IND] During R3SETUP

Set STATUS of the offending step from ERROR to OK (file `CENTRDB.R3S`) and restart R3SETUP. After installation, you have to execute the report `RADDBDIF` from transaction SE38. See SAP note 0162266 for further information.

20.7 Advanced Topics

If you are curious as to how the Linux binary compatibility works, this is the section you want to read. Most of what follows is based heavily on an email written to FreeBSD chat mailing list <freebsd-chat@FreeBSD.org> by Terry Lambert <tlambert@primenet.com> (Message ID: <199906020108.SAA07001@usr09.primenet.com>).

20.7.1 How Does It Work?

FreeBSD has an abstraction called an "execution class loader". This is a wedge into the execve(2) system call.

What happens is that FreeBSD has a list of loaders, instead of a single loader with a fallback to the #! loader for running any shell interpreters or shell scripts.

Historically, the only loader on the Unix platform examined the magic number (generally the first 4 or 8 bytes of the file) to see if it was a binary known to the system, and if so, invoked the binary loader.

If it was not the binary type for the system, the execve(2) call returned a failure, and the shell attempted to start executing it as shell commands.

The assumption was a default of "whatever the current shell is".

Later, a hack was made for sh(1) to examine the first two characters, and if they were : \n, then it invoked the csh(1) shell instead (we believe SCO first made this hack).

What FreeBSD does now is go through a list of loaders, with a generic #! loader that knows about interpreters as the characters which follow to the next whitespace next to last, followed by a fallback to /bin/sh.

For the Linux ABI support, FreeBSD sees the magic number as an ELF binary (it makes no distinction between FreeBSD, Solaris, Linux, or any other OS which has an ELF image type, at this point).

The ELF loader looks for a specialized *brand*, which is a comment section in the ELF image, and which is not present on SVR4/Solaris ELF binaries.

For Linux binaries to function, they must be *branded* as type Linux; from brandelf(1):

```
# brandelf -t Linux file
```

When this is done, the ELF loader will see the Linux brand on the file.

When the ELF loader sees the Linux brand, the loader replaces a pointer in the proc structure. All system calls are indexed through this pointer (in a traditional Unix system, this would be the sysent[] structure array, containing the system calls). In addition, the process flagged for special handling of the trap vector for the signal trampoline code, and sever other (minor) fix-ups that are handled by the Linux kernel module.

The Linux system call vector contains, among other things, a list of sysent[] entries whose addresses reside in the kernel module.

When a system call is called by the Linux binary, the trap code dereferences the system call function pointer off the proc structure, and gets the Linux, not the FreeBSD, system call entry points.

In addition, the Linux mode dynamically *reroots* lookups; this is, in effect, what the union option to FS mounts (*not* the unionfs!) does. First, an attempt is made to lookup the file in the /compat/linux/original-path directory, *then* only if that fails, the lookup is done in the /original-path directory. This makes sure that binaries that require other binaries can run (e.g., the Linux toolchain can all run under Linux ABI support). It also means that the Linux binaries can load and exec FreeBSD binaries, if there are no corresponding Linux binaries present, and that you could place a uname(1) command in the /compat/linux directory tree to ensure that the Linux binaries could not tell they were not running on Linux.

In effect, there is a Linux kernel in the FreeBSD kernel; the various underlying functions that implement all of the services provided by the kernel are identical to both the FreeBSD system call table entries, and the Linux system call table entries: file system operations, virtual memory operations, signal delivery, System V IPC, etc... The only difference is that FreeBSD binaries get the FreeBSD *glue* functions, and Linux binaries get the Linux *glue* functions (most older OS's only had their own *glue* functions: addresses of functions in a static global `sysent[]` structure array, instead of addresses of functions dereferenced off a dynamically initialized pointer in the `proc` structure of the process making the call).

Which one is the native FreeBSD ABI? It does not matter. Basically the only difference is that (currently; this could easily be changed in a future release, and probably will be after this) the FreeBSD *glue* functions are statically linked into the kernel, and the Linux glue functions can be statically linked, or they can be accessed via a kernel module.

Yeah, but is this really emulation? No. It is an ABI implementation, not an emulation. There is no emulator (or simulator, to cut off the next question) involved.

So why is it sometimes called "Linux emulation"? To make it hard to sell FreeBSD! Really, it is because the historical implementation was done at a time when there was really no word other than that to describe what was going on; saying that FreeBSD ran Linux binaries was not true, if you did not compile the code in or load a module, and there needed to be a word to describe what was being loaded—hence "the Linux emulator".

III. Appendices

Appendix A.
Obtaining FreeBSD

A.1 CDROM Publishers

A.1.1 Retail Boxed Products

FreeBSD is available as a boxed product (FreeBSD CDs, additional software, and printed documentation) from several retailers:

*   CompUSA
    WWW: `http://www.compusa.com/`

*   Frys Electronics
    WWW: `http://www.frys.com/`

*   Micro Center
    WWW: `http://www.microcenter.com/`

A.1.2 CD Sets

FreeBSD CD sets are available from many online retailers:

*   Daemon News
    2672 Bayshore Parkway, Suite 610
    Mountain View, CA 94043
    USA
    Phone: +1 650 694-4949
    Email: `<sales@daemonnews.org>`
    WWW: `http://www.bsdmall.com/`

*   Wind River Systems
    500 Wind River Way
    Alameda, CA 94501
    USA

WWW: http://www.freebsdmall.com/

A.1.3 Distributors

If you are a reseller and want to carry FreeBSD CDROM products, please contact a distributor :

* Cylogistics
  2672 Bayshore Parkway, Suite 610
  Mountain View, CA 94043
  USA
  Phone: +1 650 694-4949
  Fax: +1 650 694-4953
  Email: <sales@cylogistics.com>
  WWW: http://www.cylogistics.com/

* Ingram Micro
  WWW: http://www.ingrammicro.com/

* Navarre
  WWW: http://www.navarre.com/

A.2 DVD Publishers

FreeBSD is available on DVD from:

FreeBSD Services Ltd
11 Lapwing Close
Bicester
OX26 6XR
United Kingdom
WWW: http://www.freebsd-services.com/

A.3 FTP Sites

The official sources for FreeBSD are available via anonymous FTP from:

`ftp://ftp.FreeBSD.org/pub/FreeBSD/`.

The FreeBSD mirror sites database[11] is more accurate than the mirror listing in the Handbook, as it gets its information from the DNS rather than relying on static lists of hosts.

Additionally, FreeBSD is available via anonymous FTP from the following mirror sites. If you choose to obtain FreeBSD via anonymous FTP, please try to use a site near you.

Argentina, Australia, Brazil, Canada, China, Czech Republic, Denmark, Estonia, Finland, France, Germany, Hong Kong, Hungary, Ireland, Israel, Japan, Korea, Lithuania, Netherlands, New Zealand, Poland, Portugal, Romania, Russia, Saudi Arabia, South Africa, Spain, Slovak Republic, Slovenia, Sweden, Taiwan, Thailand, UK, Ukraine, USA.

Argentina

>In case of problems, please contact the hostmaster <hostmaster@ar.FreeBSD.org> for this domain.
>
>- `ftp://ftp.ar.FreeBSD.org/pub/FreeBSD/`

Australia

>In case of problems, please contact the hostmaster <hostmaster@au.FreeBSD.org> for this domain.
>
>- `ftp://ftp.au.FreeBSD.org/pub/FreeBSD/`
>- `ftp://ftp2.au.FreeBSD.org/pub/FreeBSD/`
>- `ftp://ftp3.au.FreeBSD.org/pub/FreeBSD/`
>- `ftp://ftp4.au.FreeBSD.org/pub/FreeBSD/`

Brazil

>In case of problems, please contact the hostmaster <hostmaster@br.FreeBSD.org> for this domain.
>
>- `ftp://ftp.br.FreeBSD.org/pub/FreeBSD/`
>- `ftp://ftp2.br.FreeBSD.org/pub/FreeBSD/`
>- `ftp://ftp3.br.FreeBSD.org/pub/FreeBSD/`
>- `ftp://ftp4.br.FreeBSD.org/pub/FreeBSD/`
>- `ftp://ftp5.br.FreeBSD.org/pub/FreeBSD/`
>- `ftp://ftp6.br.FreeBSD.org/pub/FreeBSD/`
>- `ftp://ftp7.br.FreeBSD.org/pub/FreeBSD/`

---

11 http://www.freebsdmirrors.org/

Canada

In case of problems, please contact the hostmaster <hostmaster@ca.FreeBSD.org> for this domain.

- `ftp://ftp.ca.FreeBSD.org/pub/FreeBSD/`

China

In case of problems, please contact the hostmaster <phj@cn.FreeBSD.org> for this domain.

- `ftp://ftp.cn.FreeBSD.org/pub/FreeBSD/`

Czech Republic

In case of problems, please contact the hostmaster <hostmaster@cz.FreeBSD.org> for this domain.

- `ftp://ftp.cz.FreeBSD.org/pub/FreeBSD/` Contact: <calda@dzungle.ms.mff.cuni.cz>

Denmark

In case of problems, please contact the hostmaster <hostmaster@dk.FreeBSD.org> for this domain.

- `ftp://ftp.dk.FreeBSD.org/pub/FreeBSD/`
- `ftp://ftp2.dk.FreeBSD.org/pub/FreeBSD/`
- `ftp://ftp3.dk.FreeBSD.org/pub/FreeBSD/`

Estonia

In case of problems, please contact the hostmaster <hostmaster@ee.FreeBSD.org> for this domain.

- `ftp://ftp.ee.FreeBSD.org/pub/FreeBSD/`

Finland

In case of problems, please contact the hostmaster <hostmaster@fi.FreeBSD.org> for this domain.

- `ftp://ftp.fi.FreeBSD.org/pub/FreeBSD/`

France

In case of problems, please contact the hostmaster <hostmaster@fr.FreeBSD.org> for this domain.

- `ftp://ftp.fr.FreeBSD.org/pub/FreeBSD/`
- `ftp://ftp2.fr.FreeBSD.org/pub/FreeBSD/`

- `ftp://ftp3.fr.FreeBSD.org/pub/FreeBSD/`
- `ftp://ftp4.fr.FreeBSD.org/pub/FreeBSD/`
- `ftp://ftp5.fr.FreeBSD.org/pub/FreeBSD/`
- `ftp://ftp6.fr.FreeBSD.org/pub/FreeBSD/`

Germany

In case of problems, please contact the mirror admins <`de-bsd-hubs@de.FreeBSD.org` > for this domain.

- `ftp://ftp.de.FreeBSD.org/pub/FreeBSD/`
- `ftp://ftp2.de.FreeBSD.org/pub/FreeBSD/`
- `ftp://ftp3.de.FreeBSD.org/pub/FreeBSD/`
- `ftp://ftp4.de.FreeBSD.org/pub/FreeBSD/`
- `ftp://ftp5.de.FreeBSD.org/pub/FreeBSD/`
- `ftp://ftp6.de.FreeBSD.org/pub/FreeBSD/`
- `ftp://ftp7.de.FreeBSD.org/pub/FreeBSD/`

Hong Kong

- `ftp://ftp.hk.super.net/pub/FreeBSD/` Contact: <`ftp-admin@HK.Super.NET`>.

Hungary

In case of problems, please contact the hostmaster <`mohacsi@ik.bme.hu`> for this domain.

- `ftp://ftp.hu.FreeBSD.org/pub/FreeBSD/`

Ireland

In case of problems, please contact the hostmaster <`hostmaster@ie.FreeBSD.org`> for this domain.

- `ftp://ftp.ie.FreeBSD.org/pub/FreeBSD/`

Israel

In case of problems, please contact the hostmaster <`hostmaster@il.FreeBSD.org`> for this domain.

- `ftp://ftp.il.FreeBSD.org/pub/FreeBSD/`
- `ftp://ftp2.il.FreeBSD.org/pub/FreeBSD/`

Japan

In case of problems, please contact the hostmaster <hostmaster@jp.FreeBSD.org> for this domain.

- `ftp://ftp.jp.FreeBSD.org/pub/FreeBSD/`
- `ftp://ftp2.jp.FreeBSD.org/pub/FreeBSD/`
- `ftp://ftp3.jp.FreeBSD.org/pub/FreeBSD/`
- `ftp://ftp4.jp.FreeBSD.org/pub/FreeBSD/`
- `ftp://ftp5.jp.FreeBSD.org/pub/FreeBSD/`
- `ftp://ftp6.jp.FreeBSD.org/pub/FreeBSD/`

Korea

In case of problems, please contact the hostmaster <hostmaster@kr.FreeBSD.org> for this domain.

- `ftp://ftp.kr.FreeBSD.org/pub/FreeBSD/`
- `ftp://ftp2.kr.FreeBSD.org/pub/FreeBSD/`
- `ftp://ftp3.kr.FreeBSD.org/pub/FreeBSD/`
- `ftp://ftp4.kr.FreeBSD.org/pub/FreeBSD/`
- `ftp://ftp5.kr.FreeBSD.org/pub/FreeBSD/`
- `ftp://ftp6.kr.FreeBSD.org/pub/FreeBSD/`

Lithuania

In case of problems, please contact the hostmaster <hostmaster@lt.FreeBSD.org> for this domain.

- `ftp://ftp.lt.FreeBSD.org/pub/FreeBSD/`

Netherlands

In case of problems, please contact the hostmaster <hostmaster@nl.FreeBSD.org> for this domain.

- `ftp://ftp.nl.FreeBSD.org/pub/FreeBSD/`

New Zealand

In case of problems, please contact the hostmaster <hostmaster@nz.FreeBSD.org> for this domain.

- `ftp://ftp.nz.FreeBSD.org/pub/FreeBSD/`

Poland

In case of problems, please contact the hostmaster <hostmaster@pl.FreeBSD.org> for this domain.

- ftp://ftp.pl.FreeBSD.org/pub/FreeBSD/

Portugal

In case of problems, please contact the hostmaster <hostmaster@pt.FreeBSD.org> for this domain.

- ftp://ftp.pt.FreeBSD.org/pub/FreeBSD/
- ftp://ftp2.pt.FreeBSD.org/pub/FreeBSD/

Romania

In case of problems, please contact the hostmaster <hostmaster@ro.FreeBSD.org> for this domain.

- ftp://ftp.ro.FreeBSD.org/pub/FreeBSD/

Russia

In case of problems, please contact the hostmaster <hostmaster@ru.FreeBSD.org> for this domain.

- ftp://ftp.ru.FreeBSD.org/pub/FreeBSD/
- ftp://ftp2.ru.FreeBSD.org/pub/FreeBSD/
- ftp://ftp3.ru.FreeBSD.org/pub/FreeBSD/
- ftp://ftp4.ru.FreeBSD.org/pub/FreeBSD/

Saudi Arabia

In case of problems, please contact <ftpadmin@isu.net.sa>

- ftp://ftp.isu.net.sa/pub/mirrors/ftp.freebsd.org/

South Africa

In case of problems, please contact the hostmaster <hostmaster@za.FreeBSD.org> for this domain.

- ftp://ftp.za.FreeBSD.org/pub/FreeBSD/
- ftp://ftp2.za.FreeBSD.org/pub/FreeBSD/
- ftp://ftp3.za.FreeBSD.org/FreeBSD/

Slovak Republic

In case of problems, please contact the hostmaster <hostmaster@sk.FreeBSD.org> for this domain.

- ftp://ftp.sk.FreeBSD.org/pub/FreeBSD/

Slovenia

In case of problems, please contact the hostmaster <hostmaster@si.FreeBSD.org> for this domain.

- ftp://ftp.si.FreeBSD.org/pub/FreeBSD/

Spain

In case of problems, please contact the hostmaster <hostmaster@es.FreeBSD.org> for this domain.

- ftp://ftp.es.FreeBSD.org/pub/FreeBSD/

Sweden

In case of problems, please contact the hostmaster <hostmaster@se.FreeBSD.org> for this domain.

- ftp://ftp.se.FreeBSD.org/pub/FreeBSD/
- ftp://ftp2.se.FreeBSD.org/pub/FreeBSD/
- ftp://ftp3.se.FreeBSD.org/pub/FreeBSD/

Taiwan

In case of problems, please contact the hostmaster <hostmaster@tw.FreeBSD.org> for this domain.

- ftp://ftp.tw.FreeBSD.org/pub/FreeBSD/
- ftp://ftp2.tw.FreeBSD.org/pub/FreeBSD/
- ftp://ftp3.tw.FreeBSD.org/pub/FreeBSD/
- ftp://ftp4.tw.FreeBSD.org/pub/FreeBSD/

Thailand

- ftp://ftp.nectec.or.th/pub/FreeBSD/ Contact: <ftpadmin@ftp.nectec.or.th>.

Ukraine

- `ftp://ftp.ua.FreeBSD.org/pub/FreeBSD/` Contact: <freebsd-mnt@lucky.net>.

UK

In case of problems, please contact the hostmaster <hostmaster@uk.FreeBSD.org> for this domain.

- `ftp://ftp.uk.FreeBSD.org/pub/FreeBSD/`
- `ftp://ftp2.uk.FreeBSD.org/pub/FreeBSD/`
- `ftp://ftp3.uk.FreeBSD.org/pub/FreeBSD/`
- `ftp://ftp4.uk.FreeBSD.org/pub/FreeBSD/`
- `ftp://ftp5.uk.FreeBSD.org/pub/FreeBSD/`

USA

In case of problems, please contact the hostmaster <hostmaster@FreeBSD.org> for this domain.

- `ftp://ftp2.FreeBSD.org/pub/FreeBSD/`
- `ftp://ftp3.FreeBSD.org/pub/FreeBSD/`
- `ftp://ftp4.FreeBSD.org/pub/FreeBSD/`
- `ftp://ftp5.FreeBSD.org/pub/FreeBSD/`
- `ftp://ftp6.FreeBSD.org/pub/FreeBSD/`
- `ftp://ftp7.FreeBSD.org/pub/FreeBSD/`
- `ftp://ftp8.FreeBSD.org/pub/FreeBSD/`
- `ftp://ftp9.FreeBSD.org/pub/os/FreeBSD/`
- `ftp://ftp10.FreeBSD.org/pub/FreeBSD/`
- `ftp://ftp11.FreeBSD.org/pub/FreeBSD/`
- `ftp://ftp12.FreeBSD.org/pub/FreeBSD/`
- `ftp://ftp13.FreeBSD.org/pub/FreeBSD/`

A.4 Anonymous CVS

A.4.1 Introduction

Anonymous CVS (or, as it is otherwise known, *anoncvs*) is a feature provided by the CVS utilities bundled with FreeBSD for synchronizing with a remote CVS repository. Among other things, it allows users of FreeBSD to perform, with no special privileges, read-only CVS operations against one of the FreeBSD project's official anoncvs servers. To use it, one simply sets the CVSROOT environment variable to point at the appropriate anoncvs server, provides the well-known password "anoncvs" with the cvs login command, and then uses the cvs(1) command to access it like any local repository.

While it can also be said that the CVSup and *anoncvs* services both perform essentially the same function, there are various trade-offs which can influence the user's choice of synchronization methods. In a nutshell, **CVSup** is much more efficient in its usage of network resources and is by far the most technically sophisticated of the two, but at a price. To use **CVSup**, a special client must first be installed and configured before any bits can be grabbed, and then only in the fairly large chunks which **CVSup** calls *collections*.

Anoncvs, by contrast, can be used to examine anything from an individual file to a specific program (like ls or grep) by referencing the CVS module name. Of course, **anoncvs** is also only good for read-only operations on the CVS repository, so if it is your intention to support local development in one repository shared with the FreeBSD project bits then **CVSup** is really your only option.

A.4.2 Using Anonymous CVS

Configuring cvs(1) to use an Anonymous CVS repository is a simple matter of setting the CVSROOT environment variable to point to one of the FreeBSD project's *anoncvs* servers. At the time of this writing, the following servers are available:

- *USA*: :pserver:anoncvs@anoncvs.FreeBSD.org:/home/ncvs (Use cvs login and enter the password "anoncvs" when prompted.)

Since CVS allows one to "check out" virtually any version of the FreeBSD sources that ever existed (or, in some cases, will exist, you need to be familiar with the revision (-r) flag to cvs(1) and what some of the permissible values for it in the FreeBSD Project repository are.

There are two kinds of tags, revision tags and branch tags. A revision tag refers to a specific revision. Its meaning stays the same from day to day. A branch tag, on the other hand, refers to the latest revision on a given line of development, at any given time. Because a branch tag does not refer to a specific revision, it may mean something different tomorrow than it means today.

Section A.7 contains revision tags that users might be interested in. Again, none of these are valid for the ports collection since the ports collection does not have multiple revisions.

When you specify a branch tag, you normally receive the latest versions of the files on that line of development. If you wish to receive some past version, you can do so by specifying a date with the -D date flag. See the cvs(1) manual page for more details.

A.4.3 Examples

While it really is recommended that you read the manual page for cvs(1) thoroughly before doing anything, here are some quick examples which essentially show how to use Anonymous CVS:

Example A-1. Checking Out Something from -CURRENT (ls(1)) and Deleting It Again:

```
% setenv CVSROOT :pserver:anoncvs@anoncvs.FreeBSD.org:/home/ncvs
% cvs login
At the prompt, enter the password "anoncvs".
% cvs co ls
% cvs release -d ls
% cvs logout
```

Example A-2. Checking Out the Version of ls(1) in the 3.X-STABLE Branch:

```
% setenv CVSROOT :pserver:anoncvs@anoncvs.FreeBSD.org:/home/ncvs
% cvs login
At the prompt, enter the password "anoncvs".
% cvs co -rRELENG_3 ls
% cvs release -d ls
% cvs logout
```

Example A-3. Creating a List of Changes (as unified diffs) to ls(1)

```
% setenv CVSROOT :pserver:anoncvs@anoncvs.FreeBSD.org:/home/ncvs
% cvs login
At the prompt, enter the password "anoncvs".
% cvs rdiff -u -rRELENG_3_0_0_RELEASE -rRELENG_3_4_0_RELEASE ls
% cvs logout
```

Example A-4. Finding Out What Other Module Names Can Be Used:

```
% setenv CVSROOT :pserver:anoncvs@anoncvs.FreeBSD.org:/home/ncvs
% cvs login
At the prompt, enter the password "anoncvs".
% cvs co modules
% more modules/modules
% cvs release -d modules
% cvs logout
```

A.4.4 Other Resources

The following additional resources may be helpful in learning CVS:

- CVS Tutorial[106] from Cal Poly.
- Cyclic Software[107], commercial maintainers of CVS.
- CVSWeb[108] is the FreeBSD Project web interface for CVS.

A.5 Using CTM

CTM is a method for keeping a remote directory tree in sync with a central one. It has been developed for usage with FreeBSD's source trees, though other people may find it useful for other purposes as time goes by. Little, if any, documentation currently exists at this time on the process of creating deltas, so talk to Poul-Henning Kamp <phk@FreeBSD.org> for more information should you wish to use **CTM** for other things.

A.5.1 Why Should I Use CTM?

CTM will give you a local copy of the FreeBSD source trees. There are a number of "flavors" of the tree available. Whether you wish to track the entire CVS tree or just one of the branches, **CTM** can provide you the information. If you are an active developer on FreeBSD, but have lousy or non-existent TCP/IP connectivity, or simply wish to have the changes automatically sent to you, **CTM** was made for you. You will need to obtain up to three deltas per day for the most active branches. However, you should consider having them sent by automatic email. The sizes of the updates are always kept as small as possible. This is typically less than 5K, with an occasional (one in ten) being 10-50K and every now and then a large 100K+ or more coming around.

You will also need to make yourself aware of the various caveats related to working directly from the development sources rather than a pre-packaged release. This is particularly true if you choose the "current" sources. It is recommended that you read Staying current with FreeBSD.

A.5.2 What Do I Need to Use CTM?

You will need two things: The **CTM** program, and the initial deltas to feed it (to get up to "current" levels).

The **CTM** program has been part of FreeBSD ever since version 2.0 was released, and lives in /usr/src/usr.sbin/ CTM if you have a copy of the source available.

If you are running a pre-2.0 version of FreeBSD, you can fetch the current **CTM** sources directly from:

ftp://ftp.FreeBSD.org/pub/FreeBSD/FreeBSD-current/src/usr.sbin/ctm/

---

106 http://www.csc.calpoly.edu/~dbutler/tutorials/winter96/cvs/
107 http://www.cyclic.com/
108 http://www.FreeBSD.org/cgi/cvsweb.cgi

The "deltas" you feed **CTM** can be had two ways, FTP or email. If you have general FTP access to the Internet then the following FTP sites support access to **CTM**:

`ftp://ftp.FreeBSD.org/pub/FreeBSD/CTM/`

or see section mirrors.

FTP the relevant directory and fetch the README file, starting from there.

If you wish to get your deltas via email:

Send email to <majordomo@FreeBSD.org> to subscribe to one of the **CTM** distribution lists. "ctm-cvs-cur" supports the entire CVS tree. "ctm-src-cur" supports the head of the development branch. "ctm-src-2_2" supports the 2.2 release branch, etc.. (If you do not know how to subscribe yourself using majordomo, send a message first containing the word help — it will send you back usage instructions.)

When you begin receiving your **CTM** updates in the mail, you may use the ctm_rmail program to unpack and apply them. You can actually use the ctm_rmail program directly from a entry in /etc/aliases if you want to have the process run in a fully automated fashion. Check the ctm_rmail manual page for more details.

> **Note:** No matter what method you use to get the **CTM** deltas, you should subscribe to the <ctm-\/announce@ FreeBSD.org> mailing list. In the future, this will be the only place where announcements concerning the operations of the **CTM** system will be posted. Send an email to <majordomo@FreeBSD.org> with a single line of subscribe ctm-announce to get added to the list.

A.5.3 Using CTM for the First Time

Before you can start using **CTM** deltas, you will need to get to a starting point for the deltas produced subsequently to it.

First you should determine what you already have. Everyone can start from an "empty" directory. You must use an initial "Empty" delta to start off your **CTM** supported tree. At some point it is intended that one of these "started" deltas be distributed on the CD for your convenience, however, this does not currently happen.

Since the trees are many tens of megabytes, you should prefer to start from something already at hand. If you have a -RELEASE CD, you can copy or extract an initial source from it. This will save a significant transfer of data.

You can recognize these "starter" deltas by the X appended to the number (src-cur.3210XEmpty.gz for instance). The designation following the X corresponds to the origin of your initial "seed". Empty is an empty directory. As a rule a base transition from Empty is produced every 100 deltas. By the way, they are large! 25 to 30 Megabytes of gzip'd data is common for the XEmpty deltas.

Once you have picked a base delta to start from, you will also need all deltas with higher numbers following it.

A.5.4 Using CTM in Your Daily Life

To apply the deltas, simply say:

```
# cd /where/ever/you/want/the/stuff
```

```
# ctm -v -v /where/you/store/your/deltas/src-xxx.*
```

CTM understands deltas which have been put through `gzip`, so you do not need to `gunzip` them first, this saves disk space.

Unless it feels very secure about the entire process, **CTM** will not touch your tree. To verify a delta you can also use the `-c` flag and **CTM** will not actually touch your tree; it will merely verify the integrity of the delta and see if it would apply cleanly to your current tree.

There are other options to **CTM** as well, see the manual pages or look in the sources for more information.

That is really all there is to it. Every time you get a new delta, just run it through **CTM** to keep your sources up to date.

Do not remove the deltas if they are hard to download again. You just might want to keep them around in case something bad happens. Even if you only have floppy disks, consider using `fdwrite` to make a copy.

A.5.5 Keeping Your Local Changes

As a developer one would like to experiment with and change files in the source tree. **CTM** supports local modifications in a limited way: before checking for the presence of a file `foo`, it first looks for `foo.ctm`. If this file exists, CTM will operate on it instead of `foo`.

This behavior gives us a simple way to maintain local changes: simply copy the files you plan to modify to the corresponding file names with a `.ctm` suffix. Then you can freely hack the code, while CTM keeps the `.ctm` file up-to-date.

A.5.6 Other Interesting CTM Options

Finding Out Exactly What Would Be Touched by an Update

You can determine the list of changes that **CTM** will make on your source repository using the `-l` option to **CTM**.

This is useful if you would like to keep logs of the changes, pre- or post- process the modified files in any manner, or just are feeling a tad paranoid.

Making Backups Before Updating

Sometimes you may want to backup all the files that would be changed by a **CTM** update.

Specifying the `-B backup-file` option causes **CTM** to backup all files that would be touched by a given **CTM** delta to `backup-file`.

Restricting the Files Touched by an Update

Sometimes you would be interested in restricting the scope of a given **CTM** update, or may be interested in extracting just a few files from a sequence of deltas.

You can control the list of files that **CTM** would operate on by specifying filtering regular expressions using the -e and -x options.

For example, to extract an up-to-date copy of lib/libc/Makefile from your collection of saved CTM deltas, run the commands:

```
# cd /where/ever/you/want/to/extract/it/
# ctm -e '^lib/libc/Makefile' ~ctm/src-xxx.*
```

For every file specified in a **CTM** delta, the -e and -x options are applied in the order given on the command line. The file is processed by **CTM** only if it is marked as eligible after all the -e and -x options are applied to it.

A.5.7 Future Plans for CTM

Tons of them:

- Use some kind of authentication into the CTM system, so as to allow detection of spoofed CTM updates.
- Clean up the options to **CTM**, they became confusing and counter intuitive.

A.5.8 Miscellaneous Stuff

There is a sequence of deltas for the ports collection too, but interest has not been all that high yet. Tell me if you want an email list for that too and we will consider setting it up.

A.5.9 CTM Mirrors

CTM/FreeBSD is available via anonymous FTP from the following mirror sites. If you choose to obtain CTM via anonymous FTP, please try to use a site near you.

In case of problems, please contact Poul-Henning Kamp <phk@FreeBSD.org>.

California, Bay Area, official source

- ftp://ftp.FreeBSD.org/pub/FreeBSD/development/CTM/

Germany, Trier

- `ftp://ftp.uni-trier.de/pub/unix/systems/BSD/FreeBSD/CTM/`

South Africa, backup server for old deltas

- `ftp://ftp.za.FreeBSD.org/pub/FreeBSD/CTM/`

Taiwan/R.O.C, Chiayi

- `ftp://ctm.tw.FreeBSD.org/pub/FreeBSD/CTM/`
- `ftp://ctm2.tw.FreeBSD.org/pub/FreeBSD/CTM/`
- `ftp://ctm3.tw.FreeBSD.org/pub/FreeBSD/CTM/`

If you did not find a mirror near to you or the mirror is incomplete, try FTP at `http://ftpsearch.ntnu.no/ftpsearch/`. FTP search is a great free archie server in Trondheim, Norway.

A.6 Using CVSup

A.6.1 Introduction

CVSup is a software package for distributing and updating source trees from a master CVS repository on a remote server host. The FreeBSD sources are maintained in a CVS repository on a central development machine in California. With **CVSup**, FreeBSD users can easily keep their own source trees up to date.

CVSup uses the so-called *pull* model of updating. Under the pull model, each client asks the server for updates, if and when they are wanted. The server waits passively for update requests from its clients. Thus all updates are instigated by the client. The server never sends unsolicited updates. Users must either run the **CVSup** client manually to get an update, or they must set up a `cron` job to run it automatically on a regular basis.

The term **CVSup**, capitalized just so, refers to the entire software package. Its main components are the client `cvsup` which runs on each user's machine, and the server `cvsupd` which runs at each of the FreeBSD mirror sites.

As you read the FreeBSD documentation and mailing lists, you may see references to **sup**. **Sup** was the predecessor of **CVSup**, and it served a similar purpose. **CVSup** is in used in much the same way as sup and, in fact, uses configuration files which are backward-compatible with sup's. **Sup** is no longer used in the FreeBSD project, because **CVSup** is both faster and more flexible.

A.6.2 Installation

The easiest way to install **CVSup** is to use the precompiled net/cvsup package from the FreeBSD packages collection. If you prefer to build **CVSup** from source, you can use the net/cvsup port instead. But be forewarned: the net/cvsup port depends on the Modula-3 system, which takes a substantial amount of time and disk space to download and build.

If you do not know anything about **CVSup** at all and want a single package which will install it, set up the configuration file and start the transfer via a pointy-clicky type of interface, then get the cvsupit[118] package. Just hand it to pkg_add(1) and it will lead you through the configuration process in a menu-oriented fashion.

A.6.3 CVSup Configuration

CVSup's operation is controlled by a configuration file called the supfile. There are some sample supfiles in the directory /usr/share/examples/cvsup/.

The information in a supfile answers the following questions for cvsup:

- Which files do you want to receive?
- Which versions of them do you want?
- Where do you want to get them from?
- Where do you want to put them on your own machine?
- Where do you want to put your status files?

In the following sections, we will construct a typical supfile by answering each of these questions in turn. First, we describe the overall structure of a supfile.

A supfile is a text file. Comments begin with # and extend to the end of the line. Lines that are blank and lines that contain only comments are ignored.

Each remaining line describes a set of files that the user wishes to receive. The line begins with the name of a "collection", a logical grouping of files defined by the server. The name of the collection tells the server which files you want. After the collection name come zero or more fields, separated by white space. These fields answer the questions listed above. There are two types of fields: flag fields and value fields. A flag field consists of a keyword standing alone, e.g., delete or compress. A value field also begins with a keyword, but the keyword is followed without intervening white space by = and a second word. For example, release=cvs is a value field.

A supfile typically specifies more than one collection to receive. One way to structure a supfile is to specify all of the relevant fields explicitly for each collection. However, that tends to make the supfile lines quite long, and it is inconvenient because most fields are the same for all of the collections in a supfile. **CVSup** provides a defaulting mechanism to avoid these problems. Lines beginning with the special pseudo-collection name *default can be used to set flags and values which will be used as defaults for the subsequent collections in the supfile. A default value can be overridden for an individual collection, by specifying a different value with the collection itself. Defaults can also be changed or augmented mid-supfile by additional *default lines.

With this background, we will now proceed to construct a supfile for receiving and updating the main source tree of FreeBSD-CURRENT.

---

118 ftp://ftp.FreeBSD.org/pub/FreeBSD/development/CVSup/cvsupit.tgz

- Which files do you want to receive?

  The files available via **CVSup** are organized into named groups called "collections". The collections that are available are described in the following section. In this example, we wish to receive the entire main source tree for the FreeBSD system. There is a single large collection `src-all` which will give us all of that. As a first step toward constructing our `supfile`, we simply list the collections, one per line (in this case, only one line):

  ```
  src-all
  ```

- Which version(s) of them do you want?

  With **CVSup**, you can receive virtually any version of the sources that ever existed. That is possible because the **cvsupd** server works directly from the CVS repository, which contains all of the versions. You specify which one of them you want using the `tag=` and `date=` value fields.

  > **Warning:** Be very careful to specify any `tag=` fields correctly. Some tags are valid only for certain collections of files. If you specify an incorrect or misspelled tag, **CVSup** will delete files which you probably do not want deleted. In particular, use *only* `tag=.` for the `ports-*` collections.

  The `tag=` field names a symbolic tag in the repository. There are two kinds of tags, revision tags and branch tags. A revision tag refers to a specific revision. Its meaning stays the same from day to day. A branch tag, on the other hand, refers to the latest revision on a given line of development, at any given time. Because a branch tag does not refer to a specific revision, it may mean something different tomorrow than it means today.

  Section A.7 contains branch tags that users might be interested in. When specifying a tag in **CVSup**'s configuration file, it must be preceded with `tag=` (`RELENG_4` will become `tag=RELENG_4`). Keep in mind that only the `tag=.` is relevant for the ports collection.

  > **Warning:** Be very careful to type the tag name exactly as shown. **CVSup** cannot distinguish between valid and invalid tags. If you misspell the tag, **CVSup** will behave as though you had specified a valid tag which happens to refer to no files at all. It will delete your existing sources in that case.

  When you specify a branch tag, you normally receive the latest versions of the files on that line of development. If you wish to receive some past version, you can do so by specifying a date with the `date=` value field. The cvsup(1) manual page explains how to do that.

  For our example, we wish to receive FreeBSD-CURRENT. We add this line at the beginning of our `supfile`:

  ```
  *default tag=.
  ```

  There is an important special case that comes into play if you specify neither a `tag=` field nor a `date=` field. In that case, you receive the actual RCS files directly from the server's CVS repository, rather than receiving a particular version. Developers generally prefer this mode of operation. By maintaining a copy of the repository itself on their systems, they gain the ability to browse the revision histories and examine past versions of files. This gain is achieved at a large cost in terms of disk space, however.

- Where do you want to get them from?

We use the `host=` field to tell `cvsup` where to obtain its updates. Any of the CVSup mirror sites will do, though you should try to select one that is close to you in cyberspace. In this example we will use a fictional FreeBSD distribution site, `cvsup666.FreeBSD.org`:

```
*default host=cvsup666.FreeBSD.org
```

You will need to change the host to one that actually exists before running **CVSup**. On any particular run of `cvsup`, you can override the host setting on the command line, with `-h` *hostname*.

- Where do you want to put them on your own machine?

  The `prefix=` field tells `cvsup` where to put the files it receives. In this example, we will put the source files directly into our main source tree, `/usr/src`. The `src` directory is already implicit in the collections we have chosen to receive, so this is the correct specification:

  ```
  *default prefix=/usr
  ```

- Where should `cvsup` maintain its status files?

  The **CVSup** client maintains certain status files in what is called the "base" directory. These files help **CVSup** to work more efficiently, by keeping track of which updates you have already received. We will use the standard base directory, `/usr/local/etc/cvsup`:

  ```
  *default base=/usr/local/etc/cvsup
  ```

  This setting is used by default if it is not specified in the `supfile`, so we actually do not need the above line.

  If your base directory does not already exist, now would be a good time to create it. The `cvsup` client will refuse to run if the base directory does not exist.

- Miscellaneous `supfile` settings:

  There is one more line of boiler plate that normally needs to be present in the `supfile`:

  ```
  *default release=cvs delete use-rel-suffix compress
  ```

  `release=cvs` indicates that the server should get its information out of the main FreeBSD CVS repository. This is virtually always the case, but there are other possibilities which are beyond the scope of this discussion.

  `delete` gives **CVSup** permission to delete files. You should always specify this, so that **CVSup** can keep your source tree fully up-to-date. **CVSup** is careful to delete only those files for which it is responsible. Any extra files you happen to have will be left strictly alone.

  `use-rel-suffix` is ... arcane. If you really want to know about it, see the cvsup(1) manual page. Otherwise, just specify it and do not worry about it.

  `compress` enables the use of gzip-style compression on the communication channel. If your network link is T1 speed or faster, you probably should not use compression. Otherwise, it helps substantially.

- Putting it all together:

  Here is the entire `supfile` for our example:

```
*default tag=.
*default host=cvsup666.FreeBSD.org
*default prefix=/usr
*default base=/usr/local/etc/cvsup
*default release=cvs delete use-rel-suffix compress

src-all
```

The refuse File

As mentioned above, **CVSup** uses a *pull method*. Basically, this means that you connect to the **CVSup** server, and it says, "Here's what you can download from me...", and your client responds "OK, I'll take this, this, this, and this." In the default configuration, the **CVSup** client will take every file associated with the collection and tag you chose in the configuration file. However, this is not always what you want, especially if you are synching the doc, ports, or www trees — most people cannot read four or five languages, and therefore they do not need to download the language-specific files. If you are **CVSup**ing the ports collection, you can get around this by specifying each collection individually (e.g., *ports-astrology*, *ports-biology*, etc instead of simply saying *ports-all*). However, since the doc and www trees do not have language-specific collections, you must use one of **CVSup**'s many nifty features; the *refuse file*.

The *refuse file* essentially tells **CVSup** that it should not take every single file from a collection; in other words, it tells the client to *refuse* certain files from the server. The refuse file can be found (or, if you do not yet have one, should be placed) in `base/sup/refuse`. `base` is defined in your supfile; by default, `base` is `/usr/local/etc/cvsup`, which means that by default the refuse file is in `/usr/local/etc/cvsup/sup/refuse`.

The refuse file has a very simple format; it simply contains the names of files or directories that you do not wish to download. For example, if you cannot speak any languages other than English and some German, and you do not feel the need to use the German applications, you can put the following in your *refuse file*:

```
ports/chinese
ports/german
ports/japanese
ports/korean
ports/russian
ports/vietnamese
doc/es_ES.ISO8859-1
doc/ja_JP.eucJP
```

and so forth for the other languages. Note that the name of the repository is the first "directory" in the *refuse file*.

With this very useful feature, those users who are on slow links or pay by the minute for their Internet connection will be able to save valuable time as they will no longer need to download files that they will never use. For more information on *refuse files* and other neat features of **CVSup**, please view its manual page.

A.6.4 Running CVSup

You are now ready to try an update. The command line for doing this is quite simple:

```
# cvsup supfile
```

where `supfile` is of course the name of the supfile you have just created. Assuming you are running under X11, `cvsup` will display a GUI window with some buttons to do the usual things. Press the "go" button, and watch it run.

Since you are updating your actual `/usr/src` tree in this example, you will need to run the program as `root` so that `cvsup` has the permissions it needs to update your files. Having just created your configuration file, and having never used this program before, that might understandably make you nervous. There is an easy way to do a trial run without touching your precious files. Just create an empty directory somewhere convenient, and name it as an extra argument on the command line:

```
# mkdir /var/tmp/dest
# cvsup supfile /var/tmp/dest
```

The directory you specify will be used as the destination directory for all file updates. **CVSup** will examine your usual files in `/usr/src`, but it will not modify or delete any of them. Any file updates will instead land in `/var/tmp/dest/usr/src`. **CVSup** will also leave its base directory status files untouched when run this way. The new versions of those files will be written into the specified directory. As long as you have read access to `/usr/src`, you do not even need to be root to perform this kind of trial run.

If you are not running X11 or if you just do not like GUIs, you should add a couple of options to the command line when you run cvsup:

```
# cvsup -g -L 2 supfile
```

The `-g` tells **CVSup** not to use its GUI. This is automatic if you are not running X11, but otherwise you have to specify it.

The `-L 2` tells **CVSup** to print out the details of all the file updates it is doing. There are three levels of verbosity, from `-L 0` to `-L 2`. The default is 0, which means total silence except for error messages.

There are plenty of other options available. For a brief list of them, type `cvsup -H`. For more detailed descriptions, see the manual page.

Once you are satisfied with the way updates are working, you can arrange for regular runs of **CVSup** using cron(8). Obviously, you should not let **CVSup** use its GUI when running it from cron(8).

A.6.5 CVSup File Collections

The file collections available via **CVSup** are organized hierarchically. There are a few large collections, and they are divided into smaller sub-collections. Receiving a large collection is equivalent to receiving each of its sub-collections. The hierarchical relationships among collections are reflected by the use of indentation in the list below.

The most commonly used collections are `src-all`, and `ports-all`. The other collections are used only by small groups of people for specialized purposes, and some mirror sites may not carry all of them.

`cvs-all release=cvs`

The main FreeBSD CVS repository, including the cryptography code.

`distrib release=cvs`

Files related to the distribution and mirroring of FreeBSD.

`doc-all release=cvs`

Sources for the FreeBSD Handbook and other documentation. This does not include files for the FreeBSD web site.

`ports-all release=cvs`

The FreeBSD Ports Collection.

`ports-archivers release=cvs`

Archiving tools.

`ports-astro release=cvs`

Astronomical ports.

`ports-audio release=cvs`

Sound support.

`ports-base release=cvs`

Miscellaneous files at the top of /usr/ports.

`ports-benchmarks release=cvs`

Benchmarks.

`ports-biology release=cvs`

Biology.

`ports-cad release=cvs`

Computer aided design tools.

`ports-chinese release=cvs`

Chinese language support.

`ports-comms release=cvs`

Communication software.

`ports-converters release=cvs`

character code converters.

`ports-databases release=cvs`

> Databases.

`ports-deskutils release=cvs`

> Things that used to be on the desktop before computers were invented.

`ports-devel release=cvs`

> Development utilities.

`ports-editors release=cvs`

> Editors.

`ports-emulators release=cvs`

> Emulators for other operating systems.

`ports-ftp release=cvs`

> FTP client and server utilities.

`ports-games release=cvs`

> Games.

`ports-german release=cvs`

> German language support.

`ports-graphics release=cvs`

> Graphics utilities.

`ports-irc release=cvs`

> Internet Relay Chat utilities.

`ports-japanese release=cvs`

> Japanese language support.

`ports-java release=cvs`

> Java utilities.

`ports-korean release=cvs`

> Korean language support.

`ports-lang release=cvs`

> Programming languages.

`ports-mail release=cvs`

> Mail software.

`ports-math release=cvs`

> Numerical computation software.

`ports-mbone release=cvs`

> MBone applications.

`ports-misc release=cvs`

> Miscellaneous utilities.

`ports-net release=cvs`

> Networking software.

`ports-news release=cvs`

> USENET news software.

`ports-palm release=cvs`

> Software support for 3Com Palm(tm) series.

`ports-print release=cvs`

> Printing software.

`ports-russian release=cvs`

> Russian language support.

`ports-security release=cvs`

> Security utilities.

`ports-shells release=cvs`

> Command line shells.

`ports-sysutils release=cvs`

> System utilities.

`ports-textproc release=cvs`

> text processing utilities (does not include desktop publishing).

`ports-vietnamese release=cvs`

> Vietnamese language support.

```
ports-www release=cvs
```
> Software related to the World Wide Web.

```
ports-x11 release=cvs
```
> Ports to support the X window system.

```
ports-x11-clocks release=cvs
```
> X11 clocks.

```
ports-x11-fm release=cvs
```
> X11 file managers.

```
ports-x11-fonts release=cvs
```
> X11 fonts and font utilities.

```
ports-x11-toolkits release=cvs
```
> X11 toolkits.

```
ports-x11-servers
```
> X11 servers.

```
ports-x11-wm
```
> X11 window managers.

```
src-all release=cvs
```
> The main FreeBSD sources, including the cryptography code.

```
src-base release=cvs
```
> Miscellaneous files at the top of /usr/src.

```
src-bin release=cvs
```
> User utilities that may be needed in single-user mode (/usr/src/bin).

```
src-contrib release=cvs
```
> Utilities and libraries from outside the FreeBSD project, used relatively unmodified (/usr/src/contrib).

```
src-crypto release=cvs
```
> Cryptography utilities and libraries from outside the FreeBSD project, used relatively unmodified (/usr/src/crypto).

`src-eBones release=cvs`

>   Kerberos and DES (`/usr/src/eBones`). Not used in current releases of FreeBSD.

`src-etc release=cvs`

>   System configuration files (`/usr/src/etc`).

`src-games release=cvs`

>   Games (`/usr/src/games`).

`src-gnu release=cvs`

>   Utilities covered by the GNU Public License (`/usr/src/gnu`).

`src-include release=cvs`

>   Header files (`/usr/src/include`).

`src-kerberos5 release=cvs`

>   Kerberos5 security package (`/usr/src/kerberos5`).

`src-kerberosIV release=cvs`

>   KerberosIV security package (`/usr/src/kerberosIV`).

`src-lib release=cvs`

>   Libraries (`/usr/src/lib`).

`src-libexec release=cvs`

>   System programs normally executed by other programs (`/usr/src/libexec`).

`src-release release=cvs`

>   Files required to produce a FreeBSD release (`/usr/src/release`).

`src-secure release=cvs`

>   DES (`/usr/src/secure`).

`src-sbin release=cvs`

>   System utilities for single-user mode (`/usr/src/sbin`).

`src-share release=cvs`

>   Files that can be shared across multiple systems (`/usr/src/share`).

`src-sys release=cvs`

>   The kernel (`/usr/src/sys`).

```
src-sys-crypto release=cvs
```
> Kernel cryptography code (/usr/src/sys/crypto).

```
src-tools release=cvs
```
> Various tools for the maintenance of FreeBSD (/usr/src/tools).

```
src-usrbin release=cvs
```
> User utilities (/usr/src/usr.bin).

```
src-usrsbin release=cvs
```
> System utilities (/usr/src/usr.sbin).

```
www release=cvs
```
> The sources for the FreeBSD WWW site.

```
distrib release=self
```
> The **CVSup** server's own configuration files. Used by **CVSup** mirror sites.

```
gnats release=current
```
> The GNATS bug-tracking database.

```
mail-archive release=current
```
> FreeBSD mailing list archive.

```
www release=current
```
> The pre-processed FreeBSD WWW site files (not the source files). Used by WWW mirror sites.

A.6.6 For More Information

For the **CVSup** FAQ and other information about **CVSup**, see The CVSup Home Page[119].

Most FreeBSD-related discussion of **CVSup** takes place on the FreeBSD technical discussions mailing list <freebsd-hackers@FreeBSD.org>. New versions of the software are announced there, as well as on the FreeBSD announcements mailing list <freebsd-announce@FreeBSD.org>.

Questions and bug reports should be addressed to the author of the program at <cvsup-bugs@polstra.com>.

---

119 http://www.polstra.com/projects/freeware/CVSup/

A.6.7 CVSup Sites

CVSup servers for FreeBSD are running at the following sites:

Argentina

- cvsup.ar.FreeBSD.org (maintainer <msagre@cactus.fi.uba.ar>)

Australia

- cvsup.au.FreeBSD.org (maintainer <dawes@xfree86.org>)
- cvsup3.au.FreeBSD.org (maintainer <FreeBSD@admin.gil.com.au>)

Austria

- cvsup.at.FreeBSD.org (maintainer <postmaster@wu-wien.ac.at>)

Brazil

- cvsup.br.FreeBSD.org (maintainer <cvsup@cvsup.br.FreeBSD.org>)
- cvsup2.br.FreeBSD.org (maintainer <tps@ti.sk>)
- cvsup3.br.FreeBSD.org (maintainer <camposr@matrix.com.br>)
- cvsup4.br.FreeBSD.org (maintainer <cvsup@tcoip.com.br>)

Canada

- cvsup.ca.FreeBSD.org (maintainer <dan@jaded.net>)
- cvsup2.ca.FreeBSD.org (maintainer <hostmaster@ca.freebsd.org>)

China

- cvsup.cn.FreeBSD.org (maintainer <phj@cn.FreeBSD.org>)

Czech Republic

- cvsup.cz.FreeBSD.org (maintainer <cejkar@dcse.fee.vutbr.cz>)

Denmark

- cvsup.dk.FreeBSD.org (maintainer <jesper@skriver.dk>)

Estonia

- cvsup.ee.FreeBSD.org (maintainer <taavi@uninet.ee>)

Finland

- cvsup.fi.FreeBSD.org (maintainer <count@key.sms.fi>)
- cvsup2.fi.FreeBSD.org (maintainer <count@key.sms.fi>)

France

- cvsup.fr.FreeBSD.org (maintainer <hostmaster@fr.FreeBSD.org>)
- cvsup2.fr.FreeBSD.org (maintainer <ftpmaint@uvsq.fr>)

Germany

- cvsup.de.FreeBSD.org (maintainer <cvsup@cosmo-project.de>)
- cvsup1.de.FreeBSD.org (maintainer <wosch@FreeBSD.org>)
- cvsup2.de.FreeBSD.org (maintainer <cvsup@nikoma.de>)
- cvsup3.de.FreeBSD.org (maintainer <ag@leo.org>)
- cvsup4.de.FreeBSD.org (maintainer <cvsup@cosmo-project.de>)
- cvsup5.de.FreeBSD.org (maintainer <rse@freebsd.org>)

Greece

- cvsup.gr.FreeBSD.org (maintainer <ftpadm@duth.gr>)
- cvsup2.gr.FreeBSD.org (maintainer <paschos@cs.uoi.gr>)

Iceland

- cvsup.is.FreeBSD.org (maintainer <cvsup@cvsup1.is.FreeBSD.org>)

Ireland

- cvsup.ie.FreeBSD.org (maintainer <dwmalone@maths.tcd.ie>), Trinity College, Dublin.

Japan

- cvsup.jp.FreeBSD.org (maintainer <cvsupadm@jp.FreeBSD.org>)
- cvsup2.jp.FreeBSD.org (maintainer <max@FreeBSD.org>)
- cvsup3.jp.FreeBSD.org (maintainer <shige@cin.nihon-u.ac.jp>)
- cvsup4.jp.FreeBSD.org (maintainer <cvsup-admin@ftp.media.kyoto-u.ac.jp>)
- cvsup5.jp.FreeBSD.org (maintainer <cvsup@imasy.or.jp>)
- cvsup6.jp.FreeBSD.org (maintainer <cvsupadm@jp.FreeBSD.org>)

Korea

- cvsup.kr.FreeBSD.org (maintainer <cjh@kr.FreeBSD.org>)
- cvsup2.kr.FreeBSD.org (maintainer <holywar@mail.holywar.net>)

Lithuania

- cvsup.lt.FreeBSD.org (maintainer <domas.mituzas@delfi.lt>)

New Zealand

- cvsup.nz.FreeBSD.org (maintainer <cvsup@langille.org>)

Netherlands

- cvsup.nl.FreeBSD.org (maintainer <xaa@xaa.iae.nl>)
- cvsup2.nl.FreeBSD.org (maintainer <cvsup@nl.uu.net>)

Norway

- cvsup.no.FreeBSD.org (maintainer <Per.Hove@math.ntnu.no>)

Poland

- cvsup.pl.FreeBSD.org (maintainer <Mariusz@kam.pl>)

Portugal

- cvsup.pt.FreeBSD.org (maintainer <jpedras@webvolution.net>)

Russia

- cvsup.ru.FreeBSD.org (maintainer <ache@nagual.pp.ru>)
- cvsup2.ru.FreeBSD.org (maintainer <dv@dv.ru>)
- cvsup3.ru.FreeBSD.org (maintainer <fjoe@iclub.nsu.ru>)
- cvsup4.ru.FreeBSD.org (maintainer <zhecka@klondike.ru>)
- cvsup5.ru.FreeBSD.org (maintainer <maxim@macomnet.ru>)
- cvsup6.ru.FreeBSD.org (maintainer <pvr@corbina.net>)

Slovak Republic

- cvsup.sk.FreeBSD.org (maintainer <tps@tps.sk>)
- cvsup2.sk.FreeBSD.org (maintainer <tps@tps.sk>)

Slovenia

- cvsup.si.FreeBSD.org (maintainer <blaz@si.FreeBSD.org>)

South Africa

- cvsup.za.FreeBSD.org (maintainer <markm@FreeBSD.org>)
- cvsup2.za.FreeBSD.org (maintainer <markm@FreeBSD.org>)

Spain

- cvsup.es.FreeBSD.org (maintainer <jesusr@FreeBSD.org>)
- cvsup2.es.FreeBSD.org (maintainer <jesusr@FreeBSD.org>)
- cvsup3.es.FreeBSD.org (maintainer <jose@we.lc.ehu.es>)

Sweden

- cvsup.se.FreeBSD.org (maintainer <pantzer@ludd.luth.se>)
- cvsup2.se.FreeBSD.org (maintainer <cvsup@dataphone.net>)

Taiwan

- cvsup.tw.FreeBSD.org (maintainer <jdli@freebsd.csie.nctu.edu.tw>)
- cvsup2.tw.FreeBSD.org (maintainer <ycheng@sinica.edu.tw>)
- cvsup3.tw.FreeBSD.org (maintainer <foxfair@FreeBSD.org>)

Ukraine

- cvsup2.ua.FreeBSD.org (maintainer <freebsd-mnt@lucky.net>)
- cvsup3.ua.FreeBSD.org (maintainer <ftpmaster@ukr.net>), Kiev
- cvsup4.ua.FreeBSD.org (maintainer <phantom@cris.net>)

United Kingdom

- cvsup.uk.FreeBSD.org (maintainer <ftp-admin@plig.net>)
- cvsup2.uk.FreeBSD.org (maintainer <brian@FreeBSD.org>)
- cvsup3.uk.FreeBSD.org (maintainer <ben.hughes@uk.easynet.net>)

USA

- cvsup1.FreeBSD.org (maintainer <cwt@networks.cwu.edu>), Washington state
- cvsup2.FreeBSD.org (maintainer <jdp@FreeBSD.org>), California
- cvsup3.FreeBSD.org (maintainer <wollman@FreeBSD.org>), Massachusetts
- cvsup5.FreeBSD.org (maintainer <mjr@blackened.com>), Arizona
- cvsup6.FreeBSD.org (maintainer <cvsup@cvsup.adelphiacom.net>), Illinois
- cvsup7.FreeBSD.org (maintainer <jdp@FreeBSD.org>), Washington state
- cvsup8.FreeBSD.org (maintainer <hostmaster@bigmirror.com>), Washington state
- cvsup9.FreeBSD.org (maintainer <qbsd@uswest.net>), Minnesota
- cvsup10.FreeBSD.org (maintainer <jdp@FreeBSD.org>), California
- cvsup11.FreeBSD.org (maintainer <cvsup@research.uu.net>), Virginia
- cvsup12.FreeBSD.org (maintainer <will@FreeBSD.org>), Indiana
- cvsup13.FreeBSD.org (maintainer <dima@valueclick.com>), California
- cvsup14.FreeBSD.org (maintainer <freebsd-cvsup@mfnx.net>), California
- cvsup15.FreeBSD.org (maintainer <cvsup@math.uic.edu>), Illinois
- cvsup16.FreeBSD.org (maintainer <pth3k@virginia.edu>), Virginia
- cvsup17.FreeBSD.org (maintainer <cvsup@mirrortree.com>), Washington state

A.7 CVS Tags

When obtaining or updating sources from **cvs** and **CVSup** a revision tag (reference to a date in time) must be specified. The following tags are available, each specifying different branches of FreeBSD at different points of time:

> **Note:** The ports tree does not have any tag associated with it, it is always CURRENT.

The most common tags are:

HEAD

> Symbolic name for the main line, or FreeBSD-CURRENT. Also the default when no revision is specified.
>
> In **CVSup**, this tag is represented by a . (not punctuation, but a literal . character).
>
> > **Note:** In CVS, this is the default when no revision tag is specified. It is usually *not* a good idea to checkout or update to CURRENT sources on a STABLE machine, unless that is your intent.

RELENG_4

> The line of development for FreeBSD-4.X, also known as FreeBSD-STABLE.

RELENG_4_4

> The release branch for FreeBSD-4.4, used only for security advisories and other seriously critical fixes.

RELENG_4_3

> The release branch for FreeBSD-4.3, used only for security advisories and other seriously critical fixes.

RELENG_3

> The line of development for FreeBSD-3.X, also known as 3.X-STABLE.

RELENG_2_2

> The line of development for FreeBSD-2.2.X, also known as 2.2-STABLE. This branch is mostly obsolete.

Other revision tags that are available include:

RELENG_4_4_0_RELEASE

> FreeBSD 4.4.

RELENG_4_3_0_RELEASE

> FreeBSD 4.3.

RELENG_4_2_0_RELEASE
  FreeBSD 4.2.

RELENG_4_1_1_RELEASE
  FreeBSD 4.1.1.

RELENG_4_1_0_RELEASE
  FreeBSD 4.1.

RELENG_4_0_0_RELEASE
  FreeBSD 4.0.

RELENG_3_5_0_RELEASE
  FreeBSD-3.5.

RELENG_3_4_0_RELEASE
  FreeBSD-3.4.

RELENG_3_3_0_RELEASE
  FreeBSD-3.3.

RELENG_3_2_0_RELEASE
  FreeBSD-3.2.

RELENG_3_1_0_RELEASE
  FreeBSD-3.1.

RELENG_3_0_0_RELEASE
  FreeBSD-3.0.

RELENG_2_2_8_RELEASE
  FreeBSD-2.2.8.

RELENG_2_2_7_RELEASE
  FreeBSD-2.2.7.

RELENG_2_2_6_RELEASE
  FreeBSD-2.2.6.

RELENG_2_2_5_RELEASE
  FreeBSD-2.2.5.

RELENG_2_2_2_RELEASE

    FreeBSD-2.2.2.

RELENG_2_2_1_RELEASE

    FreeBSD-2.2.1.

RELENG_2_2_0_RELEASE

    FreeBSD-2.2.0.

A.8 AFS Sites

AFS servers for FreeBSD are running at the following sites;

Sweden

    The path to the files are: `/afs/stacken.kth.se/ftp/pub/FreeBSD/`

```
stacken.kth.se          # Stacken Computer Club, KTH, Sweden
130.237.234.43          #hot.stacken.kth.se
130.237.237.230         #fishburger.stacken.kth.se
130.237.234.3           #milko.stacken.kth.se
```

    Maintainer <ftp@stacken.kth.se>

Appendix B.
Bibliography

While the manual pages provide the definitive reference for individual pieces of the FreeBSD operating system, they are notorious for not illustrating how to put the pieces together to make the whole operating system run smoothly. For this, there is no substitute for a good book on Unix system administration and a good users' manual.

B.1 Books & Magazines Specific to FreeBSD

International books & Magazines:

- Using FreeBSD (http://jdli.tw.freebsd.org/publication/book/freebsd2/index.htm) (in Chinese).
- FreeBSD for PC 98'ers (in Japanese), published by SHUWA System Co, LTD. ISBN 4-87966-468-5 C3055 P2900E.
- FreeBSD (in Japanese), published by CUTT. ISBN 4-906391-22-2 C3055 P2400E.
- Complete Introduction to FreeBSD (http://www.shoeisha.co.jp/pc/index/shinkan/97_05_06.htm) (in Japanese), published by Shoeisha Co., Ltd (http://www.shoeisha.co.jp/). ISBN 4-88135-473-6 P3600E.
- Personal UNIX Starter Kit FreeBSD (http://www.ascii.co.jp/pb/book1/shinkan/detail/1322785.html) (in Japanese), published by ASCII (http://www.ascii.co.jp/). ISBN 4-7561-1733-3 P3000E.
- FreeBSD Handbook (Japanese translation), published by ASCII (http://www.ascii.co.jp/). ISBN 4-7561-1580-2 P3800E.
- FreeBSD mit Methode (in German), published by Computer und Literatur Verlag/Vertrieb Hanser, 1998. ISBN 3-932311-31-0.
- FreeBSD Install and Utilization Manual (http://www.pc.mycom.co.jp/FreeBSD/install-manual.html) (in Japanese), published by Mainichi Communications Inc. (http://www.pc.mycom.co.jp/).
- Onno W Purbo, Dodi Maryanto, Syahrial Hubbany, Widjil Widodo *Building Internet Server with FreeBSD (http://maxwell.itb.ac.id/)* (in Indonesia Language), published by Elex Media Komputindo.

English language books & Magazines:

- The Complete FreeBSD, published by BSDi.
- The FreeBSD Corporate Networker's Guide (http://www.freebsd-corp-net-guide.com), published by Addison-Wesley (http://www.awl.com/aw/).

B.2 Users' Guides

- Computer Systems Research Group, UC Berkeley. *4.4BSD User's Reference Manual*. O'Reilly & Associates, Inc., 1994. ISBN 1-56592-075-9

- Computer Systems Research Group, UC Berkeley. *4.4BSD User's Supplementary Documents*. O'Reilly & Associates, Inc., 1994. ISBN 1-56592-076-7

- *UNIX in a Nutshell*. O'Reilly & Associates, Inc., 1990. ISBN 093717520X

- Mui, Linda. *What You Need To Know When You Can't Find Your UNIX System Administrator*. O'Reilly & Associates, Inc., 1995. ISBN 1-56592-104-6

- Ohio State University[1] has written a UNIX Introductory Course (`http://www-wks.acs.ohio-state.edu/unix_course/unix.html`) which is available online in HTML and PostScript format.

- Jpman Project, Japan FreeBSD Users Group (`http://www.jp.FreeBSD.org/`). FreeBSD User's Reference Manual (`http://www.pc.mycom.co.jp/FreeBSD/urm.html`) (Japanese translation). Mainichi Communications Inc. (`http://www.pc.mycom.co.jp/`), 1998. ISBN4-8399-0088-4 P3800E.

- Edinburgh University[2] has written an Online Guide (`http://unixhelp.ed.ac.uk/`) for newcomers to the UNIX environment.

B.3 Administrators' Guides

- Albitz, Paul and Liu, Cricket. *DNS and BIND*, 4th Ed. O'Reilly & Associates, Inc., 2001. ISBN 1-59600-158-4

- Computer Systems Research Group, UC Berkeley. *4.4BSD System Manager's Manual*. O'Reilly & Associates, Inc., 1994. ISBN 1-56592-080-5

- Costales, Brian, et al. *Sendmail*, 2nd Ed. O'Reilly & Associates, Inc., 1997. ISBN 1-56592-222-0

- Frisch, Æleen. *Essential System Administration*, 2nd Ed. O'Reilly & Associates, Inc., 1995. ISBN 1-56592-127-5

- Hunt, Craig. *TCP/IP Network Administration*, 2nd Ed. O'Reilly & Associates, Inc., 1997. ISBN 1-56592-322-7

- Nemeth, Evi. *UNIX System Administration Handbook*. 3rd Ed. Prentice Hall, 2000. ISBN 0-13-020601-6

- Stern, Hal *Managing NFS and NIS* O'Reilly & Associates, Inc., 1991. ISBN 0-937175-75-7

- Jpman Project, Japan FreeBSD Users Group[3]. FreeBSD System Administrator's Manual (`http://www.pc.mycom.co.jp/FreeBSD/sam.html`) (Japanese translation). Mainichi Communications Inc. (`http://www.pc.mycom.co.jp/`), 1998. ISBN4-8399-0109-0 P3300E.

---

1 http://www-wks.acs.ohio-state.edu/
2 http://www.ed.ac.uk/
3 http://www.jp.FreeBSD.org/

B.4 Programmers' Guides

- Asente, Paul, Converse, Diana, and Swick, Ralph. *X Window System Toolkit*. Digital Press, 1998. ISBN 1-55558-178-1

- Computer Systems Research Group, UC Berkeley. *4.4BSD Programmer's Reference Manual*. O'Reilly & Associates, Inc., 1994. ISBN 1-56592-078-3

- Computer Systems Research Group, UC Berkeley. *4.4BSD Programmer's Supplementary Documents*. O'Reilly & Associates, Inc., 1994. ISBN 1-56592-079-1

- Harbison, Samuel P. and Steele, Guy L. Jr. *C: A Reference Manual*. 4rd ed. Prentice Hall, 1995. ISBN 0-13-326224-3

- Kernighan, Brian and Dennis M. Ritchie. *The C Programming Language.*. PTR Prentice Hall, 1988. ISBN 0-13-110362-9

- Lehey, Greg. *Porting UNIX Software*. O'Reilly & Associates, Inc., 1995. ISBN 1-56592-126-7

- Plauger, P. J. *The Standard C Library*. Prentice Hall, 1992. ISBN 0-13-131509-9

- Stevens, W. Richard. *Advanced Programming in the UNIX Environment*. Reading, Mass. : Addison-Wesley, 1992 ISBN 0-201-56317-7

- Stevens, W. Richard. *UNIX Network Programming*. 2nd Ed, PTR Prentice Hall, 1998. ISBN 0-13-490012-X

- Wells, Bill. "Writing Serial Drivers for UNIX". *Dr. Dobb's Journal*. 19(15), December 1994. pp68-71, 97-99.

B.5 Operating System Internals

- Andleigh, Prabhat K. *UNIX System Architecture*. Prentice-Hall, Inc., 1990. ISBN 0-13-949843-5

- Jolitz, William. "Porting UNIX to the 386". *Dr. Dobb's Journal*. January 1991-July 1992.

- Leffler, Samuel J., Marshall Kirk McKusick, Michael J Karels and John Quarterman *The Design and Implementation of the 4.3BSD UNIX Operating System*. Reading, Mass. : Addison-Wesley, 1989. ISBN 0-201-06196-1

- Leffler, Samuel J., Marshall Kirk McKusick, *The Design and Implementation of the 4.3BSD UNIX Operating System: Answer Book*. Reading, Mass. : Addison-Wesley, 1991. ISBN 0-201-54629-9

- McKusick, Marshall Kirk, Keith Bostic, Michael J Karels, and John Quarterman. *The Design and Implementation of the 4.4BSD Operating System*. Reading, Mass. : Addison-Wesley, 1996. ISBN 0-201-54979-4

- Stevens, W. Richard. *TCP/IP Illustrated, Volume 1: The Protocols*. Reading, Mass. : Addison-Wesley, 1996. ISBN 0-201-63346-9

- Schimmel, Curt. *Unix Systems for Modern Architectures*. Reading, Mass. : Addison-Wesley, 1994. ISBN 0-201-63338-8

- Stevens, W. Richard. *TCP/IP Illustrated, Volume 3: TCP for Transactions, HTTP, NNTP and the UNIX Domain Protocols*. Reading, Mass. : Addison-Wesley, 1996. ISBN 0-201-63495-3

- Vahalia, Uresh. *UNIX Internals -- The New Frontiers*. Prentice Hall, 1996. ISBN 0-13-101908-2
- Wright, Gary R. and W. Richard Stevens. *TCP/IP Illustrated, Volume 2: The Implementation*. Reading, Mass. : Addison-Wesley, 1995. ISBN 0-201-63354-X

B.6 Security Reference

- Cheswick, William R. and Steven M. Bellovin. *Firewalls and Internet Security: Repelling the Wily Hacker*. Reading, Mass. : Addison-Wesley, 1995. ISBN 0-201-63357-4
- Garfinkel, Simson and Gene Spafford. *Practical UNIX & Internet Security*. 2nd Ed. O'Reilly & Associates, Inc., 1996. ISBN 1-56592-148-8
- Garfinkel, Simson. *PGP Pretty Good Privacy* O'Reilly & Associates, Inc., 1995. ISBN 1-56592-098-8

B.7 Hardware Reference

- Anderson, Don and Tom Shanley. *Pentium Processor System Architecture*. 2nd Ed. Reading, Mass. : Addison-Wesley, 1995. ISBN 0-201-40992-5
- Ferraro, Richard F. *Programmer's Guide to the EGA, VGA, and Super VGA Cards*. 3rd ed. Reading, Mass. : Addison-Wesley, 1995. ISBN 0-201-62490-7
- Intel Corporation publishes documentation on their CPUs, chipsets and standards on their developer web site[4], usually as PDF files.
- Shanley, Tom. *80486 System Architecture*. 3rd ed. Reading, Mass. : Addison-Wesley, 1995. ISBN 0-201-40994-1
- Shanley, Tom. *ISA System Architecture*. 3rd ed. Reading, Mass. : Addison-Wesley, 1995. ISBN 0-201-40996-8
- Shanley, Tom. *PCI System Architecture*. 4th ed. Reading, Mass. : Addison-Wesley, 1999. ISBN 0-201-30974-2
- Van Gilluwe, Frank. *The Undocumented PC*, 2nd Ed. Reading, Mass: Addison-Wesley Pub. Co., 1996. ISBN 0-201-47950-8

B.8 Unix History

- Lion, John *Lion's Commentary on UNIX, 6th Ed. With Source Code*. ITP Media Group, 1996. ISBN 1573980137
- Raymond, Eric S. *The New Hacker's Dictionary, 3rd edition*. MIT Press, 1996. ISBN 0-262-68092-0. Also known as the Jargon File[5]

---

4 http://developer.intel.com/
5 http://www.ccil.org/jargon/jargon.html

- Salus, Peter H. *A quarter century of UNIX*. Addison-Wesley Publishing Company, Inc., 1994. ISBN 0-201-54777-5

- Simon Garfinkel, Daniel Weise, Steven Strassmann. *The UNIX-HATERS Handbook*. IDG Books Worldwide, Inc., 1994. ISBN 1-56884-203-1

- Don Libes, Sandy Ressler *Life with UNIX* — special edition. Prentice-Hall, Inc., 1989. ISBN 0-13-536657-7

- *The BSD family tree*. 1997. `ftp://ftp.FreeBSD.org/pub/FreeBSD/FreeBSD-current/src/share/misc/bsd-family-tree` or local[7] on a FreeBSD-current machine.

- *The BSD Release Announcements collection*. 1997. `http://www.de.FreeBSD.org/de/ftp/releases/`

- *Networked Computer Science Technical Reports Library*. `http://www.ncstrl.org/`

- *Old BSD releases from the Computer Systems Research group (CSRG)*. `http://www.mckusick.com/csrg/`: The 4CD set covers all BSD versions from 1BSD to 4.4BSD and 4.4BSD-Lite2 (but not 2.11BSD, unfortunately). As well, the last disk holds the final sources plus the SCCS files.

B.9 Magazines and Journals

- *The C/C++ Users Journal*. R&D Publications Inc. ISSN 1075-2838

- *Sys Admin — The Journal for UNIX System Administrators* Miller Freeman, Inc., ISSN 1061-2688

---

7 file:/usr/share/misc/bsd-family-tree

Appendix B. Bibliography

Appendix C.
Resources on the Internet

The rapid pace of FreeBSD progress makes print media impractical as a means of following the latest developments. Electronic resources are the best, if not often the only, way stay informed of the latest advances. Since FreeBSD is a volunteer effort, the user community itself also generally serves as a "technical support department" of sorts, with electronic mail and USENET news being the most effective way of reaching that community.

The most important points of contact with the FreeBSD user community are outlined below. If you are aware of other resources not mentioned here, please send them to the FreeBSD documentation project mailing list `<freebsd-doc@FreeBSD.org>`so that they may also be included.

C.1 Mailing Lists

Though many of the FreeBSD development members read USENET, we cannot always guarantee that we will get to your questions in a timely fashion (or at all) if you post them only to one of the `comp.unix.bsd.freebsd.*` groups. By addressing your questions to the appropriate mailing list you will reach both us and a concentrated FreeBSD audience, invariably assuring a better (or at least faster) response.

The charters for the various lists are given at the bottom of this document. *Please read the charter before joining or sending mail to any list.* Most of our list subscribers now receive many hundreds of FreeBSD related messages every day, and by setting down charters and rules for proper use we are striving to keep the signal-to-noise ratio of the lists high. To do less would see the mailing lists ultimately fail as an effective communications medium for the project.

Archives are kept for all of the mailing lists and can be searched using the FreeBSD World Wide Web server[1]. The keyword searchable archive offers an excellent way of finding answers to frequently asked questions and should be consulted before posting a question.

C.1.1 List Summary

General lists: The following are general lists which anyone is free (and encouraged) to join:

List	Purpose
cvs-all	Changes made to the FreeBSD source tree
freebsd-advocacy	FreeBSD Evangelism
freebsd-announce	Important events and project milestones
freebsd-arch	Architecture and design discussions

---

1 http://www.FreeBSD.org/search.html

List	Purpose
freebsd-bugs	Bug reports
freebsd-chat	Non-technical items related to the FreeBSD community
freebsd-config	Development of FreeBSD installation and configuration tools
freebsd-current	Discussion concerning the use of FreeBSD-current
freebsd-isp	Issues for Internet Service Providers using FreeBSD
freebsd-jobs	FreeBSD employment and consulting opportunities
freebsd-newbies	New FreeBSD users activities and discussions
freebsd-policy	FreeBSD Core team policy decisions. Low volume, and read-only
freebsd-questions	User questions and technical support
freebsd-stable	Discussion concerning the use of FreeBSD-stable
freebsd-test	Where to send your test messages instead of one of the actual lists

Technical lists: The following lists are for technical discussion. You should read the charter for each list carefully before joining or sending mail to one as there are firm guidelines for their use and content.

List	Purpose
freebsd-afs	Porting AFS to FreeBSD
freebsd-alpha	Porting FreeBSD to the Alpha
freebsd-arm	Porting FreeBSD to ARM processors
freebsd-atm	Using ATM networking with FreeBSD
freebsd-audit	Source code audit project
freebsd-binup	Design and development of the binary update system
freebsd-cluster	Using FreeBSD in a clustered environment
freebsd-database	Discussing database use and development under FreeBSD
freebsd-doc	Creating FreeBSD related documents
freebsd-emulation	Emulation of other systems such as Linux/DOS/Windows
freebsd-fs	Filesystems
freebsd-hackers	General technical discussion
freebsd-hardware	General discussion of hardware for running FreeBSD
freebsd-i18n	FreeBSD Internationalization
freebsd-ia64	Porting FreeBSD to Intel's upcoming IA64 systems
freebsd-ipfw	Technical discussion concerning the redesign of the IP firewall code
freebsd-isdn	ISDN developers
freebsd-java	Java developers and people porting JDKs to FreeBSD
freebsd-libh	The second generation installation and package system
freebsd-mobile	Discussions about mobile computing

List	Purpose
freebsd-mozilla	Porting mozilla to FreeBSD
freebsd-multimedia	Multimedia applications
freebsd-new-bus	Technical discussions about bus architecture
freebsd-net	Networking discussion and TCP/IP source code
freebsd-platforms	Concerning ports to non-Intel architecture platforms
freebsd-ports	Discussion of the ports collection
freebsd-ppc	Porting FreeBSD to the PowerPC
freebsd-qa	Discussion of Quality Assurance, usually pending a release
freebsd-realtime	Development of realtime extensions to FreeBSD
freebsd-scsi	The SCSI subsystem
freebsd-security	Security issues
freebsd-security-notifications	Security notifications
freebsd-small	Using FreeBSD in embedded applications
freebsd-smp	Design discussions for [A]Symmetric MultiProcessing
freebsd-sparc	Porting FreeBSD to Sparc systems
freebsd-tokenring	Support Token Ring in FreeBSD

Limited lists: The following lists are for more specialized (and demanding) audiences and are probably not of interest to the general public. It is also a good idea to establish a presence in the technical lists before joining one of these limited lists so that you will understand the communications etiquette involved.

List	Purpose
freebsd-core	FreeBSD core team
freebsd-hubs	People running mirror sites (infrastructural support)
freebsd-install	Installation development
freebsd-user-groups	User group coordination
freebsd-www	Maintainers of `http://www.FreeBSD.org`

Digest lists: Many of the above lists are also available as digests. New messages posted to the list are collected and sent out as a single email when the sizes goes over 100KB. The lists available in digest form are:

List
freebsd-afs-digest
freebsd-alpha-digest
freebsd-chat-digest
freebsd-current-digest
freebsd-cvs-all-digest
freebsd-database-digest
freebsd-hackers-digest

List

freebsd-ia64-digest

freebsd-isdn-digest

freebsd-java-digest

freebsd-questions-digest

freebsd-security-digest

freebsd-sparc-digest

freebsd-stable-digest

freebsd-test-digest

CVS lists: The following lists are for people interested in seeing the log messages for changes to various areas of the source tree. They are *Read-Only* lists and should not have mail sent to them.

List	Source area	Area Description (source for)
cvs-all	/usr/src	All changes to the tree (superset)

C.1.2 How to Subscribe

All mailing lists live on `FreeBSD.org`, so to post to a given list you simply mail to <*listname*@FreeBSD.org>. It will then be redistributed to mailing list members world-wide.

To subscribe to a list, send mail to <majordomo@FreeBSD.org> and include

```
subscribe <listname> [<optional address>]
```

in the body of your message. For example, to subscribe yourself to `freebsd-announce`, you would do:

```
% mail majordomo@FreeBSD.org
subscribe freebsd-announce
^D
```

If you want to subscribe yourself under a different name, or submit a subscription request for a local mailing list (this is more efficient if you have several interested parties at one site, and highly appreciated by us!), you would do something like:

```
% mail majordomo@FreeBSD.org
subscribe freebsd-announce local-announce@example.com
^D
```

Finally, it is also possible to unsubscribe yourself from a list, get a list of other list members or see the list of mailing lists again by sending other types of control messages to majordomo. For a complete list of available commands, do this:

```
% mail majordomo@FreeBSD.org
help
^D
```

Again, we would like to request that you keep discussion in the technical mailing lists on a technical track. If you are only interested in important announcements then it is suggested that you join freebsd-announce, which is intended only for infrequent traffic.

C.1.3 List Charters

All FreeBSD mailing lists have certain basic rules which must be adhered to by anyone using them. Failure to comply with these guidelines will result in two (2) written warnings from the FreeBSD Postmaster `<postmaster@FreeBSD.org>`, after which, on a third offense, the poster will removed from all FreeBSD mailing lists and filtered from further posting to them. We regret that such rules and measures are necessary at all, but today's Internet is a pretty harsh environment, it would seem, and many fail to appreciate just how fragile some of its mechanisms are.

Rules of the road:

- The topic of any posting should adhere to the basic charter of the list it is posted to, e.g. if the list is about technical issues then your posting should contain technical discussion. Ongoing irrelevant chatter or flaming only detracts from the value of the mailing list for everyone on it and will not be tolerated. For free-form discussion on no particular topic, the freebsd-chat `<freebsd-chat@FreeBSD.org>` mailing list is freely available and should be used instead.

- No posting should be made to more than 2 mailing lists, and only to 2 when a clear and obvious need to post to both lists exists. For most lists, there is already a great deal of subscriber overlap and except for the most esoteric mixes (say "-stable & -scsi"), there really is no reason to post to more than one list at a time. If a message is sent to you in such a way that multiple mailing lists appear on the `Cc` line then the `Cc` line should also be trimmed before sending it out again. *You are still responsible for your own cross-postings, no matter who the originator might have been.*

- Personal attacks and profanity (in the context of an argument) are not allowed, and that includes users and developers alike. Gross breaches of netiquette, like excerpting or reposting private mail when permission to do so was not and would not be forthcoming, are frowned upon but not specifically enforced. *However*, there are also very few cases where such content would fit within the charter of a list and it would therefore probably rate a warning (or ban) on that basis alone.

- Advertising of non-FreeBSD related products or services is strictly prohibited and will result in an immediate ban if it is clear that the offender is advertising by spam.

Individual list charters:

FREEBSD-AFS

> *Andrew File System*

> This list is for discussion on porting and using AFS from CMU/Transarc

FREEBSD-ANNOUNCE

> *Important events / milestones*

This is the mailing list for people interested only in occasional announcements of significant FreeBSD events. This includes announcements about snapshots and other releases. It contains announcements of new FreeBSD capabilities. It may contain calls for volunteers etc. This is a low volume, strictly moderated mailing list.

FREEBSD-ARCH

Architecture and design discussions

This list is for discussion of the FreeBSD architecture. Messages will mostly be kept strictly technical in nature. Examples of suitable topics are:

- How to re-vamp the build system to have several customized builds running at the same time.
- What needs to be fixed with VFS to make Heidemann layers work.
- How do we change the device driver interface to be able to use the same drivers cleanly on many buses and architectures.
- How to write a network driver.

FREEBSD-AUDIT

Source code audit project

This is the mailing list for the FreeBSD source code audit project. Although this was originally intended for security-related changes, its charter has been expanded to review any code changes.

This list is very heavy on patches, and is probably of no interest to the average FreeBSD user. Security discussions not related to a particular code change are held on freebsd-security. Conversely, all developers are encouraged to send their patches here for review, especially if they touch a part of the system where a bug may adversely affect the integrity of the system.

FREEBSD-BINUP

FreeBSD Binary Update Project

This list exists to provide discussion for the binary update system, or **binup**. Design issues, implementation details, patches, bug reports, status reports, feature requests, commit logs, and all other things related to **binup** are fair game.

FREEBSD-BUGS

Bug reports

This is the mailing list for reporting bugs in FreeBSD Whenever possible, bugs should be submitted using the send-pr(1) command or the WEB interface[2] to it.

---

2 http://www.FreeBSD.org/send-pr.html

FREEBSD-CHAT

Non technical items related to the FreeBSD community

This list contains the overflow from the other lists about non-technical, social information. It includes discussion about whether Jordan looks like a toon ferret or not, whether or not to type in capitals, who is drinking too much coffee, where the best beer is brewed, who is brewing beer in their basement, and so on. Occasional announcements of important events (such as upcoming parties, weddings, births, new jobs, etc) can be made to the technical lists, but the follow ups should be directed to this -chat list.

FREEBSD-CORE

FreeBSD core team

This is an internal mailing list for use by the core members. Messages can be sent to it when a serious FreeBSD-related matter requires arbitration or high-level scrutiny.

FREEBSD-CURRENT

Discussions about the use of FreeBSD-current

This is the mailing list for users of freebsd-current. It includes warnings about new features coming out in -current that will affect the users, and instructions on steps that must be taken to remain -current. Anyone running "current" must subscribe to this list. This is a technical mailing list for which strictly technical content is expected.

FREEBSD-CURRENT-DIGEST

Discussions about the use of FreeBSD-current

This is the digest version of the freebsd-current mailing list. The digest consists of all messages sent to freebsd-current bundled together and mailed out as a single message. This list is *Read-Only* and should not be posted to.

FREEBSD-DOC

Documentation project

This mailing list is for the discussion of issues and projects related to the creation of documentation for FreeBSD. The members of this mailing list are collectively referred to as "The FreeBSD Documentation Project". It is an open list; feel free to join and contribute!

FREEBSD-FS

Filesystems

Discussions concerning FreeBSD filesystems. This is a technical mailing list for which strictly technical content is expected.

FREEBSD-IPFW

IP Firewall

This is the forum for technical discussions concerning the redesign of the IP firewall code in FreeBSD. This is a technical mailing list for which strictly technical content is expected.

FREEBSD-IA64

Porting FreeBSD to IA64

This is a technical mailing list for individuals actively working on porting FreeBSD to the IA-64 platform from Intel, to bring up problems or discuss alternative solutions. Individuals interested in following the technical discussion are also welcome.

FREEBSD-ISDN

ISDN Communications

This is the mailing list for people discussing the development of ISDN support for FreeBSD.

FREEBSD-JAVA

Java Development

This is the mailing list for people discussing the development of significant Java applications for FreeBSD and the porting and maintenance of JDKs.

FREEBSD-HACKERS

Technical discussions

This is a forum for technical discussions related to FreeBSD. This is the primary technical mailing list. It is for individuals actively working on FreeBSD, to bring up problems or discuss alternative solutions. Individuals interested in following the technical discussion are also welcome. This is a technical mailing list for which strictly technical content is expected.

FREEBSD-HACKERS-DIGEST

Technical discussions

This is the digest version of the freebsd-hackers mailing list. The digest consists of all messages sent to freebsd-hackers bundled together and mailed out as a single message. This list is *Read-Only* and should not be posted to.

FREEBSD-HARDWARE

General discussion of FreeBSD hardware

General discussion about the types of hardware that FreeBSD runs on, various problems and suggestions concerning what to buy or avoid.

FREEBSD-HUBS

Mirror sites

Announcements and discussion for people who run FreeBSD mirror sites.

FREEBSD-INSTALL

Installation discussion

This mailing list is for discussing FreeBSD installation development for the future releases.

FREEBSD-ISP

Issues for Internet Service Providers

This mailing list is for discussing topics relevant to Internet Service Providers (ISPs) using FreeBSD. This is a technical mailing list for which strictly technical content is expected.

FREEBSD-NEWBIES

Newbies activities discussion

We cover any of the activities of newbies that are not already dealt with elsewhere, including: independent learning and problem solving techniques, finding and using resources and asking for help elsewhere, how to use mailing lists and which lists to use, general chat, making mistakes, boasting, sharing ideas, stories, moral (but not technical) support, and taking an active part in the FreeBSD community. We take our problems and support questions to freebsd-questions, and use freebsd-newbies to meet others who are doing the same things that we do as newbies.

FREEBSD-PLATFORMS

Porting to Non-Intel platforms

Cross-platform FreeBSD issues, general discussion and proposals for non-Intel FreeBSD ports. This is a technical mailing list for which strictly technical content is expected.

FREEBSD-POLICY

Core team policy decisions

This is a low volume, read-only mailing list for FreeBSD Core Team Policy decisions.

FREEBSD-PORTS

Discussion of "ports"

Discussions concerning FreeBSD's "ports collection" (/usr/ports), proposed ports, modifications to ports collection infrastructure and general coordination efforts. This is a technical mailing list for which strictly technical content is expected.

FREEBSD-QUESTIONS

User questions

This is the mailing list for questions about FreeBSD. You should not send "how to" questions to the technical lists unless you consider the question to be pretty technical.

FREEBSD-QUESTIONS-DIGEST

User questions

This is the digest version of the freebsd-questions mailing list. The digest consists of all messages sent to freebsd-questions bundled together and mailed out as a single message.

FREEBSD-SCSI

SCSI subsystem

This is the mailing list for people working on the scsi subsystem for FreeBSD. This is a technical mailing list for which strictly technical content is expected.

FREEBSD-SECURITY

Security issues

FreeBSD computer security issues (DES, Kerberos, known security holes and fixes, etc). This is a technical mailing list for which strictly technical content is expected.

FREEBSD-SECURITY-NOTIFICATIONS

Security Notifications

Notifications of FreeBSD security problems and fixes. This is not a discussion list. The discussion list is FreeBSD-security.

FREEBSD-SMALL

Using FreeBSD in embedded applications

This list discusses topics related to unusually small and embedded FreeBSD installations. This is a technical mailing list for which strictly technical content is expected.

FREEBSD-STABLE

Discussions about the use of FreeBSD-stable

This is the mailing list for users of freebsd-stable. It includes warnings about new features coming out in -stable that will affect the users, and instructions on steps that must be taken to remain -stable. Anyone running "stable" should subscribe to this list. This is a technical mailing list for which strictly technical content is expected.

FREEBSD-USER-GROUPS

User Group Coordination List

This is the mailing list for the coordinators from each of the local area Users Groups to discuss matters with each other and a designated individual from the Core Team. This mail list should be limited to meeting synopsis and coordination of projects that span User Groups.

C.2 Usenet Newsgroups

In addition to two FreeBSD specific newsgroups, there are many others in which FreeBSD is discussed or are otherwise relevant to FreeBSD users. Keyword searchable archives[3] are available for some of these newsgroups from courtesy of Warren Toomey <wkt@cs.adfa.edu.au>.

C.2.1 BSD Specific Newsgroups

- `comp.unix.bsd.freebsd.announce`
- `comp.unix.bsd.freebsd.misc`

---

3 http://minnie.tuhs.org/BSD-info/bsdnews_search.html

C.2.2 Other Unix Newsgroups of Interest

- `comp.unix`
- `comp.unix.questions`
- `comp.unix.admin`
- `comp.unix.programmer`
- `comp.unix.shell`
- `comp.unix.user-friendly`
- `comp.security.unix`
- `comp.sources.unix`
- `comp.unix.advocacy`
- `comp.unix.misc`
- `comp.bugs.4bsd`
- `comp.bugs.4bsd.ucb-fixes`
- `comp.unix.bsd`

C.2.3 X Window System

- `comp.windows.x.i386unix`
- `comp.windows.x`
- `comp.windows.x.apps`
- `comp.windows.x.announce`
- `comp.windows.x.intrinsics`
- `comp.windows.x.motif`
- `comp.windows.x.pex`
- `comp.emulators.ms-windows.wine`

C.3 World Wide Web Servers

- `http://www.FreeBSD.org/` — Central Server.
- `http://www.au.FreeBSD.org/` — Australia/1.

- `http://www2.au.FreeBSD.org/` — Australia/2.
- `http://www3.au.FreeBSD.org/` — Australia/3.
- `http://freebsd.itworks.com.au/` — Australia/4.
- `http://www.br.FreeBSD.org/www.freebsd.org/` — Brazil/1.
- `http://www2.br.FreeBSD.org/www.freebsd.org/` — Brazil/2.
- `http://www3.br.FreeBSD.org/` — Brazil/3.
- `http://www.bg.FreeBSD.org/` — Bulgaria.
- `http://www.ca.FreeBSD.org/` — Canada/1.
- `http://www2.ca.FreeBSD.org/` — Canada/2.
- `http://www3.ca.FreeBSD.org/` — Canada/3.
- `http://www.cn.FreeBSD.org/` — China.
- `http://www.cz.FreeBSD.org/` — Czech Republic.
- `http://www.dk.FreeBSD.org/` — Denmark.
- `http://www.ee.FreeBSD.org/` — Estonia.
- `http://www.fi.FreeBSD.org/` — Finland.
- `http://www.fr.FreeBSD.org/` — France.
- `http://www.de.FreeBSD.org/` — Germany/1.
- `http://www1.de.FreeBSD.org/` — Germany/2.
- `http://www2.de.FreeBSD.org/` — Germany/3.
- `http://www.gr.FreeBSD.org/` — Greece.
- `http://www.hu.FreeBSD.org/` — Hungary.
- `http://www.is.FreeBSD.org/` — Iceland.
- `http://www.ie.FreeBSD.org/` — Ireland.
- `http://www.jp.FreeBSD.org/www.FreeBSD.org/` — Japan.
- `http://www.kr.FreeBSD.org/` — Korea/1.
- `http://www2.kr.FreeBSD.org/` — Korea/2.
- `http://www.lv.FreeBSD.org/` — Latvia.
- `http://rama.asiapac.net/freebsd/` — Malaysia.
- `http://www.nl.FreeBSD.org/` — Netherlands/1.
- `http://www2.nl.FreeBSD.org/` — Netherlands/2.
- `http://www.no.FreeBSD.org/` — Norway.
- `http://www.nz.FreeBSD.org/` — New Zealand.
- `http://www.pl.FreeBSD.org/` — Poland/1.

- `http://www2.pl.FreeBSD.org/` — Poland/2.
- `http://www.pt.FreeBSD.org/` — Portugal/1.
- `http://www2.pt.FreeBSD.org/` — Portugal/2.
- `http://www3.pt.FreeBSD.org/` — Portugal/3.
- `http://www.ro.FreeBSD.org/` — Romania.
- `http://www.ru.FreeBSD.org/` — Russia/1.
- `http://www2.ru.FreeBSD.org/` — Russia/2.
- `http://www3.ru.FreeBSD.org/` — Russia/3.
- `http://www4.ru.FreeBSD.org/` — Russia/4.
- `http://freebsd.s1web.com/` — Singapore.
- `http://www.sk.FreeBSD.org/` — Slovak Republic.
- `http://www.si.FreeBSD.org/` — Slovenia.
- `http://www.es.FreeBSD.org/` — Spain.
- `http://www.za.FreeBSD.org/` — South Africa/1.
- `http://www2.za.FreeBSD.org/` — South Africa/2.
- `http://www.se.FreeBSD.org/` — Sweden.
- `http://www.ch.FreeBSD.org/` — Switzerland.
- `http://www.tw.FreeBSD.org/www.freebsd.org/data/` — Taiwan.
- `http://www.tr.FreeBSD.org/` — Turkey.
- `http://www.ua.FreeBSD.org/www.freebsd.org/` — Ukraine/1.
- `http://www2.ua.FreeBSD.org/` — Ukraine/2.
- `http://www4.ua.FreeBSD.org/` — Ukraine/Crimea.
- `http://www.uk.FreeBSD.org/` — United Kingdom/1.
- `http://www2.uk.FreeBSD.org/` — United Kingdom/2.
- `http://www3.uk.FreeBSD.org/` — United Kingdom/3.
- `http://www6.FreeBSD.org/` — USA/Oregon.
- `http://www2.FreeBSD.org/` — USA/Texas.

C.4 Email Addresses

The following user groups provide FreeBSD related email addresses for their members. The listed administrator reserves the right to revoke the address if it is abused in any way.

Domain	Facilities	User Group	Administrator
ukug.uk.FreeBSD.org	Forwarding only	`<freebsd-users@uk.FreeBSD.org>`	Lee Johnston `<lee@uk.FreeBSD.org>`

C.5 Shell Accounts

The following user groups provide shell accounts for people who are actively supporting the FreeBSD project. The listed administrator reserves the right to cancel the account if it is abused in any way.

Host	Access	Facilities	Administrator
storm.uk.FreeBSD.org	SSH only	Read-only cvs, personal web space, email	Brian Somers `<brian@FreeBSD.org>`
dogma.freebsd-uk.eu.org	Telnet/FTP/SSH	Email, Web space, Anonymous FTP	Lee Johnston `<lee@uk.FreeBSD.org>`

Appendix D.

PGP Keys

In case you need to verify a signature or send encrypted email to one of the officers or developers a number of keys are provided here for your convenience. A complete keyring of FreeBSD.org users is available for download from http://www.FreeBSD.org/doc/pgpkeyring.txt.

D.1 Officers

D.1.1 FreeBSD Security Officer `<security-officer@FreeBSD.org>`

```
FreeBSD Security Officer <security-officer@FreeBSD.org>
Fingerprint = 41 08 4E BB DB 41 60 71  F9 E5 0E 98 73 AF 3F 11
```

D.2 Core Team Members

D.2.1 Satoshi Asami `<asami@FreeBSD.org>`

```
Satoshi Asami <asami@cs.berkeley.edu>
        aka <asami@FreeBSD.org>
Fingerprint = EB 3C 68 9E FB 6C EB 3F  DB 2E 0F 10 8F CE 79 CA
```

D.2.2 Jordan K. Hubbard `<jkh@FreeBSD.org>`

```
Jordan K. Hubbard <jkh@FreeBSD.org>
Fingerprint = 3C F2 27 7E 4A 6C 09 0A  4B C9 47 CD 4F 4D 0B 20
```

D.2.3 Warner Losh `<imp@FreeBSD.org>`

```
Warner Losh <imp@village.org>
 aka <imp@FreeBSD.org>
```

```
Fingerprint = D4 31 FD B9 F7 90 17 E8 37 C5 E7 7F CF A6 C1 B9
```

D.2.4 Peter Wemm `<peter@FreeBSD.org>`

```
Peter Wemm <peter@FreeBSD.org>
      aka <peter@spinner.dialix.com>
      aka <peter@haywire.dialix.com>
      aka <peter@perth.dialix.oz.au>
Key fingerprint = 47 05 04 CA 4C EE F8 93  F6 DB 02 92 6D F5 58 8A
```

D.2.5 Doug Rabson `<dfr@FreeBSD.org>`

```
Doug Rabson <dfr@FreeBSD.org>
Key fingerprint = 20 BB E4 38 5D 89 D2 D4  68 A6 2F DC 0A DE 10 3C
```

D.3 Developers

D.3.1 Will Andrews `<will@FreeBSD.org>`

```
pub  1024D/F81672C5 2000-05-22 Will Andrews (Key for official matters) <will@FreeBSD.org>
     Key fingerprint = 661F BBF7 9F5D 3D02 C862  5F6C 178E E274 F816 72C5
uid                        Will Andrews <will@physics.purdue.edu>
uid                        Will Andrews <will@puck.firepipe.net>
uid                        Will Andrews <will@c-60.org>
uid                        Will Andrews <will@csociety.org>
uid                        Will Andrews <will@csociety.ecn.purdue.edu>
uid                        Will Andrews <will@telperion.openpackages.org>
sub  1024g/55472804 2000-05-22
```

D.3.2 Anton Berezin `<tobez@FreeBSD.org>`

```
pub  1024D/7A7BA3C0 2000-05-25 Anton Berezin <tobez@catpipe.net>
     Key fingerprint = CDD8 560C 174B D8E5 0323  83CE 22CA 584C 7A7B A3C0
uid                        Anton Berezin <tobez@tobez.org>
uid                        Anton Berezin <tobez@FreeBSD.org>
sub  1024g/ADC71E87 2000-05-25
```

D.3.3 Jonathan M. Bresler `<jmb@FreeBSD.org>`

```
Jonathan M. Bresler <jmb@FreeBSD.org>
f16    Fingerprint16 = 31 57 41 56 06 C1 40 13  C5 1C E3 E5 DC 62 0E FB
```

D.3.4 Andrey A. Chernov `<ache@FreeBSD.org>`

```
Andrey A. Chernov <ache@FreeBSD.org>
      aka <ache@nagual.pp.ru>
Key fingerprint = 33 03 9F 48 33 7B 4A 15  63 48 88 0A C4 97 FD 49
```

D.3.5 Nik Clayton `<nik@FreeBSD.org>`

```
pub  1024D/2C37E375 2000-11-09 Nik Clayton <nik@freebsd.org>
     Key fingerprint = 15B8 3FFC DDB4 34B0 AA5F  94B7 93A8 0764 2C37 E375
uid                          Nik Clayton <nik@slashdot.org>
uid                          Nik Clayton <nik@crf-consulting.co.uk>
uid                          Nik Clayton <nik@ngo.org.uk>
uid                          Nik Clayton <nik@bsdi.com>
sub  1024g/769E298A 2000-11-09
```

D.3.6 Dima Dorfman `<dd@FreeBSD.org>`

```
pub  1024D/69FAE582 2001-09-04 Dima Dorfman <dd@freebsd.org>
     Key fingerprint = B340 8338 7DA3 4D61 7632  098E 0730 055B 69FA E582
uid                          Dima Dorfman <dima@unixfreak.org>
sub  1024g/A51DD1C0 2001-09-04 [expires: 2003-09-04]
```

D.3.7 Udo Erdelhoff `<ue@FreeBSD.org>`

```
pub  1024R/E74FA871 1994-07-19 Udo Erdelhoff <ue@nathan.ruhr.de>
     Key fingerprint = 8C B1 80 CA 2C 52 73 81  FB A7 B4 03 C5 32 C8 67
uid                          Udo Erdelhoff <ue@freebsd.org>
uid                          Udo Erdelhoff <uerdelho@eu.uu.net>
uid                          Udo Erdelhoff <uerdelho@uu.net>
uid                          Udo Erdelhoff <uer@de.uu.net>
```

D.3.8 Brian F. Feldman `<green@FreeBSD.org>`

```
pub  1024D/773905D6 2000-09-02 Brian Fundakowski Feldman <green@FreeBSD.org>
sig        773905D6 2000-09-02  Brian Fundakowski Feldman <green@FreeBSD.org>
sub  2048g/D2009B98 2000-09-02
sig        773905D6 2000-09-02  Brian Fundakowski Feldman <green@FreeBSD.org>
```

D.3.9 John-Mark Gurney `<jmg@FreeBSD.org>`

```
Type bits/keyID     Date        User ID
pub  1024/3F9951F5 1997/02/11 John-Mark Gurney <gurney_j@efn.org>
         Key fingerprint =  B7 EC EF F8 AE ED A7 31  96 7A 22 B3 D8 56 36 F4
                         John-Mark Gurney <johnmark@gladstone.uoregon.edu>
                         John-Mark Gurney <jmg@cs.uoregon.edu>
                         John-Mark Gurney <gurney_j@resnet.uoregon.edu>
```

D.3.10 Trevor Johnson `<trevor@FreeBSD.org>`

```
pub  1024D/3A3EA137 2000-04-20 Trevor Johnson <trevor@jpj.net>
     Key fingerprint = 7ED1 5A92 76C1 FFCB E5E3  A998 F037 5A0B 3A3E A137
sub  1024g/46C24F1E 2000-04-20
```

D.3.11 Poul-Henning Kamp `<phk@FreeBSD.org>`

```
Poul-Henning Kamp <phk@FreeBSD.org>
Fingerprint = A3 F3 88 28 2F 9B 99 A2  49 F4 E2 FA 5A 78 8B 3E
RSA  1024      0x0358FCBD 1995/08/01 Poul-Henning Kamp <phk@FreeBSD.org>
```

D.3.12 Josef Karthauser `<joe@FreeBSD.org>`

```
pub  1024D/E6B15016 2000-10-19 Josef Karthauser <joe@tao.org.uk>
uid                            Josef Karthauser <joe@FreeBSD.org>
uid                            Josef Karthauser <joe@uk.FreeBSD.org>
uid                            Josef Karthauser <joe@pavilion.net>
sub  2048g/1178B692 2000-10-19

pub   768R/7EBDECB1 1996-12-19 Josef L. Karthauser <joe@pavilion.net>
uid                            Josef L. Karthauser <joe@tao.org.uk>
uid                            Josef L. Karthauser <joe@uk.FreeBSD.org>
uid                            Josef L. Karthauser <joe@FreeBSD.org>
```

D.3.13 Giorgos Keramidas `<keramida@FreeBSD.org>`

```
pub   1024D/318603B6 2001-09-21 Giorgos Keramidas <keramida@FreeBSD.org>
      Key fingerprint = C1EB 0653 DB8B A557 3829  00F9 D60F 941A 3186 03B6
uid                             Giorgos Keramidas <charon@labs.gr>
uid                             Giorgos Keramidas <keramida@ceid.upatras.gr>
sub   1024g/50FDBAD1 2001-09-21
```

D.3.14 Andreas Klemm `<andreas@FreeBSD.org>`

```
pub   1024D/6C6F6CBA 2001-01-06 Andreas Klemm <andreas@klemm.gtn.com>
      Key fingerprint = F028 D51A 0D42 DD67 4109  19A3 777A 3E94 6C6F 6CBA
uid                             Andreas Klemm <andreas@FreeBSD.org>
uid                             Andreas Klemm <andreas@apsfilter.org>
uid                             Andreas Klemm <andreas.klemm@eu.didata.com>
sub   2048g/FE23F866 2001-01-06
```

D.3.15 Bruce A. Mah `<bmah@FreeBSD.org>`

```
Type Bits/KeyID     Date        User ID
pub   1024/23EC263D 1997/03/12 Bruce A. Mah <bmah@cisco.com>
                               Bruce A. Mah <bmah@freebsd.org>
                               Bruce A. Mah <bmah@employees.org>
                               Bruce A. Mah <bmah@ca.sandia.gov>
                               Bruce A. Mah <bmah@ieee.org>
                               Bruce A. Mah <bmah@acm.org>

Type Bits KeyID       Created     Expires     Algorithm       Use
sec+ 1024 0x5BA052C3 1997-12-08 ---------- DSS             Sign & Encrypt
f20     Fingerprint20 = F829 B805 207D 14C7 7197  7832 D8CA 3171 5BA0 52C3
sub  2048 0xB4E60EA1 1997-12-08 ---------- Diffie-Hellman
f20     Fingerprint20 = EF87 710B A12A 93F0 3529  E578 173D A3CD B4E6 0EA1
uid  Bruce A. Mah <bmah@ca.sandia.gov>
uid  Bruce A. Mah <bmah@acm.org>
uid  Bruce A. Mah <bmah@ieee.org>
uid  Bruce A. Mah <bmah@cisco.com>
uid  Bruce A. Mah <bmah@employees.org>
uid  Bruce A. Mah <bmah@freebsd.org>
```

D.3.16 Thomas Möstl `<tmm@FreeBSD.org>`

```
pub   1024D/419C776C 2000-11-28 Thomas Moestl <tmoestl@gmx.net>
      Key fingerprint = 1C97 A604 2BD0 E492 51D0  9C0F 1FE6 4F1D 419C 776C
uid                             Thomas Moestl <t.moestl@tu-bs.de>
uid                             Thomas Moestl <tmm@FreeBSD.org>
```

```
sub   2048g/ECE63CE6 2000-11-28
```

D.3.17 Rich Murphey `<rich@FreeBSD.org>`

```
Rich Murphey <rich@FreeBSD.org>
fingerprint = AF A0 60 C4 84 D6 0C 73  D1 EF C0 E9 9D 21 DB E4
```

D.3.18 David O'Brien `<obrien@FreeBSD.org>`

```
Type Bits KeyID       Created     Expires     Algorithm        Use
sec+ 1024 0x34F9F9D5 1995-04-23 ---------- RSA              Sign & Encrypt
f16     Fingerprint16 = B7 4D 3E E9 11 39 5F A3  90 76 5D 69 58 D9 98 7A
        David E. O'Brien <obrien@NUXI.com>
        David E. O'Brien <obrien@FreeBSD.org>
        David E. O'Brien <obrien@cs.ucdavis.edu>
        David E. O'Brien <dobrien@seas.gwu.edu>
        David E. O'Brien <obrien@elsewhere.roanoke.va.us>
        David E. O'Brien <whois Do38>

sec+ 1024 0x7F9A9BA2 1998-06-10 ---------- DSS              Sign & Encrypt
f20     Fingerprint20 = 02FD 495F D03C 9AF2 5DB7  F496 6FC8 DABD 7F9A 9BA2
sub  3072 0xBA32C20D 1998-06-10 ---------- Diffie-Hellman
f20     Fingerprint20 = 0700 6058 CE6C 1C51 D0A3  45E6 26E1 A405 BA32 C20D
        "David E. O'Brien" <obrien@NUXI.com>
        "David E. O'Brien" <obrien@FreeBSD.org>
```

D.3.19 Jim Pirzyk `<pirzyk@FreeBSD.org>`

```
Jim Pirzyk <pirzyk@FreeBSD.org>
pub  1024D/4E23DACA 2001-03-02 Jim Pirzyk <Jim.Pirzyk@disney.com>
     Key fingerprint = 07EE A1BD 32E5 C402 59B6  22D5 D846 31D1 4E23 DACA
uid                       Jim Pirzyk <pirzyk@freebsd.org>
sub  1024g/F38895F7 2001-03-02
```

D.3.20 John Polstra `<jdp@FreeBSD.org>`

```
John D. Polstra <jdp@polstra.com>
Fingerprint = 54 3A 90 59 6B A4 9D 61  BF 1D 03 09 35 8D F6 0D
```

D.3.21 Mark Pulford `<markp@FreeBSD.org>`

```
Mark Pulford <markp@FreeBSD.org>
Fingerprint = 58C9 C9BF C758 D8D4 7022  8EF5 559F 7F7B 182C 368F
```

D.3.22 Benno Rice `<benno@FreeBSD.org>`

```
pub  1024D/15BE120E 2001-01-15 Benno Rice <benno@FreeBSD.org>
     Key fingerprint = E786 5BF6 A296 5F77 E3DA  7493 6D0C 7BC6 15BE 120E
sub  1024g/313F3AF2 2001-01-15 [expires: 2002-01-15]
```

D.3.23 Guido van Rooij `<guido@FreeBSD.org>`

```
Guido van Rooij <guido@gvr.win.tue.nl>
Fingerprint = 16 79 09 F3 C0 E4 28 A7  32 62 FA F6 60 31 C0 ED
```

D.3.24 Wolfram Schneider `<wosch@FreeBSD.org>`

```
Type Bits/KeyID    Date       User ID
pub  1024/2B7181AD 1997/08/09 Wolfram Schneider <wosch@FreeBSD.org>
          Key fingerprint = CA 16 91 D9 75 33 F1 07  1B F0 B4 9F 3E 95 B6 09
```

D.3.25 Gregory Neil Shapiro `<gshapiro@FreeBSD.org>`

```
Type Bits KeyID       Created     Expires     Algorithm      Use
sec+ 1024 0x4BE2ADD 2000-10-13 ---------- RSA            Sign & Encrypt
f16     Fingerprint16 = 56 D5 FF A7 A6 54 A6 B5  59 10 00 B9 5F 5F 20 09
uid  Gregory Neil Shapiro <gshapiro@gshapiro.net>
uid  Gregory Neil Shapiro <gshapiro@FreeBSD.org>

Type Bits KeyID       Created     Expires     Algorithm      Use
sec+ 1024 0xFCE56561 2000-10-14 2001-10-14 DSS            Sign & Encrypt
f20     Fingerprint20 = 42C4 A87A FD85 C34F E77F  5EA1 88E1 7B1D FCE5 6561
sub  1024 0x285DC8A0 2000-10-14 2001-10-14 Diffie-Hellman
f20     Fingerprint20 = 69AB 26D1 A244 51E3 2B6C  7091 BD19 FA76 285D C8A0
uid  Gregory Neil Shapiro <gshapiro@gshapiro.net>
uid  Gregory Neil Shapiro <gshapiro@FreeBSD.org>
```

D.3.26 Christopher Shumway `<cshumway@FreeBSD.org>`

```
pub  1024D/3219F982 2001-05-17 Christopher Shumway <cshumway@freebsd.org>
uid                            Christopher Shumway <cshumway@titan-project.org>
sub  1024g/D215EFED 2001-05-17

pub  1024R/34879775 2001-04-24 Christopher Shumway <cshumway@freebsd.org>
uid                            Christopher Shumway <cshumway@titan-project.org>
```

D.3.27 Jesper Skriver `<jesper@FreeBSD.org>`

```
pub  1024D/F9561C31 2001-03-09 Jesper Skriver <jesper@skriver.dk>
     Key fingerprint = 6B88 9CE8 66E9 E631 C9C5  5EB4 22AB F0EC F956 1C31
uid                            Jesper Skriver <jesper@wheel.dk>
uid                            Jesper Skriver <jesper@FreeBSD.org>
sub  1024g/777C378C 2001-03-09
```

D.3.28 Ben Smithurst `<ben@FreeBSD.org>`

```
pub  1024D/2CEF442C 2001-07-11 Ben Smithurst <ben@LSRfm.com>
     Key fingerprint = 355D 0FFF B83A 90A9 D648  E409 6CFC C9FB 2CEF 442C
uid                            Ben Smithurst <ben@vinosystems.com>
uid                            Ben Smithurst <ben@smithurst.org>
uid                            Ben Smithurst <ben@FreeBSD.org>
uid                            Ben Smithurst <csxbcs@comp.leeds.ac.uk>
uid                            Ben Smithurst <ben@scientia.demon.co.uk>
sub  1024g/347071FF 2001-07-11
```

D.3.29 Daniel C. Sobral `<dcs@FreeBSD.org>`

```
Type Bits/KeyID    Date       User ID
pub  1024/488A2DD5 2000/06/07 Daniel C. Sobral <dcs@freebsd.org>
             Key fingerprint = AF 90 A6 A2 B5 8D 6C 28  37 F3 F4 47 8B 31 47 DF
                            Daniel C. Sobral <dcs@newsguy.com>
```

D.3.30 Brian Somers `<brian@FreeBSD.org>`

```
pub  1024R/666A7421 1997-04-30 Brian Somers <brian@freebsd-services.com>
     Key fingerprint = 2D 91 BD C2 94 2C 46 8F  8F 09 C4 FC AD 12 3B 21
uid                            Brian Somers <brian@awfulhak.org>
uid                            Brian Somers <brian@uk.OpenBSD.org>
uid                            Brian Somers <brian@uk.FreeBSD.org>
```

```
uid                           Brian Somers <brian@OpenBSD.org>
uid                           Brian Somers <brian@FreeBSD.org>
```

D.3.31 Murray Stokely `<murray@FreeBSD.org>`

```
pub  1024/0E451F7D 2001/02/12 Murray Stokely <murray@freebsd.org>
     Key fingerprint = E2CA 411D DD44 53FD BB4B  3CB5 B4D7 10A2 0E45 1F7D
```

D.3.32 Gregory Sutter `<gsutter@FreeBSD.org>`

```
pub  1024D/845DFEDD 2000-10-10 Gregory S. Sutter <gsutter@zer0.org>
     Key fingerprint = D161 E4EA 4BFA 2427 F3F9  5B1F 2015 31D5 845D FEDD
uid                           Gregory S. Sutter <gsutter@freebsd.org>
uid                           Gregory S. Sutter <gsutter@daemonnews.org>
uid                           Gregory S. Sutter <gsutter@pobox.com>
sub  2048g/0A37BBCE 2000-10-10
```

D.3.33 Garrett Wollman `<wollman@FreeBSD.org>`

```
pub  1024D/0B92FAEA 2000-01-20 Garrett Wollman <wollman@FreeBSD.org>
     Key fingerprint = 4627 19AF 4649 31BF DE2E  3C66 3ECF 741B 0B92 FAEA
sub  1024g/90D5EBC2 2000-01-20
```

D.3.34 Jörg Wunsch `<joerg@FreeBSD.org>`

```
Type Bits/KeyID    Date       User ID
pub  1024/76A3F7B1 1996/04/27 Joerg Wunsch <joerg_wunsch@uriah.heep.sax.de>
           Key fingerprint = DC 47 E6 E4 FF A6 E9 8F  93 21 E0 7D F9 12 D6 4E
                             Joerg Wunsch <joerg_wunsch@interface-business.de>
                             Joerg Wunsch <j@uriah.heep.sax.de>
                             Joerg Wunsch <j@interface-business.de>
```

Appendix E.
Contributing Authors

Author	Contribution
Annelise Anderson	Contributed several minor fixes.
Satoshi Asami	Contributed the Introduction/The FreeBSD Development Model (Section 1.3.3), and PPP and SLIP/Using SLIP (Section 16.6) sections.
John Baldwin	Updated several different sections of the Handbook.
Bojan Bistrovic	Contributed to the Linux Mathematica section (Section 20.3).
Neil Blakey-Milner	Contributed the Users and Basic Account Management Chapter (Chapter 8).
Wilko Bulte	Contributed to the Alpha-specific installation instructions (Chapter 2).
Andrey A. Chernov	Originally contributed the Localization Chapter (Chapter 13), and the Russian Language section (Section 13.5.1).
Peter Childs	Contributed the PPP and SLIP/User PPP section (Section 16.2).
Nik Clayton	Did the initial conversion from LinuxDoc to DocBook, wrote most of the FreeBSD Documentation Project infrastructure, and contributed to many individual sections such as the PPP and SLIP/User PPP section (Section 16.2), Unix Basics/Processes (Section 3.5), and the Install Chapter (Chapter 2).
Chris Costello	Contributed many cosmetic fixes.
Mark Dapoz	Contributed the Security/Kerberos section (Section 10.6).
Matt Dillon	Contributed the tuning(7) and security(7) man pages, which a considerable part of the Configuration and Tuning (Chapter 6) and Security (Chapter 10) chapters are based on.
Dima Dorfman	Corrected many grammar mistakes and helped respond to user feedback to improve the clarity of this text.
Udo Erdelhoff	Contributed the Advanced Networking/NIS/Netgroups (Section 17.7.7) sub-section, and revised the rest of the NIS section (Section 17.7).
Mário Sérgio Fujikawa Ferreira	Contributed the PPP and SLIP/PPPoE/3Com HomeConnect ADSL Modem Dual Link section (Section 16.4.6).
Dirk Frömberg	Provided input for the PPP and SLIP/User PPP section (Section 16.2).
Bill Fumerola	Helped keep parts of the bibliography up to date along with various other cosmetic fixes.
Andrew Gallatin	Contributed to the Alpha-specific installation instructions (Chapter 2).
Coranth Gryphon	Contributed the Advanced Networking/Gateways and Routes section (Section 17.2).
Jake Hamby	Contributed the first version of the Kernel Configuration Chapter (Chapter 9).

Author	Contribution
Brian N. Handy	Contributed the first version of the Linux Binary Compatibility Chapter (Chapter 20).
Guy Helmer	Contributed the Serial Communications/Dial-In Service section (Section 15.4), and provided info for the PPP and SLIP/SLIP section (Section 16.6).
Jordan Hubbard	Contributed most of the Introduction Chapter (Chapter 1) and several of the appendices.
Robert Huff	Contributed parts of the PPP and SLIP/Kernel PPP section (Section 16.3).
Tom Hukins	Contributed the Advanced Networking/NTP section (Section 17.10).
Yoshinobu Inoue	Contributed the Security/IPSec section (Section 10.9).
Sean Kelly	Contributed the Printing Chapter (Chapter 11), Serial Communications/Terminals section (Section 15.3), and added to the Serial Communications/Dial-In Service section (Section 15.4).
Kris Kennaway	Updated parts of the security chapter (Chapter 10).
Giorgos Keramidas	Submitted many quality patches and PRs, contributing to the whole of the doc project.
Holger Kipp	Contributed the Linux Binary Compatibility/Installing SAP/R3 section (Section 20.6).
Seth Kingsley	Contributed the X Window System/XDM section (Section 5.6).
Jun Kuriyama	Translated much of this book into Japanese.
Chern Lee	Helped in rewriting parts, standardizing technical terms, creating technical diagrams to complement the text, and other miscellaneous tasks. Associate editor for the second printed edition published by Wind River Systems. Contributed the Configuration and Tuning Chapter (Chapter 6, based on documents by others), Ports and Packages/Using Packages section (Section 4.4), Security/OpenSSH section (Section 10.10), Advanced Networking/AMD (Section 17.4.4), DNS (Section 17.9), NATD (Section 17.11), and inetd "Super-Server" (Section 17.12) sections.
Greg Lehey	Wrote the original X-Windows chapter and helped tidy up various bits of the book for printed output.
John Lind	Contributed the Advanced Networking/NFS/Problems Integrating with other Systems section (Section 17.4.5).
Bill Lloyd	Contributed the first version of the Mail Chapter (Chapter 18).
Bruce Mah	Contributed to the installation chapter (Chapter 2) and helped find grammatical errors throughout the book.
Mike Makonnen	Contributed the Advanced Networking/DNS/Running named in a Sandbox section (Section 17.9.8).
Eric Melville	Contributed to several sections.
Mike Meyer	Contributed the Storage/Creating Optical Media section (Section 12.6).
Hellmuth Michaelis	Contributed the Advanced Networking/ISDN/ISDN Cards section (Section 17.6.1).

Author	Contribution
Jim Mock	Restructured, reorganized, and rewrote parts of the Introduction (Chapter 1), Install (Chapter 2), Kernel Configuration (Chapter 9), Printing (Chapter 11), Mail (Chapter 18), and Linux Binary Compatibility (Chapter 20) chapters. Editor and project manager for the first printed edition by BSDi.
Marcel Moolenaar	Contributed the Linux Binary Compatibility/Oracle section (Section 20.5).
Moses Moore	Contributed the first version of the Sound Chapter (Chapter 14).
Rich Murphey	Contributed the first version of the Linux Binary Compatibilty Chapter (Chapter 20).
John Murphy	Helped fix many minor grammatical errors throughout the book.
Mark Murray	Contributed the Security/Kerberos section (Section 10.6).
Alex Nash	Contributed the Security/Firewalls section (Section 10.7).
Alexey V. Neyman	Contributed several minor cosmetic fixes.
David O'Brien	Contributed the Storage/Adding Disks section (Section 12.3).
Eric Ogren	Enhanced the Advanced Networking/NIS section (Section 17.7) and helped correct the grammar in many other sections.
Bill Paul	Contributed a document which the Serial Communications/Setting Up the Serial Console section (Section 15.6) is based on.
Gary Palmer	Contributed the Security/Firewalls section (Section 10.7).
Steve Peterson	Contributed the Advanced Networking/Bridging section (Section 17.3).
John Polstra	Updated the CVSup section (Section A.6) and maintainted the list of CVSup mirrors.
Randy Pratt	Wrote most of the Installation Chapter (Chapter 2).
Martin Renters	Contributed the original version of the Advanced Networking/Diskless Operation section (Section 17.5).
Hiroki Sato	Translated much of this book into Japanese.
Piero Serini	Provided input for the PPP and SLIP/SLIP section (Section 16.6).
Christopher Shumway	Rewrote the Basics Chapter (Chapter 3), contributed the X Window System/Configuration (Section 5.4) and Mail/Sendmail (Section 18.3) sections.
Mike Smith	Contributed a tutorial which part of the Configuration and Tuning Chapter (Chapter 6) is based on.
Ben Smithurst	Updated parts of the Cutting Edge/Using make world section (Section 19.4) and fixed many issues found in the PR database.
Brian Somers	Contributed the PPP and SLIP/User PPP section (Section 16.2).
Gennady B. Sorokopud	Contributed parts of the PPP and SLIP/Kernel PPP section (Section 16.3).
G. Adam Stanislav	Contributed some network diagrams along with various other cosmetic fixes.
Wylie Stilwell	Contributed the original version of the Advanced Networking/AMD section (Section 17.4.4).

Author	Contribution
Murray Stokely	Enhanced the documentation project infrastructure to support more aesthetically pleasing print output, indexed most of the book, contributed to many sections, reorganized large chunks of the text. Co-editor and project manager for the second printed edition published by Wind River Systems.
Greg Sutter	Contributed the Advanced Networking/DHCP section (Section 17.8).
Gary W. Swearingen	Contributed many minor grammar fixes.
Bill Swingle	Updated and rewrote parts of the Security/DES, MD5, and Crypt section (Section 10.4), contributed the Advanced Networking/NFS (Section 17.4) and NIS sections (Section 17.7).
Bob Van Valzah	Contributed the Storage/Bootstrapping Vinum section (Section 12.8).
Valentino Vaschetto	Contributed the Install/Advanced Installation section (Section 2.12) and X Window System/Window Managers section (Section 5.7).
Kazutaka YOKOTA	Contributed the Serial Communications/Setting Up the Serial Console section (Section 15.6).
Michael C. Wu	Rewrote the Localization Chapter (Chapter 13).
Alexey Zelkin	Helped update some of our Internet resources and fixed several minor typos.

Index

Symbols

-CURRENT, 501
   Downloading with ftp, 503
   Syncing with CTM, 503
   Syncing with CVSup, 503
-STABLE, 501, 504
   compiling, 505
   downloading with FTP, 505
   syncing with CTM, 505
   syncing with CVSup, 505
   using, 504
/etc, 145
/etc/gettytab, 378
/etc/groups, 175
/etc/login.conf, 172
/etc/mail/access, 493
/etc/mail/aliases, 493
/etc/mail/local-host-names, 493
/etc/mail/mailer.conf, 493
/etc/mail/mailertable, 493
/etc/mail/sendmail.cf, 493
/etc/mail/virtusertable, 493
/etc/remote, 384
/etc/ttys, 379
/usr, 145
/usr/bin/login, 377
/usr/local/etc, 148
/usr/local/etc/rc.d, 148
/usr/share/skel, 168
/var, 145
10 base 2, 451
10 base T, 451
386BSD, 6, 9
386BSD Patchkit, 6
4.3BSD-Lite, 6
4.4BSD-Lite, 3, 4

A

accounting
   disk space, 297
   printer, 263, 276
accounts
   adding, 168
   changing password, 171
   daemon, 167
   groups, 175
   limiting, 172
   modifying, 168
   nobody, 167
   operator, 167
   removing, 170
   superuser (root), 167
   system, 167
   user, 167
address redirection, 485
adduser, 168, 351
AIX, 452
Alpha, 14, 19, 82, 85
Alpha BIOS, 85
Amanda, 339
amd, 441
anonymous CVS, 180, 506
Apache, 5
applications
   Maple, 524
   Mathematica, 523
   Oracle, 527
   SAP R/3, 530
apsfilter, 262
ARC, 85
ASCII, 288, 348
AT&T, 6
automatic mounter daemon, 441
AutoPPP, 405

B

C

D

dangerously dedicated, 35

DCE, 368

default route, 420, 432, 433

Denial of Service (DoS), 185, 196, 201

DES, 204

DEVFS, 514

device node, 362

device nodes, 191, 361

DHCP
 configuration files, 469
 requirements, 468
 server, 469

dial-in service, 376

dial-out service, 383

directories, 94

directory hierarchy, 94

disk quotas, 172, 297
 checking, 298, 300
 limits, 298

disklabel, 340, 344

diskless operation, 443

diskless workstation, 443

disks
 adding, 294
 file-backed, 296
 memory, 296
 memory filesystem, 297
 virtual, 296

DNS, 151, 406, 470, 491, 499
 records, 476

DNS Server, 5

domain name, 421

DOS, 16, 31, 84, 354

DoS attacks
 (See Denial of Service (DoS))

DSL, 436

DTE, 367

dual homed hosts, 434

dump, 338

Dynamic Host Configuration Protocol
 (See DHCP)

E

editors, 104
 emacs, 104
 vi, 104

ee, 104

electronic mail, 5, 491

ELF, 547
 branding, 547

emacs, 104

email, 491
 configuration, 498
 receiving, 492
 troubleshooting, 495

encodings, 348

environment variables, 102

Ethernet, 425
 MAC address, 426, 432, 523

execution class loader, 547

F

fdimage, 86

fdisk, 294

file permissions, 93

filesize, 173

filesystems
 HFS, 301
 ISO-9660, 300, 301
 Joliet, 301
 mounted with fstab, 96
 mounting, 97
 unmounting, 98

finger, 198

FIPS, 84

firewall, 5, 217, 436, 437

fix-it floppies, 340

floppy disks, 344

flow control protocol, 240

fonts, 524

fortran, 257

Free Software Foundation, 6, 9, 107

FreeBSD Project
 Development Model, 8
 Goals, 7

K

Kerberos, 198, 203, 210
  installing, 210
kermit, 410
kern.maxfiles, 156
kernel, 158
  boot interaction, 162
  bootflags, 162
  building / installing, 178
  building a custom kernel, 177
  compiling, 511
  config file, 180
  configuration, 360, 424, 484
  example config file, 181
  LINT, 180
kernel configuration, 437
  options BRIDGE, 437
kernel options
  cpu, 181
  cpu type, 181
  ICMP_BANDLIM, 185
  ident, 181
  LINUX, 520
  machine, 181
  maxusers, 182
  MSDOSFS, 183
  NFS, 183
  NFS_ROOT, 183
  SMP, 185
kernel tuning, 527, 537
kernel.old, 161, 180
keymap, 352
KLD (kernel loadable object), 519
Korean localization, 358

L

language codes, 348
LCP, 405
limiting users, 172
  coredumpsize, 173
  cputime, 173
  filesize, 173
  maxproc, 173
  memorylocked, 174
  memoryuse, 174
  openfiles, 174
  quotas, 172
  sbsize, 174
  stacksize, 174
LINT, 180
Linux, 452
  /proc filesystem, 519
  ELF binaries, 522
  installing Linux libraries, 520
Linux binary compatibility, 519
LISA, 340
loader, 160
loader configuration, 160
locale, 348, 349, 351, 537
localization, 347
log files, 152
login class, 349, 351
login name, 396
loopback device, 432
LPD spooling system, 237
LPRng, 287
ls, 94

M

MacOS, 208
mail host, 492
mail server daemons
  exim, 492
  postfix, 492
  qmail, 492
  sendmail, 492
mailing list, 507
majordomo, 503, 505
make, 509
make world, 506
  timings, 511
make.conf, 507
MAKEDEV, 191, 371, 514
manual pages, 105
Master Boot Record (MBR), 158
maxproc, 173
MD5, 204

Colophon

This book is the combined work of hundreds of contributors to "The FreeBSD Documentation Project". The text is authored in SGML according to the DocBook DTD and is formatted from SGML into many different presentation formats using **Jade**, an open source DSSSL engine. Norm Walsh's DSSSL stylesheets were used with an additional customization layer to provide the presentation instructions for Jade. The printed version of this document would not be possible without Donald Knuth's **TeX** typesetting language, Leslie Lamport's **LaTeX**, or Sebastian Rahtz's **JadeTeX** macro package.

The network diagrams were created with **Dia**, an open-source diagram creation program. The cover artwork and part header illustrations were produced with **Adobe Photoshop** and **Quark Express** on a Macintosh.